W9-DFS-632

Eleventh Edition

Cultural Anthropology

The Human Challenge

WILLIAM A. HAVILAND
University of Vermont

HARALD E. L. PRINS
Kansas State University

DANA WALRATH
University of Vermont

BUNNY McBRIDE
Kansas State University

WADSWORTH

THOMSON LEARNING

Australia • Canada • Mexico • Singapore • Spain •
United Kingdom • United States

WADSWORTH

THOMSON LEARNING™

Senior Acquisitions Editor: Lin Marshall
Assistant Editor: Nicole Root
Editorial Assistant: Kelly McMahon
Technology Project Manager: Dee Dee Zobian
Marketing Manager: Matthew Wright
Marketing Assistant: Tara Pierson
Advertising Project Manager: Linda Yip
Project Manager, Editorial Production: Catherine Morris
Art Director: Robert Hugel
Print/Media Buyer: Rebecca Cross
Permissions Editor: Kiely Sexton

Production Service: Robin Lockwood Productions
Text Designer: Lisa Buckley
Photo Researcher: Sandra Lord, Sue Howard
Copy Editor: Jennifer Gordon
Illustrator: Carol Zuber-Mallison
Cover Designer: Larry Didona
Cover Image: Large photo: James Martin/Getty Images. Small photos, clockwise from top left: Bushnell/Soifer/Getty Images, Glen Allison/Getty Images, Ray Reiss, Erik Simonsen/Getty Images, Kevin Miller/Getty Images
Text and Cover Printer: Transcontinental Printing/Interglobe

COPYRIGHT © 2005 Wadsworth, a division of Thomson Learning, Inc. Thomson Learning™ is a trademark used herein under license.

ALL RIGHTS RESERVED. No part of this work covered by the copyright hereon may be reproduced or used in any form or by any means—graphic, electronic, or mechanical, including but not limited to photocopying, recording, taping, Web distribution, information networks, or information storage and retrieval systems—without the written permission of the publisher.

Printed in Canada
3 4 5 6 7 08 07 06

For more information about our products, contact us at:
Thomson Learning Academic Resource Center
1-800-423-0563
For permission to use material from this text or product, submit a request online at **http://www.thomsonrights.com**. Any additional questions about permissions can be submitted by email to **thomsonrights@thomson.com**.

ExamView® and ExamView Pro® are registered trademarks of FSCreations, Inc. Windows is a registered trademark of the Microsoft Corporation used herein under license. Macintosh and Power Macintosh are registered trademarks of Apple Computer, Inc. Used herein under license.

COPYRIGHT © 2005 Thomson Learning, Inc. All Rights Reserved. Thomson Learning WebTutor™ is a trademark of Thomson Learning, Inc.

Library of Congress Control Number: 2003116263

Student Edition: ISBN 0-534-62487-1

Instructor's Edition: ISBN 0-534-62497-9

Thomson Wadsworth
10 Davis Drive
Belmont, CA 94002-3098
USA

Asia
Thomson Learning
5 Shenton Way #01-01
UIC Building
Singapore 068808

Australia/New Zealand
Thomson Learning
102 Dodds Street
Southbank, Victoria 3006
Australia

Canada
Nelson
1120 Birchmount Road
Toronto, Ontario M1K 5G4
Canada

Europe/Middle East/Africa
Thomson Learning
High Holborn House
50/51 Bedford Row
London WC1R 4LR
United Kingdom

Latin America
Thomson Learning
Seneca, 53
Colonia Polanco
11560 Mexico D.F.
Mexico

Spain/Portugal
Paraninfo
Calle Magallanes, 25
28015 Madrid, Spain

Dedicated to

Anita de Laguna Haviland
whose efforts have helped sustain
this ever-evolving text for three decades.

About the Authors

Dr. William A. Haviland is Professor Emeritus at the University of Vermont, where he has taught since 1965. He holds a Ph.D. in Anthropology from the University of Pennsylvania and has published widely on archaeological, ethnological, and physical anthropological research carried out in Guatemala, Maine, and Vermont. Haviland is a member of many professional societies, including the American Anthropological Association and the American Association for the Advancement of Science. He has participated in many projects, including "Gender and the Anthropological Curriculum," sponsored by the American Anthropological Association in 1988.

Dr. Haviland, who has always loved teaching and writing for anthropology students was also the technical advisor for the telecourse, Faces of Culture. He has a passionate interest in indigenous rights; he worked with the Maya and Abenaki for years. He continues to work with Native Americans in the northeastern United States, does consulting, and participates in international conferences on urbanization in Mesoamerica. He is also co-editor of the series: *Tikal Reports*.

Dr. Harald Prins is Professor of Anthropology at Kansas State University. Born and raised in the Netherlands, Prins was academically trained in prehistoric archaeology, social anthropology, and comparative history at various universities in the Netherlands and the United States. He has a doctoraal degree from the University of Nijmegen and a Ph.D. from the New School for Social Research. Prins has done extensive fieldwork among indigenous peoples in South and North America. Before joining the faculty at Kansas State University in 1990, he taught at Nijmegen, Bowdoin, and Colby. He typically teaches classes on American Indians (North/South), Anthropological Theory, Ethnohistory, Visual Anthropology, Native Rights, and Introduction to Anthropology. Also professionally trained in filmmaking, Prins has consulted on numerous films, juried documentary film festivals, and served as president of the Society for Visual Anthropology (1999–2001) as well as visual anthropology editor of the journal *American Anthropologist*. His own film work includes co-producing *Our Lives in Our Hands*, a documentary on Mi'kmaq Indians and *Oh, What a Blow That Phantom Gave Me!*, about media ecology pioneer Edmund Carpenter.

Known for his spirited teaching, Prins has won his university's most prestigious teaching honors and serves as Coffman Chair for University Distinguished Teaching Scholars. On the scholarly front, his publications include *The Mi'kmaq: Resistance, Accommodation, and Cultural Survival*, various edited works, and over 75 scholarly articles, book chapters, and encyclopedia entries.

Committed to balancing teaching and scholarship with native rights advocacy, Dr. Prins played an instrumental role in the successful federal recognition and land claims case of the Aroostook Band of Micmacs and served as expert witness in several Mi'kmaq native rights cases in the U.S. Senate and Canadian courts.

Dr. Dana Walrath is an Assistant Professor of Medicine and a Women's Studies affiliated faculty member at the University of Vermont. She earned a Ph.D. in 1997 from the University of Pennsylvania in medical and biological anthropology. In her doctoral research, Walrath developed novel synthetic techniques and theories for the interpretation of the evolution of human childbirth. Her interests span biocultural aspects of reproduction, genetics, and evolutionary medicine. Her publications have appeared in *Current Anthropology, American Anthropologist*, and *American Journal of Physical Anthropology*. Walrath's work and writings often focus upon the conceptual relationship between evolutionary research and feminism.

Dr. Walrath has received grants and fellowships from the National Science Foundation, Health Resources and Services Administration, the Center for Disease

Control, Foreign Languages Area Studies, the University of Pennsylvania, and the New York Foundation for the Arts. Research sites have ranged from fieldwork at an Aurignacian site in France, to the Marine Biological Laboratory in Woods Hole, Massachusetts, to biomedical settings.

Dr. Walrath's diverse experience includes work in Yemen, Egypt, and Armenia contributing to her research and writing on her Armenian heritage. Before joining the faculty at the University of Vermont in 2000, she taught at the University of Pennsylvania, Temple University, and the Mohamed Ali Othman School in Taiz, Yemen. For the University of Vermont's College of Medicine she has developed an innovative program that brings anthropological perspectives into the study of medicine. She is presently serving on a national committee to develop women's health care learning objectives for medical education sponsored by the Association of Professors of Obstetrics and Gynecology.

Bunny McBride is an award-winning author with a master's degree in Anthropology from Columbia University. Her books include *Women of the Dawn, Molly Spotted Elk: A Penobscot in Paris,* and *Our Lives in Our Hands: Micmac Indian Basketmakers.* Working in close collaboration with Native American communities, she curated museum exhibits based on these books.

From 1978 to 1988, McBride wrote scores of articles for *The Christian Science Monitor* from Africa, Europe, and Asia. She has contributed to many other newspapers and magazines and has written introductions, articles, and chapters in a dozen books, including notable academic titles such as *Sifters: Native American Women's Lives* and *Reading Beyond Words: Contexts for Native History.* She coauthored the *Audubon Society Field Guide to African Wildlife.*

McBride is an adjunct lecturer of anthropology at Kansas State University and has been a regular visiting lecturer at Principia College in Illinois since 1981. She has also taught at the Salt Institute for Documentary Field Studies in Portland, Maine, and given dozens of guest lectures in public and academic venues.

From 1981 to 1991, McBride did historical research and community development work for the Aroostook Band of Micmacs in Maine, contributing to their successful efforts to gain federal status, establish a land base, and revitalize cultural traditions. In 1999 the Maine state legislature gave McBride a special commendation for her research and writing on the history of Native women in the state—an honor initiated by elected tribal representatives in the legislature. Currently, she serves as co-principal investigator for a National Parks Service ethnographic research project, oral history advisor for the Kansas Humanities Council, and board member of the Women's World Summit Foundation, based in Geneva, Switzerland.

Brief Contents

Contents

Features Contents

Preface

New to the eleventh edition are three co-authors. Their involvement reflects two phenomena: the senior author's own retirement from the classroom (but not from anthropology) and the fact that four-field anthropology has grown to the point where no one individual can "do it all." There has been much debate of late about the future of four-field anthropology. In our view, its future will be assured through collaboration among anthropologists with diverse backgrounds, as exemplified in this textbook. Although distinct from one another, our experiences and research interests overlap, and we all share a similar vision of what anthropology is (and should be) about.

PURPOSE

Cultural Anthropology: The Human Challenge is designed for introductory courses at the college level. While focusing on cultural anthropology, the text springs from the four-field approach to the discipline and therefore highlights the basics of physical and linguistic anthropology, as well as archaeology. This is done in the introductory chapter, which provides a historic overview of anthropology and its four fields. Moreover, the book offers an entire chapter on linguistics and another on human biology/evolution and the emergence of culture. In addition it features a series of Biocultural Connection boxes in several chapters to illustrate how cultural and biological processes work together to shape human behavior, beliefs, and biology. In short, the key concepts and terminology of each of the four fields are touched upon, providing students with a sense of how cultural anthropology fits into the larger picture of the discipline.

Most cultural anthropology instructors have two goals for their introductory classes: (1) to provide an overview of principles and processes of the discipline and (2) to plant a seed of awareness about human diversity in their students that will continue to grow and to challenge ethnocentrism long past the end of the semester. All eleven editions of *Cultural Anthropology* have tried to support and further these goals.

The majority of our students come to class intrigued with anthropology but with little more than a vague sense of what it is all about. The first and most obvious aim of the text, therefore, is to provide a comprehensive introduction to the discipline—its fundamental principles and key concepts. Drawing from the research and ideas of a number of schools of anthropological thought, this book exposes students to a mix of theoretical perspectives—in human evolution and human ecology, as well as theories about culture such as functionalism, structuralism, cultural materialism, and world systems theory. Such inclusiveness reflects our conviction that different approaches all reveal important insights about human behavior, biology, and beliefs. To employ the tools of a single approach at the expense of all others is to cut oneself off from significant insights.

If most students have little substantive concept of anthropology, they often have less clear—and potentially more destructive—views of the primacy of their own culture and its place in the world. A secondary goal of this text, then, is to prod students to appreciate the true complexity and breadth of human behavior and the human condition. Debates regarding globalization and notions of progress, the "naturalness" of the mother/father/child(ren) nuclear family, new genetic technologies, and how gender roles relate to biological variation all benefit greatly from the insights gained through anthropology. This questioning aspect of the discipline is perhaps the most relevant gift we can pass on to our students. If we, as teachers (and textbook authors), do our jobs well, students will gain a wider outlook on the world and a critical perspective on their particular culture. To paraphrase the poet T. S. Eliot: After all our explorations, they will come home and know the place for the first time.

If ever there were a time when students needed anthropological tools to step out of culture-bound ways of thinking and acting and to gain a global view of humanity, it is now. Beyond serving as a foundation for anthropology majors, this text is designed to help all students make sense of our increasingly complex and interconnected world, to perceive their particular place in it, and thereby to navigate through intertwined cultural networks with knowledge and skill, whatever professional path they take. In short, we see this book as a comprehensive guide for people entering the often bewildering maze of global crossroads in the 21st century.

ORGANIZATION OF THE BOOK

A Unifying Theme

In our own teaching, we have often found that introductory students lack a sense of the bigger picture in their studies of human beings. With this in mind, we present anthropology as the study of humankind's responses to the fundamental challenges of survival. Each chapter is framed by this theme, opening with a Challenge Issue paragraph and photograph and ending with Questions for Reflection tied to that particular challenge. In marking out the steps humans take to meet these challenges, we emphasize the biocultural connection along with the point that every culture is an integrated and dynamic system of adaptation that responds to a combination of internal and external factors. This is illustrated by what we refer to as the "barrel model" of culture—depicted in a simple but telling drawing that shows the interplay of social, ideological, and economic factors within a system along with outside influences of environment, climate, and other societies. Throughout the book examples are linked back to this point.

SPECIAL FEATURES OF THE BOOK

Accessible Language

As textbook authors, we aim to transmit and register ideas and information: to induce our readers to look at the unfamiliar as well as to look at the familiar in new ways, and then to urge them to think critically about what they see. This, of course, is easier said than done. A book may be the most content-rich, most handsomely designed, most lavishly illustrated text available on the subject, but if it is not accessible to the student, it is valueless as a teaching tool.

In this text, even the most difficult concepts are presented in prose that is clear, straightforward, and easy for today's first- and second-year students to understand, without feeling that they are being "spoken down to." Where technical terms are necessary, they appear in bold-faced type, are carefully defined in the narrative, and are defined again in the running glossary in simple, clear language.

Accessibility involves not only clear writing but also an engaging narrative voice or style. The voice of *Cultural Anthropology* is distinct among introductory texts in the discipline, for it has been thoroughly internationalized. This means we have avoided the typical "we: they" voice and used a more inclusive one that will resonate with both Western and non-Western students and professors. Moreover, the book highlights the theories and work of anthropologists from all around the world—in the general narrative as well as in special boxed features. In addition, its cultural examples come from industrial and postindustrial societies as well as nonindustrial ones.

Photographs, Maps, and Other Illustrations

The accessibility of this text is further enhanced by compelling visuals, including a uniquely large and rich array of four-color photographs, selected to catch the eye and drive home important anthropological points. Many of them are paired or clustered as "Visual Counterpoints" in order to contrast and compare cultural examples, concepts, and issues across time and around the world.

In addition, this book features a wide variety of line drawings, maps, charts, and tables, many designed exclusively for this edition. As in past editions, we expect these visual tools will effectively illustrate, emphasize, and clarify particular anthropological concepts and prove to be valuable and memorable teaching aids. Maps have been an especially popular aid through each edition of *Cultural Anthropology*, and the eleventh edition builds on this success. Many of the marginal locator maps are new or revised, and several new world maps have been added to provide an overview of important contemporary issues such as pollution, energy consumption, and refugee populations. Also of note, we have retained in the front end of the book several contrasting world map projections to illustrate the cultural messages embedded in cartography. One of the maps (the Robinson projection) locates all of the cultures mentioned in the text.

Original Studies

A special feature of this text is the Original Study that appears in each chapter. Many are new to this edition and others have been updated. These studies consist of selections from ethnographies and other original works by women and men who have done, or are doing, work of anthropological significance. Each study, integrated within the flow of the text, sheds additional light on an important anthropological concept or subject area found in the chapter. Their content is not extraneous or supplemental. The Original Studies bring specific concepts to life through concrete examples. And a number of Original Studies also demonstrate the anthropological tradition of the case study, albeit in abbreviated form.

The idea behind the Original Studies is to coordinate the two halves of the human brain, which have different functions. Whereas the left (dominant) hemisphere is logical and processes verbal inputs in a linear manner, the right hemisphere is creative and less impressed with linear logic. Psychologist James V. McConnell described it as "an analog computer of sorts—a kind of intellectual monitor that not only handles abstractions, but also organizes and stores material in terms of Gestalts [that] include the emotional relevance of the experience." Logical thinking, as well as creative problem solving, occurs when the two sides of the brain cooperate. The implication for textbook writers is obvious: To be truly effective, they must reach both sides of the brain. The Original Studies help to do this by conveying some "feel" for humans and their behavior and how anthropologists actually study them. For example, in Chapter 1 students will read a new Original Study by a

North American anthropologist who, while in graduate school, met and married a Zulu from South Africa—a personal experience that played a role in her current work with traditional healers and HIV/AIDS patients in her husband's country. In the Original Study in Chapter 5 they will read a poignant description of what it was like for the author of that study to grow up as an "intersexed" person exposed to clashing cultural views regarding her identity. Her fundamentalist Christian parents saw her intersexuality as a curse, while her Cherokee grandmother referred to it as a blessing. As with other Original Studies, the striking nature of these experiences drives the discussion of a host of issues deeply relevant to students and anthropology.

Anthropology Applied

A popular carryover from the tenth edition, this boxed feature conveys anthropology's wide-ranging relevance and gives students a glimpse into the variety of careers anthropologists enjoy. New and revised boxes include "Dispute Resolution and the Anthropologist," "Language Renewal among the Northern Ute," "Development Anthropology and Dams," "Protecting Cultural Heritages," "Anthropology in the Corporate Jungle," "Agricultural Development and the Anthropologist," "Reconciling Modern Medicine with Traditional Beliefs in Swaziland," and "Advocacy for the Rights of Indigenous Peoples." In the case of examples carried over from the previous edition, the anthropologists profiled have provided us with updates on their work.

Biocultural Connections

New to the eleventh edition, this feature illustrates how cultural and biological processes work together to shape human biology, beliefs, and behavior. It reflects the integrated biocultural approach central to the field of anthropology today. Topics include "The Anthropology of Organ Transplantation," "Paleolithic Prescriptions for the Diseases of Civilization," "The Biology of Human Speech," "African Burial Ground Project," and "Marriage Prohibitions in the United States."

Anthropologists of Note

We have increased the number of profiles in this feature (formerly Biography Boxes) and shifted the coverage to better represent the wide variety of anthropologists in the world. Featuring contemporary scholars as well as important historical figures in the field, these boxes illustrate both the history and evolution of the discipline. New profiles include Arjun Appadurai, Jomo Kenyatta, Kinji Imanishi, Eleanor Leacock, Yolanda Moses, Laura Nader, and Eric Wolf.

Integrated Gender Coverage

Unlike many introductory texts, *Cultural Anthropology* integrates rather than separates gender coverage. Thus, material on gender related issues is included in every chapter. The result of this approach is a measure of gender-related material that far exceeds the single chapter that most introductory books contain. In fact, it is the equivalent of about two full chapters.

Why is the gender-related material integrated? Anthropology is itself an integrative discipline. Concepts and issues surrounding gender are almost always too complicated to remove from their context. Moreover, spreading this material through all of the chapters emphasizes how considerations of gender enter into virtually everything people do. Much of the new content for the eleventh edition (listed below) relates to gender in some way. These changes generally fall into at least one of four categories: changes in thinking about gender within the discipline; examples that have important ramifications for gender in a particular society or culture; cross-cultural implications about gender and gender relations; and the analytic distinction between sex and gender illustrating the subtle influence of gender norms on biological theories about sex difference. New material includes expanded and updated discussions of gender roles in evolutionary discourse and studies of nonhuman primates, intersexuality, homosexual identity, same-sex marriage, and female genital mutilation. Through a steady drumbeat of such coverage, this edition avoids ghettoizing gender to a single chapter that is preceded and followed by resounding silence.

Previews and Summaries

An old and effective pedagogical technique is repetition: "Tell 'em what you're going to tell 'em, tell 'em, and then tell 'em what you've told 'em." To do this, each chapter begins with preview questions that set up a framework for studying the contents of the chapter. At the end of the chapter is a summary containing the kernels of the more important ideas presented in the chapter. The summaries provide handy reviews for students without being so long and detailed as to seduce students into thinking they can get by without reading the chapter itself.

Web Links

The Internet continues to be an increasingly important means of communication. The eleventh edition draws upon the World Wide Web both as an instructional tool and as a new set of examples of culture and cultural change. Every chapter contains several Media Trek icons integrated into the text that direct students to the CD-ROM or companion Web site for deeper exploration of topics covered in the narrative. (More on these below.)

Suggested Readings and Bibliography

Each chapter includes an annotated and up-to-date list of Suggested Readings that will supply the inquisitive student with further information about specific anthropological points that may be of interest. The books suggested are oriented toward both the general reader and the interested student who wishes to explore further the more technical aspects of the subject. In addition, the Bibliography at the end of the book contains a listing of more than 500 books, monographs, and articles from scholarly journals and popular magazines on virtually every topic covered in the text that a student might wish to investigate further.

Glossary

The running glossary is designed to catch the student's eye, reinforcing the meaning of each newly introduced term. It is also useful for chapter review, as the student may readily isolate the new terms from those introduced in earlier chapters. A complete glossary is also included at the back of the book. In the glossaries each term is defined in clear, understandable language. As a result, less class time is required for going over terms, leaving instructors free to pursue matters of greater interest.

Length

Careful consideration has been given to the length of this book. On the one hand, it had to be of sufficient length to avoid superficiality or misrepresentation of the discipline by ignoring or otherwise slighting some important aspect of anthropology. On the other hand, it could not be so long as to present more material than could be reasonably dealt with in the space of a single semester, or be prohibitively expensive. The resultant text is comparable in length to introductory texts in the sister disciplines of economics, psychology, and sociology, even though there is more ground to be covered in an introduction to cultural anthropology.

Special Features beyond the Printed Page

Recognizing that contemporary anthropology students welcome, respond to, and even expect instruction materials to include more than printed matter, we have prepared a unique multimedia teaching package for exploring the methods and findings of the discipline. These include the book in hand, as well as a CD-ROM, interactive Web site, companion videos, and PowerPoint® program.

The accompanying videos (discussed with the rest of the supplements) show culture in motion and bring action and life into the circle of ideas. The Web Links (noted above and discussed in more detail below) build skills for analysis and research and move the content of the text from standard linear textbook format to a multimedia package, while providing a media database of print and numerous nonprint resources. PowerPoint slides and overhead transparencies bring the ideas and art of the text into the classroom. And, of course, the Suggested Readings and Bibliography continue to show the rich library of anthropological texts students can utilize. The eleventh edition thus allows instructors to draw upon a broad set of instructional tools to expand their classrooms. Anthropology has been an archive of human biology, beliefs, and behavior, and it is important that the discipline shows the richness and diversity of humanity through the appropriate media.

THE ELEVENTH EDITION

The eleventh edition is one of the most radical revisions in this book's 30-year lifespan. Every chapter has been thoroughly reconsidered, reworked, and updated. Additions and deletions have been made with an eye toward building on the strengths that have made this text appeal to so many for so long. The writing has been further refined and the voice of the text "internationalized" to make it more accessible to a wider audience. A host of new photos, charts, tables, illustrations, and maps have been introduced, and every chapter has a new chapter opening photo (tied to the "challenge" theme). The summary is now presented as a series of succinct bulleted points, and we have added several Questions for Reflection at the end of each chapter. Also, we have increased the number of contemporary texts in the annotated Suggested Readings list and located many new interactive Internet sites, now labeled as "Media Treks." Major changes in the eleventh edition per chapter include:

Chapter 1: The Essence of Anthropology

The book's opening chapter offers a compelling Original Study, "Fighting HIV/AIDS in Africa: Traditional Healers on the Front Line," written by Suzanne Leclerc-Madlala for this edition. Also new among boxed features is an Anthropologists of Note profile of Yolanda Moses, and a

Biocultural Connection piece concerning the anthropology of organ transplantation. The Anthropology Applied box on forensic anthropology featuring the work of Clyde Snow has been updated to include also the work of Amy Zelson Mundorff who oversaw cataloguing the remains of those who lost their lives in the September 11, 2001, terrorist attack on the World Trade Center in New York City. In a new section titled "Anthropology and Globalization," we offer a cogent overview of one of today's most significant issues. A revised and expanded section on theory includes a discussion on the difference between theory and doctrine, which will be particularly helpful to professors who have students whose religious beliefs do not sit well with the concept of evolution. Our expanded discussion of ethnography and fieldwork now includes a narrative on the challenges anthropologists face in the field. A new illustration representing the four fields incorporates theory and applied anthropology. To enhance the text's four-field foundation, introductory passages on archaeology, linguistics, and especially physical anthropology have been fleshed out. Also, a discussion of medical anthropology has been added.

Chapter 2: The Characteristics of Culture

A new illustration we call "the barrel model," conveys the integrative and dynamic nature of culture and introduces the concepts of infrastructure/social structure/superstructure. It appears in this chapter's narrative and in a new figure/illustration, and it is referred to in subsequent chapters to clarify potentially confusing aspects of culture and to deepen student understanding of cultures as integrative and dynamic systems. A new Anthropologists of Note box profiles Eleanor Leacock and her leading role in feminist anthropology, giving context to Annette Weiner's Original Study about the contrast between her research findings among the Trobriand Islanders and those of Malinowski. A new section titled "Cross-Cultural Comparisons" includes an overview of the Human Relations Area Files, discussing how the files can be used in conjunction with original fieldwork. A reworked discussion of ethnohistory conveys the importance of thinking beyond the ethnographic present. New examples of maladaptation have been added to the discussion of adaptation.

Chapter 3: The Beginnings of Human Culture

Chapter 3 has been significantly revised and plays a key role in our effort to have the eleventh edition convey the role of biology in culture. Here, mammalian primate biology is established as a vital part of being human and is presented as a continuum rather than humans versus animals. The chapter introduction has been reshaped to show that biological anthropologists must critically reflect on their theories to avoid constructing human evolutionary history in culture-bound terms. In this vein, gender issues receive additional coverage in discussions concerning old theories about "man the hunter" and male dominance hierarchies undergoing revision in part through landmark research by women in the field.

The discussion of taxonomy has been simplified and the point made that taxonomies change with new discoveries. The chapter bypasses the terms *hominid* and *hominin* so that students do not get lost in the taxonomic disputes where scientists employ alternate taxonomies. Also of note, this edition presents new fossil finds *Homo sapiens idaltu* and their place in the out of Africa/multiregional hypotheses.

The chapter relays why the concept of race is not useful for studying human biological variation. This discussion offers a historical overview on the creation of false racial categories by scientists of the past and marks out the role of anthropology in criticizing the notion of biological race (featuring Boas and Montagu). Moreover, a new section titled "Race and Human Evolution" includes a discussion of race in the major competing theories of human evolution as well as providing a transition to the contemporary biological variation section.

Finally, this revamped chapter features several new boxed pieces. These include Frans de Waal's Original Study, "Reconciliation and Its Cultural Modification in Primates," an Anthropologists of Note profile on Kinji Imanishi, and a Biocultural Connection box titled "Paleolithic Prescriptions for the Diseases of Civilization" (featuring the work of Mel Konner and Marjorie Shostak collaborating with physician Boyd Eaton, as well as George Armelagos).

Chapter 4: Language and Communication

The Original Study on Chantek the signing orangutan has been moved here from Chapter 3, and it has been trimmed and updated by the author—making it all the more engaging. The three branches of linguistic anthropology now appear under specific subheads, and the Anthropology Applied on language renewal among the Ute has been tightened and updated with input from the researcher. A new Biocultural Connection box concerns the biology of human speech, and the section on body language has been extensively reworked, including an entirely new piece on proxemics with a brief in-text profile on its founder, Edward Hall. We have added a subsection on tonal languages, which represent 70 percent of the world's languages. In the historical linguistics section, the discussion of language change now covers language disappearance and revitalization, as well as pidgin, creole, and passive bilingualism. In the ethnolinguistic section coverage of linguistic relativity has been amplified, and the section on language and gender now features a gendered speech example from the film *Dances with Wolves*. The section on the origins of language now opens with a narrative about myths/legends on the topic. Finally, a new section, "From Speech to Writing," takes readers from traditional speech performatives and memory devices to Egyptian hieroglyphics to the conception and spread of the alphabet to the 2003 to 2012 Literacy Decade established by the United Nations.

Chapter 5: Social Identity, Personality, and Gender

The enculturation discussion in the "Self and the Behavioral Environment" section now opens with a paragraph on "wild" children. We have also added a short narrative on naming practices and the role that names play in self-awareness and social identity. We replaced the lengthy narrative about Penobscot Indians that appeared in the tenth edition with several short paragraphs of brief examples of object/spatial/temporal/normative orientation drawn cross-culturally. Commentary concerning Margaret Mead's Papua New Guinea research has been updated in terms of contemporary critiques. The section on national character has been reworked to include present-day examples of national stereotypes. Most significant among changes is a substantial new section titled "Alternative Gender Models from a Cross-Cultural Perspective"; this provides a historic overview of intersexuality, transsexuality, and transgendering, including current statistics on the incidence of intersexuality worldwide.

Chapter 6: Patterns of Subsistence

The culture area discussion has been completely rewritten, in part to put the North American Plains culture area into historical perspective. The "Food-Foraging Way of Life" section has been fully revamped, including updating the discussion and statistics of the "original affluent society" example. The "Food-Producing Society" section has been reworked and now introduces the term *Neolithic revolution.* To the concluding section of the chapter, "Nonindustrial Cities in the Modern World," we have added a very brief sketch of modern cities today, for comparative purposes and to bring home for students the

topic of cities. The content of the Anthropology Applied piece, "Agricultural Development and the Anthropologist," has been deepened and fully updated with direct input from the anthropologist.

Chapter 7: Economic Systems

The revised chapter provides fuller coverage of industrial and postindustrial societies in addition to classical examples from nonindustrial societies. The potlatch and Kula ring discussions have been expanded and sharpened. The section on labor division by gender now features new material concerning female involvement in warfare historically around the world. A new Anthropologists of Note box on Jomo Kenyatta, late president of Kenya, has been added, along with an original Anthropology Applied feature by corporate anthropologist Karen Stephenson.

Chapter 8: Sex and Marriage

Among numerous refined and updated definitions in the eleventh edition, one of the most significant is the definition of the term *marriage,* which now encompasses the real-life situations of many students in North America and Europe, as well as the rest of the world. A new discussion under the renamed heading "Regulating Sexual Relations" includes and contrasts Christian laws and Muslim Shariah laws, past and present. The section about the Nayar has been reworked to provide clarifying details about marriage practices. Eskimo hunters in northern Alaska have been added as an additional illustration of group marriage. A Biocultural Connection box written expressly for this chapter ("Marriage Prohibitions in the United States") investigates the reasons behind the outlawing of first-cousin marriage in much of the United States.

Chapter 9: Family and Household

The opening paragraphs and the "Family and Society" section have been thoroughly revamped, emphasizing family as adaptive. The definitions of family, nuclear family, and extended family have been retooled to embrace contemporary family forms. These are presented in historical anthropological context, building out from classical anthropological definitions and making it clear why revisions are necessary. Statistics on family forms, divorce rates, and intimate partner abuse have been expanded as well as updated. The impact of new reproductive technologies (NRTs) on how humans think about and form families has been added to the discussion in the general narrative, as well as the Original Study "The Ever-

Changing Family in North America," which has been revised and updated by its author. In the "Functions of the Family" section, we have added two significant anthropological terms: *family of orientation* and *family of procreation*. A new bar graph shows family forms in the United States, based on the 2002 census.

Chapter 10: Kinship and Descent

Changes in this chapter primarily involved sharpening and enlivening the narrative and trimming it down to a more digestible series of examples. That said, we added a discussion of traditional Scottish highland patriclans and their clan symbols (tartans), which appears along with the discussion of matriclans featured in the tenth edition.

Chapter 11: Grouping by Gender, Age, Common Interest, and Class

A thoroughly revised narrative on caste explores its historical context and role in Hindu culture in India and also presents examples of castelike situations from other parts of the world, including former apartheid systems in South Africa and the United States. Archaeologist Michael Blakey has contributed an original Biocultural Connection box concerning his research on New York City's African burial ground, which revealed the physical wear and tear of an entire community brought on by the social institution of slavery.

Chapter 12: Politics, Power, and Violence

This chapter has many new features. The concept of power has been defined and woven into the narrative, laying a foundation for a more extensive discussion of structural power in the book's final chapter. A new introductory discussion on state provides historical perspective and specific examples. Definitions of *band, tribe, state,* and *nation* have been revised to distinguish them more clearly for students and to reflect current perspectives. The section on tribal organization now includes an expanded historical overview of the term *tribe,* further clarifying why the word is problematic. In addition, this section features a new paragraph about female chiefs in what is now New England. Under the heading "Chiefdoms," readers will find another paragraph about female chiefs, and in the "Political Leadership and Gender" section, they will encounter several women who inherited royal leadership roles, as well as women politically elected as presidents or prime

ministers. The section on state systems has been revised to include up-to-date examples of nations struggling to free themselves from state controls not of their own choosing. The section on crime now features a discussion of new sentencing laws in Canada based on traditional Native American restorative justice techniques such as the Talking Circle. The section on war has been significantly overhauled to include a discussion of the different motives, objectives, methods, and scales of warfare as organized violence, along with a summation of wars humans have engaged in over the past 5,000 years—and a particular look at those fought over the past 30 years. Discussions of religious wars such as the Crusades and precontact intertribal warfare in the Americas have been resequenced for the sake of flow and clarity, and the lines of comparison between them are now more clearly drawn. The Anthropology Applied box about William Ury's dispute resolution work has been thoroughly revised and updated with new input from Dr. Ury. A new Anthropologists of Note box has been added featuring Laura Nader, specialist in the anthropology of law.

Chapter 13: Spirituality, Religion, and the Supernatural

The title and content of this chapter have been adjusted to reflect current distinctions among spirituality, religion, and the supernatural. A definition and discussion of worldview has been woven into the introductory paragraphs and distinguished from religion. The narrative (with a new figure) provides up-to-date statistics on the major religions of the world and the number of adherents they have, noting changes and trends. Definitions of several key terms—including religion, spirituality, animism, animatism, shaman, divination, revitalization movements—have been retooled and carefully nuanced. The section on shamanism has been significantly revised, providing a fuller historical description. A new model, titled the "shamanic complex," has been added as a figure and in the narrative, explaining how shamanic healings take place. Updates include current statistics on female genital mutilation. In the section on the functions of religion, we have added the point that people often turn to religion in the hope of reaching a specific goal, such as the healing of physical, emotional, and social ills, drawing a direct link to the chapter's Original Study, "Healing among the Ju/'hoansi of the Kalahari." This chapter's Anthropology Applied box, "Reconciling Modern Medicine with Traditional Beliefs in Swaziland," focusing on the work of Edward Green, has been updated with his input.

Chapter 14: The Arts

The key categories of art—visual (formerly referred to as pictoral), verbal, and music—have been resequenced for the sake of verbal flow. In the visual art section, the comparison of traditional and modern Western art has been expanded to include a discussion of traditional kinship motifs as described by art historian Carl Schuster and anthropologist Edmund Carpenter. Also expanded is the discussion on Navajo sand paintings. And the former "Functions of Music" section has been developed into a more inclusive "Functions of Art." A totally new section, "Art, Globalization, and Cultural Survival," investigates how threatened indigenous groups use aesthetic traditions as part of a cultural survival strategy. The role of traditional wood-splint basketry in the Aroostook Micmac Indians' federal recognition effort is presented as an example. The Anthropology Applied feature, "Protecting Cultural Heritages," profiling Richard Lerner's work with Pomo Indians in California, has been revised and updated with his input. In addition, readers will find a new and lively Original Study on a modern tattoo community by Margo DeMello and an Anthropologists of Note box about Frederica de Laguna's work among the Tlingit of Yakutat, Alaska.

Chapter 15: Processes of Change

The themes and terminology of globalization are woven through this chapter, which includes numerous retooled definitions that distinguish progress from modernization, rebellion from revolution, and acculturation from enculturation. The discussion on acculturation now includes clarifying details about the Kayapo Indians' successful push to get Brazilian authorities to recommend policy changes that could positively impact indigenous peoples. To the section on genocide, we have added recent examples, as well as the estimated total number of people who died of genocide and tyranny in the 20th century. The "Directed Change" section features an expanded exploration of practical anthropology, noting its various names—from "action" anthropology to "committed," "engaged," "involved," and "advocacy." The narrative on Skolt Lapps and the snowmobile revolution has been significantly reworked, providing historical perspective and clarifying when different cultural traditions have been practiced. Updating the various parts of the "Modernization" section, we have shifted the discussion from modernization to globalization, setting the stage for a thorough overview of today's globalized world in the book's final chapter. Changes in the boxed features include a new Anthropologist of Note on Eric Wolf, a thoroughly updated and revised Anthropology Applied piece on the work of Michael Horowitz at the Institute

for Development Anthropology, and a shorter, more reader friendly version of the Original Study "Violence against Indians in Brazil." Finally, this chapter features two new world maps: one showing refugee populations around the world and one showing country GNPs and locations of armed conflict.

Chapter 16: Global Challenges, Local Responses, and the Role of Anthropology

This extensively reworked chapter brings the text soundly into the 21st century and the age of globalization. Beginning with the preview questions and introductory paragraphs, the point is quickly driven home that anthropology has a role to play in solving the increasingly overwhelming problems brought on by globalization, as well as the opportunities presented by an evermore interconnected world. Several terms have been added or redefined: pluralistic society, multiculturalism, structural power, hard power, soft power, and structural violence. To the section on global culture we have added an overview of the counterforce to Westernization—growing nationalism and the breakup of multi-ethnic states. In the section titled "Global Culture: A Good Idea or Not?" we have added a paragraph about some of the positive aspects of globalization. The ethnic resurgence section includes several brief examples of resistance to globalization, from protests against policies of the World Trade Organization to demonstrations against the environmentally degrading practices of multinational companies. The discussion of cultural pluralism builds on revised and clear definitions of pluralistic societies and multiculturalism, presented from a historical perspective. Brief descriptions of several contrasting examples of multicultural societies (and emerging multicultural societies) have been woven into this section. The section on the rise of global corporations (changed from "multinational" corporations) now highlights the largest corporations, places them in a historical context, and presents compelling statistics, such as the fact that today's top 100 companies control 33 percent of the world's assets but employ just 1 percent of the world's workforce. This section also features two new paragraphs about the vast expansion of global media corporations and the emergence of a global media environment. This leads into a new Anthropologists of Note feature on Arjun Appadurai, who coined the term *global mediascape*. A fully new section titled "Structural Power in the Age of Globalization" paints a vivid picture of our world as it is today, revealing the ever-widening gap between those who have wealth and power and those who do not. It defines and illustrates the term *structural power* and its two branches—hard power (military and economic might) and soft power (media might that gains control through ideological influence). The section "Problems of Structural Violence" is more tangible because it comes on the heels of the new structural power section and includes a carefully crafted definition of structural violence, which is tied to structural power. The section on hunger and obesity features not only the latest statistics but includes a new paragraph on the widespread epidemic of obesity. A startling contrast to the commentary on world hunger, this section notes that there are now more overfed people in the world than those who are underfed. This section also includes a new discussion of the impact that North American and European farm subsidies have on small farmers around the world. New information about PCB poisoning has been added to the section on pollution, along with predictions concerning global warming. The section titled "The Culture of Discontent" touches on the psychological problems born of powerful marketing messages that shape cultural standards concerning the ideal human body. The Original Study "Standardizing the Body" features a new figure with the latest available statistics concerning extreme cosmetic procedures. The chapter's new conclusion focuses on the role that individuals, and anthropologists in particular, can play in addressing the many challenges of our globalized world. New figures include a bar graph comparing the wealth of states and corporations and several world maps showing global migrations, pollution, energy consumption per capita, and population density.

New Original Studies

Three of the sixteen Original Studies in the eleventh edition are entirely new, and almost all of the others have been revised and updated. The new studies are: Chapter 1—"Fighting HIV/AIDS in Africa: Traditional Healers on the Front Line," by Suzanne Leclerc-Madlala; Chapter 3—"Reconciliation and Its Cultural Modification in Primates," by Frans de Waal; Chapter 14—"The Modern Tattoo Community," by Margo DeMello.

New Anthropology Applied

The eleventh edition features fifteen Anthropology Applied boxes. Building on the strength of the profiles that appeared in the tenth edition, we contacted the anthropologists whose work was featured in order to bring their stories up to date. In addition to the resulting revisions, we feature an entirely new Anthropology Applied box, "Anthropology in the Corporate Jungle," in Chapter 7.

New Anthropologists of Note

Of the nineteen Anthropologists of Note profiles, seven are new to the eleventh edition, reflecting the global diversity of anthropologists and their perspectives: Chapter 1—Yolanda Moses; Chapter 2—Eleanor Leacock; Chapter 3—Kinji Imanishi; Chapter 7—Jomo Kenyatta; Chapter 12—Laura Nader; Chapter 15—Eric Wolf; Chapter 16—Arjun Appadurai. In addition, Chapter 1 features a large photo and lengthy caption about anthropologist Jayasinhji Jhala from northeastern India.

Biocultural Connections

Four Biocultural Connection boxes have been introduced to this edition. They cover a range of topics, illustrating how cultural and biological processes work together to shape human biology, beliefs, and behavior. Topics covered: Chapter 1—"The Anthropology of Organ Transplantation"; Chapter 4—"The Biology of Human Speech"; Chapter 8—"Marriage Prohibitions in the United States"; Chapter 11—"African Burial Ground Project."

PRINT SUPPLEMENTS

In keeping with the eleventh edition's recognition that the use of many messages requires many media, the selection of ancillaries accompanying *Cultural Anthropology* should meet most instructors' needs.

A separate Study Guide is provided to aid comprehension of the textbook material. Each chapter begins with concise learning objectives and then offers chapter exercises, review questions, and a glossary review to help students achieve these objectives. This supplement also includes hints on reading anthropology texts and studying for tests.

An Instructor's Manual offers teaching objectives and lecture and class activity suggestions that correspond to each chapter of the textbook. This manual includes a Resource Integration Guide showing how and where to use various supplements to the text including multimedia, videos, and enrichment material. Each chapter of the Instructor's Manual features a chapter synopsis; student learning objectives; a chapter review, brief descriptions of chapter feature pieces; key terms; suggestions for exercises, assignments, and research topics; as well as a list of additional resources for instructors including films and ancillary readings. Included with the manual is the book-specific MultiMedia Manager Instructor Resource CD-ROM, which contains digital media and Microsoft PowerPoint presentations for the text, placing images, lectures, and video clips at your fingertips. An extensive Test Bank, available in both printed and computerized forms, offers more than 1,200 multiple choice and true/false questions.

MULTIMEDIA SUPPLEMENTS

There are several videos available to accompany the text, including *Millennium: Tribal Wisdom and the Modern World,* hosted by anthropologist David Maybury-Lewis, which presents a thoughtful exploration of cultures across the world. Many issues are covered, including indigenous rights, definitions of gender and gender roles, and the construction of the self. Instructors can choose from ten 60-minute programs.

In addition, *Faces of Culture,* prepared by Coast Telecourses in Fountain Valley, California, through the Coastline Community College District, has been an important part of *Cultural Anthropology* since 1983. Most of the twenty-six half-hour programs focus on key anthropological concepts, while several episodes are devoted to presenting rich ethnographic detail on specific cultures. These videos are available for standalone use or in the context of a telecourse. A Telecourse Study Guide is also available.

Acknowledgments

All of us have benefited from the anthropologists with whom we studied at the University of Pennsylvania, the New School for Social Research, City University of New York, Nijmegen University, and Columbia University, not to mention those with whom we have collaborated in research or discussed issues of common interest. They are too numerous to mention here but include colleagues at the various colleges and universities where we have taught. Bill and Dana owe a particular debt to their spouses, Anita de Laguna Haviland and Peter Bingham, not to mention their children, for putting up with their preoccupation with the book. (As spouses, Harald and Bunny's debts on this front balanced each other out.) In addition, Anita has performed valiantly over three decades, doing the typing and later the word processing for previous editions and also offering valuable ideas, criticism, and encouragement as needed. Without her, this enterprise would have collapsed several editions ago.

As new co-authors, Harald, Dana, and Bunny would like to thank Bill for inviting them to participate in this enterprise, for it has brought numerous insights to all of us. Specific thanks, too, to Martin Ottenheimer who reviewed the marriage and kinship chapters; Harriet Ottenheimer for her input on the language chapter; Erin Sawicki who ably kept track of innumerable details in Chapters 2 through 13 as part of her studies in anthropology; Debbie Hedrick for her cheerful help in clerical matters; and a series of introductory anthropology teaching assistants who, through the years, have shed light on effective ways to reach new generations of students. We are grateful to Janet Benson and Donna Roper for their work on the Instructors' Manuals and helpful comments on details within various chapters, and also to M. L. Miranda for his work on the Study Guide and Test Bank. And we extend special thanks to those who wrote or revised special boxed features for the eleventh edition and those who provided visual pieces for the CD-ROM.

Thanks are also due the anthropologists who made suggestions for this edition. They include:

Brenda Benefit, New Mexico State University
Barrett P. Brenton, St. John's University
Gregory Campbell, University of Montana
AnnCorinne Freter-Abrams, Ohio University
Jeanne Humble, Lexington Community College
Barry Kass, SUNY Orange
William Loker, California State University, Chico
Ramona Perez, San Diego State University
Richard Veit, Monmouth University
Matthew Westra, Longview Community College
John Wolford, University of Missouri, St. Louis
Robert A. Wortham, North Carolina Central University

All of their comments were carefully considered; how we have responded to them has been determined by our own perspectives of anthropology, as well as our combined decades of experience with undergraduate students. Therefore, neither they nor any of the other anthropologists mentioned here should be held responsible for any shortcomings in this book.

Helpful in seeing this edition through to publication have been our editors at Wadsworth—in particular, Lin Marshall. As textbook authors, we feel extremely fortunate to have had an editor such as Lin who is trained as an anthropologist and brings unusual knowledge, passion, and social insights to her work. We also wish to thank Wadsworth's skilled editorial, design, and production team: Nicole Root, Assistant Editor; Kelly McMahon, Editorial Assistant; Dee Dee Zobian, Technology Product Manager; Matthew Wright, Senior Marketing Manager; Catherine Morris, Project Editor; Eve Howard, Vice President and Editor-in-Chief; Sean Wakely, President; and Susan Badger, CEO. In addition to their help, we had the advantage of working with several freelancers: our able, considerate copyeditor Jennifer Gordon; our diligent, go-the-distance photo researcher Sandra Lord (and her assistant Sue Howard); our illustrator Carol Zuber-Mallison who cheered up many a late night with her humorous email messages and excellent work. We hold special thanks for Robin Lockwood who brought patience, grace, and a keen eye to her coordinating tasks in production service.

William A. Haviland
Harald E. L. Prins
Dana Walrath
Bunny McBride

Putting the World in Perspective

Although all humans that we know about are capable of producing accurate sketches of localities and regions with which they are familiar, CARTOGRAPHY (the craft of mapmaking as we know it today) had its beginnings in 13th century Europe, and its subsequent development is related to the expansion of Europeans to all parts of the globe. From the beginning, there have been two problems with maps: the technical one of how to depict on a two-dimensional, flat surface a three-dimensional spherical object, and the cultural one of whose worldview they reflect. In fact, the two issues are inseparable, for the particular projection one uses inevitably makes a statement about how one views one's own people and their place in the world. Indeed, maps often shape our perception of reality as much as they reflect it.

In cartography, a PROJECTION refers to the system of intersecting lines (of longitude and latitude) by which part or all of the globe is represented on a flat surface. There are more than 100 different projections in use today, ranging from polar perspectives to interrupted "butterflies" to rectangles to heart shapes. Each projection causes distortion in size, shape, or distance in some way or another. A map that shows the shape of land masses correctly will of necessity misrepresent the size. A map that is accurate along the equator will be deceptive at the poles.

Perhaps no projection has had more influence on the way we see the world than that of Gerhardus Mercator, who devised his map in 1569 as a navigational aid for mariners. So well suited was Mercator's map for this purpose that it continues to be used for navigational charts today. At the same time, the Mercator projection became a standard for depicting land masses, something for which it was never intended. Although an accurate navigational tool, the Mercator projection greatly exaggerates the size of land masses in higher latitudes, giving about two-thirds of the map's surface to the northern hemisphere. Thus, the lands occupied by Europeans and European descendants appear far larger than those of other people. For example, North America (19 million square kilometers) appears almost twice the size of Africa (30 million square kilometers), while Europe is shown as equal in size to South America, which actually has nearly twice the land mass of Europe.

A map developed in 1805 by Karl B. Mollweide was one of the earlier equal-area projections of the world. Equal-area projections portray land masses in correct rel-

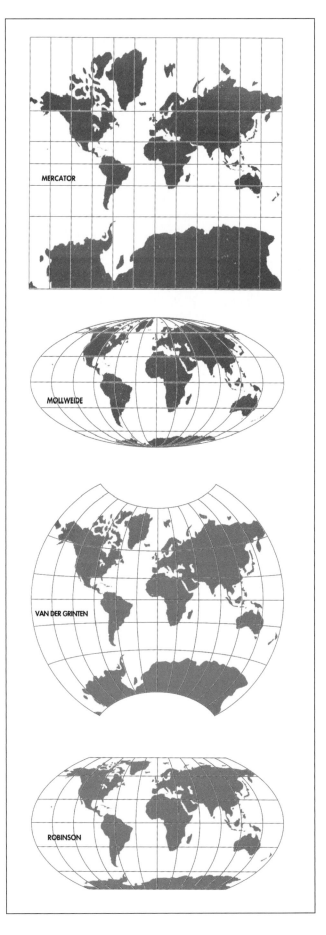

ative size, but, as a result, distort the shape of continents more than other projections. They most often compress and warp lands in the higher latitudes and vertically stretch land masses close to the equator. Other equal-area projections include the Lambert Cylindrical Equal-Area Projection (1772), the Hammer Equal-Area Projection (1892), and the Eckert Equal-Area Projection (1906).

The Van der Grinten Projection (1904) was a compromise aimed at minimizing both the distortions of size in the Mercator and the distortion of shape in equal-area maps such as the Mollweide. Allthough an improvement, the lands of the northern hemisphere are still emphasized at the expense of the southern. For example, in the Van der Grinten, the Commonwealth of Independent States (the former Soviet Union) and Canada are shown at more than twice their relative size.

The Robinson Projection, which was adopted by the National Geographic Society in 1988 to replace the Van der Grinten, is one of the best compromises to date between the distortion of size and shape. Although an improvement over the Van der Grinten, the Robinson projection still depicts lands in the northern latitudes as proportionally larger at the same time that it depicts lands in the lower latitudes (representing most third-world nations) as proportionally smaller. Like European maps before it, the Robinson projection places Europe at the center of the map with the Atlantic Ocean and the Americas to the left, emphasizing the cultural connection between Europe and North America, while neglecting the geographical closeness of northwestern North America to northeast Asia.

The following pages show four maps that each convey quite different "cultural messages." Included among them is the Peters Projection, an equal-area map that has been adopted as the official map of UNESCO (the United Nations Educational, Scientific, and Cultural Organization), and a map made in Japan, showing us how the world looks from the other side.

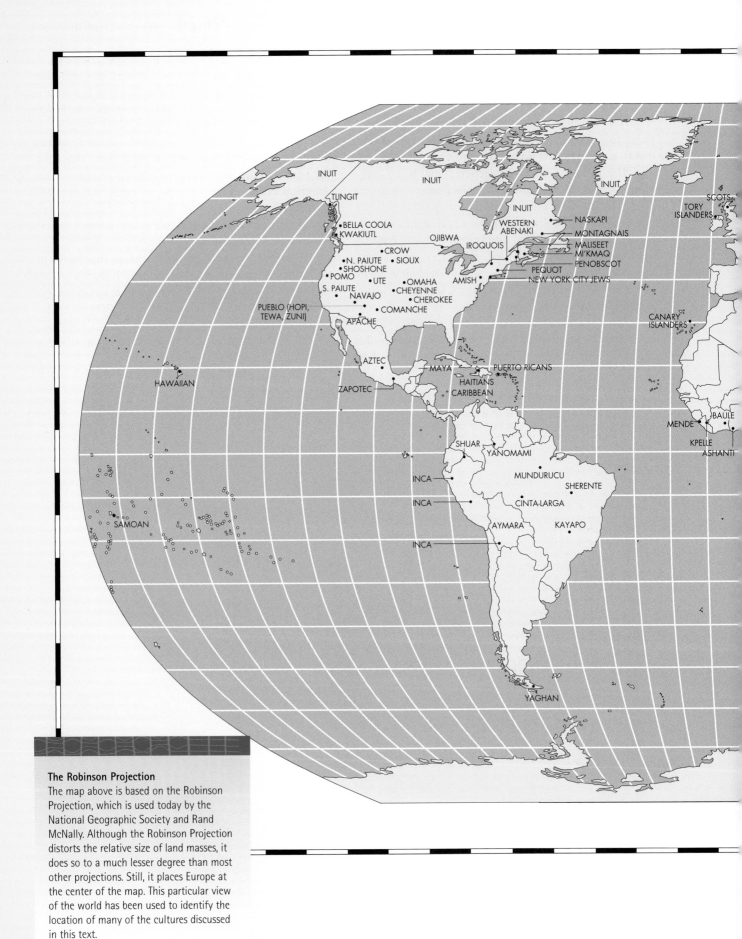

The Robinson Projection
The map above is based on the Robinson Projection, which is used today by the National Geographic Society and Rand McNally. Although the Robinson Projection distorts the relative size of land masses, it does so to a much lesser degree than most other projections. Still, it places Europe at the center of the map. This particular view of the world has been used to identify the location of many of the cultures discussed in this text.

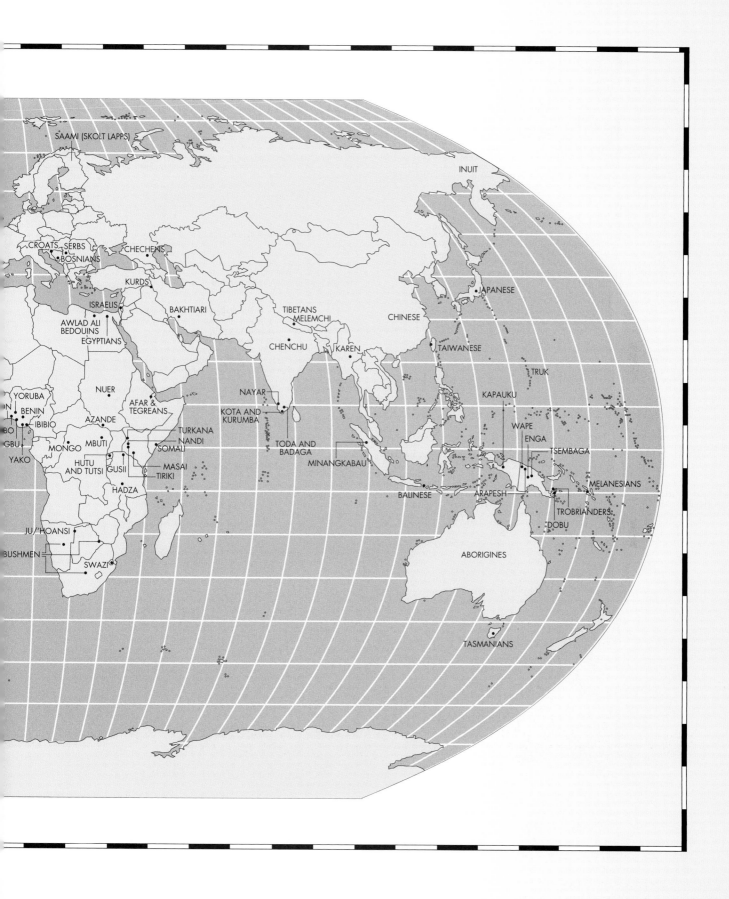

The Peters Projection

The map above is based on the Peters Projection, which has been adopted as the official map of UNESCO. While it distorts the shape of continents (countries near the equator are vertically elongated by a ratio of two to one), the Peters Projection does show all continents according to their correct relative size. Though Europe is still at the center, it is not shown as larger and more extensive than the third world.

CZECHOSLOVAKIA
STRIA
SWEDEN
FINLAND
ESTONIA
AZERBAIJAN
LATVIA
ARMENIA
LITHUANIA
POLAND BELARUS
GEORGIA
ROMANIA
UKRAINE
HUNGARY
MOLDOVA
SERBIA
BULGARIA
MONTENEGRO
MACEDONIA
ALBANIA
GREECE
TURKEY
BOSNIA-
HERZEGOVINA SYRIA
CROATIA
LEBANON
ISRAEL
LIBYA
JORDAN
KUWAIT
EGYPT
QATAR
SAUDI
ARABIA
OMAN
UNITED
ARAB
EMIRATES
YEMEN
DJIBOUTI
CHAD
SUDAN
CENTRAL
AFRICAN
REPUBLIC
ETHIOPIA
CAMEROON
SOMALIA
GABON
UGANDA
CONGO
KENYA
RWANDA
BURUNDI
DEMOCRATIC
REPUBLIC OF
TANZANIA
CONGO
MALAWI
ANGOLA
ZAMBIA
NAMIBIA
MADAGASCAR
BOTS-
WANA
ZIMBABWE
MOZAMBIQUE
SWAZILAND
LESOTHO
SOUTH
AFRICA

IRAQ
IRAN
BAHRAIN
PAKISTAN

UZBEKISTAN
TURKMENISTAN
AFGHAN-
ISTAN

KAZAKHSTAN
KIRGHIZSTAN
TAJIKISTAN

RUSSIA

MONGOLIA

PEOPLE'S REPUBLIC
OF CHINA

NORTH
KOREA
SOUTH
KOREA
JAPAN

BHUTAN
NEPAL
INDIA
MYANMAR
TAIWAN
BANGLA-
DESH
LAOS
THAILAND
VIETNAM
PHILIPPINES
CAMBODIA
SRI LANKA
BRUNEI
MALAYSIA
SINGAPORE
INDONESIA

PAPUA
NEW
GUINEA

AUSTRALIA

NEW ZEALAND

ANTARCTICA

xxix

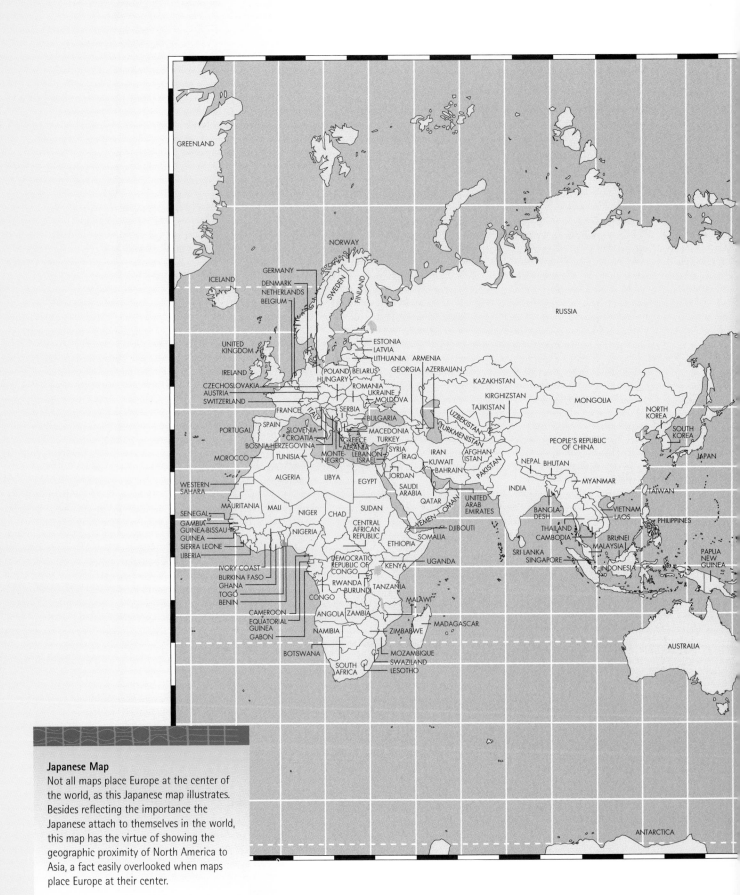

Japanese Map

Not all maps place Europe at the center of the world, as this Japanese map illustrates. Besides reflecting the importance the Japanese attach to themselves in the world, this map has the virtue of showing the geographic proximity of North America to Asia, a fact easily overlooked when maps place Europe at their center.

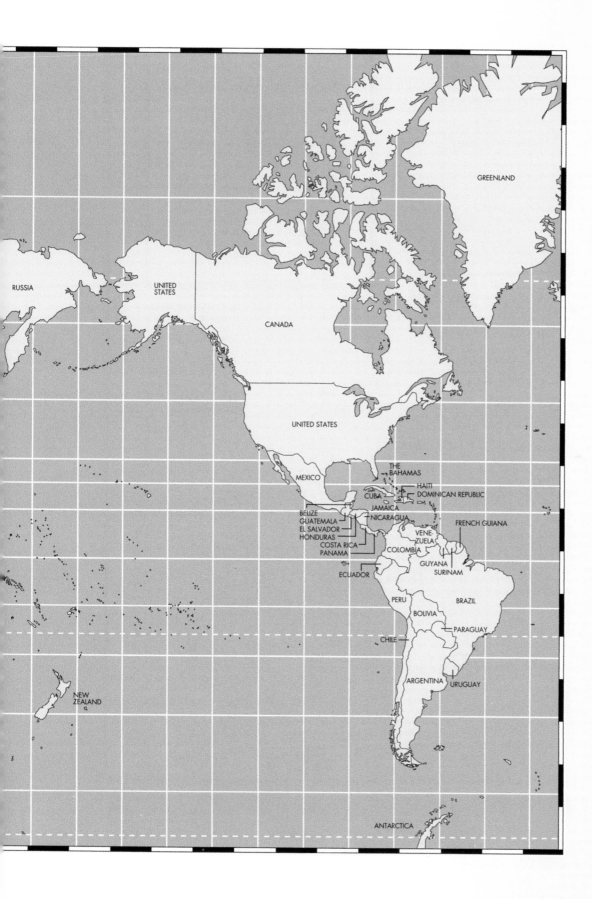

RUSSIA

UNITED
STATES

CANADA

GREENLAND

UNITED STATES

MEXICO

THE
BAHAMAS

HAITI
DOMINICAN REPUBLIC

CUBA

JAMAICA

BELIZE
GUATEMALA
EL SALVADOR
HONDURAS
COSTA RICA
PANAMA

NICARAGUA

VENE-
ZUELA

COLOMBIA

FRENCH GUIANA

GUYANA
SURINAM

ECUADOR

PERU

BRAZIL

BOLIVIA

PARAGUAY

CHILE

NEW
ZEALAND

ARGENTINA

URUGUAY

ANTARCTICA

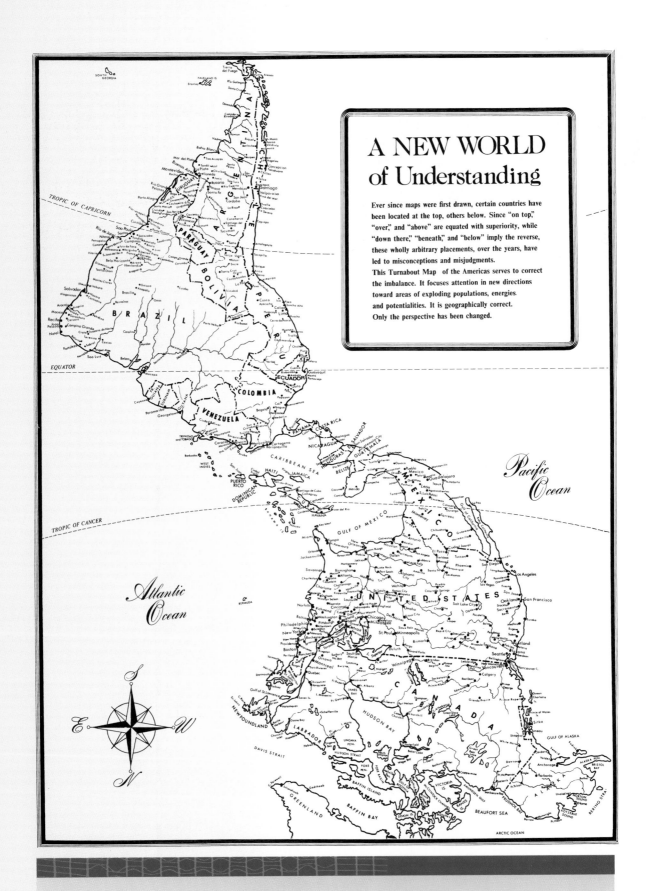

A NEW WORLD of Understanding

Ever since maps were first drawn, certain countries have been located at the top, others below. Since "on top," "over," and "above" are equated with superiority, while "down there," "beneath," and "below" imply the reverse, these wholly arbitrary placements, over the years, have led to misconceptions and misjudgments.

This Turnabout Map of the Americas serves to correct the imbalance. It focuses attention in new directions toward areas of exploding populations, energies and potentialities. It is geographically correct. Only the perspective has been changed.

The Turnabout Map

The way maps may reflect (and influence) our thinking is exemplified by the "Turnabout Map," which places the South Pole at the top and the North Pole at the bottom. Words and phrases such as "on top," "over," and "above" tend to be equated by some people with superiority. Turning things upside down may cause us to rethink the way North Americans regard themselves in relation to the people of Central America. © 1982 by Jesse Levine Turnabout Map™—Dist. by Laguna Sales, Inc., 7040 Via Valverde, San Jose, CA 95135

Cultural Anthropology
The Human Challenge

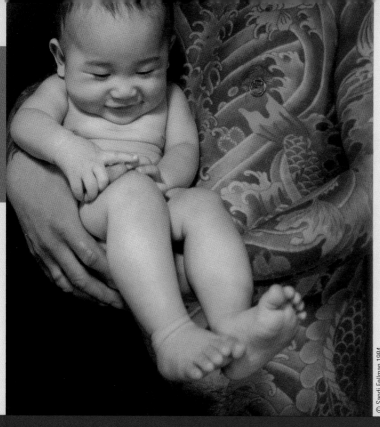

© Sandi Fellman 1984

PART 1

Anthropology
The Challenge of Knowing Humanity

Chapter 1
The Essence of Anthropology

Chapter 2
The Characteristics of Culture

Chapter 3
The Beginnings of Human Culture

Introduction

Anthropology is the most liberating of all the sciences. Not only has it exposed the fallacies of racial and cultural superiority, but its devotion to the study of all peoples, everywhere and throughout time, has cast more light on human nature than all the reflections of sages or the studies of laboratory scientists. This may sound like the assertion of an overly enthusiastic anthropologist; however, it is a statement made by the philosopher Grace de Laguna in her 1941 presidential address to the Eastern Division of the American Philosophical Association.

The subject matter of anthropology is vast, as we shall see in the first three chapters of this book: It includes everything that has to do with human beings, past and present. Of course, many other disciplines are concerned in one way or another with humans. Some, such as anatomy and physiology, study our species as biological organisms. The social sciences are concerned with the distinctive forms of human relationships, while the humanities examine the achievements in human cultures. Anthropologists are interested in all of these things, too, but they try to deal with them all together, in all places and times. It is this unique, broad, and holistic perspective that equips anthropologists so well to deal with that elusive thing called human nature.

Needless to say, no single anthropologist is able to investigate personally everything that has to do with humanity. For practical purposes, the discipline is divided into various subfields, and individual anthropologists specialize in one or more of these. Whatever their specialization, though, they retain a commitment to a broader, overall perspective on humankind. For example, cultural anthropologists specialize in the study of human ideas, values, and behavior, while physical anthropologists specialize in the study of humans as biological organisms. Yet neither can afford to ignore the work of the other, for human culture and nature are inextricably intertwined, with each affecting the other in important ways. The fact that we are nature-culture beings is evident in the photograph of the famous Japanese tattoo artist Horiyoshi III holding his newborn son. Every one of us comes into the world in a natural state with a biological profile, but over time we acquire cultural identity—etched

Scala/Art Resource, NY

into our minds and sometimes into our very skin.

There are countless examples of our species' biocultural connection. For example, in certain parts of Africa and Asia, when humans took up the practice of farming, they altered the natural environment in a way that, by chance, created ideal conditions for the breeding of mosquitoes. As a result, malaria became a serious problem (mosquitoes carry the malarial parasite), and a biological response to this was the spread of certain genes that, in those people living in malarial areas who inherit the gene from one parent, produced a built-in resistance to the disease. Although those who inherit the gene from both parents contract a poten-

tially lethal anemia, such as sickle-cell anemia, those without the gene are vulnerable to malaria. Biology in turn impacts cultural practices, including food choice and folklore. For instance, consider the relationship between fava beans and malaria. Although fava beans contain substances that are potentially toxic to humans, these substances also interfere with the development of the parasite that causes malaria in human red blood cells. In cultures around the Mediterranean Sea where malaria is common, fava beans are incorporated into the diet through foods eaten at the height of the malaria season. The simultaneous toxic effect of fava beans in some genetically susceptible individuals has led to a rich folklore about this simple food, including the ancient Greek belief that fava beans contain the souls of the dead. So it is that we humans have one leg in culture and the other in nature, and in the interplay of both our destinies unfold.

To begin our study of cultural anthropology, we will look at how it fits within the general field of anthropology. Chapter 1 surveys the scope of anthropology, marking out its main subfields and showing how they relate to one another and to the other sciences and humanities. In Chapter 2 we will turn our attention to our discipline's core concept of culture, exploring the meaning of the term and its significance for human individuals and societies. We will conclude Part 1 with a chapter that investigates how culture originated and gained primacy over biological change as our species' mechanism for solving the problems of existence. We will see how cultural evolution has its roots in biological evolution and how the dynamic interplay between cultural and biological processes is fundamental in making humans the kind of creatures they are today. With these concerns covered, we will have set the stage for a detailed look at the subject matter of cultural anthropology.

CHAPTER 1

The Essence of Anthropology

Bani Malek Dist.

Always Remember That Your Family Is Waiting For You

© Jodi Cobb/National Geographic Image Collection

©Anup and Manoj Shah

© James L. Stanfield/National Geographic Image Collection

© George H. H. Huey/Corbis

CHALLENGE ISSUE

IT IS A CHALLENGE TO DISCERN ONE'S PLACE IN THE WORLD. Humans are just one of 10 million species. But among these, including 4,000 fellow mammals, we humans are the only ones biologically capable of studying ourselves and the world around us. We do this not only because we are curious, but also because knowledge helps us create and improve our living conditions and make adjustments necessary for survival. Adaptations based on knowledge are essential in every culture, and culture is our species' ticket to survival. Made possible by means of sophisticated communication, human cultures emerged as our ancestors developed the physical capacity for complex language and tool use. The comprehensive study of human development and cultures, past and present, is the business of anthropology.

1 What Is Anthropology?

Anthropology, the study of humankind everywhere, throughout time, seeks to produce reliable knowledge about the things that make people different from one another and the things they all share in common.

2 What Do Anthropologists Do?

Anthropologists do their work within four basic subfields of the discipline. Physical anthropologists focus on humans as biological organisms, tracing the evolutionary development of humankind and looking at biological variations within the species, past and present. Cultural anthropologists are concerned with human cultures, past and present. Meanwhile, archaeologists try to recover information about human cultures—usually from the past and especially those that have left no written records—by studying material objects, skeletal remains, and settlements. Finally, linguists study languages, human communication systems by which cultures are maintained and passed on to succeeding generations. Though each of these four subfields has its own research strategies, they rely upon one another and are united by a common anthropological perspective on the human condition.

3 How Do Anthropologists Do What They Do?

Anthropologists, like other scholars, are concerned with the description and explanation of reality. They formulate and test hypotheses—tentative explanations of observed phenomena—concerning humankind. Their aim is to develop reliable theories—explanations supported by bodies of data—about our species. In order to frame objective hypotheses that are as free of cultural bias as possible, anthropologists typically develop them through "fieldwork," a particular kind of hands-on research that makes them so familiar with the minute details of the situation that they can begin to recognize patterns inherent in the data. It is also through fieldwork that anthropologists test existing hypotheses.

For as long as they have been on earth, people have sought answers to questions about who they are, where they come from, and why they act as they do. Throughout most of human history, though, people relied on myth and folklore for answers, rather than the systematic testing of data obtained through careful observation. Anthropology, over the last 150 years, has emerged as a tradition of scientific inquiry with its own approach to answering these questions. Simply stated, **anthropology** is the study of humankind in all times and places. The anthropologist is concerned primarily with a single species, *Homo sapiens*—the human species, its ancestors, and near relatives. Because anthropologists are members of the species being studied, it can be difficult for them to maintain a scientific detachment toward those they study. This, of course, is part of a larger problem in science where our own cultural ideas and values may impact our approaches to research. In the words of the great German writer-naturalist Goethe: "We see only what we know."

If it's true, as the old saying goes, that we are prone to see what lies behind our eyes rather than what appears before them, can anthropologists who are part of the very humanity they study ever hope to gain truly objective knowledge about people? While concerned about this, anthropologists have found that by maintaining a critical awareness of their assumptions, and constantly testing their conclusions against new sources of data, they can achieve a useful understanding of human thought and behavior. By scientifically approaching how people live and think, anthropologists have learned a great deal about human differences, as well as the many things humans have in common.

MEDIATREK

For information on subdisciplines—such as urban, feminist, and ecological anthropology—plus profiles of theorists, see MediaTrek 1.1 on the companion Web site or CD-ROM.

THE DEVELOPMENT OF ANTHROPOLOGY

Although works of anthropological significance have a considerable antiquity—two examples being cross-cultural accounts of people written by the Greek historian Herodotus about 2,500 years ago and the North African scholar Ibn Khaldun nearly 700 years ago—anthropology as a distinct field of inquiry is a relatively

anthropology The study of humankind in all times and places.

recent product of Western civilization. In the United States, for example, the first course in general anthropology to carry credit in a college or university (at the University of Rochester in New York) was not offered until 1879. If people have always been concerned about themselves and their origins, and those of other people, why then did it take such a long time for a systematic discipline of anthropology to appear?

The answer to this is as complex as human history. In part, it relates to the limits of human technology. Throughout most of history, people have been restricted in their geographical horizons. Without the means of traveling to distant parts of the world, observation of cultures and peoples far from one's own was a difficult—if not impossible—undertaking. Extensive travel was usually the exclusive privilege of a few; the study of foreign peoples and cultures was not likely to flourish until improved modes of transportation and communication could be developed.

This is not to say that people have always been unaware of the existence of others in the world who look and act differently from themselves. The Old and New Testaments of the Bible, for example, are full of references to diverse ancient peoples, among them Babylonians, Egyptians, Greeks, Jews, and Syrians. However, the differences among these people pale by comparison to those between any of the more recent European nations and (for example) traditional indigenous peoples of the Pacific islands, the Amazon rainforest, or Siberia. Using new inventions such as the compass aboard better-equipped sailing ships, it became easier to travel to truly faraway places and meet for the first time such radically different groups. It was the massive encounter with hitherto unknown peoples—which began 500 years ago as Europeans sought to extend their trade and political domination to all parts of the world—that focused attention on human differences in all their amazing variety.

Another significant element that contributed to the emergence of anthropology was that Europeans gradually came to recognize that despite all the differences, they might share a basic "humanity" with people everywhere. Initially, Europeans labeled societies that did not share their fundamental cultural values as "savage" or "barbarian." In the course of time, however, Europeans came to recognize such highly diverse groups as fellow members of one species and therefore relevant to an understanding of what it is to be human and of their collective place in world history. This growing interest in human diversity, coming at a time when there were increasing efforts to explain things in scientific terms of natural laws, cast doubts on the traditional explanations based on authoritative texts such as the Torah, Bible, or Koran and helped set the stage for the birth of anthropology.

Although anthropology originated within the historical context of European culture, it has long since gone global. Today, it is an exciting, transnational discipline whose practitioners come from a wide array of societies all around the world. Even societies that have long been studied by European and North American anthropologists—several African and Native American societies, for example—have produced anthropologists who have made and continue to make a mark on the discipline. Their distinct perspectives shed new light not

only on their own cultures, but also on those of others. It is noteworthy that in one regard diversity has long been a hallmark of the discipline: From its earliest days both women and men have entered the field. Throughout this text, we will be featuring the work of individual anthropologists, illustrating their diversity, as well as that of their work.

ANTHROPOLOGY AND OTHER ACADEMIC DISCIPLINES

Anthropologists are not the only scholars who study people, but they are uniquely holistic in their approach. They do not think of their findings in isolation from those of other social or natural scientists— psychologists, economists, sociologists, biologists, and so on. Rather, they welcome the contributions researchers from these other disciplines have to make to the common goal of understanding humanity, and they gladly offer their own findings for the benefit of these other disciplines. Anthropologists do not expect, for example, to know as much about the structure of the human eye as anatomists, or as much about the perception of color as psychologists. As synthesizers, however, they are better prepared than any of their fellow scientists to understand how these relate to color-naming practices in different human societies. Because they look for the broad basis of human ideas and practices without limiting themselves to any single social or biological aspect, anthropologists can acquire an especially expansive and inclusive overview of the complex biological and cultural organism that is the human being.

One could say physical anthropology is closely related to the biological sciences just as cultural anthropology is closely related to the other social sciences and the humanities, however it is the integration of these two approaches that characterizes anthropology. The social science to which cultural anthropology has most often been compared is sociology, since both are concerned with describing and explaining the behavior of people within a social context. Sociologists, however, have concentrated heavily on studies of contemporary people living in industrialized North American and European (commonly known as Western) societies, while anthropologists have traditionally focused on non-Western tribal peoples and cultures, past and present. As anthropology developed, its practitioners found that to fully understand the complexities of human ideas, behavior, and biology, all humans, wherever and whenever, must be studied. More than any other feature, this unique cross-cultural and long-term historical perspective distinguishes anthropology from the other social sciences. It guards against the danger that theories of

© Documentary Educational Resources

Anthropologists come from many corners of the world and carry out research in a huge variety of cultures all around the globe. Dr. Jayasinhji Jhala hails from the old city of Dhrangadhra in Gujarat, northeast India. A member of the Jhala clan of Rajputs, an aristocratic caste of warriors, he grew up in the royal palace of his father, the maharaja. After earning a bachelor of arts degree in India, he came to the United States and earned a master's degree in visual studies from the Massachusetts Institute of Technology, followed by a Ph.D. in anthropology from Harvard. Currently a professor and director of the programs of Visual Anthropology and the Visual Anthropology Media Laboratory at Temple University, he returns regularly to India with students to film cultural traditions in his own caste-stratified society.

Anthropologists of Note

Matilda Coxe Stevenson (1849–1915) ▪ Yolanda Moses (1946–)

Among the founders of North American anthropology were a number of women, whose work was highly influential among 19th-century women's rights advocates. One such pioneering anthropologist was Matilda Coxe Stevenson, who also did field-work among the Zuni. In 1885, she founded the Women's Anthropological Society, the first professional association for women scientists. Three years later, hired by the Bureau of American Ethnology, she became one of the first women in the United States to receive a full-time position in science.

The tradition of women being active in anthropology continues. In fact, since World War II more than half the presidents of the now 12,000-member American Anthropological Association have been women. In 1996, Dr. Yolanda Moses became the first African American to hold that high office. A specialist on cultural diversity, she has done field-work in Alaska, the Caribbean, and East Africa. Since earning her Ph.D. from the University of California, Riverside, in 1976, Dr. Moses has taught at various universities. In 1993, she became president of The City College of New York, followed by three years as president of the American Association of Higher Education. She serves on the boards of numerous international associations and corporations, as well as editorial boards of major academic journals, and she remains tireless in her conviction that anthropologists have a major role to play in educating a wider public about cultural pluralism, notions of race, and diversity in education.

---

human behavior will be **culture-bound:** that is, based on assumptions about the world and reality that are part of the researcher's own particular culture. It provides a distinctly rich body of comparative data on humankind that can shed light on countless issues, past or present. As a case in point, consider the fact that infants in the United States typically sleep apart from their parents. To most North Americans, this may seem quite normal, but cross-cultural research shows that "co-sleeping," of mother and baby in particular, is the rule. Only in the past two hundred years, generally in Western industrialized societies, has it been considered proper for them to sleep apart. In fact, it amounts to a cultural experiment in child rearing.

Recent studies have shown that this unusual degree of separation of mother and infant in Western societies has important biological and cultural consequences. For one thing, it increases the length of the infant's crying bouts, which may last in excess of 3 hours a day in the child's second and third month. Some mothers incorrectly interpret the cause as a deficiency in breast milk and switch to less healthy bottle formulas, and in extreme cases, the crying may provoke physical abuse, sometimes with lethal effects. But the benefits of co-sleeping go beyond significant reductions in crying: Infants also nurse more often and three times as long per feeding; they receive more stimulation (important for brain development); and they are apparently less suscep-

tible to sudden infant death syndrome ("crib death"). There are benefits to the mother as well: Frequent nursing prevents early ovulation after childbirth, and she gets at least as much sleep as mothers who sleep without their infants.[1]

These benefits may lead one to ask: Why do so many mothers continue to sleep apart from their infants? In North America the cultural values of independence and consumerism come in to play. To begin building unique individual identities, babies are provided with rooms (or at least space) of their own. This room of one's own also provides a place to put all the toys, furniture, and other paraphernalia that signify that the parents are "good" and "caring" (and help keep the consumer economy humming along).

The emphasis anthropology places on studies of traditional, non-Western peoples has often led to findings that run counter to generally accepted opinions derived from Western studies. Thus, anthropologists were the first to demonstrate

> that the world does not divide into the pious
> and the superstitious; that there are sculptures
> in jungles and paintings in deserts; that politi-
> cal order is possible without centralized power
> and principled justice without codified rules;
> that the norms of reason were not fixed
> in Greece, the evolution of morality not

---

culture-bound Theories about the world and reality based on the assumptions and values of one's own culture.

[1]Barr, R. G. (1997, October). The crying game. *Natural History,* 47. Also, McKenna, J. J. (2002, September–October). Breastfeeding and bedsharing. *Mothering,* 28–37.

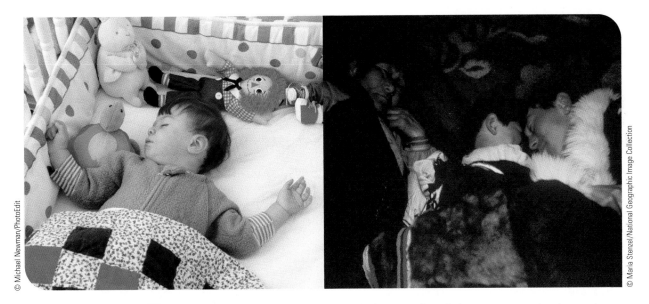

VISUAL COUNTERPOINT Although infants in the United States typically sleep apart from their parents, cross-cultural research shows that co-sleeping, of mother and baby in particular, is the rule. The photo on the right shows a Nenet family sleeping together in their *chum* (reindeer-skin tent). Nenet people are arctic reindeer pastoralists living in Siberia, Russia.

consummated in England. . . . We have, with no little success, sought to keep the world off balance; pulling out rugs, upsetting tea tables, setting off firecrackers. It has been the office of others to reassure; ours to unsettle.[2]

Although the findings of anthropologists have often challenged the conclusions of sociologists, psychologists, and economists, anthropology is absolutely indispensable to them, as it is the only consistent check against culture-bound assertions. In a sense, anthropology is to these disciplines what the laboratory is to physics and chemistry: an essential testing ground for their theories.

ANTHROPOLOGY AND ITS SUBFIELDS

As noted above, anthropology is traditionally divided into four fields: physical anthropology, archaeology, linguistic anthropology, and cultural anthropology (Figure 1.1). Each is distinct, yet they are all closely related. For example, while linguistic anthropology focuses primarily on the cultural aspects of language, it has deep connections to the evolution of human language and the biological basis of speech and language studied within physical anthropology. As anthropolo-

gists, we aim to know how biology and culture do and do not influence each other, certain that understanding what people think and do involves knowing how they are made. Each of anthropology's subfields may take a distinct approach to the study of humans, but all of them gather and analyze data that are essential to explaining similarities and differences among humans, as well as ways that people everywhere have developed and continue to change. Moreover, all of them generate knowledge that has numerous practical applications. In fact, within all four subfields we find individuals who practice **applied anthropology,** which means using anthropological knowledge and methods to solve practical problems. Examples of how anthropology is used in a wide range of problem-solving challenges appear in many chapters of this book in boxes titled Anthropology Applied.

Physical Anthropology

Physical anthropology, also called *biological anthropology,* focuses on humans as biological organisms. Traditionally, biological anthropologists concentrated on human evolution, primatology, growth and development,

---

[2]Geertz, C. (1984). Distinguished lecture: Anti anti-relativism. *American Anthropologist, 86,* 275.

applied anthropology The use of anthropological knowledge and methods to solve practical problems, often for a specific client.
physical anthropology Also known as biological anthropology. The systematic study of humans as biological organisms.

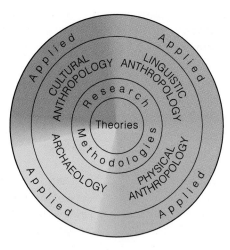

FIGURE 1.1

The four fields of anthropology. Note that the divisions between them are not sharp, indicating that their boundaries overlap. Moreover, each operates on the basis of a common body of knowledge. All four are involved in theory building, developing their own research methodologies, and solving practical problems through applied anthropology.

and human adaptation. Today, **molecular anthropology,** or the anthropological study of genes and genetic relationships, is another vital component of biological anthropology. Comparisons among groups separated by time, geography, or the frequency of a particular gene are critical to biological anthropology. As experts in the anatomy of human bones and tissues, physical anthropologists lend their knowledge about the body to applied areas such as gross anatomy laboratories and to criminal investigations.

Paleoanthropology

Human evolutionary studies focus on the biological changes through time that led to the emergence of our species. Anthropological approaches differ from other evolutionary studies in that the biological basis of human culture is its special emphasis. Whatever other distinctions people may claim for themselves, they are mammals—specifically primates—and, as such, they share a common ancestry with other primates, most specifically apes. Physical anthropologists try to reconstruct the biology and behavior of the human species in order to understand how, when, and why we became the kind of creature we

molecular anthropology A branch of biological anthropology that uses genetic and biochemical techniques to test hypotheses about human evolution, adaptation, and variation.
paleoanthropology The study of the origins and predecessors of the present human species.
primatology The study of living and fossil primates.

are today. In human evolutionary studies, physical anthropologists, known as **paleoanthropologists,** look back to the earliest primates from 55 million years ago, or even the earliest mammals some 225 million years ago, to reconstruct the complex path of human evolution.

Paleoanthropologists investigating human evolution depend principally upon analysis of the fossilized skeletons of our ancestors. Comparison of the size and shape of these fossils to the bones of living species form the basis of these analyses. Today, biochemical and genetic studies add considerably to this approach. As we will see in later chapters, genetic evidence established the close relationship between humans and ape species—chimpanzees, bonobos, and gorillas. DNA analysis has helped to estimate the origins of the human lineage some 5 to 8 million years ago. Physical anthropology therefore deals with time spans much greater than archaeology or other branches of anthropology.

Primatology

Studying the anatomy and behavior of our closest living relatives helps us understand what is unique about human nature. Therefore, **primatology,** or the study of living and fossil primates is a vital part of physical anthropology. Primates include the Asian and African apes, as well as monkeys, lemurs, lorises, and tarsiers. Biologically, humans are apes—large-bodied, broad-shouldered primates with no tail. Detailed studies of ape behavior in the wild indicate that the sharing of learned behavior is a significant part of the apes' social life. Some primatologists designate the shared, learned behavior of nonhuman apes as culture. For example, tool use and communication systems indicate the elementary basis of language in some ape societies.

© 1998 Jim Leachman

Monkeys and apes have long fascinated humans, owing to our many shared anatomical and behavioral characteristics. The study of other primates provides us with important clues as to what life may have been like for our own ancestors.

Primate studies offer scientifically grounded perspectives on the behavior of our ancestors as well as greater appreciation and respect for the sophistication of our closest living relatives. Considering that the evolution of life on earth is a fascinating story of divergence and differentiation, comparisons of the behavior and biology among living primate groups helps refine our understanding of ongoing evolutionary processes.

Human Growth, Adaptation, and Variation

Another area of research that is of interest to physical anthropologists is the study of human growth and development. Anthropologists examine biological mechanisms of growth as well as the impact of the environment on the growth process. For example, Franz Boas, a pioneer of four-field anthropology of the early 20th century, compared the heights of European immigrants who spent their childhood in "the old country" to the increased heights obtained by their children who grew up in the United States. Today, physical anthropologists study the impacts of disease, pollution, and poverty on growth. Comparisons between human and nonhuman primate growth patterns can provide clues to the evolutionary history of humans. Detailed studies of the hormonal, genetic, and physiological basis of healthy growth in living humans contribute not only to our understanding of the growth patterns of our ancestors but also contribute significantly to the health of children today.

Studies of human adaptation focus on the capacity of humans to adapt, or adjust to their material environment—biologically and culturally. This branch of physical anthropology takes a comparative approach to humans living today in a variety of environments. Humans are remarkable among the primates in that they now inhabit the entire earth. Though cultural adaptations make it possible for humans to live in some environmental extremes, biological adaptations also contribute to survival in extreme cold, heat, and high altitude. Such biological adaptation contributes to present-day human variation.

Although we are all members of a single species, we humans differ from one another in many obvious and not so obvious ways. Our differences include visible traits such as height, body build, and skin color, as well as biochemical factors such as blood type and susceptibility to certain diseases. The physical anthropologist applies all the techniques of modern biology to achieve fuller understanding of human variation and its relationship to the different environments in which people have lived. Research in this branch of anthropology has debunked false notions of racial categories born of widespread misinterpretation of human variation, a subject addressed more fully in upcoming pages. By making systematic comparisons among humans and between humans and other primates, physical anthropologists seek to arrive at scientific conclusions concerning the function and operation of human biology and culture in all times and places.

Physical anthropology has many practical applications, such as forensics. **Forensic anthropology** specializes in the identification of human skeletal remains for legal purposes. Law enforcement authorities call upon forensic anthropologists to identify murder victims, missing persons, or people who have died in disasters, such as plane crashes. From skeletal remains, the forensic anthropologist can establish the age, sex, population affiliation, and stature of the deceased, and often whether the person was right- or left-handed, exhibited any physical abnormalities, or had evidence of trauma (broken bones and the like). In addition, some details of an individual's health and nutritional history can be read from the bones (see Anthropology Applied, next page).

Archaeology

Archaeology is the branch of anthropology that studies material remains in order to describe and explain human behavior. Traditionally, it has focused on the prehistoric human past—the period before writing was invented or introduced. Since material products and traces of human practices, rather than the practices themselves, are all that survive of that past, archaeologists study the tools, pottery, and other enduring features such as hearths and enclosures that remain as the testimony of earlier cultures, some of them as many as 2.5 million years old. Surviving structures and objects, and the way they are situated in or on the ground, reflect aspects of human ideas and behavior. For example, shallow, restricted concentrations of charcoal that include oxidized earth, bone fragments, and charred plant remains, and near which are pieces of fire-cracked rock, pottery, and tools suitable for food preparation, are indicative of cooking and associated food processing. Such remains reveal much about a people's diet and subsistence practices. Moreover, the interpretation of such material remains in conjunction with skeletal remains allows for a complete biocultural reconstruction of human life in the past. Thus the archaeologist is able reach back for

forensic anthropology Field of applied physical anthropology that specializes in the identification of human skeletal remains for legal purposes.
archaeology The study of material remains, usually from the past, to describe and explain human behavior.

Anthropology Applied | Forensic Anthropology

Physical anthropologists do not just study fossil skulls. Here Clyde Snow holds the skull of a Kurd who was executed by Iraqi security forces. Snow specializes in forensic anthropology, and is widely known for his work identifying victims of state-sponsored terrorism.

Among the best-known forensic anthropologists is Clyde C. Snow. He has been practicing in this field for 40 years, first for the Federal Aviation Administration

and more recently as a freelance consultant. In addition to the usual police work, Snow has studied the remains of General George Armstrong Custer and his men from the 1876 battlefield at Little Big Horn, and in 1985, he went to Brazil, where he identified the remains of the notorious Nazi war criminal Josef Mengele.

He was also instrumental in establishing the first forensic team devoted to documenting cases of human rights abuses around the world. This began in 1984 when he went to Argentina at the request of a newly elected civilian government to help with the identification of remains of the *desaparecidos*, or "disappeared ones," the 9,000 or more people who were eliminated by government death squads during seven years of military rule. A year later, he returned to give expert testimony at the trial of nine junta members and to teach Argentineans how to recover, clean, repair, preserve, photograph, x-ray, and analyze bones. Besides providing factual accounts of the fate of victims to their surviving kin and refuting the assertions of "revisionists" that the massacres never happened, the work of Snow and his Argentinean associates was crucial in convicting several military officers of kidnapping, torture, and murder.

Since Snow's pioneering work, forensic anthropologists have become increasingly

Amy Zelson Mundorff, a forensic anthropologist for New York City's Office of the Chief Medical Examiner, was injured in the September 11, 2001, terrorist attack on the World Trade Center. Two days later she returned to work to supervise and coordinate the management, treatment, and cataloguing of people who lost their lives in the attack.

involved in the investigation of human rights abuses in all parts of the world, from Chile to Guatemala, Haiti, the Philippines, Rwanda, Iraq, Bosnia, and Kosovo. Meanwhile, they continue to do important work for more typical clients. In the United States these clients include the Federal Bureau of Investigation and city, state, and county medical examiners' offices. ■ ■ ■

clues to human behavior far beyond the mere 5,000 years to which historians are confined by their dependence upon written records.

That said, archaeologists are not limited to the study of prehistoric societies; they may also study those for which historical documents are available to supplement the material remains. In most literate societies, written records are associated with governing elites rather than farmers, fishers, laborers, slaves and other folks at the "grass roots." Thus, although they can tell archaeologists much that might not be known from archaeological evidence alone, it is equally true that archaeological remains can tell historians much about a society that is not apparent from its written documents.

Although most archaeologists concentrate on the human past, some of them study material objects in contemporary settings. One example is the Garbage Project, founded by William Rathje at the University of Arizona in 1973. This carefully controlled study of household waste continues to produce thought-provoking information about contemporary social issues. Among its accomplishments, the project has tested the validity of interview-survey techniques, upon which sociologists, economists, other social scientists and policymakers rely heavily for their data. The tests clearly show a significant difference between what people believe or say they do and what garbage analysis shows they actually do. For example, in 1973, conventional techniques were used to construct and administer a questionnaire to find out

Archaeological investigation of the African burial ground in New York City revealed the horror of slavery in North America, showing that even young children were worked so far beyond their ability to endure that their spines were fractured. Biological archaeologist Michael Blakey, who led the research team, notes: "Although *bioarchaeology* and forensics are often confused, when skeletal biologists use the population as the unit of analysis (rather than the individual), and incorporate cultural and historical context (rather than simply ascribing biological characteristics), and report on the lifeways of a past community (rather than on a crime for the police and courts), it is bioarchaeology rather than forensics."[3]

about the rate of alcohol consumption in Tucson. In one part of town, 15 percent of respondent households affirmed consumption of beer, but no household reported consumption of more than eight cans a week. Analysis of garbage from the same area, however, demonstrated that some beer was consumed in over 80 percent of households, and 50 percent discarded more than eight empty cans a week. Another interesting finding of the Garbage Project is that when beef prices reached an all-time high in 1973, so did the amount of beef wasted by households (not just in Tucson but in other parts of the country as well). Although common sense would lead us to suppose just the opposite, high prices and scarcity correlate with more, rather than less, waste. Such findings are important, for they demonstrate that ideas about human behavior based on conventional interview-survey techniques alone can be seriously in error. Likewise, they show what people actually do does not always match what they think they do.

In 1987, the Garbage Project began a program of excavating landfills in different parts of the United States and Canada. From this work came the first reliable data on what materials actually go into landfills and what happens to them there. And once again, common beliefs

turned out to be at odds with the actual situation. For example, biodegradable materials such as newspapers take far longer to decay when buried in deep compost landfills than anyone had previously expected. This kind of information is a vital step toward solving waste-disposal problems. (Details about the Garbage Project's past and present work can be seen on its Web site: *http://info-center.ccit.arizona.edu/~bara/report.htm.*)

Linguistic Anthropology

Perhaps the most distinctive feature of the human species is language. Studies have shown that the sounds and gestures made by some other animals—especially by apes—may serve functions comparable to those of human language; yet no other animal has developed a system of symbolic communication as richly complex as that of humans. Ultimately, language is what allows people to preserve and transmit their culture from generation to generation.

The branch of anthropology that studies human languages is called **linguistic anthropology.** Linguists may deal with the description of a language (the way a sentence is formed or a verb conjugated), the history of languages (the way languages develop and change with the passage of time), or with the relation between language and culture. All three approaches yield valuable information about how people communicate and how they understand the world around them. The everyday language of English-speaking North Americans, for example, includes a number of slang words, such as *dough, greenback, dust, loot, bucks, change,* and *bread,* to identify what an indigenous inhabitant of Papua New Guinea would recognize only as "money." Such phenomena help identify things that are considered of special importance to a culture. Through the study of language in its social setting, the anthropologist is able to understand how people perceive themselves and the world around them.

Anthropological linguists also make a significant contribution to our understanding of the human past. By working out the genealogical relationships among languages and examining the distributions of those languages, they may estimate how long the speakers of those languages have lived where they do. By identifying those words in related languages that have survived from an ancient ancestral tongue, they can also suggest both where, and how, the speakers of the ancestral language lived.

---
[3]Blakey, M. Personal communication, October 29, 2003.

linguistic anthropology The study of human languages.

Cultural Anthropology

Cultural anthropology (sometimes referred to as *socio-cultural anthropology*) is the study of customary patterns in human behavior, thought, and feelings. It focuses on humans as culture-producing and culture-reproducing creatures. Thus, in order to understand the work of the cultural anthropologist, we must clarify what we mean by "culture." The concept is discussed in detail in Chapter 2, but for our purposes here, we may think of culture as the often unconscious standards by which societies—structured groups of people—operate. These standards are socially learned rather than acquired through biological inheritance. Since they determine, or at least guide, the normal day-to-day behavior, thought, and emotional patterns of the members of a society, human activities, ideas, and feelings are above all culturally acquired and influenced. The manifestations of culture may vary considerably from place to place, but no person is "more cultured" in the anthropological sense than any other.

Cultural anthropology has two main components: ethnography and ethnology. An **ethnography** is a detailed description of a particular culture primarily based on **fieldwork,** which is the term anthropologists use for on-location research. Because the hallmark of fieldwork is a combination of social participation and personal observation within the community being studied, as well as interviews and discussion with individual members of the cultural group in question, the ethnographic method is commonly referred to as **participant observation.** Ethnographies provide the basic information used to make systematic comparisons between different cultures all across the world. Known as **ethnology,** such cross-cultural research allows anthropologists to develop anthropological theories that help explain why certain important differences or similarities occur between groups.

Ethnography

Through participant observation—eating a people's food, sleeping under their roofs, speaking their language, and personally experiencing their habits and customs—the ethnographer seeks to understand their way of life to a far greater extent than any nonparticipant researcher ever could. One learns a culture best by learning how to speak and behave acceptably in the society in which one is doing fieldwork. Being a participant observer does not mean that the anthropologist must join in a people's battles in order to study a culture in which warfare is prominent; but by living among a warlike people, the ethnographer should be able to understand how warfare fits into the overall cultural framework. He or she must be a careful observer to gain an in-depth overview of a culture without placing undue emphasis on one of its parts at the expense of another. Only by discovering how all aspects of a culture—its social, political, economic, and religious practices and institutions—relate to one another can the ethnographer begin to understand the cultural system. Anthropologists refer to this as the **holistic perspective,** and it is one of the fundamental principles of anthropology. Robert Gordon, an anthropologist from Namibia, speaks of it this way: "Whereas the sociologist or the political scientist might examine the beauty of a flower petal by petal, the anthropologist is the person that stands on the top of the mountain and looks at the beauty of the field. In other words, we try and go for the wider perspective."[4]

MEDIATREK
For a Smithsonian Institution virtual tour of Alice Fletcher's fieldwork among Sioux Indian women in the 1880s, see MediaTrek 1.2 on the companion Web site or CD-ROM.

An ethnographer's most essential tools are notebooks, pen/pencil, camera, tape recorder, and, increasingly, a laptop computer. Most important of all, he or she needs flexible social skills. When participating in an unfamiliar culture, the ethnographer does not just blunder about blindly but enlists the assistance of **informants**—members of the society being studied, who provide information that helps the researcher make sense of activities taking place. Just as parents guide a child

cultural anthropology The study of customary patterns in human behavior, thought, and feelings. It focuses on humans as culture-producing and culture-reproducing creatures.
ethnography A detailed description of a particular culture primarily based on fieldwork.
fieldwork The term anthropologists use for on-location research.
participant observation In ethnography, the technique of learning a people's culture through social participation and personal observation within the community being studied, as well as interviews and discussion with individual members of the group over an extended period of time.
ethnology The study and analysis of different cultures from a comparative or historical point of view, utilizing ethnographic accounts and developing anthropological theories that help explain why certain important differences or similarities occur among groups.
holistic perspective A fundamental principle of anthropology, that the various parts of culture must be viewed in the broadest possible context in order to understand their interconnections and interdependence.
informants Members of a society being studied who provide information that helps the ethnographer make sense of what is being said and done.

[4]Gordon, R. (1981, December). [Interview for Coast Telecourses Inc.]. Los Angeles.

Sociologists conduct structured interviews and administer questionnaires to *respondents*, while psychologists experiment with *subjects*. Anthropologists, by contrast, learn from *informants*. The researcher in the third photo is Dutch anthropologist Harald Prins, co-author of this book. Doing fieldwork among the Plains Apache Indians in Oklahoma, he is using a camera to document an oral history project with tribal chief Alfred Chalepah.

toward proper behavior, so do informants help the anthropologist in the field unravel the "mysteries" of what at first seems to be a strange culture, full of puzzling things.

So basic is ethnographic fieldwork to cultural anthropology that British anthropologist C. G. Seligman once asserted, "Field research in anthropology is what the blood of the martyrs is to the church."[5] Certainly anthropological fieldwork often involves at least a measure of strain and pain, for it requires the researcher to step out of his or her cultural comfort zone into a world that is unfamiliar and sometimes unsettling. Anthropologists in the field are likely to face a host of challenges—physical, social, mental, political, and ethical. They may have to deal with the physical challenge of adjusting to food, climate, and hygiene conditions that are vastly different from what they are accustomed to. Socially, they are likely to encounter the challenge of not being accepted or trusted and of being unable to communicate until they learn the local language. Typically, anthropologists in the field struggle with such mental challenges as loneliness, feeling like a perpetual outsider, being socially clumsy and clueless in their new cultural setting, and having to be

[5]Lewis, I. M. (1976). *Social anthropology in perspective* (p. 27). Harmondsworth, England: Penguin.

alert around the clock because anything that is happening or being said may be significant to their research. Political challenges include the possibility of unwittingly letting oneself be used by factions within the community, or being viewed with suspicion by government authorities who may suspect the anthropologist is a spy. And there are ethical dilemmas galore: what to do if faced with a cultural practice one finds troubling, such as female circumcision; how to deal with demands for food supplies and/or medicine; the temptation to use deception to gain vital information; and so on.

On the positive side, the ethnographic endeavor often leads to tangible and meaningful personal, professional, and social rewards, ranging from lasting friendships to vital knowledge and insights concerning the human condition that make positive contributions to people's lives. Something of the meaning of anthropological fieldwork—its usefulness and its impact on researcher and subject—is conveyed in the following Original Study by Suzanne Leclerc-Madlala, an anthropologist who left her familiar New England surroundings 20 years ago to do AIDS research among Zulu-speaking people in South Africa. Her research interest has changed the course of her own life, not to mention the lives of individuals who have AIDS/HIV and the type of treatment they receive.

Original Study

Fighting HIV/AIDS in Africa: Traditional Healers on the Front Line

In the 1980s, as a North American anthropology graduate student at George Washington University in St. Louis, I met and married a Zulu-speaking student from South Africa. It was the height of apartheid, and upon moving to that country I was classified as "honorary black" and forced to live in a segregated township with my husband. The AIDS epidemic was in its infancy, but it was clear from the start that an anthropological understanding of how people

[CONTINUED]

[CONTINUED]

perceive and engage with this disease would be crucial for developing interventions. I wanted to learn all that I could to make a difference, and this culminated in earning a Ph.D. from the University of Natal on the cultural construction of AIDS among the Zulu. The HIV/AIDS pandemic in Africa became my professional passion.

Faced with overwhelming global health-care needs, the World Health Organization passed a series of resolutions in the 1970s promoting collaboration between traditional and modern medicine. Such moves held a special relevance for Africa, where traditional healers typically outnumber practitioners of modern medicine by a ratio of 100 to 1 or more. Given Africa's disproportionate burden of disease, supporting partnership efforts with traditional healers makes sense. But what sounds sensible today was once considered absurd, even heretical. For centuries Westerners generally viewed traditional healing as a whole lot of primitive mumbo jumbo practiced by witchdoctors with demonic powers who perpetuated superstition. Yet, its practice survived. Today, as the African continent grapples with an HIV/AIDS epidemic of crisis proportion, millions of sick people who are either too poor or too distant to access modern health care are proving that traditional healers are an invaluable resource in the fight against AIDS.

Of the world's estimated 40 million people currently infected by HIV, 70 percent live in sub-Saharan Africa, and the vast majority of children left orphaned by AIDS are African. From the 1980s onward, as Africa became synonymous with the rapid spread of HIV/AIDS, a number of prevention programs involved traditional healers. My initial research in South Africa's KwaZulu-Natal province—where it is estimated that 36 percent of the population is HIV infected—revealed that traditional Zulu healers were regularly consulted for the treatment of sexually transmitted dis-

eases (STD). I found that such diseases, along with HIV/AIDS, were usually attributed to transgressions of taboos related to birth, pregnancy, marriage, and death. Moreover, these diseases were often understood within a framework of pollution and contagion, and like most serious illnesses, ultimately believed to have their causal roots in witchcraft.

In the course of my research, I investigated a pioneer program in STD and HIV education for traditional healers in the province. The program aimed to provide basic biomedical knowledge about the various modes of disease transmission, the means available for prevention, the diagnosing of symptoms, the keeping of records, and the making of patient referrals to local clinics and hospitals. Interviews with the healers showed that many maintained a deep suspicion of modern medicine. They perceived AIDS education as a one-way street intended

© Kerry Cullinan

Medical anthropologist Suzanne Leclerc-Madlala visits with "Doctor" Koloko in KwaZulu-Natal, South Africa. This Zulu traditional healer proudly displays her official AIDS training certificate.

to press them into formal health structures and convince them of the superiority of modern medicine. Yet, today, few of the 6,000-plus KwaZulu-Natal healers who have been trained in AIDS education say they would opt for less collaboration; most want to have more.

Treatments by Zulu healers for HIV/AIDS often take the form of infusions of bitter herbs to "cleanse" the body, strengthen the blood, and remove misfortune and "pollution." Some treat-

ments provide effective relief from common ailments associated with AIDS, such as itchy skin rashes, oral thrush, persistent diarrhea, and general debility. Indigenous plants such as *unwele (Sutherlandia frutescens)* and African potato *(Hypoxis hemerocallidea)* are well-known traditional medicines that have proven immuno-boosting properties. Both have recently become available in modern pharmacies packaged in tablet form. With modern anti-retroviral treatments still well beyond the reach of most South Africans, indigenous medicines that can delay or alleviate some of the suffering caused by AIDS are proving to be valuable and popular treatments.

Knowledge about potentially infectious bodily fluids has led healers to change some of their practices. Where porcupine quills where once used to give a type of indigenous injection, patients are now advised to bring their own sewing needles to consultations. Patients provide their own individual razor blades for making incisions on their skin, where previously healers reused the same razor on many clients. Some healers claim they have given up the practice of biting clients' skin to remove foreign objects from the body. It is not uncommon today, especially in urban centers like Durban, to find healers proudly displaying AIDS training certificates in their inner-city "surgeries" where they don white jackets and wear protective latex gloves.

Politics and controversy have dogged South Africa's official response to HIV/AIDS. But back home in the waddle-and-daub, animal-skin-draped herbariums and divining huts of traditional healers, the politics of AIDS holds little relevance. Here the sick and dying are coming in droves to be treated by healers who have been part and parcel of community life (and death) since time immemorial. In many cases traditional healers have transformed their homes into hospices for AIDS patients. Turned away from provincial hospitals unable to cope with the rising tide of AIDS, the sick are returning home to die. Because of the strong stigma that still plagues the disease, those with AIDS symptoms are often abandoned or sometimes chased away from their homes by family members. They seek refuge with healers who provide them with comfort in their final days. Healers' homes are also becoming orphanages as healers respond to what has been called the "third wave" of AIDS destruction: the growing legions of orphaned children.

The practice of traditional healing in Africa is adapting to the changing face of health and illness in the context of HIV/AIDS. But those who are suffering go to traditional healers not only in search of relief for physical symptoms.

They go to learn about the ultimate cause of their disease—something other than the immediate cause of a sexually transmitted "germ" or "virus." They go to find answers to the "why me and not him" questions, the "why now" and "why this." As with most traditional healing systems worldwide, healing among the Zulu and most all African ethnic groups cannot be separated from the spiritual concerns of the individual and the cosmological beliefs of the community at large. Traditional healers help to restore a sense of balance between the individual and the community, on one hand, and between the individual and the cosmos, or ancestors, on the other hand. They provide health care that is personalized, culturally appropriate, holistic, and tailored to meet the needs and

expectations of the patient. In many ways it is a far more satisfactory form of healing than that offered by modern medicine.

Traditional healing in Africa is flourishing in the era of AIDS, and understanding why this is so requires a shift in the conceptual framework by which we understand, explain, and interpret health. Anthropological methods and its comparative and holistic perspective can facilitate, like no other discipline, the type of understanding that is urgently needed to address the AIDS crisis. *(By Suzanne Leclerc-Madlala. Adapted in part from Leclerc-Madlala, S. (2002). Bodies and politics: Healing rituals in the democratic South Africa. In V. Faure (Ed.), Les cahiers de 'l'IFAS, No. 2. Johannesburg: The French Institute.)*

The popular image of ethnographic fieldwork is that it occurs among people who live in far-off, isolated places. To be sure, much ethnographic work has been done in the remote villages of Africa or South America, the islands of the Pacific Ocean, the deserts of Australia, and so on. During the heyday of colonialism (1880s–1940s) many European anthropologists did indeed focus on the study of traditional cultures in the colonies overseas. Meanwhile, their North American colleagues were engaged primarily in fieldwork on Indian reservations, documenting endangered Native American cultures. That said, anthropologists have recognized from the start that a generalized understanding of human ideas and behavior depends upon knowledge of all cultures and peoples, including those in the industrialized West. During the years of the Great Depression and World War II, for example, many anthropologists in the United States worked in settings ranging from factories to whole communities.

The conditions and priorities of fieldwork altered dramatically after World War II (1939–1945) in response to changes in the world political order. By the 1960s, European colonial powers had lost almost all of their overseas territorial possessions. A significant number of anthropologists turned their attention to South and Central America, while others focused on changes in the newly independent countries in Africa and Asia. However, as political unrest made fieldwork increasingly difficult in many parts of the world, many anthropologists zeroed in on important cross-cultural issues that needed to be dealt with inside Europe and North America. Many of these issues, which remain focal points

to this day, involve immigrants and refugees who come from places where anthropologists have conducted research. Some anthropologists have gone beyond studying such groups to playing a role in helping them adjust to their new circumstances—an example of applied anthropology. Simultaneously, anthropologists are using the same research techniques that served them so well in the study of non-Western peoples to research such diverse subjects as religious cults, street gangs, schools, corporate bureaucracies, health-care delivery systems, and how people deal with consumer complaints in Western cultures.

Although it has much to offer, anthropological study within one's own society may present special problems. Sir Edmund Leach, a major figure in British anthropology, once put it this way:

> Surprising though it may seem, fieldwork in a cultural context of which you already have intimate firsthand experience seems to be much more difficult than fieldwork which is approached from the naïve viewpoint of a total stranger. When anthropologists study facets of their own society their vision seems to become distorted by prejudices which derive from private rather than public experience.[6]

For this reason, the most successful anthropological studies of societies to which the researchers

[6]Leach, E. (1982). *Social anthropology* (p. 124). Glasgow, Scotland: Fontana Paperbacks.

themselves belong are usually those carried out by individuals who first worked in some other culture. The more one learns of other cultures, the more one gains a different perspective on one's own.

Ethnology

Although ethnographic fieldwork is basic to cultural anthropology, it is not the sole occupation of the cultural anthropologist. Largely descriptive in nature, ethnography provides the basic data needed for ethnology—the branch of cultural anthropology that makes cross-cultural comparisons and develops theories that explain why certain important differences or similarities occur between groups.

Intriguing insights into one's own beliefs and practices may come from cross-cultural comparisons. Consider, for example, a comparison between industrialized peoples and traditional food foragers (people who rely on wild plant and animal resources for subsistence) concerning the amount of time spent on domestic chores. In the United States, there is a widespread belief that the ever-increasing output of household appliances has resulted in a steady reduction in housework, with a consequent increase in leisure time. Thus, consumer appliances have become important indicators of a high standard of living.

Anthropological research among food foragers, however, has shown that they work far less at household tasks, and indeed less at all subsistence pursuits, than do people in industrialized societies. Aboriginal Australian women, for example, traditionally devote an average of 20 hours per week to collecting and preparing food, as well as other domestic chores. By contrast, women in the rural United States in the 1920s, without the benefit of labor-saving appliances, devoted approximately 52 hours a week to their housework. One might suppose that this has changed over the decades since, yet some 50 years later, urban U.S. women who were not working for wages outside their homes were putting 55 hours a week into their housework—this despite all their "labor-saving" dishwashers, washing machines, clothes dryers, vacuum cleaners, food processors, and microwave ovens.[7]

Considering such cross-cultural comparisons, one may think of ethnology as the study of alternative ways of doing things. But more than that, by making systematic comparisons, ethnologists seek to arrive at scientific

conclusions concerning the function and operation of culture in all times and places.

Medical Anthropology

In part due to the growing importance of global health organizations, which face a wide cross-cultural array of healing traditions and practices, medical anthropology has emerged as a significant specialization within the discipline of anthropology. In the past, medical anthropologists were individuals trained as physicians and ethnographers who investigated health beliefs and practices of people in exotic places while also providing them with "Western" medicine. Medical anthropologists during this early period translated local experiences of sickness into the scientific language of Western biomedicine. Following a re-evaluation of this ethnocentric approach in the 1970s, medical anthropology emerged as a unified discipline that incorporated theories and practices of anthropology. Today, **medical anthropology** is defined as a specialization that brings theoretical and applied approaches from cultural and biological anthropology to the study of human health and disease. Medical anthropologists study medical systems as cultural systems similar to any other social institution. They use cross-cultural and scientific models drawn from biological anthropology to understand and improve human health. They have also turned their attention toward biomedicine, contributing a wide-ranging perspective to the social and cultural aspects of health care in their own societies. Their work sheds light on the connections between human health and political and economic forces, both globally and locally. Many of the Biocultural Connections featured throughout this text present the work of medical anthropologists.

ANTHROPOLOGY AND SCIENCE

The foremost concern of all anthropologists is the detailed and comprehensive study of humankind in all its rich diversity. Some people refer to anthropology as a social or behavioral science. Others speak of it as a natural science or as one of the humanities. Can the work of the anthropologist properly be labeled "scientific"? What exactly do we mean by the term *science*?

Science, a carefully honed way of producing objective knowledge, aims to reveal and explain the underlying logic, the structural processes, that make the world "tick." It is a creative endeavor that seeks testable explanations for observed phenomena, ideally in terms of the workings of hidden but universal and unchanging principles, or laws. Two basic ingredients are essential for

---

[7]Bodley, J. H. (1985). *Anthropology and contemporary human problems* (2nd ed., p. 69). Palo Alto, CA: Mayfield.

medical anthropology A specialization in anthropology that brings theoretical and applied approaches from cultural and biological anthropology to the study of human health and disease.

VISUAL COUNTERPOINT To many people, a scientist is someone who works in a laboratory, carrying out experiments with the aid of specialized equipment. Contrary to the stereotypical image, not all scientists work in laboratories, nor is experimentation the only technique they use. On the right, villagers in Papua New Guinea watch themselves on a video shown by anthropologist Michael Wesch.

this: imagination and skepticism. Imagination, though capable of leading us astray, is required to help us recognize unexpected ways phenomena might be ordered and think of old things in new ways. Without it, there can be no science. Skepticism is what allows us to distinguish **fact** (an observation verified by several skilled observers) from fancy, to test our speculations, and to prevent our imaginations from running away with us.

In their search for explanations, scientists do not assume that things are always as they appear on the surface. After all, what could be more obvious than that the earth is a stable entity, around which the sun travels every day? And yet, it isn't so.

Like other scientists, anthropologists often begin their research with a **hypothesis** (a tentative explanation or hunch) about the possible relationships between certain observed facts or reported events. By gathering various kinds of data that seem to ground such suggested explanations on evidence, anthropologists come up with **theories**—explanations for natural or cultural phenomena, supported by a reliable body of data. In their effort to demonstrate linkages between known facts or events, anthropologists may discover unexpected facts, events, or relationships. In other words, an important function of theory is that it guides us in our explorations and may result in new knowledge. Equally important, the newly discovered facts may provide evidence that certain explanations, however popular or firmly believed to be true, are unfounded. When the evidence is lacking or fails to support the suggested explanations, anthropologists are forced to drop promising hypotheses or attractive hunches. Moreover, no scientific theory, no matter how widely accepted by the international community of schol-

ars, is beyond challenge. Like other scientists, anthropologists do not view any theory as the final truth. Rather, they measure its validity and soundness by varying degrees of probability; what is considered to be "true" is what is most probable. But while anthropologists cannot claim anything as proven absolutely true, they can and do provide evidence that assumptions widely thought to have been true are unfounded or contrary to the observed facts of reality. Thus a theory, contrary to widespread misuse of the term, is much more than mere speculation; it is a closely examined and critically checked out explanation of observed reality.

In this respect, it is important to distinguish between scientific theories—which are always open to future challenges born of new evidence or insights—and doctrine. A **doctrine,** or dogma, is an assertion of opinion or belief formally handed down by an authority as true and indisputable. Examples of such authority can be found in all religious movements, from the Iroquois Indians and their longhouse tradition in northeast America to Buddhists in Tibet, Orthodox Jews in Israel, Sunni Muslims in Egypt, Roman Catholics in Italy, and so on. For instance, Judaism, Christianity, and Islam each

fact An observation verified by several observers skilled in the necessary techniques of observation.
hypothesis A tentative explanation of the relation between certain phenomena.
theory In science, an explanation of natural phenomena, supported by a reliable body of data.
doctrine An assertion of opinion or belief formally handed down by authority as true and indisputable.

hold as sacred certain ancient writings. Respectively known as the Torah, Bible, and Koran, these holy texts are believed to contain divine wisdom and eternal truths. All three speak of the origin of the human species in a way very similar to that found in the Bible's first chapter, Genesis: *God created the world in seven days, and on day six He created the first human beings, Adam and Eve, in the Garden of Eden.* But while these religions share a creationist doctrine, there are also significant differences among them. Moreover, within each of these religions, major divisions have emerged over doctrine. For instance, not all Christians subscribe to the doctrine of the Virgin Mary's Immaculate Conception. Those who accept this doctrine do so on the basis of religious authority, conceding that this sacred story is contrary to human biology. Such doctrines cannot be tested or proved one way or another: They are accepted as matters of faith.

In contrast to religious doctrine, however, scientific theory depends on demonstrable evidence and testing before an explanation can be accepted as "true." So it is that, as our knowledge expands, the odds in favor of some theories over others are generally increased, even though old "truths" sometimes must be discarded as alternative theories are shown to be more probable.

By way of illustration, we may compare two competing theories that sought to explain the fact of biological evolution: those of Jean Baptiste Lamarck (1744–1829) and Charles R. Darwin (1809–1882). While Lamarck theorized that evolution took place through inheritance of acquired characteristics, Darwin claimed that it was the result of natural selection. Lamarck's theory was laid to rest in the late 1800s due to experiments conducted by August Weismann and other scientists. Breeding twenty generations of mice, Weismann cut off the tails in each generation, only to find them still present in the 21st. By contrast, countless attempts to falsify Darwin's theory have failed to do so. Moreover, as our knowledge of genetics, geology, and paleontology has increased, our understanding of how natural selection works has advanced accordingly. Thus, while Lamarck's theory to account for biological change over time had to be abandoned, evidence has increased the probability that Darwin's is correct.

Difficulties of the Scientific Approach

Straightforward though the scientific approach may seem, there are serious difficulties in its application in anthropology. For instance, once a hypothesis has been proposed, the person who suggested it is strongly motivated to verify it, and this can cause one to unwittingly overlook negative evidence and unanticipated findings.

This is a familiar problem in science in general. In the words of paleontologist Stephen Jay Gould, "The greatest impediment to scientific innovation is usually a conceptual lock, not a factual lock."[8] The anthropological perspective highlights an additional difficulty: In order to arrive at useful theories concerning human behavior and its evolution, one must begin with hypotheses that are as objective and as little culture-bound as possible. And here lies a major—some people would say insurmountable—problem: It is difficult for someone who has grown up in one culture to frame hypotheses about others that are not culture-bound.

As one example of this sort of problem, we may look at attempts by archaeologists to understand the nature of settlement in the Classic period of Maya civilization. This civilization flourished between 1,750 and 1,100 years ago in what is now northern Guatemala, Belize, and neighboring portions of Mexico and Honduras. Today much of this region is covered by a dense tropical forest that is thinly inhabited by villagers, who sustain themselves through slash-and-burn farming. (After cutting and burning the natural vegetation, crops are grown for two years or so before fertility is exhausted, and a new field must be cleared.) Yet in these now sparsely populated forests there are numerous archaeological sites, featuring towering temples as tall as modern 20-story buildings, plus other sorts of monumental architecture and carved stone monuments.

Because of their cultural bias against tropical forests as places to prosper, and against slash-and-burn farming as a means of raising sufficient food, North American and European archaeologists were puzzled. How could the Maya have maintained large, permanent settlements on the basis of slash-and-burn farming? At first, the answer seemed self-evident—they couldn't; therefore, the great archaeological sites must have been ceremonial centers inhabited by few, if any, people. Periodically a rural peasantry, living scattered in small hamlets over the countryside, must have gathered in these places for rituals or to provide labor for their construction and maintenance.

This was the generally accepted scholarly view until 1960. That year a group of young University of Pennsylvania archaeologists working at Tikal, one of the largest of all Maya sites in Guatemala, dared to ask some simple, unbiased questions: Did anyone live at this particular site on a permanent basis; if so, how many, and how were they supported? Throwing preconceived notions overboard and working intensively over the next decade, the archaeologists established that Tikal had actually been inhabited on a permanent basis

[8]Gould, S. J. (1989). *Wonderful life* (p. 226). New York: Norton.

Anthropologists of Note

Franz Boas (1858–1942) ▪ Fredric Ward Putnam (1839–1915)   John Wesley Powell (1834–1902)

In North America, anthropology among the social sciences has a unique character, owing in large part to the natural science (rather than social science) background of the three men pictured here. **Boas**, educated in physics, was not the first to teach anthropology in the United States, but it was he and his students, with their insistence on scientific rigor, who made such courses a common part of college and university curricula.

Putnam, a zoologist specializing in the study of birds and fishes, and permanent secretary of the American Association for the Advancement of Science, made a decision in 1875 to devote himself to the promotion of anthropology. It was through his efforts that many of the great anthropology museums were established: the Phoebe Hearst Museum at the University of California, the Peabody Museum at Harvard University, and the Field Museum in Chicago. Putnam also founded the anthropology department of the American Museum of Natural History in New York.

Powell was a geologist and founder of the United States Geological Survey, but he also carried out ethnographic and linguistic research. (His classification of Indian languages north of Mexico is still consulted by scholars today.) In 1879, he founded the Bureau of American Ethnology (ultimately absorbed by the Smithsonian Institution), thereby establishing anthropology within the U.S. government.

---

by tens of thousands of people! The society was supported by intensive forms of agriculture more productive than slash-and-burn alone. This work at Tikal proved wrong the older, culture-bound hypotheses and paved the way for an improved understanding of Classic Maya civilization.

When anthropologists do research in different cultures, they make an effort to be as objective as possible. To accomplish that goal, they recognize the importance of trying to frame their research strategies in ways that avoid culture-boundedness. In so doing, they rely heavily on a technique that has proved successful in other natural science disciplines. As did the archaeologists working at Tikal, they immerse themselves in the data to the fullest extent possible. In the process, anthropologists become so thoroughly familiar with even the smallest details that they can begin to recognize underlying patterns in the data, many of which might easily have been overlooked. Recognition of such patterns enables the anthropologist to frame meaningful hypotheses, which then may be subjected to further testing in the field.

Unlike many other social scientists, the anthropologist usually does not go into the field armed with prefigured questionnaires; rather, he or she recognizes that there are probably all sorts of things that can be found out only by maintaining as open a mind as one can. As fieldwork proceeds, anthropologists sort their complex observations into a meaningful whole, some-

times by formulating and testing limited or low-level hypotheses, but just as often by making use of intuition and playing hunches. What is important is that the results are constantly checked for consistency, for if the parts fail to fit together in a manner that is internally consistent, then the anthropologist knows that a mistake may have been made and that further inquiry is necessary.

Two studies of a village in Peru illustrate the contrast between anthropological and other social science approaches. One was carried out by a sociologist who, after conducting a survey by questionnaire, concluded

Tikal, one of the largest of all Maya sites in Guatemala was at its height between 1,450 and 1,150 years ago.

that people in the village invariably worked together on one another's privately owned plots of land. By contrast, a cultural anthropologist who lived in the village for over a year (including the brief period when the sociologist did his study) observed that particular practice only once. The anthropologist's sustained fieldwork showed that although a belief in labor exchange relations was important for the people's understanding of themselves, it was not a regular economic practice.[9] This is not to say that all sociological research is bad and all anthropological research is good. The point is that relying exclusively on questionnaire surveys is a risky business, no matter who does it. That is because questionnaires all too easily embody the concepts and categories of the researcher, who is an outsider, rather than those of the subjects themselves. Even where this is not a problem, questionnaire surveys alone are not good ways of identifying causal relationships. They tend to concentrate on what is measurable, answerable, and acceptable as a question, rather than probing the less obvious and more complex, qualitative aspects of society. Moreover, for a host of reasons—fear, prudence, wishful thinking, ignorance, exhaustion, hostility, hope of benefit—people may give partial, false, or self-serving information.[10] Keeping culture-bound ideas out of research methods, as illustrated through the example of standardized questionnaires, is an important point in all of anthropology's subfields.

Another issue in scientific anthropology is the matter of validity. In the natural sciences, replication of observations and/or experiments is a major means of establishing the reliability of a researcher's conclusions. Thus, one can see for oneself if one's colleague has "gotten it right." In anthropology, validation is uniquely challenging because observational access is often limited. Access to a particular research site can be constrained by a number of factors. Difficulty of getting there and obtaining necessary permits, insufficient funding, and the fact that social, political, and environmental conditions often change mean that what could be observed in a certain context at one particular time cannot be at others, and so on. Thus, one researcher cannot easily confirm the reliability or completeness of another's account. For this reason, an anthropologist bears a special responsibility for accurate reporting. In the final research report, she or he must be clear about several basic things: Why was a particular location selected as a

research site? What were the research objectives? What were the local conditions during fieldwork? Which local individuals provided the key information and major insights? How were the data collected and recorded? Without such background information, it is difficult for others to judge the validity of the account and the soundness of the researcher's conclusions.

ANTHROPOLOGY'S COMPARATIVE METHOD

The end product of anthropological research, if properly carried out, is a coherent statement about culture or human nature that provides an explanatory framework for understanding the ideas and actions of the people who have been studied. And this, in turn, is what permits the anthropologist to frame broader hypotheses about human beliefs, behavior, and biology. Plausible though such hypotheses may be, however, the consideration of a single society is generally insufficient for their testing. Without some basis for comparison, the hypothesis grounded in a single case may be no more than a particular historical coincidence. On the other hand, a single case may be enough to cast doubt on, if not refute, a theory that had previously been held to be valid. For example, the discovery in 1948 that aborigines living in Australia's northern Arnhem Land put in an average workday of less than 6 hours, while living well above a level of bare sufficiency, was enough to call into question the widely accepted notion that food-foraging peoples are so preoccupied with finding scarce food that they lack time for any of life's more pleasurable activities. The observations made in the Arnhem Land study have since been confirmed many times over in various parts of the world.

Hypothetical explanations of cultural and biological phenomena may be tested by the comparison of archaeological, biological, linguistic, historical, and/or ethnographic data for several societies found in a particular region. Carefully controlled comparison provides a broader basis for drawing general conclusions about humans than does the study of a single culture or population. The anthropologist who undertakes such a comparison may be more confident that events or features believed to be related really are related, at least within the area under investigation; however, an explanation that is valid in one area is not necessarily so in another.

Ideally, theories in anthropology are generated from worldwide comparisons. The cross-cultural researcher examines a global sample of societies in order to discover whether or not hypotheses proposed to explain cultural

---

[9]Chambers, R. (1983). *Rural development: Putting the last first* (p. 51). New York: Longman.

[10]Sanjek, R. (1990). On ethnographic validity. In R. Sanjek (Ed.), *Fieldnotes* (p. 395). Ithaca, NY: Cornell University Press.

Biocultural
Connection

The Anthropology of Organ Transplantation

In 1954, the first organ transplant occurred in Boston when surgeons removed a kidney from one identical twin to place it inside his sick brother. Though some transplants rely upon living donors, routine organ transplantation depends largely upon the availability of organs obtained from individuals who have died.

From an anthropological perspective, the meanings of death and the body vary cross-culturally. While death could be said to represent a particular biological state, social agreement about this state's significance is of paramount importance. Anthropologist Margaret Lock has explored differences between Japanese and North American acceptance of the biological state of "brain death" and how it affects the practice of organ transplants.

Brain death relies upon the absence of measurable electrical currents in the brain and the inability to breathe without technological assistance. The brain-dead individual, though attached to machines, still seems alive with a beating heart and pink cheeks. North Americans find brain death acceptable, in part, because personhood and individuality are culturally located in the brain. North American comfort with brain death has allowed for the "gift of life" through organ donation and subsequent transplantation.

By contrast, in Japan, the concept of brain death is hotly contested and organ transplants are rarely performed. The Japanese do not incorporate a mind-body split into their models of themselves and locate personhood throughout the body rather than in the brain.

They resist accepting a warm pink body as a corpse from which organs can be "harvested." Further, organs cannot be transformed into "gifts" because anonymous donation is not compatible with Japanese social patterns of reciprocal exchange.

Organ transplantation carries far greater social meaning than the purely biological movement of an organ from one individual to another. Cultural and biological processes are tightly woven into every aspect of this new social practice. *(Based on Lock, M. (2001). Twice dead: Organ transplants and the reinvention of death. Berkeley: University of California Press.)*

phenomena or biological variation are universally applicable. Ideally the sample is selected at random, thereby enhancing the probability that the theoretical conclusions will be valid. However, the greater the number of societies being compared, the less likely it is that the investigator will have a detailed understanding of all the societies encompassed by the study. Therefore, the cross-cultural researcher depends upon data gathered by other scholars as well as his or her own. A key resource for this is the Human Relations Area Files, a vast cross-cultural catalogue discussed in detail in Chapter 2. This resource provides cross-cultural data on a variety of cultural and biological characteristics. Similarly, archaeologists and biological anthropologists rely on artifacts and skeletal collections housed in museums, as well as published descriptions of these collections.

ANTHROPOLOGY AND THE HUMANITIES

Although the sciences and humanities are often thought to be mutually exclusive approaches to learning, they share methods for critical thinking, mental creativity, and deepening knowledge about the substance of reality.[11] In anthropology, both come together, which is

why, for example, anthropological research in the United States is funded not only by such "hard science" agencies as the National Science Foundation but also by such organizations as the National Endowment for the Humanities. To paraphrase Roy Rappaport, a past president of the American Anthropological Association:

> The combination of scientific and humanistic approaches is and always has been a source of tension. It has been crucial to anthropology because it truly reflects the condition of a species that lives and can only live in terms of meanings that it must construct in a world devoid of intrinsic meaning, yet subject to natural law. Without the continued grounding in careful observation that scientific aspects of our tradition provide, our interpretive efforts may float off into literary criticism and speculation. But without the interpretive tradition, the scientific tradition that grounds us will never get off the ground.[12]

[11]Shearer, R. R., & Gould, S. J. (1999). Of two minds and one nature. *Science, 286,* 1093.

[12]Rappaport, R. A. (1994). Commentary, *Anthropology Newsletter, 35,* 76.

The humanistic side of anthropology is perhaps most immediately evident in its concern with other cultures' languages, values, achievements in the arts and literature (including oral literature among peoples who lack writing), and how they make sense of their lives. Beyond this, anthropologists remain committed to the proposition that one cannot fully understand another culture by simply observing it; as the term *participant observation* implies, one must *experience* it as well. Thus, ethnographers spend prolonged periods of time living with the people they study, sharing their joys and suffering, their hardships, including sickness and, sometimes, premature death. They are not so naïve as to believe that they can be, or even should be, dispassionate about the people whose trials and tribulations they share. As Robin Fox put it, "our hearts, as well as our brains, should be with our men and women."[13]

The humanistic side of anthropology is evident as well in its emphasis on qualitative—in contrast to quantitative—research. This is not to say that anthropologists are unaware of the value of quantification and statistical procedures; they do make use of them for various purposes. Nevertheless, reducing people and the things they do and think to numbers may have a certain "dehumanizing" effect (it is easier to ignore the concerns of "impersonal numbers" than it is those of flesh-and-blood humans) and keep us from dealing with important issues less susceptible to abstract calculation. For all these reasons, anthropologists tend to place less emphasis on statistical data than do other social scientists.

Given their intense involvement with other peoples, it should come as no surprise that anthropologists have amassed considerable information about human failure and success, weakness and greatness—the real stuff of the humanities. Small wonder, too, that above all anthropologists steer clear of a "cold" impersonal scientific approach that would blind them to the fact that human societies are made up of individuals with rich assortments of emotions and aspirations that demand respect. Anthropology has sometimes been called the most humane of the sciences and the most scientific of the humanities—a designation that most anthropologists accept with considerable pride.

MEDIATREK
To learn more about the American Anthropological Association, including its code of ethics, see MediaTrek 1.3 on the companion Web site or CD-ROM.

---

[13]Fox, R. (1968). *Encounter with anthropology* (p. 290). New York: Dell.

QUESTIONS OF ETHICS

The kinds of research carried out by anthropologists, and the settings within which they work, raise a number of important moral questions about the potential uses and abuses of our knowledge. Who will utilize our findings and for what purposes? Who, if anyone, will profit from them? For example, in the case of research on an ethnic or religious minority whose values or lifeways may be at odds with dominant mainstream society, will governmental or corporate interests use anthropological data to suppress that group? And what of traditional communities around the world? Who is to decide what changes should, or should not, be introduced for community "betterment"? And who defines what constitutes betterment—the community, its national government, or an international agency like the World Health Organization? Then there is the problem of privacy. Anthropologists deal with matters that are private and sensitive, including things that individuals would prefer not to have generally known about them. How does one write about such important but delicate issues and at the same time protect the privacy of informants? Not surprisingly, because of these and other questions, there has been much discussion among anthropologists over the past three decades on the subject of ethics.

Anthropologists recognize that they have special obligations to three sets of people: those whom they study, those who fund the research, and those in the profession who expect us to publish our findings so that they may be used to further our collective knowledge. Because fieldwork requires a relationship of trust between fieldworker and informants, the anthropologist's first responsibility clearly is to his or her informants and their community. Everything possible must be done to protect their physical, social, and psychological welfare and to honor their dignity and privacy. In other words, *do no harm*. Although early ethnographers often provided colonial administrators with the kind of information needed to control the "natives," they have long since ceased to be comfortable with such work and regard as basic a people's right to maintain their own culture.

ANTHROPOLOGY AND GLOBALIZATION

Anthropology has been shaped by a holistic perspective and a long-term commitment to understanding the human species in all its variety. This given, it is better equipped than any other scientific discipline to grapple with an issue that has overriding importance for all of us

VISUAL COUNTERPOINT A major feature of globalization is the communications revolution. Cell phones are used by a vast array of people all around the world, from urban bankers engaged in international investments, to semi-nomadic Khampa herders who may never venture beyond their native region of highland Tibet.

at the beginning of the 21st century: **globalization.** The term refers to worldwide interconnectedness, evidenced in global movements of natural resources, trade goods, human labor, finance capital, information, and infectious diseases. Although worldwide travel, trade relations, and information flow have existed for several centuries, the pace and magnitude of these long-distance exchanges has picked up enormously in recent decades; the Internet, in particular, has greatly expanded information exchange capacities.

The powerful forces driving globalization are technological improvements, lower transport and communication costs, faster knowledge transfers, and increased trade and financial integration among countries. Touching almost everybody's life on the planet, globalization is about economics as much as politics, and it changes human relations and ideas as well as our natural environments. Even geographically remote countries are quickly becoming more interdependent through globalization. For these reasons, globalization has been defined as "the intensification of worldwide social relations which link distant localities in such a way that local happenings are shaped by events occurring many miles away and vice versa."[14]

Doing research in all corners of the world, anthropologists are confronted with the impact of globaliza-tion on human communities wherever they are located. As participant observers, they describe and try to explain how individuals and organizations respond to the massive changes confronting them. Anthropologists may also find out how local responses sometimes change the global flows directed at them.

Dramatically increasing every year, globalization can be a two-edged sword. It generates economic growth and prosperity, but it also undermines long-established institutions. Generally, globalization has brought significant gains to higher-educated groups in wealthier countries, while doing little to boost developing countries and actually contributing to the erosion of traditional cultures. Upheavals born of globalization are key causes for rising levels of ethnic and religious conflict throughout the world.

Obviously, since all of us now live in a "global village," we can no longer afford the luxury of ignoring our neighbors no matter how distant they still may seem to most of us. Based on 150 years of cross-cultural research throughout the world, anthropologists have accumulated vitally important knowledge about our species in all its amazing variety. In this age of globalization, anthropology may not only provide humanity with useful insights concerning diversity,

globalization Worldwide interconnectedness, evidenced in global movements of natural resources, trade goods, human labor, finance capital, information, and infectious diseases.

[14]Giddens, A. (1990). *The consequences of modernity* (p. 64). Stanford, CA: Stanford University Press.

it may also assist us in avoiding or overcoming significant problems born of that diversity. In countless social arenas, from schools to businesses to hospitals, anthropologists have done cross-cultural research that makes it possible for educators, businesspeople, and doctors to do their work more effectively. (For example, the brief Biocultural Connection box in this chapter is an important alert for surgeons who carry out organ transplants for patients outside of their cultural niche.)

The wide-ranging relevance of anthropological knowledge for the contemporary world may be illustrated by three quite different examples. In the United States today, discrimination based on notions of race continues to be a serious issue affecting economic, political, and social relations. What anthropology has shown, however, is the fallacy of racial categories themselves. Far from being the biological reality it is supposed to be, the concept of race emerged in the 18th century as a device for justifying European dominance over Africans, American Indians, and other "people of color." In fact, differences of skin color are simply surface adaptations to differing amounts of ultraviolet radiation and have nothing to do with physical or mental capabilities. Nor does its variance correspond to other biological characteristics; a German, for example,

may have more in common with a "black" person from Congo than with someone from Greece, Italy, or even Germany itself, depending on what genetically based characteristics other than skin color are considered. Indeed, geneticists find far more biological variation *within* any given human population than *between* them. In short, human "races" are divisive categories based on prejudice, false ideas of differences, and erroneous notions of the superiority of one's own group. The sooner everyone recognizes that the categories lack scientific merit, the better off we will all be.[15]

A second example involves the issue of same-sex marriage. In 1989, Denmark became the first country to enact a comprehensive set of legal protections for same-sex couples, known as the Registered Partnership Act. At this writing, more than a half-dozen other countries have passed similar laws, variously named, and numerous countries around the world are considering legislation that would provide people in homosexual unions some of the benefits and protections afforded by marriage. In 2001 the Netherlands went a step farther and legalized same-sex marriage. In 2003, Belgium did the

---

[15]Haviland, W. A. (2000). *Human evolution and prehistory* (5th ed., pp. 348–368). Fort Worth, TX: Harcourt Brace.

These boys—one from an East African cattle-herding family, the other from northern Europe—share the genetically based ability to digest milk, something that sets them apart from the majority of the world's inhabitants. Because genetic traits are inherited independently, humans cannot be classified into races having any biological validity.

These people are protesting Vermont's "civil union" legislation, which gave legal status to same-sex unions in 2000.

Alden Pellett/The Image Works

same, followed by the Canadian provinces of Ontario and British Columbia. In the United States, Vermont legalized "civil unions" between same-sex couples in 2000, providing *some* of the benefits and protections of heterosexual marriages. In 2003 the Massachusetts Supreme Judicial Court ruled that same-sex marriage was a constitutional right in that state.[16] Those opposed to same-sex unions often argue that marriage has always been between one man and one woman and that only heterosexual relations are "normal." Yet, as we will see in upcoming chapters, neither assertion is true. Anthropologists have documented same-sex marriages in many human societies in various parts of the world, where they are regarded as acceptable under appropriate circumstances. As for homosexual behavior, it is quite common in the animal world, including among humans.[17] The key difference between people and other animals is that human societies specify when, where, how, and with whom it is appropriate or normal (just as they do for heterosexual behavior).

A final example relates to the common confusion of *nation* with *state.* The distinction is important: States are politically organized territories that are internationally recognized, whereas nations are socially organized bodies of people, who share ethnicity—a common origin, language, and cultural heritage. For example, the homeland of the Kurds, known as Kurdistan, is divided between several states, primarily Turkey, Iraq, and Iran. The modern boundaries between these three states were drawn up after World War I and the collapse of the Turkish Ottoman Empire. With the Turks defeated by Britain and her allies, much of the old empire was carved up in 1918. With little regard for the region's ethnic groups or nations such as the Kurds, who had long struggled for self-rule, arbitrary lines were drawn right through Kurdistan, and new political boundaries were imposed. In the process, new countries were created and internationally recognized as independent states.

Similar processes have taken place throughout the world, especially in Asia and Africa, often making the political condition in these countries inherently unstable. As we will see in Chapters 12 and 16, states and nations rarely coincide, nations being split between different states and states typically being controlled by members of one nation who commonly use their control to gain access to the land, resources, and labor of other nationalities. Rarely is the consent of the other nationals obtained, nor are their interests given much (if any) consideration by those who control the government. As a consequence, oppressed nationals often resort to force to defend their land, resources, and even their very identities, feeling they have no other options. Most of the armed conflicts in the world today are of this sort and are not the mere acts of "tribalism" or "terrorism," as commonly asserted.

In numerous ways, our ignorance about other peoples and their ways is a cause of serious problems. In the

[16]Merin, Y. (2002). *Equality for same-sex couples: The legal recognition of gay partnerships in Europe and the United States.* Chicago: University of Chicago Press. "Court says same-sex marriage is a right." *San Francisco Chronicle.* Feb. 5, 2004. Up-to-date overviews and breaking news on the global status of same-sex marriage is posted on the Internet by the Partners Task Force for Gay & Lesbian Couples at *www.buddybuddy.com.*

[17]Kirkpatrick, R. C. (2000). The evolution of human homosexual behavior. *Current Anthropology, 41,* 384.

Violence triggered by the Kurd struggle for self-determination in Iraq and neighboring countries exemplifies the problem of multinational states in which members of a more powerful nationality or ethnic group tries to control those of another through brutal force.

words of Edwin Reischauer, U.S. ambassador to Japan from 1961 to 1966, "Education is not moving rapidly enough in the right directions to produce the knowledge about the outside world and attitudes toward other peoples that may be essential for human survival."[18] His comment is all the more true today, and anthropology is part of the answer. It offers a way of looking at and understanding the world's peoples—insights that are nothing less than basic skills for survival in this age of globalization.

---

[18]Quoted in Haviland, W. A. (1997). Cleansing young minds, or what should we be doing in introductory anthropology? In C. P. Kottack, J. J. White, R. H. Furlow, & P. C. Rice (Eds.), *The teaching of anthropology: problems, issues and decisions* (p. 35). Mountain View, CA: Mayfield.

Chapter Summary

■ Throughout human history, people have needed to know who they are, where they came from, and why they believe and behave as they do. Traditionally, myths and legends provided the answers to these fundamental questions. Anthropology, as it has emerged over the last 150 years, offers a more scientific approach to answering the questions people ask about themselves and others.

■ Anthropology is the study of humankind. In employing a scientific approach, anthropologists seek to produce a reasonably objective understanding of both human diversity and those things all humans have in common.

■ Anthropology contains four major subfields: physical anthropology, archaeology, linguistic anthropology, and cultural anthropology. Physical anthropology focuses on humans as biological organisms. Particular emphasis is given by physical anthropologists to tracing the evolutionary development of the human animal and studying biological variation within the species today. Forensics is an example of applied physical anthropology. Archaeologists study material objects, usually from past cultures, to explain human behavior. Linguists, who study human languages, may deal with the description of a language, with the history of languages, or how languages are used in particular social settings. Cultural anthropologists study humans in terms of their cultures, the often-unconscious standards by which social groups operate. Medical anthropology is a growing specialization.

■ Within all of anthropology's subfields, one can find applied anthropologists who utilize the discipline's unique research methodology toward solving practical problems.

■ Some cultural anthropologists are ethnographers, who do a particular kind of hands-on fieldwork known as participant observation. They produce a detailed record of a specific culture in writing (and/or visual imagery) known as an ethnography. Other cultural anthropologists are also ethnologists, who study and analyze cultures from a comparative or historical point of view, utilizing ethnographic accounts. Often, they focus on a particular aspect of culture, such as religious or economic practices.

■ Unique among the modern sciences, anthropology has long been concerned specifically with traditional tribal societies outside Europe. Today, anthropology stands out among the social and natural sciences for its holistic approach, which aims to formulate theoretically valid explanations of human diversity based on detailed studies of all aspects of human biology, behavior, and beliefs in all known societies, past and present.

■ Anthropologists are concerned with the objective and systematic study of humankind. The anthropologist employs the methods of other scientists by developing hypotheses, or assumed explanations, using other data to test these hypotheses, and ultimately arriving at theories—explanations supported by reliable bodies of data. The comparative method is key to all branches of anthropology. Anthropologists make broad comparisons between peoples and cultures past and present, related species, and fossil groups.

■ In anthropology, the humanities, social sciences, and natural sciences come together into a genuinely human science. Anthropology's link with the humanities can be seen in its concern with people's beliefs, values, languages, arts, and literature—oral as well as written—but above all in its attempt to convey the experience of living in different cultures. As both science and humanity, anthropology has essential insights to offer the modern world, particularly in this era of globalization, when understanding our neighbors in the global village has become a matter of survival for all.

Questions for Reflection

1. Considering the challenge of discerning one's place in the world, what insights have you gained in this chapter that help with this challenge?

2. From the holistic anthropological perspective, humans have one leg in culture and the other in nature, and in the interaction between them our destiny unfolds. Think of examples from your life that illustrate this idea.

3. Globalization can be described as a two-edged sword. How does it foster growth and destruction simultaneously?

4. The textbook definitions of *state* and *nation* are based on scientific distinctions between both organizational types. However, this distinction is sometimes lost in everyday language. Consider, for instance, the names *United States of America* and the *United Nations*.

5. The Biocultural Connection in this chapter contrasts different cultural perspectives on "brain death," while the Original Study featured a discussion about traditional Zulu healers and their role in dealing with AIDS victims. What do these two accounts suggest about the role of applied anthropology in dealing with cross-cultural health issues across the world?

Key Terms

Anthropology	Fieldwork
Culture-bound	Participant observation
Applied anthropology	Ethnology
Physical anthropology	Holistic perspective
Molecular anthropology	Informants
Paleoanthropology	Medical Anthropology
Primatology	Fact
Forensic anthropology	Hypothesis
Archaeology	Theory
Linguistic anthropology	Doctrine
Cultural anthropology	Globalization
Ethnography	

Multimedia Review Tools

Companion Web Site

Visit **http://www.wadsworth.com/anthropology_d/** and click on the companion Web site for this textbook to access a wide range of material to aid your study of anthropology. Among the options for self-study in each chapter are learning objectives, flash cards, Internet activities, Web links, InfoTrac College Edition exercises, and practice tests that can be scored and e-mailed to your instructor.

CD-ROM

The *Doing Anthropology Today* CD-ROM supplied with your textbook provides unique and valuable information designed to enhance your learning experience. This interactive multimedia resource includes video clips, interviews with renowned anthropologists, map and timeline exercises, chapter study quizzes, and much more. *Doing Anthropology Today* will not only help you in achieving your grade goals, but it will also make your learning experience fun and exciting!

Suggested Readings

Bernard, H. R. (2002). *Research methods in anthropology: Qualitative and quantitative approaches* (3rd ed.). Walnut Creek, CA: Altamira Press.

Written in a conversational style and rich with examples, this extremely useful and accessible book has twenty chapters divided into three sections: preparing for fieldwork, data collection, and data analysis. It touches on all the basics, from literature search and research design to interviewing, fieldnote management, multivariate analysis, ethics, and much more.

Bonvillain, N. (2000). *Language, culture, and communication: The meaning of messages* (3rd ed.). Upper Saddle River, NJ: Prentice-Hall.

An up-to-date text on language and communication in a cultural context.

Erickson, P. A., & Murphy, L. D. (2003). *A history of anthropological theory* (2nd ed.). Peterborough, Ontario: Broadview Press.

A clear and concise survey that spans from antiquity to the modern era, effectively drawing the lines between the old and the new. This edition features several new and expanded sections on topics including feminist anthropology, globalization, and medical anthropology.

Fagan, B. M. (1999). *Archeology: A brief introduction* (7th ed.). New York: Longman.

This primer offers an overview of archaeological theory and methodology, from field survey techniques to excavation to analysis of materials.

Jones, S., Martin R., & Pilbeam, D. (Eds.). (1992). *Cambridge encyclopedia of human evolution*. New York: Cambridge University Press.

This comprehensive introduction to the human species covers the gamut from genetics, primatology, and the fossil evidence to a detailed exploration of contemporary human ecology, demography, and disease. Each topic covered, written by an expert in the field, provides a comprehensive summary of this area of biological anthropology. Over seventy scholars from throughout the world contributed to this encyclopedia.

Peacock, J. L. (2002). *The anthropological lens: Harsh light, soft focus.* (2nd ed.). New York: Cambridge University Press.

This lively and innovative book gives the reader a good understanding of the diversity of activities undertaken by cultural anthropologists, while at the same time identifying the unifying themes that hold the discipline together. Additions to the second edition include topics such as globalization, gender, and postmodernism.

CHAPTER 2

The Characteristics of Culture

© David Wells/The Image Bank

CHALLENGE ISSUE

CULTURE IS INSCRIBED ALMOST EVERYWHERE WE LOOK. One of its most visible expressions is self-adornment—the distinctive ways groups of people dress, style their hair, and otherwise decorate their bodies. Beyond individual style, the function of such shared visual expression is to mark group identities, to signal who is insider and who is outsider. This photograph, taken in front of the western city wall of Jerusalem, includes people from three different religious/cultural groups. For each, that ancient holy city has distinct symbolic meaning, and their clothing reveals what the particular perspective and behavior of each person is likely to be. This is very useful, because part of the challenge of survival is knowing each other.

1 What Is Culture?

Culture consists of the abstract ideas, values, and perceptions of the world that inform and are reflected in people's behavior. Culture is shared by members of a society and produces behavior that is intelligible to other members of that society. Cultures are learned rather than inherited biologically, and all the different parts of a culture function as an integrated whole.

2 How Is Culture Studied?

Anthropologists, like children, learn about a culture by experiencing it and talking about it with those who live by its rules. Of course, anthropologists have less time to learn, but they take a systematic approach to the endeavor. Through careful observation and discussion with informants who are especially knowledgeable in the ways of their particular culture, the anthropologist detects the often hidden social rules and worldview that guide human behavior in the society being investigated.

3 Why Do Cultures Exist?

Every culture provides a blueprint for thought and action that helps people deal with problems and other matters of concern. To endure, a culture must satisfy the basic needs of those who live by its rules, and it must provide an orderly existence for the members of a society. In doing so, a culture must strike a balance between the self-interests of individuals and the needs of society as a whole. Moreover, it must have the capacity to change in order to adapt to new circumstances or to alter perceptions of existing circumstances.

Students of anthropology are bound to find themselves studying a seemingly endless variety of human societies, each with its own distinctive environment and system of economics, politics, and religion. Yet for all this variation, these societies have one thing in common: Each is a group of people cooperating to ensure their collective survival and well-being. For this to work, some degree of predictable behavior is required of each person within the society, for group living and cooperation are impossible unless individuals know how others are likely to behave in any given situation. In humans, it is culture that sets the limits of behavior and guides it along predictable paths that are generally acceptable to a certain group of people.

THE CONCEPT OF CULTURE

Anthropologists conceived the modern concept of culture toward the end of the 19th century. The first really clear and comprehensive definition came from the British anthropologist Sir Edward Tylor. Writing in 1871, he defined culture as "that complex whole which includes knowledge, belief, art, law, morals, custom, and any other capabilities and habits acquired by man as a member of society." Since Tylor's time, definitions of culture have proliferated, so that by the early 1950s, North American anthropologists A. L. Kroeber and Clyde Kluckhohn were able to collect over a hundred of them from the academic literature. Recent definitions tend to distinguish more clearly between actual behavior on the one hand and the abstract ideas, values, and perceptions of the world that inform that behavior on the other. To put it another way, **culture** goes deeper than observable behavior; it is a society's shared and socially transmitted ideas, values, and perceptions, which are used to make sense of experience and generate behavior—and which are reflected in behavior.

MEDIATREK

For a debate on what culture is and to find out about some of humankind's more intriguing learned behaviors, go to MediaTrek 2.1 on the companion Web site or CD-ROM.

culture A society's shared and socially transmitted ideas, values, and perceptions—which are used to make sense of experience and generate behavior and which are reflected in behavior.
society An organized group or groups of interdependent people who generally share a common territory, language, and culture and who act together for collective survival and well-being.

CHARACTERISTICS OF CULTURE

Through the comparative study of many cultures, past and present, anthropologists have arrived at an understanding of the basic characteristics that all human cultures share. A careful study of these helps us to see the importance and the function of culture itself.

Culture Is Shared

As a shared set of ideas, values, perceptions, and standards of behavior, culture is the common denominator that makes the actions of individuals intelligible to other members of their society. It enables them to predict how others are most likely to behave in a given circumstance, and it tells them how to react accordingly. A group of people from different cultures, stranded over a period of time on a desert island, might appear to become a society of sorts. They would have a common interest—survival—and would develop techniques for living and working together. Each member of this group, however, would retain his or her own identity and cultural background, and the group would disintegrate without further ado as soon as its members were rescued from the island. The group would have been merely an aggregate in time and not a cultural entity. **Society** may be defined as an organized group or groups of interdependent people who generally share a common territory, language, and culture and who act together for collective survival and well-being. The way in which these people depend upon one another can be seen in such features as their family relationships and their economic, communication, and defense systems. They are also bound together by a general sense of common identity.

Because culture and society are such closely related concepts, anthropologists study both. Obviously, there can be no culture without a society. Conversely, there are no known human societies that do not exhibit culture. This cannot be said for all other animal species. Ants and bees, for example, instinctively cooperate in a manner that clearly indicates a degree of social organization, yet this instinctual behavior is not a culture. Whether or not there exist animals other than humans that exhibit cultural behavior is a question that will be dealt with shortly.

Although a culture is shared by members of a society, it is important to realize that all is not invariable uniformity. For one thing, no two people share the exact same version of their culture. And there are bound to be other variations. At the very least, there is some difference between the roles of men and women. This stems from the fact that women give birth but men do not and that there are obvious differences between male and female reproductive anatomy and physiology. Every culture gives meaning to sexual differences by explaining them and specifying what is to be done about them. Moreover, every culture stipulates how the kinds of people resulting from the differences should relate to others. Because each culture does this in its own way, there can be tremendous variation from one society to another. Anthropologists use the term **gender** to refer to the cultural elaborations and meanings assigned to the biological differentiation between the sexes. So, although one's sex is biologically determined, one's sexual identity or gender is socially constructed within the context of one's particular culture.

The distinction between sex, which is biological, and gender, which is cultural, is an important one. Presumably, gender differences are as old as human culture—about 2.5 million years—and arose from the biological differences between early human males and females. Back then, sex differences and body size appears to have been greater in the earliest human ancestors compared to humans today. In chimps and gorillas, the species most closely related to humans, the males are on average somewhat and substantially larger respectively than females. Moreover, technological advancements in the home and workplace over the last century or two have greatly diminished the cultural significance of most remaining biological differences in many societies all across the world. Thus, apart from sexual differences directly related to reproduction, any biological basis for contrasting gender roles has largely disappeared in modern industrialized societies. Nevertheless, all cultures exhibit at least some role differentiation based on biology—some far more so than others.

Paradoxically, gender differences were more extreme in late 19th- and early 20th-century Western (European and European-derived) societies, when women were expected to submit unquestioningly to male authority, than they are among most historically known and contemporary food-foraging peoples whose lifeways resemble those of our late Stone Age ancestors. Among food foragers, relations between men and women tend to be relatively egalitarian, and although they may not typically carry out the same tasks, such arrangements tend to be flexible. In other words, differences between the behavior of men and women in North American and other Western societies today, which are thought by many to be rooted in human biology, are not so rooted at all. Rather, they appear to have been recently elaborated in the course of history.

In addition to cultural variation associated with gender, there is also variation related to differences in age. In any society, children are not expected to behave as adults, and the reverse is equally true. But then, who is a child and who is an adult? Again, although the age differences are "natural," cultures give their own meaning and timetable to the human life cycle. In North America, for example, individuals are generally not regarded as adults until the age of 18; in many others, adulthood begins earlier—often around age 12. That said, the status of adulthood often has less to do with age than with passage through certain prescribed rituals. Besides age and gender variation, there may be cultural variation between subgroups in societies. These may be occupational groups, where there is a complex division of labor, or social classes in a stratified society, or ethnic groups in some other societies (more will be said of these in subsequent chapters). When such groups exist within a society, each functioning by its own distinctive standards of behavior while still sharing some common standards, we speak of **subcultures.** The word *subculture,* it should be noted, carries no connotation of lesser status relative to the word *cultural.*

Amish communities comprise one example of a subculture in North America.[1] Specifically, they are an

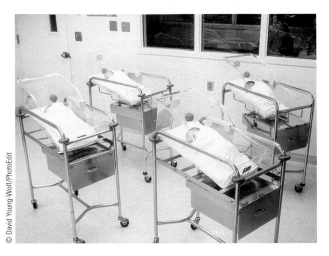

In the United States, European American culture requires that newborn infants be assigned a sexual identity of either male or female. Yet, significant numbers of infants are born each year whose genitalia do not conform to cultural expectations. Because only two genders are recognized, the usual reaction is surgery to make the young bodies conform to cultural requirements. In most cases, male genitals are constructed, merely because they are easier. This is in contrast to many Native American cultures in which more than two genders are recognized and socially acceptable.

[1]Hostetler, J., & Huntington, G. (1971). *Children in Amish society.* New York: Holt, Rinehart and Winston.

gender The cultural elaborations and meanings assigned to the biological differentiation between the sexes.
subculture A distinctive set of standards and behavior patterns by which a group within a larger society operates.

© Elizabeth Crews/The Image Works

© Michael Newman/PhotoEdit

VISUAL COUNTERPOINT In all human societies, children's play is used both consciously and unconsciously to teach gender roles.

ethnic group—people who collectively and publicly identify themselves as a distinct group based on various cultural features such as shared ancestry and common origin, language, customs, and traditional beliefs. The Amish originated in Central Europe during the Christian Protestant revolutions that swept through Europe in the 16th century. Today members of this group number about 100,000 and live mainly in Pennsylvania, Ohio, Illinois, and Indiana in the United States, and in Ontario, Canada. They are pacifistic, rural people, who base their lives on their traditional fundamentalist religion and prohibit marriage outside their faith. Among themselves they usually speak a German dialect known as Pennsylvania Dutch (*Deutsch* meaning German). They use High German for religious purposes, and children learn English in school. They value simplicity, hard work, and a high degree of neighborly cooperation. They dress in a distinctive plain garb, and even today rely on the horse for transportation as well as agricultural work. As such, they share the same **ethnicity.** This term, rooted in the Greek word *ethnikos* ("nation") and related to *ethnos* ("custom") is the expression of the set of cultural ideas held by an ethnic group.

The goal of Amish education is to teach youngsters reading, writing, and arithmetic, as well as Amish values.

ethnic group People who collectively and publicly identify themselves as a distinct group based on various cultural features such as shared ancestry and common origin, language, customs, and traditional beliefs.
ethnicity This term, rooted in the Greek word *ethnikos* ("nation") and related to *ethnos* ("custom") is the expression of the set of cultural ideas held by an ethnic group.

Adults in the community reject what they regard as "worldly" knowledge and the idea of schools producing good citizens for the state. Resisting all attempts to force their children to attend regular public schools, they insist that education take place near home and that teachers be committed to Amish ideals. Their nonconformity to many standards of mainstream culture has caused frequent conflict with state authorities, as well as legal and personal harassment. Pressed to compromise, they have introduced "vocational training" beyond the elementary level to fulfill state requirements, but they have managed to retain control of their schools and maintain their way of life. A besieged community, more distrustful than ever of the dominant North American culture surrounding them, they mingle as little as possible with non-Amish people.

The Amish are but one example of the way a subculture may be dealt with by the larger culture within which it functions. Different as they are, the Amish actually put into practice many values that other North Americans primarily respect in the abstract: thrift, hard work, independence, a close family life. The degree of tolerance accorded to them, in contrast to some other ethnic groups, is also due in part to the fact that the Amish are "white" Europeans; they are defined as being of the same "race" as those who comprise dominant mainstream society. Although the concept of race has been shown to have no biological validity when applied to humans, it still persists as a powerful social classification. This can be seen in the general lack of tolerance shown toward American Indians, typically viewed as racially different by members of the dominant society.

Implicit in the discussion thus far is that subcultures may develop in different ways. On the one hand, Amish subculture in the United States emerged as the product of

Anthropology Applied ▸ New Houses for Apache Indians

The United States, in common with other industrialized countries of the world, contains a number of more or less separate subcultures. Those who live by the standards of one particular subculture have their closest relationships with one another, receiving constant reassurance that their perceptions of the world are the only correct ones, and coming to take it for granted that the whole culture is as they see it. As a consequence, members of one subcultural group frequently have trouble understanding the needs and aspirations of other such groups. For this reason anthropologists, with their special understanding of cultural differences, are frequently employed as go-betweens in situations requiring interaction between peoples of differing cultural traditions.

As an example, George S. Esber, Jr., while still a graduate student in anthropology, was hired to work with architects and a band of Apache Indians in designing a new community for the Apaches.[a] Although architects began with an awareness that cross-cultural differences in the use of space exist,

they had no idea of how to get relevant information from the Indians. For their part, the Apaches had no explicit awareness of their needs, for these were based on unconscious patterns of behavior. Moreover, the idea that patterns of behavior could be acted out unconsciously was an alien one to them.

Esber's task was to persuade the architects to hold back on their planning long enough for him to gather, through fieldwork and review of written records, the kind of data from which Apache housing needs could be abstracted. At the same time, he had to overcome Apache anxieties over an outsider coming into their midst to learn about matters as personal as their daily lives. With these things accomplished, Esber was able to identify and successfully communicate to the architects features of Apache life with important implications for community design. At the same time, discussions of findings with the Apaches themselves enhanced awareness of their own unique needs.

As a result of Esber's work, in 1981 the Apaches were able to move into

houses that had been designed with *their* participation, for *their* specific needs. Among other things, account was taken of their need to ease into a social situation rather than to jump right in. Apache etiquette requires that all people be in full view of one another so each can assess from a distance the behavior of others in order to act appropriately with them. This requires a large, open living space. At the same time, hosts must be able to offer food to guests as a prelude to further social interaction. Thus, cooking and dining areas cannot be separated from living space. Nor can standard middle-class Anglo kitchen equipment be installed; the need for handling large quantities of food requires large pots and pans, for which extra-large sinks and cupboards are necessary. In such ways were the new houses made to accommodate long-standing native traditions. ■ ■ ■

[a]See Esber, G. (1987). Designing Apache houses with Apaches. In R. M. Wulff & S. J. Fiske (Eds.), *Anthropological praxis: Translating knowledge into action.* Boulder, CO: Westview.

the way these European immigrants have communicated and interacted in pursuit of their common goals within the wider society. On the other hand, North American Indian subcultures are formerly independent cultural groups that underwent colonization by European settlers and were forcibly brought under the control of federal governments in the United States and Canada. Although all American Indian groups have undergone enormous changes due to colonization, many have held on to traditions significantly different from those of the dominant Euramerican culture surrounding them, so that it is sometimes difficult to decide whether they remain as distinct

The Amish people have held on to their traditional agrarian way of life in the midst of industrialized North American society. By maintaining their own schools to instill Amish values in their children, prohibiting mechanized vehicles and equipment, and dressing in their distinctive plain clothing, the Amish proclaim their own special identity.

© Dennis MacDonald/PhotoEdit

cultures as opposed to subcultures. In this sense, *culture* and *subculture* represent opposite ends of a continuum, with no clear dividing line in the "gray area" between.

This raises the issue of the multi-ethnic or **pluralistic society,** in which two or more ethnic groups or nationalities are politically organized into one territorial state but maintain their cultural differences. Pluralistic societies could not have existed before the first politically centralized states arose a mere 5,000 years ago. With the rise of the state, it became possible to bring about the political unification of two or more formerly independent societies, each with its own culture, thereby creating what amounts to a more complex order that transcends the theoretical one culture–one society linkage. Pluralistic societies, which are common in the world today (Figure 2.1), all face the same challenge: They are comprised of groups that, by virtue of their high degree of cultural variation, are all essentially operating by different sets of rules. Since social living requires predictable behavior, it may be difficult for the members of any one subgroup to accurately interpret and follow the different standards by which the others operate. This can lead to significant misunderstandings, such as the following case reported in the *Wall Street Journal* of May 13, 1983:

> Salt Lake City—Police called it a cross-cultural misunderstanding. When the man showed up to buy the Shetland pony advertised for sale, the owner asked what he intended to do with the animal. "For my son's birthday," he replied, and the deal was closed.
>
> The buyer thereupon clubbed the pony to death with a two-by-four, dumped the carcass in his pickup truck and drove away. The horrified seller called the police, who tracked down the buyer. At his house they found a birthday party in progress. The pony was trussed and roasting in a *luau pit.* "We don't ride horses, we eat them," explained the buyer, a recent immigrant from Tonga [an island in the Pacific Ocean].

Unfortunately, the difficulty members of one subgroup within a pluralistic society may have making sense of the standards by which members of other groups operate can go far beyond mere misunderstanding. It can intensify to the point of anger and violence.

The difficulties of making pluralistic societies work is illustrated here by violent uprisings in Chechnya, seeking independence from the Russian Federation.

Among many examples of this is the pluralistic society of Guatemala, where a government distrustful of the country's large indigenous Maya populations unleashed a deadly reign of terror against them. We will look at this in some detail in Chapter 16.

Every culture includes individuals who behave in abnormal ways that earn them such labels as "oddball," "eccentric," or "crazy." Typically, because they differ too much from the acceptable standard, they are looked upon with disapproval by their society. And if their behavior becomes too peculiar, they are sooner or later excluded from participating in the activities of the group. Such exclusion acts to keep what is defined as deviant behavior outside the group. Interestingly, behavior viewed as deviant in one society may not be in another. In many American Indian societies, for example, a few exceptional individuals were permitted to assume for life the role normally associated with people of the opposite sex. Thus, a man could dress as a woman and engage in what were conventionally defined as female activities; conversely, women could achieve renown in activities normally in the masculine domain. In effect, four different gender identities were available: masculine men, feminine men, feminine women, and masculine women. Furthermore, masculine women and feminine men were not merely accepted, but were highly respected.

Culture Is Learned

All culture is learned rather than biologically inherited, prompting anthropologist Ralph Linton to refer to it as humanity's "social heredity." One learns one's culture by growing up with it, and the process whereby culture is transmitted from one generation to the next is called **enculturation.**

pluralistic society A society in which two or more ethnic groups or nationalities are politically organized into one territorial state but maintain their cultural differences.
enculturation The process by which a society's culture is transmitted from one generation to the next and individuals become members of their society.

FIGURE 2.1

Shown here are some of the ethnic groups of the Russian Federation, which is by far the largest and most important part of the former Union of Soviet Socialist Republics. Contrary to popular belief, the ethnic conflicts that have broken out since the collapse of the Soviet Union stem not from a conflictive nature of ethnicity but from Stalin's policy of emphasizing ethnicity while preventing its expression and forcibly removing populations from their homelands to new localities.

VISUAL COUNTERPOINT

In the United States, a man dressing as a woman (cross-dressing) has traditionally been regarded as abnormal behavior, but in some cultures, it is considered perfectly normal. Not only does culture define what is normal and abnormal, but such definitions may change over time. Although male cross-dressers in the United States are still mocked or looked down upon by many, women today throughout North America commonly wear men's clothing without being regarded as at all odd.

Most animals eat and drink whenever the urge arises. Humans, however, are enculturated to do most of their eating and drinking at certain culturally prescribed times and feel hungry as those times approach. These eating times vary from culture to culture, as does what is eaten, how it is prepared, how it is eaten, and where. To add complexity, food is used to do more than merely satisfy nutritional requirements. For example, when used to celebrate rituals and religious activities, as it often is, food "establishes relationships of give and take, of cooperation, of sharing, of an emotional bond that is universal."[2]

Through enculturation every person learns the socially appropriate way of satisfying the basic biologically determined needs of all humans: food, sleep, shelter, companionship, self-defense, and sexual gratification. It is important to distinguish between the needs themselves, which are not learned, and the learned ways in which they are satisfied—for each culture determines in its own way how these needs will be met. For instance, a North American's idea of a comfortable way to sleep may vary greatly from that of a Japanese person.

Learned behavior is exhibited in some degree by most, if not all, mammals. Several species may even be said to have elementary culture, in that local populations share patterns of behavior that, just like humans, each generation learns from the one before and that differ from one population to another. Elizabeth Marshall Thomas, for example, has described a distinctive pattern of behavior among lions of southern Africa's Kalahari Desert—behavior that regulates interaction with the region's indigenous people and that each generation passes on to the next.[3] She has shown as well how that Kalahari lion culture changed over a 30-year period in response to new circumstances. That said, it is important to note that not all learned behavior is cultural. For instance, a pigeon may learn tricks, but this behavior is reflexive, the result of conditioning by repeated training, not the product of enculturation.

Beyond our species, examples of cultural behavior are particularly evident among other primates. A chimpanzee, for example, will take a twig, strip it of all leaves, and smooth it down to fashion a tool for extracting termites from their nest. Such tool making, which juveniles learn from their elders, is unquestionably a form of cul-

tural behavior once thought to be exclusively human. In Japan, macaques that learned the advantages of washing sweet potatoes before eating them passed the practice on to the next generation. And so it goes; what is interesting is that within any given primate species, the culture of one population often differs from that of others, just as it does among humans. We have discovered both in captivity and in the wild that primates in general and apes in particular "possess a near-human intelligence generally, including the use of sounds in representational ways, a rich awareness of the aims and objectives of others, the ability to engage in tactical deception, and the ability to use symbols in communication with humans and each other."[4]

Given the remarkable degree of biological similarity between apes and humans, it should come as no surprise to find that they are like us in other ways as well. In fact, in all respects the differences between apes and humans are differences of degree rather than kind (although the degree *does* make a major difference). All of this knowledge has come as something of a shock, as it contradicts a belief that is deeply embedded in Western cultures: the idea that there is a vast and unbridgeable gap between humans and animals. It has not been easy to overcome this bias, and indeed we still have not come to grips fully with the moral implications with respect to the way humans treat fellow primates in research laboratories.

Culture Is Based on Symbols

Much of human behavior is mediated by **symbols**—signs, sounds, emblems, and other things that represent something else in a meaningful way. Because there is no inherent or necessary relationship between a thing and its representation, symbols are arbitrary. They only acquire specific meaning when people agree on usage in their communications. In fact, symbols—ranging from national flags to wedding rings to money—enter into every aspect of culture, from social life and religion to politics and economics. We're all familiar with the fervor and devotion that a religious symbol can elicit from a believer. An Islamic crescent, Christian cross, or a Jewish Star of David, as well as the sun among the Inca, a cow among the Hindu, a white buffalo calf among Plains Indians, or any other object of worship may bring to mind years of struggle and persecution or may stand for a whole philosophy or creed.

The most important symbolic aspect of culture is language—using words to represent objects and ideas. Through language humans are able to transmit culture from one generation to another. In particular, language

[2]Caroulis, J. (1996). Food for thought. *Pennsylvania Gazette*, 95(3), 16.

[3]Thomas, E. M. (1994). *The tribe of the tiger* (pp. 109–186). New York: Simon & Schuster.

symbols Signs, emblems, and other things that represent something else in a meaningful but arbitrary way.

[4]Reynolds, V. (1994). Primates in the field, primates in the lab. *Anthropology Today*, 10(2), 4.

makes it possible to learn from cumulative, shared experience. Without it, one could not inform others about events, emotions, and other experiences to which they were not a party. We will explore the important relationship between language and culture in greater detail in Chapter 4.

Culture Is Integrated

For purposes of comparison and analysis, anthropologists customarily imagine a culture as a well-structured system made up of distinctive parts that function together as an organized whole. While they may sharply distinguish each part as a clearly defined unit with its own characteristic features and special place within the larger system, anthropologists recognize that reality is more convoluted, and divisions between cultural units are often blurry. However, because all aspects of a culture must be reasonably well integrated in order to function properly, anthropologists seldom focus on an individual feature in isolation. Instead, they view each in terms of its larger context and carefully examine its connections to related cultural features.

Broadly speaking, a society's cultural features fall within three categories: social structure, infrastructure, and superstructure. **Social structure** concerns the rule-governed relationships that hold members of a society together, with all their rights and obligations. Households, families, associations, and power relations, including politics, are all part of social structure. It establishes group cohesion and enables people to consistently satisfy their basic needs, including food and shelter for themselves and their dependents, by means of work. So, there is a direct relationship between a group's social structure and its economic foundation, which includes subsistence practices and the tools and other material equipment used to make a living. Because subsistence practices involve tapping into available resources to satisfy a society's basic needs, this aspect of culture is known as **infrastructure.** Supported by this economic foundation, a society is also held together by a shared sense of identity and worldview. This collective body of ideas, beliefs, and values by which a group of people makes sense of the world—its shape, challenges, and opportunities—and their place in it is known as ideology or **superstructure.** Including religion and national ideology, it structures the overarching ideas that people in a society have about themselves and everything else that exists around them—and it gives meaning and direction to their lives. Influencing and reinforcing one another, these three interdependent structures together form part of a cultural system (Figure 2.2).

The integration of economic, social, and ideological aspects of a culture can be illustrated by the Kapauku Papuans, a mountain people of western New Guinea

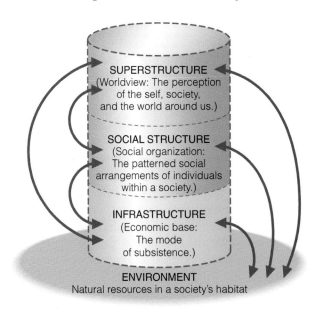

FIGURE 2.2

The barrel model of culture. Every culture is an integrated and dynamic system of adaptation that responds to a combination of internal factors (economic, social, ideological) and external factors (environmental, climatic). Within a cultural system, there are functional relationships among the economic base (infrastructure), the social organization (social structure), and the ideology (superstructure). A change in one leads to a change in the others.

(Figure 2.3), studied in 1955 by the North American anthropologist Leopold Pospisil.[5] The Kapauku economy relies on plant cultivation, along with pig breeding, hunting, and fishing. Although plant cultivation provides most of the people's food, it is through pig

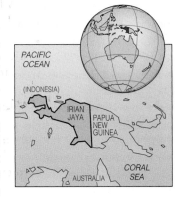

FIGURE 2.3

[5]Pospisil, L. (1963). *The Kapauku Papuans of west New Guinea.* New York: Holt, Rinehart and Winston.

social structure The rule-governed relationships—with all their rights and obligations—that hold members of a society together. This includes households, families, associations, and power relations, including politics.
infrastructure The economic foundation of a society, including its subsistence practices, and the tools and other material equipment used to make a living.
superstructure A society's shared sense of identity and worldview. The collective body of ideas, beliefs, and values by which a group of people makes sense of the world—its shape, challenges, and opportunities—and their place in it. This includes religion and national ideology.

breeding that men achieve political power and positions of legal authority.

Among the Kapauku, pig breeding is a complex business. Raising lots of pigs, obviously, requires lots of food to feed them. The primary fodder is sweet potatoes, grown in garden plots. Since Kapauku culture defines some essential gardening activities as women's work, these tasks can be performed only by women. Furthermore, pigs must be cared for by women. So, to raise lots of pigs, a man has to have lots of women in the household. Thus, in Kapauku society, multiple wives (polygyny) are not only permitted, they are highly desired. For each wife, however, a man must pay a bride price, and this can be expensive. Furthermore, wives have to be compensated for their care of pigs. Put simply, it takes pigs, by which wealth is measured, to get wives, without whom pigs cannot be raised in the first place. Needless to say, this requires considerable entrepreneurship. It is this ability that produces leaders in Kapauku society.

The interrelatedness of the various parts of Kapauku culture is even more complicated. For example, one condition that encourages polygyny is a surplus of adult females, sometimes caused by loss of males through warfare. Among the Kapauku, recurring warfare is a fact of life and has long been viewed as a necessary evil. By the rules of Kapauku warfare, men may be killed but women may not. This system works to promote the kind of imbalanced sex ratio that fosters polygyny. Polygyny tends to work best if a man's wives all come to live in his village, which is the case among the Kapauku, rather than the other way around. Thus, the men of a village are typically "blood" relatives of one another, and this enhances their ability to cooperate in warfare. Considering all of this, it makes sense that Kapauku typically reckon descent (ancestry) through men.

Descent reckoning through men coupled with near-constant warfare tend to promote male dominance. So it is not surprising to find that positions of leadership in Kapauku society are held exclusively by men, who appropriate the products of women's labor in order to play their political "games." Such male dominance is by no means characteristic of all human societies, despite assertions to the contrary (see Anthropologists of Note on Eleanor Leacock). Rather, as in the Kapauku case, it arises only under particular sets of circumstances that, if changed, will alter the way in which men and women relate to each other.

In sum, for a culture to function properly, its various parts must be consistent with one another. But consistency is not the same as harmony. In fact, there is often friction and potential for conflict within every culture—among individuals, factions, and competing institutions. Even on the most basic level of a society, individuals rarely experience the enculturation process in precisely the same way, nor do they perceive their reality in precisely identical fashion. Moreover, conditions may change, brought on by inside or outside forces. A society will function reasonably well as long as its culture is capable of handling the daily strains and tensions. However, when a culture no longer provides adequate solutions or when its component parts are no longer consistent, a situation of cultural crisis ensues. These ideas were explored with considerable depth by British anthropologist A. R. Radcliffe-Brown (see Anthropologists of Note).

Culture Is Dynamic

Cultures are dynamic systems that respond to motions and actions within and around them. When one element within the system shifts or changes, the entire system gears to adjust, just as it does when an outside force applies pressure. To function adequately, a culture must be flexible enough to allow such adjustments in the face of unstable or changing circumstances. All cultures are, of necessity, dynamic, but some are far less so than others. When a culture is too rigid or static and fails to provide its members with the means required for long-term survival under changing conditions, it is not likely to endure. On the other hand, some cultures are so fluid and open to change that they may lose their distinctive character. The Amish mentioned earlier in this chapter typically resist change as much as possible but are constantly making balanced decisions to adjust when absolutely necessary. North Americans in general, however, have created a culture in which change has become a positive ideal. This dynamic aspect of culture is discussed further later in this chapter.

MEDIATREK
To visit an award-winning Web site that presents the ins and outs of anthropological fieldwork from start to finish, go to MediaTrek 2.2 on the companion Web site or CD-ROM.

STUDYING CULTURE IN THE FIELD

Equipped now with some basic knowledge about culture, we can raise the question, How does an anthropologist study culture in the field? Since every culture is comprised of rules or standards that cannot be directly observed, an anthropologist faces the challenge of gleaning those rules through an analysis of observed behavior. By carefully watching, questioning, listening, and analyzing over a period of time, one can usually identify, explain, and often predict a group's social behavior. The task is similar to that of a linguist who tries to develop a set of rules to account for the ways a

Anthropologists of Note

A. R. Radcliffe-Brown (1881–1955) ▪ Eleanor Burke Leacock (1922–1987)

The British anthropologist A. R. Radcliffe-Brown was the originator of what has come to be known as the structural-functionalist school of thought. He and his followers maintained that each custom and belief of a society has a specific function that serves to perpetuate the structure of that society—its ordered arrangements of parts—so that the society's continued existence is possible. The job of the anthropologist, therefore, is to study the ways in which customs and beliefs function to solve the problem of maintaining the system. From such studies, he claimed, universal laws of human behavior would emerge.

© Bettmann/Corbis

The value of the structural-functionalist approach is that it caused anthropologists to analyze societies and their cultures as systems and to examine the interconnections between their various parts. However, Radcliffe-Brown's universal laws of social behavior have not emerged, for anthropology is not an experimental science like physics or chemistry, and human activities are not the product of natural laws that always operate in predictable ways. In the natural sciences, scholars may engage in carefully controlled experimentation in their laboratories where they can accurately observe and exactly describe what happens under which circumstances. Finding out how nature really functions, they may discover a fundamental principle and formulate a natural law—such as the law of gravity—that allows them to explain and precisely predict how something in nature will behave under given conditions. In contrast, anthropologists study human cultures as they function in reality, not in the laboratory. And because cultures are complex and historically conditioned, anthropologists are forced to come to terms with a degree of uncertainty in their theories. This is why anthropologists may successfully explain why something happened or is likely to happen but can rarely predict exactly what will happen.

A pioneer in feminist anthropology, Eleanor Burke Leacock was among the first to critically examine anthropological writings from a woman's perspective. Her doctoral research among Innu Indians in Labrador investigated the impact that fur trade with European colonizers had on tribal gender relations and revealed that it lowered the status of women. Earning her Ph.D. in 1952, Leacock first raised a family and then began teaching anthropology in 1963. She went on to chair the anthropology

Vance Allen

department at City College of New York from 1972 until her death. A founder of the New York Women's Anthropology Caucus in 1972 and author of many publications, she challenged academia's false assumptions about the universality of female inferiority, arguing that these misconceptions reflect class-based prejudices of the researchers' own societies. In 1980, she co-organized a groundbreaking international conference of female anthropologists to review how colonialism and global capitalism had contributed to the subordination of women in peasant and nonindustrial societies of the poor countries. Interested in a critical anthropology that could contribute to radical social change, Leacock became a Marxist feminist. Fighting sex, class, and race discrimination, she sought to bridge the gap between academia and activism and became a respected advocate for a socially committed anthropology that helps break the shackles of repression.

---

group of people combine sounds into meaningful phrases.

To further explore the anthropologist's task of identifying the rules that underlie each culture, consider the following discussion of exogamy—marriage outside one's own group—among the Trobriand Islanders, as described by Polish anthropologist Bronislaw Malinowski:

> If you were to inquire into the matter among the Trobrianders, you would find that . . . the natives show horror at the idea of violating the rules of exogamy and that they believe that sores, diseases, even death might follow clan incest. [But] from the viewpoint of the native libertine, *suvasova* (the breach of exogamy) is indeed a specially interesting and spicy form of erotic experience. Most of my informants would not only admit but did actually boast about having committed this offense.[6]

[6]Malinowski, B. (1922). *Argonauts of the western Pacific*. New York: Dutton.

Describing another culture is like trying to describe a new game. The people in this picture look as though they are playing baseball, but they are playing cricket. To describe cricket in the language of baseball would be at best a caricature of the game as the British know it. The challenge in anthropology is how to describe another culture for an audience unfamiliar with it, so that the description is not a caricature.

Malinowski himself determined that although such breaches did occur, they were much less frequent than gossip would have it. Had he relied solely on what the Trobrianders told him, his description of their culture would have been inaccurate. The same sort of discrepancy between cultural ideals and the way people actually behave can be found in any culture, as illustrated in our Chapter 1 discussion of William Rathje's Garbage Project.

From these examples, it is obvious that an anthropologist must be cautious if aiming for an accurate description of a culture. To play it safe, he or she needs to seek out and consider three kinds of data:

1. The people's own understanding of their culture and the general rules they share—that is, their ideal sense of the way their own society ought to be.
2. The extent to which people believe they are observing those rules—that is, how they think they really behave.
3. The behavior that can be directly observed—that is, what the anthropologist actually sees happening. (In the example of the Trobrianders, one would watch to see whether or not the rule of *suvasova* is actually violated.)

Clearly, the way people think they *should* behave, the way in which they think they *do* behave, and the way in which they *actually* behave may be distinctly different. By carefully examining and comparing these elements, the anthropologist can draw up a set of rules that may explain the acceptable range of behavior within a culture. Of course, the anthropologist is only human. As discussed in Chapter 1, it is difficult to completely cast aside one's personal feelings and biases, which have been shaped by one's own culture, as well as gender and age. Yet it is important to recognize this challenge and make every effort to overcome it, for otherwise one may seriously misinterpret what one sees. As a case in point, we may see how the male bias of the Polish culture in which Malinowski was raised caused him to miss important things in his pioneering study of the Trobriand Islanders. Unlike today, when anthropologists receive special training before going into the field, Malinowski set out to do fieldwork early in the 20th century with little formal preparation.

The following Original Study is by anthropologist Annette Weiner, who ventured to the Trobriand Islands 60 years after Malinowski. It reveals how gender may impact one's research findings—both in terms of the bias that may affect the researcher's outlook and in terms of what informants may feel comfortable sharing with the researcher.

Original Study

The Importance of Trobriand Women

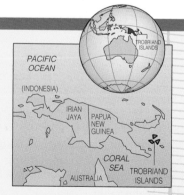

Walking into a village at the beginning of fieldwork is entering a world without cultural guideposts. The task of learning values that others live by is never easy. The rigors of fieldwork involve listening and watching, learning a new language of speech and actions, and most of all, letting go of one's own cultural assumptions in order to understand the meanings others give to work, power, death, family, and friends. As my fieldwork in the Trobriand Islands of Papua New Guinea was no exception, I wrestled doggedly with each of these problems.

Doing research in the Trobriand Islands created one additional obstacle. I was working in the footsteps of a celebrated anthropological ancestor, Bronislaw Kasper Malinowski. . . .

In 1971, before my first trip to the Trobriands, I thought I understood many things about Trobriand customs and beliefs from having read Malinowski's exhaustive writings. Once there, however, I found that I had much more to discover about what I thought I already knew. For many months I worked with these discordant realities, always conscious of Malinowski's shadow, his words, his explanations. Although I found significant differences in areas of importance, I gradually came to understand how he reached certain conclusions. The answers we both received from informants were not so dissimilar, and I could actually trace how Malinowski had analyzed what his informants told him in a way that made sense and was scientifically significant—given what anthropologists generally then recognized about such societies. Sixty years separate our fieldwork, and any comparison of our studies illustrates not so much Malinowski's mistaken interpretations but the developments in anthropological knowledge and inquiry from his time to mine.

This important point has been forgotten by those anthropologists who today argue that ethnographic writing can never be more than a kind of fictional account of an author's experiences. Although Malinowski and I were in the Trobriands at vastly different historical moments, and there also are many areas in which our analyses differ, a large part of what we learned in the field was similar. From the vantage point that time gives to me, I can illustrate how our differences, even those that are major, came to be. Taken together, our two studies profoundly exemplify the scientific basis that underlies the collection of ethnographic data. Like all such data, however, whether researched in a laboratory or a village, the more we learn about a subject, the more we can refine and revise earlier assumptions. This is the way all sciences create their own historical developments. Therefore, the lack of agreement between Malinowski's ethnography and mine must not be taken as an adversarial attack against an opponent. Nor should it be read as an example of the writing of ethnography as "fiction" or "partial truths." Each of our differences can be traced historically within the discipline of anthropology.

My most significant point of departure from Malinowski's analyses was the attention I gave to women's productive work. In my original research plans, women were not the central focus of study, but on the first day I took up residence in a village I was taken by them to watch a distribution of their own wealth—bundles of banana leaves and banana fiber skirts—which they exchanged with other women in commemoration of someone who had recently died. Watching that event forced me to take women's economic roles more seriously than I would have from reading Malinowski's studies. Although Malinowski noted the high status of Trobriand women, he attributed their importance to the fact that Trobrianders reckon descent through women, thereby giving them genealogical significance in a matrilineal society. Yet he never considered that this significance was underwritten by women's own wealth because he did not systematically investigate the women's productive activities. Although in his field notes he mentions Trobriand women making these seemingly useless banana bundles to be exchanged at a death, his published work only deals with men's wealth.

My taking seriously the importance of women's wealth not only brought women as the neglected half of society clearly into the ethnographic picture but also forced me to revise many of Malinowski's assumptions about Trobriand men. For example, Trobriand kinship as described by Malinowski has always been a subject of debate among anthropologists. For Malinowski, the basic relationships within a Trobriand family were guided by the matrilineal principle of "mother-right" and "father-love." A father was called "stranger" and had little authority over his own children. A woman's brother was the commanding figure and exercised

Estate of Annette B. Weiner

In the Trobriand Islands, women's wealth consists of skirts and banana leaves, large quantities of which must be given away on the death of a relative.

[CONTINUED]

[CONTINUED]

control over his sister's sons because they were members of his matrilineage rather than their father's matrilineage.

According to Malinowski, this matrilineal drama was played out biologically by the Trobrianders' belief that a man has no role as genitor. A man's wife is thought to become pregnant when an ancestral spirit enters her body and causes conception. Even after a child is born, Malinowski reported, it is the woman's brother who presents a harvest of yams to his sister so that her child will be fed with food from its own matrilineage, rather than its father's matrilineage. In this way, Malinowski conceptualized matrilineality as an institution in which the father of a child, as a member of a different matrilineage, was excluded not only from participating in procreation but also from giving any objects of lasting value to his children, thus provisioning them only with love.

In my study of Trobriand women and men, a different configuration of matrilineal descent emerged. A Trobriand

father is not a "stranger" in Malinowski's definition, nor is he a powerless figure as the third party to the relationship between a woman and her brother. The father is one of the most important persons in his child's life, and remains so even after his child grows up and marries. Even a father's procreative importance is incorporated into his child's growth and development. A Trobriand man gives his child many opportunities to gain things from his matrilineage, thereby adding to the available resources that he or she can draw upon. At the same time, this giving creates obligations on the part of a man's children toward him that last even beyond his death. Therefore, the roles that men and their children play in each other's lives are worked out through extensive cycles of exchanges, which define the strength of their relationships to each other and eventually benefit the other members of both their matrilineages. Central to these exchanges are women and their wealth.

That Malinowski never gave equal time to the women's side of things, given the deep significance of their role in societal and political life, is not surprising. Only recently have anthropologists begun to understand the importance of taking women's work seriously. In some cultures, such as the Middle East or among Australian aborigines, it is extremely difficult for ethnographers to cross the culturally bounded ritual worlds that separate women from men. In the past, however, both women and men ethnographers generally analyzed the societies they studied from a male perspective. The "women's point of view" was largely ignored in the study of gender roles, since anthropologists generally perceived women as living in the shadows of men—occupying the private rather than the public sectors of society, rearing children rather than engaging in economic or political pursuits. *(By Annette B. Weiner. (1988).* The Trobrianders of Papua New Guinea *(pp. 4–7). Wadsworth, a division of Thomson Learning.)*

CROSS-CULTURAL COMPARISONS

Ideally, as noted in Chapter 1, theories in cultural anthropology are generated from worldwide comparisons. A key resource that makes this possible is the **Human Relations Area Files (HRAF),** a vast collection of cross-indexed ethnographic and archaeological data catalogued by cultural characteristics and geographic location. Initiated by George Peter Murdock at Yale University in 1949, this ever-growing data bank classifies more than 700 cultural characteristics and includes nearly 400 societies, past and present, from all around the world. Available on the Internet and approaching a million pages of information, the HRAF facilitates comparative research on almost any cultural feature imaginable—warfare, subsistence practices, settlement patterns, marriage, rituals, and so on. Among other things, anthropologists interested in finding explanations for certain cultural beliefs and practices can use HRAF to test their hypotheses. For example, Peggy Reeves Sanday

examined a sample of 156 societies drawn from HRAF in an attempt to answer such questions as: Why do women play a more dominant role in some societies than others? Why, and under what circumstances, do men dominate women? Her study, published in 1981 (*Female Power and Male Dominance*), disproves the common misperception that women are universally subordinate to men, sheds light on the way men and women relate to each other, and ranks as a major landmark in the study of gender.

Although HRAF is a valuable research tool, it should be used with caution. For instance, the files only allow us to establish correlations between cultural features; they do not permit conclusions about cause and effect. In other words, while HRAF makes it possible to develop functional explanations (how things work), it does not provide us with causal explanations. For that, anthropologists must engage in more in-depth historical analysis of particular cultural practices.

Cultural comparisons are not restricted to contemporary ethnographic data. Indeed, anthropologists frequently turn to archaeological or historical data to test hypotheses about culture change. Cultural characteristics thought to be caused by certain specified conditions can be tested archaeologically by investigating similar situations where such conditions actually occurred. Also useful are data provided by the ethnohistorian.

Human Relations Area Files (HRAF) An ever-growing catalogue of cross-indexed ethnographic data, filed by geographic location and cultural characteristics. Housed at Yale University, HRAF is also electronically available on the Internet.

Ethnohistory is a kind of historical ethnography that studies cultures of the recent past through oral histories, the accounts of explorers, missionaries, and traders, and through analysis of such records as land titles, birth and death records, and other archival materials. The ethnohistorical analysis of cultures, like archaeology, is a valuable approach to understanding change.

Ethnohistorical research is also valuable for assessing the reliability of data used for making cross-cultural comparisons. For example, some anthropologists working with data from such resources as HRAF have concluded that, among foragers (people who subsist on hunting/fishing/gathering), it is (and was) the practice for married couples to live in or near the household of the husband's parents (anthropologists call this patrilocal residence). To be sure, many of the ethnographic reports now held at HRAF note this cultural feature among foragers. But the sweeping conclusion about residence patterns fails to take into account the fact that most such ethnographies were done among foragers whose traditional practices had been severely altered by pressures brought on by European traders and settlers invading their territories.

A case in point is the Western Abenaki people of northwestern New England. Ethnographic accounts of the 19th- and early 20th-centuries reported that they practiced patrilocal residence at that time and must also have done so prior to the actual invasion of their homeland by English colonists. However, more recent ethnohistorical research paints a different picture. It shows that Abenaki participation in the fur trade with Europeans, coupled with intensified warfare to hold back the aggressive intrusions of newcomers, increased the value placed on male activities and prompted a change from flexible to patrilocal residence patterns.[7] Upon close examination, other cases of patrilocal residence among foragers turn out to be similar responses to circumstances associated with the rise of colonialism and worldwide trade relations.

Ethnohistorical research, like the field studies of archaeologists, is valuable for testing hypotheses about culture. And like much of anthropology, it has practical use as well. In the United States, ethnohistorical research has flourished, for it often provides the key evidence necessary for deciding legal cases involving Native American land claims and hunting and fishing rights.

CULTURE AND ADAPTATION

In the course of their evolution, humans, like all animals, have continually faced the challenge of adapting to their environment. The term *adaptation* refers to a gradual

[7]Haviland, W. A., & Power, M. W. (1994). *The original Vermonters* (rev. and exp. ed., pp. 174–175, 215–261, 297–299). Hanover, NH: University Press of New England.

process by which organisms adjust to the conditions of the locality in which they live. With the exception of humans, organisms have generally adapted biologically, relying on advantageous anatomical and physiological mechanisms through a process known as natural selection. For example, body hair coupled with certain other physiological traits protects mammals from extremes of temperature; specialized teeth help them to procure the kinds of food they need; and so on. Humans, however, have increasingly come to depend on cultural adaptation, using a unique combination of brain power and physical skills to alter their circumstances. For example, biology has not provided them with built-in fur coats to protect them in cold climates, but it has given them the ability to make their own coats, build fires, and construct shelters to shield themselves against the cold. They may not be able to run as fast as a cheetah, but they are able to invent and build vehicles that can carry them faster and further than any other creature. Through culture and its many constructions, the human species has secured not just its survival but its expansion as well. By manipulating environments through cultural means, people have been able to move into a vast range of environments, from the icy Arctic to the Sahara Desert. They have even set foot on the moon.

This is not to say that everything that humans do they do *because* it is adaptive to a particular environment. For one thing, people do not just react to an environment as given; rather, they react to it as they perceive it, and different groups of people may perceive the same environment in radically different ways. They also react to things other than the environment: their own biological natures; their beliefs and attitudes; and the short and long-term consequences of their behavior for themselves and other life forms that share their habitats. Although people maintain cultures to deal with problems, it is clear that some cultural practices prove to be maladaptive and actually create new problems—such as toxic water and air caused by certain industrial practices or North America's obesity epidemic brought on by the culture of cars, fast food, and television.

A further complication is the relativity of any given adaptation: What is adaptive in one context may be seriously maladaptive in another. For example, the sanitation practices of food-foraging peoples—their toilet habits and methods of garbage disposal—are appropriate to contexts of low population levels and some degree of residential mobility. These same practices, however, become serious health hazards in the context of large, fully sedentary

ethnohistory The study of cultures of the recent past through oral histories; accounts left by explorers, missionaries, and traders; and through analysis of such records as land titles, birth and death records, and other archival materials.

© Alec Duncan

What is adaptive at one time may not be at another. In the United States, the principal source of fruits, vegetables, and fiber is the Central Valley of California, where irrigation works have made the desert bloom. As happened in ancient Mesopotamia, evaporation concentrates salts in the water, but here pollution is made even worse by chemical fertilizers. These poisons are now accumulating in the soil and threaten to make the valley a desert again.

populations. Similarly, behavior that is adaptive in the short run may be maladaptive over the long run. Thus, the development of irrigation in ancient Mesopotamia (modern-day Iraq) made it possible over the short run to increase food production, but over time it favored the gradual accumulation of salts in the soils. This, in turn, contributed to the collapse of civilization there about 4,000 years ago. Similarly, the development of prime farmland today in places like the eastern United States for purposes other than food production makes us increasingly dependent on food raised in marginal environments. High yields are presently possible through the application of expensive technology, but continuing loss of topsoil, increasing salinity of soils through evaporation of irrigation waters, and silting of irrigation works, not to mention impending shortages of water and fossil fuels, make continuing high yields over the long term unlikely. All of this said, it should be clear that for a culture to survive, it must produce behavior that is generally adaptive to the natural environment.

Functions of Culture

Polish anthropologist Bronislaw Malinowski put forth the idea that every successful culture resolves three fundamental levels of needs, which he referred to as biological, instrumental, and integrative (see Anthropologists of Note). Others have marked out different categories, but the idea is basically the same: A culture cannot survive if it does not deal effectively with primary problems. It must provide for the production and distribution of goods and services considered necessary for life. It must meet the bio-

logical and psychological needs of its members and provide some structure for reproduction in order to ensure the biological continuity of its members. It must enculturate new members so they can become functioning adults. It must facilitate conflict resolution and the maintenance of order among its members, as well as between them and outsiders. It must motivate its members to survive and engage in those activities necessary for survival. On top of all of this, a culture must be able to change if it is to remain adaptive under shifting conditions.

Culture and Change

Cultures have always changed over time, although rarely as rapidly or as massively as many are doing today. Changes take place in response to such events as population growth, technological innovation, environmental crisis, the intrusion of outsiders, or modification of behavior and values within the culture. Changes are often signified by apparel. For example, in North America, where swift change is driven by capitalism and the need for incessant market growth, clothing fashions change quickly. Over the past half-century or so, as advertisers increasingly utilized sexuality to promote sales, it became culturally permissible for men and women alike to wear clothing that revealed more and more of their bodies. Along with this has come greater permissiveness about body exposure in photographs, movies, and television, as well as less restrictive sexual attitudes and practices among many.

Although cultures must have some flexibility to remain adaptive, culture change can also bring unexpected and often disastrous results. For example, consider the relationship between culture and the droughts that periodically afflict so many people living in Africa just south of the Sahara Desert. Native to this region are some 14 million pastoral nomadic people whose lives are centered on cattle and other livestock, which are herded from place to place as required for pasturage and water. For thousands of years these people have been able to go about their business, efficiently utilizing vast areas of arid lands in ways that allowed them to survive severe droughts many times in the past. Unfortunately for them, their nomadic lifestyle annoys the central governments of modern states in the region. This is because the age-old seasonal migration patterns of pastoralists take them across relatively new international boundaries and make them difficult to track for purposes of taxation and other governmental controls.

Seeing nomads as a challenge to their authority, these governments have gone all out to stop them from ranging through their traditional grazing territories and to convert them into sedentary villagers. Overgrazing has resulted from this loss of mobility; moreover, the

Anthropologists of Note

Bronislaw Malinowski (1884–1942)

Courtesy Phoebe Apperson Hearst Museum of Anthropology

Polish-born Bronislaw Malinowski argued that people everywhere share certain biological and psychological needs and that the ultimate function of all cultural institutions is to fulfill those needs. Everyone, for example, needs to feel secure in relation to the physical universe. Therefore, when science and technology are inadequate to explain certain natural phenomena—such as eclipses or earthquakes—people develop religion and magic to account for those phenomena and to establish a feeling of security. The nature of the institution, according to Malinowski, is determined by its function.

Malinowski outlined three fundamental levels of needs that he claimed had to be resolved by all cultures:

1. A culture must provide for biological needs, such as the need for food and procreation.
2. A culture must provide for instrumental needs, such as the need for law and education.
3. A culture must provide for integrative needs, such as religion and art.

If anthropologists could analyze the ways in which a culture fills these needs for its members, Malinowski believed that they could also deduce the origin of cultural traits. Although this belief was never justified, the quality of data called for by Malinowski's approach set new standards for ethnographic fieldwork. He was the first to insist on the necessity to join in native life to really understand it. He himself showed the way with his work in the Trobriand Islands between 1915 and 1918. Never before had such in-depth work been done, nor had such insights been gained into the workings of another culture. Such was the quality of Malinowski's Trobriand research that, with it, ethnography can be said to have come of age as a scientific enterprise.

© Bettmann/Corbis

AP/Wide World Photos

AP/Wide World Photos

VISUAL COUNTERPOINT In the United States before 1950, matters pertaining to the human body were not considered suitable for polite conversation, so mention of President Roosevelt's paralyzed legs was scrupulously avoided in the 1930s and 1940s. By the 1980s, attitudes had changed so dramatically that the president's colon was discussed in great detail when President Reagan was hospitalized for cancer. By the late 1990s even President Clinton's genitals were discussed in public.

problem has been compounded by government efforts to involve the pastoralists in a market economy by encouraging them to raise many more animals than required for their own needs in order to have a surplus to sell. The resultant devastation, where there had previously been no significant overgrazing or erosion, now makes droughts far more disastrous than they would otherwise be. In fact, it places the very existence of the nomads' traditional way of life in jeopardy.

CULTURE, SOCIETY, AND THE INDIVIDUAL

Ultimately, a society is no more than a union of individuals, all of whom have their own special needs and interests. If a society is to survive, it must succeed in balancing the self-interest of its members against the demands of the society as a whole. To accomplish this, a society offers rewards for adherence to its cultural standards. In most cases, these rewards assume the form of social acceptance. In contemporary North American society, a man who holds a good job, is faithful to his wife, and goes to church, for example, may be elected "Model Citizen" by his neighbors. To ensure the survival of the group, each person must learn to postpone certain immediate personal satisfactions. Yet the needs of the individual cannot be suppressed too far, lest levels of stress become too much to bear. Hence, a delicate balance always exists between an individual's interests and the demands made upon each person by the group.

Take, for example, the matter of sexual expression, which, like anything that people do, is shaped by culture. Sexuality is important in any society, for it helps to strengthen cooperative bonds between members of society ensuring the perpetuation of society itself. Yet sex can be disruptive to social living. If the issue of who has sexual access to whom is not clearly spelled out, competition for sexual privileges can destroy the cooperative bonds on which human survival depends. Uncontrolled sexual activity, too, can result in reproductive rates that cause a society's population to outstrip its resources. Hence, as it shapes sexual behavior, every culture must balance the needs of society against the need for sufficient individual gratification, so that frustration does not build up to the point of being disruptive in itself. Of course, cultures vary widely in the way they go about this. On one end of the spectrum, societies such as the Amish in North America or groups in Saudi Arabia have taken an extremely restrictive approach, specifying no sex outside of marriage. On the other end are societies such as the Norwegians in Europe who often create families without marriage, or even more extreme, the Canela Indians in Brazil, whose social codes guarantee that, sooner or later, everyone in a given village has had sex with just about everyone of the opposite sex. Yet, even as permissive as the latter situation may sound, there are nonetheless strict rules as to how the system operates.[8]

Not just in sex, but in all things, cultures must strike a balance between the needs of individuals and those of society. When those of society take precedence, then people experience excessive stress. Symptomatic of this are increased levels of mental illness and behavior regarded as antisocial: violence, crime, abuse of alcohol and other drugs, depression, suicide, or simply alienation. If not corrected, the situation can result in cultural breakdown. But just as problems develop if the

In the United States, the rise of private militia groups reflects the frustration of people whose needs are poorly satisfied by the culture.

needs of society take precedence over those of the individual, so too do they develop if the balance is upset in the other direction.

EVALUATION OF CULTURE

We have knowledge of numerous highly diverse cultural solutions to the challenges of human existence. The question often arises, Which is best? In the 19th century, Europeans—like the Asian peoples of China and Japan—had no doubts about the answer. Each saw its own civilization as the peak of human development. At the same time, though, anthropologists were intrigued to find that all cultures with which they had any familiarity saw themselves as the best of all possible worlds. This was commonly reflected in each society's name for itself, which almost invariably translated roughly into "true human beings." In contrast their names for outsiders typically translated into various versions of "subhumans," including "monkeys," "dogs," "weird-looking people," "funny talkers," and so forth. We now know that any adequately functioning culture regards its own ways as the only proper ones, a view known as **ethnocentrism.** Anthropologists have been actively engaged in the fight against ethnocentrism ever since they started to live among traditional peoples with radically different cultures and learned by personal experience that they were no less human than anyone else. Resisting the common urge to rank cultures, anthropologists have instead aimed to understand individual cultures and the general concept of culture. To do so, they examined each culture on its own terms, aiming to discern whether or not the culture

---

[8]Crocker, W. A., & Crocker, J. (1994). *The Canela, bonding through kinship, ritual and sex* (pp. 143–171). Fort Worth, TX: Harcourt Brace.

ethnocentrism The belief that the ways of one's own culture are the only proper ones.

satisfies the needs and expectations of the people themselves. If a people practiced human sacrifice or capital punishment, for example, they asked about the circumstances that made the taking of human life acceptable according to their values. The idea that one must suspend judgment on other peoples' practices in order to understand them in their own cultural terms is called **cultural relativism.** Only through such an approach can one gain an undistorted view of another people's ways, as well as insights into the practices of one's own society.

Take, for example, the 16th-century Aztec practice of sacrificing humans for religious purposes. Few (if any) North Americans today would condone such practices, but by suspending judgment one can get beneath the surface and discern how it functioned to reassure the populace that the Aztec state was healthy and that the sun would remain in the heavens. Beyond this, one can understand how the death penalty functions in the same way in the United States today. Numerous studies by a variety of social scientists have clearly shown that the death penalty does not deter violent crime, any more than Aztec sacrifice really provided sustenance for the sun. In fact, cross-cultural studies show that homicide rates mostly decline after its abolition.[9] Just like Aztec human sacrifice, capital punishment is an institutionalized magical response to perceived disorder. As U.S. anthropologists Anthony Paredes and Elizabeth D. Purdum point out, it "reassures many that society is not out of control after all, that the majesty of the law reigns and that God is indeed in his heaven."[10]

MEDIATREK
To view an interactive cross-cultural workbook created by the Peace Corps to teach volunteers how to work successfully in other cultures, go to MediaTrek 2.3 on the companion Web site or CD-ROM.

Clearly, cultural relativism is essential as a research tool. However, employing it as a tool does not mean suspending judgment forever, nor does it require the anthropologist to defend a people's right to engage in any cultural practice, no matter how destructive. All that is necessary is that we avoid *premature* judgments until we have a full understanding of the culture in which we are interested. Then, and only then, may the anthropologist adopt a critical stance. As David Maybury-Lewis emphasizes, "one does not avoid making judgments, but

rather postpones them in order to make informed judgments later."[11]

Forty years ago anthropologist Walter Goldschmidt devised a still-useful formula to help colleagues avoid the pitfalls of ethnocentrism without ending up in the "anything goes" position of cultural relativism pushed to absurdity.[12] In his view the important question to ask is, How well does a given culture satisfy the physical and psychological needs of those whose behavior it guides? Specific indicators are to be found in the nutritional status and general physical and mental health of its population; the incidence of violence, crime, and delinquency; the demographic structure, stability, and tranquility of domestic life; and the group's relationship to its resource base. The culture of a people who experience high rates of malnutrition, violence, crime, delinquency, suicide, emotional disorders and despair, and environmental degradation may be said to be operating less well than that of another people who exhibit few such problems. In a well-working culture, people "can be proud, jealous, and pugnacious, and live a very satisfactory life without feeling '*angst*,' 'alienation,' 'anomie,' 'depression,' or any of the other pervasive ills of our own inhuman and civilized way of living."[13] When traditional ways of coping no longer seem to work and people feel helpless to shape their own lives in their own societies, symptoms of cultural breakdown become prominent.

A culture is essentially a maintenance system to ensure the continued well-being of a group of people. Therefore, it may be deemed successful as long as it secures the survival of a society in a way that its members find to be reasonably fulfilling. What complicates matters is that any society is made up of groups with different interests, raising the possibility that some people's interests may be served better than those of others. Therefore, a culture that is quite fulfilling for one group within a society may be less so for another. For this reason, the anthropologist must always ask: Whose needs and whose survival are best served by the culture in question? Only by looking at the overall situation can a reasonably objective judgment be made as to how well a culture is working.

[9]Ember, C. J., & Ember, M. (1996). What have we learned from cross-cultural research? *General Anthropology*, 2(2), 5.

[10]Paredes, J. A., & Purdum, E. D. (1990). "Bye, bye Ted . . ." *Anthropology Today*, 6(2), 9.

[11]Maybury-Lewis, D. H. P. (1993). A special sort of pleading. In W. A. Haviland & R. J. Gordon (Eds.), *Talking about people* (2nd. ed.) (p. 17). Mountain View, CA: Mayfield.

[12]Bodley, J. H. (1990). *Victims of progress* (3rd ed., p. 138). Mountain View, CA: Mayfield.

[13]Fox, R. (1968). *Encounter with anthropology* (p. 290). New York: Dell.

cultural relativism The thesis that one must suspend judgment of other people's practices in order to understand them in their own cultural terms.

VISUAL COUNTERPOINT One sign that a culture is not adequately satisfying a people's needs and expectations is a high incidence of crime and delinquency. It is sobering to note that 25 percent of all imprisoned people in the world are incarcerated in the United States, where the numbers of prisoners quadrupled from 500,000 to 2 million between 1980 and 2000. School shootings have been on the rise, as have gated communities where those who can afford it withdraw from the outside world.

Chapter Summary

■ Culture, to the anthropologist, includes the socially transmitted ideas, values, and perceptions that are shared by members of a society, which they use to interpret experience and to generate behavior and which is reflected in their behavior. All cultures share certain basic characteristics; study of these sheds light on the nature and function of culture itself. Culture cannot exist without society: an organized group or groups of interdependent people who generally share a common territory, language, and culture and who act together for collective survival and well-being. Culture, which is learned, is distinct from shared instinctive behavior.

■ Although culture has to do with a group's shared values/ideas/behavior, everything within a culture is not uniform. For instance, in all cultures there is some difference between men's and women's roles. Anthropologists use the term *gender* to refer to the elaborations or meanings cultures assign to the biological differences between men and women. Age variation is also universal, and in some cultures there are other subcultural variations as well. A subculture (for example, the Amish) shares certain overarching assumptions of the larger culture, while observing its own set of distinct rules. Pluralistic societies are those in which cultural variation is particularly marked. They are characterized by a number of groups operating under different sets of rules, while following to a certain degree the society's overarching culture.

■ All cultures have the following characteristics: In addition to being shared, they are learned, with individual members learning the accepted norms of social behavior through the process of enculturation; culture is based on symbols—transmitted through the communication of ideas, emotions, and desires expressed in symbols, especially language; culture is integrated, so that all aspects function as an integrated whole, although total harmony of all elements is approximated rather than completely achieved in a properly functioning culture; finally, all cultures are dynamic and changeable.

■ As illustrated in the barrel model, all aspects of a culture fall into one of three broad, interrelated categories: infra-structure (the subsistence practices or economic system), social structure (the rule-governed relationships), and super-structure (the ideology or worldview).

■ The job of the anthropologist is to abstract a set of rules from what he or she observes in order to explain social behavior. To arrive at a realistic description of a culture free from personal and cultural biases, the anthropologist must examine a people's notion of how their society ought to function, determine how a people think they behave, and compare these with how a people actually do behave. It is also the anthropologist's job to free him- or herself as much as possible from the biases of his or her own culture. As well, anthropologists must acknowledge that gender can slant research findings. The Human Relations Area Files (HRAF), a vast collection of cross-indexed ethnographic and archaeological data catalogued by cultural characteristics and geographic location, assists anthropologists in making worldwide comparison.

■ Cultural adaptation has enabled humans to survive and expand into a wide variety of environments. Sometimes what is adaptive in one set of circumstances or over the short run is maladaptive over time. To survive, a culture must satisfy the basic biological and psychological needs of its members, provide some structure for reproduction to ensure their continuity, and maintain order among its members as well as between its members and outsiders.

■ Culture change takes place in response to such events as population growth, technological innovation, environmental crisis, intrusion of outsiders, or modification of values and behavior within the culture. Although cultures must change to adapt to new circumstances, sometimes the unforeseen consequences of change are disastrous for a society. As well, a society must strike a balance between the self-interest of individuals and the needs of the group.

■ Ethnocentrism is the belief that one's own culture is superior to all others. To avoid making ethnocentric judgments, anthropologists adopt the approach of cultural relativism, which requires that each culture be examined in its own terms, according to its own standards.

■ The least biased measure of a culture's success may be based on answering this question: How well does a particular culture satisfy the physical and psychological needs of those whose behavior it guides? These indicators provide answers: the nutritional status and general physical and mental health of the population, the incidence of violence, the stability of domestic life, and the group's relationship to its resource base.

Questions for Reflection

1. Anthropologists not only try to accurately describe different cultures all across the world, but also wrestle with explaining them in an unbiased fashion. Why do you think their work is so challenging?

2. Anthropological fieldwork is based on participant observation. Imagine a foreign anthropologist choosing your town or neighborhood for such research. Would you, your family, or your friends react differently to a female researcher than to a male? If so, how and why? And what if this male or female anthropologist came from Congo or Ireland? Which would play a more significant role in terms of acceptance and research findings—the researcher's gender or his/her national origin?

3. Many large modern societies are pluralistic. Are you familiar with any subcultures in your own society? How different are these subcultures from one another? Could you make friends or even marry someone from another subculture? What kind of problems would you be likely to encounter?

4. Although all cultures across the world display some degree of ethnocentrism, some are more ethnocentric than others. In what ways is your own society ethnocentric? Considering the modern fact of globalization (as described in Chapter 1), do you think ethnocentrism poses more of a problem in today's world than in the past?

5. The barrel model offers you a simple framework to imagine what a culture looks like from an analytical point of view. How would you apply that model to your own community?

Key Terms

Culture	Social structure
Society	Infrastructure
Gender	Superstructure
Subculture	Human Relations Area Files
Ethnic Group	(HRAF)
Ethnicity	Ethnohistory
Pluralistic society	Ethnocentrism
Enculturation	Cultural relativism
Symbols	

Multimedia Review Tools

Companion Web Site

Visit **http://www.wadsworth.com/anthropology_d/** and click on the companion Web site for this textbook to access a wide range of material to aid your study of anthropology. Among the options for self-study in each chapter are learning objectives, flash cards, Internet activities, Web links, InfoTrac College Edition exercises, and practice tests that can be scored and emailed to your instructor.

CD-ROM

The *Doing Anthropology Today* CD-ROM supplied with your textbook provides unique and valuable information designed to enhance your learning experience. This interactive multimedia resource includes video clips, interviews with renowned anthropologists, map and timeline exercises, chapter study quizzes, and much more. *Doing Anthropology Today* will not only help you in achieving your grade goals, but it will also make your learning experience fun and exciting!

Suggested Readings

Brown, D. E. (1991). *Human universals.* New York: McGraw-Hill.

The message of this book is that we should not let our fascination with the diversity of cultural practices interfere with the study of human universals: those things that all cultures share in spite of their differences. Important though the differences are, the universals have special relevance for our understanding of the nature of all humanity and raise issues that transcend the boundaries of biological and social science, as well as the humanities.

Gamst, F. C., & Norbeck, E. (1976). *Ideas of culture: Sources and uses.* New York: Holt, Rinehart and Winston.

This is a book of selected writings, with editorial comments, about the culture concept. From these selections one can see how the concept has grown, as well as how it has given rise to narrow specializations within the field of anthropology.

Goodenough, W. H. (1970). *Description and comparison in cultural anthropology.* Chicago: Aldine.

The major question Goodenough addresses is how anthropologists are to avoid ethnocentric bias when studying culture. His approach relies on models of descriptive linguistics. A large part of the book is concerned with kinship and terminology, with a discussion of the problems of a universal definition of marriage and the family. This is a particularly lucid discussion of culture, its relation to society, and the problem of individual variance.

Hatch, E. (1983). *Culture and morality: The relativity of values in anthropology.* New York: Columbia University Press.

This book is about cultural relativism, often used as a cover term for the quite different concepts of relativity of knowledge, historical relativism, and ethical relativism. It traces the attempts of anthropologists to grapple with these concepts, beginning with the rise of the discipline in the 19th century.

Mascia-Lees, F. E., & Black, N. J. (2000). *Gender and anthropology.* Prospect Heights, IL: Waveland Press.

Directed to undergraduate students, this short book offers a useful guide to anthropological research on gender issues since the 1970s. Organized in short, well-written chapters, this valuable resource provides a critical appraisal of "how anthropologists using different theoretical orientations have approached the study of gender roles and gender inequality" (p. xii).

CHAPTER 3

The Beginnings of Human Culture

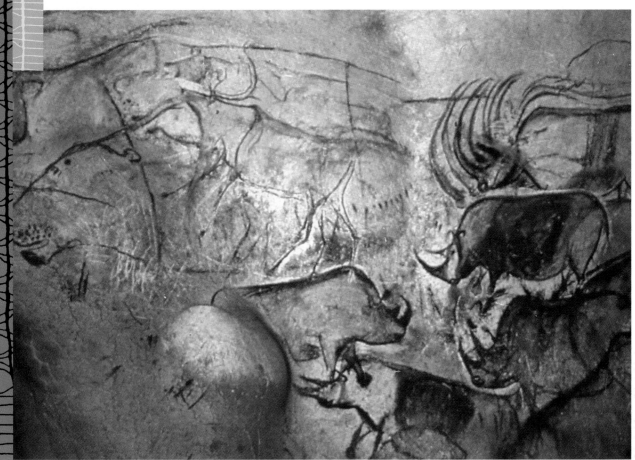

© Austin J. Stevens/Animals Animals

CHALLENGE ISSUE

THIS WALL, PAINTED **32,000** YEARS AGO IN THE CHAUVET CAVE AT THE FOOT OF A CLIFF IN SOUTHEASTERN FRANCE, PROVIDES SPECTACULAR EVIDENCE OF EARLY ARTISTIC CREATIVITY AMONG OUR ANCESTORS. The Ice Age images depicted on the full wall include bears, bison, horses, panthers, mammoths, and rhinoceroses plus various symbolic figures. As a culture-making species, humans have always faced the challenge of understanding where and how we fit in the larger natural system of all life forms, past and present. Today, anthropologists play a key role in unlocking the answers to such complex questions.

1. To What Group of Animals Do Humans Belong?

Biologists classify humans as *Homo sapiens,* members of the primates—a subgroup of mammals. Biological species are defined by reproductive isolation and designated by a two-part name including genus (*Homo*) and species (*sapiens*). Other primates include lemurs, lorises, tarsiers, monkeys, and apes. Because human culture is rooted in our mammalian primate biology, studying the anatomy and behavior of other primates, particularly our closest living ape relatives, helps us understand how and why early humans developed as they did.

2. When and How Did Humans Evolve?

Present evidence suggests that humans evolved from small African apes between 8 and 5 million years ago. Bipedalism, or walking on two feet, was the first change to distinguish the human evolutionary line. The behavior of these early bipeds was comparable to that of modern-day chimpanzees. Several million years after the evolution of bipedalism, brain size began to expand, along with the development of cultural activities such as making stone tools. The earliest stone tools date to between 2.5 and 2.6 million years ago, coinciding with the appearance of the first members of the genus *Homo* in the fossil record. From then on, shared, learned behavior—culture—played an increasingly important role in human survival.

3. Is the Biological Concept of Race Useful for Studying Physical Variation in Humans?

No. Biologically defined, *race* refers to subspecies, and no subspecies exist within modern *Homo sapiens.* The vast majority of biological variation within our species occurs *within* populations rather than among them. Furthermore, the differences that do exist among populations occur in gradations from one neighboring population to another without sharp breaks. For these and other reasons, anthropologists have actively worked to expose the fallacy of race as a biological concept while recognizing the significance of race as a social category.

Anthropologists gather information from a variety of sources to piece together an understanding of evolutionary history and humankind's place in the animal kingdom. Studies of living primates (our closest mammal relatives), ancient fossils, and even molecular biology contribute to the story of how humans evolved. On one level, human evolutionary studies are wholly scientific, formulating and testing hypotheses about biological and behavioral processes in the past. At the same time, like all scientists, anthropologists are influenced by changing cultural values. Thus, **paleoanthropologists,** who study human evolutionary history, and **primatologists,** who study living primates, as well as the biological anthropologists who study contemporary biological diversity, must be critically aware of their personal beliefs and cultural assumptions as they construct their theories.

EVOLUTION THROUGH ADAPTATION

In a general sense, **evolution** (from the Latin word *evolutio,* literally meaning "unrolling" or "rolling forth") refers to change through time. Biologically, it refers to changes in the genetic makeup of a population over generations. (**Genes** are the inherited molecular code that specifies the biological traits and characteristics of each individual.) While some evolution takes place through a process known as **adaptation**—a series of beneficial adjustments of organisms to their environment—random forces also contribute critically to evolutionary change. Adaptation is the cornerstone of the theory of evolution by **natural selection,** originally formulated by English naturalist Charles Darwin in 1859. In this theory, individuals having characteristics best suited to a particular environment survive and reproduce with greater frequency than do individuals without those characteristics. Today, scientists understand that random genetic mutation is the source of variation that gives organisms this reproductive edge.

In this chapter, we will discuss examples of anatomical and behavioral adaptations in the evolutionary history of our species. The biology and behavior of our closest living relatives, the other primates, will complement our examination of the past. We will also explore some aspects of human biological variation and the cultural meanings given to this variation.

Unique among humans is the biological capacity to produce a rich array of *cultural adaptations,* a complex of ideas, activities, and technologies that enable people to survive and even thrive in their environment. Early forerunners of humanity, like all other creatures, greatly depended on physical attributes for survival. But in the course of time, humans came to rely increasingly on culture as an effective way of adapting to the environment. They learned to manufacture and utilize tools; they organized into social units that made food-foraging more successful; and they learned to preserve and share their traditions and knowledge through the use of symbols.

The ability to solve a vast array of challenges through culture has made our species unusual among creatures on this planet. Humans do not merely adapt to the environment through biological change; we shape the environment to suit human needs and desires. Today, computer technology enables us to organize and manipulate an ever-increasing amount of information to keep pace with the environmental changes we have wrought. Space technology may enable us to propagate our species in extraterrestrial environments. If we manage to avoid self-destruction through misuse of our sophisticated tools, biomedical technology may eventually enable us to control genetic inheritance and thus the future course of our biological evolution.

The fundamental elements of human culture came into existence about 2.5 million years ago. Using scientific know-how to reach far back in time, we can trace the roots of our species and reconstruct the origins of human culture.

paleoanthropologists Anthropologists specializing in the study of human evolutionary history.

primatologists Specialists in the behavior and biology of living primates and their evolutionary history.

evolution Changes in the genetic makeup of a population over generations.

genes The inherited molecular code that specifies the biological traits and characteristics of each individual.

adaptation Both a process and a result of a series of beneficial adjustments of organisms to their environment.

natural selection The principle or mechanism by which individuals having biological characteristics best suited to a particular environment survive and reproduce with greater frequency than individuals without those characteristics.

species A population or group of populations having common attributes and the ability to interbreed and produce live, fertile offspring. Different species are reproductively isolated from one another.

HUMANS AND OTHER PRIMATES

As noted in the beginning of this book, humans are one of 10 million species on earth, 4,000 of which are fellow mammals. **Species** are populations or groups of populations having common attributes and the ability to interbreed and produce live, fertile offspring. Different species are reproductively isolated from one another. Biologists organize or classify species into larger groups of biologically related organisms. The

The Kobal Collection/Hammer

Though popular media depict the coexistence of humans and dinosaurs, in reality the extinction of the dinosaurs occurred 65 million years ago while the first bipeds ancestral to humans appeared between 8 and 5 million years ago.

human species is one kind of **primate,** a subgroup of mammals that also includes lemurs, lorises, tarsiers, monkeys, and apes. Among fellow primates, humans are most closely related to apes—chimpanzees, bonobos, gorillas, orangutans, and gibbons—all of particular interest to primatologists.

European scientists have argued long and hard over issues of species classification, especially since the start of the Age of Exploration 500 years ago led to the discovery of distant lands inhabited by life forms they had never before seen, including apes. Most vexing was the question concerning the difference between these apes and humans. In 1698, after dissecting a young male chimpanzee captured in West Africa and brought to Europe, an English physician concluded the creature was almost human and classified it as *Homo sylvestris* ("man of the forest"). A few decades later, Swedish naturalist Carolus Linnaeus (1707–1778) published the first edition of his famous *System of Nature* (1735). In it he classified humans with sloths and monkeys in the same order: Anthropomorpha ("human-shaped"). By the time Linnaeus published the tenth edition of his famous book in 1758, he had replaced the name "Anthropomorpha" with "Primate" and included bats, lemurs, monkeys, and humans in that category. Moreover, he now recognized not just one human species but two: *Homo sapiens* or *Homo diurnus* ("active during daylight") and an apelike human he called *Homo nocturnus* ("active during night"). He also referred to the latter as *Homo troglodytes* ("human cave-dweller"). And so went the challenge of classifying humans within the natural system. Perhaps the best illustration of the perplexity involved is a comment made by an 18th-century French bishop upon seeing an orangutan in a menagerie. Uncertain whether the creature before him was human or beast, he proclaimed: "Speak and I shall baptize thee!"[1]

Early scientific struggles to classify great apes, and to identify and weigh the significance of the similarities and differences between them and humans, is reflected in early European renderings of apes, including this 18th-century image of a chimpanzee portrayed as a biped equipped with a walking stick.

[1]Corbey, R. (1995). Introduction: Missing links, or the ape's place in nature (p. 1). In R. Corbey & B. Theunissen (Eds.), *Ape, man, apeman: Changing views since 1600*. Leiden: Department of Prehistory, Leiden University.

primate An individual belonging to subgroup of mammals including, lemurs, lorises, tarsiers, monkeys, apes, and humans.

In the course of the 18th century, European scientists continued to debate the proper classification of the great apes (as well as human "savages" encountered overseas) and placed chimpanzees and orangutans (gorillas were not recognized as a separate species until 1847) squarely between humans and the other animals. Perhaps going further than any other reputable scholar in Europe at the time, the famous Scottish judge Lord Monboddo argued in several widely read scholarly publications in the 1770s and 1780s that orangutans should be considered part of the human species. He pointed out that they could walk erect and construct shelters and that they used sticks to defend themselves. He even suggested that at least in principle these "savages" were capable of speech.[2] Still, most Europeans clung to the notion of a marked divide between humans on the one hand and animals on the other. Debates about the exact relationship between humans and other animals continue to this day. These debates include biological data on ancient fossils and genetics, as well as philosophical stances on the "humane" treatment of our closest ape relatives.

One could question the value of including nonhuman primates in this textbook when the distinctive cultural capacities of humans are our major concern. However, humans have a long evolutionary history as mammals and primates that set the stage for the cultural beings we are today. By studying our evolutionary history as well as the biology and behavior of our closest living relatives, we gain a better understanding of how and why humans developed as they did.

Evidence from ancient skeletons indicates the first mammals appeared over 200 million years ago as small nocturnal (night-active) creatures. The earliest primate-like creatures came into being about 65 million years ago when a new, mild climate favored the spread of dense tropical and subtropical forests over much of the earth. The change in climate and habitat, combined with the sudden extinction of dinosaurs, favored mammal diversification, including the evolutionary development of arboreal (tree-living) mammals from which primates evolved.

The ancestral primates possessed biological characteristics that allowed them to adapt to life in the forests. Their relatively small size enabled them to use tree branches not accessible to larger competitors and predators. Arboreal life opened up an abundant new food supply. The primates were able to gather leaves, flowers, fruits, insects, birds' eggs, and even nesting birds, rather than having to wait for them to fall to the ground.

Natural selection favored those who judged depth correctly and gripped the branches tightly. Those individuals who survived life in the trees passed on their genes to the succeeding generations. Although the earliest primates were nocturnal, today most primate species are diurnal (active in the day). The transition to diurnal life in the trees required important biological adjustments that helped shape the biology and behavior of humans today.

Anatomical Adaptation

Ancient and modern primate groups possess a number of anatomical characteristics that are described below. However, compared to other mammals, primates possess only a few anatomical specializations while their behavior patterns are very diverse and flexible.

Primate Dentition

The varied diet available to arboreal primates—shoots, leaves, insects, and fruits—required relatively unspecialized teeth, compared to those found in other mammals. Comparative anatomy and the fossil record reveal that mammals ancestral to primates possessed three incisors, one canine, four premolars, and three molars on each side of the jaw, top and bottom, for a total of forty-four teeth. The incisors (in the front of the mouth) were used for gripping and cutting, canines (behind the incisors) for tearing and shredding, and molars and premolars (the "cheek teeth") for grinding and chewing food.

The evolutionary trend for primate dentition (Figure 3.1) has been toward a reduction in the number and size of the teeth. In the early stages, one incisor on each side of the upper and lower jaws was lost, further differentiating primates from other mammals. The canines of most of the primates, especially males, are daggerlike and useful for ripping into tough foods. They also serve well in social communication: All an adult male gorilla needs to do to get a youngster to be submissive is to raise his upper lip to display his sharp canines. Over the millennia, the first and second premolars became smaller and eventually disappeared altogether; the third and fourth premolars grew larger and gained a second pointed projection, or cusp, thus becoming "bicuspid." The molars also evolved from a three-cusp to a four- and even five-cusp pattern. Thus the functions of grasping, cutting, and grinding were served by different kinds of teeth.

Sensory Organs

The primates' adaptation to arboreal life involved changes in the form and function of their sensory organs. The sense of smell was vital for the earliest

---

[2]Barnard, A. (1995). Monboddo's *Orang Outang* and the definition of man (pp. 71–85). In Corbey & Theunissen.

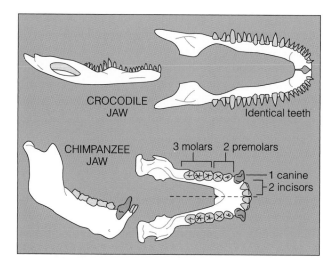

FIGURE 3.1

As seen in all reptiles, this crocodile jaw contains a series of identically shaped teeth. If a tooth breaks or falls out, a new tooth will emerge in its place. By contrast, primates, like all mammals, have only two sets of teeth; "baby" and adult teeth. Apes and humans possess precise numbers of specialized teeth, each with a particular shape, as indicated on this chimpanzee jaw: Incisors in front are shown in blue, canines behind in red, followed by two premolars and three molars in yellow (the last being the wisdom teeth in humans).

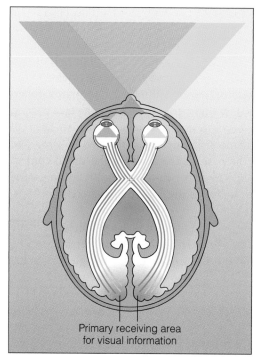

FIGURE 3.2

Anthropoid primates possess binocular stereoscopic vision. Binocular vision refers to overlapping visual fields due to forward-facing eyes. Three-dimensional or stereoscopic vision comes from binocular vision and the transmission of information from each eye to both sides of the brain.

ground-dwelling, night-active mammals. It enabled them to operate in the dark, to sniff out their food, and to detect hidden predators. However, for active tree life during daylight, good vision is a better guide than smell in judging the location of the next branch or tasty morsel. Accordingly, the sense of smell declined in primates, while vision became highly developed.

Traveling through trees demands judgments concerning depth, direction, distance, and the relationships of objects hanging in space, such as vines or branches. Monkeys, apes, and humans achieved this through stereoscopic color vision (Figure 3.2), the ability to see the world in the three dimensions of height, width, and depth. Stereoscopic vision comes from binocular vision (in which two eyes sit next to each other on the same plane so that their visual fields overlap) and nerve connections that run from each eye to both sides of the brain. This arrangement allows nerve cells to integrate the images derived from each eye. Increased brain size in the visual area in primates and a greater complexity at nerve connections also contributes to stereoscopic color vision.

Tree-living primates also possess an acute sense of touch. An effective feeling and grasping mechanism helps keep them from falling and tumbling while speeding through the trees. The early mammals from which primates evolved possessed tiny touch-sensitive hairs at the tips of their hands and feet. In primates, sensitive pads backed up by nails on the tips of the animals' fin-

gers and toes replaced these hairs. In monkeys from Central and South America, this feeling and grasping ability extends to the tail.

The Primate Brain

An increase in brain size, particularly in the cerebral hemispheres—the areas supporting conscious thought—occurred in the course of primate evolution. In monkeys, apes, and humans the cerebral hemispheres completely cover the cerebellum, the part of the brain that coordinates the muscles and maintains body balance. One of the most significant outcomes of this is the flexibility seen in primate behavior. Rather than relying on reflexes controlled by the cerebellum, primates constantly react to a variety of features in the environment. Messages from the hands and feet, eyes and ears, as well as from the sensors of balance, movement, heat, touch, and pain, are simultaneously relayed to the cerebral cortex. Obviously the cortex had to develop considerably in order to receive, analyze, and coordinate these impressions and transmit the appropriate response back down to the motor nerves. The enlarged, responsive, cerebral cortex provides the biological basis for flexible behavior patterns found in all primates, including humans.

The Primate Skeleton

The skeleton gives vertebrates—animals with internal backbones—their basic shape or silhouette, supports the soft tissues, and helps protect vital internal organs (Figure 3.3). Some evolutionary trends are evident in the primate skeleton. For example, as primates relied increasingly on vision rather than smell, the eyes rotated forward to become enclosed in a protective layer of bone. Simultaneously, the snout reduced in size. The opening at the base of the skull for the spinal cord to pass assumed a more forward position, reflecting some degree of upright posture rather than a constant four-footed stance.

The limbs of the primate skeleton follow the same basic ancestral plan seen in the earliest vertebrates. The upper portion of each arm or leg has a single long bone, the lower portion has two bones, and then hands or feet with five radiating digits. Other animals possess limbs specialized to optimize a particular behavior, such as speed. In nearly all of the primates, the big toe and thumb are *opposable,* making it possible to grasp and manipulate objects such as sticks and stones with both the hands and feet. Humans and their direct ancestors are the only exceptions, having lost the opposable big toe. The generalized limb pattern allows for flexible movements by primates.

In the apes, a sturdy collarbone (clavicle) orients the arms at the side rather than the front of the body, allowing for heightened flexibility. With their broad flexible shoulder joints, apes can hang suspended from tree branches and swing from tree to tree.

The retention of the flexible vertebrate limb pattern in primates was a valuable asset to evolving humans. It was, in part, having hands capable of grasping that enabled our own ancestors to manufacture and use tools and thus alter the course of their evolution.

Behavioral Adaptation

Primates adapt to their environments not only anatomically but also through a wide variety of behaviors. Young apes spend more time reaching adulthood than do most other mammals. During their lengthy growth and development, they learn the behaviors of their social group. While biological factors play a role in the duration of primate dependency, many of the specific behaviors learned during childhood derive solely from the traditions of the group. The behavior of primates, particularly apes, provides anthropologists with clues about the earliest development of human cultural behavior.

Many studies of ape behavior in their natural habitat have been undertaken to provide models for the reconstruction of behavior of evolving humans. While no living primate lives exactly as our ancestors did, these

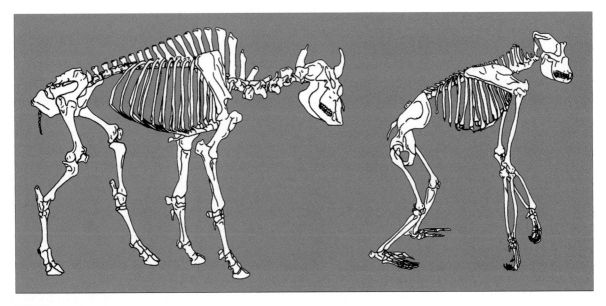

FIGURE 3.3

All primates possess the same ancestral vertebrate limb pattern as seen in reptiles and amphibians, consisting of a single upper long bone, two lower long bones, and five radiating digits (fingers and toes), as seen in this gorilla (right) skeleton. Other mammals such as bison (left) have a modified version of this pattern. In the course of evolution bison have lost all but two of their digits, which form their hooves. The second long bone in the lower part of the limb is reduced. Note also the joining of the skull and vertebral column in these skeletons. In bison (as in most mammals) the skull projects forward from the vertebral column, but in semi-erect gorillas, the vertebral column is further beneath the skull.

© Jeff Greenberg/Photo Researchers, Inc.

© D. Chivers/Anthro-Photo

VISUAL COUNTERPOINT All apes, as well as humans, possess widely spaced flexible shoulder joints for hanging suspended from the branches or swinging from branch to branch.

studies have revealed remarkable variation and sophistication in ape behavior. Primatologists increasingly interpret these variations as cultural because they are learned rather than genetically programmed or instinctive. We shall look at the behavior of two closely related African species of chimpanzee: common chimpanzees and bonobos.

MEDIATREK

For information about living and fossil primates, as well as the people who study them, go to MediaTrek 3.1 on the companion Web site or CD-ROM.

Chimpanzee and Bonobo Behavior

Like nearly all primates, chimpanzees and bonobos are highly social animals. Among chimps, the largest social organizational unit is the community, usually composed of fifty or more individuals who collectively inhabit a large geographical area. Rarely, however, are all of these animals together at one time. Instead, they are usually found ranging singly or in small subgroups consisting of adult males, or females with their young, or males and females together with young. In the course of their travels, subgroups may join forces and forage together, but sooner or later these will break up again into smaller units. Typically, when some individuals split off others join, so the composition of subunits shifts frequently.

Relationships among individuals within the ape communities are relatively harmonious. In the past, primatologists believed that male dominance hierarchies, in which some animals outrank and can dominate others, formed the basis of primate social structures. They noted that physical strength and size play a role in determining an animal's rank. By this measure males generally outrank females. However, the male-biased cultures of many primatologists may have contributed to this theoretical perspective with its emphasis on domination through superior size and strength. Male dominance hierarchies seemed "natural" to these early researchers. With the benefit of detailed field studies over the last forty years, including cutting-edge research by female primatologists such as Jane Goodall (see Anthropologists of Note), the nuances of primate social behavior and the importance of female primates has been documented. High-ranking female chimpanzees may dominate low-ranking males. And among bonobos, female rank determines the social order of the group far more than male rank. While greater strength and size do contribute to an animal's higher rank, several other factors also come into play in determining its social position. These include the rank of its mother, which is largely determined through her cooperative social behavior and how effective each individual animal is at creating alliances with others.

On the whole, bonobo females form stronger bonds with one another than do chimpanzee females.

Anthropologists of Note

Jane Goodall (1934–) ▪ Kinji Imanishi (1902–1992)

In July 1960 Jane Goodall arrived with her mother at the Gombe Chimpanzee Reserve on the shores of Lake Tanganyika in Tanzania. The first of three women Kenyan anthropologist Louis Leakey sent out to study great apes in the wild (the others were Dian Fossey and Birute Galdikas, who were to study gorillas and orangutans, respectively), her task was to begin a long-term study of chimpanzees. Little did she realize that, more than 40 years later, she would still be at it.

Born in London, Goodall grew up and was schooled in Bournemouth, England. As a child, she had always dreamed of going to Africa to live among animals, so when an invitation arrived to visit a friend in Kenya, she jumped at the opportunity. Once in Kenya, she met Leakey, who gave her a job as an assistant secretary. Before long, she was on her way to Gombe. Within a year, the outside world began to hear the most extraordinary things about this pioneering woman and her work: tales of tool-making apes, cooperative hunts by chimpanzees, and what seemed like exotic chimpanzee rain dances. By the mid-1960s, her work had earned her a Ph.D. from Cambridge University, and Gombe was on its way to becoming one of the most dynamic field stations for the study of animal behavior anywhere in the world.

Although Goodall is still very much involved with her chimpanzees, she spends a good deal of time these days lecturing, writing, and overseeing the work of others. She also is heavily committed to primate conservation, and no one is more dedicated to efforts to halt the illegal trafficking in captive chimps nor a more eloquent champion of humane treatment of captive chimpanzees.

Kinji Imanishi, a naturalist, explorer, and mountain climber, profoundly influenced primatology in Japan and throughout the world. Like all Japanese scholars, he was fully aware of Western methods and theories but developed a radically different approach to the scientific study of the natural world. He dates his transformation to a youthful encounter with a grasshopper: "I was walking along a path in a valley, and there was a grasshopper on a leaf in a shrubbery. Until that moment I had happily caught insects, killed them with chloroform, impaled them on pins, and looked up their names, but I realized I knew nothing at all about how this grasshopper lived in the wild."[a] In his most important work, *The World of Living Things,* first published in 1941, Imanishi developed a comprehensive theory about the natural world rooted in Japanese cultural beliefs and practices.

Imanishi's work challenged Western evolutionary theory in sev-

eral ways. First, Imanishi's theory, like Japanese culture, does not emphasize differences between humans and other animals. Second, rather than focusing on the biology of individual organisms, Imanishi suggested that naturalists examine "specia" (a species society) to which individuals belong as the unit of analysis. Rather than focusing on time, Imanishi emphasized space in his approach to the natural world. He highlighted the harmony of all living things rather than conflict and competition among individual organisms. Imanishi's research techniques, now standard worldwide, developed directly from his theories: long-term field study of primates in their natural societies using methods from ethnography.

Imanishi and his many students conducted pioneering field studies of African apes, as well as studies of Japanese and Tibetan macaques, long before Louis Leakey sent the first Western primatologists into the field. Japanese primatologists were the first to document the importance of kinship, the complexity of primate societies, patterns of social learning, and the unique character of each primate social group. Because of the work by Imanishi and his students, we now think about the distinct cultures of primate societies.

[a] Heita, K. (1999). Imanishi's world view. *Journal of Japanese Trade and Industry,* 18(2), 15.

Moreover, the strength of the bond between mother and son interferes with bonds among males. Not only do bonobo males defer to females in feeding, but *alpha* (high-ranking) females have been observed chasing alpha males; such males may even yield to low-ranking females, particularly when groups of females form alliances.[3]

Widening his gaze beyond social ranking and attack behavior among great apes, Japanese primatologist Kinji Imanishi (see Anthropologists of Note) initiated field studies of bonobos, investigating and demonstrating the importance of social cooperation rather than competition. Likewise, Dutch primatologist Frans de Waal's research, highlighted in the following Original Study, shows that reconciliation after an attack may be even more important from an evolutionary perspective than the actual attacks.

---

[3] de Waal, F., Kano, T., & Parish, A. R. (1998). Comments. *Current Anthropology, 39,* 408, 410, 413.

Original Study

Reconciliation and Its Cultural Modification in Primates

Despite the continuing popularity of the struggle-for-life metaphor, it is increasingly recognized that there are drawbacks to open competition, hence that there are sound evolutionary reasons for curbing it. The dependency of social animals on group life and cooperation makes aggression a socially costly strategy. The basic dilemma facing many animals, including humans, is that they sometimes cannot win a fight without losing a friend.

This photo shows what may happen after a conflict—in this case between two female bonobos. About 10 minutes after their fight, the two females approach each other, with one clinging to the other and both rubbing their clitorises and genital swellings together in a pattern known as genito-genital (or GG) rubbing. This sexual contact, typical of bonobos, constitutes a so-called reconciliation. Chimpanzees, which are closely related to bonobos (and to us: bonobos and chimpanzees are our closest animal relatives), usually reconcile in a less sexual fashion, with an embrace and mouth-to-mouth kiss.

There is now evidence for reconciliation in more than twenty-five different primate species, not just in apes but also in many monkeys. The same sorts of studies have been conducted on human children in the schoolyard, and of course children show reconciliation as well. Researchers have even found reconcilia-

tion in dolphins, spotted hyenas, and some other nonprimates. Reconciliation seems widespread: a common mechanism found whenever relationships need to be maintained despite occasional conflict.[a, b]

The definition of reconciliation used in animal research is a friendly reunion between former opponents not long after a conflict. This is somewhat different from definitions in the dictionary, primarily because we look for an empiri-

© Amy Parish/Anthro-Photo

Two adult female bonobos engage in so-called GG-rubbing, a sexual form of reconciliation typical of this species.

cal definition that is useful in observational studies—in our case, the stipulation that the reunion happen not long after the conflict. There is no intrinsic reason that a reconciliation could not occur after hours or days, or, in the case of humans, generations.

Let me describe two interesting elaborations on the mechanism of reconciliation. One is *mediation*. Chimpanzees are the only animals to use mediators in conflict resolution. In order to be able to mediate conflict, one needs to understand relationships

outside of oneself, which may be the reason why other animals fail to show this aspect of conflict resolution. For example, if two male chimpanzees have been involved in a fight, even on a very large island as where I did my studies, they can easily avoid each other, but instead they will sit opposite from each other, not too far apart, and avoid eye contact. They can sit like this for a long time. In this situation, a third party, such as an older female, may move in and try to solve the issue. The female will approach one of the males and groom him for a brief while. She then gets up and walks slowly to the other male, and the first male walks right behind her.

We have seen situations in which, if the first male failed to follow, the female turned around to grab his arm and make him follow. So the process of getting the two males in proximity seems intentional on the part of the female. She then begins grooming the other male, and the first male grooms her. Before long, the female disappears from the scene, and the males continue grooming: She has in effect brought the two parties together.

There exists a limited anthropological literature on the role of conflict resolution, a process absolutely crucial for the maintenance of the human social fabric in the same way that it is crucial for our primate relatives. In human society,

[CONTINUED]

mediation is often done by high-ranking or senior members of the community, sometimes culminating in feasts in which the restoration of harmony is celebrated.[c]

The second elaboration on the reconciliation concept is that it is not purely instinctive, not even in our animal relatives. It is a learned social skill subject to what primatologists now increasingly call "culture" (meaning that the behavior is subject to learning from others as opposed to genetic transmission.[d]) To test the learnability of reconciliation, I conducted an experiment with young rhesus and stumptail monkeys. Not nearly as conciliatory as stumptail monkeys, rhesus monkeys have the reputation of being rather aggressive and despotic. Stumptails are considered more laid-back and tolerant. We housed members of the two species together for 5 months. By the end of this period, they were a fully integrated group: They slept, played, and groomed together. After 5 months, we separated them again, and measured the effect of their time together on conciliatory behavior.

The research controls—rhesus monkeys who had lived with one another, without any stumptails—showed absolutely no change in the tendency to reconcile. Stumptails showed a high rate of reconciliation, which was also expected, because they also do so if living together. The most interesting group was the experimental rhesus monkeys, those who had lived with stumptails. These monkeys started out at the same low level of reconciliation as the rhesus controls, but after they had lived with the stumptails, and after we had segregated them again so that they were now housed only with other rhesus monkeys who had gone through the same experience, these rhesus monkeys reconciled as much as stumptails do. This means that we created a "new and improved" rhesus monkey, one that made up with its opponents far more easily than a regular rhesus monkey.[e]

This was in effect an experiment on social culture: We changed the culture of a group of rhesus monkeys and made it more similar to that of stumptail monkeys by exposing them to the practices of this other species. This experiment also shows that there exists a great deal of flexibility in primate behavior. We humans come from a long lineage of primates with great social sophistication and a well-developed potential for behavioral modification and learning from others. *(By Frans B. M. de Waal, Living Links, Yerkes National Primate Research Center, Emory University)*

a de Waal, F. B. M. (2000). Primates—A natural heritage of conflict resolution. *Science, 28,* 586–590.

b Aureli, F., & de Waal, F. B. M. (2000). *Natural conflict resolution.* Berkeley: University of California Press.

c Reviewed by Frye, D. P. (2000). Conflict management in cross-cultural perspective. In F. Aureli & F. B. M. de Waal, *Natural conflict resolution* (pp. 334–351). Berkeley: University of California Press.

d See de Waal, F. B. M. (2001). *The ape and the sushi master.* New York: Basic Books, for a discussion of the animal culture concept.

e de Waal, F. B. M., & Johanowicz, D. L. (1993). Modification of reconciliation behavior through social experience: An experiment with two macaque species. *Child Development, 64,* 897–908.

Grooming, the ritual cleaning of another animal to remove parasites and other matter from its skin or coat, is a common pastime for both chimpanzees and bonobos. Besides serving hygienic purposes, it can be a gesture of friendliness, closeness, appeasement, reconciliation, or even submission. Bonobos and chimpanzees have favorite grooming partners. Group sociability, an important behavioral trait undoubtedly also found among human ancestors, is further expressed in embracing, touching, and the joyous welcoming of other members of the ape community. Group protection and coordination of group efforts are facilitated by visual and vocal communication, including special calls for warnings, threats, and gathering. Unique to bonobos is the use of large leaves as trail signs to indicate their whereabouts to others not immediately present.[4]

Prior to the 1980s most primates were thought to be vegetarian while humans alone were considered meat-eating hunters. Pioneering research by Jane Goodall, among others, revealed that the diets of monkeys and apes were extremely varied. Goodall's fieldwork among chimpanzees in their natural habitat at Gombe, a wildlife reserve on the eastern shores of Lake Tanganyika in Tanzania, revealed that these apes supplement their primary diet of fruits and other plant foods with insects and also meat. Even more surprising, she found that in addition to killing small invertebrate animals for food, they also hunted and ate monkeys. In the course of four decades of work at Gombe, this British researcher observed chimpanzees grabbing adult red colobus monkeys and flailing them to death.

Chimpanzee females sometimes hunt, but males do so far more frequently. When on the hunt, they may spend up to 2 hours watching, following, and chasing intended prey. Moreover, in contrast to the usual primate practice of each animal finding its own food, hunting frequently involves teamwork to trap and kill prey, particularly when hunting for baboons. Once a potential victim has been isolated from its troop, three or more adult chimps will carefully position themselves so as to block off escape routes while another pursues the prey. Following the kill, most who are present get a share of

[4]Recer, P. (1998, February 16). Apes are shown to communicate in the wild. *Burlington Free Press,* p. 12A.

© Anita de Laguna Haviland

© Anita de Laguna Haviland

VISUAL **COUNTERPOINT**
Grooming is an important activity among monkeys and apes. It strengthens bonds between individual members of the group.

the meat, either by grabbing a piece as chance affords or by begging for it.

Whatever the nutritional value of meat, hunting is not done purely for dietary purposes, but for social and sexual reasons as well. U.S. anthropologist Craig Stanford, who has done fieldwork among the chimpanzees of Gombe since the early 1990s, found that these sizable apes (100-pound males are common) frequently kill animals weighing up to 25 pounds and eat much more meat than previously believed. Their preferred prey is the red colobus monkey that shares their forested habitat. Annually, chimpanzee hunting parties at Gombe kill about 20 percent of these monkeys, many of them babies, often shaking them out of the tops of 30-foot trees. They may capture and kill as many as seven victims in a raid. These hunts usually take place during the dry season when plant foods are less readily available and female chimps display genital swelling, which signals that they are ready to mate. Moreover, fertile females are more successful than others at begging for meat, and males often share the meat after copulation. According to Stanford, "Males are giving meat to the females not to be nice or to help the group or the species, but to further their own selfish, political, and manipulative goals. They want more mating."[5] On average, each chimp at Gombe eats about a quarter-pound of meat per day during the dry season, about the same amount consumed by contemporary human foragers in the region. For female chimps ready for pregnancy, a supply of protein-rich food benefits her physical condition during a period of increased nutritional requirements. Beyond sharing meat to attract sexual partners, males use their catch to reward friends and allies, gaining status in the process. In other words, although Stanford links male hunting and food-sharing behavior with female reproductive biology, these behaviors are part of a complex social system that may be rooted more in the cultural traditions and history of Gombe than in chimpanzee biology.

Somewhat different chimpanzee hunting practices have been observed in West Africa. At Tai National Park in the Ivory Coast, for instance, chimpanzees engage in highly coordinated team efforts to chase monkeys hiding in very tall trees in the dense tropical forest. Individuals who have especially distinguished themselves in a successful hunt see their contributions rewarded with more meat. Recent research shows that bonobos in Congo's rainforest also supplement their diet with meat obtained by means of hunting. Although their behavior resembles that of the chimpanzees, there are crucial differences. Among bonobos hunting is primarily a female activity. Also, female hunters regularly share carcasses with other females, but less often with males. Even when the most dominant male throws a tantrum nearby, he may still be denied a share of meat.[6] Such discriminatory sharing among female bonobos is also evident when it comes to other foods such as fruits.

Chimpanzees and bonobos have not only developed different hunting strategies, but also different sexual practices. For chimps, sexual activity—initiated by

[5]C. B. Stanford, cited in Sullivan, M. (1999). Chimpanzee hunting habits yield clues about early ancestors. *The Chronicle for Higher Education;* Stanford, C. B. (2001). *Chimpanzee and red colobus: The ecology of predator and prey.* Cambridge, MA: Harvard University Press.

[6]Ingmanson, E. J. (1998). Comment. *Current Anthropology, 39,* 409.

VISUAL COUNTERPOINT This gelada (left), a kind of African monkey who spends much of her day sitting on the ground and feeding, signals ovulation through swelling of glands on her chest. Chimpanzees (right) display their fertility through swelling of the genitalia at the time of ovulation. Animals with time limited displays are sexually receptive only during these times of fertility.

either the male or the female—occurs only during the periods when females signal their fertility through genital swelling. By most human standards, chimp sexual behavior is promiscuous. A dozen or so males have been observed to have as many as fifty copulations in one day with a single female. Dominant males try to monopolize females when the latter are most receptive sexually, although cooperation from the female is usually required for this to succeed. In addition, an individual female and a lower-ranking male sometimes form a temporary bond, leaving the group together for a few private days during the female's fertile period. Thus, dominant males do not necessarily father all (or even most) of the offspring in a social group. Social success, achieving alpha male status, does not translate neatly into the evolutionary currency of reproductive success.

In contrast to chimpanzees, bonobos (like humans) do not limit their sexual behavior to times of female fertility. Whereas the genitals of chimpanzee females are swollen only at times of fertility, bonobo female genitals are perpetually swollen. The constant swelling, in effect, conceals the females' ovulation, or moment when an egg released into the womb is receptive for fertilization. As among humans, concealed ovulation in bonobos may play a role in the separation of sexual activity for social reasons and pleasure from the purely biological task of reproduction. In fact, among bonobos (as among humans) sexuality goes far beyond male–female mating for purposes of biological reproduction. Primatologists have observed virtually every

possible combination of ages and sexes engaging in a remarkable array of sexual activities, including oral sex, tongue-kissing, and massaging each other's genitals. Male bonobos may mount each other, or one may rub his scrotum against that of the other. They have also been observed "penis fencing"—hanging face to face from a branch and rubbing their erect penises together as if crossing swords. Among females, genital rubbing is particularly common. As described in this chapter's Original Study, the primary function of most of this sex, both hetero- and homosexual, is to reduce tensions and resolve social conflicts. Notably, although rape among chimpanzees (and humans) is known to occur, forced copulation has never been observed among bonobos.[7]

Bonobo and chimpanzee dependence on learned social behavior is related to their extended period of childhood development. Born without built-in responses dictating specific behavior in complex situations, the young chimp or bonobo, like the young human, learns how to strategically interact with others and even manipulate them for his or her own benefit—by trial and error, observation, imitation, and practice. Young primates make mistakes along the way, learning to modify their behavior based on the reactions of other members of the group. Each member of the community has a unique physical appearance and personality. Youngsters learn

---

[7]de Waal, F. (1998). Comment. *Current Anthropology, 39,* 407.

This bonobo figured out by himself how to make stone tools like those our own ancestors made 2.5 million years ago.

to match their interactive behaviors according to each individual's social position and temperament. Anatomical features such as a free upper lip (unlike lemurs or cats, for example) allow monkeys and apes varied facial expression, contributing to greater communication among individuals.

Young chimpanzees also learn other functional behaviors from adults, such as how to make and use tools. Beyond deliberately modifying objects to make them suitable for particular purposes, chimps can to some extent modify them to regular patterns and may even prepare objects at one location in anticipation of future use at another place. For example, chimps have been observed to select a long, slender branch, strip off its leaves, and carry it on a "fishing" expedition to a termite nest. Reaching their destination, they insert the stick into the nest, wait a few minutes, and then pull it out to eat the insects clinging to it. Bonobos in the wild have not been observed making and using tools to the extent that chimpanzees do. However, their use of large leaves as trail markers may be considered a form of tool use. Tool-making capabilities have also been demonstrated by a captive bonobo who independently made stone tools remarkably similar to the earliest tools made by our own ancestors.

As researchers uncover increasing evidence of the remarkable behavioral sophistication and intelligence of chimpanzees and other apes—including a capacity for conceptual thought previously unsuspected by most scientists—the widespread practice of caging our primate "cousins" and exploiting them for entertainment or medical experimentation becomes increasingly controversial.

HUMAN ANCESTORS

Classifying humans within the animal kingdom is as controversial and challenging in the 21st century as it was in the 18th when Linnaeus was working on his *System of Nature.* Today, paleoanthropologists working out taxonomic or classification schemes for humans and their ancestors reach beyond Linnaeas' focus on shared morphology or physical characteristics to consider genetic makeup. Humans are classified as **hominoids,** the broad-shouldered tailless group of primates that includes all living and extinct apes and humans. Humans and their ancestors are distinct among the hominoids for **bipedalism**—a special form of locomotion on two feet.

In the past 30 years, genetic and biochemical studies have confirmed that the African apes—chimpanzees, bonobos, and gorillas—are our closest living relatives (Figure 3.4). By comparing genes and proteins among all the apes, scientists have estimated that gibbons, followed by orangutans, were the first to diverge from a very ancient common ancestral line. At some time between 8 and 5 million years ago, humans, chimpanzees, and gorillas began to follow separate evolutionary courses. Chimpanzees later diverged into two separate species: the common chimpanzee and the bonobo. Early human evolutionary development followed a path that produced,

hominoids The broad-shouldered tailless group of primates that includes all living and extinct apes and humans.
bipedalism A special form of locomotion on two feet found in humans and their ancestors.

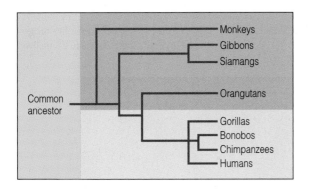

FIGURE 3.4

The relationship among monkeys, apes, and humans can be established by molecular similarities and differences. Molecular evidence indicates that the split between the human and African ape lines took place between 8 and 5 million years ago. Several important fossil finds dating from between 7 to 5 million years ago have been discovered over the last few years.

eventually, only one surviving bipedal species: *Homo sapiens.* Larger brains and bipedal locomotion constitute the most striking differences between humans and our closest primate relatives. Although we might like to think that it is our larger brains that make us special among fellow primates, it is now clear that bipedalism appeared at the beginning of the ancestral line leading to humans and played a pivotal role in setting us apart from the apes. Brain expansion came later.

The First Bipeds

Between 15 and 5 million years ago, various kinds of hominoids lived throughout Africa, Asia, and Europe. One of these apes living in Africa between 8 and 5 million years ago was a direct ancestor to the human line. Each new fossil from this critical time period (such as the 6 million-year-old *Orrorin* fossils discovered in Kenya in 2001[8] or the 6 to 7 million-year-old skull discovered in Chad, Central Africa[9]) is proposed as the latest "missing link" in the evolutionary chain leading to humans.

For a hominoid fossil to be definitively classified as part of the human evolutionary line, certain evidence of

---

[8]Senut, B., et al. (2001). First hominid from the Miocene (Lukeino formation, Kenya). *C. R. Academy of Science, Paris, 332,*137–144.

[9]Brunett, M., et al. (2002). A new hominid from the Upper Miocene of Chad, Central Africa. *Nature 418,* 145–151.

Australopithecus The genus including several species of early bipeds from southern and eastern Africa living between 4 .2 and about 1 million years ago, one of whom was directly ancestral to humans.

bipedalism is required. However, all early bipeds are not necessarily direct ancestors to the humans. Consider, for example, fossils of the genus *Ardipithecus* that lived between 5.8 and 4.4 million years ago. Found in Ethiopia, East Africa, this genus was much smaller than a modern chimpanzee, but it was chimpanzeelike in other features, such as the shape and enamel thickness of its teeth. On the other hand, a partially complete skeleton of one *Ardipithecus* individual suggests that unlike chimpanzees, and like all other species in the human line, this creature was bipedal. Given the combination of bipedalism and chimpanzeelike characteristics, many paleoanthropologists consider it a side branch on the human evolutionary tree.

Between 5 and 4 million years ago, the environment of eastern and southern Africa was mostly a mosaic of open country with pockets of closed woodland. Some early bipeds seem to have lived in one of the woodland pockets. Later human ancestors inhabited more open country known as savannah—grasslands with scattered trees and groves—and are assigned to one or another species of the genus *Australopithecus* (from Latin *australis,* meaning "southern," and Greek *pithekos,* meaning "ape"). Opinions vary on just how many species there were in Africa between about 4 and 1 million years ago. For our purposes and the sake of simplicity, it suffices to refer to them collectively as "australopithecines." The earliest definite australopithecine fossils date back 4.2 million years,[10] whereas the most recent ones are only about 1 million years old. They have been found up and down the length of eastern Africa from Ethiopia to South Africa and westward into Chad (Figure 3.5).

None of the australopithecines were as large as most modern humans, although all were much more muscular for their size. Males seem to have been quite a bit larger than females, with size differences between the sexes less than those found in living apes such as gorillas and orangutans but greater than those seen among living humans. Because larger animals tend to have larger brains, when comparing brain size among individuals or species body size must be taken into account. Taking their relative body size into consideration, australopithecines possessed brains comparable to those of modern African apes. However, the structure and size of the teeth were more like those of modern people than they are like those of apes.

Bipedalism is considered an important adaptive feature in the savannah environment for many reasons.[11] A

---

[10]Wolpoff, M. (1996). *Australopithecus:* A new look at an old ancestor. *General Anthropology, 3*(1), 2.

[11]Lewin, R. (1987). Four legs bad, two legs good. *Science, 235,* 969.

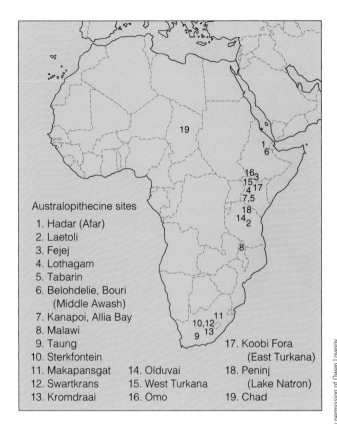

1985 David L. Brill by permission of Owen Lovejoy

FIGURE 3.5

Australopithecine fossils have been found in South Africa, Malawi, Tanzania, Kenya, Ethiopia, and Chad.

Australopithecine sites

1. Hadar (Afar)
2. Laetoli
3. Fejej
4. Lothagam
5. Tabarin
6. Belohdelie, Bouri
   (Middle Awash)
7. Kanapoi, Allia Bay
8. Malawi
9. Taung
10. Sterkfontein
11. Makapansgat
12. Swartkrans
13. Kromdraai
14. Olduvai
15. West Turkana
16. Omo
17. Koobi Fora
    (East Turkana)
18. Peninj
    (Lake Natron)
19. Chad

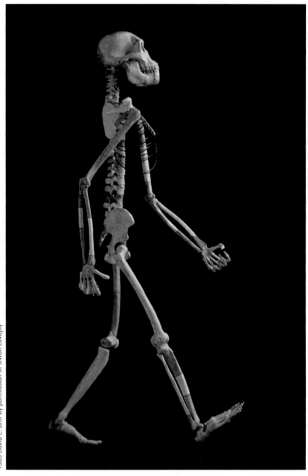

A 40 percent complete skeleton "Lucy" (named after the Beatles' song "Lucy in the Sky with Diamonds"—popular at the time of discovery) indicates these australopithecine ancestors were bipedal. This adult female *Australopithecus* was only 3½ feet tall, typical of the small size of female australopithecines.

biped could not run as fast as a quadruped but could travel long distances in search of food and water without tiring. With free hands, a biped could take food to places where it could be eaten in relative safety and could carry infants rather than relying on the babies hanging on for themselves. As bipeds, australopithecines could use their hands to wield sticks or other objects effectively in threat displays and to protect themselves against predators. Also, erect posture exposes a smaller area of the body to the direct heat of the sun than a quadrupedal position, helping to prevent overheating on the open savannah. Furthermore, a biped with its head held high could see further, spotting food as well as predators from a distance.

Although adapted fully to bipedalism, curved toe bones and relatively long arms indicate australopithecines had not given up tree climbing altogether. One reason may be that sparsely distributed trees continued to be important places of refuge on the African savannah, a land teeming with dangerous predatory animals. Chimpanzees today build their night nests in trees, suggesting a habit that may have been part of the australopithecine pattern as well. In addition, trees provide rich sources of food such as fruits, seeds, and nuts. However, to survive in their savannah environment, early bipeds may have been forced to try out supplementary sources

of food on the ground, as they likely did around the time when the first members of the genus *Homo* appeared about 2.5 million years ago. In addition to whatever plant foods were available, the major new source was animal protein. This was not protein from monkey meat obtained as a result of coordinated hunting parties like those of the chimpanzees and bonobos of today, but rather the fatty marrow and whatever other edible leftover flesh remained in and on the bones of dead animals.

Homo habilis

Increased meat consumption by our early ancestors was important for human evolution. On the savannah, it is hard for a primate with a humanlike digestive system to satisfy its protein requirements from available plant resources. Moreover, failure to do so has serious consequences: stunted growth, malnutrition, starvation, and

The earliest stone tools dated to between 2.6 and 2.5 million years ago were discovered by Ethiopian paleoanthropologist Sileshi Semaw at Gona, located in the west-central Afar region of Ethiopia.

death. Leaves and legumes (nitrogen-fixing plants, familiar modern examples being beans and peas) provide most readily accessible plant sources of protein. The problem is that these are hard for primates like us to digest unless they are cooked. The leaves and legumes available contain substances causing the proteins to pass right through the gut without being absorbed.

Chimpanzees have a similar problem today when out on the savannah. In such a setting, they spend more than a third of their time going after insects like ants and termites on a year-round basis, while at the same time increasing their predation on eggs and small vertebrate animals. Not only are such animal foods easily digestible, but they provide high-quality proteins that contain all the essential amino acids, the building blocks of protein, in just the right percentages. No single plant food does this by itself. Only the right combination of plants can supply the balance of amino acids provided by meat alone. Our ancestors probably solved their dietary problems in much the same way that chimps on the savannah do today. However, without the daggerlike teeth for ripping and cutting flesh, they were at a disadvantage. Even chimpanzees, whose canine teeth are far larger and sharper than ours, frequently have trouble tearing through the skin of other

animals. It appears then that for more efficient utilization of animal protein, our ancestors needed sharp tools for butchering carcasses.

The earliest identifiable tools consist of a number of stone implements made by striking sharp-edged flakes, useful for cutting meat, from the surface of a stone core. In the process, cores were transformed into choppers. These flakes and choppers are from Olduvai Gorge in Tanzania and are known as implements in the **Oldowan** tool tradition. They mark the beginning of the **Lower Paleolithic,** or Old Stone Age, which lasted from about 2.5 million until approximately 250,000 or 200,000 years ago. The earliest tools of this sort, which were recently found in Ethiopia, are perhaps even 2.6 million years old. Before this time, australopithecines probably used tools such as heavy sticks to dig up roots or ward off animals, unmodified stones to hurl as weapons or to crack open nuts and bones, and simple carrying devices made of hollow gourds or knotted plant fibers. These tools, however, are not traceable in the long-term archaeological record.

Since the late 1960s, a number of sites in southern and eastern Africa have been discovered with fossil remains of a lightly built biped with a body all but indistinguishable from that of the earlier australopithecines, except that the teeth are smaller and the brain is significantly larger relative to body size.[12] Furthermore, the inside of the skull shows a pattern in the left cerebral hemisphere that, in contemporary people, is associated

Oldowan The first stone tool industry beginning between 2.5 and 2.6 million years ago.
Lower Paleolithic Old Stone Age spanning from about 2.5 million to 250,000 or 200,000 years ago and characterized by Oldowan and Acheulean tools.

---

[12]Conroy, G. C. (1997). *Reconstructing human origins: A modern synthesis* (pp. 264–265, 269–270). New York: Norton.

© 1999 David L. Brill

with a language area. While this does not prove that these bipeds could speak, it suggests a marked advance in information-processing capacity over that of australopithecines. Since major brain-size increase and tooth-size reduction are important trends in the evolution of the genus *Homo,* paleoanthropologists designated these fossils as a new species: ***Homo habilis*** ("handy man").[13] Significantly, the earliest fossils to exhibit these trends appeared around 2.5 million years ago, about the same time as the earliest evidence of stone tool making.

MEDIATREK

To visit the Web site of the famous Leakey Foundation and access an interactive timeline of key discoveries in paleoanthropology, go to MediaTrek 3.2 on the companion Web site or CD-ROM.

Paleoanthropological depictions of early *Homo* from the 1960s and 1970s profiled "man the hunter" wielding tools with a killer instinct in a savannah teeming with meat, while females stayed at home tending their young. However, this theoretical reconstruction of ancient human life was flawed due to insufficient evidence and to male-centered bias in both the discipline's earlier accounts, and in the ethnographic record of still-existing foraging cultures used for comparative purposes. Until then, most anthropologists doing fieldwork among foragers stressed the role of male hunters and underreported the significance of female gatherers in providing food for the community. Since the 1960s, however, female anthropologists began to set the record straight, documenting the vital role of "woman the gatherer" in provisioning the social group in foraging cultures, past and present.

Moreover, new evidence suggests that early humans may have depended more on scavenging than on hunting. Indeed, microscopic analysis of cut marks on fossil bones, which commonly overlie marks made by the teeth of carnivores, suggest that the lightly built *Homo habilis* may have been what is known as *tertiary scavengers:* third in line to feed off an animal killed by a predator. Fortunately, these tool-wielding ancestors could break open the shafts of long bones to get at the fat and protein-rich marrow inside. Although this scavenging hypothesis regarding our earliest human ancestors has attracted considerable attention and endorsement among a majority of experts, it might be questioned on the basis of evidence from recent research among wild chimpanzees at Gombe, Tanzania. This work suggests that our closest primate "cousins" have little interest in dead animals as food, but when scavenging actually does take place, female chimpanzees show more interest in it than do males. That *H. habilis* behaved similarly seems unlikely, however, in view of the evidence just noted on the fossil animal bones, as well as the fact that *H. habilis* was a different kind of primate, living in a different environment from chimpanzees.

Becoming scavengers put *Homo habilis* in competition with formidable adversaries like hyenas.

© J & B Photos/Animals, Animals

---

[13]Although some have argued that *habilis* was not the only species of early *Homo,* evidence supporting such an idea is problematic.

Homo habilis "Handy man." The first fossil members of the genus *Homo* appearing 2.5 million years ago, with larger brains and smaller faces than australopithecines.

Biocultural Connection

Paleolithic Prescriptions for the Diseases of Civilization

Though increased life expectancy is often hailed as one of modern civilization's greatest accomplishments, in some ways people in industrialized countries lead far less healthy lifestyles than their ancestors. Throughout most of their evolutionary history, humans led more physically active lives and ate a more varied low-fat diet than many do now. They did not drink or smoke. They spent their days scavenging or hunting for animal protein while gathering vegetable foods with some insects thrown in for good measure. They stayed fit through traveling great distances each day over the savannah and beyond. Today many people survive longer but in old age are beset by chronic disease. Heart disease, diabetes, high blood pressure, and cancer shape the experience of old age in wealthy industrialized nations. The prevalence of these "diseases of civilization" has increased rapidly over the past 50 years. Anthropologists Melvin Konner and Marjorie Shostak and physician Boyd

Eaton have suggested that our Paleolithic ancestors have provided us with a prescription for a cure. They propose that as "stone-agers in a fast lane," the health of people in industrialized countries will improve by returning to the lifestyle to which our bodies are adapted. Such Paleolithic prescriptions

© Gusto/Photo Researchers

are an example of evolutionary medicine—a branch of medical anthropology that uses evolutionary principles to contribute to human health.

Evolutionary medicine bases its prescriptions on the idea that rates of cultural change exceed the rates of biological change. Our hunter–gatherer physiology was shaped over millions of years, while the cultural changes leading to contemporary lifestyles have occurred rapidly. Anthropologist George Armelagos suggests that the downward trajectory for human health began with the earliest human village settlements some 10,000 years ago. When humans began farming rather than gathering, they often switched to single-crop diets. In addition, settlement into villages led directly to an increase in infectious disease. While the more recent cultural invention of antibiotics has cured many infectious diseases, it also led to an increase in chronic diseases. In many cases, alternative treatments for these conditions stem from evolutionary medicine. ■ ■ ■

Tools, Food, and Brain Expansion

Evolutionary transformations often occur suddenly as large random mutations produce novel organisms that, by chance, are well adapted to a particular environment. Sometimes natural selection produces change more gradually. This appears to have taken place following the arrival of *Homo habilis,* the first species in the genus *Homo;* with the demonstrated use of tools, our human ancestors began a course of gradual brain expansion that continued until some 200,000 years ago. By then, brain size had approximately tripled and reached the levels of today's humans.

Many scenarios proposed for the adaptation of early *Homo,* such as the relationship among tools, food, and brain expansion, rely upon a feedback loop between brain size and behavior. The behaviors made possible by larger brains confer advantages to large-brained individuals, contributing to their increased reproductive success. Over time, their genetic variance becomes more common in successive generations, and the population gradually evolves to acquiring a larger-brained form. In

the case of tool making, the archaeological record provides us with tangible data concerning our ancestors' cultural abilities fitting with the simultaneous biological expansion of the brain. Tool making itself puts a premium on manual dexterity as opposed to hand use emphasizing power. In addition, the patterns of stone tools and fossilized animal bones at Oldowan sites in Africa suggest improved organization of the nervous system. The sources for stone used to make cutting and chopping tools were often far from the sites where tools were used to process parts of animal carcasses. Also, the high density of fossil bones at some Oldowan sites and patterns of seasonal weathering indicate such sites were repeatedly used over a period of years. It appears that the Oldowan sites were places where tools and the raw materials for making them were stockpiled for later use in butchering. This implies advanced preparation for meat processing and thereby attests to the growing importance of foresight and the ability to plan ahead. Beginning with *Homo habilis* in Africa about 2.5 million years ago, human evolution began a sure course of increasing brain size relative to body size and increasing

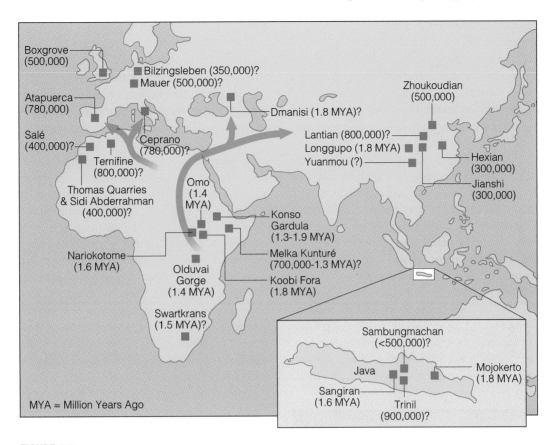

FIGURE 3.6

Paleoanthropological sites, with dates, at which *Homo erectus* remains have been found. The arrows indicate the proposed routes by which *Homo* spread from Africa to Eurasia.

cultural development, each acting upon and thereby promoting the other.

Homo erectus

Shortly after 2 million years ago, at a time that *Homo habilis* and Oldowan tools had become widespread in Africa, a new species, **Homo erectus** ("upright man"), appeared on that continent. Unlike *H. habilis,* however, *H. erectus* did not remain confined to Africa. In fact, evidence of *H. erectus* fossils almost as old as those discovered in Africa have been found in the Caucasus Mountains of Georgia (between Turkey and Russia), south-central China, and on the island of Java, Indonesia. These fossils indicate that it was not long before members of the genus *Homo* spread widely throughout much of Asia and Europe (Figure 3.6).

The emergence of *H. erectus* as a new species in the long course of human evolution coincided with the beginning of the Pleistocene epoch or Ice Age, which spanned from almost 2 million to 10,000 years ago. During this period of global cooling, Arctic cold conditions and abundant snowfall in the earth's Northern Hemisphere created vast ice sheets that temporarily cov-

ered much of Eurasia and North America. These fluctuating but major glacial periods often lasted tens of thousands of years, separated by intervening warm periods. During interglacial periods the world warmed up to the point that the ice sheets melted and sea levels rose, but during much of this time sea levels were much lower than today, exposing large surfaces of low-lying lands now under water.[14]

Of all the epochs in the earth's 4.6 *billion*-year history, the Pleistocene is particularly significant for our species, for this era of dramatic climatic shifts is the period in which humans—from *H. erectus* to *H. sapiens*—evolved and spread all across the globe. Confronted by environmental changes due to climatic fluctuations or movements into different geographic areas, our early human ancestors were constantly challenged to make

[14]Fagan, B. M. (2000). *Ancient lives: An introduction to archaeology.* (pp. 125–133). Englewood Cliffs, NJ: Prentice-Hall.

Homo erectus "Upright man." A species within the genus *Homo* first appearing just after 2 million years ago in Africa and ultimately spreading throughout the Old World.

biological and, more especially, cultural adaptations in order to survive and successfully reproduce. In the course of this long evolutionary process, random mutations introduced new characteristics into evolving populations in different regions of the world. The principle of natural selection was at work on humans as it was on all forms of life, favoring the perpetuation of certain characteristics within particular environmental conditions. At the same time, other characteristics that conferred no particular advantage or disadvantage also appeared by random mutation in geographically removed populations. The end result was a gradually growing physical variation in the human species. In this context, it is not surprising that *H. erectus* fossils found in Africa, Asia, and Europe reveal levels of physical variation not unlike those seen in modern human populations living across the globe today.

Available fossil evidence indicates that *H. erectus* had a body size and proportions similar to modern humans, though with heavier musculature. Differences in body size between the sexes diminished considerably compared to earlier bipeds, perhaps to facilitate successful childbirth. Based on fossil skull evidence, *H. erectus*

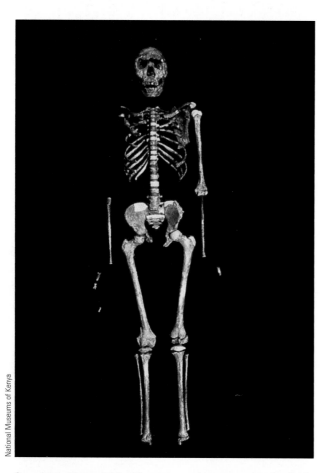

One of the oldest—at 1.6 million years—and most complete fossils of *Homo erectus* is the "strapping youth" from Lake Turkana, Kenya: a tall and muscular boy who was already 5 feet 3 inches tall when he died at about the age of 13.

average brain size fell within the higher range of *H. habilis* and within the lower range of modern human brain size. The dentition was fully human, though relatively large by modern standards.

As one might expect, given its larger brain, *H. erectus* outstripped its predecessors in cultural development. In Africa and Eurasia, the Oldowan chopper was replaced by the more sophisticated hand axe. At first the hand axes—shaped by regular blows giving them a larger and finer cutting edge than chopper tools—were probably all-purpose implements for food procurement and processing, and defense. But *H. erectus* also developed cleavers (like hand axes but without points) and various scrapers to process animal hides for bedding and clothing. In addition, this early human relied on flake tools used "as is" to cut meat and process vegetables, or refined by "retouching" into points and borers for drilling or punching holes in materials. Improved technological efficiency is also evident in *H. erectus'* use of raw materials. Instead of making a few large tools out of big pieces of stone, these ancestors placed a new emphasis on smaller tools, thus economizing their raw materials.

Remains found in southern Africa suggest that *H. erectus* may have learned to use fire by 1 million years ago. Although there exists considerable variation in physiological conditioning among different human groups and even among individuals within each group, studies of modern humans indicate that most people can remain reasonably comfortable down to 50 degrees Fahrenheit (10 degrees Celsius) with minimal clothing so long as they keep active. Below that temperature, hands and feet cool to the point of pain. Without controlled use of fire, it is unlikely that early humans could have moved successfully into regions where winter temperatures regularly dropped below that point—as they must have in northern China and most of Europe, where *H. erectus* spread some 780,000 years ago.

Fire gave our human ancestors more control over their environment. It permitted them to continue activities after dark and provided a means to frighten away predators. It supplied them with the warmth and light needed for cave dwelling, and it enabled them to cook food. The ability to modify food culturally through cooking may have paved the way for reduction in the tooth size and jaws of later fossil groups since raw food is tougher and requires more chewing. However, cooking does more than this. It detoxifies a number of otherwise poisonous plants. In addition, it alters substances in plants, allowing important vitamins, minerals, and proteins to be absorbed from the gut rather than passing unused through the intestines. And, finally, it makes high-energy complex carbohydrates, such as starch, digestible. In short, when our human ancestors learned to employ fire to warm and protect themselves and to

National Museums of Kenya

cook their food, they dramatically increased their geographical range and nutritional options.

With *H. erectus* we also have evidence of organized hunting as the means for procuring meat, animal hides, horn, bone, and sinew. Early evidence demonstrating the hunting technology of these ancestors includes 400,000-year-old wooden spears discovered in a peat bog (what was originally marsh or swamp land) in northern Germany although it is likely that evolving humans had begun to hunt before then. Increased organizational ability is also indicated in prehistoric sites such as Ambrona and Torralba in Spain where group hunting techniques were used to drive a variety of large animals (including elephants) into a swamp for killing.[15]

With *H. erectus,* then, we find a clearer manifestation than ever before of the complex interplay among biological, cultural, and ecological factors. Social organization and technology developed along with an increase in brain size and complexity and a reduction in tooth and jaw size. The appearance of cultural adaptations such as controlled use of fire, cooking, and more complex tool kits may have facilitated language development. (See Chapter 4 for more on language origins.) Improvements in communication and social organization brought about by language undoubtedly contributed to better methods for food gathering and hunting, to a population increase, and to territorial expansion. Continuous biological and cultural change through natural selection in the course of hundreds of thousands of years gradually transformed *H. erectus* into the next emerging species: *Homo sapiens.*

Homo sapiens

At various sites in Africa, Asia, and Europe, a number of fossils have been found that date between roughly 400,000 and 200,000 years ago. The best population sample, bones of about thirty individuals of both sexes and all ages (but none older than about 40) comes from Atapuerca, a 400,000-year-old site in Spain. Overall, these bones show a mixture of characteristics of *Homo erectus* with those of early *Homo sapiens,* exactly what one would expect of fossil remains transitional between the two. For example, brain size overlaps the upper end of the *H. erectus* range and the lower end of the range for *H. sapiens.* Whether one chooses to call these or any other contemporary fossils early *H. sapiens,* late *H. erectus,* or *Homo antecessor,* as did the Spanish anthropologists who discovered them, is more than a name game. Fossil names indicate researchers' perspectives about

[15]Freeman, L. G. (1992). *Ambrona and Torralba: New evidence and interpretation.* Paper presented at the 91st Annual Meeting, American Anthropological Association.

At the site Sima de los Huesos ("Pit of Bones") in the Sierra de Atapuerca, Spain, paleoanthropologist Juan Luis Arsuaga and his team have discovered the remains of about thirty individuals.

evolutionary relationships among groups. When specimens are given separate species names, it signifies that they form part of a reproductively isolated group.

Some paleoanthropologists approach the fossil record with the perspective that making such detailed biological determinations is arbitrary. Arguing that it is impossible to prove whether or not a collection of ancient bones and teeth represents a distinctive species, they tend to be "lumpers," placing more or less similar-looking fossil specimens together in more inclusive groups. "Splitters," by contrast, may interpret even minor differences in the shape of skeletons or skulls as evidence of distinctive biological species with corresponding cultural capacities. Referring to the variable shape of the boney ridge above ancient eyebrows, South African paleoanthropologist Philip Tobias has quipped, "Splitters will create a new species at the drop of a brow ridge."

Archaic Homo sapiens

As we proceed along the human evolutionary trajectory, the fossil record provides us with many more human specimens compared to earlier periods. The record is particularly rich when it comes to the **Neandertals,** perhaps the most controversial ancient member of the genus *Homo.* Typically, they are represented as the classic "cave men," stereotyped in Western popular media and even in natural history museum displays as wild and hairy club-wielding brutes.

Based on abundant fossil evidence, we now know that Neandertals were an extremely muscular group of humans living from about 125,000 to approximately 30,000 years ago in Europe, Southwest Asia, and south-central Asia. While having brains of modern size, Neandertals often possessed faces and skulls quite different from those of later fossilized remains referred to as anatomically modern humans. Their large noses and teeth projected forward more than is the case with modern people. They generally had a sloping forehead and prominent bony brow ridges over their eyes, and on the back of the skull, a bony mass provided for attachment of powerful neck muscles. These features, while not exactly in line with modern ideals of European beauty, are common in Norwegian and Danish skulls dating to about 1,000 years ago—the time of the Vikings.[16] Nevertheless, these anatomical features do little to negate the popular image of Neandertals as cave-dwelling brutes. Their rude reputation may also derive from the time of their discovery, as

the first widely publicized Neandertal skull was found in 1856, well before scientific theories to account for human origins had gained acceptance. This odd-looking old skull, happened upon near Düsseldorf in Germany's Neander "Valley" (*Tal* in German), took German scientists by surprise. Initially, they explained its extraordinary features as evidence of some disfiguring disease in an invading "barbarian" from the east who had crawled into a deep cave to die. Although it became evident that the skull belonged to an ancient human fossil, Neandertals are still surrounded by controversy. That said, we now know that many aspects of this species' unique skull shape and body form represent its biological adaptation to an extremely cold climate. We also know that the Neandertal's intellectual capacity for cultural adaptation was noticeably superior to that of earlier members of the genus *Homo.*

One of the most hotly debated arguments in paleoanthropology today is the relationship of Neandertals to anatomically modern humans. Were they a separate species that became extinct about 30,000 years ago? Or were they a subspecies of *Homo sapiens?* And if they were not a dead-end and inferior side branch in human evolution, did they actually contribute to our modern human gene pool? In that case, so the argument goes, their direct descendants walk the earth today (and you could be one of them).

> *Neandertals* A distinct group of archaic *Homo sapiens* inhabiting Europe, Southwest Asia, and south-central Asia from approximately 125,000 to 30,000 years ago.

[16]Ferrie, H. (1997). An interview with C. Loring Brace. *Current Anthropology* 38, 861.

VISUAL COUNTERPOINT
Perceptions about the capabilities of fossil groups are expressed in visual representations of fleshed-out versions of fossil remains. The Neandertal diorama from the 1920s exhibit in the Field Museum of Chicago contains a message about their evolutionary distance from us, while positive cultural attributes are given to anatomically modern specimens.

© Bettmann/CORBIS

The Field Museum, John Weinstein

As this face-off between U.S. paleoanthropologist Milford Wolpoff and his reconstruction of a Neandertal shows, the latter did not differ all that much from modern humans of European descent.

Meanwhile, other parts of the world were inhabited by other variants of archaic *H. sapiens,* lacking the mid-facial projection and massive muscle attachments on the back of the skull common among the Neandertals. Human fossil skulls found near the Solo River in Java are a prime example. Dates for these specimens range anywhere between about 200,000 and 27,000 years ago. The fossils, with their modern-sized brains, display certain features of *H. erectus* combined with those of archaic as well as more modern *H. sapiens.* Human fossils from various parts of Africa, the most famous being a skull from Kabwe in Zambia, also show a combination of ancient and modern traits. Finally, similar remains have been found at several places in China.

Adaptations to a wide range of different natural environments by archaic *Homo sapiens* were, of course, both biological and cultural, but their capacity for cultural adaptation was predictably superior to what it had been in earlier members of the genus *Homo.* Neandertals' extensive use of fire, for example, was essential to survival in a cold climate like that of Europe during the various glacial periods. They lived in small bands or single-family units, both in the open and in caves, probably communicating

through language (see Chapter 4). Evidence of deliberate burials of the deceased among Neandertals reflects a measure of ritual behavior in their communities. Moreover, the fossil remains of an amputee discovered in Iraq and an arthritic man excavated in France imply that Neandertals took care of the disabled, something not seen previously in the human fossil record.

The tool-making tradition of all but the latest Neandertals is called the **Mousterian** tradition after a site (Le Moustier) in the Dordogne region of southern France. *Mousterian* refers to a tradition of the Middle Paleolithic stone tool industries of Europe and Southwest Asia, generally dating from about 125,000 until about 40,000 years ago. Although considerable variability exists, Mousterian tools are generally lighter and smaller than those of earlier traditions. Whereas previously only two or three flakes could be obtained from the entire stone core, Mousterian toolmakers

Mousterian The tool industry of the Middle Paleolithic used by all people in Europe, the Middle East, and Africa from 125,000 to 40,000 years ago.

obtained many smaller flakes, which they skillfully retouched and sharpened. Their tool kits also contained a greater variety of types than the earlier ones: hand axes, flakes, scrapers, borers, notched flakes for shaving wood, and many types of points that could be attached to wooden shafts to make spears. This variety of tools facilitated more effective use of food resources and enhanced the quality of clothing and shelter. These types of stone tools were used by *all* people, Neandertals and their contemporaries elsewhere, including North Africa and Southwest Asia during this time period.

For archaic *H. sapiens,* improved cultural adaptive abilities relate to the fact that the brain had achieved modern size. Such a brain made possible not only sophisticated technology but also conceptual thought of considerable intellectual complexity. Decorative pendants and objects with carved and engraved markings also appear in the archaeological record from this period. Objects were also commonly colored with pigments such as manganese dioxide and red or yellow ocher. The ceremonial burial of the dead and nonutilitarian, decorative objects provide additional evidence supporting theoretical arguments in favor of symbolic thinking and language use in these ancient populations.

In the course of the Middle Paleolithic, individuals with a somewhat more anatomically modern human appearance began to appear in Africa and Southwest Asia. Like Neandertals, these particular *Homo sapiens* used Mousterian tools. In Europe, the transition to the tools of the Upper Paleolithic occurred between 40,000 and 35,000 years ago. By this time, Neandertal technology was also comparable to the industries used by these anatomically modern *H. sapiens*.[17]

Anatomically Modern Peoples and the Upper Paleolithic

A veritable explosion of tool types and other forms of cultural expression beginning about 40,000 years ago constitutes what is known as the **Upper Paleolithic** transition. Upper Paleolithic tool kits include increased prominence of "blade" tools: long, thin, precisely shaped pieces of stone demonstrating the considerable skill of their creators. The Upper Paleolithic, lasting until about 10,000 years ago, is best known from archaeological evidence found in Europe where numerous distinctive tool industries from successive time periods have been documented. In addition, the European archaeological record is rich with cave wall paintings, engravings, and bas-relief sculptures as well as many portable nonutilitarian artifacts from this period.

In Upper Paleolithic times, humans began to manufacture tools for more effective hunting, fishing, as well as gathering. Cultural adaptation also became more highly specific and regional, thus enhancing human chances for survival under a wide variety of environ-

© Gianni Dagli Orti/Corbis

© 1985 David L. Brill

The techniques of the Upper Paleolithic allowed for the manufacture of a variety of tool types. The finely wrought Solutrean bifaces of Europe are shaped like plant leaves. Tools such as eyed needles and harpoons began to be manufactured out of bone and antler.

Upper Paleolithic The last part (40,000–10,000 years ago) of the Old Stone Age, featuring tool industries characterized by long slim blades and an explosion of creative symbolic forms.

[17]Mellars, P. (1989). Major issues in the emergence of modern humans. *Current Anthropology, 30,* 356–357.

mental conditions. Instead of manufacturing all-purpose tools, Upper Paleolithic populations inhabiting a wide range of environments—mountains, marshlands, tundra, forests, lake regions, river valleys, and seashores—all developed specialized devices suited to the resources of their particular habitat and to the different seasons. This versatility also permitted human spread by crossing open water and Arctic regions to places never previously inhabited by humans, most notably Australia (between 60,000 and 40,000 years ago) and the Americas (about 30,000 to 15,000 years ago).

This degree of specialization required improved manufacturing techniques. The blade method of manufacture (Figure 3.7), invented by archaic *H. sapiens* and later used widely in Europe and western Asia, required less raw material than before and resulted in smaller and lighter tools with a better ratio between weight of flint and length of cutting edge. The pressure-flaking technique—in which a bone, antler, or a wooden tool is used to press off small flakes from a larger flake or blade—gave the Upper Paleolithic toolmaker greater control over the shape of the tool than was possible with percussion flaking.

Invented by Mousterian toolmakers, the *burin* (a stone tool with chisel-like edges) came into common use in the Upper Paleolithic. The burin provided an excellent means of working bone and antler used for tools such as fishhooks and harpoons. The spear-thrower, or *atlatl* (a Nahuatl word used by Aztec Indians in Mexico, referring to a wooden device, 1–2 feet long, with a hook on the end for throwing a spear), also appeared at this time. By

effectively elongating the arm, the atlatl gave hunters increased force behind the spear throw.

Art was an important aspect of Upper Paleolithic culture. As far as we know, humans had not produced representational artwork before. In some regions, tools and weapons were engraved with beautiful animal figures; pendants were made of bone and ivory, as were female figurines; and small sculptures were modeled out of clay. Spectacular paintings and engravings depicting humans and animals of this period have been found on the walls of caves and rock shelters in Spain, France, Australia, and Africa. Because the southern African rock art tradition spanned 27,000 years and lasted into historic times, we know that much of it depicts artists' visions when in altered states of consciousness related to spiritual practices. Along with the animals, the art also includes a variety of geometric motifs spontaneously generated by the human nervous system when in trance. Australian cave art, some of it older than European cave art and also associated with trancing, includes similar motifs. The occurrence of the same geometric designs in the cave art of Europe suggests trancing was a part of these prehistoric foraging cultures as well. The geometric motifs in Paleolithic art have also been interpreted as stylized human figures and patterns of descent. Given the great importance of kinship in all historically known communities of hunters, fishers, and gatherers, this should not be surprising (Chapter 2).

Whether or not a new kind of human, anatomically modern with correspondingly superior intellectual and creative abilities, is responsible for this cultural

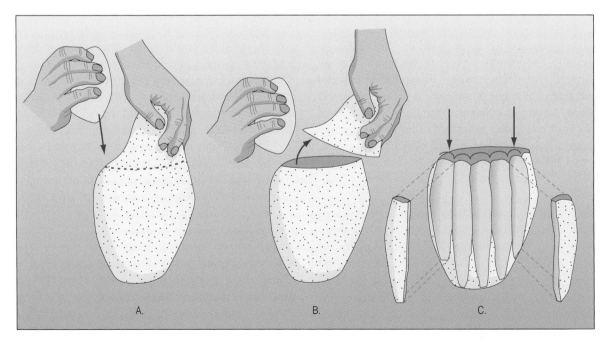

FIGURE 3.7
During the Upper Paleolithic, a technique used to manufacture blades became common. The stone was broken to create a striking platform, then vertical blades were flaked off to form sharp-edged tools.

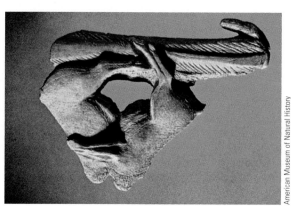

Shown here is part of a tool known as an atlatl or spear-thrower carved in the late Ice Age between 15,000 and 11,000 years ago. The entire atlatl would have been a foot or two long, with a handle on one end and a hook on the other that fitted into the blunt end of the spear. Extending a person's throwing arc, an atlatl increased the distance and speed a hunter could send a spear. The upside-down ibexes carved to ornament this particular atlatl would have flipped rightside-up every time it was used. The tumbling motion of these wild mountain goats may have given the Upper Paleolithic hunter aesthetic pleasure and may also have had spiritual significance as a charm to ensure a successful hunt.

American Museum of Natural History

explosion is hotly debated within paleoanthropology. The biological and cultural evidence preserved in fossil and archaeological records does not tell a simple story.

On a biological level the great debate can be distilled to a question of whether one, some, or all populations of the archaic groups played a role in the evolution of modern *H. sapiens*. Those supporting the **multiregional hypothesis** argue that the fossil evidence suggests a simultaneous local transition from *H. erectus* to modern *H. sapiens* throughout the parts of the world inhabited by early members of the genus *Homo*. By contrast, those supporting the **recent African origins hypothesis** (also known as the "Eve" or "Out of Africa" hypothesis) use genetic evidence to argue that all anatomically modern humans living today descend directly from one single population of archaic *H. sapiens* in Africa. Improved cultural capabilities then allowed members of this group to replace other archaic human forms as they began to spread out of Africa some time after 100,000 years ago. So while both models place

human origins firmly in Africa, the first argues that our human ancestors began moving into Asia and Europe as early as 1.8 million years ago, whereas the second maintains that anatomically modern *H. sapiens* evolved only in Africa, completely replacing other members of the genus *Homo* as they spread throughout the world.

For many years, the absence of good fossil evidence from Africa to support the second hypothesis has been a major problem. In 2003, however, skulls of two adults and one child discovered in 1997 in the Afar region of Ethiopia and described as anatomically modern were reconstructed and dated to 160,000 years ago.[18] The discoverers of these fossils called them *Homo sapiens idaltu* (meaning "elder" in the local Afar language). Convinced that they have conclusively proved the recent African origins hypothesis, they argue that their latest evidence verifies that Neandertals represent a dead-end side branch of human evolution. Not everyone agrees.

Though the recent African origins hypothesis is accepted by many paleoanthropologists, not every scholar supports it. Among those with opposing views, Chinese paleoanthropologists generally favor the multiregional hypothesis in part because it fits better with the fossil discoveries from Australia and Asia. The claim of ancient human roots in eastern Asia also resonates well with the region's traditional ethnocentric ideas about China as the place of human origins and the world's most ancient civilization—the center of humanity on

multiregional hypothesis The hypothesis that modern humans originated through a process of simultaneous local transition from *Homo erectus* to *Homo sapiens* throughout the inhabited world.

recent African origins hypothesis The hypothesis that all modern people are derived from one single population of archaic *H. sapiens* from Africa who migrated out of Africa after 100,000 years ago, replacing all other archaic forms due to their superior cultural capabilities. Also called the "Eve" or "Out of Africa" hypothesis.

[18]White, T., et al. (2003). Pleistocene *Homo sapiens* from the Middle Awash, Ethiopia. *Nature, 423,* 742–747.

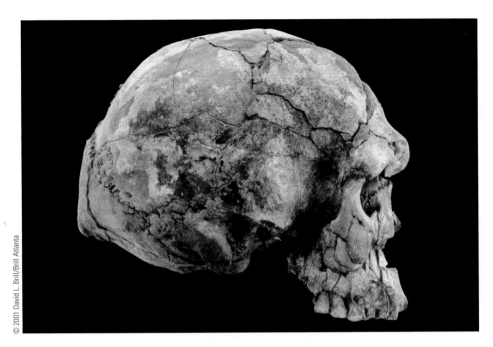

© 2001 David L. Brill/Brill Atlanta

The newly discovered, well-preserved specimens found near the Ethiopian village of Herto in the Afar region provide the best fossil evidence in support of the recent African origins hypothesis. Though these fossils unquestionably possess an anatomically modern appearance, they are still relatively robust. In addition, the question of whether the higher skull and forehead indicate superior cultural abilities remains open.

earth, China is traditionally imagined as "the Middle Kingdom." By contrast, the recent African origins hypothesis depends more upon the interpretation of genetic evidence, fossils, and cultural remains from Europe, Africa, and Southwest Asia. However, this model can be critiqued on several grounds. For example, the molecular evidence upon which it is based has been strongly criticized as more recent genetic studies indicate that Africa was not the sole source of DNA in modern humans.[19]

Recent African origins proponents argue that anatomically modern people coexisted for a time with other archaic populations until the superior cultural capacities of the moderns resulted in extinction of the archaic peoples. Especially clear evidence of this is said to have been found in Europe, where Neandertals and moderns supposedly coexisted between 40,000 and 30,000 years ago. However, defining fossils as either Neandertals or moderns illustrates the difficulty with distinguishing a distinct biological species given the presence of considerable physical variation found in humans living today. The latest Neandertals show features (such as chins) more commonly seen in modern humans, while "early moderns" show features (such as brow ridges and bony masses at the back of the skull) reminiscent of Neandertals. This mix of modern and Neandertal features is so strong in a child's skeleton recently found in Portugal as to lead several specialists to regard it as clear evidence of hybridization, or successful

sexual mating between both human populations.[20] This, of course, would mean that the two human forms belonged to one single species rather than to separate ones. In fact, an explanation that accounts for all this evidence is that all of these fossils belong to a single varied population, with some individuals showing features more typical of Neandertals than others. This accords with archaeological evidence that the cultural achievements of late Neandertals were not fundamentally different from those of "early moderns."[21]

Nevertheless, by 30,000 years ago, many of the distinctive anatomical features seen in archaic groups like Neandertals seem to disappear from the fossil record in Europe. Instead, individuals more generally with higher foreheads, smoother brow ridges, and more distinct chins seemed to have Europe to themselves. However, a comparative examination of skulls representing the full range of individual human variation found in every part of the world today reveals now living people with skulls not meeting the anatomical definition of "modernity" proposed in the recent African origins model.[22]

---

[19]Gibbons, A. (1997). Ideas on human origins evolve at anthropology gathering. *Science, 276,* 535–536; Pennisi, E. (1999). Genetic study shakes up out of Africa theory. Science, 283, 1,828.

---

[20]Holden, C. (1999). Ancient child burial uncovered in Portugal. *Science, 283,* 169.

---

[21]D'Errico, F., Zilhão, J., Julien, M., Baffier, D., & Pelegrin, J. (1998). Neandertal acculturation in Western Europe? *Current Anthropology, 39,* 521. See also Henry, D. O., et al. (2004). Human behavioral organization in the Middle Paleolithic: Were Neandertals different? *American Anthropologist, 107*(1), 17–31.

---

[22]Wolpoff, M., & Caspari, R. (1997). *Race and human evolution* (pp. 344-345, 393). New York: Simon & Schuster.

Some living people, such as this indigenous Australian, do not all meet the problematic definition of anatomical modernity according to skull shape proposed in the recent African origins model. Therefore, some paleoanthropologists suggest that this narrow definition of anatomical modernity is flawed, perhaps even ethnocentric, because all living people are clearly full-fledged members of the species *Homo sapiens.*

© Michael Coyne/Getty Images

RACE AND HUMAN EVOLUTION

The Neandertal debate raises fundamental questions about the complex relationship between biological and cultural human variation. As we reviewed the human fossil record throughout this chapter, inferences were made about the cultural capabilities of our ancestors partially based on biological features. For instance, the argument of a significantly increased brain size of *Homo habilis* 2.5 million years ago compared to earlier australopithecines was used to support the claim that these ancestors were capable of more complex cultural activities, including the manufacture of stone tools. Can we make the same kinds of assumptions about other more recent biological developments? Can we say that only the anatomically modern humans with higher foreheads and reduced brow ridges were capable of making sophisticated tools and beautiful art due to fundamental biological difference? Supporters of the multiregional hypothesis argue we cannot.

Such questions are deeply embedded within a discipline that has a long history of studying cultural and biological variation within the human species and how it relates to the concept of **race** as a subspecies or discrete biological division within a species. Today, anthropologists agree that no subspecies exist within currently surviving *Homo sapiens.* Consequently, as far as contemporary humanity is concerned, race is not a valid biological category. In fact, anthropologists work actively to expose the concept of race as scientifically inapplicable to humans. At the same time, they recognize the powerful

symbolic significance of race as a socio-political category in many countries, including the United States, Germany, Brazil, and South Africa.

Race as a Social Construct

To deal with the politically divisive aspects of racial symbolism, we must begin by understanding how the notion of distinct human races came to be. Earlier in this chapter, we discussed how European scholars struggled to make sense of the massive amounts of new information generated since the Age of Exploration, beginning about 500 years ago. Coming to them from the most remote corners of the world, this information forced them to critically rethink deeply rooted ideas about humanity and its relationship to other forms of life. In the quest for understanding, they reasoned not only on the basis of scientific facts but also from the perspective of their particular religious beliefs and cultural traditions. Looking back on their writings, we are now painfully aware of how ethnocentrism and other prejudices clouded their findings.

Among the most telling examples of this is the racial categorizing done by German anatomist Johann Blumenbach (1752–1840), sometimes called the father of physical anthropology. Initially, Blumenbach adopted the classification system devised by the Swedish naturalist Linnaeus in 1758, which divided the human species into four major groups according to geographic area and classified all Europeans as "white," Africans as "black," American Indians as "red," and Asians as "yellow." Later, in the 1795 edition of his book *On the Natural Variety of Mankind,* Blumenbach introduced some significant changes to this four-race scheme. Based on a comparative examination of his human skull collection, he

race In biology, a subgroup within a species, not applicable to humans.

judged as most beautiful the skull of a woman from the Caucasus Mountains between Russia and Turkey. It was more symmetrical than the others, and he thought it reflected nature's ideal form: the circle. Surely, Blumenbach reasoned, this perfect specimen resembled God's original creation. Moreover, he thought that the living inhabitants of the Caucasus region were the most "beautiful" in the world. Based on these criteria, he concluded that this high mountain range not far from the Biblical lands was near the place of human origins.

Building on his idea that the southeastern Europeans inhabiting the Caucasus looked most like the first humans, Blumenbach decided that all light-skinned peoples in Europe and adjacent parts of western Asia and northern Africa belonged to the same race. On this basis, he dropped the European race label and replaced it with "Caucasian." Although he continued to distinguish American Indians as a separate race, he regrouped dark-skinned Africans as "Ethiopian" and split those Asians not considered Caucasian into two separate races: "Mongolian" (referring to most inhabitants of Asia, including China and Japan) and "Malay" (indigenous Australians, Pacific Islanders, and others).

But, Blumenbach did more than change labels: He also introduced a formal hierarchical ordering of the races he delineated. Convinced that Caucasians were closest to the original ideal humans created in God's image, he ranked them as superior. The other races, he argued, were the result of "degeneration"; moving away from their place of origin and adapting to different environments and climates, they had degenerated physically and morally into what many Europeans came to think of as inferior races.[23]

Critically reviewing this and other early historical efforts in classifying humanity in higher and lower forms, we now clearly recognize their factual errors and ethnocentric biases with respect to the concept of race. Especially disastrous is the notion of superior and inferior races, as this has been used as justification for brutalities ranging from repression to slavery to mass murder or genocide. It has also been employed to justify stunning levels of mockery, as painfully illustrated in the tragic story of Ota Benga, an African pygmy man who in the early 1900s was caged in a New York zoo with an orangutan.

Captured in a raid in the Congo, Ota Benga somehow came into the possession of a North American missionary-explorer looking for exotic "savages" for exhibition in the United States. In 1904, Ota and a group of fellow pygmies were shipped across the Atlantic and exhibited at a World's Fair in Saint Louis, Missouri. About 23 years old at the time, Ota was 4 feet 11 inches in height and weighed 103 pounds. Throngs of visitors came to see displays of dozens of indigenous peoples from around the globe, shown in their traditional dress and living in replica villages doing their customary things. The fair was a success for the organizers, and all the pygmies survived to be shipped back to their homeland. The enterprising missionary also returned to Congo and with Ota's help collected artifacts to be sold to the American Museum of Natural History in New York City. In the summer of 1906 he returned to the United States, along with Ota. Soon thereafter, the missionary went bankrupt and lost his entire collection to the bank. Left stranded in the big city, Ota was placed in the care of the museum and then taken to the Bronx Zoo where he was put on exhibit in the monkey house, with an orangutan as company. Ota's sharpened teeth (a cultural practice among his own people) were seen as evidence of his supposedly cannibal nature. After intensive protest, zoo officials released the unfortunate pygmy from his cage and during the day let him roam free in the park, where he was often harassed by teasing visitors. Ota (usually referred to as a "boy") was then turned over to an orphanage for African American children. In 1916, upon hearing that he would never return to his homeland, he took a revolver and shot himself through the heart.[24]

The racist display at the Bronx Zoo almost a century ago was by no means unique. Just a tip of the ethnocentric iceberg, it was the manifestation of a powerful ideology in which one small part of humanity sought to demonstrate and justify its claims of biological and cultural superiority. This had particular resonance in North America, where people of European descent were thrown together in a society with Native Americans, African slaves, and (later) Asians imported as a source of cheap labor. Indeed, such claims, based on false notions of race, have resulted in the oppression and genocide of millions of humans because of the color of their skin or the shape of their skulls.

MEDIATREK
To visit the American Anthropological Association Web site and read the discipline's statement on race, go to MediaTrek 3.3 on the companion Web site or CD-ROM.

Fortunately, by the early 20th century, some scholars began to challenge the concept of racial superiority. Among the strongest critics was Franz Boas (1858–1942), a Jewish scientist who immigrated to the United States because of rising anti-Semitism in his German homeland and went on to become the founder of North America's academic anthropology. As president of the American Association for the Advancement of Science, Boas criticized hierarchical notions of race in an important speech titled "Race and Progress," published in the prestigious

---

[23]Gould, S. J. (1994). The geometer of race. *Discover, 15*(11), 65–69.

[24]Bradford, P. V., & Blume, H. (1992). *Ota Benga: The pygmy in the zoo.* New York: St. Martin's Press.

journal *Science* in 1909. Ashley Montagu (1905–1999), a student of Boas and one of the best-known anthropologists of his time, devoted much of his career to combating scientific racism. Like Boas, he was born into a Jewish family. Born in England and originally named Israel Ehrenberg, he also felt the sting of anti-Semitism. After changing his name in the 1920s, he immigrated to the United States, where he went on to fight racism in his writing and in academic and public lectures. Of all his works, none is more important than his book *Man's Most Dangerous Myth: The Fallacy of Race*. Published in 1942, it took the lead in exposing, on purely scientific grounds, the fallacy of human races as clearly bounded biological categories. The book has since gone through six editions, the last in 1999. Although Montagu's once controversial ideas have now become mainstream, his text remains the most comprehensive treatment of its subject.

Race as a Biological Construct

Social constructions of race are often tied up in the false but tenacious idea that there really is a biological foundation to the concept of human races. As already mentioned, in biology a race is defined as a subspecies: a population within a species that differs in terms of genetic variance from other populations of the same species. Simple and straightforward though such a definition may seem, there are three very important things to note about it. First, it is arbitrary; there is no agreement on how many differences it takes to make a race. For some who are interested in the topic, different frequencies in the variants of one gene are sufficient; for others, different frequencies involving several genes are necessary. Ultimately, it proved impossible to reach agreement not just on the number of genes, but also on precisely which ones are the most important for defining races.

After arbitrariness, the second important thing to note about the biological definition of *race* is that it does not mean that any one so-called race has exclusive possession of any particular variant of any gene or genes. In human terms, the frequency of a trait like type O blood, for example, may be high in one "race" population and low in another, but it is present in both. In other words, populations are genetically "open," meaning that genes flow between them. Because human populations are genetically open, no fixed racial groups have developed within our modern species.

The third important thing to note about the scientifically inappropriate use of the term *race* with respect to humans is that the differences among individuals within a particular population are generally greater than the differences among populations. As the science writer James Shreeve puts it, "most of what separates me genetically from a typical African or Eskimo also separates me from another average American of European ancestry."[25]

© Kit Kittle/CORBIS

Many people have become accustomed to viewing so-called racial groups as natural and separate divisions within our species based on visible physical differences. However, the broadly defined geographic "racial" groupings differ from one another in only 6 percent of their genes. Having exchanged genes throughout history, different groups have continued to do so. Instead of leading to the development of distinctive subspecies (biologically defined races), this genetic exchange has maintained all of humankind as a single species. This continued sharing is effectively illustrated by this picture of children born of a European American mother and an African American father.

In sum, the biological concept of race does not apply to *Homo sapiens*. That said, to dismiss race as a biologically invalid category is not to deny the reality of human biological diversity. The task for anthropologists is to explain that diversity and the social meanings given to it rather than to try to falsely split our species into discrete categories called races.

Skin Color: A Case Study in Adaptation

The popular idea of race is commonly linked to skin color, a complex biological trait. Skin color is subject to great variation and is attributed to several key factors: the transparency or thickness of the skin; a copper-

---

[25]Shreeve, J. (1994) Terms of estrangement. *Discover, 15*(11), 60.

VISUAL COUNTERPOINT The Andaman Islanders on the left are the traditional inhabitants of a group of isolated tropical islands in the Bay of Bengal east of India. Short, dark-skinned, and frizzy-haired, they represent a population once widespread in Southeast Asia. The people on the right are descendants of southern Chinese migrants who spread into Vietnam and other parts of the region after the invention of agriculture. In the course of a few hundred generations, the newcomers interbred with Southeast Asia's original inhabitants (who looked more like today's indigenous Andamanese), giving rise to people we now view as "typically" Vietnamese.

colored pigment called carotene; reflected color from the blood vessels (responsible for the rosy color of lightly pigmented people); and, most significantly, the amount of melanin (from *melas,* a Greek word meaning "black")—a dark pigment in the skin's outer layer. People with dark skin have more melanin-producing cells than those with light skin, but everyone (except albinos) has a measure of melanin. Exposure to sunlight increases melanin production, causing skin color to deepen. Melanin is known to protect skin against damaging ultraviolet solar radiation;[26] consequently, dark-skinned peoples are less susceptible to skin cancers and sunburn than are those with less melanin. They also seem to be less susceptible to destruction of certain vitamins under intense exposure to sunlight. Because the highest concentrations of dark-skinned people tend to be found in the tropical regions of the world, it appears that natural selection has favored heavily pigmented skin as a protection against exposure where ultraviolet radiation is most constant.[27]

In northern latitudes light skin has an adaptive advantage related to the skin's important biological function as the manufacturer of vitamin D through a chemical reaction dependent upon sunlight. Vitamin D is vital for maintaining the balance of calcium in the body. In northern climates with little sunshine, light skin allows enough sunlight to penetrate the skin and stimulate the formation of vitamin D, essential for healthy bones. Dark pigmentation interferes with this process. The severe consequences of vitamin D deficiency can be avoided through culture. Until recently, children in northern Europe and North America were regularly fed a spoonful of cod liver oil during the dark winter months. Today, pasteurized milk is often fortified with vitamin D.

Given what we know about the adaptive significance of human skin color, and the fact that, until 800,000 years ago, members of the genus *Homo* were exclusively creatures of the tropics, it is likely that lightly pigmented skins are a recent development in human history. Conversely, and consistent with humanity's African origins, darkly pigmented skins likely are quite ancient. The enzyme tyrosinase, which converts the amino acid tyrosine into the compound that forms melanin, is present in lightly pigmented peoples in sufficient quantity to make them very "black." The reason it does not is that they have genes that inactivate or inhibit it.[28] Human skin, more liberally endowed with sweat glands and lacking heavy body hair compared to other primates, effectively eliminates excess body heat in a hot climate. This would have been especially advantageous to our ancestors on the savannah, who could have avoided confrontations with large carnivorous animals by carrying out most of their activities in the heat of the day. For the most part, tropical predators rest during this period, hunting primarily from dusk until early morning.

[26]Neer, R. M. (1975). The evolutionary significance of vitamin D, skin pigment, and ultraviolet light. *American Journal of Physical Anthropology, 43,* 409–416.

[27]Branda, R. F., & Eatoil, J. W. (1978). Skin color and photolysis: An evolutionary hypothesis. *Science, 201,* 625–626.

[28]Wills, C. (1994). The skin we're in. *Discover, 15*(11), 79.

Without much hair to cover their bodies, selection would have favored dark skin in our human ancestors. In short, based on available scientific evidence, all humans appear to have a "black" ancestry, no matter how "white" some of them may appear to be today.

Obviously, one should not conclude that, because it may be a more recent development, lightly pigmented skin is better, or more highly evolved, than heavily pigmented skin. The latter is clearly better evolved to the conditions of life in the tropics or at high altitudes, although with cultural adaptations like protective clothing, hats, and more recently invented sunscreen lotions, lightly pigmented peoples can survive there. Conversely, the availability of supplementary sources of vitamin D allows more heavily pigmented peoples to do quite well

far away from the tropics. In both cases, culture has rendered skin color differences largely irrelevant from a purely biological perspective. With time and with the efforts we see being made in many cultures today, skin color may lose its social significance as well.

Over the course of our long evolutionary history, we have become an amazingly diverse and yet still unified single species inhabiting the entire earth. Biological adaptation to a wide geographic range of natural environments is responsible for some aspects of human variation. However, while biological evolution continues into the present, our different cultures shape both the expression and the interpretation of human biological variation at every step. Human bipeds do indeed stand with one foot in nature and another in culture.

Chapter Summary

■ As a four-field discipline, anthropology includes not only research on human cultures and languages worldwide and through time, but also the study of our biological nature. Paleoanthropologists unearth and analyze ancient fossil humans and their ancestors. Primatologists study the behaviors of our closest animal relatives (the apes) and other primates. Others specialize in molecular research, investigating our genetic heritage and the genetic basis for variations within and among different human populations. New discoveries in these specializations force us to rethink ideas about the origin of our species.

■ As the early primates became daytime active tree dwellers, they came to rely on vision rather than the sense of smell. In addition, learned social behavior became increasingly important. Through the study of the behavior of present-day primates, anthropologists seek clues for reconstructing behavioral patterns that may have characterized human ancestors.

■ Like nearly all primates, bonobos and chimpanzees live in structured social groups expressing their sociability through communication by visual and vocal signals. In-depth field studies have led primatologists to recognize the distinct "cultures" of these primate groups. The young members of the social group learn to behave appropriately through observation and practice. In addition, chimpanzees and bonobos can make and use tools.

■ The earliest members of the bipedal human line diverged from the African apes (chimpanzees, bonobos, and gorillas) sometime between 8 and 5 million years ago. Best known are the australopithecines, well equipped for generalized foraging in a relatively open savannah environment. Although many theories propose that bipedalism reinforced brain expansion by freeing the hands for activities other than locomotion, the increase in brain size did not appear in human evolutionary history until much later with the appearance of the genus *Homo*.

■ With the appearance of the first members of genus *Homo*— *Homo habilis*—about 2.5 million years ago, stone tools begin to appear in the archaeological record. Possible earlier tools made

of perishable materials such as plant fibers are not preserved. Throughout the course of the evolution of the genus *Homo*, the critical importance of culture as the human mechanism for adaptation imposed selective pressures favoring a larger brain, which in turn made possible improved cultural adaptation.

■ *Homo erectus*, appearing shortly after 2 million years ago, had a brain close in size to that of modern humans and sophisticated behaviors including controlled use of fire for warmth, cooking, and protection. *H. erectus* remains are found throughout Africa, Asia, and Europe, ultimately reaching the colder northern areas about 780,000 years ago. The technological efficiency of *H. erectus* is evidenced in improved tool making—first the hand axe and later specialized tools for hunting, butchering, food processing, hide scraping, and defense. Hunting techniques developed by *H. erectus* reflected a considerable advance in organizational ability.

■ Between 400,000 and 200,000 years ago, evolving humans achieved the brain capacity of true *Homo sapiens*. Apparently several local variations of archaic *H. sapiens* existed, including the Neandertals. Their capacity for cultural adaptation was considerable, doubtless because their fully modern brains made sophisticated technology and conceptual thought possible. Those who lived in Europe used fire extensively in their Arctic climate, lived in small bands, and communicated through language. Remains testify to ritual behavior and caretaking for the aged and infirm.

■ Evidence indicates that at least one population of archaic *H. sapiens* evolved into modern humans. Whether this involved the biological evolution of a new species with improved cultural capabilities or a simultaneous worldwide process involving all archaic forms remains one of the most contentious issues in paleoanthropology. The stone tool industries and artwork of Upper Paleolithic cultures surpassed any previously undertaken by humans. Cave paintings and rock art found in Spain, France, Australia, and Africa, which served a religious purpose, attest to a highly sophisticated aesthetic sensibility.

■ Race is a cultural construction that varies culture to culture. Although biological variation exists in the human species, biological races or distinct subspecies do not. Some variation such as differences in skin color is the result of genetic adaptation processes to a variety of different natural environments. Human variation appears in continuous gradations from one population to another without sharp breaks. Moreover, because of the independent inheritance of individual traits and the genetic openness of human populations, the vast majority of human variation exists within populations rather than among populations.

Questions for Reflection

1. Over the course of their evolutionary history, humans increasingly used the medium of culture to face the challenges of existence. How does studying the biological basis of human culture through living primates and human evolution help address the challenge of knowing ourselves?

2. Given your understanding of the concept of culture, do you think that chimps and bonobos possess culture?

3. How might you relate the Neandertal debates to stereotyping or racism in contemporary society?

4. Some aspects of human variation derive clearly from biological adaptations to the environment. As humans came to rely more upon cultural adaptations, what were the effects on our biology? How has culture shaped our interpretations of our biology?

Key Terms

Paleoanthropologists	Oldowan
Primatologists	Lower Paleolithic
Evolution	*Homo habilis*
Genes	*Homo erectus*
Adaptation	Neandertals
Natural selection	Mousterian
Species	Upper Paleolithic
Primate	Multiregional hypothesis
Hominoids	Recent African origins hypothesis
Bipedalism	Race
Australopithecus	

Multimedia Review Tools

Companion Web Site

Visit **http://www.wadsworth.com/anthropology_d/** and click on the companion Web site for this textbook to access a wide range of material to aid your study of anthropology. Among the options for self-study in each chapter are learning objectives, flash cards, Internet activities, Web links, InfoTrac College Edition exercises, and practice tests that can be scored and emailed to your instructor.

CD-ROM

The *Doing Anthropology Today* CD-ROM supplied with your textbook provides unique and valuable information designed to enhance your learning experience. This interactive multimedia resource includes video clips, interviews with renowned anthropologists, map and timeline exercises, chapter study quizzes, and much more. *Doing Anthropology Today* will not only help you in achieving your grade goals, but it will also make your learning experience fun and exciting!

Suggested Readings

De Waal, F. (2001). *The ape and the sushi master*. New York: Basic Books.

In an accessible style, one of the world's foremost experts on bonobos demonstrates ape culture and challenges theories that exclude animals from the "culture club." His discussion takes the concept of ape culture beyond anthropocentrism and ties it to communication and social organization.

Goodall, J. (2000). *Reason for hope: A spiritual journey*. New York: Warner Books.

A personal memoir linking this famous primatologist's life-work with chimpanzees in Tanzania's Gombe wildlife preserve to her spiritual convictions. Exploring difficult topics such as environmental destruction, animal abuse, and genocide, Goodall expands the concept of humanity and advocates basic human rights for chimpanzees.

Jones, S., Martin, R., & Pilbeam, D. (1992). *Cambridge encyclopedia of human evolution* New York: Cambridge University Press.

Over seventy scholars contributed to this comprehensive introduction to the human species, covering the gamut—from genetics, primatology, and the fossil evidence to contemporary human ecology, demography, and disease.

Marks, J. (2002). *What it means to be 98 percent chimpanzee: Apes, people, and their genes*. Berkeley: University of California Press.

This provocative book places the ongoing study of the relationship between genes and behavior in historical and cultural contexts. Marks uses the close genetic relationship of chimps and humans to demonstrate the limits of genetics for explaining differences in complex traits such as behavior or appearance. His discussion of the absence of a genetic basis for race is particularly good.

Wolpoff, M., & Caspari, R. (1997). *Race and human evolution: A fatal attraction*. New York: Simon & Schuster.

A historical account of efforts to develop a scientific theory of race in Western societies is joined with an analysis of the fossil evidence for modern human origins in this fascinating book. Its authors, champions of the multiregional hypothesis, document the social processes leading to the division of contemporary humans into racial groups suggesting that the division of fossil groups into separate species represents a similar application of the false concept of biological race.

© Napoleon Chagnon/Anthro-Photo

PART 2

Culture and Survival
The Challenge of Communicating, Raising Children, and Staying Alive

Introduction

All living creatures face a fundamental challenge in common—that of survival. Simply put, unless they adapt themselves to some available environment, they cannot survive. Adaptation requires the development of behaviors that will help an organism use the environment to its advantage—to find food and sustenance, avoid hazards, and (if the species is to continue) reproduce its own kind. In turn, organisms need to have the biological equipment that allows development of appropriate patterns of behavior. For the hundreds of millions of years of life on earth, biological adaptation has been the primary means by which the challenge of survival has been met. This is accomplished as organisms of a particular kind, whose biological equipment is best suited to a particular environment and way of life, produce more offspring than those whose equipment is not. In this way, advantageous characteristics become more common in succeeding generations, at the same time that less advantageous ones become increasingly rare.

One characteristic that ultimately did become common among mammals, to one degree or another, was the ability to learn new patterns of behavior to solve at least limited problems of existence. This problem-solving ability became particularly well developed among the last common ancestors of apes and humans, and by 2.5 million years ago (long after the human and ape lines of evolution had diverged), early members of the genus *Homo* began to rely increasingly on what their minds could invent rather than on what their bodies could do. Although the human species has not freed itself entirely, even today, from the forces of biological adaptation, it has come to rely primarily on culture—a body of learned traditions that, in essence, tells people how to live—as the medium through which the challenges of human existence may be solved.

The consequences of this are profound. As the evolving genus *Homo* unconsciously came to rely more on cultural solutions to its problems as opposed to biological ones, its chances of survival improved. So it was that when members of this genus added scavenging to their subsistence practices some 2.5 million years ago, the resources available to them increased substantially. More-over, the tools and techniques that enabled this new way of life made our ancient ancestors less vulnerable to predators than they had been before. Thus, life became a bit easier, and with humans, as with other animals, this generally makes for easier reproduction. A slow but steady growth of human populations followed the development of scavenging and gathering.

Among most mammals, population growth frequently leads to the spillover of fringe populations into regions previously uninhabited by a species. There they find new environments, to which they must adapt or face extinction. This pattern of dispersal seems to have been followed by early humans, for soon after the invention of scavenging and gathering, they began to spread geographically, inhabiting new and even harsh environments. As they did so, they devised cultural rather than biological solutions to their new problems of existence.

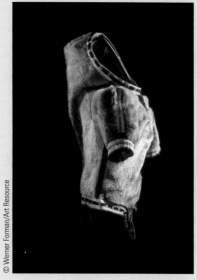

© Werner Forman/Art Resource

Because culture is learned and not inherited biologically, its transmission from one person to another, and from one generation to the next, depends on an effective system of communication far more complex than that of any other animal. Thus, a first requirement for any culture is providing a means of communication among individuals. All cultures do this through some form of language, one of human-kind's most distinctive characteristics and the subject of Chapter 4.

In human societies each generation must learn its culture anew. The learning process itself is thus crucial to a culture's survival. A second requirement of culture, then, is the development of reliable ways to teach children the behavior that is expected of them as members of their community—a social structure that ensures that individuals growing up in a society will contribute to its survival. Since adult personality is in large part the product of life experiences, the ways children are raised and educated play a major part in the shaping of their later selves. The ability of individuals to function properly as adults depends, to a degree, upon how effectively their personalities have been shaped to fit their culture. As we will see in Chapter 5, findings have emerged from anthropological investigations in these areas that have implications for human behavior that go beyond anthropology.

As important as effective communication and education are for the survival of a culture, they are of no avail unless the culture is able to satisfy the basic needs of the individuals who live by its rules. A third requirement of culture, therefore, is the ability to provide its members with food, water, and protection from the elements. Chapter 6 discusses the ways in which cultures handle people's basic needs and the ways societies adapt through culture to the environment. Since this leads to the production, distribution, and consumption of goods—the subject matter of economic anthropology—we conclude this section with Chapter 7, focusing on economic systems.

CHAPTER 4

Language and Communication

© Yavuz Arslan/Peter Arnold

CHALLENGE ISSUE

Humans communicate in many ways, including touch, gesture, and posture. Our most distinctive and complex form of communication, however, is language. It is the foundation stone of culture, which is our species' primary means of meeting the challenge of survival.

1. What Is Language?

A language is a system of symbolic communication using sounds or gestures that are put together according to certain rules, resulting in meanings that are based on agreement by a society and intelligible to all who share that language. Although humans rely heavily on spoken language, or speech, to communicate with one another, it is not their sole means of communication. Human language is embedded in an age-old gesture-call system in which body motions and facial expressions, along with vocal features such as tone and volume, play vital roles in conveying messages.

2. How Is Language Related to Culture?

Without our capacity for complex language, human culture as we know it could not exist. Languages are shared by people who belong to societies that have their own distinctive cultures. Social variables, such as age, gender, and economic status, may influence how people use language. Moreover, people communicate what is meaningful to them, and that is largely defined by their particular culture. In fact, our use of language has an effect on, and is influenced by, our culture.

3. How Did Language Begin?

Anthropologists theorize that human language probably began as a system of gestures with elementary patterns or rules that grew more complex over time. A key factor in its growing complexity may have been an emerging awareness among our ancient ancestors that planning ahead for a variety of possible circumstances increased the likelihood of survival. Because speech is a product of muscular movements, spoken language may have emerged as the muscles of the mouth and vocal tract were favored through natural selection; speaking would have increased survivability because it allowed people to use their hands for other things as they talked, and it permitted communication with others without having to be in full view.

All normal humans are born with the ability to communicate through language and may spend a considerable part of each day doing so. Indeed, language is so much a part of our lives that it involves everything we do, and everything we do involves language. There is no doubt that our ability to communicate, whether through sounds or gestures (sign languages, such as the American Sign Language used by the hearing impaired, are fully developed languages in their own right), rests squarely upon our biological makeup. We are "programmed" for language, although only in a general sort of way. Beyond the cries of babies, which are not learned but which do communicate, humans must learn their language. And so it is that any normal child from anywhere in the world readily learns the language of his or her culture.

As noted above, **language** is a system of communication using sounds and/or gestures that are put together according to certain rules, resulting in meanings that are intelligible to all who share that language. These sounds and gestures fall into the category of symbols, defined in Chapter 2 as things that arbitrarily and by convention represent something else in a meaningful way. For example, the word *crying* is a symbol, a combination of sounds to which we assign the meaning of a particular action and which we can use to communicate that meaning, whether or not anyone around us is actually crying. **Signals,** unlike culturally learned symbols, are instinctive sounds and gestures that have a natural or self-evident meaning. A scream, a cough, and the sound of crying itself are signals that convey some kind of emotional or physical state.

> **language** A system of communication using sounds or gestures that are put together in meaningful ways according to a set of rules.
> **signals** Instinctive sounds or gestures that have a natural or self-evident meaning.

Today's language experts are not certain how much credit to give to animals, such as dolphins or chimpanzees, for the ability to use symbols as well as signals, even though these animals and many others have been found to communicate in remarkable ways. Several chimpanzees, gorillas, and orangutans have been taught American Sign Language, and researchers have discovered that even vervet monkeys utilize distinct calls for communication. These calls go beyond merely signaling levels of fear or arousal. Among other things, these small African monkeys have specific calls to signify the type of predator threatening the group. According to primatologist Allison Jolly,

> [The calls] include which direction to look in or where to run. There is an audience effect: calls are given when there is someone appropriate to listen . . . monkey calls are far more than involuntary expressions of emotion.[1]

What are the implications for our understanding of the nature and evolution of language? No final answer will be evident until we gain more knowledge about the various systems of animal communication. What we can be sure of is that communication among nonhuman species cannot be dismissed as a set of simple instinctive reflexes or fixed action patterns, even though debate continues over just how human and animal communication relate to each other.[2] A particularly remarkable example of the many scientific efforts underway on this subject is the story of an orangutan named Chantek, featured in the following Original Study.

[1]Jolly, A. (1991). Thinking like a vervet. *Science, 251,* 574. See also Seyfarth, R. M., et al. (1980). Monkey responses to three different alarm calls: evidence for predator classification and semantic communication. *Science, 210,* 801–803.

[2]Armstrong, D. F., Stokoe, W. C., & Wilcox, S. E. (1993). Signs of the origin of syntax. *Current Anthropology, 34,* 349–368; Burling, R. (1993). Primate calls, human language, and nonverbal communication. *Current Anthropology, 34,* 25–53.

Original Study

The Intellectual Abilities of Orangutans

In 1978, after researchers began to use American Sign Language for the deaf to communicate with chimpanzees and gorillas, I began the first long-term study of the language ability of an orangutan named Chantek. There was criticism that symbol-using apes might just be imitating their human caregivers, but there is now growing agreement that orangutans, gorillas, and both chimpanzee species can develop language skills at the level of a 2- to 3-year-old human child. The goal of Project Chantek was to investigate the mind of an orangutan through a devel-

H. Lyn Miles

Though the orangutans diverged from humans, chimps, and gorillas about 12 million years ago, all of these ape species share a number of qualities. Orangutans have an insightful, humanlike thinking style characterized by longer attention spans and quiet, deliberate action. Orangutans make shelters, tie knots, recognize themselves in mirrors, use one tool to make another, and are the most skilled of the apes in manipulating objects. In this photo, an orangutan named Chantek, now an adult, begins the sign for tomato.

opmental study of his cognitive and linguistic skills. It was a great ethical and emotional responsibility to engage an orangutan in what anthropologists call "enculturation," since I would not only be teaching a form of communication, I would be teaching aspects of the culture upon which that language was based. If my project succeeded, I would create a symbol-using creature that would be somewhere between an ape living under natural conditions and an adult human. This threatened to raise as many questions as I sought to answer.

A small group of caregivers at the University of Tennessee, Chattanooga, began raising Chantek when he was 9 months old. They communicated with him by using gestural signs based on the American Sign Language for the deaf. After a month, Chantek produced his own first sign and eventually learned to use approximately 150 different signs, forming a vocabulary similar to that of a very young child. Chantek learned names for people (LYN, JOHN), places (YARD, BROCK-HALL), things to eat (YOGURT, CHOCOLATE), actions (WORK, HUG), objects (SCREW-DRIVER, MONEY), animals (DOG, APE), colors (RED, BLACK), pronouns (YOU, ME), location (UP, POINT), attributes

(GOOD, HURT), and emphasis (MORE, TIME-TO-DO). We found that Chantek's signing was spontaneous and nonrepetitious. He did not merely imitate his caregivers as had been claimed for the sign language-trained chimpanzee Nim; rather, Chantek actively used his signs to initiate communications and meet his needs. Almost immediately, he began to use his signs in combinations and modulated their meanings with slight changes in how he articulated and arranged his signs. He commented "COKE DRINK" after drinking his coke, "PULL BEARD" while pulling a caregiver's hair through a fence, "TIME HUG" while locked in his cage as his caregiver looked at her watch, and "RED BLACK PAINT" for a group of colored paint jars. At first he used signs to manipulate people and objects to meet his needs, rather than to refer to them. But, could he use these signs as symbols, that is, more abstractly to represent a person, thing, action, or idea, even apart from its context or when it was not present?

One indication of the capacity to use symbolic language in both deaf and hearing human children is the ability to point, which some researchers argued that apes could not do spontaneously. Chantek began to point to objects when he was 2 years old, somewhat later than human children, as we might expect. First, he showed and gave us objects, and then he began pointing to where he wanted to be tickled and to where he wanted to be carried. Finally, he could answer questions like WHERE HAT? WHICH DIFFERENT? and WHAT WANT? by pointing to the correct object.

As Chantek's vocabulary increased, the ideas that he was expressing became more complex, such as when he signed BAD BIRD at noisy birds giving alarm calls, and WHITE CHEESE FOOD-EAT for cottage cheese. He understood that things had characteristics or attributes that could be described. He also created combinations of signs that we had never used before. In the way that a child learns language, Chantek began to over- or under-extend the meaning of his signs, which gave us insight into his emotions and how he was beginning to classify his world. For

example, he used the sign DOG for actual dogs, as well as for a picture of a dog in his viewmaster, orangutans on television, barking noises on the radio, birds, horses, a tiger at the circus, a herd of cows, a picture of a cheetah, and a noisy helicopter that presumably sounded like it was barking. For Chantek, the sign BUG included crickets, cockroaches, a picture of a cockroach, beetles, slugs, small moths, spiders, worms, flies, a picture of a graph shaped like a butterfly, tiny brown pieces of cat food, and small bits of feces. He signed BREAK before he broke and shared pieces of crackers, and after he broke his toilet. He signed BAD to himself before he grabbed a cat, when he bit into a radish, and for a dead bird.

We also discovered that Chantek could comprehend our spoken English (after the first couple of years we used speech as well as signing). When he was 2 years old, Chantek began to sign for things that were not present. He frequently asked to go to places in his yard to look for animals, such as his pet squirrel and cat, who served as playmates. He also made requests for ICE CREAM, signing CAR RIDE and pulling us toward the parking lot for a trip to a local ice-cream shop. We learned that an orangutan can tell lies. Deception is an important indicator of language abilities since it requires a deliberate and intentional misrepresentation of reality. In order to deceive, you must be able to see events from the other person's perspective and negate his or her perception. Chantek began to deceive from a relatively early age, and we caught him in lies about three times a week. He learned that he could sign DIRTY to get into the bathroom to play with the washing machine, dryer, soap, and so on, instead of using the toilet. He also used his signs deceptively to gain social advantage in games, to divert attention in social interactions, and to avoid testing situations and coming home after walks on campus. On one occasion, Chantek stole food from my pocket while he simultaneously pulled my hand away in the opposite direction. On another occasion, he stole a pencil eraser, pretended to swallow it, and "supported" his case

[CONTINUED]

[CONTINUED]

by opening his mouth and signing FOOD-EAT, as if to say that he had swallowed it. However, he really held the eraser in his cheek, and later it was found in his bedroom where he commonly hid objects.

We carried out tests of Chantek's mental ability using measures developed for human children. Chantek reached a mental age equivalent to that of a 2- to 3-year-old child, with some skills of even older children. On some tasks done readily by children, such as using one object to represent another and pretend play, Chantek performed as well as children, but less frequently. He engaged in chase games in which he would look over his shoulder as he darted about, although no one was chasing him. He also signed to his toys and offered them food and drink.

Like children, Chantek showed evidence of animism, a tendency to endow objects and events with the attributes of living things. Chantek also experimented in play and problem solving. For example, he tried vacuuming himself and investigated a number of clever ways to short out the electric fence that surrounded his yard. He learned how to use several tools, such as hammers, nails, and screwdrivers, and he was able to complete tasks using tools with up to twenty-two problem-solving steps. By the time he was 2 years old, he was imitating signs and actions. We would perform an action and ask him to copy it by signing DO SAME. He would immediately imitate the behavior, sometimes with novel twists, as when he winked by moving his eyelid up and down with his finger. Chantek also liked to use paints, and his own free-style drawings resembled those of 3-year-old human children. He learned to copy horizontal lines, vertical lines, and circles. By 4$^{1}/_{2}$ years of age, Chantek could identify himself in the mirror and use it to groom himself. He showed evidence of planning, creative simulation, and the use of objects in novel relations to one another to invent new meanings. For example, he simulated the context for food preparation by giving his caregiver two objects needed to prepare his milk

formula and staring at the location of the remaining ingredient.

A further indication that Chantek had mental images is found in his ability to respond to his caregiver's request that he improve the articulation of a sign. When his articulation became careless, we would ask him to SIGN BETTER. Looking closely at us, he would sign slowly and emphatically, taking one hand to put the other into the proper shape. Evidence for mental images also comes from Chantek's spontaneous execution of signs with his feet, which we did not teach him to do. Chantek even began to use objects in relation to each other to form signs. For example, he used the blades of scissors instead of his hands to make the sign for biting.

Chantek was extremely curious and inventive. When he wanted to know the name of something, he offered his hands to be molded into the shape of the proper sign. But language is a creative process, so we were pleased to see that Chantek began to invent his own signs. He invented: NO-TEETH (to show us that he would not use his teeth during rough play); EYE-DRINK (for contact lens solution used by his caregivers); DAVE-MISSING-FINGER (a name for a favorite university employee who had a hand injury); VIEWMASTER (a toy that displays small pictures); and BALLOON. Like our ancestors, Chantek had become a creator of language, the criterion that 200 years earlier Lord Monboddo had said would define orangutans as persons.

This photo shows Chantek using his mouth as well as his hands to string a bead necklace.

We had a close relationship with Chantek. He became extremely attached to his caregivers and began to show empathy and jealousy toward us. He would quickly "protect" us from an "attacking" toy animal or other pretense. We have lived day to day with Chantek and have shared common experiences, as if he were a child. We have healed his hurts, comforted his fears of stray cats, played keep-away games, cracked nuts in the woods with stones, watched him sign to himself, felt fooled by his deceptions and frustrated when he became bored with his tasks. We have dreamed about him, had conversations in our imagination with him, and loved him. Through these rare events shared with another species, I have no doubt I was experiencing Chantek as a person. *(Adapted from H. L. W. Miles. (1993). Language and the orangutan: The old "person" of the forest. In P. Cavalieri & P. Singer (Eds.), The great ape project (pp. 45–50). New York: St. Martin's Press.)*

2003 update: My relationship and research with Chantek continues, through the Chantek Foundation in Atlanta, Georgia. Chantek now uses several hundred signs and has invented new signs for CAR WATER (bottled water that I bring in my car), KATSUP, and ANNOYED. He makes stone tools, arts and crafts, necklaces, and other jewelry, and small percussion instruments used in my rock band Animal Nation. He even co-composes songs with the band. Plans are in the making for Chantek and other enculturated apes to live in culture-based preserves where they have more range of choices and learning opportunities than in zoos or research centers. An exciting new project under the auspices of ApeNet will give Chantek an opportunity to communicate with other apes via the Internet. It is of special note that based on great ape language skills, efforts will be underway in the next decade to obtain greater legal rights for these primates, as well as greater recognition of them as another type of "person." For more information, see *www.chantek.org*

All of this said, the fact remains that human culture is ultimately dependent on an elaborate system of communication far more complex than that of any other species. The reason for this is the sheer amount of what must be learned by each individual from other individuals in order to control the knowledge and rules for behavior necessary for full participation in his or her society. Of course, a significant amount of learning can and does take place in the absence of language by way of observation and imitation, guided by a limited number of meaningful signs or symbols. However, all known human cultures are so rich in content that they require communication systems that not only can give precise labels to various classes of phenomena but also permit people to think and talk about their own and others' experiences and expectations—past, present, and future. The central and most highly developed human system of communication is language. Knowledge of the workings of language, then, is essential to a full understanding of what culture is about and how it operates.

THE NATURE OF LANGUAGE

Any human language—Chinese, English, Swahili, or whatever—is obviously a means of transmitting information and sharing with others both collective and individual experiences. Because we tend to take language for granted, it is perhaps not so obvious that language is also a system that enables us to translate our concerns, beliefs, and perceptions into symbols that can be understood and interpreted by others. In spoken language, this is done by taking a few sounds—no language uses more than about fifty—and developing rules for putting them together in meaningful ways. Sign languages, such as American Sign Language, do the same thing but with gestures rather than sounds. The many languages presently in existence all over the world—some 6,000 or so different ones—may well astound and mystify us by their great variety and complexity, but this should not blind us to the fact that all languages, as far back as we can trace them, are organized in the same basic way.

The roots of **linguistics**—the systematic study of all aspects of language—go back a long way, to the works of ancient language specialists in India more than 2,000 years ago. The European age of exploration from the 16th through the 18th centuries set the stage for a great leap forward in the scientific study of language. Explorers, invaders, and missionaries accumulated information about a huge diversity of languages from all around the world. An estimated 10,000 languages still existed when they began their inquiries. Nineteenth-century linguists, including anthropologists, made a significant contribution in discovering systems, regularity, and relationships in the

data and tentatively formulating laws and regular principles concerning language. In the 20th century, while still collecting data, they made considerable progress in unraveling the reasoning process behind language construction, testing and working from new and improved theories. Insofar as theories and facts of language are verifiable by independent researchers looking at the same materials, there may now be said to be a science of linguistics. This science has three main branches: descriptive linguistics, historical linguistics, and ethnolinguistics.

MEDIATREK

To *hear* as well as read about languages around the world, go to MediaTrek 4.1 on the companion Web site or CD-ROM.

Descriptive Linguistics

How can an anthropologist, a trader, a missionary, a diplomat, or anyone else approach and make sense of a language that has not yet been described and analyzed, or for which there are no readily available written materials? There are hundreds of such undocumented languages in the world; fortunately, effective methods have been developed to help with the task. **Descriptive linguistics** involves unraveling a language by recording, describing, and analyzing all of its features. It is a painstaking process, but it is ultimately rewarding in that it provides deeper understanding of a language—its structure, its unique linguistic repertoire (figures of speech, word plays, and so on), and its relationship to other languages.

The process of unlocking the underlying rules of a spoken language requires a trained ear and a thorough understanding of the way multiple different speech sounds are produced. Without such know-how, it is extremely difficult to write out or make intelligent use of any data concerning a particular language. To satisfy this preliminary requirement, most people need special training in phonetics.

Phonology

Rooted in the Greek word *phone,* **phonetics** is defined as the systematic identification and description of the distinctive sounds of a language. Phonetics is basic to

linguistics The modern scientific study of all aspects of language.
descriptive linguistics The branch of linguistics that involves unraveling a language by recording, describing, and analyzing all of its features.
phonetics The systematic identification and description of distinctive speech sounds in a language.

Biocultural Connection

The Biology of Human Speech

While other primates have shown some capacity for language (a socially agreed-upon code of communication), actual speech is unique to humans. It comes at a price, for the anatomical organization of the human throat and mouth that make speech possible also increase the risk of choking.

Of particular importance are the positions of the human larynx or voice box and the epiglottis. The larynx is the anatomical structure that vibrates and resonates to produce sounds as air is passed from the nose through the trachea or wind pipe to the lungs. The epiglottis is the structure that separates the esophagus or food pipe from the wind pipe as food passes from the mouth to the stomach. (See Figure 4.1 for comparative diagrams of the anatomy of this region in chimps and humans.)

The overlapping routes of passage for food and air can be seen as a legacy of our evolutionary history. Fish, the earliest vertebrates (animals with back-

bones), obtained both food and oxygen from water entering through their mouths. As land animals evolved, separate means for obtaining food and air developed out of the preexisting combined system. As a result, the pathways for air and food overlap. In most mammals, including human infants and apes of all ages, choking on food is not a problem because the larynx is relatively high in the throat so that the epiglottis seals the windpipe from food with every swallow. The position of the larynx and trachea make it easy for babies to coordinate breathing with eating.

However, as humans mature and develop the neurological and muscular coordination for speech, the larynx and epiglottis shift to a downward position. The human tongue bends at the back of the throat and is attached to the pharynx, the region of the throat where the food and airways share a common path. Sound occurs as air exhaled from the lungs passes over the vocal cords and causes them to vibrate.

Through continuous interactive movements of the tongue, pharynx, lips, and teeth, as well as nasal passages, the sounds are alternately modified to produce speech—the uniquely patterned sounds of a particular language. Based on long-standing socially learned patterns of speech, different languages stress certain distinctive types of sounds as significant and ignore others. For instance, languages belonging to the Iroquoian family, such as Mohawk, Seneca, and Cherokee, are among the few in the world that have no bilabial stops (*b* and *p* sounds). They also lack the labio-dental spirants (*f* and *v* sounds), leaving the bilabial nasal *m* sound as the only consonant requiring lip articulation.

It takes many years of practice for people to master the muscular movements needed to produce the precise sounds **of any particular language.** But no human could produce the finely controlled **speech** sounds without a lowered position of the larynx and epiglottis. ■ ■ ■

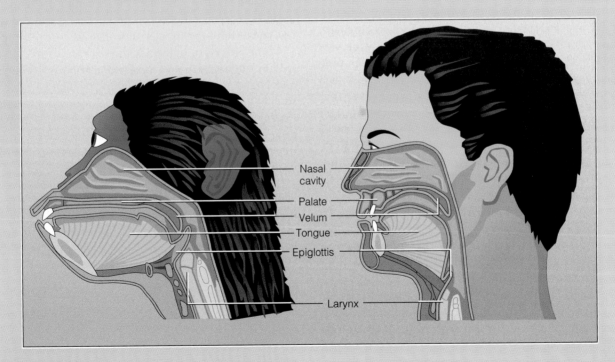

Nasal cavity
Palate
Velum
Tongue
Epiglottis
Larynx

FIGURE 4.1

For linguists studying another language in the field, tape recorders and laptops have become indispensable tools.

© Richard Lord/The Image Works

phonology, the study of language sounds. In order to analyze and describe any language, one needs first an inventory of all its distinctive sounds. While some of the sounds used in other languages may seem very much like those of the researcher's own speech pattern, others may be unfamiliar. For example, the "th" sound common in English does not exist in the Dutch language and is difficult for most Dutch speakers to pronounce, just as the "r" sound used in numerous languages is tough for Japanese speakers. And the unique "click" sound used in Bushman languages in southern Africa is difficult for speakers of just about every other language. Sometimes words that feature sounds notoriously difficult for outsiders to pronounce are used as passwords to identify foreigners. For instance, because Germans find it hard to pronounce the sound "sch" the way their Dutch neighbors do, resistance fighters in the Netherlands during World War II chose the place name *Scheveningen* as a test word to identify Dutch-speaking German spies trying to infiltrate their groups. Such a password is known as a shibboleth.

While collecting speech sounds or utterances, the linguist works to isolate the **phonemes**—the smallest units of sound that make a difference in meaning. This isolation and analysis may be done by a process called the minimal-pair test. The researcher tries to find two short words that appear to be exactly alike except for one sound, such as *bit* and *pit* in English. If the substitution of *b* for *p* in this minimal pair makes a difference in meaning, as it does in English, then those two sounds have been identified as distinct phonemes of the language and will require two different symbols to record. If, however, the linguist finds two different pronunciations (as when "butter" is pronounced "budder") and

then finds that there is no difference in their meaning for a native speaker, the sounds represented will be considered variants of the same phoneme. In such cases, for economy of representation only one of the two symbols will be used to record that sound wherever it is found. Obviously, a systematic way of recording phonemes in writing is essential. For greater accuracy and to avoid confusion with the various sounds of one's own language, the symbols of a phonetic alphabet (such as the one originally developed by anthropologist Edward Sapir, shown in Table 4.1) can be used to clearly distinguish between the sounds of most languages in a way comprehensible to anyone familiar with the system.

Morphology

While making and studying an inventory of distinctive sounds, linguists also look into **morphology,** the study of the patterns or rules of word formation in a language (including such things as rules concerning verb tense, pluralization, and compound words). They do this by marking out specific sounds and sound combinations that seem to have meaning. These are called **morphemes**—the

---

phonology The study of language sounds.
phonemes The smallest units of sound that make a difference in meaning in a language.
morphology The study of the patterns or rules of word formation in a language (including such things as rules concerning verb tense, pluralization, and compound words).
morphemes The smallest units of sound that carry a meaning in language. They are distinct from phonemes, which can alter meaning, but have no meaning by themselves.

TABLE 4.1   PHONETIC VOWEL SYMBOLS (SAPIR SYSTEM)*

i	*ü*	*ɨ*	*u̇*	*ï*	*u*
i	ü	ɨ	u̇	ï	u
(Fr. *fini*)	(Fr. *lune*)		(Swed. *hus*)		(Ger. *gut*)
ɩ	ü̇	ι	v̇	ï	ʋ
(Eng. *bit*)	(Ger. *Mütze*)				(Eng. *put*)
e	ö	—	ȯ	α	o
(Fr. *été*)	(Fr. *peu*)			(Eng. *but*)	(Ger. *so*)
ε	ɜ	—	ɜ	a	ɔ
(Eng. *men*)	(Ger. *Götter*)			(Ger. *Mann*)	(Ger. *Volk*)
—	ω̈	—	ω̇	—	ω
	(Fr. *peur*)				(Eng. *law*)
ä	—	ȧ	—	—	—
(Eng. *man*)		(Fr. *patte*)			

* The symbol ∂ is used for an "indeterminate" vowel.

SOURCE: G. L. Trager. (1972). *Language and languages* (p. 304). San Francisco: Chandler.

smallest units of sound that carry a meaning in a language. Morphemes are distinct from phonemes, which can alter meaning but have no meaning by themselves. Such units may consist of words or parts of words. For example, a linguist studying English in a North American farming community would soon learn that *cow* is a morpheme—a meaningful combination of the phonemes *c, o,* and *w.* Pointing to two of these animals, the linguist would elicit the word *cows* from local speakers. This would reveal yet another morpheme—the *s*—which can be added to the original morpheme to indicate "plural." In time, discovering that the *s* does not occur in the language on its own or unattached, the linguist identifies it as a "bound morpheme." *Cow,* however, is noted as a "free morpheme" because it can occur unattached. A linguist faces numerous challenges during this stage of the research, including the fact that an informant may pretend not to be able to say certain words considered in their culture to be impolite, vulgar, sacrilegious, or otherwise inappropriate for mention to outsiders. It may even be unacceptable to point, in which case the fieldworker may have to devise roundabout ways of finding out the precise words for objects, ideas, or actions.

Grammar and Syntax

The next step in unraveling a language is to see how morphemes are put together to form phrases or sentences. This process is known as identifying the syntactic units of the language, or the way morphemes are put together into larger chains or strings that have meaning. One way to do this is to use a method called **frame substitution.** By proceeding slowly at first and relying on pointing or gestures, the fieldworker can elicit such strings as *my cow, your cow,* or *her cow,* and *I see your cow, she sees my cow.* This begins to establish the rules or principles of phrase and sentence making, the **syntax** of the language. The **grammar** of the language will ultimately consist of all observations about its morphemes and syntax. Further work may include the establishment, by means of substitution frames, of all the **form classes** of the language: that is, the parts of speech or categories of words that function the same way in any sentence. For example, there exists a category we call "nouns," defined as any word that will fit the substitution frame "I see a _____." The linguist simply makes the frame, tries out a number of words in it, and has a native speaker indicate yes or no for whether the words work. In English, the words *house* and *cat* will fit this frame and will be said to belong to the same form class, but the word *think* will not. Another possible substitution frame for nouns might be "The _____ died," in which the word *cat* will

frame substitution A method used to identify the syntactic units of language. For example, a category called "nouns" may be established as anything that will fit the substitution frame "I see a _____."
syntax The patterns or rules for the formation of phrases and sentences in a language.
grammar The entire formal structure of a language, including morphology and syntax.
form classes The parts of speech or categories of words that work the same way in any sentence, such as nouns, verbs, and adjectives.

VISUAL COUNTERPOINT Humans talk, while other primates communicate mostly through gesture and body language, including facial expression. Still, humans have by no means abandoned these other forms of communication, as we see here.

fit, but not the word *house*. Thus, we can identify subclasses of our nouns—in this case what we call "animate" or "inanimate" subclasses. The same procedure may be followed for all the words of the language, using as many different frames as necessary, until we have a lexicon, or dictionary, that accurately describes the possible uses of all the words in the language.

One of the strengths of modern descriptive linguistics is the objectivity of its methods. For example, an English-speaking anthropologist who specializes in this will not approach a language with the idea that it must have nouns, verbs, prepositions, or any other of the form classes identifiable in English. She or he instead sees what turns up in the language and makes an attempt to describe it in terms of its own inner workings. This allows for unanticipated discoveries. For instance, unlike many other languages, English does not distinguish between feminine and masculine nouns. So it is that English speakers use the article *the* in front of any noun, while the French require two types of articles: *la* for feminine nouns and *le* for masculine—as in *la lune* (the moon) and *le soleil* (the sun). German speakers go one step further, utilizing three types of articles: *der* in front of masculine nouns, *die* for feminine, and *das* for neutral. It is also interesting to note that in contrast to their French neighbors, Germans consider the moon as masculine, so they say *der Mon,* and the sun as feminine, which makes it *die Sonne.*

Beyond Words: The Gesture-Call System

Efficient though languages are at naming and talking about ideas, actions, and things, all are insufficient to some degree in communicating certain kinds of information that people need to know in order to fully understand what is being said. For this reason, human language is always embedded within a gesture-call system of a type that we share with monkeys and apes. The various sounds and gestures of this system serve to "key" speech, providing listeners with the appropriate frame for interpreting what a speaker is saying. Messages about human emotions and intentions are effectively communicated by this gesture-call system: Is the speaker happy, sad, mad, enthusiastic, tired, or in some other emotional state? Is he or she requesting information, denying something, reporting factually, or lying? Very little of this information is conveyed by spoken language alone. In English, for example, at least 90 percent of emotional information is transmitted not by the words spoken but by "body language" and tone of voice.

As something that we have inherited from our primate ancestors, our gesture-call system includes sounds and body language that are to a degree genetically determined. This accounts for the universality of various cries and facial expressions, as well as for the great difficulty people have in bluffing or especially lying through gesture-calls. This is not to say that the system is entirely immune to deliberate control or manipulation, but rather that screams, laughter, tears, blushing, goose bumps, and the like are less subject to control or manipulation than is speech.

Body Language

The **gesture** component of the gesture-call system consists of facial expressions and bodily postures and motions that convey intended as well as subconscious messages. The method for notating and analyzing this

> **gesture** Facial expressions and bodily postures and motions that convey intended as well as subconscious messages.

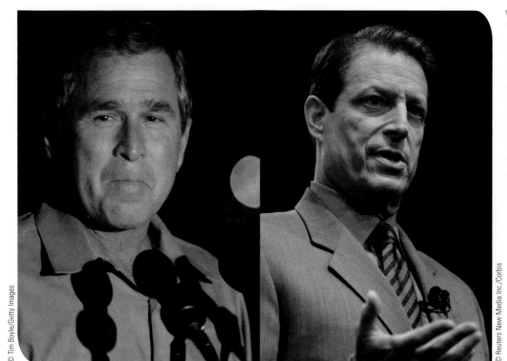

© Tim Boyle/Getty Images

© Reuters New Media Inc./Corbis

VISUAL COUNTERPOINT
The importance of body language is shown by the role it played in the United States 2000 presidential election. George W. Bush's facial expression was taken as a sign of condescension and was a factor in his loss of the New Hampshire primary. Similarly, some voters were put off by Al Gore's seemingly "wooden" body language.

"body language" is known as **kinesics.** Humankind's repertoire of body language is enormous. This is evident if you consider just one aspect of it: the fact that a human being has eighty facial muscles and is thereby capable of making more than 7,000 facial expressions! This given, it should not be surprising to hear that at least 60 percent of our total communication takes place nonverbally. Often, gestural messages complement spoken messages—for instance, nodding the head while affirming something verbally, raising eyebrows when asking a question, or using hands to illustrate or emphasize what is being talked about. However, nonverbal signals are sometimes at odds with verbal ones, and they have the power to override or undercut them. For example, a person may say the words "I love you" a thousand times to someone, but if it's not true, their nonverbal signals will likely communicate that and will probably be perceived as what really matters. Even individuals who do not say much verbally are more often than not communicating when in the presence of others. For example, in North America scratching one's scalp, biting one's lip, or knitting one's brows usually indicate feelings of doubt, just as leaning forward during a conversation typically conveys interest and slouching back suggests disinterest.

Body stance carries a host of meanings. Among other things, the way a person stands often reveals some-

thing about his or her gender. In North America, although there is some regional and class variation, women generally bring their legs together when standing, sometimes bending one knee and tucking it behind the other or crossing their legs so that the outer sides of the feet abut each other. The pelvis is rolled slightly forward, and the upper arms are held close to the body. Men, by contrast, typically stand with legs apart, pelvis in a slightly rolled back position, and arms held out at 10 to 15 degrees from the body.

Such gender markers are conventions inscribed on the body during childhood through imitation and subtle training. By the time individuals become adults, they have acquired an array of gender markers that impact all

© Esbin-Anderson/The Image Works

Learned gestures to which different cultures assign different meanings are known as conventional gestures. An example is this sign, which in North America means "OK." In Brazil, it is an obscene gesture.

---

kinesics A system of notating and analyzing postures, facial expressions, and body motions that convey messages.

VISUAL COUNTERPOINT There is a great deal of similarity around the world in such basic expressions as smiling, laughing, crying, and anger, as one can see from the expressions of these children from Africa, South America, and Asia. Expressions such as these are part of the human inheritance from their primate ancestry.

aspects of their lives in ways that they may not even be aware of. Consider, for example, philosopher Marilyn Frye's description of the role these markers play in social interaction:

> To discover the differences in how you greet a woman and how you greet a man, for instance, just observe yourself, paying attention to the following sorts of things: frequency and duration of eye contact, frequency and type of touch, . . . physical distance maintained between bodies, how and whether you smile . . . , whether your body dips into a shallow curtsey or bow. That I have two repertories for handling introductions to people was vividly confirmed for me when a student introduced me to his friend, Pat, and I really could not tell what sex Pat was. For a moment I was stopped cold, completely incapable of action. I felt myself helplessly caught between two paths—the one I would take if Pat were female and the one I would take if Pat were male. Of course the paralysis does not last. One is rescued by one's ingenuity and good will: one can invent a way to behave as one says "How do you do?" to a human being. But the habitual ways are not for humans: they are one way for women and another for men.[3]

_____

[3]Frye, M. (1983). Sexism. In *The politics of reality* (p. 20). New York: Crossing Press.

Little scientific notice was taken of body language prior to the 1950s, but since then a great deal of research has been devoted to this intriguing subject. Cross-cultural studies in this field have shown that there are many similarities around the world in such basic facial expressions as smiling, laughing, crying, and displaying shock or anger. The smirks, frowns, and gasps that we have inherited from our primate ancestry require little learning and are harder to "fake" than conventional or socially obtained gestures that are shared by members of a group, albeit not always consciously so. Routine greetings are also similar around the world. Europeans, Balinese, Papuans, Samoans, Bushmen, and at least some South American Indians all smile and nod, and if the individuals are especially friendly, they will raise their eyebrows with a rapid movement, keeping them raised for a fraction of a second. By doing so, they signal a readiness for contact. The Japanese, however, suppress the eyebrow flash, regarding it as indecent, which goes to show that there are important differences, as well as similarities, cross-culturally. This can be seen in gestural expressions for yes and no. In North America, one nods the head down then up for yes or shakes it left and right for no. The people of Sri Lanka also nod to answer yes to a factual question, but if asked to do something, a slow sideways movement of the head means yes. In Greece, the nodded head means yes, but no is indicated by jerking the head back so as to lift the face, usually with the eyes closed and the eyebrows raised.

Another aspect of body language has to do with social space: how people position themselves physically in

VISUAL COUNTERPOINT Cultures around the world have noticeably different attitudes concerning proxemics or personal space—how far apart people should position themselves in nonintimate social encounters. How does the gap between the U.S. businessmen pictured here compare with that of the berobed men of Saudi Arabia?

relation to others. **Proxemics,** the cross-cultural study of humankind's perception and use of space, came to the fore through the work of anthropologist Edward Hall, who coined the term. Growing up in the culturally diverse southwestern United States, Hall glimpsed the complexities of intercultural relations early on in life. As a young man in the 1930s, he worked with construction crews of Hopi and Navajo Indians, building roads and dams. In 1942 he earned his doctorate in anthropology under the famous Franz Boas, who stressed the point that "communication constitutes the core of culture." This idea was driven home for Hall during World War II, when he commanded an African American regiment in Europe and the Philippines, and again when he worked with the U.S. State Department to develop the new field of intercultural communication at the Foreign Service Institute (FSI). It was during his years at FSI (1950–1955), while training some 2,000 Foreign Service workers, that Hall's ideas about proxemics began to crystallize. He articulated them and other aspects of nonverbal communication in his 1959 book, *The Silent Language,* now recognized as the founding document for the field of intercultural communication. His work showed that people from different cultures have different frameworks for defining and organizing space—the personal space they establish around their bodies, as well as the macrolevel sensibilities that shape cultural expectations

about how streets, neighborhoods, and cities should be arranged. Among other things, his investigation of personal space revealed that every culture has distinctive norms for closeness. (You can see this for yourself if you are watching a foreign film, visiting a foreign country, or find yourself in a multicultural group. How close to one another do the people you are observing stand when talking in the street or riding in a subway or elevator? Does the pattern match the one you are accustomed to in your own cultural corner?) Hall identified four categories of proxemically relevant spaces or body distances: intimate (0–18 inches), personal-casual (1½–4 feet), social-consultive (4–12 feet), and public distance (12 feet and beyond). Hall warned that different cultural definitions of socially accepted use of space within these categories can lead to serious failures of communication and understanding in cross-cultural settings. His research has been a foundation stone for the present-day training of international businesspeople, diplomats, and others involved in intercultural work.

Paralanguage

The second component of the gesture-call system is **paralanguage**—specific voice effects that accompany speech and contribute to communication. These include vocalizations such as giggling, groaning, or sighing, as well as voice qualities such as pitch and tempo. The importance of paralanguage is suggested by the comment, "It's not so much *what* was said as *how* it was said." Recent studies have shown, for example, that subliminal messages communicated below the threshold of conscious perception by seemingly minor differences in phrasing, tempo, length of answers, and the like are far more important in courtroom proceedings than even the most perceptive trial lawyer may have realized. Among other things, how

proxemics The cross-cultural study of humankind's perception and use of space.
paralanguage Voice effects that accompany language and convey meaning. These include vocalizations such as giggling, groaning, or sighing, as well as voice qualities such as pitch and tempo.

a witness gives testimony alters the reception it gets from jurors and influences the witness' credibility.[4]

Voice qualities operate as the background characteristics of a speaker's voice. These involve pitch range (from low to high pitched); lip control (from closed to open); glottis control (sharp to smooth transitions in pitch); articulation control (forceful and relaxed speech); rhythm control (smooth or jerky setting off of portions of vocal activity); resonance (from resonant to thin); and tempo (an increase or decrease from the norm).

Voice qualities are capable of communicating much about the state of being of the person who is speaking, quite apart from what is being said. An obvious example of this is slurred speech, a lack of articulation that may indicate that the speaker is intoxicated. Or, if someone says rather languidly, coupled with a restricted pitch range, that she or he is delighted with something, it probably indicates that the person is not delighted at all. The same thing said more rapidly, with rising pitch, might indicate that the speaker is genuinely excited about the matter.

While voice qualities operate as background characteristics of speech, **vocalizations** are actual identifiable noises that are turned on and off at perceivable and relatively short intervals. They are sometimes similar to but nonetheless separate from language sounds. One category of vocalizations is **vocal characterizers**—the sounds of laughing or crying, yawning or belching, and the like. One "talks through" vocal characterizers, and they are generally indicative of the speaker's attitude. For example, if a person yawns while speaking to someone, this may indicate boredom on the part of the speaker. Breaking—an on–off tensing and relaxing of the vocal musculature that makes speech tremble—may indicate great emotion on the part of the speaker.

Another category of vocalizations consists of **vocal qualifiers.** These are of briefer duration than vocal characterizers, being limited generally to the space of a single intonation rather than over whole phrases. They modify utterances in terms of intensity (loud versus soft), pitch (high versus low), and extent (drawl versus clipping). These indicate the speaker's attitude to specific phrases such as "get out." The third category consists of **vocal segregates.** Sometimes called "oh oh expressions," these resemble the actual sounds of language, but they do not appear in the kinds of sequences that can be called words. Examples of vocal segregates familiar to English-speaking peoples are such substitutes for language as *shh, uh-huh,* or *uh-uh.* Unlike such par-

alinguistic vocalizations as sobs, giggles, and screams, vocal segregates are socially shared and learned and far more variable from culture to culture.

MEDIATREK
To test your cross-cultural gesture literacy, go to MediaTrek 4.2 on the companion Web site or CD-ROM.

Tonal Languages

There is an enormous diversity in the ways languages are spoken. In addition to hundreds of vowels and consonants, sounds can be divided into tones—rises and falls in pitch that play a key role in distinguishing one word from another. About 70 percent of the world's languages are **tonal languages** in which the various distinctive sound pitches of spoken words are not only an essential part of their pronunciation but also key to their meaning, and at least one-third of the people in the world speak a tonal language. Many languages in Africa, Central America, and East Asia are tonal. For instance, the tone or pitch level of a spoken word is an essential part of its pronunciation in Mandarin Chinese, the most common language in China. Mandarin has four contrasting tones: flat, rising, falling, and falling then rising. These tones are used to distinguish among normally stressed syllables that are otherwise identical. Thus, depending on intonation, *ba* can mean "to uproot," "eight," "to hold," or "a harrow" (farm tool).[5] Cantonese, the primary language

---

[5]Catford, J. C. (1988). *A practical introduction to phonetics* (p. 183). Oxford, England: Clarendon Press.

---

voice qualities In paralanguage, the background characteristics of a speaker's voice, including pitch, articulation, tempo, and resonance.
vocalizations Identifiable paralinguistic noises that are turned on and off at perceivable and relatively short intervals. These include vocal characterizers (giggling, sighing, and so on), vocal qualifiers (volume, tempo, and so on) and vocal segregates ("oh oh," for example).
vocal characterizers In paralanguage, vocalizations such as laughing, crying, yawning, or "breaking," which the speaker "talks through."
vocal qualifiers In paralanguage, vocalizations of brief duration that modify utterances in terms of intensity. These include volume, pitch, tempo.
vocal segregates In paralanguage, vocalizations that resemble the sounds of language but do not appear in sequences that can properly be called words. Sometimes called "oh oh expressions."
tonal language A language in which the sound pitch of a spoken word is an essential part of its pronunciation and meaning.

---

[4]O'Barr, W. M., & Conley, J. M. (1993). When a juror watches a lawyer. In W. A. Haviland & R. J. Gordon (Eds.), *Talking about people* (2nd. ed., pp. 42–45). Mountain View, CA: Mayfield.

in southern China and Hong Kong, uses six contrasting tones, and some Chinese dialects have as many as nine. In nontonal languages such as English, tone can be used to convey an attitude or to change a statement into a question, but tone alone does not change the meaning of individual words as it does in Mandarin, where careless use of tones with the syllable *ma* could cause one to call someone's mother a horse!

Historical Linguistics

In contrast to descriptive linguistics, which focuses on all features of a particular language as it is at any one moment in time, **historical linguistics** deals with the fact that languages change. In addition to deciphering "dead" languages that are no longer spoken, specialists in this field investigate relationships between earlier and later forms of the same language, study older languages for developments in modern ones, and examine interrelationships among older languages. For example, they attempt to sort out the development of Latin (spoken almost 1,500 years ago in southern Europe) into Italian, Spanish, Portuguese, French, and Romanian by identifying natural shifts in the original language, as well as modifications brought on by direct contact during the next few centuries with Germanic-speaking invaders from northern Europe. That said, historical linguists are not limited to the faraway past, for even modern languages are constantly transforming—adding new words, dropping others, or changing meaning. Over the last decade or so, Internet use has widened the meaning of a host of already existing English words—from *hacking* to *surfing* to *spam*.

🖥️ **MEDIATREK**
For a chart of the twenty most spoken languages in the world, plus information on language families and the history of English, go to MediaTrek 4.3 on the companion Web site or CD-ROM.

Especially when focusing on long-term processes of change, historical linguists depend on written records of languages. They have achieved considerable success in

historical linguistics The branch of linguistics that studies the histories of and relationships among languages, both living and dead.
language family A group of languages descended from a single ancestral language.
linguistic divergence The development of different languages from a single ancestral language.
glottochronology In linguistics, a method for identifying the approximate time that languages branched off from a common ancestor. It is based on analyzing core vocabularies.

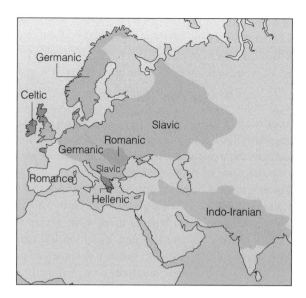

FIGURE 4.2
The Indo-European languages. (For a world map of language families, see MediaTrek 4.3.)

working out the relationships among different languages, and these are reflected in schemes of classification. For example, English is one of approximately 140 languages classified in the larger Indo-European **language family** (Figure 4.2). This family is subdivided into some eleven subgroups, which reflects the fact that there has been a long period (6,000 years or so) of **linguistic divergence** from an ancient unified language (reconstructed as Proto-Indo-European) into separate "daughter" languages. English is one of several languages in the Germanic subgroup (Figure 4.3), all of which are more closely related to one another than they are to the languages of any other subgroup of the Indo-European family. So it is that, despite the differences between them, the languages of one subgroup share certain features when compared to those of another. As an illustration, the word for "father" in the Germanic languages always starts with an *f* or closely related *v* sound (Dutch *vader*, German *Vater*, Gothic *Fadar*). Among the Romance languages, by contrast, the comparable word always starts with a *p*: French *père*, Spanish and Italian *padre*—all derived from the Latin *pater*. The original Indo-European word for "father" was *p'te̅r*, so in this case, the Romance languages have retained the earlier pronunciation, whereas the Germanic languages have diverged. Thus, many words that begin with *p* in the Romance languages, like Latin *piscis* and *pes,* become words like English *fish* and *foot* in the Germanic languages.

In addition to describing the changes that have taken place as languages have diverged from ancient parent languages, historical linguists have also developed methods to estimate when such divergences occurred. One such technique is known as **glottochronology,** a

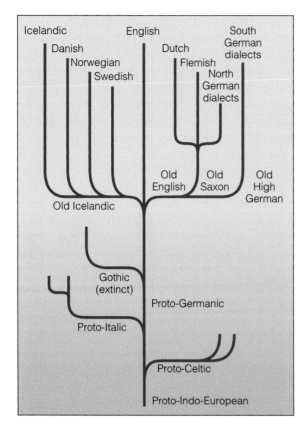

FIGURE 4.3

English is one of a group of languages in the Germanic sub-group of the Indo-European family. This diagram shows its relationship to other languages in the same subgroup. The root was Proto-Indo-European, an ancestral language originally spoken by early farmers and herders who spread north and westward over Europe, bringing with them both their customs and their language.

term derived from the Greek word *glottis*, which means "language." This method compares the **core vocabularies** of languages—pronouns, lower numerals, and names for body parts and natural objects. It is based on the assumption that these basic vocabularies change more slowly than other words and at a more or less constant rate of 14 to 19 percent per 1,000 years. (Linguists determined this rate by calculating changes documented in thirteen historic written languages.) By applying a logarithmic formula to two related core vocabularies, one can determine how many years the languages have been separated. Although not as precise as this might suggest, glottochronology, in conjunction with other chronological methods such as those based on archaeological and genetic data, can help determine the time of linguistic divergence.

Studying modern languages in their particular cultural contexts can help us understand the processes of change that may have led to linguistic divergence. Clearly, one force for change is selective borrowing by

one language from another. This is evident in the many French words present in the English language—and in the growing number of English words cropping up in languages all around the world due to modern-day globalization. Technological breakthroughs resulting in new equipment and products also prompt linguistic shifts. For instance, the electronic revolution that brought us radio, television, and computers has created entirely new vocabularies. Increasing professional specialization is another driving force. We see one of many examples in the field of Western medicine where today's students must learn the specialized vocabulary and idioms of the profession—over 6,000 new words in the first year of medical school. There is also a tendency for any group within a larger society to create its own unique vocabulary, whether it is a street gang, sorority, religious group, prison inmates, or platoon of soldiers. By changing the meaning of existing words or inventing new ones, members of the "in-group" can communicate with fellow members while effectively excluding outsiders who may be within hearing range. Finally, there seems to be a human tendency to admire the person who comes up with a new and clever idiom, a useful word, or a particularly stylish pronunciation, as long as these do not seriously interfere with communication. All of this means that no language stands still.

Phonological differences among groups may be regarded in the same light as vocabulary differences. In a class-structured society, for example, members of the upper class may try to keep their pronunciation distinct from that of lower classes, or vice versa, as a means of demonstrating class solidarity. An example of this is Cockney, an English working-class dialect from London's East End, characterized by loss of initial *h,* use of an intrusive *r,* and extreme diphthongization in which these speakers glide from the position of one vowel sound to that for another within the same syllable, as "oi" in *boy,* and "ou" in *down.*

Perhaps the most powerful force for linguistic change is the domination of one society over another, as demonstrated during 500 years of European colonialism. Such dominations persist in many parts of the world to the present time, such as Taiwan's aboriginal peoples being governed by Mandarin-speaking Chinese, Tarascan Indians by Spanish-speaking Mexicans, West New Guinea's Papuas by Malay-speaking Indonesians, Lapland's Saami by Norwegians, or Bushmen by English-speaking Namibians. In many cases, such political power has resulted in linguistic erosion or even complete

core vocabularies The most basic and long-lasting words in any language—pronouns, lower numerals, and names for body parts and natural objects.

disappearance, sometimes only leaving a faint trace in old names for geographic features such as hills and rivers. In fact, over the last 500 years 4,000 of the world's 10,000 or so languages have become extinct as a direct result of warfare, epidemics, and forced assimilation brought on by colonial powers and other aggressive outsiders. Most of the remaining 6,000 languages are spoken by very few people, and many of them are losing speakers rapidly due to globalization. In fact, half have fewer than 10,000 speakers each, and a quarter have fewer than 1,000. In North America, for instance, only 150 of the original 300 indigenous languages still exist, and many of these surviving tongues are seriously threatened.

Some anthropologists predict that the number of languages still spoken in the world today will be cut in half by the year 2100, in large part due to printed and electronic media. The printing press, radio, satellite television, Internet, and instant messaging on cellular phones are driving the need for sharing languages that many understand, and increasingly that is English. In the past 500 years, this language originally spoken by about 2.5 million people living only in part of the British Isles in northwestern Europe has spread around the world. Today more than 375 million people claim English as their native tongue. Another 375 million people speak it as a second language and 700 million as a foreign language. While a common language allows people to communicate easily, linguists contend that a global tongue should not come at the cost of language diversity. With the disappearance of each language, they warn, a measure of humankind's richly varied cultural heritage, including countless insights on life, is lost.

Culture contact does not always lead to language extinction. For instance, when speakers from different language groups are involved in regular trade relations, they may create **pidgin** languages in which the syntax and vocabulary of two distinct languages are simplified and combined. In some cases, pidgin replaces the original language of the native community altogether, developing into what is known as **creole.**

Sometimes, in reaction to a real or perceived threat of cultural dominance by powerful foreign societies, ethnic groups and even entire countries may seek to maintain or reclaim their unique identity by purging

pidgin A language in which the syntax and vocabulary of two other languages are simplified and combined.
creole A pidgin language that has become the mother tongue of society.
linguistic nationalism The attempt by ethnic minorities and even countries to proclaim independence by purging their language of foreign terms.

their vocabularies of "foreign" terms. Emerging as a significant force for linguistic change, such **linguistic nationalism** is particularly characteristic of the former colonial countries of Africa and Asia today. It is by no means limited to those countries, however, as one can see by periodic French attempts to purge their language of such Americanisms as *le hamburger.* A recent example of this is France's decision to substitute the word *email* with the newly minted government-approved term *couriel.* Also in the category of linguistic nationalism are revivals of languages long out of common use by ethnic minorities and sometimes even whole countries. Examples include the Ute Indian tribe's current effort to restore their language (see Anthropology Applied) and Greece's successful revival of Greek after many centuries of Turkish domination. Perhaps the most remarkable example is the revival of ancient Hebrew as the basis for the national language of the newly formed state of Israel in 1948, almost 2,000 years after Jews were forced into an exile that eventually scattered their population around the world and resulted in the disappearance of their language from everyday use.

For many ethnic minorities, efforts to counter the threat of linguistic extinction or to resurrect already extinct languages form part of their struggle to maintain their sense of cultural identity and dignity. Furthermore, language preservation may protect their communities against outside intrusions, allowing people to pursue traditional livelihoods and interests they choose for themselves. By the same token, a prime means by which powerful countries try to assert their dominance over minorities living within their borders is to actively suppress their languages. A dramatic illustration of this is a series of forced assimilation policies concerning Native Americans, carried out by the U.S. and Canadian governments until a few decades ago. These policies included taking Indian children away from their parents and putting them in boarding schools where use of English was mandatory. Often required to stay in these schools for many years, Indian youngsters were punished for speaking their traditional languages. When they finally returned to their communities, many could often no longer communicate with their own families. While these institutions have been abolished, the historical policies that shaped them did lasting damage to American Indian groups struggling to maintain their cultural heritage. Especially since the 1980s, many of these besieged indigenous communities are now actively involved in language preservation efforts.

In many societies throughout the world, it is not unusual for individuals to be fluent in two, three, or more different languages. They succeed in this in large part because they experience training in multiple

Language Renewal among the Northern Ute*

On April 10, 1984, the Northern Ute tribe became the first community of American Indians in the United States to affirm the right of its members to regain and maintain fluency in their ancestral language, as well as their right to use it as a means of communication throughout their lives. Like many other Native Americans, they had experienced a decline in fluency in their native tongue, as they were forced to interact more and more intensively with outsiders who spoke only English. Once the on-reservation boarding school was closed in 1953, Ute children had to attend schools where teachers and most other students were ignorant of the Ute language. Outside the classroom as well, children and adults alike were increasingly bombarded by English as they sought employment off reservation, traded in non-Indian communities, or were exposed to television and other popular media. By the late 1960s, although Ute language fluency was still highly valued, many members of the community could no longer speak it.

Alarmed by this situation, a group of Ute parents and educators that supervises federally funded tutorial services to Indian students decided that action needed to be taken, lest their native language be lost altogether. With the help of other community leaders, they organized meetings to discuss how to remedy the situation. Anthropologist William Leap, who had worked on language education with other tribes, was invited to participate in the discussions, and subsequently the Utes hired him to assist with

their linguistic renewal efforts. One result of his work was the official statement of policy by the tribe's governing body, noted above.

The first thing Leap did when he began working with the Utes in 1978 was to conduct a first-ever, reservation-wide language survey. Among other things, the survey revealed that many individuals had retained a "passive fluency" in the language and could understand it, even though they couldn't speak it.[a] Furthermore (and quite contrary to expectations), it showed that children who were still able to speak Ute had fewer problems with English in school than did nonspeakers.

Over the next few years, Leap helped set up a Ute language renewal program within the tribe's Division of Education, wrote several grants to provide funding, led staff training workshops in linguistic transcription and grammatical analysis, provided technical assistance in designing a practical writing system for the language, and supervised data-gathering sessions with already fluent speakers of the language. In 1980, the local public school established an in-school program to provide instruction in English and developmental Ute for Indian and other interested children. Agreeing to be the staff linguist, Leap helped train the language teachers (all of whom were Ute and none of whom had degrees in education). He also carried out research that resulted in numerous technical reports, publications, and in-service workshops; helped prepare a practical Ute language handbook for home use so that parents

and grandparents might enrich the children's language learning experience; and prepared the preliminary text for the tribe's statement of policy on language. By 1984, this policy was official, and several language development projects were in place on the reservation, all monitored and coordinated by a tribally sanctioned language and culture committee. Although writing in Ute was not a goal, practical needs resulted in development of writing systems, and a number of people in fact became literate in the language. Such success, Leap notes, was possible because Ute people were involved in all stages of the effort. The projects began in response to the tribal community's own expressed needs, and all along the way members of the community participated in all discussions and decisions.

Today, Ute language and culture instruction is part of the curriculum in a tribally operated high school, and community programs have been established to build language awareness and literacy. Leap's involvement with this effort continues. He is now working with a Ute language staff to develop a dictionary and complete a grammar of sentence and paragraph structures.[b] ■ ■ ■

[a]See Leap, W. L. (1987). Tribally controlled culture change: The Northern Ute language renewal project. In R. M. Wulff & S. J. Fiske (Eds.), *Anthropological praxis: Translating knowledge into action.* Boulder, CO: Westview Press.

[b]Update based on authors' personal communication with Leap (2003).

* Pronounced "yute."

languages as children—not as high school or college students, which is the educational norm in the United States. In some regions where groups speaking different languages coexist and interact, people often understand one another but may choose not to speak the other's language. Such is the case in the borderlands of northern Bolivia and southern Peru where Quechua-speaking and Aymara-speaking Indians are neighbors. When an Aymara farmer speaks to a Quechua herder in Aymara, the Quechua will reply in Quechua, and vice versa, each knowing that the other understands both languages

even if speaking just one. The ability to comprehend two languages but express oneself in only one is known as "receptive" or "passive" bilingualism.

In the United States, perhaps reflecting the country's enormous size and power, many citizens are not interested in learning a second or foreign language. This is especially significant given the country's multicultural diversity. In fact, the United States is one of the world's most ethnically diverse countries, inhabited primarily by descendants of European immigrants and African slaves, in addition to many other groups, including American

FIGURE 4.4

Linguistic nationalism in the United States: states with "English only" laws.

Indians whose ancestors traditionally owned all the land. A never-ending stream of newcomers from throughout the globe contribute daily to this complex ethnic mosaic. Together, all of these contrasting cultural groups have forged a common national identity as "Americans," a general idea broad enough to provide a sense of belonging to many millions in spite of their differences. A telling illustration of uneasiness about linguistic diversity in the United States can be seen in efforts to make "English only" a national policy (Figure 4.4). Proponents of this policy argue that multilingualism is divisive and often cite the example of French-speaking inhabitants in the Canadian province of Quebec who threatened to split from Canada's English-speaking provinces to form a separate country. What they do not cite are examples such as Bosnia-Herzegovina or Northern Ireland, both instances where a single common language has not prevented violent fighting between factions. Nor do they mention multilingual countries like Belgium and Finland, where three languages are spoken without people being

at one another's throats. The fact is, where linguistic diversity is divisive, it is often *because* official policies favor monolingualism.

Ethnolinguistics

As the discussion above suggests, language is not simply a matter of combining sounds according to certain rules to come up with meaningful utterances. It is important to remember that languages are spoken by people who are members of distinct societies. In addition to the fact that each society has its own unique culture, individuals within a society tend to vary in the ways they use language based on social variables such as gender, class, and ethnicity. We choose words and sentences to communicate meaning, and what is meaningful in one community or culture may not be in another. The fact is that our use of language reflects, and is reflected by, the rest of our culture. The whole question of the relationships between language and other aspects of culture is the intellectual domain of **ethnolinguistics.** One of the three branches of linguistic anthropology, this specialization concerns every aspect of the language that relates to its particular cultural context and social use.

ethnolinguistics A branch of linguistics that studies the relationship between language and culture.

Language and Thought

An important ethnolinguistic concern that came to the fore in the 1930s and 1940s was the question of whether language might influence or even determine how its speakers think and act, thereby shaping culture itself. This idea that language shapes thought and action is expressed in the principle of **linguistic relativity,** sometimes called the Sapir-Whorf hypothesis after its originators Edward Sapir and his student Benjamin Lee Whorf. According to these two anthropologists, each language provides particular grooves of linguistic expression that predispose speakers of that language to see the world in a certain way. In Whorf's words, "The structure of the language one habitually uses influences the manner in which one understands his environment. The picture of the universe shifts from tongue to tongue."[6]

Many of Whorf's insights on this came while translating English into Hopi, a North American Indian language still spoken in Arizona. Doing this work, he discovered that Hopi differs from English not only in vocabulary, but also in terms of its grammatical categories such as nouns and verbs. For instance, Hopi use numbers for counting and measuring things that have physical existence, but they do not apply numbers to abstractions like time. They would have no problem translating an English sentence such as, "I see fifteen sheep grazing on three acres of grassland," but an equally simple sentence such as, "Three weeks ago, I enjoyed my fifteen minutes of fame," would require a much more complex translation into Hopi. It is also of note that Hopi verbs do not express tenses in the same way that English verbs do. Rather than marking past, present, and future, with *-ed*, *-ing*, or *will*, Hopi requires additional words to indicate if an event is completed, still ongoing, or is expected to take place. So instead of saying, "Three strangers stayed for fifteen days in our village," a Hopi would say something like, "We remember three strangers stay in our village until the sixteenth day." In addition, the Hopi language can express the fact that the event talked about is a regular thing that generally occurs. Considering such linguistic distinctions in connection with observed Hopi behavior, Whorf concluded that the Hopi language structures thinking and behavior with a focus on the present—on getting ready and carrying out what needs to be done right. He summed it up like this: "A characteristic of Hopi behavior is the emphasis on preparation. This includes announcing and getting ready for events well beforehand, elaborate precautions to ensure persistence of desired conditions, and stress on good will as the preparer of good results."[7]

Until recently, there was little followup to Sapir and Whorf's pioneering research in cognitive anthropology. Linguistic anthropologists are now devising new methods to actually test their original hypothesis.[8] To cite one example, speakers of Swedish and Finnish (neighboring peoples but speaking radically different languages) working at similar jobs in similar regions under similar laws and regulations show significantly different rates of on-the-job accidents. The rates are substantially lower among the Swedish speakers. What emerges from comparison of the two languages is that Swedish (one of the Indo-European languages) emphasizes information about movement in three-dimensional space. Finnish (a Ural-Altaic language, like Estonian and Hungarian, unrelated to Indo-European languages) emphasizes more static relations among coherent temporal entities. As a consequence, it seems that Finns organize the workplace in a way that favors the individual person over the temporal organization in the overall production process. This in turn leads to frequent production disruptions, haste, and (ultimately) accidents. Intriguing though such studies may be, they are not sufficient by themselves for a full understanding of the relation between language and thought. Supplementary approaches are necessary and are being developed.

A closely related point of view is that language mirrors or reflects, rather than determines, cultural reality. Aymara Indians living in the Bolivian highlands, for example, depend on the potato (or *luki*) as their major source of food. Their language has over 200 words for potatoes, reflecting the many varieties they traditionally grow and the many different ways that they preserve and prepare this food. In contrast, the language of the Ayoreo Indians in Paraguay's tropical shrub lands contains about twenty distinctive words for different types of honey, indicating the importance of this sweet substance in their daily lives.

If language does mirror cultural reality, it would follow that changes in a culture will sooner or later be reflected in changes in the language. We see this is happening all around the world today, including in the English language. Consider, for example, the cultural practice of marriage. Historically, English-speaking North Americans have defined marriage as a legally binding union between one man and one woman. However, a growing tolerance toward homosexuals over the past two decades or so,

[6]Quoted in Hoebel, E. A. (1958). *Man in the primitive world: An introduction to anthropology* (p. 571). New York: McGraw-Hill.

[7]Carroll, J. B. (Ed.). (1956). *Language, thought and reality: Selected writings of Benjamin Lee Whorf* (p. 148). Cambridge, MA: MIT Press.

[8]Lucy, J. A. (1997). Linguistic relativity. *Annual Review of Anthropology, 26,* 291–312.

linguistic relativity The proposition that language plays a fundamental role in shaping the way members of a society think and behave.

This photo illustrates so-called "collateral damage"—a phrase used to sanitize or mask the tragedy of the innocent victims of war. It shows Iraqi civilians taking shelter after being caught in a fierce engagement between the United States and Iraqi forces on the outskirts of Baghdad, Iraq.

coupled with legislation prohibiting sexual discrimination, resulted in a ruling by Canada's Supreme Court in summer 2003 that it is illegal to exclude same-sex unions from the definition of marriage. Consequently, the meaning of the word *marriage* is now being stretched. It is no longer possible to automatically assume that the term refers to the union of a man and a woman—or that a woman who mentions her "spouse" is speaking of a man. Such changes in the English language reflect the wider process of change in North America's cultural reality.

Linguists have found that although language is generally flexible and adaptable, established terminologies do tend to perpetuate themselves, reflecting and revealing the social structure and worldview of groups and people.

For example, American English has a wide array of words having to do with conflict and warfare. It also features an abundance of militaristic metaphors, such as "conquering" space, "fighting" the "battle" of the budget, carrying out a "war" against drugs, making a "killing" on the stock market, "shooting down" an argument, "torpedoing" a plan, "spearheading" a movement, "decapitating" a foreign government, or "bombing" on an exam, to mention just a few. An observer from an entirely different and perhaps less aggressive culture, such as the Hopi in Arizona or the Jain in India, could gain considerable insight into the importance of open competition and winning in American society simply by tuning into such commonly used phrases. Similarly, anthropologists have noted that the language of the Nuer, a nomadic African people of southern Sudan, is rich in words and expressions having to do with cattle; not only are more than 400 words used to describe cattle, but Nuer boys actually take their names from them. Thus, by studying the language we can determine the significance of cattle in Nuer culture and the whole etiquette of human and cattle relationships.

Kinship Terms

Ethnolinguists are also interested in the kinship terms people use when referring to their relatives, for these words can reveal much about a culture. By looking at names people in a particular society use for their relatives, an anthropologist can glean how families are structured, what relationships are considered especially important, and sometimes what the prevailing attitudes are concerning various relationships. Kinship terminology varies considerably across cultures. For instance, a number of languages use the same word to denote a brother and a cousin, and others have a single word for

So important are cattle to the Nuer of southern Sudan that they have more than 400 words to describe them.

Orion Pictures Corp/Everett Collection

Makers of the 1990 feature film *Dances with Wolves* aimed for cultural authenticity by casting Native American actors and hiring a language coach to teach Lakota to those who did not know how to speak it. However, the lessons did not include the "gendered speech" aspect of Lakota—the fact that females and males follow different rules of syntax. Consequently, when native speakers of the language later saw the finished film, they were amused to hear the actors who portrayed the Lakota warriors speaking like women.

cousin, niece, and nephew. Some cultures find it useful to distinguish an oldest brother from his younger brothers and have different words for these brothers. And unlike English, many languages distinguish between an aunt who is mother's sister and one who is father's sister. In Chapter 10 we will discuss in detail the meanings behind these and other contrasting kinship terminologies.

Language and Gender

Numerous intriguing and thought-provoking topics fall under the category of language and gender. Among these is the sometimes heated discussion about whether North American women generally exhibit less decisive speech styles than men—and if so, why? If true, it may be because they have been enculturated to see themselves as comparatively weak and needing confirmation, or perhaps because they have been enculturated to maintain family ties, in which case such unassertive speech styles better facilitate this. Or is it something else altogether?

Another area of interest is **gendered speech**—distinct male and female syntax exhibited in various languages around the world, including Lakota, as spoken at the Pine Ridge and Rosebud Indian reservations in South Dakota. When a Lakota woman asks someone, "How are you?" she says, "*Tonikthkahe?*" But when her brother poses the same question, he says, "*Toniktukahwo?*" As explained by Michael Two Horses, "Our language is gender-specific in the area of commands, queries, and a couple of other things."[9]

Learning these nuances of language is not difficult for a child growing up surrounded by Lakota speakers, but it can be hard for newcomers. So it was for Kevin Costner and other actors in the 1990 film *Dances with Wolves,* which tells the fictional story of a white soldier's relationship with a Lakota Indian community in the 1800s. Since Costner (who plays the soldier) and several of the Native American actors did not speak Lakota, the producers hired a Lakota woman to coach them, aiming to make the feature film as culturally authentic as possible. Upon release, the film won critical acclaim and drew crowds to cinemas all across the country. When it showed in a theater in Rapid City, South Dakota, Lakota people from the nearby reservations arrived on the scene eager to see this movie about their ancestors. But when they heard Costner and his on-screen warrior friends talk, they began to snicker. As the dramatic scenes unfolded, their laughter grew. What was so hilarious? While it was true that Lakota in the audience were generally pleased to hear their own language in a major Hollywood film, they thought it very funny to hear the white hero, along with some non-Lakota Indian actors dressed as warriors, speak Lakota like women. Because the language coach had had to teach both male and female actors, and because they found the language difficult to learn, she had decided not to bother them with the complexities of gendered speech.

Social Dialects

Ethnolinguists are also interested in **dialects**—varying forms of a language that are similar enough to be mutually intelligible. Technically, all dialects are languages—there is nothing partial or sublinguistic about them—and the point at which two different dialects become distinctly different languages is roughly the point at which speakers of one are almost totally unable to communicate with speakers of the other. Boundaries may be psychological, geographical, social, or economic, and they are not always very clear. In the case of regional dialects, there is frequently a transitional territory, or perhaps a buffer zone, where features of both are found and understood, as between central and southern China. The fact is that if you learn the Chinese of Beijing, you cannot communicate with someone who comes from Canton or Hong Kong, although both languages—or dialects—are usually lumped together as Chinese.

A classic example of the kind of dialect that may set one group apart from others within a single society

---

[9]Personal communication, April 2003.

gendered speech Distinct male and female syntax exhibited in various languages around the world.
dialects Varying forms of a language that reflect particular regions, occupations, or social classes and that are similar enough to be mutually intelligible.

is one spoken by many inner-city African Americans. Technically known as African American Vernacular English (AAVE), it has often been referred to as "black English" and (more recently) as "Ebonics." Unfortunately, there is a widespread perception among upper- and middle-class whites and blacks alike that this dialect is somehow substandard or defective, which it is not. A basic principle of linguistics is that the selection of a prestige dialect—in this case, what we may call "Standard English" as opposed to Ebonics—is determined by social historical forces such as wealth and power and is not dependent on virtues or shortcomings of the dialects themselves. In fact, African American Vernacular English is a highly structured mode of speech, capable of expressing anything its speakers care to express, often in extremely creative ways (as in rapping). Many of its distinctive features stem from retention of sound patterns, grammatical devices, and even words of the West African languages spoken by the ancestors of present-day African Americans.[10] Compared to the richness of black English, the Standard English dialect lacks certain sounds; contains some unnecessary sounds; doubles and drawls some of its vowel sounds in sequences that are unusual and difficult to imitate; lacks a method of forming an important tense (the habitual); requires more ways than necessary of indicating tense, plurality, and gender; and does not mark negatives in such a way as to make a strong negative statement.

Because the AAVE dialect differs so much from Standard English and has been discredited by mainstream society, those who speak it frequently find themselves at a disadvantage outside of their own communities. Schoolteachers, for example, often view African American children as deficient in verbal skills and have even misdiagnosed some of them as "learning impaired." The great challenge for the schools is to find ways of teaching these children how to use Standard English in those situations where it is to their advantage to do so, without detracting from their ability to use the dialect of their own community. This has been achieved with considerable success in several other countries that have similar challenges. In Scotland, for example, Scots English is now recognized in the schools as a valid and valued way of speaking and is utilized in the teaching of Standard English. As a consequence, individuals become

Martin Luther King, Jr. Part of his effectiveness as a civil rights leader was his skill at code switching between Standard English and African American Vernacular English.

skilled at switching back and forth between the two dialects, depending on the situation in which one is speaking. Without being conscious of it, we all do the same sort of thing when we switch from formality to informality in our speech, depending upon where we are and to whom we are talking. The process of changing from one level of language to another as the situation demands, whether from one language to another or from one dialect of a language to another, is known as **code switching,** and it has been the subject of a number of ethnolinguistic studies.

THE ORIGINS OF LANGUAGE

Cultures all around the world have sacred stories or myths addressing the age-old question of the origin of human languages. Anthropologists collecting these stories have often found that cultural groups tend to locate the place of origin in their own ancestral homelands and believe that the first humans also spoke their language. For example, the Incas of Peru tell the story of Pachamacac, the divine creator, who came to the valley of Tiwanaku in the Andean highlands in ancient times. As the story goes, Pachamacac drew people up from the earth, making out of clay a person of each nation, painting each with particular clothing, and giving to each a language to be spoken and songs to be sung. On the other side of the globe, ancient Israelites believed that it

[10]Monaghan, L., Hinton, L., & Kephart, R. (1997). Can't teach a dog to be a cat? The dialogue on ebonics. *Anthropology Newsletter, 38* (3), 1, 8, 9.

code switching The process of changing from one language or dialect to another.

was Yahweh, the divine creator and one true God, who had given them Hebrew, the original tongue spoken in Paradise. Later, when humans began building the massive Tower of Babel to signify their own power and to link earth and heaven, Yahweh intervened. He created a confusion of tongues so that people could no longer understand one another, and he scattered them all across the face of the earth, leaving the tower unfinished.

The question of the origin of language has also been a popular subject among scientists, who have put forth some reasonable and some not so reasonable ideas on the subject: Exclamations became words, sounds in nature were imitated, or people simply got together and assigned sounds to objects and actions. The main trouble with early efforts to explain the origin of language is that so little data were available. Today, there is more scientific evidence to work with—better knowledge of primate brains, new studies of primate communication, more information on the development of linguistic competence in children, more human fossils that can be used to tentatively reconstruct what ancient brains and vocal tracts were like, and a better understanding of the lifeways of early human ancestors. We still cannot conclusively prove how, when, and where human language first developed, but we can now theorize reasonably on the basis of more and better information.

Anthropologists have gained considerable insight on human language by observing the communication systems of fellow primates (especially apes)—comparing their physiology with that of humans past and present and testing their ability to learn and use forms of human language such as American Sign Language. Attempts to teach other primates to actually speak like humans have not been successful. In one famous experiment in communication that went on for 7 years, for example, the chimpanzee Viki learned to voice only a very few words, such as *up*, *mama*, and *papa*. This inability to speak is not the result of any obvious sensory or perceptual deficit, and apes can in fact produce many of the sounds used in speech. Evidently, their failure to speak has to do with either a lack of motor control mechanisms to articulate speech or to the virtually complete preoccupation of the throat and mouth for expressing emotional states, such as anger, fear, or joy.

Better results have been achieved through nonvocal methods. Chimpanzees and gorillas free in nature make a variety of vocalizations, but these are often emotional rather than propositional. In this sense, these sounds are equivalent to human paralanguage. Much of ape communication takes place through use of specific gestures and postures. Indeed, some of these, such as grimacing, kissing, and embracing, are in virtually universal use today among apes as well as humans. Recognizing the importance of gestural communication to apes, psychologists Allen and Beatrice Gardner began teaching American Sign Language (ASL), used by the deaf in North America, to their young chimpanzee Washoe, the first of several who have since learned to sign. (See this chapter's Original Study about Chantek, an orangutan taught to sign.) With vocabularies of over 400 signs, chimps have shown themselves to be able to transfer each sign from its original referent to other appropriate

The unfinished Tower of Babel, described in the first book of the Bible, symbolizes an ancient West Asian myth about the origins of language diversity.

© Archivo Iconografico, S.A./Corbis

Several species of apes have been taught to use American Sign Language. Some chimpanzees have acquired signing vocabularies surpassing 400 words, and Koko the lowland gorilla has a working vocabulary of more than 1,000 words.

© Susan Kuklin/Photo Researchers, Inc.

objects and even pictures of objects. Their vocabularies include verbs, adjectives, and such words as *sorry* and *please;* furthermore, they can string signs together properly to produce original sentences, even inflecting their signs to indicate person, place, and instrument. More impressive still, Washoe was observed spontaneously teaching her adopted son Loulis how to sign by deliberately manipulating his hand. For 5 years, humans had refrained from signing when in sight of Loulis, over which time he learned no fewer than fifty signs. Today, Loulis and Washoe live with three other signing chimpanzees, all of whom are shown by remote videotaping to use ASL signs to communicate among themselves when no humans are present.

Some chimpanzees have been taught to communicate by other symbolic means. One named Sarah learned to converse by means of pictographs—basic designs such as squares and triangles—on brightly colored plastic chips. Each pictograph stands for a noun or a verb. Sarah can also produce new sentences of her own. Another chimpanzee, Lana, learned to converse by means of a computer with a keyboard somewhat like that of a typewriter, but with symbols rather than letters. One of the most adept with this system is a bonobo named Kanzi, who picked up signing early in life from his mother and the humans with whom she communicated. After beginning to sign spontaneously, Kanzi went on to become more fluent than his mother, who had learned to sign as an adult.

Chimps have not been the only subjects of ape language experiments. Gorillas and orangutans have also

been taught American Sign Language with results that replicate those obtained with chimps. As a consequence, there is now a growing agreement among researchers that all of the great apes can develop language skills at least to the level of a 2- to 3-year-old human, as noted in this chapter's Original Study. Not only are comprehension skills similar, but so is acquisition order: *What* and *where, what-to-do* and *who,* as well as *how* questions are acquired in that order by both apes and humans. Like humans, apes are capable of referring to events removed in time and space, a phenomenon known as **displacement** and one of the distinctive features of human language.

In view of apes' demonstrated abilities in the use of sign language, it is not surprising that a number of anthropologists, psychologists, and other linguists have shown new interest in an old hypothesis: that human language began as a gestural rather than vocal system. Certainly, the potential to communicate through gestures must have been as well developed among our earliest ancestors as it is among today's apes, since they share it as a consequence of a common ancestry that predates the divergence of the human line of development. Moreover, the bipedalism of our earliest ancestors would have enabled them to use their hands more freely to gesture. Manual signing and gesturing are skilled activities in which hand preference plays a major role, and evidence for the pronounced "handedness" found only among humans is provided by the external configuration of the brain of *Homo habilis* as well as by the tools made by this human ancestor. Furthermore, among modern children learning ASL, hand preference appears in signing *before* it does in object manipulation. Thus, not only is it likely that *Homo habilis* used gestures to communicate, but this may have played a role in the

displacement The ability to refer to things and events removed in time and space.

development of the manual dexterity involved in early tool making.

One of the most difficult problems for students dealing with the origin of language is the origin of syntax, which was necessary to enable our ancestors to articulate and communicate more complex ideas. Here, a look at the physical nature of gestures is helpful, for in fact, they can be construed not just as words but as sentences. This can be illustrated with the modern ASL gesture meaning "seize": The hand begins fully open or slightly bent, the elbow is slightly flexed, and the upper arm rotates at the shoulder to bring the forearm and hand across the body until the moving hand closes around the upright forefinger of the other hand. What we have here is not just the word seize but a complete transitive sentence with a verb and a direct object, or in semantic terms, an agent, an action, and a patient.[11] In this case, there is a clear relation between the sign and what is signified, suggesting that syntax could have its origin in signs that mimic the things and actions they represent.

Another problem involves the shift from manual gestures to spoken language. Two things to keep in mind here are that: (1) the manual signs of a sign language are typically accompanied by facial gestures, and (2) just as making a sign is the outcome of a particular motor act, so is speech the outcome of a series of motor acts, in this case concentrated in the mouth and throat. In other words, *all* language, signed or spoken, can be analyzed as gesture. Furthermore, research on hearing-impaired users of ASL suggests that areas of the brain critical for speech may be critical to signing as well. Thus, early continuity exists between gestural and spoken language; the latter could have emerged from the former through increasing emphasis on finely controlled movements of the mouth and throat—a scenario consistent with the appearance of neurological structures underlying language in the earliest representatives of the genus *Homo* and steady enlargement of the human brain *before* the alteration of the vocal tract began that allows us to speak the way we do.

The advantage of spoken over gestural language to a species increasingly dependent on tool use for survival is obvious. To talk with your hands, you must stop whatever else you are doing with them; speech does not interfere with that. Other benefits include being able to talk in the dark, past opaque objects, or among speakers whose attention is diverted. Just when the changeover to spoken language took place is not known, although all would agree that spoken languages are at least as old as "anatomically modern" *Homo sapiens*. There is, however, no anatomical evidence to support arguments that

Far from being simple or primitive, the languages of nonliterate people are often the opposite. For example, in World War II, the complexity of the Navajo Indian language was such that, when used for a code by U.S. Marines in the Pacific, it defied all deciphering attempts by the Japanese enemy.

Neandertals and other representatives of archaic *H. sapiens* were incapable of speech. Perhaps its emergence began with *Homo erectus,* the first human ancestor to live in regions with cold climates. The ability to plan ahead for changes in seasonal conditions crucial to survival under such conditions would not have been possible without use of a grammatically structured language, whether it be gestural or vocal. Having the use of fire, we do know that *H. erectus* would not have had to cease all activity when darkness fell. We also know that the vocal tract and brain of *H. erectus* were intermediate between that of *H. sapiens* and earlier *Australopithecus*. It may be that the expansion from gestural to spoken language was a driving force in these evolutionary changes.

Early anthropologists searched for a truly "primitive" language spoken by a living people that might show the processes of language just beginning or developing. That search has now been abandoned, for anthropologists have come to realize that there is no such thing as a "primitive" language in the world today, or even in the recent past. So far, all human languages that have been described and studied, even among people with something approximating a Stone Age technology, are highly developed, complex, and capable of expressing infinite meanings. The truth is that humans have been talking in this world for an extremely long time, and every known language, wherever it is, now has a long history and has developed subtleties and complexities that do not permit any label of "primitive." What a language may or may not express is not a measure of its age but of its speakers' way of life, reflecting what they want or need to communicate with others.

---

[11]Armstrong, D. F., Stokoe, W. C., & Wilcox, S. E. (1994). Signs of the origin of syntax. *Current Anthropology, 35,* 355.

FROM SPEECH TO WRITING

When anthropology developed as an academic discipline over a century ago, it concentrated its attention on small traditional communities that relied primarily on personal interaction and oral communication for survival. Cultures that depend on talking and listening often have rich traditions of storytelling and speechmaking. For them, oration (from the Latin *orare,* "to speak") plays a central role in education, conflict resolution, political decision making, spiritual or supernatural practices, and many other aspects of life. Consequently, people capable of making expressive and informed speeches usually enjoy great prestige in such societies. Traditional orators were typically trained from childhood in memorizing genealogies, ritual prayers, customary laws, and diplomatic agreements. In ceremonies that could last many hours, even days, they eloquently recited the oral traditions by heart. Their extraordinary memories were often enhanced by oral devices such as rhyme, rhythm, and melody. Orators also employed special objects to help them remember proper sequences and points to be made—memory devices such as notched sticks, knotted strings, bands embroidered with shells, and so forth. Traditional Iroquois Indian orators, for example, performed their formal speeches often with wampum belts made of hemp string and blue and white shell beads woven into distinctive patterns. More than artful motifs, these designs could represent any of a variety of important messages, including treaties with other nations. Such symbolic designs are found all over the world, some dating back more than 30,000 years. When ancient artifacts of bone, antler, stone, or some other material have been etched or painted, anthropologists try to determine if these markings were created to symbolize specific ideas such as seasonal calendars, kinship relations, trade records, and so forth. From basic visual signs such as these emerged a few writing systems, including the alphabet.

Although thousands of languages, past and present, have existed only in spoken form, many have long been documented in one form of writing or another. Archaeologists suggest writing emerged after humans began cultivating crops, breeding animals, and establishing towns and trade networks—as an instrument of power. With it, elites could keep track of exchanges, inventories, debts, and possessions, as well as devise calendars to know when to plant crops. It was also valuable

> *writing system* A set of visible or tactile signs used to represent units of language in a systematic way.
> *alphabet* A series of symbols representing the sounds of a language arranged in a traditional order.

Inscriptions carved about 3,800 years ago by Semitic people in Egypt's western desert at Wadi el-Hol are now thought to represent the first writing in the alphabet. Similar Proto-Sinaitic inscriptions from about the same period have been identified across the Red Sea in the western Sinai Peninsula, at the ancient Egyptian-controlled turquoise mines at Serabit el-Khadem.

as a symbolic means of proclaiming elite power and ideological indoctrination. Over time, graphic representations in the form of simplified pictures of things (pictographs) evolved into more stylized symbolic forms. Although different peoples invented a variety of graphic styles, anthropologists distinguish an actual **writing system** as a set of visible or tactile signs used to represent units of language in a systematic way. Recently discovered symbols carved into 8,600-year-old tortoise shells found in western China may represent the earliest evidence of elementary writing found anywhere. A fully developed early writing system is Egyptian hieroglyphics, developed some 5,000 years ago and in use for about 3,500 years. One of the other oldest systems in the world is cuneiform, an arrangement of wedge-shaped imprints developed in Mesopotamia (mostly present-day Iraq), which lasted nearly as long. About 1,500 years or so after these systems were established, others began to appear, developing independently in distant locations around the world, such as Chinese (about 3,500 years ago) and Maya hieroglyphics (almost 2,500 years ago).

Inscriptions recently discovered in Egypt's western desert at the Wadi el-Hol ("Gulch of Terror") suggest that the **alphabet** (a series of symbols representing the *sounds* of a language) was invented almost 4,000 years ago by Semitic-speaking peoples in that region. Analysis of the Semitic inscriptions, which were carved into a natural limestone wall alongside hundreds of Egyptian hieroglyphs, reveals that these early Semites adopted a limited number of Egyptian hieroglyphs as symbols for sounds in their own language. For instance, they took the Egyptian glyph for "ox" and determined that it would stand for the sound at the start the Semitic word for "ox," which is *aleph.* (This symbol looks like the horned head of an ox—and like the letter *A* upside down.) Likewise, they chose the Egyptian glyph for "house" to stand for the opening sound of the Semitic word for "house," which is *beth.* (This symbol looks like a two-room house—and like the letter *B* tipped back.) The result was a writing system with characters based on a selection of Egyptian glyphs but used to represent sounds in an early Semitic language. Over the next 1,000 years, Semites inhabiting the Sinai desert and the Mediterranean (including Canaanites, Hebrews, and Phoenicians) adopted this system and developed the script into a more linear form.[12]

Most of the alphabets used today descended from the Phoenician one. The Greeks adopted it about 2,800 years ago, modifying the characters to suit sounds in their own language. The word *alphabet* comes from the first two letters in the Greek writing system, *alpha* and *beta* (otherwise meaningless words in Greek). From Greek colonies in southern Italy, the writing system spread north to Rome. Then, when Latin-speaking Romans expanded their empire throughout much of Europe, northern Africa, and western Asia, small groups of formally educated people from dozens of different nations in the realm communicated in the Latin language and used its associated alphabet. The Roman alphabet, slightly modified from Greek, spread even further from the 15th century onward as European nations expanded their trade networks and built colonial empires overseas. The 15th-century invention of the printing press fueled worldwide diffusion of the alphabet, making it possible to mechanically reproduce writings in any human language.

In North America variations of the Roman alphabet have emerged to distinguish the unique phonetic values of some Native American languages that have been put in written form relatively recently. Such is the case with Cree syllabics, a writing system developed in the 19th century and still used by many indigenous groups throughout eastern Canada. Another writing system inspired by the alphabet is the Cherokee Indian syllabary. Invented by a Cherokee named Sequoya around 1821, it is still used among some Cherokee in Oklahoma and North Carolina. Although other writing systems, such as Chinese, are very widely used by millions of people, North American inventions—such as the Internet in the late 20th century—help solidify the use of the alphabet as a global writing system.

It has been nearly 5,000 years since literacy emerged in Egypt and Iraq. Yet, today more than 860 million adults worldwide cannot read and write. Illiteracy condemns already disadvantaged people to ongoing poverty—migrant rural workers, refugees, ethnic minorities, and those living in the rural backlands and urban slums throughout the world. For example a third of India's 1 billion inhabitants cannot read and write, and some 113 million children around the world are not enrolled in school. Declaring literacy a human right, the United Nations has proclaimed the period 2003 to 2012 as the Literacy Decade, with the objective of extending literacy to all humanity.

---

[12]Himmelfarb, E. J. (2000). First alphabet found in Egypt. Newsbrief. *Archaeology 53* (1), January/February.

Chapter Summary

■ Anthropologists need to understand the workings of language, because it is through language that people in every society are able to share their experiences, concerns, and beliefs, over the past and in the present, and to communicate these to the next generation. Language makes communication of infinite meanings possible by employing a few sounds or gestures that, when put together according to certain rules, result in meanings that are intelligible to fellow speakers.

■ Linguistics is the modern scientific study of all aspects of language by anthropologists, psychologists, and other specialists. Phonetics focuses on the production, transmission, and reception of speech sounds, or phonemes. Phonology studies the sound patterns of language in order to extract the rules that govern the way sounds are combined. Morphology is concerned with the smallest units of meaningful combinations of sounds—morphemes—in a language. Syntax refers to the principles according to which phrases and sentences are built. The entire formal structure of a language, consisting of all observations about its morphemes and syntax, constitutes the grammar of a language.

■ There are three main branches of linguistics. Descriptive linguists mark out and explain the features of a language at a particular time in its history. Historical linguists investigate relationships between earlier and later forms of the same language—including identifying the forces behind the changes that have taken place in languages in the course of linguistic divergence. Their work provides a means of roughly dating certain migrations, invasions, and contacts of people. Ethnolinguists study language as it relates to society, the rest of culture, and human behavior.

■ Human language is embedded in a gesture-call system inherited from our primate ancestors that serves to "key" speech, providing the appropriate frame for interpreting linguistic form. The gestural component of this system consists of body motions (including facial expressions) used to convey messages. The system of notating and recording these motions is known as kinesics. Another aspect of body language is proxemics, the study of how people perceive and use space. The call component of the gesture-call system is represented by paralanguage, consisting of extralinguistic sounds involving various voice qualities and vocalizations.

■ About 70 percent of the world's languages are tonal, in which the musical pitch of a spoken word is an essential part of its pronunciation and meaning.

■ All languages change—borrowing terms from other languages or inventing new words for new technologies or social realities. A major cause of language change is the domination of one society over another, which over the last 500 years led to the disappearance of about 4,000 of the world's 10,000 languages. A reaction to this loss and to the current far-reaching spread and domination of the English language is linguistic nationalism—purging foreign terms from a language's vocabulary and pressing for the revitalization of lost or threatened languages.

■ Some linguistic anthropologists, following Edward Sapir and Benjamin Lee Whorf, have proposed that language shapes the way people think and behave. Others have argued that language reflects reality. Although language is flexible and adaptable, a terminology once established tends to perpetuate itself and to reflect much about the speakers' beliefs and social relationships. Kinship terms, for example, help reveal how a family is structured, what relationships are considered close or distant, and certain attitudes toward relationships. Similarly, gender language reveals how the men and women in a society relate to each other.

■ A social dialect is the language of a group of people within a larger one, all of whom may speak more or less the same language. Ethnolinguists are concerned with whether dialect differences reflect cultural differences. They also study code switching—the process of changing from one level of language to another as the situation demands—for much the same reason.

■ One theory of language origins is that early human ancestors, having their hands freed by bipedalism, began using gestures as a tool to communicate within a social setting. In early *Homo's* development of stone tools, preserved in the archaeological record, we see evidence of handedness indicating structural changes in the brain that may be related to linguistic abilities. With the movement of *Homo erectus* out of the tropics, planning for the seasons of cold temperatures required the grammar and syntax to communicate information about events removed in time and space. By the time archaic *Homo sapiens* appeared, emphasis on finely controlled movements of the mouth and throat had probably given rise to spoken language.

■ All languages that have been studied, including those of people with supposedly primitive cultures, are complex, sophisticated, and able to express a wide range of experiences.

■ Writing emerged after humans began cultivating crops, breeding animals, and establishing towns and trade networks—as it became necessary to keep track of exchanges, inventories, debts, and possessions, as well as to devise calendars to know when to plant crops. Over time, graphic representations in the form of simplified pictures of things (pic-tographs) evolved into more stylized forms. The first actual writing systems—Egyptian hieroglyphics and cuneiform—developed about 5,000 years ago, Chinese perhaps earlier. The alphabet was invented almost 4,000 years ago by early Semitic-speaking peoples in that region.

Questions for Reflection

1. If apes can learn to use sign language in a meaningful way beyond mimicking, how does that challenge the idea of a boundary between humans and apes?

2. Up to 4,000 languages have disappeared over the last 500 years, most of them vanishing without a trace. Only 6,000 languages remain. If the same rate of extinction continues, and just one or two languages exist in the year 2500, would that be a loss or a gain? How so?

3. Applying the principle of linguistic relativity to your own language, consider how your perceptions of objective reality might have been shaped by your language and how your sense of reality might have been different if you grew up speaking Hopi.

4. Think about the gestures commonly used in your own family. Are they more or less powerful than words expressed?

5. From its earliest days, writing was linked to political power. How does that apply to modern media and globalization?

Key Terms

Language	Vocal qualifiers
Signals	Vocal segregates
Linguistics	Tonal language
Descriptive linguistics	Historical linguistics
Phonetics	Language family
Phonology	Linguistic divergence
Phonemes	Glottochronology
Morphology	Core vocabularies
Morphemes	Pidgin
Frame substitution	Creole
Syntax	Linguistic nationalism
Grammar	Ethnolinguistics
Form classes	Linguistic relativity
Gesture	Gendered speech
Kinesics	Dialects
Proxemics	Code switching
Paralanguage	Displacement
Voice qualities	Writing system
Vocalizations	Alphabet
Vocal characterizers	

Multimedia Review Tools

Companion Web Site

Visit **http://www.wadsworth.com/anthropology_d/** and click on the companion Web site for this textbook to access a wide range of material to aid your study of anthropology. Among the options for self-study in each chapter are learning objectives, flash cards, Internet activities, Web links, InfoTrac College Edition exercises, and practice tests that can be scored and emailed to your instructor.

CD-ROM
The *Doing Anthropology Today* CD-ROM supplied with your textbook provides unique and valuable information designed to enhance your learning experience. This interactive multimedia resource includes video clips, interviews with renowned anthropologists, map and timeline exercises, chapter study quizzes, and much more. *Doing Anthropology Today* will not only help you in achieving your grade goals, but it will also make your learning experience fun and exciting!

Suggested Readings

Duranti, A. (2001). Linguistic anthropology: History, ideas, and issues. In A. Duranti (Ed.), *Linguistic anthropology: A reader* (pp. 1–38). Oxford, England: Blackwell.

A good summary of the development of the field of linguistic anthropology.

Farnell, B. (1995). *Do you see what I mean? Plains Indian sign talk and the embodiment of action.* Austin: University of Texas Press.

Excellent book on Plains Indian sign language.

Gardner, R. A., Gardner, B. T., & Van Cantfort, T. E. (Eds.). (1989). *Teaching sign language to chimpanzees.* Albany: State University of New York Press.

Using accessible, jargon-free prose, the authors detail their methods and results. Psychologists and anthropologists who reviewed the book agree that it represents a milestone in ape language research, and as one put it, should be read by all interested in the evolution of human behavior.

Hall, E. T. (1959). *The silent language.* Garden City, NY: Anchor Press/Doubleday.

Written for a general audience but recognized as the founding document on intercultural communication, this classic explores culture and communication, with particular focus on proxemics, as well as cross-cultural concepts of time and public space.

Key, M. R. (1975). *Paralanguage and kinesics: Nonverbal communication.* Metuchen, NJ: Scarecrow Press.

Thorough discussion of elements of both paralanguage and kinesics.

Morse, D., et al. (1979). *Gestures: Their origins and distribution.* New York: Stein & Day.

A fascinating, well-illustrated text that discusses dozens of gestures—from the fingertips kiss and the V-sign to the nose thumb. It explores the derivations and distributions of gestures, as well as the sometimes startlingly different meanings they have in different parts of the world.

Ruhlen, M. (1994). *The origin of language: Tracing the evolution of the mother tongue.* New York: Wiley.

Scholarly in substance but written for a popular audience, this makes a good introduction to comparative linguistics for beginning anthropology students. With an evolutionary theme, it cuts through the difficult problems of our linguistic ancestors with plausible though still controversial results.

Yip, M. (2002). *Tone.* Cambridge, England: Cambridge University Press.

A clearly organized introduction to tone and tonal phonology. Comprehensive in scope, it examines the main types of tonal systems found in Africa, the Americas, and Asia.

CHAPTER 5

Social Identity, Personality, and Gender

© Henry S. Hamlin

CHALLENGE ISSUE

E VERY SOCIETY FACES THE CHALLENGE OF HUMANIZING ITS CHILDREN, TEACHING THEM THE VALUES AND SOCIAL CODES THAT WILL ENABLE THEM TO BE FUNCTIONING AND CONTRIBUTING MEMBERS IN THE COMMUNITY. This is essential, for it helps ensure that the society will perpetuate itself biologically and culturally. Ethnographic research has revealed a wide range of approaches to raising children in order to meet this goal. These different child-rearing methods and their possible effects on adult personalities have long been of interest to anthropologists.

1

What Is Enculturation?

Enculturation is the process by which culture is passed from one generation to the next and through which individuals become members of their society. It begins soon after birth with the development of self-awareness—the ability to perceive oneself as a unique phenomenon in time and space and to judge one's own actions. For self-awareness to function, the individual must be provided with a behavioral environment. The way a person perceives and gets oriented to surrounding objects is specified by the culture in which he or she grows up. Along with object orientation, a behavioral environment includes spatial, temporal, and normative orientations.

2

How Does Enculturation Influence Personality?

Studies have shown that there is some kind of structural relationship between enculturation and personality development, although it is also clear that each individual begins with certain broad potentials and limitations that are genetically inherited. In some cultures, particular child-rearing practices seem to promote the development of compliant personalities, while in others different practices seem to promote more independent, self-reliant personalities.

3

Are Different Personalities Characteristic of Different Cultures?

Every culture emphasizes certain personality traits as good and others as bad—and has distinct ways of encouraging or discouraging those traits accordingly. Nonetheless, it is difficult to characterize cultures in terms of particular personalities. Of the several attempts made, the concept of modal personality is the most satisfactory. This recognizes that any human society has a range of individual personalities, but some will be more "typical" than others. Those that approximate the modal personality of a particular culture are thought of as normal. Since modal personalities may differ from one culture to another and since cultures may differ in the range of variation they will accept, it is clear that abnormal personality is a relative concept.

In 1690 English philosopher John Locke presented his *tabula rasa* theory in his book *An Essay Concerning Human Understanding*. This notion held that the newborn human was like a blank slate, and what the individual became in life was written on the slate by his or her life experiences. The implication is that all individuals are biologically identical at birth in their potential for personality development and that their adult personalities are exclusively the products of their postnatal experiences, which will differ from culture to culture. Locke's idea offered high hopes for the all-embracing impact of education on a child's character formation, but it missed the mark, for it did not take into consideration what we now know: that each person is born with unique inherited tendencies that will help determine his or her adult personality. Our current understanding of how individual personalities are shaped is that genetic inheritance sets certain broad potentials and limitations, and that life experiences, particularly in the early years, also play a significant role in this formation. Since different cultures handle the raising and education of children in different ways, these practices and their effects on personalities are important subjects of anthropological inquiry. Such studies gave rise to the specialization of psychological anthropology and are the subjects of this chapter.

THE SELF AND THE BEHAVIORAL ENVIRONMENT

From the moment of birth, a person faces multiple challenges to survive as an individual human being. Obviously, newborns cannot yet take care of their own biological needs. Only in myths and romantic fantasies do we encounter stories about children successfully coming of age alone in the wilderness or accomplishing this feat having been raised by animals in the wild. Italians in Rome today, for example, still celebrate the mythological founders of their city, the twin brothers Romulus and Remus, who, according to legend, were suckled as infants by a she-wolf. Also, millions of children around the world have been fascinated by stories about Tarzan and the apes or the jungle boy Mowgli and the wolves. Moreover, young and old alike have been captivated by newspaper hoaxes about "wild" children, such as the 10-year-old boy reported to have been found running among gazelles in the Syrian desert in 1946.

Fanciful imaginations aside, human children are biologically ill-equipped to survive without culture. This point has been driven home by several documented cases about feral children who grew up deprived of human contact. None of them had a happy ending. For instance, there was nothing romantic about the girl

Kamala, supposedly rescued from a wolf den in India in 1920: She moved about on all fours and could not feed herself. And everyone in Paris considered the naked "wild boy" captured in the woods outside Aveyron village in 1800 an incurable idiot. Clearly, the biological capacity for what we think of as human, which entails culture, must be nurtured to be realized.

Because culture is socially constructed and learned rather than biologically inherited, all societies must somehow ensure that culture is adequately transmitted from one generation to the next. This process of transmission through which individuals become accepted members of their society is known as enculturation, as discussed in Chapter 2. Since each group lives by a particular set of cultural rules, a child will have to learn the rules of his or her society in order to survive. Most of that learning takes place in the first few years when a child learns how to feel, think, speak, and, ultimately, act like an adult who embodies being Japanese, Kikuyu, Lakota, Norwegian, or whatever ethnic or national group it was born into.

The first agents of enculturation in all societies are the members of the household into which a person is born. Initially, the most important member of this household is the newborn's mother. (In fact, cultural factors are at work even before a child is born, through what a pregnant mother eats, drinks, and inhales.) Soon thereafter, other household members come to play roles in the enculturation process. Just who these others are depends on how households are structured in the particular society. In the United States, households ideally include the father or stepfather and the child's siblings in addition to the mother—although this is no longer the case in many instances. In other societies, the North American ideal of a father having contact with his chil-

In the United States, the need for two paychecks to sustain desired standards of living means that large numbers of children spend time at home fending for themselves without adults present.

dren in their early years is nonexistent. Indeed, there are societies where men never live with the mothers of their children. In such instances, brothers of the child's mother usually have important responsibilities toward their nieces and nephews. In many societies, grandparents, other wives of the father, brothers of the father, or sisters of the mother, not to mention their children, are also likely to be key players in the enculturation process. We will discuss various household arrangements in detail in Chapter 9, on family and household.

As the young person matures, individuals outside the household are brought into the enculturation process. These usually include other relatives and certainly the individual's peers. The latter may be included informally in the form of playgroups or formally in age associations, where children actually teach other children. In some societies, and the United States is a good example, professionals are brought into the process to provide formal instruction. In many societies, however, children are pretty much allowed to learn through observation and participation, at their own speed.

The Self

Enculturation begins with the development of **self-awareness**—the ability to identify oneself as an individual creature, to reflect on oneself, and to evaluate and react to oneself. Humans do not have this ability at birth, even though it is essential for their successful social functioning. It is self-awareness that permits one to assume

responsibility for one's conduct, to learn how to react to others, and to assume a variety of roles in society. An important aspect of self-awareness is the attachment of positive value to one's self. Without this, individuals cannot be motivated to act to their advantage rather than disadvantage; self-identification by itself is not sufficient for this.

Self-awareness does not come all at once. In modern industrial and postindustrial societies, for example, self and non-self are not clearly distinguished until a child is about 2 years of age. This development of self-awareness in children growing up in such large-scale societies, however, may lag somewhat behind other cultures. Self-awareness develops in concert with neuromotor development, which is known to proceed at a slower rate in infants from industrial societies than in infants in many, perhaps even most, small-scale farming or foraging communities. The reasons for this slower rate are not yet clear, although the amount of human contact and stimulation that infants receive seems to play an important role. In the United States, for example, infants generally do not sleep with their parents, most often being put in rooms of their own. This is seen as an important step in making them into individuals, "owners" of themselves and their capacities, rather than part of some social whole. As a consequence, they

self-awareness The ability to identify oneself as an individual, to reflect on oneself, and to evaluate oneself.

© James Balog

Self-awareness is not restricted to humans. This chimpanzee knows that the individual in the mirror is himself and not some other chimp.

do not experience the steady stream of stimuli, including touch, smell, movement, and warmth, that they would if co-sleeping. Private sleeping also deprives them of the opportunity for frequent nursing through the night.

In traditional societies, infants routinely sleep with their parents, or at least their mothers. What's more (unlike practices in most of Europe and North America), they are carried or held most other times, usually in an upright position. The mother typically responds to a cry or "fuss" literally within seconds, usually offering the infant her breast. Thus, among traditional Ju/'hoansí (of whom more in a moment) of southern Africa's Kalahari Desert, infants are nursed about four times an hour, for 1 or 2 minutes at a time. Overall, a 15-week-old Ju/'hoansí infant is in close contact with its mother about 70 percent of the time, as compared with 20 percent for home-reared infants in the United States. Moreover, their contacts are not usually limited to their mothers; they include numerous other adults and children of virtually all ages. In modern industrial and postindustrial societies, day-care centers now approximate these same conditions. The catch here is that their personnel must remain stable and (ideally) be recruited from the child's neighborhood if these centers are to have a positive effect on the cognitive and social development of the very young children enrolled in them. Unfortunately, these conditions are not usually met. Among other reasons, low pay for caregivers all but guarantees a high rate of personnel turnover.

From the above, it is obvious that infants in traditional societies are exposed to a steady stream of various stimuli far more than most babies in contemporary North America and most other industrial and postindustrial societies. This is important, for recent studies show that stimulation plays a key role in the "hard wiring" of the brain—it is necessary for development of the neural circuitry. Looking at breastfeeding in particular, studies show that the longer a child is breastfed, the higher it will score on cognitive tests and the lower its risk of attention deficit hyperactivity disorder. Furthermore, breastfed children have fewer allergies, fewer ear infections, less diarrhea, and are at less risk of sudden infant death syndrome. Nonetheless breastfeeding tends to be relatively short-lived at best in the industrialized world, in part due to workplace conditions that rarely facilitate it.[1]

In the development of self-awareness, *perception* (a kind of vague awareness of one's existence) precedes *conception* (more specific knowledge of the interrelated needs, attitudes, concerns, and interests that define what one is). Conception involves a cultural definition of self, and in this definition language plays a crucial role. This is why in all cultures individuals become competent at using personal and possessive pronouns at an early age.

Social Identity through Personal Naming

Personal names, too, are important devices for self-definition in all cultures. It is through naming that a social group acknowledges a child's birthright and establishes its social identity. Without a name, an individual has no identity, no self. For this reason, many cultures consider name selection to be an important issue and mark the naming of a child with a special **naming ceremony.** For instance,

---

[1]Dettwyler, K. A. (1997, October). When to wean. *Natural History, 49*; Stuart-MacAdam, P., & Dettwyler, K. A. (Eds.). (1995). *Breastfeeding: Biocultural perspectives.* New York: Aldine de Gruyter.

VISUAL COUNTERPOINT In traditional societies around the world, infants are never left by themselves and so receive constant stimulation, an important element in their development. In the United States, by contrast, many infants spend considerable time isolated from human interaction.

Aymara Indians in the Bolivian highland village of Laymi do not consider an infant truly "human" until they have given it a name. And naming does not happen until the child begins to speak the Aymara language, typically around the age of 2. Once the child shows the ability to speak like a human, he or she is considered fit to be recognized as such with a proper name. The naming ceremony marks their social transition from a state of "nature" to "culture" and consequently to full acceptance into the Laymi community.

There are countless contrasting approaches to naming. Icelanders still follow an ancient naming custom in which children use their father's personal given name as their last name. A son adds the suffix *sen* to the name and a daughter adds *dottir*. Thus, a brother and sister whose father is named Sven Olafsen would have the last names Svensen and Svendottir. In some Nigerian ethnic groups, parents and other relatives often give a child three or more names at birth. The first is a personal name that may relate to the family's circumstances; the second expresses what the family hopes the child will become; the third relates to the child's lineage or clan and may refer to a founding ancestor such as a legendary hero or a god, or even a thing considered sacred by the family. When the child has matured, she or he may take two of these given names and use them in combination with the name of her or his father or some other forefather's name.

Among Iroquois Indians, naming a child was traditionally the right of the clan mother, the senior-ranking female elder in a cluster of related families. In their estimation, naming was so important that they codified the custom in their constitution:

> The women of the Forty-Eight (now fifty) Royaneh [noble] families shall be the heirs of the Authorized Names for all time to come. When an infant of the Five Nations is given an Authorized Name at the Midwinter Festival or at the Ripe Corn Festival, one in the cousinhood of which the infant is a member shall be appointed a speaker. He shall then announce to the opposite cousinhood the names of the father and the mother of the child together with the clan of the mother. Then the speaker shall announce the child's name twice. The uncle of the child shall then take the child in his arms and walking up and down the room shall sing: "My head is firm, I am of the Confederacy." As he sings the opposite cousinhood shall respond by chanting, "Hyenh, Hyenh, Hyenh, Hyenh," until the song is ended.[2]

In many cultures, a person receives a name soon after birth but may acquire new names during subsequent phases in their lives. A Hopi child, for instance, is born into its mother's clan. Cared for by the elder women, the newborn spends the first 19 days of its life wrapped in a blanket and secluded indoors. Placed next to the infant are two perfectly shaped ears of corn, referred to as "Mother Corn." On the 20th day, the father's sister gives the baby its name in a sunrise ceremony. At age 6, the child receives another name in a religious ceremony. Reaching adulthood, the person gets yet another name and keeps that one till the end of her or his life. Yet one more name is bestowed upon a Hopi at death, a name that is not to be mentioned after it is given.

Finally, among the Netsilik Inuit in Arctic Canada, women experiencing a difficult delivery would call out the names of deceased people of admirable character. The name being called at the moment of birth was thought to enter the infant's body and help the delivery, and the child would bear that name thereafter. Inuit parents may also name their children for deceased relatives in the belief that the spiritual identification will help shape their character.[3]

Among the many cultural rules that exist in each society, those having to do with naming are unique because they individualize a person while at the same time identify one as part of a group and even connect the person to the spirit world. In short, name-giving customs play an important role in a person's life journey as a socially accepted member of a culture.

MEDIATREK
For an interactive look at learned behaviors and the relationship between environment and culture, go to MediaTrek 5.1 on the companion Web site or CD-ROM.

The Behavioral Environment

For self-awareness to emerge and function, basic orientations are necessary to structure the psychological field in which the self acts. These include object orientation, spatial orientation, temporal orientation, and normative orientation.

First, each individual must learn about a world of objects other than the self. Each culture singles out for attention certain environmental attributes, while ignoring

---

[2]The Iroquois Constitution can be seen online at: *http://www.law.ou.edu/hist/iroquois.html*

---

[3]Balikci, A. (1970). *The Netsilik Eskimo.* Garden City, NY: Natural History Press.

naming ceremony A special event or ritual to mark the naming of a child.

other features or lumping them together into broad categories. A culture also *explains* the perceived environment. This is important, for a cultural explanation of one's surroundings imposes a measure of order and provides the individual with a sense of direction needed to act meaningfully and effectively. Behind this lies a powerful psychological drive to reduce uncertainty—part of the common human need for a balanced and integrated perspective on the relevant universe. When confronted with ambiguity and uncertainty, people invariably strive to clarify and give structure to the situation; they do this, of course, in ways that their particular culture deems appropriate. Thus, we should not be surprised to find that explanations of the universe are never entirely objective in nature but are culturally constructed. In fact, everything in the physical environment varies in the way it is *perceived and experienced* by humans, for the environment is organized culturally and mediated symbolically through language. Putting it another way, we might say that the world around us is perceived through cultural lenses.

The behavioral environment in which the self acts also involves *spatial orientation,* or the ability to get from one object or place to another. In all societies, the names and significant features of places are important references for spatial orientation. Traditionally, geographic place names often contain references to significant features in the landscape. For instance, the name of the great Chinese port city of Shanghai means literally "above the sea"; the English coastal city of Plymouth is located at the mouth of the river Plym; and the riverside city of Bamako, Mali, in West Africa translates as "crocodile river."

Temporal orientation, which gives people a sense of their place in time, is also part of the behavioral environment. Connecting past actions with those of the present and future, it provides a sense of self-continuity. This is the function of calendars, for example. Derived from the Latin word *kalendae,* which originally referred to a public announcement at the first day of a new month, or moon, such a chart gives people a sense of where they are in the annual cycle. Just as the perceived environment of objects is organized in cultural terms, so too are time and space.

A final aspect of the behavioral environment is the *normative orientation.* Moral values, ideals, and principles, which are purely cultural in origin, are as much a part of the individual's behavioral environment as are trees, rivers, and mountains. Without them people would have nothing by which to gauge their own actions or those of others. In short, the self-evaluation aspect of self-awareness could not be made functional. Normative orientation includes standards that indicate what ranges of behavior are acceptable for males and females in a particular society. Such behavior is embedded in biology but modified by culture, so it should not be surprising that they vary cross-culturally, as revealed in the following Original Study, written by Rhonda Kay Williamson while an undergraduate student of philosophy at Bryn Mawr College in Pennsylvania.

VISUAL COUNTERPOINT
The Ituri forest in the geographical heart of Africa is viewed in two very different ways by the people who live there. Mbuti foragers view it with affection; like a benevolent parent, it provides them with all they ask for: sustenance, protection, and security. Village-dwelling farmers, by contrast, view the forest with a mixture of fear, hostility, and mistrust—something they must constantly struggle to control.

© Devore/Anthro-Photo

© Hart/Anthro-Photo

Original Study

The Blessed Curse

One morning not so long ago, a child was born. This birth, however, was no occasion for the customary celebration. Something was wrong: something very grave, very serious, very sinister. This child was born between sexes, an "intersexed" child. From the day of its birth, this child would be caught in a series of struggles involving virtually every aspect of its life. Things that required little thought under "ordinary" circumstances were, in this instance, extraordinarily difficult. Simple questions now had an air of complexity: "What is it, a girl or a boy?" "What do we name it?" "How shall we raise it?" "Who (or what) is to blame for this?"

A Foot in Both Worlds

The child referred to in the introductory paragraph is myself. As the great-granddaughter of a Cherokee woman, I was exposed to the Native American view of people who were born intersexed, and those who exhibited transgendered characteristics. This view, unlike the Euro-American one, sees such individuals in a very positive and affirming light. Yet my immediate family (mother, father, and brothers) were firmly fixed in a negative Christian Euro-American point of view. As a result, from a very early age I was presented with two different and conflicting views of myself. This resulted in a lot of confusion within me about what I was, how I came to be born the way I was, and what my intersexuality meant in terms of my spirituality as well as my place in society.

I remember, even as a small child, getting mixed messages about my worth as a human being. My grandmother, in keeping with Native American ways, would tell me stories about my birth. She would tell me how she knew when I was born that I had a special place in life, given to me by God, the Great Spirit, and that I had been given "a great strength that girls never have, yet a gentle tenderness that boys never know" and that I was "too pretty and beautiful to be a boy only and too strong to be a girl only." She rejoiced at this "special gift"

and taught me that it meant that the Great Spirit had "something important for me to do in this life." I remember how good I felt inside when she told me these things and how I soberly contemplated, even at the young age of five, that I must be diligent and try to learn and carry out the purpose designed just for me by the Great Spirit.

My parents, however, were so repulsed by my intersexuality that they would never speak of it directly. They would just refer to it as "the work of Satan." To them, I was not at all blessed with a "special gift" from some "Great Spirit," but was "cursed and given over to the Devil" by God. My father treated me with contempt, and my mother wavered between contempt and distant indifference. I was taken from one charismatic church to another in order to have the "demon of mixed sex" cast out of me. At some of these "deliverance" services I was even given a napkin to cough out the demon into!

In the end, no demon ever popped out of me. Still I grew up believing that there was something inherent within me that caused God to hate me, that my intersexuality was a punishment for this something, a mark of condemnation.

Whenever I stayed at my grandmother's house, my fears would be allayed, for she would once again remind me that I was fortunate to have been given this special gift. She was distraught that my parents were treating me cruelly and pleaded with them to let me live with her, but they would not let me stay at her home permanently. Nevertheless, they did let me spend a significant portion of my childhood with her. Had it not been for that, I might not have been able to survive the tremendous trials that awaited me in my walk through life.

Blessed Gift: The Native American View

It is now known that most, if not all, Native American societies had certain individuals that fell between the categories of "man" and "woman."

The various nations had different names for such people, but a term broadly used and recognized is *berdache*, a word of French origin that designated a male, passive homosexual. [The preferred term today is *two-spirit*.] Some of these individuals were born physically intersexed. Others appeared to be anatomically normal males, but exhibited the character and the manners of women—or vice versa. The way native people treated such individuals reveals some interesting insights into Native American belief systems.

The Spirit

The extent to which Native Americans see spirituality is reflected in their belief that all things have a spirit: "Every object—plants, rocks, water, air, the moon, animals, humans, the earth itself—has a spirit. The spirit of one thing (including a human) is not superior to the spirit of any other. . . . The function of religion is not to try to condemn or to change what exists, but to accept the realities of the world and to appreciate their contributions to life. Everything that exists has a purpose."

This paradigm is the core of Native American thought and action. Because everything has a spirit, and no spirit is superior to that of another, there is no "above" or "below," no "superior" or "inferior," no "dominant" and "subordinate." These are only illusions that arise from unclear thinking. Thus, an intersexed child is not derided or viewed as a "freak of nature" in many traditional Native American cultures. Intersexuality (as well as masculinity in a female or effeminacy in a male) is seen as the manifestation of the spirit of the child, so an intersexed child is respected as much as a girl child or a boy child. It is the spirit of the child that determines what the gender of the child will ultimately be. According to a Lakota, Lame Deer, "the Great Spirit made them *winktes* [two-spirit], and we accepted them as such." In this sense, the child has no control over what her or his gender will be. It follows that where there is no

[CONTINUED]

[CONTINUED]

choice, there can be no accountability on the part of the child. Indeed, the child who is given the spirit of a *winkte* is unable to resist becoming one.

"When an Omaha boy sees the Moon Being [a feminine Spirit] on his vision quest, the spirit holds in one hand a man's bow and arrow and in the other a woman's pack strap. . . . 'When the youth tried to grasp the bow and arrows, the Moon Being crossed hands very quickly, and if the youth was not very careful he seized the pack strap instead of the bow and arrows, thereby fixing his lot in later life. In such a case he could not help acting [like a] woman, speaking, dressing, and working just as . . . women . . . do.'"

The Curse: The Euro–American View

In contrast to the view of respect and admiration of physical intersexuality and transgendered behavior traditionally held by Native Americans, the Europeans who came to "Turtle Island" (the Cherokee name for North America) brought with them their worldview, shaped by their Judeo-Christian beliefs. According to this religious perspective, there had to be, by mandate of God, a complete dichotomy of the sexes. . . .

Will Roscoe, in his book *The Zuni Man-Woman,* reports (pp. 172–73): "Spanish oppression of 'homosexual' practices in the New World took brutal forms. In 1513, the explorer Balboa had some forty berdaches thrown to his dogs [to be eaten alive]—'a fine action by an honorable and Catholic Spaniard,' as one Spanish historian commented. In Peru, the Spaniards burned 'sodomites, . . . and in this way they frightened them in such a manner that they left this great sin.'"

It is abundantly clear that Christian Euro-Americans exerted every effort to destroy Native American culture: "In 1883, the U.S. Office of Indian Affairs issued a set of regulations that came to be known as the Code of Religious offenses, or Religious Crimes Code. . . . Indians who refused to adopt the habits of industry, or to engage in 'civilized pursuits or employments' were subject to arrest and punishment. . . . By interfering with native sexuality [and culture], the agents of assimilation effectively undermined the social fabric of entire tribes" (Roscoe, p. 176).

A Personal Resolution

For me, the resolution to the dual message I was receiving was slow in coming, largely due to the fear and

self-hatred instilled in me by Christianity. Eventually, though, the Spirit wins out. I came to adopt my Grandmother's teaching about my intersexuality. Through therapy, and a new, loving home environment, I was able to shed the constant fear of eternal punishment I felt for something I had no control over. After all, I did not create myself.

Because of my own experience, and drawing on the teaching of my grandmother, I am now able to see myself as a wondrous creation of the Great Spirit—but not only me. All creation is wondrous. There is a purpose for everyone in the gender spectrum. Each person's spirit is unique in her or his or her-his own way. It is only by living true to the nature that was bestowed upon us by the Great Spirit, in my view, that we are able to be at peace with ourselves and be in harmony with our neighbor. This, to me, is the Great Meaning and the Great Purpose . . . (*Adapted from R. K. Williamson. (1995). The blessed curse: Spirituality and sexual difference as viewed by Euro-American and Native American cultures. The College News, 18(4).)* Reprinted with permission of the author.

PERSONALITY

In the process of enculturation, we have seen that each individual is introduced to the ideas of self and the behavioral environment characteristic of his or her culture. The result is the creation of a kind of cognitive or mental map of how the world looks and operates in which the individual will think and act. It is his or her particular map of how to run the maze of life. It is an integrated, dynamic system of perceptual assemblages, including the self and its behavioral environment. When we speak of someone's personality, we are generalizing about that person's cognitive map over time. Hence, personalities are products of enculturation, as experienced by individuals, each with his or her distinctive genetic makeup. **Personality** does not lend itself to a formal def-

inition, but for our purposes we may take it as the distinctive way a person thinks, feels, and behaves. The term is derived from the Latin word for "mask" and as such relates to the idea of learning to play one's role on the stage of daily life. Gradually, the mask, as it is placed on the face of a child, begins to shape the latter until there is little sense of the mask as a superimposed alien force. Instead it feels natural, as if one were born with it. The individual has successfully internalized the culture.

The Development of Personality

Although *what* one learns is important to personality development, most anthropologists assume that *how* one learns is no less important. Along with the psychoanalytic theorists, anthropologists view childhood experiences as strongly influencing adult personality. Indeed, many anthropologists have been attracted to Freudian psychoanalytic theory, but with a critical eye. Psychoanalytic literature tends to be long on speculative

personality The distinctive way a person thinks, feels, and behaves.

concepts, clinical data, and studies that are culture-bound. Anthropologists, for their part, are most interested in studies that seek to prove, modify, or at least shed light on the cultural differences in shaping personality. For example, the traditional ideal in Western societies has been for men to be tough, aggressive, assertive, dominant, and self-reliant; whereas women have been expected to be gentle, passive, obedient, and caring. To many, these personality contrasts between the sexes seem so natural that they are thought to be biologically grounded and therefore fundamental, unchangeable, and universal. But are they? Have anthropologists identified any psychological or personality characteristics that universally differentiate men and women?

North American anthropologist Margaret Mead is well known as a pioneer in the cross-cultural study of both personality and gender (see Anthropologists of Note, page 133). Her research on gender suggested that whatever biological differences exist between men and women, they are extremely malleable. In short, biology is not destiny. Studying three ethnic groups in Papua New Guinea in the early 1930s, Mead found that among the Arapesh, relations between men and women were expected to be equal, with both genders exhibiting what most North Americans traditionally consider feminine traits (cooperative, nurturing, and gentle).[4] And although she also discovered gender equality among the Mundugamor (now generally called Biwat), in that community both genders displayed masculine traits (individualistic, assertive, volatile, aggressive). Among the Tchambuli (now called Chambri), however, Mead found that women dominated over men.

Recent anthropological research suggests that some of Mead's interpretations of gender roles were incorrect—for instance, Chambri women neither dominate Chambri men, nor vice versa. Yet, overall her research generated new insights into the human condition, showing that male dominance is a cultural construct and, consequently, that alternative gender arrangements can be created. Although biological influence in male–female behavior cannot be ruled out (in fact, debate continues about the genetic and hormonal factors at play), it has nonetheless become clear that each culture provides different opportunities and has different expectations for ideal or acceptable male–female behavior.[5]

To understand the importance of child rearing practices for the development of gender-related personality characteristics, we may look briefly at how children grow up among the Ju/'hoansi (pronounced "zhutwasi"), a people native to the Kalahari Desert of Namibia and Botswana in southern Africa. The Ju/'hoansi are one of a number of groups traditionally referred to as Bushmen, who were once widespread through much of southern Africa. In recent times, anthropologists began referring to these groups collectively as the San, thinking the word *Bushman* insulting. Unfortunately, as researchers soon discovered, *San,* a Nama word, is highly contemptuous. In fact, these indigenous people themselves now prefer Bushman as the generic name covering all groups.[6]

Traditionally subsisting as nomadic hunter–gatherers ("foragers"), in the past three decades many Ju/'hoansi have been forced to settle down—tending small herds of goats, planting gardens for their livelihood, and engaging in occasional wage labor.[7] Among those who traditionally forage for a living, equality is stressed, and dominance and aggressiveness are not tolerated in either gender. Ju/'hoansi men are as mild-mannered as the women, and women are as energetic and self-reliant as the men. By contrast, among the Ju/'hoansi who have recently settled in permanent villages, men and women exhibit personality characteristics approximating those traditionally thought of as typically masculine and feminine in North America and other industrial societies.

Among the food foragers, each newborn child receives lengthy, intensive care from its mother during the first few years of life, for the space between births is typically 4 to 5 years. This is not to say that mothers are constantly with their children. For instance, when women go to collect wild plant foods in the bush, they

---

[4]Mead, M. (1950) (orig. 1935). *Sex and temperament in three primitive societies.* New York: New American Library.

[5]Errington, F. K., & Gewertz, D. B. (2001). *Cultural alternatives and a feminist anthropology: An analysis of culturally constructed gender interests in Papua New Guinea.* Cambridge, England, and New York: Cambridge University Press.

[6]Gordon, R. J. (1992). *The bushman myth* (p. 6). Boulder, CO: Westview Press; Griffin, B. (1994). CHAGS 7. *Anthropology Newsletter, 35* (1), 13; Lewis-Williams, J. D., Dowson, T. A., & Deacon, J. (1993). Rock art and changing perceptions of Southern Africa's past: Ezeljagdspoort reviewed. *Antiquity, 67,* 273.

[7]Draper, P. (1975). !Kung women: Contrasts in sexual egalitarianism in foraging and sedentary contexts. In R. Reiter (Ed.), *Toward an anthropology of women* (pp. 77–109). New York: Monthly Review Press.

© Gallo Images/Corbis

In traditional Ju/'hoansi society, fathers as well as mothers show great indulgence to children, who do not fear or respect men more than women.

do not always take their offspring with them. At such times, the children are supervised by their fathers or other community adults, one-third to one-half of whom are always found in camp on any given day. Because these include men as well as women, children are as much habituated to the male as to the female presence.

Ju/'hoansi fathers spend much time with their offspring, interacting with them in nonauthoritarian ways. Although they may correct their children's behavior, so may women who neither defer to male authority nor use the threat of paternal punishment. Thus, among Ju/'hoansi foragers, no one grows up to respect or fear male authority any more than that of women. In fact, instead of being punished, a child who misbehaves will simply be carried away and introduced to some other more agreeable activity. Neither boys nor girls are assigned chores. In fact, children of both sexes do equally little work. Instead, they spend much of their time in play groups that include members of both sexes of widely different ages. Thus, Ju/'hoansi children have few experiences that set one sex apart from the other. Although older ones do amuse and keep an eye on younger ones, this is done spontaneously rather than as

an assigned task, and the burden does not fall any more heavily on girls than boys.

The situation is different among Ju/'hoansi who are sedentary villagers: Women spend much of their time in and around the home preparing food, attending to other domestic chores, and tending the children. Men, meanwhile, spend many hours outside the household growing crops, raising animals, or doing wage labor. As a result, children are less habituated to their presence. This remoteness of the men, coupled with their more extensive knowledge of the outside world and their cash, tends to strengthen male influence within the household.

Within village households, gender typecasting begins early. As soon as girls are old enough, they are expected to attend to many of the needs of their younger siblings, thereby allowing their mothers more time to deal with other domestic tasks. This not only shapes but also limits the behavior of girls, who cannot range as widely or explore as freely and independently as they could without little brothers and sisters in tow. Indeed, they must stay close to home and be more careful, more obedient, and more sensitive to the wishes of others than they otherwise might be. Boys, by contrast, have little to do with the handling of infants, and when they are assigned work, it generally takes them away from the household. Thus, the space that girls occupy becomes restricted, and they are trained in behaviors that promote passivity and nurturance, whereas boys begin to learn the distant, controlling roles they will later play as adult men.

From this comparison, we may begin to understand how a society's economy helps structure the way a child is brought up, and how this, in turn, influences the adult personality. It also shows that alternatives exist to the way that children are raised—which means that changing the societal conditions in which one's children grow up can alter significantly the way men and women act and interact.

Dependence Training

Some years after Margaret Mead's pioneering comparative research on gender in three Papua communities, psychological anthropologists carried out a significant and more wide-ranging series of cross-cultural studies on the effects of child rearing on personality. Among other things, their work showed that it is possible to distinguish between two general patterns of child rearing, which we may label for convenience "dependence training" and "independence training."[8]

Dependence training socializes people to think of themselves in terms of the larger whole. Aiming to cre-

dependence training Child-rearing practices that foster compliance in the performance of assigned tasks and dependence on the domestic group, rather than reliance on oneself.

[8]Whiting, J. W. M., & Child, I. L. (1953). *Child training and personality: A cross-cultural study.* New Haven, CT: Yale University Press.

ate community members whose idea of selfhood transcends individualism, it promotes compliance in the performance of assigned tasks and favors keeping individuals within the group. This pattern is typically associated with extended families, which consist of several husband-wife-children units within the same household. It is most likely to be found in societies with an economy based on subsistence farming, but also in foraging groups where several family groups may live together for at least part of the year. Big extended families are important, for they provide the labor force necessary to till the soil, tend whatever flocks are kept, and carry out other part-time economic pursuits considered necessary for existence. These large families, however, have built into them certain potentially disruptive tensions. For example, important family decisions must be collectively accepted and followed. In addition, the in-marrying spouses—husbands and/or wives who come from other groups—must conform themselves to the group's will, something that may not be easy for them.

Dependence training helps to keep these potential problems under control and involves both supportive and corrective aspects. On the supportive side, indulgence is shown to young children, particularly in the form of prolonged breastfeeding. Nursing continues for several years and is provided virtually on demand. This may be interpreted as rewarding the child for seeking support within the family, the main agent in meeting the child's needs. Also on the supportive side, children at a relatively early age are assigned a number of child-care and domestic tasks, all of which make significant and obvious contributions to the family's welfare. Thus, family members all actively work to help and support one another. On the corrective side, behavior the adults interpret as aggressive or selfish is likely to be actively discouraged. Moreover, the adults tend to be insistent on overall obedience, which is seen as rendering the individual subordinate to the group. This combination of encouragement and discouragement in the socialization process ideally produces individuals who are obedient, supportive, noncompetitive, generally responsible, and who will stay within the fold and not do anything potentially disruptive. Indeed, their very definition of self comes from their being a part of a larger social whole rather than from their mere individual existence.

Independence Training

By contrast, **independence training** emphasizes individual independence, self-reliance, and personal achievement. It is typically associated with societies in which a basic social unit consisting of parent(s) and offspring fends for itself. Independence training is particularly characteristic of mercantile (trading), industrial, and postindustrial societies where self-sufficiency and per-

sonal achievement are important traits for success, if not survival—especially for men, increasingly for women. Again, this pattern of training involves both encouragement and discouragement. On the negative side, infant feeding is prompted more by schedule than demand. In North America, as noted above, babies are typically nursed for only several months if at all. Many parents resort to an artificial nipple or teething ring (pacifier) to satisfy the baby's sucking instincts—typically doing so to calm the child rather than out of an awareness that infants need sucking to strengthen and train coordination in the muscles used for feeding and speech. In addition, North American parents are comparatively quick to start feeding infants baby food and even try to get them to feed themselves. Many are delighted if they can prop their infants up in the crib or playpen so that they can hold their own bottles. Moreover, as soon after birth as possible, children are given their own private space, away from their parents. As already noted, infants do not receive the amount of attention they so often do in nonindustrial societies. In the United States a mother may be very affectionate with her 15-week-old infant during the 20 percent of the time she is in contact with it, but for the other 80 percent of the time the baby is more or less on its own. Collective responsibility is not encouraged in children; they are not given responsible tasks to perform until later in childhood, and these are often carried out for personal benefit rather than as contributions to the family's welfare.

Displays of individual will, assertiveness, and even aggression are encouraged, or at least tolerated to a

In North American society, independence training pits individuals against one another through games and other forms of competition.

independence training Child-rearing practices that promote independence, self-reliance, and personal achievement on the part of the child.

greater degree than where dependence training is the rule. In schools, and even in the family, competition and winning are emphasized. Schools in the United States, for example, devote considerable resources to competitive sports. Competition is fostered within the classroom as well: overtly through such devices as spelling bees and awards, covertly through such devices as grading on a curve. In addition, there are various popularity contests, such as crowning a prom queen and king or holding an election to choose the classmate who is "best looking" or "most likely to succeed." Thus, by the time individuals have grown up in U.S. society, they have received a clear message: Life is about winning or losing, and losing is equal to failure. Often, success is viewed as something that comes at someone else's expense. As anthropologist Colin Turnbull observed, "Even the team spirit, so loudly touted" in U.S. school athletics (or out of school in Little League baseball and the like), "is merely a more efficient way, through limited cooperation, to 'beat' a greater number of people more efficiently."[9]

In sum, independence training generally encourages individuals to seek help and attention rather than to give it, and to try to exert individual dominance. Such qualities are useful in societies with hierarchical social structures that emphasize personal achievement and where individuals are expected to look out for their own interests.

Combined Dependence/Independence Training

In actuality, dependence and independence training represent extremes along a continuum, and particular

---

[9]Turnbull, C. M. (1983). *The human cycle* (p. 74). New York: Simon & Schuster.

situations may include elements of both. This is the case in child-rearing practices in food-foraging societies, for example. "Share and share alike" is the order of the day, so competitive behavior, which can interfere with the cooperation on which all else depends, is discouraged. Thus, infants receive much in the way of positive, affectionate attention from adults, including extended breastfeeding. This, as well as low pressure for compliance and a lack of emphasis on competition, encourages individuals to be more supportive of one another than is often the case in modern industrial and postindustrial societies. At the same time, personal achievement and independence are encouraged, for those individuals most capable of self-reliance are apt to be the most successful in the food quest.

In the United States the argument is sometimes made that "permissive" child rearing produces irresponsible adults. Yet the practices of food foragers seem to be about as "permissive" as they can get, and socially responsible adults are produced. The fact is, no particular system of child rearing is inherently better or worse than any other; what matters is whether the system is functional or dysfunctional in the context of a particular society. If compliant adults who are accepting of authority are required, then independence training will not work well in that society. Nor will dependence training serve very well a society whose adults are expected to be self-reliant, questioning of authority, and ready to explore and embrace new ways of doing things.

Sometimes, however, inconsistencies develop, and here we may look again at the situation in North America. As we have seen, independence training generally tends to be stressed in the United States, where

In the 1950s, in an effort to end its special relationship with the North American Indians, the U.S. federal government terminated its establishment of and aid to some Native reservations. This termination policy led many Natives to relocate to urban areas. Because they were a people whose definition of self springs from the group they were born into, separation from family and relatives led many to severe depression and related problems.

Estate of Jerome Tiger

people often speak in glowing terms about the worth of personal independence, the dignity of the individual, and so on. Their pronouncements, however, do not always suit their actions. In spite of the professed desire for personal independence and emphasis on competition, a strong underlying desire for compliance seems to exist. This is reflected, for example, in decisions handed down by the U.S. Supreme Court, which often sway between affirming the rights of individuals and privileging the authority of the government and other powerful institutions or corporations. It is reflected, too, by the fate of whistleblowers in both government and industry, who, if they do not lose their jobs, are at least accused of disloyalty, shunted to one side, and passed by when the rewards are handed out. They are not "team players." In business as well as in government, the rewards tend to be given to those who go along with the system, while criticism, no matter how constructive, is a risky business. In corporate and government bureaucracies, the ability to please, not shake up the system, is what is required for success. Yet, in spite of pressures for compliance, which would be most effectively served by dependence training, we continue to raise our children to be independent and then wonder why they so often refuse to behave in ways adults would have them behave.

GROUP PERSONALITY

From studies such as those reviewed here, it is clear that personality, child-rearing practices, and other aspects of culture are systematically interrelated. The existence of a close, if not causal, relationship between child-rearing practices and personality development, coupled with variation in child-rearing practices from one society to another, have led to a number of attempts to characterize whole societies in terms of particular kinds of personalities. Indeed, common sense suggests that personalities appropriate for one culture may be less appropriate for others. For example, an egocentric, aggressive personality would be out of place where cooperation and sharing are the keys to success.

Unfortunately, common sense, like conventional wisdom in general, is not always the truth. A question worth asking is: Can we describe a group personality without falling into stereotyping? The answer appears to be a qualified yes; in an abstract way, we may speak of a generalized "cultural personality" for a society, so long as we do not expect to find a uniformity of personalities within that society. Put another way, each individual develops certain personality characteristics that, from common experience, resemble those of other people. Yet, each human being also acquires distinct personality traits because every individual is exposed to unique sets of experiences and may react to shared experiences in novel ways. Moreover, each person brings to these experiences a one-of-a-kind genetic potential (except in the case of identical twins) that plays a role in determining personality.

This is evident, if not obvious, in every society—including even the most traditional ones. Consider for example the Yanomami people, who subsist on foraging and horticulture in the tropical forests of northern Brazil and southern Venezuela. Typically, Yanomami men strive to achieve a reputation for fierceness and

Yanomami men display their fierceness. While flamboyant, belligerent personalities are especially compatible with the Yanomami ideal that men should be fierce, some are quiet and retiring.

© N. Chagon/Anthro-Photo

aggressiveness, and they defend that reputation at the risk of serious personal injury and death. Yet, among the Yanomami there are men who have quiet and somewhat retiring personalities. It is all too easy for an outsider to overlook these individuals when other, more typical Yanomami are in the front row, pushing and demanding attention.

Modal Personality

Obviously, any fruitful approach to the problem of group personality must recognize that each individual is unique to a degree in both inheritance and life experiences and must expect a range of personality types in any society. In addition, personality traits that may be regarded as appropriate in men may not be so regarded in women, and vice versa. Given all this, we may focus our attention on the **modal personality** of a group, defined as the body of character traits that occur with the highest frequency in a culturally bounded population. Modal personality is a statistical concept, and, as such, it opens up for investigation the questions of how societies organize diversity and how diversity relates to culture change. Such questions are easily missed if one associates one particular type of personality with one particular culture, as did some earlier anthropologists (see Anthropologists of Note on Ruth Benedict). At the same time, modal personalities of different groups can be compared.

Data on modal personality are best gathered by means of psychological tests administered to a sample of the population in question. Those most often used include the Rorschach, or "ink blot," test and the Thematic Apperception Test (TAT). The latter consists of pictures, which the individual being tested is asked to describe and explain. These and other sorts of projective tests that have been used at one time or another have in common a purposeful ambiguity that forces the individual being tested to structure the situation before responding. The idea is that one's personality is reflected in the sort of structure or definition that he or she projects into the ambiguous situation. Along with such tests, observations recording the frequency of certain behaviors, the collection and analysis of life histories and dreams, and the analysis of popular tales, jokes, folkloric legends, and traditional myths are helpful in eliciting data on modal personality.

While having much to recommend it, the concept of modal personality as a means of dealing with group personality nevertheless presents certain difficulties. One is the complexity of the measurement techniques, which may be difficult to do in the field. For instance, an adequate representative sample of subjects is necessary. The problem here is twofold: making sure the sample is really representative and having the time and personnel necessary to administer the tests, conduct interviews, and so on, all of which can be lengthy proceedings. Also, the tests themselves constitute a problem, for those devised in one cultural setting may not be appropriate in another. This is more of a problem with the TAT than with some other tests, although different pictures have been devised for other cultures. Still, to minimize any cultural bias, it is best not to rely on projective tests alone. In addition to all this, language differences or conflicting cultural values between the researcher and the individuals being studied may inhibit communication and/or lead to misinterpretation. Finally, what is being measured must be questioned. Just what, for example, is aggression? Does everyone define it the same way? Is it a legitimate entity, or does it involve other variables?

National Character

In summer 2003, Italy's tourism minister publicly commented on "typical characteristics" of Germans, referring to them as "hyper-nationalistic blondes" and "beer drinking slobs" holding "noisy burping contests" on his country's beaches.[10] Outraged (and proud of his country's excellent beer), Germany's prime minister canceled his planned vacation to Italy and demanded an official apology. Of course, many Germans think of Italians as dark-eyed, hot-blooded spaghetti eaters. To say so in public, however, might cause uproar. Unflattering stereotypes about foreigners are deeply rooted in cultural traditions everywhere. Many Japanese believe Koreans are stingy, crude, and aggressive, while many Koreans see the Japanese as cold and arrogant. Similarly, we all have in mind some image, perhaps not well defined, of the typical citizen of Russia or Japan or

---

modal personality The body of character traits that occur with the highest frequency in a culturally bounded population.

[10]Italy-Germany verbal war hots up. (2003, July 9). *Deccan Herald.* (Bangalore, India).

Anthropologists of Note

Margaret Mead (1901–1978) ▪ Ruth Fulton Benedict (1887–1947)

Although all of the academic sciences are able to look back and honor certain "founding fathers," anthropologists take pride in the fact that they have a number of "founding mothers" whose pioneering work they celebrate. One is Margaret Mead, who was encouraged by her professor, Franz Boas, to pursue a career in anthropology when few other professions accepted women into their ranks. As a 24-year-old doctoral candidate, she set out for the Pacific Ocean island of Samoa to test the theory (then widely accepted) that the biological changes of adolescence were always fraught with social, psychological, and emotional stress. Based on her fieldwork there, she later wrote the book *Coming of Age in Samoa: A Psychological Study of Primitive Youth for Western Civilization*, explaining that adolescence does not have to be a time of stress and strain, but cultural conditions may make it so. Published in 1928, this book is generally credited as marking the beginning of psychological anthropology (culture and personality).

Pioneering works, however, are rarely without their faults, and *Coming of Age* is no exception. For one, Mead's time in the field (9 months) was not enough to understand fully the nuances of native speech and body language necessary to comprehend the innermost feelings of her informants. Furthermore, her sample of Samoan adolescents was a mere fifty, half of whom had not yet passed puberty. That

she exaggerated her findings is suggested by her dismissal as "deviant" those girls who did not fit her ideal and by inconsistencies with data collected elsewhere in Polynesia.

Despite its faults, Mead's book stands as a landmark for several reasons: Not only was it a deliberate test of a Euroamerican psychological hypothesis, but it also showed psychologists the value of modifying intelligence tests to make them appropriate for the population under study. Furthermore, by emphasizing the lesson to be drawn for Mead's own society, it laid the groundwork for the popularization of anthropology and advanced the cause of applied anthropology.

Ruth Benedict came late to anthropology; after her graduation from Vassar College, she taught high school English, published poetry, and tried her hand at social work. At age 31, she began studying anthropology, first at the New School for Social Research in New York City, and then at Columbia University. Having earned her doctorate under Boas, she joined his department. One of her own first students was Margaret Mead.

As Benedict herself once said, the main purpose of anthropology is "to make the world safe for human differences." In anthropology, she developed the idea that culture was a collective projection of the personality of those who created it. In her most famous book *Patterns of Culture* (1934), she compared the cultures of three peoples—the

Kwakiutl Indians of the Pacific Northwest coast in Canada, the Zuni Indians of the Arizona desert in the United States, and the Melanesians of Dobu Island off the southern shore of Papua New Guinea. She held that each was comparable to a great work of art, with an internal coherence and consistency of its own. Seeing the Kwakiutl as egocentric, individualistic, and ecstatic in their rituals, she labeled their cultural configuration "Dionysian" (named after the Greek God of wine and noisy feasting). The Zuni, whom she saw as living by the golden mean, wanting no part of excess or disruptive psychological states and distrusting of individualism, she characterized as "Apollonian" (named after the Greek God of poetry who exemplified beauty). The Dobuans, whose culture seemed to her magic-ridden, with everyone fearing and hating everyone else, she characterized as "paranoid."

Another theme of *Patterns of Culture* is that deviance should be understood as a conflict between an individual's personality and the norms of the culture to which the person belongs. Still in print today, *Patterns* has sold close to 2 million copies in a dozen languages. It had great influence on Mead during her cross-cultural gender studies among the Papuans in New Guinea. Although *Patterns of Culture* still enjoys popularity in some nonanthropological circles, anthropologists have long since abandoned its approach as impressionistic and not susceptible to replication. To compound the problem, Benedict's characterizations of cultures are misleading (the supposedly "Apollonian" Zunis, for example, indulge in such seemingly "Dionysian" practices as sword swallowing and walking over hot coals), and the use of such value-laden terms as *paranoid* prejudices others against the culture so labeled. Nonetheless, the book did have an enormous and valuable influence by focusing attention on the problem of the interrelation between culture and personality and by popularizing the reality of cultural variation.

England. Essentially, these are simply stereotypes. We might well ask, however, if these stereotypes have any basis in fact. In reality, does such a thing as national character exist?

Some anthropologists have thought that the answer may be yes. Accordingly, they embarked upon national character studies aiming to discover basic personality traits shared by the majority of the people of modern countries. Their research emphasized child-rearing practices and education as the factors theoretically responsible for such characteristics. Central figures in what came to be known as the culture and personality movement (especially Ruth Benedict, Margaret Mead, Weston LaBarre, and Geoffrey Gorer) conducted pioneering studies of national character using relatively small samples of informants. During World War II, techniques were developed for studying "culture at a distance" through the analysis of newspapers, books, photographs, popular films, and interviews with refugees and emigrants from the enemy countries in question. By investigating memories of childhood and cultural attitudes, and by examining graphic material for the appearance of recurrent themes and values, researchers attempted to portray national character.

The Japanese

At the height of World War II, quite a few anthropologists worked for the U.S. Office of War Information. In that context, Columbia University anthropology professor Ruth Benedict wrote a study of Japanese national character, published in 1946 as *The Chrysanthemum and the Sword*. Meanwhile, fellow anthropologist Geoffrey Gorer attempted to determine the underlying reasons for what he described as a contrast between the all-pervasive gentleness of family life in Japan, which has charmed nearly every visitor, and the overwhelming brutality and sadism of the Japanese military at war. Strongly under the influence of Freud, Gorer sought his causes in the toilet-training practices of the Japanese, which he believed were severe and threatening. He suggested that because Japanese infants were forced to control their bowel movements before they had acquired the necessary muscular or neurological development, they grew up filled with repressed rage. As adults, the Japanese were able to express this rage in their ruthlessness in war.[11]

Because Benedict and Gorer were not able to do fieldwork in Japan during the war, they helped break ground in the study of "culture at a distance." After the war was over, though, the toilet-training hypothesis was tested, and it was found that the severity of Japanese toilet training was a myth. Children were not subject to threats of severe punishment. Nor were all Japanese soldiers brutal and sadistic in war; some were, but then so were some North Americans. Also, the participation of many Japanese in postwar peace movements in the Far East hardly conformed to the wartime image of brutality. Studies by Benedict and Gorer, along with others, were most important not in revealing the importance of Japanese bowel control to the national character but in pointing out the dangers of generalizing from insufficient evidence and employing simplistic individual psychology to explain complex social phenomena.

Objections to National Character Studies

Critics of national character theories have emphasized the tendency for such work to be based on unscientific and overgeneralized data. The concept of modal personality has a certain statistical validity, they argue, but to generalize the qualities of a complex country on the basis of such limited data is to lend insufficient recognition to the countless individuals who vary from the generalization. Further, such studies tend to be highly subjective; for example, the tendency during the late 1930s and 1940s for anthropologists to characterize the German people as aggressive paranoids was obviously a reflection of wartime hostility rather than scientific objectivity. Finally, it has been pointed out that occupation and social status tend to cut across national boundaries. A French farmer may have less in common with a French lawyer than he does with a German farmer.

An alternative approach to national character—one that allows for the fact that not all personalities will conform to cultural ideals—is that of anthropologist Francis Hsu. His approach was to study the **core values** of a country's culture and related personality traits. The Chinese, he suggested, value kin ties and cooperation above all else. To them, mutual dependence is the very essence of personal relationships and has been for thousands of years. Compliance and subordination of one's will to that of family and kin transcend all else, while self-reliance is neither promoted nor a source of pride.

Perhaps the core value held in highest esteem by North Americans of European descent is "rugged individualism," traditionally for men but in recent decades for women as well. Each individual is supposed to be able to achieve anything he or she likes, given a willingness to work hard enough. From their earliest years, individuals are subjected to relentless pressures to excel, and as we have already noted, competition and winning are seen as crucial to this. Undoubtedly, this contributes

---

[11]Gorer, G. (1943). Themes in Japanese culture. *Transactions of the New York Academy of Sciences, Series II, 5.*

core values Those values especially promoted by a particular culture.

VISUAL COUNTERPOINT The core values of Chinese culture promote the integration of the individual into a larger group. By contrast, the core values of Euroamerican culture promote the separation of the individual from the group.

to the restlessness and drivenness of North American society, and to the degree that it motivates individuals to work hard and to go where the jobs are, it fits well with the demands of a modern market. Thus, while individuals in Chinese traditional society are firmly bound into a larger group to which they have lifelong obligations, most urban North Americans are isolated from all other relatives other than their young children and spouse—and even the commitment to marriage has lessened.[12] Many couples live together without being married or having plans for marriage (Figure 5.1). Increasingly, when couples do marry, prenuptial agreements are made to protect individual assets in case of divorce—and something like 50 percent of marriages do end in divorce. Even parents and children have no legal obligations to one another once the latter have reached the age of majority. Indeed, many North American parents seem to "lose" their children in their teenage years.

ALTERNATIVE GENDER MODELS FROM A CROSS-CULTURAL PERSPECTIVE

As we have already discussed, the gender roles assigned to each sex vary from culture to culture and have an impact on personality formation. But what if the sex of an individual is not self-evident, as in this chapter's Original Study? The biological facts of human nature are not always as clear-cut as most people assume. At the level of chromosomes (the paired intracellular structures that contain our genes), biological sex is determined according to whether a person's 23rd chromosomal set is

Unmarried couples cohabiting continues to rise

Year	Number
1960	439,000
1970	523,000
1980	1.6 million
1990	3.2 million
2000	5.5 million

FIGURE 5.1

Number of unmarried couples cohabiting in the United States, by year. In the year 2000, 8.5 percent of all cohabiting couples in the United States were unmarried.

[12]Observations on North American culture in this paragraph are drawn primarily from Natadecha-Sponsal, P. (1993). The young, the rich and the famous: Individualism as an American cultural value. In P. R. DeVita & J. D. Armstrong (Eds.), *Distant mirrors: America as a foreign culture* (pp. 46–53). Belmont, CA: Wadsworth.

XX (female) or XY (male). Some of the genes on these chromosomes control sexual development. This standard biological package does not apply to all humans, for a considerable number of **intersexuals** are born with reproductive organs, genitalia, and/or sex chromosomes that are not exclusively male or female. These people do not fit neatly into a binary gender standard.[13]

For example, some people are born with a genetic mutation that gives biological females only one X chromosome instead of the usual two. A person with this chromosomal complex, known as Turner's syndrome, develops female external genitalia, but has nonfunctional ovaries and is therefore infertile. Other individuals are born with the XY sex chromosomes of a male but have an abnormality on the X chromosome that affects the body's sensitivity to androgens (male hormones). This is known as androgen insensitivity syndrome (AIS). An adult XY person with complete AIS appears fully female with a normal clitoris, labia, and breasts. Internally, these individuals possess testes, but they are otherwise born without a complete set of either male or female internal genital organs. They generally possess a short, blind-ended vagina.

"Hermaphrodites" comprise a distinct category of intersexuality—although the terms *male pseudohermaphrodite* and *female pseudohermaphrodite* are often used to refer to a range of intersex conditions. The name, objected to by many, comes from a figure in Greek mythology: Hermaphroditus (son of Hermes, messenger of the gods, and Aphrodite, goddess of beauty and love) who became half-male and half-female when he fell in love with a nymph and his body fused with hers. True hermaphrodites have both testicular and ovarian tissue. They may have a separate ovary and testis, but more commonly they have an ovotestis—a gonad containing both sorts of tissue. About 60 percent of hermaphrodites possess XX (female) sex chromosomes, and the remainder may have XY or a mosaic (a mixture). Their external genitalia may be ambiguous or female, and they may have a uterus or (more commonly) a hemi-uterus (half uterus).

Biologist Anne Fausto-Sterling, a specialist in this area, notes that the concept of intersexuality is "rooted in the very ideas of male and female," in an idealized biological world in which:

> human beings are divided into two kinds: a perfectly dimorphic species. Males have an X and a Y chromosome, testes, a penis and all of the appropriate internal plumbing for delivering urine and semen to the outside world. They also have well-known secondary sexual characteristics, including a muscular build and facial hair. Women have two X chromosomes, ovaries, all of the internal plumbing to transport urine and ova to the outside world, a system to support pregnancy and fetal development, as well as a variety of recognizable secondary sexual characteristics.
>
> That idealized story papers over many obvious caveats: some women have facial hair, some men have none; some women speak with deep voices, some men veritably squeak. Less well known is the fact that on close inspection, absolute dimorphism disintegrates even at the level of basic biology. Chromosomes, hormones, the internal sex structures, the gonads and external genitalia all vary more than most people realize. Those born outside of the . . . dimorphic mold are called intersexuals.[14]

Intersexuality may be unusual but is not uncommon. In fact, about 1 percent of all humans are intersexed in some way—in other words, about 60 million people worldwide.[15] Until recently, it was rarely discussed publicly in many societies. Since the mid-20th century, individuals with financial means in postindustrial parts of the world have had the option of reconstructive surgery and hormonal treatments to alter such conditions, and many parents faced with raising a visibly intersexed child in a culture unaccepting of such minorities have chosen this option for their baby. However, there is a growing movement to put off such irreversible procedures indefinitely or until the child becomes old enough to be the one to make the choice. Obviously, a society's attitude toward these individuals can impact their personality—their fundamental sense of self and how they express it.

MEDIATREK

To learn more about the challenges faced by intersexed individuals, go to MediaTrek 5.2 on the companion Web site or CD-ROM.

---

[13]This paragraph and the two following are based on several sources: Chase, C. (1998). Hermaphrodites with attitude. *Gay and Lesbian Quarterly, 4*(2), 189–211; Dumurat-Dreger, A. (1998, May/June). "Ambiguous sex" or ambivalent medicine? *The Hastings Center Report, 28*(3), 2, 435 (posted on the Intersex Society of North America Web site: *www.isna.org*); Fausto-Sterling, A. (1993). The five sexes: Why male and female are not enough. *The Sciences, 33*(2), 20–24; the Mayo Clinic Web site.

intersexuals People born with reproductive organs, genitalia, and/or sex chromosomes that are not exclusively male or female.

---

[14]Fausto-Sterling, A. (2000, July). The five sexes revisited. *The Sciences*, 20–24.

---

[15]Fausto-Sterling, A. (2003, August 2). Personal email communication.

In addition to people who are genetically intersexed, throughout history some individuals have been subjected to a surgical removal of some of their sexual organs. In many cultures, male prisoners or war captives have undergone forced castration, crushing or cutting the testicles. Archaeological evidence from Egypt, Mesopotamia, Persia, and China suggests that the cultural practice of castrating war captives may have begun several thousand years ago. Young boys captured during war or slave-raiding expeditions were often castrated before being sold and shipped off to serve in foreign households, including royal courts. In the Ottoman Empire, where they could occupy a variety of important functions in the sultan's household from the mid-15th century onward, they became known as *eunuchs.* As suggested by the original meaning of the word, which is Greek for "guardian of the bed," castrated men were often put in charge of a ruler's harem, the women's quarters in a household. Eunuchs could also rise to high status as priests and administrators and were even appointed to serve as army commanders. Some powerful lords, kings, and emperors kept hundreds of eunuchs in their castles and palaces.

In addition to forced castration, there were also men who engaged in self-castration or underwent voluntary castration. For example, early Christian monks in Egypt and neighboring regions voluntarily abstained from sexual relationships and sometimes castrated themselves for the sake of the kingdom of heaven. Such genital mutilation was also practiced among Coptic monks, until the early 20th century.[16] In the late 15th century, Europe saw the emergence of a category of musical eunuchs known as *castrati.* These eunuchs sang female parts in church choirs after Roman Catholic authorities banned women singers on the basis of Saint Paul's instruction, "Let your women keep silence in the churches." Simultaneously, castrati began performing female roles in operas. Castrated before they reached puberty so as to retain their high voices, these selected boys were often orphaned or came from poor families. Without a functioning testis to produce male sex hormones, physical development into manhood is aborted, so deeper voices, as well as body hair, semen production, and other usual male attributes, were not part of a castrati's biology. During the 1700s, at the height of castrati popularity, an estimated 4,000 boys a year were castrated in Italy alone. Some became celebrated performers, drawing huge fees, adopting fantastic stage names, and gaining notoriety for their eccentricity on and off stage. Not necessarily homosexual, castrati were "gender benders" who could engage in sexual relations with men or women, or both. The phenomenon of castrati continued until about 1900, when Roman Catholic authorities

in the Vatican banned their role in church music. By then, the eunuch systems in the Chinese and Ottoman Empires were also about to be abolished.[17]

Although human castration was not practiced among North American Indians, many indigenous communities in the Great Plains and Southwest created alternative social space for intersexed or transgendered individuals. (**Transgenders** are people who crossover or occupy a culturally accepted intermediate position in the binary male—female gender construction.) For example, the Lakota of the northern Plains had an intermediate category of culturally accepted transgendered males who dressed as women and were thought to possess both male and female spirits. They called (and still call) these third-gender individuals *winkte,* applying the term to a male "who wants to be a woman." Thought to have special curing powers, *winktes* traditionally enjoyed considerable prestige in their communities. Among the

Shown here is the famous Zuni Indian two-spirit named We'wha. For a man to assume a feminine identity was not regarded as abnormal by the Zuni. In fact, such individuals were regarded as special in that they bridged the gap between the purely feminine and purely masculine.

[16]Abbot, E. (2001). *A history of celibacy.* Cambridge, MA: Da Capo Press.

[17]Taylor, G. (2000). *Castration: Abbreviated history of western manhood.* (pp. 38–44, 252–259). New York: Routledge.

transgenders People who cross-over or occupy a culturally accepted intermediate position in the binary male—female gender construction.

neighboring Cheyenne, such a person was called *hemanah,* literally meaning "half-man, half-woman."[18]

French traders who came to the Great Plains in the 1600s eventually encountered cross-dressing Native American men, whom they called *berdache* (also spelled *burdash*). The name derived from the Persian word *bardah,* which referred to eunuchs or slaves. The French term *berdache* had acquired obvious contemptuous applications for effeminacy and celibacy, as well as cowardice, and it was broadly used for eunuchs, castrati, cross-dressers, and homosexuals alike. Although early anthropological literature adopted the word, the preferred term for North American Indians today is "two-spirits," which avoids the negative connotations associated with the term *berdache.*[19]

Mapping the sexual landscape, anthropologists have come to realize that gender bending exists in many cultures all around the world, playing a significant role in shaping behaviors and personalities. For instance, third-gender individuals are well known in Samoa, where males who take on the identity of females are referred to as *fa'afafines* ("the female way"). Becoming a *fa'afafine* is an accepted option for boys who prefer to dance, cook, clean house, and care for children and the elderly. In large families, it is not unusual to find two or three boys being raised as girls to take on domestic roles in their households. As American anthropologist Lowell Holmes recently reported,

> In fact, they tend to be highly valued because they can do the heavy kinds of labor that most women find difficult. A Samoan nun once told me how fortunate it is to have a fa'afafine in the family to help with the household chores. [There] is also the claim made that fa'afafines never have sexual relations with each other but, rather, consider themselves to be "sisters." [They] are religious and go to church regularly dressed as women and . . . some are even Sunday school teachers. Fa'afafines often belong to women's athletic teams, and some even serve as coaches.[20]

Among many other third genders, the best known may be the *hijra* (or *hijadas*) in India. *Hijra* is an Urdu term that covers transgendered men, castrated males,

Photography Hugh Hartshorne. Copyright Re Angle Picture

Transgendering occurs in many cultures, but is not always publicly tolerated. Among Polynesians inhabiting Pacific Ocean islands such as Tonga and Samoa, however, such male transvestites are culturally accepted. Samoans refer to these third genders as *fa'afafines* ("the female way").

and hermaphrodites who dress and behave like women in an exaggerated way. As Hindu devotees of the Mother Goddess Bahuchara Mata, their cultural role is to perform blessings for young married couples and male babies. Beyond small earnings for those rituals, they survive by begging, chanting, running bathhouses, and sometimes prostitution.[21]

None of these transgendered cultural types can be simply lumped together as homosexuals. For example, the Tagalog-speaking people in the Philippines use the word *bakla* to refer to a man who views himself "as a male with a female heart." These individuals cross-dress on a daily basis, often becoming more female than females in their use of heavy makeup, in the clothing they wear, and in the way they walk. Like the Samoan *fa'afafines,* they are generally not sexually attracted to other *bakla* but are drawn to heterosexual men instead.

In sum, human cultures in the course of thousands of years have creatively dealt with a wide range of inherited and artificially imposed sexual features. The impor-

[18]Medicine, B. (1994). Gender. In M. B. Davis (Ed.), *Native America in the twentieth century.* New York: Garland.

[19]Jacobs, S. E. (1994). Native American two-spirits. *Anthropology Newsletter, 35*(8), 7.

[20]Holmes, L. D. (2000). Paradise bent (film review). *American Anthropologist, 102*(3), 604–605.

[21]Nanda, S. (1990). *Neither man nor woman: The hijras of India.* Belmont, CA: Wadsworth.

Anthropology Applied

Anthropologists and Mental Health

One consequence of "development" in the recently emerged states of Africa, Asia, and Central and South America is a rising incidence of mental disturbances among their people. Similarly, mental health problems abound among ethnic minorities living within industrialized countries. Unfortunately, orthodox approaches to mental health have not been successful at dealing with these problems for a number of reasons. For one, the various ethnic groups have different attitudes toward mental disorders than do medical practitioners trained in Western (Euroamerican) medicine. For another, the diverse lifeways of different ethnic groups produce culturally patterned health conditions including culture-bound syndromes not recognized by the orthodox medical profession. Among Puerto Ricans, for example, a widely held belief is that spirits are active in the world and that they influence human behavior. Thus, for someone with a psychiatric problem, it makes sense to go to a native spiritist for help rather than to a psychiatrist. In a Puerto

Rican community, going to a spiritist is normal. Not only does the client not understand the symbols of psychiatry, but to go to a psychiatrist implies that he or she is crazy and requires restraint or removal from the community.

Although practitioners of Western medicine have traditionally regarded spiritists and other folk healers as ignorant, if not charlatans, experimentation began in the 1950s with community-based treatment in which psychiatrists cooperated with traditional healers. Since then, this approach has gained widespread acceptance in many parts of the world, as when (in 1977) the World Health Organization advocated cooperation between health professionals and native specialists (including herbalists and midwives). As a consequence, many anthropologists have found work as cultural brokers, studying the cultural system of the client population and explaining this to the health professionals while also explaining the world of the psychiatrists to the folk healers and the client population.

To cite one example, as a part of Miami Community Mental Health Program in Florida, a field team led by an anthropologist was established to work with the Puerto Rican community of Dade County.[a] Like other ethnic communities in the area, this one was characterized by low incomes, high rents, and a plethora of health (including mental health) problems, yet health facilities and social service agencies were underused. Working in the community, the team successfully built up support networks among the Puerto Ricans involving extended families, churches, clubs, and spiritists. At the same time, they gathered information about the community, providing it to appropriate social service agencies. At the Dade County Hospital, team members acted as brokers between the psychiatric personnel and their Puerto Rican clients, and a training program was implemented for the mental health staff. ■ ■ ■

[a]See Willigan, J. V. (1986). *Applied anthropology* (pp. 128–129, 133–139). South Hadley, MA: Bergin and Garvey.

---

tance of studying complex categories involving intersexuality and transgendering is that doing so enables us to recognize the existing range of gender alternatives and to debunk false stereotypes. It is one more piece of the human puzzle—an important one that prods us to rethink social codes and the range of forces that shape personality as well as each society's definition of normal.

NORMAL AND ABNORMAL PERSONALITY

The standards that define normal behavior for any culture are determined by that culture itself. So it is that in mainstream North American culture, in contrast to those just noted, transgender behavior has traditionally been regarded as abnormal. If a North American man dresses as a woman, it is still widely viewed as a cause for concern and is likely to lead to psychiatric intervention. There are countless examples of the fact that what seems normal in one culture is often considered abnormal in another.

The father of this book's senior author as a little boy. In the United States, boys spent their earliest years in the company of women and were commonly dressed like girls. Adoption of a masculine identity required rejection of an earlier feminine identity. Not until well into the 20th century did this change.

© William A. Haviland

Consider, for instance, contrasting attitudes toward individuals who enter into altered states of consciousness. Among the Yolmo people of Melemchi, Nepal, the shaman (*bombo*) calls the gods or spirits into the room to let them speak through him.[22] To do this, he symbolically rides into their world. Through drumming and chanting, he enters an altered state of consciousness, or trance. This allows him to communicate with the gods. To outsiders, it appears the shaman is hallucinating—seeing visions, smelling smells, hearing sounds, and experiencing bodily sensations that seem real, but are not seen, smelled, heard, or felt by others who are present but have not entered into trance.

In contemporary North American society, behavior like that of the Melemchi shaman is generally regarded as deviant, and the practice of entering altered states is apt to be seen as a sign of mental instability or even unlawful activity if it involves the use of hallucinogenic substances. Yet, there is nothing abnormal per se about the ability to enter trancelike states and experience a wide range of hallucinations. To the contrary, "The desire to alter consciousness periodically is an innate, normal drive analogous to hunger or the sexual drive."[23] There is even good evidence that chimpanzees, various monkeys, cats, dogs, and other animals hallucinate and that the ability is a function of the mammalian, not just human, nervous system.[24] Thus, the ability to enter altered states and experience visions and other sensations appears to predate the appearance of *Homo sapiens,* and it is not surprising that the ability to enter trance is a human universal. Although some societies try to suppress the practice, the vast majority (like the Yolmo people) accepts trancing and shapes it to their own ends. One study, for example, found that as

Melemchi shaman in Nepal. Although the ability to enter trance is a consequence of having a normal human nervous system, some societies, such as that of the United States, define entering trance as abnormal, while many others accept it as normal. Among the Yolmo people of Nepal, men are trained to enter into a trance state through drumming and chanting. While in trance, they can communicate with the spirit world, bringing messages that help heal people and animals.

many as 437 out of a sample of 488 historically known societies had some form of institutionalized altered states of consciousness.[25]

It is also true that the abnormal may become normal. In this vein, anthropologist Emily Martin cites changing attitudes toward manic depression and attention deficit hyperactivity disorder (ADHD).[26] Commonly regarded as dreaded liabilities, she suggests that, in North America, the manic and hyperactivity aspects

---

[22]Womack, M. (1994). Program 5: Psychological anthropology. *Faces of culture.* Fountain Valley, CA: Coast Telecourses, Inc.

[23]Furst, P. T. (1976). *Hallucinogens and culture* (p. 7). Novato, CA: Chandler and Sharp.

[24]Lewis-Williams, J. D., & Dowson, T. A. (1988). Signs of all times: Entoptic phenomena in Upper Paleolithic art. *Current Anthropology, 29,* 202.

[25]Lewis-Williams, J. D., & Dowson, T. A. (1993). On vision and power in the Neolithic: Evidence from the Decorated Monuments. *Current Anthropology, 34,* 55.

[26]Martin, E. (1999). Flexible survivors. *Anthropology News, 40* (6), 5–7.

are coming to be seen as assets in the quest for success. More and more, they are interpreted as indicative of "finely wired, exquisitely alert nervous systems" that make one constantly alert for signs of change, able to fly from one thing to another while pushing the limits of everything, and doing it all with an intense level of energy focused totally in the future. These are extolled as high virtues in the corporate world, and to be called "hyper" or "manic" is increasingly an expression of approval.

Is all this to suggest that "normalcy" is a meaningless concept when applied to personality? Within the context of a particular culture, the concept of normal personality is quite meaningful. Irving Hallowell, a major figure in the development of psychological anthropology, somewhat ironically observed that it is normal to share the delusions traditionally accepted by one's society. Abnormality involves the development of a delusional system of which the culture does not approve. The individual who is disturbed because he or she cannot adequately measure up to the norms of society and be happy may be termed *neurotic*. When a person's delusional system is so different that it in no way reflects his or her society's norms, the individual may be termed *psychotic*.

If severe enough, culturally induced conflicts can produce psychosis and also determine the form of the psychosis. In a culture that encourages aggressiveness and suspicion, the insane person may be one who is passive and trusting. In a culture that encourages passivity and trust, the insane person may be the one who is aggressive and suspicious. Just as each society establishes its own norms, each individual is unique in his or her perceptions. Many anthropologists see the only meaningful criterion for personality evaluation as the correlation between personality and social conformity. From their point of view, insanity is a culturally constructed mental illness, and people are considered insane when they fail to conform to a culturally defined range of normal behavior.

Although it is true that each particular culture defines what is and is not normal behavior, the situation is complicated by findings suggesting that major categories of mental disorders may be universal types of human affliction. Take, for example, schizophrenia, probably the most common of all psychoses, and one that may be found in any culture, no matter how it may manifest itself. Individuals afflicted by schizophrenia experience distortions of reality that impair their ability to function adequately, so they withdraw from the social world into their own psychological shell. Although environmental factors play a role, evidence exists that schizophrenia is caused by a biochemical disorder for which

there is an inheritable tendency. One of its more severe forms is paranoid schizophrenia. Those suffering from it fear and mistrust most everyone. They hear voices that whisper dreadful things to them, and they are convinced that someone is "out to get them." Acting on this conviction, they engage in bizarre sorts of behavior, which lead to their removal from society.

A precise image of paranoid schizophrenia is one of the so-called **ethnic psychoses** known as Windigo. Such psychoses involve symptoms of mental disorders specific to particular ethnic groups (Table 5.1). Windigo psychosis is limited to northern Algonquian Indian groups such as the Cree and Ojibwa. In their

© David Young-Wolff

Anorexia nervosa, a psychological eating disorder evidenced in self-induced starvation, occurs most frequently among females in Western countries, but can now be seen in some other industrializing countries, such as Korea.

ethnic psychoses Mental disorders specific to particular ethnic groups.

| TABLE 5.1 | ETHNIC PSYCHOSES AND OTHER CULTURE-BOUND SYNDROMES |

Name of Disorder	Culture	Description
Amok	Malasia (also observed in Java, Philippines, Africa, and Tierra del Fuego)	A disorder characterized by sudden, wild outbursts of homicidal aggression in which the afflicted person may kill or injure others. The rage disorder is usually found in males who are rather withdrawn, quiet, and inoffensive prior to the onset of the disorder. Stress, sleep deprivation, extreme heat, and alcohol are among the conditions thought to precipitate the disorder. Several stages have been observed: Typically in the first stage the person becomes more withdrawn; then a period of brooding follows in which a loss of reality contact is evident. Ideas of persecution and anger predominate. Finally, a phase of automatism, or *amok,* occurs, in which the person jumps up, yells, grabs a knife, and stabs people or objects within reach. Exhaustion and depression usually follow, with amnesia for the rage.
Anorexia nervosa	Western countries	A disorder occurring most frequently among young women in which a preoccupation with thinness produces a refusal to eat. This condition can result in death.
Latah	Malasia	A fear reaction often occurring in middle-aged women of low intelligence who are subservient and self-effacing. The disorder is precipitated by the word *snake* or by tickling. It is characterized by echolalia (repetition of the words and sentences of others). The disturbed individual may also react with negativism and the compulsive use of obscene language.
Koro	Southeast Asia (particularly Malasia)	A fear reaction or anxiety in which the person fears that his penis will withdraw into his abdomen and he will die. This reaction may appear after sexual overindulgence or excessive masturbation. The anxiety is typically very intense and of sudden onset. The condition is "treated" by having the penis held firmly by the patient or by family members or friends. Often the penis is clamped to a wooden box.
Windigo	Algonquian Indians of Canada and northern United States	A fear reaction in which a hunter becomes anxious and agitated, convinced that he is bewitched. Fears center on his being turned into a cannibal by the power of a monster with an insatiable craving for human flesh.
Kitsunetsuki	Japan	A disorder in which victims believe that they are possessed by foxes and are said to change their facial expressions to resemble foxes. Entire families are often possessed and banned by the community.
Pibloktoq and other Arctic hysterias	Circumpolar peoples from Lapland eastward across Siberia, northern Alaska, and Canada to Greenland	A disorder brought on by fright, which is followed by a short period of bizarre behavior; victim may tear clothes off, jump in water or fire, roll in snow, try to walk on the ceiling, throw things, thrash about, and "speak in tongues." Outburst followed by return to normal behavior.

SOURCE: Based on Carson, R. C., Butcher, J. N., & Coleman, J. C. (1990). *Abnormal psychology and modern life* (8th ed., p. 85). Glenview, IL: Scott Foresman.

traditional belief systems, these northern Indians recognized the existence of cannibalistic monsters called Windigos. Individuals afflicted by the psychosis developed the delusion that, falling under control of these monsters, they themselves were being transformed into Windigos, with a craving for human flesh. As this happened, they saw people around them turning into various edible animals—fat, juicy beavers, for instance. Although no instances where sufferers of Windigo psychosis actually ate another human being are known, they nonetheless developed an acute fear of doing so.

Furthermore, other members of their group genuinely feared that they might.

At first, Windigo psychosis seems different from clinical cases of paranoid schizophrenia found in Euroamerican cultures, but a closer look suggests otherwise; the disorder was merely being expressed in ways compatible with traditional northern Algonquian culture. Ideas of persecution, instead of being directed toward other humans, are directed toward supernatural beings (the Windigo monsters); cannibalistic panic replaces panic expressed in other forms. The northern

Algonquian Indian, like Euroamericans, expresses his or her problem in terms compatible with the appropriate view of the self and its behavioral environment. Traditionally though, the northern Algonquian was removed from society not by being committed to a mental institution but by being killed.

Windigo behavior has seemed exotic and dramatic to Euroamericans. When all is said and done, however, the imagery and symbolism that a psychotic person has to draw upon is that which his or her culture has to offer, and in northern Algonquian culture, these involve myths in which cannibal giants figure prominently. By contrast, the delusions of Irish schizophrenics draw upon the images and symbols of Irish Catholicism, and feature Virgin and Savior motifs. Euroamericans, on the other hand, tend toward secular or electromagnetic persecution delusions. The underlying structure of the mental disorder is the same in all cases, but its expression is culturally specific.

Chapter Summary

■ Enculturation, the process by which individuals become members of their society, begins soon after birth. Its first agents are the members of an individual's household, but later, other members of society become involved. For enculturation to proceed, individuals must possess self-awareness, the ability to perceive and reflect upon themselves as individuals. For self-awareness to emerge and function, four basic orientations are necessary to structure the behavioral environment in which the self acts. First among these is object orientation, learning about a world of objects other than the self. Also required is a sense of both spatial and temporal orientation. Finally, the growing individual needs a normative orientation, or an understanding of the values, ideals, and standards that constitute the behavioral environment.

■ A child's birthright and social identity is established through personal naming, a universal practice with numerous cross-cultural variations. A name is an important device for self-definition—without one, an individual has no identity, no self. Many cultures mark the naming of a child with a special ceremony.

■ Personality refers to the distinctive ways a person thinks, feels, and behaves. Along with psychoanalysts, most anthropologists believe early childhood experiences play a key role in shaping adult personality. A prime goal of anthropologists has been to produce objective studies that test this theory. Cross-cultural studies of gender-related personality characteristics, for example, show that whatever biologically based personality differences exist between men and women, they are extremely malleable. A society's economy helps structure the way children are brought up, which in turn influences their adult personalities.

■ Psychological anthropologists, on the basis of cross-cultural studies, have established the interrelation of personality, child-rearing practices, and other aspects of culture. For example, dependence training, usually associated with traditional farming societies, tries to ensure that members of society will willingly and routinely work for the benefit of the group, performing the jobs assigned to them. At the opposite extreme, independence training, typical of societies characterized by independent nuclear families, puts a premium on self-reliance and independent behavior. Although a society may emphasize one sort of behavior over the other, it may not emphasize it to the same degree in both sexes. Some psychological anthropologists contend that child-rearing practices have their roots in a society's customs for meeting the basic physical needs of its members, and that these practices produce particular kinds of adult personalities.

■ Gender behaviors and relations are extremely malleable and vary cross-culturally. Each culture presents different opportunities and expectations concerning ideal or acceptable male–female behavior. In some cultures, male–female relations are based on equal status, with both genders expected to behave similarly. In others, however, male–female relations are based on inequality and are marked by different standards of expected behavior. Anthropological research demonstrates that gender dominance is a cultural construct and, consequently, that alternative male–female social arrangements can be created if so desired.

■ Early on, anthropologists began to work on the problem of whether it is possible to delineate a group personality without falling into stereotyping. Each culture chooses, from the vast array of possibilities, those traits that it sees as normative or ideal. Individuals who conform to these traits are rewarded; the rest are not. The modal personality of a group is the personality typical of a culturally bounded population, as indicated by the central tendency of a defined frequency distribution. As a statistical concept, it opens up for investigation how societies organize the diverse personalities of their members, some of which conform more than others to the modal "type."

■ National character studies have focused on the modal characteristics of modern countries. They have attempted to determine the child-rearing practices and education that shape such a group personality. Many anthropologists believe national character theories are based on unscientific and overgeneralized data; others have chosen to focus on the core values promoted in particular societies while recognizing that success in instilling these values in individuals may vary considerably.

■ Intersexuals are individuals who do not fit neatly into either a male or female biological standard or into a binary gender standard. Many cultures have created social space for transgendered individuals who are culturally accepted as a third gender category.

■ What defines normal behavior in any culture is determined by the culture itself, and what may be acceptable, or even admirable, in one may not be in another. Abnormality involves developing personality traits not accepted by a culture. Culturally induced conflicts not only can produce psychological disturbance but can determine the form of the disturbance as well. Similarly, mental disorders that have a biological cause, like schizophrenia, will be expressed by symptoms specific to the culture of the afflicted individual.

Questions for Reflection

1. Every society faces the challenge of humanizing its children. What child-rearing practices did you experience that embody the values and social codes of your society?

2. Considering the cultural significance of naming ceremonies in so many societies, what do you think motivated your parents when they named you? Does that have any influence on your sense of self?

3. Margaret Mead's cross-cultural research on gender relations showed that male dominance is a cultural construct and, consequently, that alternative gender arrangements can be created. Looking at your grandparents, parents, and siblings, do you see any changes in your own family? What about your own community? Do you think such changes are positive?

4. Do you fit within the acceptable range of your society's modal personality? How so?

5. Given that about 60 million people currently are intersexed, and in light of the fact that a very small fraction of these people have access to reconstructive sexual surgery, what do you think of societies that have created cultural space for a third gender option?

Key Terms

Self-awareness	Modal personality
Naming ceremony	Core values
Personality	Intersexuals
Dependence training	Transgenders
Independence training	Ethnic psychoses

Multimedia Review Tools

Companion Web Site

Visit **http://www.wadsworth.com/anthropology_d/** and click on the companion Web site for this textbook to access a wide range of material to aid your study of anthropology. Among the options for self-study in each chapter are learning objectives, flash cards, Internet activities, Web links, InfoTrac College Edition exercises, and practice tests that can be scored and emailed to your instructor.

CD-ROM

The *Doing Anthropology Today* CD-ROM supplied with your textbook provides unique and valuable information designed to enhance your learning experience. This interactive multimedia resource includes video clips, interviews with renowned anthropologists, map and timeline exercises, chapter study quizzes, and much more. *Doing Anthropology Today* will not only help you in achieving your grade goals, but it will also make your learning experience fun and exciting!

Suggested Readings

Barnouw, V. (1985). *Culture and personality* (4th ed.). Homewood, IL: Dorsey Press.

This is a revision of a well-respected text designed to introduce students to psychological anthropology.

Brettell, C. B., & Sargent, C. F. (Eds.). (2000). *Gender in cross-cultural perspective* (3rd. ed.). Upper Saddle River, NJ: Prentice-Hall.

A collection of classic and contemporary gender readings on a range of topics, including the cultural construction of femininity and masculinity and the impact of globalization on gender issues.

Gottlieb, A., & DeLoache, J. S. (Eds.). (2000). *A world of babies: Imagined childcare guides for seven societies.* Cambridge, England, and New York: Cambridge University Press.

A highly engaging and instructive book that presents and answers questions about the nature and nurture of infants in the form of advice to parents in seven world societies. A rich fund of ethnographic knowledge couched in a creative format.

LaFont, S. (Ed.). (2003). *Constructing sexualities: Readings in sexuality, gender and culture.* Upper Saddle River, NJ: Prentice-Hall.

The essays in this broad yet detailed look at sexuality and gender behavior offer statistics, ethnographic examples, and theoretical insights concerning numerous aspects of the topic—from the biological basics and sex categories to sexual orientation and transsexuality.

Shore, B. (1996). *Culture in mind: Meaning, construction, and cultural cognition.* New York: Oxford University Press.

A readable exploration of developmental and cognitive psychology and the cultural context of individual psychology.

Suárez-Orozoco, M. M., Spindler, G., & Spindler, L. (1994). *The making of psychological anthropology, II.* Fort Worth, TX: Harcourt Brace.

This collection of articles consists of firsthand accounts of the objectives, accomplishments, and failures of well-known specialists in psychological anthropology.

Wallace, A. F. C. (1970). *Culture and personality* (2nd ed.). New York: Random House.

The logical and methodological foundations of culture and personality as a science form the basis of this book. The study is guided by the assumptions that anthropology should develop a scientific theory about culture and that a theory pretending to explain or predict cultural phenomena must reckon with noncultural phenomena (such as personality) as well.

Whiting, J. W. M., & Child, I. (1953). *Child training and personality: A cross-cultural study.* New Haven, CT: Yale University Press.

How culture is integrated through the medium of personality processes is the main concern of this classic study. It covers the influence of culture on personality and personality on culture. It is oriented toward testing general hypotheses about human behavior in any and all societies, rather than toward a detailed analysis of a particular society.

CHAPTER 6

Patterns of Subsistence

© Leslie Hugh Stone/The Image Works

CHALLENGE ISSUE

FACING THE CHALLENGE OF GETTING FOOD, SHELTER, AND OTHER NECESSITIES, HUMANS MUST GATHER OR PRODUCE RESOURCES TO SATISFY SUCH NEEDS. This is true for Nigerian farmers and Icelandic fishers, as much as it is for these Indonesians who are foraging for food and other goods at a city dump. The basic function of culture is securing the survival of those who live by its rules, and so the study of subsistence is an important aspect of anthropological inquiry.

1 What Is Adaptation?

Adaptation refers to beneficial adjustments of organisms to their environment, a process that not only leads to changes in the organisms but also impacts their environment. Such dynamic interaction is necessary for the survival of all life forms, including human beings.

2 How Do Humans Adapt?

In the course of evolution, humans came to rely increasingly on culture rather than biological change as a means of effectively adapting to different and changing environments. Through cultural adaptation, humans develop ways of doing things that are compatible with the resources they have available to them and within the limitations of the various habitats in which they live. In a particular region, people living in similar environments tend to borrow from one another customs that work well in those settings. Once achieved, adaptations may be remarkably stable for long periods of time, even thousands of years. Humankind's unique creative capacity to adapt by means of culture has enabled our species to inhabit an extraordinary variety of environments.

3 What Sorts of Cultural Adaptations Have Humans Achieved through the Ages?

Food foraging is the oldest and most universal type of human adaptation and typically involves geographical mobility. Other adaptations, involving domestication of plants and animals, began to develop in some parts of the world about 10,000 years ago. Horticulture (cultivating plants with hand tools) led to more permanent settlements (villages and towns) while pastoralism (herding grazing animals) required mobility to seek out pasture and water. Cities began to develop as early as 5,000 years ago in some world regions, as intensive agriculture and long-distance trading produced sufficient resources to support larger populations and various full-time specialists. These changes led to increasingly complex and large-scale social organizations.

Several times today you will interrupt your activities to eat or drink. You may take this very much for granted, but if you went totally without food for as long as a day, you would begin to feel the symptoms of hunger: weakness, fatigue, and headache. After a month of starvation, your body would probably never repair the damage. A mere week to 10 days without water would be enough to kill you.

All living beings, and people are no exception, must satisfy certain basic needs in order to stay alive. Among these needs are food, water, and shelter. Humans may not "live by bread alone," but nobody can live for long without any bread at all; and no creature could long survive if its relations with its environment were random and chaotic. Living beings must have regular access to a supply of food and water and a reliable means of obtaining and using it. A lion might die if all its prey disappeared, if its teeth and claws grew soft, or if its digestive system failed. Although people face these same sorts of problems, they have an overwhelming advantage over other creatures: People have culture. If our meat supply dwindles, we can turn to some vegetable, like the soybean, and process it to taste like meat. When our tools fail, we replace them or invent better ones. Even when our stomachs are incapable of digesting a particular food, we can predigest it by boiling or pureeing. We are, nonetheless, subject to the same needs and pressures as all living creatures, and it is important to understand human behavior from this point of view. The crucial concept that underlies such a perspective is adaptation or how humans adjust to and act upon the burdens and opportunities presented in daily life.

ADAPTATION

As defined in an earlier chapter, adaptation is a process—the process organisms undergo to achieve a beneficial adjustment to a particular environment, which not only leads to biological changes in the organisms but also impacts their environment. This dynamic interaction is necessary for the survival of all life forms, including human beings. What makes human adaptations unique among all other species is our capacity to produce and reproduce culture, enabling us to creatively adapt to an extraordinary range of radically different environments. How humans adjust to and deal with the burdens and

opportunities presented in daily life is the basic business of all cultures. A people's **cultural adaptation** consists of a complex of ideas, activities, and technologies that enable them to survive and even thrive.

The process of adaptation establishes a moving balance between the needs of a population and the potential of its environment. This process can be illustrated by the Tsembaga people of Papua New Guinea, one of about twenty local groups of Maring speakers who support themselves chiefly through **horticulture**—the cultivation of crops carried out with simple hand tools such as digging sticks or hoes.[1] Although the Tsembaga also raise pigs, they eat them only under conditions of illness, injury, warfare, or celebration. At such times the pigs are sacrificed to ancestral spirits, and their flesh is ritually consumed. (This guarantees a supply of high-quality protein when it is most needed.)

Traditionally, the Tsembaga and their neighbors are bound together in a unique cycle of pig sacrifices that serves to mark the end of hostilities between groups. Hostilities are periodically fueled by ecological pressures in which pigs play a significant role. Pigs are rarely slaughtered because they fulfill important roles: omnivorous eaters, they keep the village free of garbage and even human feces; moreover, they serve as status symbols for their owners who reserve them for significant rituals. But keeping them alive and allowing them to multiply comes at a cost since their numbers grow quickly. Invading the village gardens, the hungry pigs eat the sweet potatoes and other crops, leaving almost nothing for their human owners. In short, they become a problem. The need to expand food cultivation in order to feed the prestigious but pesky pigs puts a strain on the land best suited for farming. Sooner or later, fighting breaks out between the Tsembaga and their neighbors. Hostilities usually end after several weeks, followed by a pig feast ritual. For this event, the Tsembaga butcher and roast almost all of their pigs and feast heartily on them with invited allies. By means of this feast, the Tsembaga not only pay their debts to their allies and gain prestige, but also eliminate a major source of irritation and com-

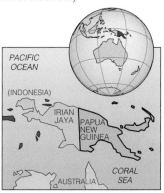

cultural adaptation A complex of ideas, activities, and technologies that enable people to survive and even thrive.
horticulture The cultivation of crops with simple hand tools such as digging sticks or hoes.

[1]Rappaport, R. A. (1969). Ritual regulation of environmental relations among a New Guinea people. In A. P. Vayda (Ed.), *Environment and cultural behavior* (pp. 181–201). Garden City, NY: Natural History Press.

plaint between neighbors. Moreover, the feast leaves everyone well fed and physically strengthened as a result of the animal protein intake. Even without hostilities over scarce land, such large pig feasts have been held whenever the pig population has become unmanageable—every 5 to 10 years, depending on the groups' success in growing crops and raising animals. Thus, the cycle of fighting and feasting keeps the ecological balance among humans, land, and animals.

As noted, the term *adaptation* refers to the process of interaction between changes an organism makes in its environment and those that the environment makes in the organism. A good example of this is the spread of the gene for sickle-cell anemia, noted earlier in this textbook. To recap briefly, long ago, in the tropics of central Africa, a genetic mutation appeared in human populations, causing the manufacture of red blood cells that take on a sickle shape under conditions of low oxygen pressure. Since people who inherit the varient for this trait from both parents usually develop severe anemia and die in childhood, selective pressure was exerted against its spread in the local population. Then came the introduc-

tion of slash-and-burn horticulture in this region. This reduced the natural vegetative cover and transformed the environment into a habitat conducive to the breeding of mosquitoes that carry the parasite that causes falciparum malaria. When transmitted to humans, this parasite lives in the red blood cells, and the resulting disease is always debilitating and very often fatal. However, individuals who inherit the gene for the sickle-cell trait from only one parent (receiving one "normal" gene from the other) turn out to have a natural defense against the parasite. Since these individuals do not succumb to malaria, they are favored by natural selection, and the sickling trait has become more and more common in the population.

Sickle-cell anemia is a revealing illustration of the relativity of any adaptation. In malarial areas, the genetic varient responsible for this condition is adaptive for human populations, even though some individuals suffer as a result of its presence. In nonmalarial regions, however, it is highly maladaptive. There, the varient confers no advantage at all on human populations, and some individuals die as a result of its presence.

© Mark Richards

Human adaptations impact environments in various ways. In California, native food foragers regularly burned vast areas, thereby favoring the growth of oak trees (acorns were a staple food) and deer browse. Once "white" settlers stopped the practice, highly flammable brush and conifers flourished at the expense of oaks. As a consequence, disastrous outbreaks of wildfires periodically sweep through parts of the state, causing millions of dollars in property loss.

VISUAL COUNTERPOINT Although Hopi and Navajo Indians inhabit the same region and are neighbors, their cultures are quite different. Originally food foragers, Navajos became pastoral nomads, while the Hopi are village-dwelling farmers. Environments do not determine culture but do set certain potentials and limitations.

The Unit of Adaptation

The unit of adaptation includes both organisms and environment. Organisms, including human beings, exist as members of a population; populations, in turn, must have the flexibility to cope with variability and change within the natural environment that sustains them. In biological terms, this flexibility means that different organisms within the population have somewhat differing genetic endowments. In cultural terms, it means that variation occurs among individual skills, knowledge, and personalities. Organisms and environments form dynamic interacting systems. People might as easily farm as fish, but we do not expect to find farmers in Siberia's frozen tundra or people who fish for a living in the middle of North Africa's Sahara Desert. In other words, although environments do not determine culture, they do present certain possibilities and limitations.

Some anthropologists have adopted the ecologists' concept of **ecosystem,** defined as a system composed of both the natural environment and all the organisms liv-

ecosystem A system, or a functioning whole, composed of both the natural environment and all the organisms living within it.
cultural ecology The dynamic interaction of specific cultures with their environments.
progress The ethnocentric notion that humans are moving forward to a higher, more advanced stage in their development toward perfection.

ing within it. The system is bound by the activities of the organisms, as well as by such physical processes as erosion and evaporation. **Cultural ecology** is a term that refers to the dynamic interaction of specific cultures with their natural environments. Cultural ecologists are generally concerned with detailed microstudies of particular human ecosystems. They emphasize that all aspects of human culture must be considered, not just the most obvious technological ones. They would be among the first to point out that the Tsembaga's attitude toward pigs and the cycle of sacrifices have important economic and biological functions—whether or not the Tsembaga themselves see it that way. Interestingly, whatever awareness the Tsembaga may have of these adaptive functions, they explain the feasting ritual as an event motivated by their belief in the power and needs of their ancestral spirits. Although the pigs are consumed *by* the living, they are sacrificed *for* ancestors, say the Tsembaga.

Adaptation in Cultural Evolution

Human groups adapt to their environments by means of their cultures. However, cultures may change over the course of time; they evolve. This is called *cultural evolution,* which is sometimes confused with the idea of **progress**—the notion that humans are moving forward to a higher, more advanced stage in their development toward perfection. Yet, not all innovations turn out to be positive in the long run, nor do they improve conditions for every member of a society even in the short run.

Adaptation must also be understood from a historical point of view. To fit into an ecosystem, humans (like all organisms) must have the potential to adjust to or become a part of it. A good example of this is the Comanche, whose history begins in the highlands of southern Idaho.[2] Living in that harsh, arid region, these North American Indians traditionally subsisted on wild plants, small animals, and occasionally larger game. Their material equipment was simple and limited to what they (and their dogs) could carry or pull. The size of their groups was restricted, and what little social power could develop was in the hands of the shaman, who was a combination of healer and spiritual guide.

At some point in their nomadic history, the Comanche moved east onto the Great Plains, where buffalo were abundant and the Indians' potential as hunters could be fully developed. As larger groups could be supported by the new and abundant food supply, the need arose for a more complex political organization. Hunting ability thus became a means of gaining political power and prestige.

Eventually the Comanche acquired horses and guns from whites. This enhanced their hunting capabilities significantly, and the great hunting chiefs became powerful indeed. The Comanche became raiders in order to get horses, which they did not breed for themselves, and their hunting chiefs evolved into war chiefs. The once "poor" and peaceful hunter–gatherers of the dry highlands became wealthy, and raiding became a way of life. In the late 18th and early 19th centuries they dominated the southern Plains from the borders of New Spain (Mexico) in the south to those of New France (Louisiana) and the fledgling United States in the east and north. In moving from one environment to another, and in changing from one way of life to another, the Comanche were able to capitalize on existing cultural capabilities to flourish in their new situation.

Sometimes societies that developed independently of one another find similar solutions to similar problems. For example, the Cheyenne Indians moved out onto the Great Plains and took up a form of Plains Indian culture resembling that of the Comanche even though their cultural background differed significantly. (Before they transformed into horse-riding buffalo hunters, the Cheyenne had cultivated crops and gathered wild rice in the woodlands of the Great Lakes region, which fostered a distinct set of social, political, and religious practices.) This is an example of **convergent evolution**—the development of similar cultural adaptations to similar environmental conditions by dif-

A Comanche bison hunt as painted by artist George Catlin. Plains Indians such as the Comanche, Cheyenne, Crow, and Lakota developed similar cultures, as they had to adapt to similar environmental conditions. (For a map of Native American culture areas, see Figure 6.1 on page 153.)

ferent peoples with different ancestral cultures. Especially interesting is that the Cheyenne completely gave up crop cultivation and focused exclusively on hunting and gathering after their move into the vast grasslands of the northern High Plains. Contrary to the popular notion of evolution as a progressive movement toward increased control over the environment, this ethnographic example shows that cultural historical changes in subsistence practices do not always go from dependence on wild food to farming; it may go the other way as well.

Somewhat similar to the phenomenon of convergent evolution is **parallel evolution,** in which similar cultural adaptations to similar environmental conditions are achieved by peoples whose ancestral cultures were already somewhat alike. For example, the development of farming in Southwest Asia and Mesoamerica took place independently, as people in both regions, whose ways of life were already comparable, became dependent on a narrow range of plant foods that required human intervention for their protection and reproductive success. Both developed intensive forms of agriculture, built large cities, and created complex social and political organizations.

It is important to recognize that stability as well as change is involved in evolutionary adaptation, and that

---

[2]Wallace, E., & Hoebel, E. A. (1952). *The Comanches.* Norman: University of Oklahoma Press.

convergent evolution In cultural evolution, the development of similar cultural adaptations to similar environmental conditions by different peoples with different ancestral cultures.
parallel evolution In cultural evolution, the development of similar cultural adaptations to similar environmental conditions by peoples whose ancestral cultures were already somewhat alike.

© National Museum of American Art, Washington, DC

© Nathan Benn/Corbis

Saying that a society is stable is not to say it is changeless. Descendants of people who maintained a stable way of life for 5,000 years, Western Abenakis nevertheless incorporated new elements into their culture, including longhouses such as the one here. Today, 400 years after first contact with Europeans, Abenaki houses are like those of European Americans, but many traditional values and practices endure.

once a satisfactory adaptation is achieved, too much in the way of change may cause it to break down. Thus, episodes of major change may be followed by long periods of relative stability. For example, about 5,500 years ago a way of life had evolved in northwestern New England and southern Quebec that was well attuned to the environmental conditions of the times.[3] Since those conditions remained more or less stable over the next 5,000 years or so, it is understandable that people's lifeways remained so as well. This is not to say that change was entirely absent, for it was not. (*Stable* does not mean *static*.) Periodically, people refined and enhanced their way of life—replacing spears and spear-throwers with more far-reaching bows and arrows; improving cooking by using pottery vessels instead of containers made from animal hide, wood, or bark; substituting heavy and cumbersome dugouts with lightweight birch-bark canoes; and supplementing the products of hunting, gathering, and fishing with limited cultivation of corn, beans, and squash.

Despite these changes, however, the native peoples of the region retained the basic structure of their culture and tended toward a balance with their resource base well into the 17th century, when the culture had to adjust to pressures associated with European invasions of North America. Such long-term stability by no means implies "stagnation," "backwardness," or "failure to

progress." Rather, it suggests success. Had this culture not effectively satisfied people's physical and psychological needs, it never would have endured as it did for thousands of years. That said, not every group has implemented the changes needed for long-term survival—and some have made changes that failed to bring the expected benefits. Moreover, not everybody benefits from changes, especially if change is forced upon them. As world history painfully demonstrates, all too often humans have made changes that have had disastrous results, leading to the deaths of thousands, even millions of people—not to mention other creatures and the destruction of the natural environment. In short, we must avoid falling into the ethnocentric trap of equating change with progress or seeing everything as adaptive.

Culture Areas

From early on, anthropologists recognized that ethnic groups living within the same broad habitat often share certain culture traits. This reflects the fact that neighboring peoples may easily borrow from each other, and that there exists a basic relationship among their similar natural environment, available resources, and subsistence practices. Classifying groups according to their culture traits, anthropologists have mapped culture clusters known as **culture areas**—geographic regions in which a number of societies have similar ways of life. Such areas often correspond to ecological areas. In sub-Arctic North America, for example, migratory caribou herds graze across the vast tundra. For dozens of different groups that have made this region their home, these animals provide a major source of food as well as mate-

---

[3]Haviland, W. A., & Power, M. W. (1994). *The original Vermonters* (rev. and exp. ed.). Hanover, NH: University Press of New England.

culture area A geographic region in which a number of societies follow similar patterns of life.

rial for shelter and clothing. Adapting to more or less the same ecological resources in this sub-Arctic landscape, these groups have developed similar subsistence technologies and practices in the course of generations. They may speak very different languages, but they may all be said to form part of the same culture area.

Because everything in nature is always in a state of flux—daily, seasonal, and annual cycles of abundance and scarcity, as well as permanent changes in the environment due to destruction of habitat and extinction of plant and animal species—culture areas are not always stable. Moreover, new species may be introduced and technologies invented or introduced from more distant cultures. Such was the case with the indigenous culture area of the Great Plains in North America (Figure 6.1). For thousands of years, many indigenous groups with similar ways of life existed in this vast ecological area between the Mississippi River and the Rocky Mountains. Until the mid-1800s, when European immigrants invaded the region and almost completely annihilated the millions of free-ranging buffalo, these large grazing herds provided an obvious and practical source of food and materials for clothing and shelter.

The efficiency of indigenous groups in the southern plains increased greatly in the 1600s, when they

gained access to Spanish horses on the northern Mexican frontier, and became mounted buffalo hunters. During the next century, the new horse complex spread northward to almost every indigenous group ranging in the Great Plains culture area. A total of thirty-one politically independent peoples, including the Cheyenne and Comanche, reached a similar adaptation to this particular grassland region. So it was that by the time of the Euroamerican invasion of their vast hunting territories in the 19th century, the Indians of the Great Plains were all buffalo hunters, dependent upon this animal for food, clothing, shelter, and bone tools. Each native nation was organized into a number of warrior societies, and prestige came from hunting and fighting skills. Their villages were typically arranged in a distinctive circular pattern, and many religious rituals, such as the Sun Dance, were practiced throughout the region. During the 1870s and 1880s, railroads were built across the Great Plains, and mass slaughter of buffalo followed. More than one million of these animals were killed every year, mostly by non-Indians only interested in their hides and tongues (tongues were a luxury meat commodity, easily removed and compact to ship). With their herds almost exterminated, Indians of the Plains faced starvation, which made effective defense of their homelands impossible. This resulted in the near collapse of their traditional cultures from the 1890s onward.

Sometimes geographic regions are not uniform in climate and landscape, so new discoveries do not always spread from one group to another. Moreover, within a culture area, there are variations between local environments, and these favor variations in adaptation. The Great Basin of the western United States is an intermontane dry highland area embracing the states of Nevada and Utah, with adjacent portions of California, Oregon, Wyoming, and Idaho.[4] The Shoshone Indians who live there are divided into a northern and a western group. Traditionally, both subsisted as nomadic hunters and gatherers, but there were certain distinctions between them. In the north, a relative abundance of game animals made hunting primary and provided for the maintenance of large human populations, requiring a great deal of cooperation among local groups. In the west, by contrast, game was less plentiful so the western Shoshone depended especially upon rabbit hunting and the gathering of wild plants such as pine nuts for their subsistence. Since plants varied considerably in their seasonal and local availability, the western Shoshone were forced to cover vast distances in search of food. Under such conditions, it was most efficient to travel in groups

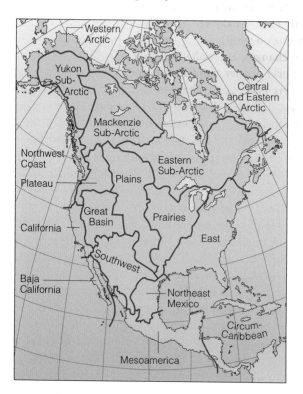

FIGURE 6.1

The culture area concept was developed by anthropologists in the early part of the 20th century. This map shows the culture areas that have been defined for North and Central America. Within each, there is an overall similarity of native cultures, as opposed to the differences that distinguish the cultures of one area from those of all others.

---

[4]Steward, J. H. (1972). *Theory of culture change: The methodology of multilinear evolution.* Urbana: University of Illinois Press.

of but a few families, only occasionally coming together with other groups and not always with the same ones.

The Shoshone were not the only inhabitants of the Great Basin. To the south lived the closely related Paiutes. They, too, were foragers (hunter–gatherers) living under similar environmental conditions as the Shoshone, but some Paiute bands inhabiting areas with swampy lowlands managed their food resources more actively by diverting small streams to irrigate wild crops such as wild hyacinth, nutgrass, and spikerush. These bulbs and seeds were the mainstay of their food supply. Because this ecological adaptation provided them with higher yields than their northern neighbors, their populations were larger than those of the Shoshone, and they led a less nomadic existence.

To deal with variations within a given region, anthropologist Julian Steward (see Anthropologists of Note) proposed the concept of **culture type.** This refers to a collection of elements in a culture that generally occurs cross-culturally and concerns a particular technology and its relationship with certain environmental features. It is illustrated in the Great Basin accounts noted above, which show how technology—such as surface irrigation of noncultivated food crops in swampy lowlands—helps determine just which environmental features will be useful.

Culture Core

Environment and technology are not the only factors that determine a society's pattern of subsistence; social and political organization also influence how technology is applied to the problem of staying alive. This given, if we wish to understand the rise of irrigation agriculture in the great centers of ancient civilization (such as Egypt, China, Peru, and Mesopotamia), we need to know not only the technological and environmental factors that made the building of large-scale irrigation works possible but also the social and political organization that made it possible to mobilize the many workers necessary to build and maintain the systems. We must examine the monarchies and priesthoods that coordinated the work and decided where the water would be used and how the agricultural products of this collective venture would be distributed.

© Joe Carini/The Image Works

In Bali, gatherings for rituals at water temples allowed farmers to arrange schedules for flooding their rice paddies.

The cultural features that are fundamental in the society's way of making its living are called its **culture core.** This includes the society's food-producing techniques and knowledge of available resources in its environment. It also encompasses the work arrangements involved in applying those techniques to the local environment. For example, do people work every day for a fixed number of hours, or is most work concentrated during certain times of the year? The culture core comprises other aspects of culture that bear on the production and distribution of food. Among these is worldview or ideology, evidenced in the ways religious beliefs sometimes prohibit the use of certain readily available and highly nutritious foods. For example, the Tutchone people native to the Yukon Territory of northwestern Canada have taboos against eating otters, young ravens, or crows, even though their meat is perfectly edible. In their northern forest homeland, seasonal food shortages are always a threat, but even when faced with famine, these Athapaskan-speaking Indians adhere to their taboo. Instead of eating these animals, they resort to techniques such as finding an area previously used by mice and lighting a fire over it to melt the frozen soil, providing access to bare roots previously stored by the mice.[5] Better known contemporary examples of such food taboos include pigs (traditionally not eaten by most Muslims and Jews), horses (regularly part of French fare but abhorred in England), cows (not eaten by most Hindus in southern Asia), dogs (not eaten by Europeans but a regular part of Korean meals), monkeys (appreciated by Amazonian Indians but excluded from North American menus), and humans (not eaten by most humans).[6]

[5]Legros, D. (1997). Comment. *Current Anthropology, 38,* 617.

[6]Pelto, G. H., Goodman, A. H., & Dufour, D. L. (Eds.). (2000). *Nutritional anthropology: Biocultural perspectives on food and nutrition.* Mountain View, CA: Mayfield.

culture type Concerns a particular technology and its relationship with certain environmental features.
culture core Cultural features that are fundamental in the society's way of making its living—including food-producing techniques, knowledge of available resources, and work arrangements involved in applying those techniques to the local environment.

Anthropologists of Note

Julian H. Steward (1902–1972)

Courtesy University of Illinois/Urbana-Champaign

North American anthropologist Julian H. Steward developed an approach he called *cultural ecology*—that is, the interaction of specific cultures with their environments.

Initially, Steward was struck by a number of similarities in the development of urban civilizations in both Peru and Mesoamerica and noted that certain developments were paralleled in the ancient urban civilizations of the Old World. He identified the constants and abstracted from this his laws of cultural development. Steward proposed three fundamental procedures for cultural ecology:

1. The interrelationship of a culture's technology and its environment must be analyzed. How effectively does the culture take advantage of available resources to provide food and housing for its people?

2. The patterns of behavior associated with a culture's technology must be analyzed. How do members of the culture perform the work necessary for their survival?

3. The relation between those behavior patterns and the rest of the cultural system must be determined. How does the work people do to survive affect their attitudes and outlooks? How is their survival behavior linked to their social activities and their personal relationships?

A number of anthropologists, known as ethnoscientists, focus on identifying the principles behind native idea systems, how they inform a people about their environment, and what role they play in survival. For example, on the Indonesian island of Bali ritual meetings were held regularly at water temples, located at the forks of rivers. Part of the ritual included negotiating seasonal schedules for flooding the farmers' rice fields. When the Indonesian government forced abandonment of this traditional system in an effort to promote more productive growing techniques, disaster ensued. Without the water temple rituals, irrigation coordination fell apart, and water shortages and pest infestation became the norm. This led to lower and uneven field yields, plus resentment toward those with better harvests.[7] Eventually, the old system was restored because it worked better. The point of this example is that cultural beliefs, no matter how irrelevant they may seem to outsiders, are often anything but irrelevant if one is to understand another society's subsistence practices.

THE FOOD-FORAGING WAY OF LIFE

At the present time, perhaps a quarter of a million people—less then 0.005 percent of the world population of about 6 billion—still support themselves mainly through **food foraging,** defined as hunting, fishing, and gathering wild plant foods. Yet, before the domestication of plants and animals, which began a mere 10,000 years ago, all people supported themselves through some combination of wild plant harvesting, hunting, and fishing. It was as food foragers that our species became truly human, acquiring the basic habits of dealing with one another and with the surrounding world that still guide the behavior of individuals, groups, nations, and even the global community at large. Thus, if we would know who we are and how we came to be, if we would understand the relationship between environment and culture, and if we want to comprehend the institutions of the food-producing societies that have arisen since the development of farming and animal husbandry, we should turn first to the oldest and most universal of fully human lifestyles: the food-foraging adaptation.

MEDIATREK

To learn about hunter–gatherer societies and about the agricultural revolution and its impact on humankind, go to MediaTrek 6.1 on the companion Web site or CD-ROM.

When food foragers had the world to themselves about 10,000 years ago, they had their pick of the best environments. But gradually, through time, areas with rich soils and ample supplies of water were appropriated by farming and, more recently, by industrial societies. As a result, small foraging communities were edged out of their traditional habitats by the sheer numbers and overwhelming force of these expanding groups. Today, most food foragers are found only in the world's marginal areas—frozen Arctic tundra, deserts, and inaccessible forests. These habitats, although they may not support large or dense agricultural societies, provide a good living

---

[7]Fountain, H. (2000, January 30). Now the ancient ways are less mysterious. *New York Times,* News of the Week, 5.

food foraging Hunting, fishing, and gathering wild plant foods.

for foragers. Traditional foragers typically lead a migratory existence that makes it impractical to accumulate too many material possessions. Many outsiders have misinterpreted their unburdened existence as backward, impoverished, and inferior—a negative stereotype reinforced by the ideology of progress that emerged in Europe in the mid-1800s. In this ideology, industrialism and capitalism were represented as the height of success in humanity's journey towards perfection. By the same token, foragers were considered savage primitives who struggled hard to stay alive in an unforgiving wilderness and whose lives were "nasty, brutish, and short."

In the mid-1960s, anthropologists began to seriously question and investigate this negative stereotype. Based on new studies and a critical review of existing ethnographic evidence, they determined that it was ill-founded. The research showed that forager diets were well balanced and ample, and that these people were less likely to experience severe famine than were farmers. Their material possessions were limited, but so were their desires to amass things. On the other hand, they had plenty of leisure time for concentrating on family ties, social life, and spiritual development—apparently far more than people living in agricultural and industrial societies. Such findings clearly challenged the idea that food foragers lived a miserable existence. In fact, research results prompted anthropologist Marshall Sahlins to refer to them as "the original affluent society." In his 1972 book *Stone Age Economics,* he wrote:

> Hunter-gatherers consume less energy per capita per year than any other group of human beings. Yet when you come to examine it the original affluent society was none other than the hunter's—in which all the people's material wants were easily satisfied. To accept that hunters are affluent is therefore to recognize that the present human condition of [the industrial] man slaving to bridge the gap between his unlimited wants and his insufficient means is a tragedy of modern times.[8]

Replacing the old stereotype of the miserable forager, Sahlins' "affluent" forager became the new standard idea widely accepted among fellow anthropologists. More recent cross-cultural research into work and leisure issues, however, suggests a more complex picture.[9]

All modern food foragers have had some degree of interaction with neighbors whose ways of life often differ radically from their own. For example, the food-foraging Mbuti pygmies of the Republic of Congo's Ituri rainforest live in a complex dependency relationship with their neighbors, Bantu- and Sudanic-speaking peoples who are farmers. They exchange meat and other products of the forest for farm produce and manufactured goods. During part of the year, these pygmies live in their trading partner's village and are incorporated into his kin group, even to the point of allowing him to initiate their sons.

Although some contemporary food foragers, such as the Mbuti, have continued to maintain traditional ways while adapting to neighbors and traders, various other groups have turned to this way of life after giving up other modes of subsistence. Some, like the Cheyenne Indians of the Great Plains, were once crop cultivators, while others, such as some of the Bushmen of southern Africa, have at times been farmers and at other times pastoral nomads. Nor are such transformations things of the past. In the 1980s, when a world economic recession led to the abandonment of many sheep stations in the Australian outback, a number of aboriginal peoples returned to food foraging, thereby freeing themselves from a dependency on the government into which they had been forced.

An important point that emerges from the preceding discussion is this: People in the world today who subsist by hunting, fishing, and wild plant collection are not following an ancient way of life because they do not know any better. Rather, they are doing it either because they have been forced by circumstances into a situation where foraging is the best means of survival or because they simply prefer to live this way. In many cases, they find such satisfaction in living the way they do that, like the Hadza of northern Tanzania, they go to great lengths to avoid adopting other ways of life.[10] The fact is, foraging constitutes a rational response to particular ecological, economic, and sociopolitical realities. Moreover, for at least 2,000 years, a need has existed for specialized market hunters, fishers, and gatherers to supply commodities such as furs, hides, feathers, ivory, pearls, fish, nuts, and honey that have helped feed east-west trade since ancient times.[11] Like everyone else, food foragers are part of a larger world system.

---

[8]Sahlins, M. (1972). *Stone Age economics* (p. 1). Chicago: Aldine. See also Cashdan, E. (1989). Hunters and gatherers: Economic behavior in bands. In S. Plattner (Ed.), *Economic anthropology* (pp. 23–24). Stanford, CA: Stanford University Press.

[9]Kaplan, D. (2000). The darker side of the original affluent society. *Journal of Anthropological Research, 53*(3), 301–324.

---

[10]Hawkes, K., O'Connell, J. F., & Blurton Jones, N. G. (1997). Hadza women's time allocation, offspring provisioning, and the evolution of long postmenopausal life spans. *Current Anthropology, 38,* 552.

---

[11]Stiles, D. (1992). The hunter–gatherer 'revisionist' debate. *Anthropology Today, 8* (2), 15.

Human groups (including food foragers) do not exist in isolation except occasionally, and even then not for long. The bicycle this Bushman of southern Africa is riding is indicative of his links with the wider world. For 2,000 years, Bushmen have been interacting regularly with neighboring farmers and pastoralists. Much of the elephant ivory used for the keyboards on pianos so widely sought in 19th-century North America came from the Bushmen.

Characteristics of the Food-Foraging Life

Food foragers are by definition people who do not farm or practice animal husbandry. Hence, they must seek to fit their places of residence to naturally available food sources. Thus, it is no wonder they move about a great deal. Such movement is not aimless wandering but is done within a fixed territory or home range. Some groups, such as the Bushmen known as Ju/'hoansi, who depend on the reliable and highly drought-resistant Mongongo nut, may keep to fairly fixed annual routes and cover only a restricted territory. Others, such as the traditional Shoshone in the western highlands of North America, had to cover a wider territory, their course determined by the local availability of the erratically productive pine nut.

VISUAL COUNTERPOINT Food foraging has by no means disappeared, even in industrial societies such as that of the United States. Some do it occasionally for pleasure, as this textbook's senior author is shown doing—gathering wild blueberries. Some, such as commercial fishers, forage full-time, as do many homeless people in order to survive.

A crucial factor in this mobility is availability of water. The distance between the food supply and water must not be so great that more energy is required to fetch water than can be obtained from the food.

Another characteristic of the food-foraging adaptation is the small size of local groups, typically fewer than a hundred people. Although no completely satisfactory explanation of group size has yet been offered, it seems certain that both ecological and social factors are involved. Among those suggested are the **carrying capacity** of the land (the number of people that the available resources can support at a given level of food-getting techniques) and the **density of social relations** (the number and intensity of interactions among camp members). Higher social density means more opportunities for conflict.

Both carrying capacity and social density are complex variables. Carrying capacity involves not only the immediate presence of food and water but also the tools and work necessary to secure them, as well as short- and long-term fluctuations in their availability. Social density involves not only the number of people and their interactions but also the circumstances and quality of those interactions as well as the mechanisms for regulating them. A mob of a hundred angry strangers has a different social density than the same number of neighbors enjoying themselves at a block party.

Among food-foraging populations, social density always seems in a state of flux as people spend more or less time away from camp and as they move to other camps, either on visits or more permanently. Among the Ju/'hoansi of southern Africa, for example, exhaustion of local food resources, conflict within the group, or the desire to visit friends or relatives living elsewhere cause people to leave one group for another. As Canadian anthropologist Richard Lee notes, "Ju love to go visiting, and the practice acts as a safety valve when tempers get frayed. In fact, the Ju usually move, not when their food is exhausted, but rather when only their patience is exhausted."[12] If a camp has so many children as to create a burden for the working adults, some young families may be encouraged to join others where fewer children live. Conversely, groups with few children may actively recruit families with young offspring in order to ensure the group's survival. Redistribution of people, then, is an important mechanism for regulating social density, as well as for assuring that the size and composition of local groups is suited to local variations in resources. Thus, cultural adaptations help transcend the limitations of the physical environment.

In addition to seasonal or local adjustments, food foragers must make long-term adjustments to resources. Most food-foraging populations seem to stabilize at numbers well below the carrying capacity of their land. In fact, the home ranges of most food foragers could support from three to five times as many people as they typically do. In the long run, it may be more adaptive for a group to keep its numbers low rather than to expand indefinitely and risk destruction by a sudden and unexpected natural reduction in food resources. The population density of foraging groups surviving in marginal environments today rarely exceeds one person per square mile, a very low density, even though their resources could support greater numbers.

How food-foraging peoples regulate population size relates to two things: how much body fat they accumulate and how they care for their children. Ovulation requires a certain minimum of body fat, and in traditional foraging societies, this is not achieved until early adulthood. Hence, female fertility peaks between the early and mid-20s, and teenage pregnancies—at least, successful ones—are virtually unknown.[13] Once a child is born, its mother nurses it several times each hour, even at night, and this continues over a period of as many as 4 or 5 years. The constant stimulation of the mother's nipple suppresses the level of hormones that promote ovulation, making conception less likely, especially if work keeps the mother physically active, and she does not have a large store of body fat to draw on for energy.[14] By continuing to nurse for several years, women give birth only at widely spaced intervals. Thus, the total number of offspring remains low but sufficient to maintain stable population size.

[12]Lee, R. (1993). *The Dobe Ju/'hoansi* (p. 65). Fort Worth: Harcourt Brace.

[13]Hrdy, S. B. (1999). Body fat and birth control. *Natural History, 108*(8), 88.

[14]Small, M. F. (1997). Making connections. *American Scientist, 85,* 503. See also Konner, M., & Worthman, C. (1980). Nursing frequency, gonadal function, and birth spacing among !Kung hunter-gatherers. *Science, 207,*788–791.

carrying capacity The number of people that the available resources can support at a given level of food-getting techniques.
density of social relations The number and intensity of interactions among the members of a camp.

© Anthony Bannister/ABPL

Frequent nursing of children over as many as 4 or 5 years acts to suppress ovulation among food foragers such as Bushmen. As a consequence, women give birth to relatively few offspring at widely spaced intervals.

The Impact of Food Foraging on Human Society

Although much has been written on the theoretical importance of hunting for shaping the supposedly competitive and aggressive nature of the human species, most anthropologists are unconvinced by these arguments. To be sure, warlike behavior on the part of food-foraging people is known, but such behavior is a relatively recent phenomenon in response to pressure from expansionist states. In the absence of such pressures, food-foraging peoples are remarkably non-aggressive and place more emphasis on peacefulness and cooperation than they do on competition. It does seem likely, however, that three crucial elements of human social organization developed with food foraging. The first of these is the division of labor by gender. Some form of this, however variable and modified, has been observed

in all human societies and is probably as old as human culture. Postindustrial societies are now moving away from such division, and one may ask what the implications are for future cooperative relationships between men and women. We will discuss this issue further in the coming chapters.

Subsistence and Gender

The hunting and butchering of large game as well as the processing of hard or tough raw materials are almost universally masculine occupations. By contrast, women's work in foraging societies usually focuses on collecting and processing a variety of plant foods, as well as other domestic chores that can be fit to the demands of breast-feeding and do not endanger pregnancy and childbirth. This pattern appears to have its origin in an earlier era, in which males—substantially larger and more muscular than females—scavenged meat from the carcasses of dead animals, butchered it with stone tools, and shared it with females, who primarily tended to the gathering of wild plant foods. As the hunting of live animals replaced scavenging as a source of meat, technology lessened the adaptive advantage of male physical power. Notwithstanding the multiple changes that have occurred over the course of many thousands of years, elements of this original division of labor remain and can be found in every culture.

Among food foragers today, the work of women is no less arduous than that of men. Ju/'hoansi women, for example, may walk as many as 12 miles a day two or three times a week to gather food, carrying not only their children but also, on the return home, anywhere from 15 to 33 pounds of food. Still, they do not have to travel quite so far afield as do men on the hunt, and their work is usually less dangerous than hunting. Also, their tasks require less rapid mobility, do not need complete and undivided attention, and are readily resumed after interruption. All of this is compatible with those biological differences that remain between the sexes. Certainly women who are pregnant or have infants to nurse cannot travel long distances in pursuit of game as easily as men can. By the same token, of course, women may have preferred and been better at the less risky task of gathering. In addition to wide-ranging mobility, the successful hunter must also be able to mobilize rapidly high bursts of energy. Although some women can certainly run faster than some men, it is a fact that in general men can outrun women, even when women are not pregnant, breastfeeding, or otherwise encumbered with infants. Because human females must be able to give birth to infants with relatively large heads, their pelvic structure differs from that of human males. As a consequence, the human female is not as well equipped as is the human male for rapid mobility.

To say that differing gender roles among food foragers are compatible with the biological differences between men and women is *not* to say that they are biologically determined. Among the Great Plains Indians of North America, for example, are quite a few reported cases of women who gained fame as hunters and warriors, both historically regarded as men's activities. There is even one 19th-century case of an Atsina Indian girl who was captured by Crow (Absaroke) warriors and became one of their chiefs because she was so accomplished at what were considered to be masculine pursuits. Conversely, any young Crow man who disliked masculine pursuits could assume the dress and demeanor of women, providing he acquired the necessary skills to achieve success in non-male activities. As detailed in the previous chapter, sexual preference might enter into the decision to assume a feminine identity, but not all such transgendered individuals are homosexuals, nor do all homosexuals assume a woman's role. Clearly, sexual preference is of lesser importance than social status, occupation, and appearance. In fact, the division of labor by gender is often far less rigid among food foragers than it is in most other types of society. Thus, Ju/'hoansi males, willingly and without embarrassment, as the occasion demands, will gather wild plant foods, build huts, and collect water, even though all are regarded as women's work.

The nature of women's work in food-foraging societies is such that it can be done while taking care of children. They also can do it in company with other women, which provides adult companionship and opportunities for sharing useful ideas, venting frustrations, idle chatter, gossip, and laughter. In the past, the gender biases of their own male-dominated cultures caused European and North American anthropologists to underestimate the contribution the food-gathering activities of women made to the survival of their group.

We now know that modern food foragers may obtain up to 60 or 70 percent of their diets from plant foods, with perhaps some fish and shellfish provided by women (the exceptions tend to be food foragers living in Arctic regions, where plant foods are not available for much of the year).

Although women in food-foraging societies may spend some time each day gathering plant food, men do not spend all or even the greatest part of their time hunting. The amount of energy expended in hunting, especially in hot climates, is often greater than the energy return from the kill. Too much time spent searching out game might actually be counterproductive. Energy itself is derived primarily from plant carbohydrates, and it is usually the female gatherers who bring in the bulk of the calories. A certain amount of meat in the diet, though, guarantees high-quality protein that is less easily obtained from plant sources, for meat contains exactly the right balance of all of the amino acids (the building blocks of protein) the human body requires. No one plant food does this, and in order to get by without meat, people must hit on exactly the right combination of plants to provide the essential amino acids in the correct proportions.

Food Sharing

A second key feature of human social organization associated with food foraging is the sharing of food among adults. It is easy enough to see why sharing takes place, with women supplying one kind of food and men another. Among the Ju/'hoansi, women have control over the food they collect and can share it with whomever they choose. Men, by contrast, are constrained by rules that specify how much meat is to be distributed and to whom. Thus, a hunter has little effective control over the meat he brings into camp. For the individual hunter, meat sharing is really a way of storing it for the future: His generosity, obligatory though it might

© Anthony Bannister/ABPL

© Anthony Bannister/ABPL

VISUAL COUNTERPOINT
Food foragers such as the Ju/'hoansi have a division of labor in which women gather and prepare "bush" food (here an ostrich egg omelette), but hunting is usually done by men.

be, gives him a claim on the future kills of other hunters. As a cultural trait, food sharing has the obvious survival value of distributing resources needed for subsistence.

A final distinctive feature of the food-foraging economy is the importance of the camp as the center of daily activity and the place where food sharing actually occurs. Among nonhuman primates (and probably among human ancestors until they controlled the use of fire), activities tend to be divided between feeding areas and sleeping areas, and the latter tend to be shifted each evening. Historically known food-foraging people, however, live in camps of some permanence, ranging from the dry-season camps of the Ju/'hoansi, which serve for the entire winter, to the wet-season camps of the Hadza in Tanzania, which are centered on berry picking and honey collection and serve for a few weeks at most. Moreover, human camps are more than sleeping areas; people are in and out all day, eating, working, and socializing in camps to a greater extent than any other primates.

Cultural Adaptations and Material Technology

The mobility of food-foraging groups may depend on the availability of water, as among the Ju/'hoansi; of pine nuts, as in the Shoshone example; or of game animals and other seasonal resources, as among the Hadza in Tanzania or the Mbuti in the Republic of Congo. Different hunting techniques may also play a role in determining sexual division of labor, population size, and movement. Among the Mbuti pygmies in the Ituri tropical forest, all bands hunt elephants with spears. For other game, however, they either use large nets or bows. In those Mbuti bands equipped with large nets there exists a cooperative division of labor in which men, women, and children collaborate in driving and killing antelope and other game. Mbuti net hunting usually involves very long hours and covers great distances. Mbuti net hunters pursue their prey communally, surrounding the animal(s) and beating the woods noisily to chase the game in one direction toward large nets. This sort of "beat-hunt" requires the cooperation of seven to thirty families, so their camps are relatively large. Among Mbuti bow hunters, on the other hand, only men participate. These archers tend to stay closer to the village for shorter periods of time and live in smaller groups, typically no more than six families. While there exists no significant difference in population densities of net and bow hunting areas, archers generally harvest a greater diversity of animal species, including monkeys.[15]

---

[15]Bailey, R. C., & Aunger, R. (1989). Net hunters vs. archers: Variation in women's subsistence strategies in the Ituri forest. *Human Ecology, 17,* 273–297; Terashima, H. (1983). Mota and other hunting activities of the Mbuti archers: A socio-ecological study of subsistence technology. *African Studies Monograph* (Kyoto), 71–85.

Egalitarian Society

An important characteristic of the food-foraging society is its egalitarianism. Food foragers are usually highly mobile, and, lacking animal or mechanical transportation, they must be able to travel without many encumbrances, especially on food-getting expeditions. The average weight of an individual's personal belongings among the Ju/'hoansi, for example, is just under 25 pounds. The material goods of food foragers moving about on foot are, by necessity, limited to the barest essentials, which include implements for hunting, gathering, fishing, building, and cooking. In this context, it makes little sense for them to accumulate luxuries or surplus goods, and the fact that no one owns significantly more than another helps to limit status differences. Age and sex are usually the only sources of important status differences.

It is important to realize that status differences by themselves do not constitute inequality, a point that is all too easily misunderstood, especially where relations between men and women are concerned. In most traditional food-foraging societies, women did not and do not defer to men. To be sure, women may be excluded from some rituals that males participate in, but the reverse is also true. Moreover, the fruits of women's labor are not controlled by men but by the women themselves. Nor do women sacrifice their autonomy even in societies in which male hunting, rather than female gathering, brings in the bulk of the food. Such was the case, for example, among the Innu (Montagnais) Indians of Labrador. Theirs was a society in which the hunt was of overwhelming importance. For their part, women manufactured clothing and other necessities but provided much less of the food than is common among food foragers. Until recently, women as well as men could be shamans. Nevertheless, women were excluded from ritual feasts having to do with hunting—but then, so were men excluded from ritual feasts held by women. Basically, each gender carried out its own activities, with neither meddling in those of the other. Early missionaries to the Innu hunting bands lamented that men had no inclination to make their wives obey them and worked long and hard to convince the Indians that civilization required men to impose their authority on women. But after 300 years of pressing this point, missionaries achieved only limited success.

Food foragers make no attempt to accumulate surplus foodstuffs, often an important source of status in agrarian societies. This does not mean that they live constantly on the verge of starvation, for their environment is their natural storehouse. Except in the coldest climates (where a surplus must be set aside to see people through the long, lean winter season), or in times of acute ecological disaster, some food can almost always be found in a group's territory. Because food resources are typically distributed equally throughout the group (share and share alike is the order of the day), no one achieves the wealth or status that hoarding might bring. In such a society, wealth is a sign of deviance rather than a desirable characteristic.

The food forager's concept of territory contributes as much to social equality as it does to the equal distribution of resources. Most groups have home ranges within which access to resources is open to all members. What is available to one is available to all. If a Mbuti hunter discovers a honey tree, he has first rights; but when he has taken his share, others have a turn. In the unlikely possibility that he does not take advantage of his discovery, others will. No individual within the community privately owns the tree; the system is first come, first served. Therefore, knowledge of the existence of food resources circulates quickly throughout the entire group.

Families move easily from one group to another, settling in any group where they have a previous kinship tie. (Although the idea of food foragers being patrilocal—that is, a wife moving to her husband's group—is still held by some, as discussed in a previous chapter, this represents a historic response to European exploration and colonization.) As noted earlier, the composition of groups among food foragers is always shifting. This loose attitude toward group membership promotes the widest access to resources while maintaining a balance between populations and resources.

The food-forager pattern of generalized exchange, or sharing without any expectation of a direct return, also serves the ends of resource distribution and social equality. A Ju/'hoansi man or woman spends as much as two-thirds of his or her day visiting others or receiving guests; during this time, many exchanges of gifts take place. In their view, hoarding and refusing to share is morally wrong. By sharing whatever is at hand, the Ju/'hoansi achieve social balance. Those who share in their time of plenty will have others to turn to in times of want—and vice versa.

Neolithic revolution The profound culture change associated with the early domestication of plants and animals.

FOOD-PRODUCING SOCIETY

As discussed in earlier chapters, it was tool making that allowed humans to consume significant amounts of meat as well as plant foods. The next truly momentous event in human history was the domestication of plants and animals. The transition from food foraging to food production first took place about 10,000 years ago in Southwest Asia (the Fertile Crescent, including the Jordan River Valley and neighboring regions in the Middle East). Within the next few thousand years, similar early transitions to agricultural economies took place independently in other faraway parts of the world where human groups began to grow, and (later) alter wild cereal plants such as wheat, maize (corn), and rice; legumes such as beans; gourds such as squash; and tubers such as potatoes. They did the same with a number of wild animal species ranging in their hunting territories and began to domesticate goats, sheep, pigs, cattle, and llamas (Figure 6.2).

Because these activities brought about a radical transformation in almost every aspect of their cultural systems, Australian-born archaeologist Gordon Childe introduced the term **Neolithic revolution** to refer to the profound culture change associated with the early domestication of plants and animals. Marking the beginning of what is traditionally known as the New Stone Age, this revolution changed the very nature of human society. As humans became increasingly dependent on domesticated crops, they mostly gave up their mobile way of life and settled down to till the soil, sow, weed, protect, harvest, and safely store their crops. No longer on the move, they could build more permanent dwellings and began to make pottery for storage of water, food, and so on.

Just why this change came about is one of the important questions in anthropology. Since food production by and large requires more work than food foraging, is more monotonous, is often a less secure means of subsistence, and requires people to eat more of the foods that foragers eat only when they have no other choice, it is unlikely that people voluntarily became food producers. Initially, it appears that food production arose as a largely unintended by-product of existing food-management practices. Earlier in this chapter, we offered the ethnographic example of the Paiute, an American Indian group whose habitat in the western desert of North America includes marshlands. These foragers discovered how to irrigate wild crops in their otherwise very dry homeland, thus increasing the quantity of wild seeds and bulbs to be harvested. Although their ecological intervention was very limited, it allowed them to settle down for longer periods in greater numbers than otherwise would have been possible. Unlike the Paiute, who just stopped short of a Neolithic revolu-

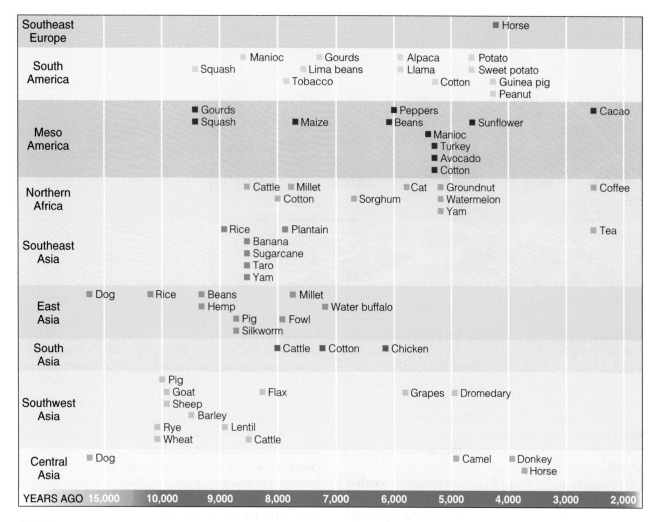

FIGURE 6.2

Appearance of domesticates in the archaeological record.

tion, other groups elsewhere in the world continued to transform their landscapes in ways that favored the appearance of new varieties of particular plants and animals, which came to take on increasing importance for people's subsistence. Although probably at first accidental, it became a matter of necessity as growth outstripped people's ability to sustain themselves through food foraging. For them, food production became a subsistence option of last resort.

The Settled Life of Farmers

Whatever the causes, one of the most significant correlates of this new way of life was the development of fixed settlements, in which families of farmers lived together. As food foragers stay close to their food by moving around to follow nature's seasonal fluctuations, farmers stay close to their food by staying near their gardens. The task of food production lent itself to a different kind of social organization. Because the

hard work of some members of the group could provide food for all, others became free to devote their time to inventing and manufacturing the equipment needed for a new sedentary way of life. Tools for

While it supports larger and more sedentary populations than food foraging, farming generally requires longer and more monotonous work.

© 1980 James D. Nations/DDB Stock

This swidden plot in Chiapas, Mexico, shows what such gardens look like after slash has been burned but before the crops have begun to grow. Although it looks destructive, if properly carried out, swidden farming is an ecologically sound way of growing crops in the tropics.

digging and harvesting, pottery for storage and cooking, clothing made of woven textiles, and housing made of stone, wood, or sun-dried bricks all grew out of the new sedentary living conditions and the altered division of labor.

The transition also brought important changes in social structure. At first, social relations were egalitarian and hardly different from those that prevailed among food foragers. As settlements grew, however, and large numbers of people had to share important resources such as land and water, society became more elaborately structured. Most likely, the organizing units were multifamily kinship groups such as lineages, to which people belong by virtue of descent from a common ancestor but which do not commonly play a large part in the social order of food foragers. As will be discussed in Chapter 10, they provide a convenient way to handle the distinctive problems of land use and ownership that arise in food-producing societies.

Humans adapted to this new settled life in a number of ways. For example, some societies became horticultural—small communities of gardeners working with simple hand tools and using neither irrigation nor the plow. Horticulturists typically cultivate several varieties of crops together in small gardens they have cleared by hand. Because these gardeners commonly use a given garden plot for only a few years before abandoning it in favor of a new one, horticulture may be said to constitute an *extensive* form of agriculture. Production is

for subsistence rather than to produce a surplus for sale. However, the politics of horticultural communities commonly involve periodic feasts (as described early on in this chapter), in the course of which substantial amounts of produce and other gifts are given away in order to gain prestige. Such prestige is the basis for the political power of leaders, who play important roles in production, exchange, and resource allocation—as detailed in the next chapter on economics.

One of the most widespread forms of horticulture, especially in the tropics, is **swidden farming** (also known as slash-and-burn). Unfortunately, widespread use of fire in connection with the clearing of vast tracts of Amazonian or Indonesian forest for cattle raising and other development schemes has led many people to see this kind of farming in a negative light. In fact, it is an ecologically sophisticated and sustainable way of raising food, especially in the tropics, when carried out under the right conditions: low population densities and adequate amounts of land. Only when pursued in the absence of these conditions does the practice lead to environmental degradation and destruction. Swidden farming mimics the diversity of the natural ecosystem, growing several different crops in the same field. Mixed together, the crops are less vulnerable to pests and plant diseases than single ones. Not only is the system ecologically sound, but it is far more energy efficient than the sort of high-tech farming carried out in developed countries such as the United States. While modern, high-tech farming requires more energy input than it yields, swidden farming produces between 10 and 20 units of energy for every unit expended. A good example of how such a system works is provided by the Mekranoti Kayapo Indians of Brazil's Amazon forest, profiled in the following Original Study.

swidden farming Also known as slash-and-burn. An extensive form of horticulture in which the natural vegetation is cut, the slash is subsequently burned, and crops then planted among the ashes.

Original Study

Gardens of the Mekranoti Kayapo

The planting of a Mekranoti garden always follows the same sequence. First, men clear the forest and then burn the debris. In the ashes, both men and women plant sweet potatoes, manioc, bananas, corn, pumpkins, papaya, sugar cane, pineapple, cotton, tobacco, and annatto, whose seeds yield achiote, the red dye used for painting ornaments and people's bodies. Since the Mekranoti don't bother with weeding, the forest gradually invades the garden. After the second year, only manioc, sweet potatoes, and bananas remain. And after three years or so there is usually nothing left but bananas. Except for a few tree species that require hundreds of years to grow, the area will look like the original forest twenty-five or thirty years later.

This gardening technique, known as slash-and-burn agriculture, is one of the most common in the world. The early European settlers in North America adopted the method from the surrounding Indians, although it had been used in an earlier period in Europe as well. At one time critics condemned the technique as wasteful and ecologically destructive, but today we know that, especially in the humid tropics, slash-and-burn agriculture may be one of the best gardening techniques possible.

Anthropologists were among the first to note the possibly disastrous consequences of U.S.-style agriculture in the tropics. Continuous high temperatures encourage the growth of the microorganisms that cause rot, so organic matter quickly breaks down into simple minerals. The heavy rains dissolve these valuable nutrients and carry them deep into the soils, out of the reach of plants. The tropical forest maintains its richness because the heavy foliage shades the earth, cooling it and inhibiting the growth of the decomposers. A good deal of the rain is captured by leaves before ever reaching the ground. When a tree falls in the forest and begins to rot, other plants quickly absorb the nutrients that are released. With open-field agriculture, the sun heats the earth, the decomposers multiply, and the rains quickly leach the soils of their nutrients. In a few years a lush forest, if cleared for open one-crop agriculture, can be transformed into a barren wasteland.

A few months after the Mekranoti plant banana and papaya, these trees shade the soil, just as the larger forest trees do. The mixing of different kinds of plants in the same area means that minerals can be absorbed as soon as they are released; corn picks up nutrients very fast, while manioc is slow. Also, the small and temporary clearings mean that the forest can quickly reinvade its lost territory.

Because decomposers need moisture as well as warmth, the long Mekranoti dry season could alter this whole picture of soil ecology. But soil samples from recently burned Mekranoti fields and the adjacent forest floor showed that, as in most of the humid tropics, the high fertility of the Indians' garden plots comes from the trees that are burned there, not from the soil, as in temperate climes.

Getting a good burn is a tricky operation. Perhaps for this reason its timing was left to the more experienced and knowledgeable members of the community. If the burn is too early, the rains will leach out the minerals in the ash before planting time. If too late, the debris will be too wet to burn properly. Then, insects and weeds that could plague the plants will not die and few minerals will be released into the soil. If the winds are too weak, the burn will not cover the entire plot. If they are too strong, the fire can get out of hand.

Shortly after burning the plots and clearing away of some of the charred debris, people began the long job of planting, which took up all of September and lasted into October. In the center of the circular garden plot the women dug holes and threw in a few pieces of sweet potatoes. After covering the tubers with dirt they usually asked a male—one of their husbands or anyone else who happened to be nearby—to stomp on the mound and make a ritual noise resembling a Bronx cheer. This magic would ensure a large crop, I was told. Forming a large ring around the sweet potatoes, the Indians rapidly thrust pieces of manioc stems into the ground, one after the other.

When grown, the manioc stems form a dense barrier to the sweet potato patch, and some of the plants must be cut down to gain entrance. Outside of the ring of manioc, the women plant yams, cotton, sugar cane, and annatto. Banana stalks and papaya trees, planted by simply throwing the seeds on the ground, form the outermost circle. The Indians also plant corn, pumpkins, watermelons, and pineapple throughout the garden. These grow rapidly and are harvested long before the manioc matures. The garden appears to change magically from corn and pumpkins to sweet potatoes and manioc without replanting.

Mekranoti gardens grew well. A few Indians complained now and then about a peccary that had eaten a watermelon they were looking forward to eating, or that had reduced their corn harvest. Capybara, large rodents usually found near the river banks, were known for their love of sugar cane, but in general the animals seemed to leave the crops alone. Even the leaf-cutting ants that are problems in other areas did not bother the Mekranoti. Occasionally a neighbor who had not planted a new garden would make off with a prized first-year crop, such as pumpkin, watermelon, or pineapple. But even these thefts were rare. In general, the Mekranoti could depend on harvesting whatever they planted.

Eventually, I wanted to calculate the productivity of Mekranoti gardens. Agronomists knew very little about slash-and-burn agriculture. They were accustomed to experiments in which a field

[CONTINUED]

[CONTINUED]

was given over to one crop only, and in which the harvest happened all at once. Here, the plants were all mixed together, and people harvested piecemeal whenever they needed something. The manioc could stay in the ground, growing for several years before it was dug up.

I began measuring off areas of gardens to count how many manioc plants, ears of corn, or pumpkins were found there. The women thought it strange to see me struggling through the tangle of plants to measure off areas, 10 meters by 10 meters, placing string along the borders, and then counting what was inside. Sometimes I asked a woman to dig up all of the sweet potatoes within the marked-off area. The requests were bizarre, but the women cooperated just the same, holding on to the ends of the measuring tapes, or sending their children to help. For some plants,

like bananas, I simply counted the number of clumps of stalks in the garden, and the number of banana bunches I could see growing in various clumps. By watching how long it took the bananas to grow, from the time I could see them until they were harvested, I could calculate a garden's total banana yield per year.

After returning from the field, I was able to combine the time allocation data with the garden productivities to get an idea of how hard the Mekranoti need to work to survive. The data showed that for every hour of gardening one Mekranoti adult produces almost 18,000 kilocalories of food. (As a basis for comparison, people in the United States consume approximately 3,000 kilocalories of food per day.) As insurance against bad years, and in case they receive visitors from other villages, they grow far more

produce than they need. But even so, they don't need to work very hard to survive. A look at the average amount of time adults spend on different tasks every week shows just how easy going life in horticultural societies can be:

8.5 hours	Gardening
6.0 hours	Hunting
1.5 hours	Fishing
1.0 hour	Gathering wild foods
33.5 hours	All other jobs

Altogether, the Mekranoti need to work less than 51 hours a week, and this includes getting to and from work, cooking, repairing broken tools, and all of the other things we normally don't count as part of our work week.
(Adapted from D. Werner. (1990). Amazon journey (pp. 105–112). Englewood Cliffs, NJ: Prentice-Hall.)

Technologically more complex than horticulture is intensive agriculture, which usually results in far more modification of the landscape and the natural environment than does horticulture. **Intensive agriculture** involves more technology, such as irrigation, fertilizers, and the wooden or metal plow pulled by harnessed draft animals. In the so-called developed countries of the world, it relies on fuel-powered tractors to produce food on larger plots of land. Agriculturalists, in contrast to horticulturalists, are able to grow surplus food—providing not only for their own needs but for those of various full-time specialists and nonproducing consumers as well. This surplus may be sold for cash, or it may be coerced out of the farmers through tribute, taxes, or rent paid to landowners. These landowners and other specialists typically reside in substantial towns or cities, where political power is centralized in the hands of a socially elite class of people. The distinction between horticulture and intensive agriculture is not always an easy one to make. For example, the Hopi Indians of the North American Southwest, in addition to flood plain farming, also irrigate plots near springs, while using simple hand tools. Moreover, they produce for their own immediate needs and live in towns without centralized political government.

MEDIATREK
To find out about the roles that women around the world play in food production today, go to MediaTrek 6.2 on the companion Web site or CD-ROM.

As food producers, people have developed several major crop complexes: two adapted to dry uplands and two to tropical wetlands. In the dry uplands of Southwest Asia, for example, farmers time their agricultural activities with the rhythm of the changing seasons, cultivating wheat, barley, flax, rye, and millet. In the tropical wetlands of Southeast Asia, rice and tubers such as yams and taro are cultivated. In the Americas, people have adapted to environments similar to those of the Old World but have cultivated different plants. Maize, beans, squash, and the potato are typically grown in drier areas, whereas manioc is extensively grown in the tropical wetlands.

MEDIATREK
For a glimpse at life in Russian Siberia, where reindeer herders subsist in one of the earth's harshest climates, go to MediaTrek 6.3 on the companion Web site or CD-ROM.

Pastoralism

Before further discussion of agriculturalists, we should examine one of the more striking examples of human adaptation to the environment: **pastoralism**—breeding and managing herds of domesticated grazing animals, such as goats, sheep, cattle, llamas, or camels. Migrating with their herds, pastoralists regard movement of all or

intensive agriculture Crop cultivation using technologies other than hand tools, such as irrigation, fertilizers, and the wooden or metal plow pulled by harnessed draft animals.
pastoralism Breeding and managing of herds of domesticated grazing animals, such as goats, sheep, cattle, llamas, or camels.

In Mongolia, pastoral production has increased dramatically following the collapse of communism. Today, some 2.2 million people herd 2 million animals, and 79 percent of the land is under pasture—the largest common grazing land in the world.

part of the society as a normal and natural part of life. This cultural aspect is vitally important, for although some (but not all) pastoral nomads are dependent on nearby farmers for some of their supplies, and may even earn more from non-pastoral sources than from their own herds, the concept of nomadic pastoralism remains central to their identities. These societies are built around a pastoral economic specialization but imbued with values far beyond just doing a job. This distinguishes them from North American ranchers, who likewise have a pastoral economic specialization but who are not nomadic and identify culturally with a larger society.[16] It also sets them apart from food foragers, migrant farm workers, corporate executives, or others who are nomadic but not pastoralists.

Pastoralism is an effective way of living—far more so than ranching—in places that are too dry, too cold, too steep, or too rocky for farming, such as the arid grasslands that stretch eastward from northern Africa through the Arabian Desert, across the plateau of Iran and into Turkistan and Mongolia. In Africa and Southwest Asia alone, more than 21 million people follow pastoral nomadic ways of life.

The Bakhtiari Pastoralists

One group living in this belt of arid lands is the Bakhtiari, a fiercely independent people who live in the Zagros Mountains of western Iran, where they have tended herds of goats and fat-tailed sheep for many

thousands of years.[17] For transport, some of the Bakhtiari own horses and most own donkeys. But sheep and goats are the center of their pastoral way of life.

The harsh, bleak environment dominates the lives of the Bakhtiari: It determines when and where they move their flocks, the clothes they wear, the food they eat, and even their dispositions—they have been called "mountain bears" by Iranian townspeople. In the Zagros are snow-covered ridges that reach altitudes of

12,000 to 14,000 feet. Their steep, rocky trails and escarpments challenge the hardiest and ablest climbers; jagged peaks, deep chasms, and watercourses with thunderous torrents also make living and traveling hazardous.

The pastoral life of the Bakhtiari revolves around two seasonal migrations to find better grazing lands for the flocks. Twice a year the people move: in the spring to their summer quarters in the mountains and in the fall to their winter quarters in the lowlands. This pattern of strict seasonal movement between highlands and lowlands is known as **transhumance.** In the fall, before the harsh winter comes to the mountains, the nomads load their tents and other belongings on donkeys and drive their flocks down to the warm plains that border Iraq in the west. Here the grazing land is excellent and well watered during

---

[16]Barfield, T. J. (1984). Introduction. *Cultural Survival Quarterly, 8* (2).

---

[17]Material on the Bakhtiari is drawn mainly from Barth, F. (1960). Nomadism in the mountain and plateau areas of Southwest Asia. *The problems of the arid zone* (pp. 341–355). UNESCO; Coon, C. S. (1958). *Caravan: The story of the Middle East* (2nd ed., ch. 13). New York: Holt, Rinehart and Winston; Salzman, P. C. (1967). Political organization among nomadic peoples. *Proceedings of the American Philosophical Society, 111,* 115–131.

---

transhumance Among pastoralists, the grazing of animals in low steppe lands in the winter and then moving to high pastures on the plateaus in the summer.

the winter months. In the spring, when the low-lying pastures dry up, the Bakhtiari return to the mountain valleys, where a new crop of grass is sprouting. For this trek, they split into five groups, each containing about 5,000 individuals and 50,000 animals.

The return trip north is especially dangerous because the mountain snows are melting and the gorges are full of turbulent, ice-cold water rushing down from the mountain peaks. This long trek is further burdened by the newborn spring lambs and goat kids. Where the watercourses are not very deep, the nomads ford them. Deeper channels, including one river that is a half-mile wide, are crossed with the help of inflatable goatskin rafts, on which they place infants and elderly or infirm family members, as well as lambs and kids. Men swim alongside the rafts, pushing them through the icy water. If they work from dawn to dusk, the nomads can get all of the people and animals across the river in 5 days. Not surprisingly, dozens of animals drown each day.

In the mountain passes, where a biting wind numbs the skin and brings tears to the eyes, the Bakhtiari trek a rugged slippery trail. Climbing the steep escarpments is dangerous, and often the stronger men must carry their children and the baby goats on their shoulders as they make their way over the ice and snow to the lush mountain valley that is their destination. During each migration the nomads may cover as many as 200 miles. They have fixed routes and a somewhat definite itinerary, knowing about where they should be and when they should be there. The journey is familiar but not predictable. It can take weeks, for the flocks travel slowly

Pastoral nomadism is a cultural ecological adaptation that is effective in many parts of the world that are too hot, too cold, too dry, too rocky, or too rugged for farming. In the unforgiving Zagros Mountains region of Iran, Bakhtiari herders follow seasonal pastures, migrating with their flocks over perilously steep snowy passes and fast ice-cold rivers.

and require constant attention. Men and older boys walk the route, driving the sheep and goats as they go. Women and children usually ride atop donkeys, along with tents and other equipment.

When they reach their destination, the Bakhtiari live in tents—traditionally black goat-hair tents woven by the women. Inside, the furnishings are sparse and functional, but also artful. Heavy felt pads or elaborate wool rugs woven by the women cover the ground, and pressed against the inside walls of the tent are stacks of blankets, goatskin containers, copper utensils, clay jugs, and bags of grain. Traditional Bakhtiari tents provide an excellent example of adaptation to a changing environment. The goat-hair cloth retains heat and repels water during the winter and keeps out heat during the summer. These portable homes are easy to erect, take down, and transport.

Central to Bakhtiari subsistence, sheep and goats provide milk, cheese, butter, meat, hides, and wool. Women and girls spend considerable time spinning wool into yarn—sometimes doing so while riding atop donkeys on the less rugged parts of their migration. They use the yarn not only to make rugs and tents, but also clothing, storage bags, and other essentials. Bakhtiari people also engage in very limited horticulture; they own lands that contain orchards, producing fruit for themselves and to sell to townspeople. The division of labor is according to gender. The men, who take great pride in their marksmanship and horsemanship, engage in a limited amount of hunting on horseback, but their chief task is the tending of the flocks. The women cook, sew, weave, care for the children, and carry fuel and water.

With men owning and controlling the animals, which are of primary importance in Bakhtiari life, women have generally lacked both economic and political power. The Bakhtiari live in Iran but have their own traditional system of justice, including laws and a penal code. They are governed by tribal leaders, or *khans,* men who are elected or inherit their office. Most of the Bakhtiari *khans* grew wealthy when oil was discovered in their homeland around the start of the 20th century, and many of them are well educated, having attended Iranian or foreign universities. Despite this, and although some of them own houses in cities, the *khans* spend much of their lives among their people in the mountains. Such prominence of men in both economic and political affairs is common among pastoral nomads; theirs is very much a man's world. That said, elderly Bakhtiari women eventually may gain a good deal of power. And some women of all ages today are gaining a measure of economic power, bringing cash into the household by making and selling rugs traditionally created for their own domestic use.

© Reinhold Loeffler

Anthropology Applied

Agricultural Development and the Anthropologist

Gaining insight into the traditional practices of indigenous peoples, anthropologists have often been impressed by the ingenuity of their knowledge. This awareness has spread beyond the profession to the Western public at large, giving birth to the popular notion that indigenous groups invariably live in some sort of blissful oneness with the environment. But this was never the message of anthropologists, who know that traditional people are only human, and like all human beings, are capable of making mistakes. Yet, just as we have much to learn from their successes, so can we learn from their failures.

Archaeologist Ann Kendall is doing just this in the Patacancha Valley in the Andes Mountains of southern Peru. Kendall is director and founder of the Cusichaca Trust, near Oxford, England, a rural development organization that revives ancient farming practices. In the late 1980s, after working for 10 years on archaeological excavations and rural development projects, she invited botanist Alex Chepstow-Lusty of Cambridge University to investigate climatic change and paleoecological data. His findings, along with Kendall's, provided evidence of intensive farming in the Patacancha Valley, beginning about 4,000 years ago. The research showed that over time widespread clearing to establish and maintain farm plots, coupled with minimal terracing of the hillsides, had resulted in tremendous soil loss through erosion. By 1,900 years ago, soil degradation and a cooling climate had led to a dramatic reduction in farming. Then, about 1,000 years ago, farming was revived, this time with soil-sparing techniques. Kendall's investigations have documented intensive irrigated terrace construction over two periods of occupation,

including Inca development of the area. It was a sophisticated system, devised to counteract erosion and achieve maximum agricultural production. The effort required workers to haul load after load of soil up from the valley floor. In addition, they planted alder trees to stabilize the soil and to provide both firewood and building materials. So successful was this farming system by Inca times that the number of people living in the valley quadrupled to some 4,000, about the same as it is now. However, yet another reversal of fortune occurred when the Spanish took over Peru and the terraces and trees here and elsewhere were allowed to deteriorate.

Armed with these research findings and information and insights gathered through interviews and meetings with locals, the Cusichaca Trust supported the restoration of the terraces and 5.8 km of canal. The effort relied on local labor working with traditional methods and

materials—clay (with a cactus mix to keep it moist), stone, and soil. Local families have replanted 160 hectares of the renovated pre-conquest terraces with maize, potatoes, and wheat, finding the plots up to ten times more productive than they were. Among other related accomplishments, twenty-one water systems have been installed, which reach more than 800 large families, and a traditional concept of home-based gardens has been adapted to introduce European-style vegetable gardens to improve diet and health and to facilitate market gardening. Since 1997, these projects have been under a new and independent local rural development organization known as ADESA.

The Cusichaca Trust is now continuing its pioneering work in areas of extreme poverty in Peru further to the north, such as Apurimac and Ayacucho, using tried and tested traditional technology in the restoration of ancient canal and terrace systems. *(Adapted from K. Krajick. (1998). Greenfarming by the Incas? Science, 281, 323. The 2003 update and elaboration by textbook authors is based on personal communication with Kendall and Cusichaca Trust reports. For more information see www.cusichaca.org.)* ▪ ▪ ▪

Intensive Agriculture and Nonindustrial Cities

With the intensification of agriculture, some farming villages grew into towns and even cities (Figure 6.3). In these larger population centers, individuals who had previously been engaged in farming were freed to specialize in other activities. Thus, craft specialists such as carpenters, blacksmiths, sculptors, basket makers, and stonecutters contribute to the vibrant, diversified life of the city.

Unlike horticulturists and pastoralists, city dwellers are only indirectly concerned with adapting to their natural environment. Far more important is the need to adapt to living and getting along with their fellow urbanites. To a significant degree, this is true as well for the farmers who provide the city dwellers with their food. Under the political control of an urban elite, much of what the farmers do is governed by economic forces over which they have little, if any, control. Urbanization brings with it a new social order: Marked inequality develops as society becomes more complex, and people are ranked according to how much control they hold over resources, the kind of work they do, their gender, or the family they are born into. As social institutions cease to operate in simple, face-to-face groups of relatives, friends, and acquaintances, they become more formal and bureaucratic, with specialized political institutions.

With urbanization came a sharp increase in the tempo of human cultural evolution. Writing was invented, trade intensified and expanded, the wheel and the sail were invented, and metallurgy and other crafts were developed. In many early cities, monumental buildings, such as royal palaces and temples, were built by thousands of men, often slaves taken in war. These feats of engineering still amaze modern architects and engineers. The inhabitants of these buildings—the ruling class composed of nobles and priests—formed a central government that dictated social and religious rules were carried out by the merchants, soldiers, artisans, farmers, and other citizens.

Aztec City Life

The Aztec empire, which flourished in Mexico in the 16th century, is a good example of a highly developed urban society among America's indigenous peoples.[18] The capital city of the empire, Tenochtitlán (modern-day Mexico City), was located in a fertile valley 7,000 feet above sea level. Its population, along with that of its sister city, Tlatelolco, was about 200,000 in 1519, when the Spanish conqueror Hernan Cortes first saw it. This makes it five times more populous than the city of London at the same time. The Aztec capital sat on an island in the middle of a lake, which has since been drained and filled, and two aqueducts brought in fresh

---

[18]Most of the following information is taken from Berdan, F. F. (1982). *The Aztecs of Central Mexico.* New York: Holt, Rinehart and Winston.

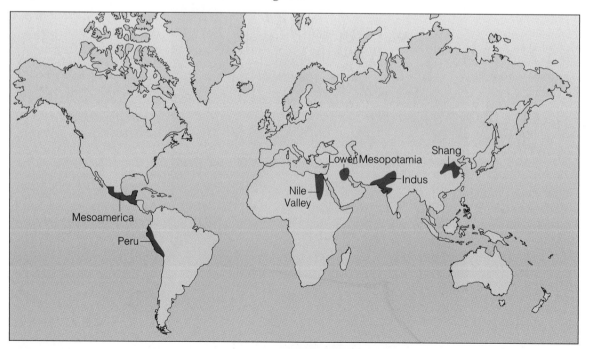

FIGURE 6.3

Locations of major early civilizations. Those of North and South America developed wholly independently of those in Africa, Asia, and Europe. Chinese civilization may have developed independently of those that developed earlier in Mesopotamia, the Egyptian Valley, and the Indus Valley.

water from springs on the mainland. A 10-mile dike rimmed the eastern end of the city to prevent nearby salty waters from entering the lake around Tenochtitlán.

As in the early cities of Southwest Asia, the foundation of Aztec society was intensive agriculture. Corn was the principal crop. Each family, allotted a plot of land by its lineage, cultivated any of a number of crops, including beans, squash, gourds, peppers, tomatoes, cotton, and tobacco. Unlike Old World societies, however, only a few animals were domesticated; these included dogs and turkeys (both for eating). Many (but not all) crops were grown in plots that were artificially constructed in the shallow waters of the lake surrounding Tenochtitlán. Canals between these *chinampas,* or raised fields, not only facilitated transport but were also a source of water plants used for heavy mulching. In addition, muck rich in fish feces was periodically dredged from the canals and spread over the gardens to maintain their fertility. Because they were incredibly productive as well as sustainable, *chinampas* are still in use today at Xochimilco, on the outskirts of Mexico City.

Aztec agricultural success provided for an increasingly large population and the diversification of labor. Skilled artisans, such as sculptors, silversmiths, stone workers, potters, weavers, feather workers, and painters could make good livings by pursuing these crafts exclusively. Since religion was central to the operation of the Aztec social order, these craftspeople were continuously engaged in the manufacture of religious artifacts, clothing, and decorations for buildings and temples. Other nonagricultural specialists included some of the warriors, the traveling merchants or *pochteca,* the priests, and the government bureaucracy of nobles.

As specialization increased, both among individuals and cities of the Aztec empire, the market became an extremely important economic and social institution. In addition to the daily markets in each city, larger markets were held in the various cities at different times of year. Buyers and sellers traveled to these from the far reaches of the empire. The market at Tlatelolco, Tenochtitlán's sister city, was so huge that the Spanish compared it to

One form of intensive agriculture, the *chinampa* (raised field), was perfected in ancient Mexico. This picture is of a modern *chinampa* garden on the Gulf Coast of Mexico.

those of Rome and Constantinople. At the Aztec markets barter was the primary means of exchange. At times, however, cacao beans and cotton cloaks were used as currency. In addition to its obvious economic use, the market served social functions. People went there not only to buy or to sell but also to meet other people and to hear the latest news. A law actually required that each person go to market at least once within a specified number of days. This ensured that the citizenry stayed informed on all important news. The other major economic institution, trade networks between the Aztec capital and other cities, brought goods such as chocolate, vanilla beans, and pineapples into Tenochtitlán.

The Aztec social order was stratified into three main classes: nobles, commoners, and serfs. The nobles, among whom gender inequality was most marked, operated outside the lineage system on the basis of land and serfs that the ruler allotted them from conquered peoples. The commoners were grouped into lineages, on which they were dependent for land. Within each of these, individual status was based on the degree of descent from the founder. Those more closely related to the lineage founder had higher status than those whose kinship was more distant. The third class in Aztec society consisted of serfs bound to the land and porters employed as carriers by merchants. Lowest of this class were the slaves. Some had sold themselves into bondage; others were captives taken in war.

The Aztecs were governed by a semi-divine king, chosen from among candidates of royal lineage by a council of nobles, priests, and leaders. Although the king was an absolute monarch, the councilors advised him on affairs of state. A vast number of government officials oversaw various functions, such as maintenance of the tax system and the courts of justice, management of government storehouses, and control of military training.

The typical Aztec city was rectangular and reflected the way the land was divided among the lineages. In the center was a large plaza containing the temple and the house of the city's ruler. At Tenochtitlán, with a total area of about 20 square miles, a huge temple and two lavish palaces stood in the central plaza, also called the Sacred Precinct. Surrounding this area were other ceremonial buildings belonging to each lineage.

As in a modern city, housing in Tenochtitlán ranged from squalid to magnificent. On the outskirts of the city, on *chinampas,* were the farmers' huts built of wooden posts, thatched straw, and wattle plastered with mud. In the city proper were the houses of the more affluent—graceful, multiroomed, one- and two-story stone and mortar buildings, each surrounding a flower-filled patio and built on a stone platform for protection against floods. It is estimated that there were about 60,000 houses in Tenochtitlán. The focal points of the city were the *teocallis,* or pyramidal temples, where religious ceremonies, including human sacrifice, were held. The 100-foot-high double temple dedicated to the war god and the rain god was made of stone and featured a steep staircase leading to a platform with an altar, a chamber containing shrines, and an antechamber for the priests.

The palace of the emperor Moctezuma boasted a menagerie, hanging gardens, a swimming pool, and numerous rooms for attendants and concubines. Since Tenochtitlán sat in the middle of a lake, it was unfortified and connected to the mainland by three causeways. Communication among different parts of the city was easy, and people could travel either by land or by water. A series of canals, with footpaths beside them, ran throughout the city. The Spaniards who came to the Aztec capital reported that thousands of canoes plied the canals, carrying passengers and cargo around the city. While the Spanish invaders were very impressed by

The American Museum of Natural History

Model of the center of Tenochtitlán, the Aztec capital city.

The modern industrial city is a very recent human development, although its roots lie in the so-called preindustrial city. The widespread belief that preindustrial cities are things of the past and that industrial cities are things of the future is based upon culture-bound assumptions rather than established facts.

Tenochtitlán's magnificence as one of the largest cities in the world, that did not prevent them from completely destroying it.

NONINDUSTRIAL CITIES IN THE MODERN WORLD

Tenochtitlán is a good example of the kind of urban settlement characteristic of most ancient, nonindustrial civilizations. Commonly termed **preindustrial cities,** they are likely to be thought of as part of the past, or as little more than stages in some sort of inevitable progression toward the kinds of industrial cities found today in places like Asia, Europe, and North America. This essentially ethnocentric view obscures the fact that preindustrial cities are far from uncommon in the world today—especially in the so-called underdeveloped countries of the world. Furthermore,

industrial cities have not yet come close to demonstrating they have the long-term viability shown by nonindustrial cities, which in some parts of the world have been around for not just hundreds but thousands of years. Today, about half of the world's entire population lives in cities, many of which are severely polluted. All the fastest-growing cities are in so-called developing countries. By the year 2015, six of the seven cities with more than 20 million inhabitants will be outside Europe and North America. Primarily due to massive flight from rural plight, the explosive population growth in many cities has led to the formation of vast urban slums where millions of malnourished and poverty-stricken people are forced to live in overcrowded, unsanitary, and disease-infested dwellings.

> *preindustrial cities* The kinds of urban settlements that are characteristic of nonindustrial civilizations.

Chapter Summary

■ Adaptation, essential for survival, is the ongoing process organisms undergo to achieve beneficial adjustments to a particular environment. It results in biological changes in the organisms, which in turn impact the environment. Humans are unique in that they adapt through culture, which has made it possible for them to inhabit an extraordinary range of environments. Cultural adaptation is the complex of ideas, activities, and technologies that enables people to survive in a certain environment.

■ A culture area is a region in which different societies follow similar patterns of life. Since geographic regions are not always uniform in climate and topography, new discoveries do not always spread to every group. Environmental variation

also favors variation in technology, since needs may differ from area to area. Julian Steward used the concept of cultural ecology to explain variations within geographical regions. In this view a culture is considered in terms of a particular technology and of the particular environmental features for which that technology is best suited.

■ The social and political organization of a society is another factor that influences how technology can be used to ensure survival. Those features of a culture that play a part in the way the society makes a living are its culture core. Anthropologists can trace direct relationships between types of culture cores and types of environments.

■ The food-foraging way of life, the oldest and most universal type of human adaptation, requires that people move their residence according to changing food sources. Local group size is kept small, possibly because small numbers fit the land's capacity to sustain the groups. Another possible reason for small size is that the fewer the people, the less the chance of social conflict. The primary mechanisms for regulation of population size among food foragers are absence of sufficient reserves of fat in females before early adulthood and frequent nursing of infants, which prevents ovulation.

■ Three important elements of human social organization probably developed along with scavenging and hunting for meat. These are a division of labor by gender, food sharing, and the camp as the center of daily activity and food sharing. A characteristic of food-foraging societies is their egalitarianism. Since this way of life requires mobility, people accumulate only the material goods necessary for survival, so that status differences are limited to those based on age and gender. Status differences associated with sex, however, do not imply subordination of women to men. Food resources are distributed equally throughout the groups; thus no individual can achieve the wealth or status that hoarding might bring.

■ The transition from food foraging to food production was probably the unforeseen consequence of increased management of wild food resources. Known as the Neolithic revolution, it began about 10,000 years ago. With it came the development of permanent settlements as people practiced horticulture using simple hand tools. One common form of horticulture is slash-and-burn, or swidden farming. Intensive agriculture, a more complex activity, requires irrigation, fertilizers, and draft animals. Pastoralism is a means of subsistence that relies on raising herds of domesticated grazing animals, such as cattle, sheep, and goats. Pastoralists are usually nomadic, moving to different pastures as required for grass and water.

■ Cities developed as intensified agricultural techniques created a surplus, freeing individuals to specialize full-time in other activities. Social structure became increasingly stratified with the development of cities, and people were ranked according to gender, the work they did, and the family they were born into. Social relationships grew more formal, with centralized political institutions. The sequence from food foraging, through horticultural/pastoral, to intensive agricultural nonindustrial urban, and then industrial societies is not inevitable. Where older adaptations continue to prevail, it is because conditions are such that they continue to work so well and provide such satisfaction that the people who maintain them prefer them to the alternatives of which they are aware. Contemporary food-foraging, horticultural, pastoral, nonindustrial, and industrial urban societies are all highly evolved adaptations, each in its own particular way.

Questions for Reflection

1. Since the beginning of human history, humans have been challenged to adapt to the resources available. Although you have read in this chapter about successful adaptations, failures have also happened. Do you know of any failures? From an ecological point of view, what are some of the causes?

2. What was so radical about the Neolithic revolution? Can you think of any equally radical changes going on in the world today?

3. Consider the ideas of change and progress in light of the agricultural development project described in the Anthropology Applied box. Come up with your own definition of progress that goes beyond the standard idea of technological and material advancement.

4. In light of what you have read about "the original affluent society," what is the role of advertising in your own society? Do you know of advertisements that actually create needs where there were none? How do these advertisements target potential consumers?

Key Terms

Cultural adaptation	Food foraging
Horticulture	Carrying capacity
Ecosystem	Density of social relations
Cultural ecology	Neolithic revolution
Progress	Swidden farming
Convergent evolution	Intensive agriculture
Parallel evolution	Pastoralism
Culture area	Transhumance
Culture type	Preindustrial cities
Culture core	

Multimedia Review Tools

Companion Web Site

Visit **http://www.wadsworth.com/anthropology_d/** and click on the companion Web site for this textbook to access a wide range of material to aid your study of anthropology. Among the options for self-study in each chapter are learning objectives, flash cards, Internet activities, Web links, InfoTrac College Edition exercises, and practice tests that can be scored and emailed to your instructor.

CD-ROM

The *Doing Anthropology Today* CD-ROM supplied with your textbook provides unique and valuable information designed to enhance your learning experience. This interactive multimedia resource includes video clips, interviews with renowned anthropologists, map and timeline exercises, chapter study quizzes, and much more. *Doing Anthropology Today* will not only help you in achieving your grade goals, but it will also make your learning experience fun and exciting!

Suggested Readings

Bates, D. G. (2001). Human adaptive strategies: *Ecology, culture and politics* (2nd ed.). Boston: Allyn & Bacon.

Taking an ecological approach to understanding human cultural diversity, this book explores different adaptive practices and their correlative political structures. Theoretical issues are made accessible through use of readable ethnographic case studies.

Bogucki, P. (1999). *The origins of human society.* Oxford, England: Blackwell.

In this well-written and comprehensive global history of the human species, the author traces the process of cultural evolution from our prehistoric beginnings as foragers to the creation of agricultural economies leading to complex societies and empires. As a record of human achievements, this book successfully incorporates the explosion in archaeological data accumulated during the last five decades.

Chatty, D. (1996). *Mobile pastoralists: Development planning and social change in Oman.* New York: Columbia University Press.

This study looks at the forces of modernization in a nomadic community and the resulting shift from herding to wage labor, as well as the changing role of women.

Lee, R. B., & Daly, R. H. (1999). *The Cambridge encyclopedia of hunters and gatherers.* New York: Cambridge University Press. Essential reference text on foragers.

Lustig-Arecco, V. (1975). *Technology: Strategies for survival.* New York: Holt, Rinehart and Winston.

Although the early anthropologists devoted a good deal of attention to technology, the subject fell into neglect early in the 20th century. This is one of the few relatively recent studies of the subject. The author's particular interest is the technoeconomic adaptation of hunters, pastoralists, and farmers.

Schrire, C. (Ed.). (1984). *Past and present in hunter gatherer studies.* Orlando: Academic Press.

This collection of papers demolishes many a myth (including several held by anthropologists) about food-foraging societies. Especially recommended is the editor's introduction, "Wild Surmises on Savage Thoughts."

CHAPTER 7

Economic Systems

© 1991 Richard Lord

CHALLENGE ISSUE

ALL HUMANS FACE THE CHALLENGE OF GAINING AND MAINTAINING ACCESS TO RESOURCES NEEDED FOR IMMEDIATE AND LONG-TERM SURVIVAL. Whatever they lack, they may seek to get by peaceful means through exchange or trade. In such economic transactions, humans forge and affirm their social networks. These friendships, partnerships, and alliances, in turn, are essential in their search for safety and well-being. A fundamental characteristic of the market in nonindustrial societies is that it always means a specific place where people meet in person to exchange goods at certain designated times. At this market in the highlands of Guatemala, people from the region exchange items they have produced for things they need but can only get from others.

1 How Do Anthropologists Study Economic Systems?

Anthropologists study the means by which goods are produced, distributed, and consumed in the context of the total culture of particular societies. Although they have adopted theories and concepts from economists, most anthropologists understand that theoretical principles derived from the study of capitalist market economies have limited applicability to economic systems where people do not produce and exchange goods for profit.

2 How Do the Economies of Nonindustrial Peoples Work?

In nonindustrial societies there is always a division of labor by age and gender, with some additional craft specialization. Land and other valuable resources are usually controlled by groups of relatives, and individual ownership is rare. Production takes place in the quantity and at the time required, and most goods are consumed by the group that produces them. Leveling mechanisms ensure that no one accumulates significantly more goods than anyone else.

3 How and Why Are Goods Exchanged?

People exchange goods through reciprocity, redistribution, and/or market exchange. Reciprocity involves the exchange of goods and services of roughly equivalent value and is often undertaken for ritual or prestige purposes. Redistribution requires a government and/or religious elite to collect and reallocate resources, in the form of either goods or services. Market exchange in nonindustrial societies takes place in designated locations where people trade goods, meet friends and strangers, and find entertainment. In industrial and postindustrial societies, market exchange may be indirect, impersonal, and mediated by money or capital in the form of shares or stock. With the advent of digital technology, trading is increasingly conducted on the Internet in an entirely impersonal manner.

An **economic system** may be defined as a means of producing, distributing, and consuming goods. Since a people, in pursuing a particular means of subsistence, necessarily produces, distributes, and consumes things, it is obvious that our discussion of subsistence patterns in Chapter 6 involved economic matters. Yet economic systems encompass much more than we have covered so far. Now comes the rest of the story.

ECONOMIC ANTHROPOLOGY

Studying the economies of traditional small-scale societies, researchers from industrial and postindustrial societies run the danger of interpreting anthropological data in terms of their own technologies, their own values of work and property, and their own determination of what is rational. Take, for example, the following statement from just one respected textbook in economics: "In all societies, the prevailing reality of life has been the inadequacy of output to fill the wants and needs of the people."[1] This ethnocentric assertion fails to realize that in many societies people's wants are maintained at levels that can be fully and continuously satisfied, and without jeopardizing the environment. In such societies, people gather or produce goods in the quantity and at the time required, and to do more than this makes no sense at all. Thus, no matter how hard they may work when hard work is called for, at other times they will have available hours, days, or even weeks on end to devote to "unproductive" (in the economic sense) activities. To observers from the industrial and postindustrial corners of the world, such people may seem lazy—and if they happen to be hunters and gatherers, even the skillful or strenuous work they do is likely to be misinterpreted. To those whose livelihoods depend on farming, trading, factory or office work, hunting is typically defined as a "sport." Hence, the male hunters in foraging societies are often perceived as spending virtually all of their time in "recreational pursuits," while the female food gatherers are seen as working themselves to the bone.

To understand how the schedule of wants or demands of a given society is balanced against the supply of goods and services available, it is necessary to introduce a noneconomic variable—the anthropological variable of culture. In any given economic system, economic processes cannot be interpreted without culturally defining the demands and understanding the conventions that dictate how and when they are satisfied. The fact is, the economic sphere of behavior is *not* separate from the social, religious, and political spheres and thus is not completely free to follow its own purely economic logic. To be sure, economic behavior and institutions can be analyzed in strictly economic terms, but to do so is to ignore crucial noneconomic considerations, which do, after all, have an impact on the way things are in real life.

As a case in point, we may look briefly at yam production among the Trobriand Islanders, who inhabit a group of coral islands in the southern Pacific that lie off the eastern tip of New Guinea.[2] Trobriand men spend a great deal of their time and energy raising yams–not for themselves or their own households, but to give to others, normally their sisters and married daughters. The purpose of this yam production is not to provision the households that receive them, because most of what people eat they grow for themselves in gardens where they plant taro, sweet potatoes, tapioca, greens, beans, and squash, as well as breadfruit and banana trees. The

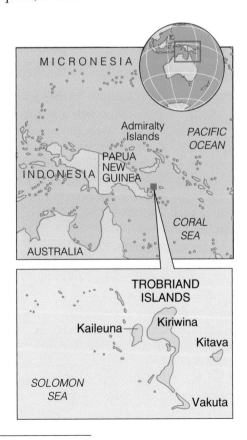

---

[1]Heilbroner, R. L., & Thurow, L. C. (1981). *The economic problem* (6th ed., p. 327). Englewood Cliffs, NJ: Prentice-Hall.

economic system A means of producing, distributing, and consuming goods.

[2]Weiner, A. B. (1988). *The Trobrianders of Papua New Guinea*. New York: Holt, Rinehart and Winston.

A crowd of protesters demonstrating against World Trade Organization (WTO) policies that favor rich countries over poor ones during the organization's 2003 meeting in Cancun, Mexico. While the field of economics is about markets, economic anthropology is about people and the defining role of culture in economic processes. Established in 1995 and headquartered in Geneva, WTO is the successor to the General Agreement on Tariffs and Trade, founded in 1947. With nearly 150 member-countries, it is the only global international organization dealing with rules of trade among countries.

reason a man gives yams to a woman is to show his support for her husband and to enhance his own influence.

Once received by the woman, the gift yams are loaded into her husband's yam house, symbolizing his worth as a man of power and influence in his community. Some of these yams he may use to purchase a variety of things, including arm shells, shell necklaces and earrings, betel nuts, pigs, chickens, and locally produced goods such as wooden bowls, combs, floor mats, lime pots, and even magic spells. Some he must use to fulfill social obligations. For instance, a man is expected to present yams to the relatives of his daughter's husband when she marries and again when death befalls a member of the husband's lineage (an organized group of relatives descended, in this case, through women, from a common ancestor). Finally, any man who aspires to high status and power is expected to show his worth by organizing a yam competition, during which he gives away huge quantities of yams to invited guests. As anthropologist Annette Weiner explains: "A yam house, then, is like a bank account; when full, a man is wealthy and powerful. Until yams are cooked or they rot, they may circulate as limited currency. That is why, once harvested, the usage of yams for daily food is avoided as much as possible."[3]

By giving yams to his sister or daughter, a man not only expresses his confidence in the woman's husband, but he also makes the latter indebted to him. Although the recipient rewards the gardener and his helpers by throwing a feast, at which they are fed cooked yams, taro, and—what everyone especially looks forward to—ample pieces of pork, this in no way pays off the debt.

Trobriand Island men devote a great deal of time and energy to raising yams, not for themselves but to give to others. These yams, which have been raised by men related through marriage to a chief, are about to be loaded into the chief's yam house.

[3]Weiner, p. 86.

Nor does the gift of a stone axe blade (another valuable in the Trobriand system), which may reward an especially good harvest. The debt can only be repaid in women's wealth, which consists of bundles of banana leaves and skirts made of the same material dyed red.

Although the banana leaf bundles are of no utilitarian value, extensive labor is invested in their production, and large quantities of them, along with skirts, are regarded as essential for paying off all the members of other lineages who were close to a recently deceased relative in life and who assisted with the funeral. Also, the wealth and vitality of the dead person's lineage is measured by the quality and quantity of the bundles and skirts so distributed. Because a man has received yams from his wife's brother, he is obligated to provide his wife with yams for purchasing the necessary bundles and skirts, beyond those she has produced, to help with payments following the death of a member of her lineage. Because deaths are unpredictable, and can occur at any time, a man must have yams available for his wife when she needs them. This, and the fact she may require all of his yams, acts as an effective check on a man's wealth.

Like people the world over, the Trobriand Islanders assign meanings to objects that make those objects worth far more than their cost in labor or materials. Yams, for example, establish long-term relationships that lead to other advantages, such as access to land, protection, assistance, and other kinds of wealth. Thus, yam exchanges are as much social and political transactions as they are economic ones. Banana leaf bundles and skirts, for their part, are symbolic of the political state of lineages and of their immortality. In their distribution, which is related to rituals associated with death, we see how men in Trobriand society are ultimately dependent on women and their valuables. So important are these matters to Trobrianders that even with the infiltration of industrial-world money, education, religion, and law, they remain committed to yam cultivation and the production of women's wealth. Looked at in terms of modern capitalist economics, these activities appear to make little sense, but viewed in terms of Trobriand values and concerns, they make a great deal of sense.

PRODUCTION AND ITS RESOURCES

In every society customs and rules govern the kinds of work done, who does the work, how it is accomplished, and who controls the resources and tools. Labor, raw materials, and technology are the primary resources that a social group may use to produce desired goods and services. The rules surrounding the use of these are embedded in the culture and determine the way the economy operates.

Labor Resources and Patterns

Labor is a key resource in any economic system. A look around the world reveals many different labor patterns, but there are two features almost always present in human cultures: a basic division of labor by gender and by age categories. Division by gender is not only effective when women and men are also raising offspring together, but it may actually expedite learning the necessary skills, since only half the adult repertoire needs to be learned by any one individual. Division by age provides necessary time for developing those skills.

Division of Labor by Gender

Anthropologists have studied extensively the division of labor by gender in societies of all sorts, and we discussed some aspects of this in earlier chapters. Whether men or women do a particular job varies from group to group, but much work has been set apart as the work of either one or the other. For example, we have seen that the tasks most often regarded as "women's work" tend to be those that can be carried out near home and that are easily resumed after interruption. The tasks most often regarded as "men's work" tend to be those requiring physical strength, rapid mobilization of high bursts of energy, frequent travel at some distance from home, and assumption of high levels of risk and danger. However, plenty of exceptions occur, as in those societies where women regularly carry burdensome loads or put in long hours of hard work cultivating crops in the fields.

In some societies, women perform almost three-quarters of all work, and in several societies they have served as warriors. For example, in the 19th-century West African kingdom of Dahomey, in what is now called Benin, thousands of women served in the armed forces of the Dahomean king and in the eyes of some observers were better fighters than their male counterparts. Also, there are references to female warriors in ancient Ireland, archaeological evidence indicates their presence among Vikings, and female Abkhasians of the Caucasus were trained in weaponry until quite recently. During World War II in the early 1940s, some 58,000 Soviet women engaged in frontline combat defending their homeland against German invaders, a volunteer women's platoon formed part of Fidel Castro's revolutionary forces in Cuba in the late 1950s, and North Vietnamese women fought in mixed-gender army units during the Vietnam War in the 1960s and early 1970s. Whether or not women should participate in direct combat operations is an ongoing issue in the United States, where women are still banned from combat

VISUAL **COUNTERPOINT** Often, work that is considered inappropriate for men (or women) in one society is performed by them in another. Here, a Uigir man in China sews, and a woman in neighboring Bhutan carries concrete for bridge construction.

infantry but do serve as combat pilots and on combat ships. Clearly, the division of labor by gender cannot be explained simply as a consequence of sex differences, whether they be of male strength and expendability or female reproductive biology.

Instead of looking for key biological factors to explain the division of labor, a more useful strategy is to examine the kinds of work that men and women do in the context of specific societies to see how it relates to other cultural and historical factors. Researchers find a continuum of patterns, ranging from flexible integration of men and women to rigid segregation by gender.[4] The *flexible/integrated pattern* is exemplified by people such as the Ju/'hoansi of the Kalahari Desert in southern Africa (whose practices we examined in previous chapters) and is seen most often among food foragers and subsistence farmers. In such societies, men and women perform up to 35 percent of activities with approximately equal participation, and tasks deemed especially appropriate for one gender may be performed by the other, without loss of face, as the situation warrants. Where these practices prevail, boys and girls grow up in much the same way, learn to value cooperation over competition, and become equally habituated to adult men and women, who interact with one another on a relatively equal basis.

Societies segregated by gender rigidly define almost all work as either masculine or feminine, so men and women rarely engage in joint efforts of any kind. In such societies, it is inconceivable that someone would even think of doing something considered the work of the opposite sex! This pattern is frequently seen in pastoral nomadic, intensive agricultural, and industrial societies, where men's work keeps them outside the home for much of the time. Thus, boys and girls alike are raised primarily by women, who encourage compliance in their offspring. At some point, however, boys must undergo a role reversal to become like men, who are supposed to be tough, aggressive, and competitive. To do this, they must prove their masculinity in ways women do not have to prove their feminine identity. Commonly, this involves assertions of male superiority, and hence authority, over women. Historically, societies segregated by gender often have imposed their control on those featuring integration, upsetting the egalitarian nature of the latter.

In the third pattern of labor division by gender, sometimes called the *dual sex configuration*, men and women carry out their work separately, as in societies segregated by gender, but the relationship between them is one of balanced complementarity rather than inequality. Although competition is a prevailing ethic, each gender manages its own affairs, and the interests of both men and women are represented at all levels. Thus, as in integrated societies, neither gender exerts dominance over the other. The dual sex orientation may be seen among certain American Indian peoples whose economies were based upon subsistence farming, as well as among several West African kingdoms, including that of the aforementioned Dahomeans.

Division of Labor by Age

Division of labor according to age is also typical of human societies. Among the Ju/'hoansi, for example, children are not expected to contribute significantly to

---

[4]Sanday, P. R. (1981). *Female power and male dominance: On the origins of sexual inequality* (pp. 79–80). Cambridge, England: Cambridge University Press.

© Eric Kroll

© D. Donne Bryant/DDB Stock

VISUAL COUNTERPOINT In nonindustrial societies, households produce much of what they consume. Among the Maya, men work in the fields to produce foods for the household; women prepare the food and take care of other chores that can be performed in or near the house.

subsistence until they reach their late teens. Indeed, until they possess adult levels of strength and endurance, many "bush foods"—edible tubers, for example—are not readily accessible to them. The Ju/'hoansi equivalent of "retirement" comes somewhere around the age of 60. Elderly people, while they will usually do some foraging for themselves, are not expected to contribute much food. However, older men and women alike play an essential role in spiritual matters. Freed from food taboos and other restrictions that apply to younger adults, they may handle ritual substances considered dangerous to those still involved with hunting or having children. By virtue of their old age, they also remember

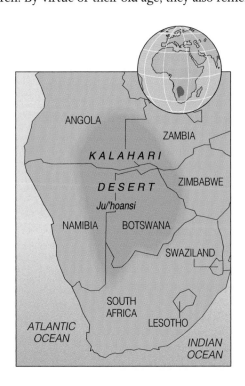

things that happened far in the past. Thus, they are repositories of accumulated wisdom—the "libraries" of a nonliterate people—and are able to suggest solutions to problems younger adults have never before had to face. Considered useful for their knowledge, they are far from being unproductive members of society.

In some food-foraging societies, women do continue to make a significant contribution to provisioning in their older years. Among the Hadza of East Africa, their input is critical to their daughters, whose foraging abilities are significantly impaired when they have new infants to nurse. This is because lactation is energetically expensive, along with the fact that holding, carrying, and nursing an infant all interfere with the mother's foraging efficiency. Those most immediately affected by this are a woman's weaned children not yet old enough to forage effectively for themselves. The problem is solved by the foraging efforts of grandmothers.[5]

In many traditional farming societies, children as well as older people may make a greater contribution to the economy in terms of work and responsibility than is common in industrial or postindustrial societies. For instance, in Maya peasant communities in southern Mexico and Guatemala, children not only look after their younger brothers and sisters but also help with housework. Girls begin to make a substantial contribution to the work of the household by age 7 or 8. By age 11 they are constantly busy with an array of chores—grinding corn, making tortillas, fetching wood and water, sweeping, and so forth. Young boys have less to

[5]Hawkes, K., O'Connell, J. F., & Blurton Jones, N. G. (1997). Hadza women's time allocation, offspring, provisioning, and the evolution of long postmenopausal life spans. *Current Anthropology, 38,* 551–577.

do but are given small tasks, such as bringing in the chickens or playing with a baby. However, by age 12 they are carrying toasted tortillas to the men out working in the fields and returning with loads of corn.[6]

Similar situations are not unknown in industrial societies. In Naples, Italy, children play a significant role in the economy. At a very young age, girls begin to take on responsibilities for housework, leaving their mothers and older sisters free to earn money for the household. Nor is it long before little girls are apprenticed out to neighbors and kin, from whom they learn the skills that enable them, by age 14, to enter a small factory or workshop. Typically, girls turn over earned wages to their mothers. Boys, too, are apprenticed out at an early age, but they may achieve more freedom from adult control by becoming involved in various street activities not available to girls.[7]

The use of child labor has become a matter of increasing concern as large capitalist corporations rely more and more on the low-cost manufacture of goods in the world's poorer countries. Although reliable figures are hard to come by, it is estimated that there are some 15 million bonded child laborers in South Asia alone, including some as young as 4 years old. Although the United States long ago passed laws prohibiting institutionalized child labor, the country imports at least $100 million worth of products manufactured by poorly paid children, ranging from rugs and carpets to clothing and soccer balls.[8] In the mid-1990s U.S. President Bill Clinton signed into law legislation aimed at preventing importation of products made by children who are forced into wage labor, but identifying violations and implementing such laws is difficult.

Cooperative Labor

Cooperative work groups can be found everywhere—in foraging as well as food producing, and in nonindustrial as well as industrial societies. Often, if the effort involves the whole community, a festive spirit permeates the work. Jomo Kenyatta, who became president of the East African country of Kenya after it won independence from British colonial rule in 1963, describes the time of enjoyment after a day's labor in his country:

> If a stranger happens to pass by, he will have no idea that these people who are singing and dancing have completed their day's work. This is why most Europeans have erred by not realizing that the African in his own environment does not count hours or work by the movement of the clock, but works with good spirit and enthusiasm to complete the tasks before him.[9]

In some parts of East Africa, work parties begin with the display of a pot of millet beer to be consumed after the tasks have been finished. Yet, the beer is not payment for the work; indeed, the labor involved is worth far more than the beer consumed. Rather, the beverage is more of a symbol, whereas recompense comes as individuals sooner or later participate in work parties for others.

Among the Ju/'hoansi in southern Africa, women's work is frequently highly social. About three times a week, they go out to gather wild plant foods away from the camp. Although they may do this alone, they more often go out in groups, talking loudly all the while. This not only turns what might otherwise seem a monotonous task into a social occasion, it also causes large animals—potential sources of danger—to move elsewhere.

---

[6]Vogt, E. Z. (1990). *The Zinacantecos of Mexico, a modern Maya way of life* (2nd ed., pp. 83–87). Fort Worth: Holt, Rinehart and Winston.

---

[7]Goddard, V. (1993). Child labor in Naples. In W. A. Haviland & R. J. Gordon (Eds.), *Talking about people* (pp. 105–109). Mountain View, CA: Mayfield.

© PhotoEdit

This Thai girl exemplifies the use of child labor in many parts of the world, often by large corporations. Even in Western countries, child labor plays a major economic role.

---

[8]It's the law: Child labor protection. (1997, November/December). *Peace and Justice News*, 11.

---

[9]Herskovits, M. (1952). *Economic anthropology: A study in comparative economics* (2nd ed., p. 103). New York: Knopf.

Jomo Kenyatta (1889–1978)

Jomo Kenyatta, Kenya's first president, was academically trained in anthropology and took the concept of cooperation from the local level and applied it to the state. His national slogan was *Harambee* ("Pull Together"), and with that sentiment he led his country to freedom from British colonial rule.

Born a Kikuyu, Kenya's largest ethnic group, he was originally named Kamau Ngengi. Later in life he adopted the name Jomo Kenyatta—Jomo meaning "burning spear" in his own language and Kenyatta referring to the beaded belt (*kinyata*) that he always wore. After his father died in 1896, he went to live with his grandfather, a medicine man. As a teenager, he attended primary school at a Scottish mission, followed by work as an apprentice carpenter. In 1915, he found work on a sisal farm, and in 1917 he moved to Narok where he lived with Maasai relatives while employed by an Asian contractor. A year later he found a job as a storekeeper in the capital city of Nairobi and took evening classes at another mission school. In 1919 he and his new wife turned part of their home into a little shop, which became a gathering place for friends from different ethnic groups who, like Kenyatta, were hungry for independence. Living outside of Nairobi, he also kept a small farm.

© Bruce Dale/National Geographic Image Collection

In the late 1920s, while working for the Nairobi City Council water department, Kenyatta became actively involved in the politics of land control and edited a newspaper on Kikuyu culture and new farming methods. As president of the Kikuyu Central Association, he traveled to London in 1929 and again in 1931 to argue for his people's right to the land on which British colonials had settled. Staying on in England, he completed studies at a Quaker college. In the mid-1930s he studied anthropology at the London School of Economics under the famous Bronislaw Malinowski. During this time he also penned various anti-colonialism articles, taught at

University College in London, and wrote anthropological studies about his people. Most significantly he published an autobiography titled *Facing Mount Kenya*, sometimes referred to as the bible of independence.

After serving as a key organizer of the 1945 Pan African Congress held in Manchester, England, Kenyatta went home to Kenya. In 1946 he became president of the Kenya African Union, which pressed for voting rights, an end to racial discrimination, and the return of indigenous lands. Dissatisfied with what appeared to be dead-end diplomacy, radical natives launched the "Mau Mau" uprising against British colonial rule. Responding with brutal force to guerrilla attacks that claimed about 100 British lives, British forces killed many thousands of native people and arrested those they suspected as instigators—including Kenyatta. During his 7 years of imprisonment, Kenyatta gained all the more influence, and in 1960—just before his release—fellow natives in the colony elected him president of the newly founded Kenya African National Union. After his country finally won independence in 1963, he was elected as the republic's first president, holding that office until his death in 1978.

In most human societies, the basic unit within which cooperation takes place is the household. It is both a unit of production and consumption; only in industrial societies have these two things been separated. The Maya farmer in Guatemala, for example, unlike his North American counterpart (but like peasant and subsistence farmers everywhere), is not so much running a commercial enterprise as he is a household. He is motivated by a desire to provide for the welfare of his own family; each family, as an economic unit, works as a group for its own good. Cooperative work may be undertaken outside the household, however, for other reasons, though not always voluntarily. It may be part of fulfilling duties to in-laws, or it may be performed for

political officials or priests by command. Thus, institutions of family, kinship, religion, and the state all may act as organizing elements that define the nature and condition of each worker's cooperative obligations.

As anthropologist Magdalena Hurtado points out, the spatial separation of work from household requires especially cruel trade-offs. Working outside the home and caring for children full-time are equally beneficial to a mother and her offspring. The problem is that inflexible work hours and commuting make them mutually exclusive.[10]

---

[10]Hurtado, A. M. (2000). Origins of trade-offs in maternal care. *Science, 287,* 434.

© 1996 Joel Gordon

The separation of wage work from the household presents women with a cruel trade-off: caring for children versus earning an income. For some women, the rise of the Internet has restored work to the home.

Craft Specialization

In contemporary industrial and postindustrial societies there is a great diversity of specialized tasks to be performed, and no individual can even begin to know all of those customarily seen as fitting for his or her age and gender. However, although specialization has increased in these societies, modern technologies are making labor divisions based on gender less relevant. By contrast, in foraging and traditional crop-cultivating societies, where division of labor occurs along lines of age and gender, each person has knowledge and competence in all aspects of work appropriate to his or her age and gender. Yet even in nonindustrial societies there is some specialization of craft. This is often minimal in food-foraging societies, but even here the arrow points of one man may be in some demand because of his particular skill at making them. Among people who produce their own food, specialization is more apt to occur. In the Trobriand Islands, for example, if a man wanted stone to make axe blades, he had to travel some distance to a particular island where the appropriate kind of stone was quarried; clay pots, on the other hand, were made by people living on yet another island.

One example of specialization is afforded by the Afar people of the desolate Danakil Depression of northeastern Ethiopia, one of the lowest and hottest places on earth. Afar men are miners of salt, which since ancient times has been traded widely in East Africa. It is mined from the crust of an extensive salt plain, and to get to it is a risky and difficult business. L. M. Nesbitt, the first European to successfully cross this desert, called it "the hell-hole of creation."[11] The heat is extreme during the day, with shade temperatures of 140° to 156° Fahrenheit not unusual. Shade is not found on the salt plain, however, unless a shelter of salt blocks is built. Nor is there food or water for man or beast. To add to the difficulty, until recently the Muslim Afars and the Christian Tigrians, who also mine salt, were sworn enemies.

Successful mining, then, requires specialized skill at planning and organization, as well as physical strength and the will to work under the most trying conditions.[12] Pack animals to carry the salt have to be fed in advance, for carrying sufficient fodder for them interferes with their ability to carry out salt. Food and water must be carried for the miners, who usually number thirty to forty per group. Travel is planned to take place at night to avoid the intense heat of day. In the past, measures to protect against attack had to be taken. Finally, timing is critical; a party has to return to sources of food and water before their own supplies are too long exhausted and before their animals are unable to continue.

Control of Land and Water Resources

All societies have regulations that determine the way valuable natural resources—especially land and water—will be allocated. Food foragers must determine who can hunt game and gather plants and where these activities take place. Similar problems are faced by those who fish on large bodies of water. Horticulturists must decide how their farmland is to be acquired, worked, and passed on. Pastoralists require a system that determines rights to watering places and grazing land, as well as the right of access to land where they move their herds. Full-time or intensive agriculturalists must have some means of determining title to land and access to water supplies for irrigation. In industrialized Western societies, a system of private ownership of land and rights to natural resources generally prevails. Although elaborate laws have been enacted to regulate the buying, owning, and selling of land and water resources, if individuals wish to reallocate valuable farmland to some other purpose, for instance, they generally can.

In traditional nonindustrial societies, land is often controlled by kinship groups such as the band or lineage (discussed in Chapter 10) rather than by individuals. For example, among the Ju/'hoansi, each band of anywhere from ten to thirty people lives on roughly 250 square miles of land, which they consider to be their territory—

---

[11]Nesbitt, L. M. (1935). *Hell-hole of creation*. New York: Knopf.

[12]Mesghinua, H. M. (1966). Salt mining in Enderta. *Journal of Ethiopian Studies, 4*(2); O'Mahoney, K. (1970). The salt trade. *Journal of Ethiopian Studies, 8*(2).

A Ju/'hoansi water hole. The practice of defining territories on the basis of core features such as water holes is typical of food foragers, such as these people of the Kalahari.

their own country. These territories are defined not in terms of boundaries but in terms of water holes that are located within them. The land is said to be "owned" by those who have lived the longest in the band, usually a group of brothers and sisters or cousins. Their concept of ownership, however, is not something easily translated in modern Western terms. Within their traditional worldview, no part of their homeland can be sold for money or traded away for goods. However, their permission must be asked by outsiders to enter the territory. To refuse such permission, though, would be unthinkable.

The practice of defining territories on the basis of core features—be they water holes (as among the Ju/'hoansi), distinctive features of the landscape where ancestral spirits are thought to dwell (as among Aborigines in Australia), watercourses (as among Indians of the northeastern United States), or whatever, is typical of food foragers. Territorial boundaries are left typically rather vaguely defined. To avoid friction, they may designate part of their territory as a buffer zone between them and their neighbors. The adaptive value of this is obvious—the size of band territories, as well as the size of the bands, can adjust to keep in balance with availability of resources in any given place. Such adjustment would be more difficult under a system of individual ownership of clearly bounded land.

Among some West African farmers, a tributary system of land ownership prevails. All land is said to belong to the head chief. He allocates it to various subchiefs,

who in turn distribute it to lineages; lineage leaders then assign individual plots to each farmer. Just as in medieval Europe, these African people owe allegiance to the subchiefs (or nobles) and the head chief (or king). The people who work the land must pay tribute in the form of products or special services such as fighting for the king when necessary.

These people do not really own the land; rather, it is a form of lease. Yet as long as the land is kept in use, rights to such use will pass to their heirs. No user, however, can give away, sell, or otherwise dispose of a plot of land without approval from the elder of the lineage. When an individual no longer uses the allocated land, it reverts to the lineage head, who reallocates it to some other member of the lineage. The important operative principle here is that the system extends the individual's right to use land for an indefinite period, but the land is not "owned" outright. This serves to maintain the integrity of valuable farmland as such, preventing its loss through subdivision and conversion to other uses.

Technology Resources

All societies have some means of creating and allocating tools used to produce goods and that are passed on to succeeding generations. The number and kinds of tools a society uses—which, together with knowledge about how to make and use them constitute its **technology**—are related to the lifestyles of its members. Food foragers and pastoral nomads, who are frequently on the move, are apt to have fewer and simpler tools than the more sedentary farmer, in part because a great number of complex tools would interfere with their mobility.

technology Tools and other material equipment, together with the knowledge of how to make and use them.

Among the Ju/'hoansi, game belongs to the man whose arrow killed it. But because arrows are freely loaned or given, the man who owns the kill may not even have been present on the hunt.

Food foragers make and use a variety of tools, many of which are ingenious in their effectiveness. Some of these they make for their individual use, but codes of generosity are such that a person may not refuse to give or loan what is requested. Thus, tools may be given or loaned to others in exchange for the products resulting from their use. For example, a Ju/'hoansi who gives his arrow to another hunter has a right to a share in any animals the hunter kills. Game is considered to "belong" to the man whose arrow killed it, even when he is not present on the hunt.

Among horticulturists, the axe, digging stick, and hoe are the primary tools. Since these are relatively easy to produce, every person can make them. Although the maker has first rights to their use, when that person is not using them, any family member may ask to use them and usually is granted permission to do so. Refusal would cause people to treat the tool owner with scorn for this singular lack of concern for others. If a relative helps raise the crop traded for a particular tool, that relative becomes part owner of the implement, and it may not be traded or given away without his or her permission.

In permanently settled communities, which farming makes possible, tools and other productive goods are more complex, more difficult, and costlier to make. Where this happens, individual ownership in them usually is more absolute, as are the conditions under which people may borrow and use such equipment. It is easy to replace a knife lost by a relative during palm cultivation but much more difficult to replace an iron plow or a diesel-fueled harvesting machine. Rights to the ownership of complex tools are more rigidly applied; generally the person who has funded the purchase of a complex piece of machinery is considered the sole owner and may decide how and by whom it will be used.

LEVELING MECHANISMS

Despite the increased opportunities that exist in permanently settled farming communities for people to accumulate belongings, limits on property acquisition may be as prominent in them as among nomadic peoples. In such communities, social obligations compel people to divest themselves of wealth, and no one is permitted to accumulate too much more than others. Greater wealth simply brings greater obligation to spend and give. Anthropologists refer to such an obligation as a **leveling mechanism.**

Leveling mechanisms are found in communities where property must not be allowed to threaten a more-or-less egalitarian social order, as in many Maya Indian villages and towns in the highlands of southern Mexico and Guatemala. In these communities, *cargo systems* function to siphon off any excess wealth people may accumulate. A cargo system (not to be confused with cargo cults, discussed in Chapter 13) is a civil-religious hierarchy that, on a revolving basis, combines most of a community's civic and ceremonial offices. All offices are open to all men, and eventually virtually every man serves at least one term in office, each term lasting for 1 year. The scale is pyramidal, which means that more offices exist at the lower levels, with progressively fewer toward the top. For example, a community of about 8,000 people may have four levels of offices, with thirty-two on the lowest level, twelve on the next one up, six on the next, and two at the apex. Positions at the lowest

leveling mechanism A societal obligation compelling a family to distribute goods so that no one accumulates more wealth than anyone else.

level include those for the performance of various menial chores, such as sweeping and carrying messages. The higher offices are councilmen, judges, mayors, and ceremonial positions. All positions are regarded as "burdens" (or *cargos* in Spanish) for which the holders are not paid. In fact, the officeholder is expected to pay for the food, liquor, music, fireworks, or whatever is required for community festivals or for banquets associated with the transmission of office. For some cargos, the cost is as much as a man can earn in 4 years! After holding a cargo position, a man usually returns to normal life for a period, during which he may accumulate sufficient resources to campaign for a higher office. Each male citizen of the community is socially obligated to serve in the system at least once, and social pressure to do so is such that it drives individuals who have once again accumulated excess wealth to apply for higher offices in order to raise their social status. Ideally, while some individuals gain appreciably more prestige than others in their community, no one has appreciably more wealth in a material sense than anyone else. In actuality, the ideal is not always achieved, in which case service in the cargo system functions to legitimize wealth differences, thereby preventing disruptive envy.

In addition to equalizing (or legitimizing) wealth, the cargo system accomplishes other results. Through its system of offices, it ensures that necessary services within the community are performed. It also keeps goods in circulation rather than sitting around gathering dust. Moreover, members are pressured into investing their resources in their own community rather than elsewhere. Likewise, the costs of holding office require participants to produce and sell a surplus or seek work outside the community in order to secure sufficient funds, thereby benefiting outside interests. To the degree that outsiders can control the goods and wages cargo holders require, the basic system's function may be subverted to serve as a means of drawing wealth and labor *out* of the community.

DISTRIBUTION AND EXCHANGE

The money economy of industrial societies involves a two-step process between labor and consumption. The money received for labor must be translated into something else before it is directly consumable. In societies with no such medium of exchange, the rewards for labor are usually direct. The workers in a family group consume what they harvest; they eat what the hunter or gatherer brings home, and they use the tools they themselves make. But even where there is no formal medium of exchange, some distribution of goods takes place. Karl Polanyi, an Austrian economic historian who immigrated to North America, classified the cultural systems of distributing material goods into three modes: reciprocity, redistribution, and market exchange.[13]

Reciprocity

Reciprocity refers to a transaction between two parties whereby goods and services of roughly equivalent value are exchanged. This may involve gift giving, but in nonindustrial societies pure selflessness in gift giving is as rare as it is in Japan, France, the United States, or any other industrial or postindustrial society. The overriding motive is to fulfill social obligations and perhaps to gain a bit of prestige in the process. It might be best compared in North American society to someone who gives a party. He or she may go to great lengths to impress others by the excellence of the food and drink served, not to mention the quality of wit and conversation of those in attendance. The expectation is that, sooner or later, he or she will be invited to similar parties by some, although perhaps not all, of the guests.

Social customs dictate the nature and occasion of exchange. When an animal is killed by a group of indigenous hunters in Australia, the meat is divided among the hunters' families and other relatives. Each person in the camp gets a share, the size depending on the nature of the person's kinship tie to the hunters. The least desirable parts may be kept by the hunters themselves. When a kangaroo is killed, for example, the left hind leg goes to the brother of the hunter, the tail to his father's brother's son, the loins and the fat to his father-in-law, the ribs to his mother-in-law, the forelegs to his father's younger sister, the head to his wife, and the entrails and the blood to the hunter. If arguments were to arise over the apportionment, it would be because the principles of distribution were not followed properly. The hunter and his family seem to fare badly in this arrangement, but they have their turn when another man makes a kill. The giving and receiving is obligatory, as is the particularity of the distribution. Such sharing of food reinforces community bonds and ensures that everyone eats. It also might be viewed as a way of saving perishable goods. By giving away part of his kill, the hunter gets a social credit for a similar amount of food in the future. It is a little bit like putting money in a time-deposit savings account.

reciprocity The exchange of goods and services, of approximately equal value, between two parties.

[13]Polanyi, K. (1968). The economy as instituted process. In E. E. LeClair, Jr., & H. K. Schneider (Eds.), *Economic anthropology: Readings in theory and analysis* (pp. 127–138). New York: Holt, Rinehart and Winston.

These Ju/'hoansi are cutting up meat, which will be shared by others in the camp. The food distribution practices of such food foragers are an example of generalized reciprocity.

The food-distribution practices just described for indigenous hunters in Australia constitute an example of **generalized reciprocity.** This may be defined as exchange in which the value of what is given is not calculated, nor is the time of repayment specified. Gift giving, in the unselfish sense, also falls in this category. So, too, does the act of a kindhearted soul who stops to help a stranded motorist or someone else in distress and refuses payment with the admonition: "Pass it on to the next person in need." Most generalized reciprocity, though, occurs among close kin or people who otherwise have very close ties with one another. Typically, participants will deny that the exchanges are economic, and will couch them explicitly in terms of kinship and friendship obligations.

Balanced reciprocity differs in that it is not part of a long-term process. The giving and receiving, as well as the time involved, are more specific. One has a direct obligation to reciprocate promptly in equal value in order for the social relationship to continue. Examples of balanced reciprocity in North American society include such practices as trading baseball cards or buying drinks when one's turn comes at a gathering of friends or associates. Examples from a nonindustrial society include those related by anthropologist Robert Lowie in his classic account of the Crow (or Absaroke) in Montana.[14] A woman skilled in the tanning of buffalo hides might offer her services to a neighbor who needed a new cover for her tepee. It took an expert to design a tepee cover,

which required from fourteen to twenty skins. The designer might need as many as twenty collaborators, whom she instructed in the sewing together of the skins and whom the tepee owner might remunerate with a feast. The designer herself would be given some kind of property by the tepee owner. In another example from these Plains Indians, Lowie reports that if a married Crow woman brought her brother a present of food, he might reciprocate with a present of ten arrows for her husband, which rated as the equivalent of a horse.

Giving, receiving, and sharing as so far described constitute a form of social security or insurance. A family contributes to others when they have the means and can count on receiving from others in time of need. A leveling mechanism is at work in the process of generalized or balanced reciprocity, promoting an egalitarian distribution of wealth over the long run.

Negative reciprocity is a third form of exchange, in which the giver tries to get the better of the deal. The parties involved have opposing interests, usually are members of different communities, and are not closely related. The ultimate form of negative reciprocity is to take something by force. Less extreme forms involve

generalized reciprocity A mode of exchange in which the value of the gift is not calculated, nor is the time of repayment specified.
balanced reciprocity A mode of exchange in which the giving and the receiving are specific as to the value of the goods and the time of their delivery.
negative reciprocity A form of exchange in which the giver tries to get the better of the exchange.

[14]Lowie, R. (1956). *Crow Indians* (p. 75). New York: Holt, Rinehart and Winston. (orig. ed. 1935)

Political fundraising in the United States involves elements of both balanced and negative reciprocity. Large contributors expect that their "generosity" will buy influence with a candidate, resulting in considerations and benefits of equal value. The recipient of the contribution, however, may seek to do as little as possible in return, but not so little as to jeopardize future contributions.

guile and deception, or at the least, hard bargaining. In the United States, an example would be the stereotype of the car salesman who claims a car was "driven by a little old lady to church" when in fact it was not and is likely to develop problems soon after it leaves the sales lot. Among the Navajo Indians of the southwestern United States, according to anthropologist Clyde Kluckhohn, "to deceive when trading with foreign peoples is morally accepted."[15]

Barter and Trade

Exchanges that occur within a group of people generally take the form of generalized or balanced reciprocity. When they occur between two groups, a potential for hostility and competition is apt to exist. Therefore, such exchanges may well be in the form of negative reciprocity, unless some sort of arrangement has been made to ensure at least an approach to balance. *Barter* is one form of negative reciprocity by which scarce items from one group are exchanged for desirable goods from another group. Relative value is calculated, and despite an outward show of indifference, sharp trading is more the rule, when compared to the more balanced nature of exchanges within a group.

An arrangement that combined elements of balanced reciprocity as well as barter existed between the Kota, in India, and three neighboring peoples who traded their surplus goods and certain services with the Kota. The Kota were the musicians and blacksmiths for

---

[15]Kluckhohn, C. (1972). Quoted in Sahlins, M. (1972). *Stone Age economics* (p. 200). Chicago: Aldine.

silent trade A form of barter in which no verbal communication takes place.

the region. They exchanged their iron tools with the other three groups and provided the music essential for ceremonial occasions. The Toda furnished to the Kota *ghee* (a kind of butter) for certain ceremonies and buffalo for funerals; relations between the two peoples were amicable. The Badaga were agricultural and traded their grain for music and tools. Between the Kota and Badaga there was a feeling of great competition, which sometimes led to one-sided trading practices; usually the Kota procured the advantage. The forest-dwelling Kurumba, who were renowned as sorcerers, had honey, canes, and occasionally fruits to offer, but their main contribution was protection against the supernatural. The Kota feared the Kurumba, and the Kurumba took advantage of this in their trade dealings, so that they always got more than they gave. Thus, great latent hostility existed between these two peoples.

Silent trade is a specialized form of barter in which no verbal communication takes place. In fact, it may involve no actual face-to-face contact at all. Such cases have often characterized the dealings between food-foraging peoples and their food-producing neighbors, as over the past 2,000 or so years, the former have supplied various commodities in demand in a wider economy. A classic description of such trade follows:

> The forest people creep through the lianas to the trading place, and leave a neat pile of jungle products, such as wax, camphor, monkeys' gall bladders, birds' nests for Chinese soup. They creep back a certain distance, and wait in a safe place. The partners to the exchange, who are usually agriculturalists with a more elaborate and extensive set of material possessions but who cannot be bothered stumbling through the jungle after wax when they have someone else to do it for them, discover the little pile, and lay

down beside it what they consider its equivalent in metal cutting tools, cheap cloth, bananas, and the like. They too discreetly retire. The shy folk then reappear, inspect the two piles, and if they are satisfied, take the second one away. Then the opposite group comes back and takes pile number one, and the exchange is completed. If the forest people are dissatisfied, they can retire once more, and if the other people want to increase their offering they may, time and again, until everyone is happy.[16]

To speculate about the reasons for silent trade, in some situations it may be silent for lack of a common language. More often silent trade may serve to control situations of distrust so as to keep relations peaceful. Good relations are maintained by preventing direct contact. Another possibility that does not exclude the others is that it makes exchange possible where problems of status might make verbal communication unthinkable. In any event, it provides for the exchange of goods between groups despite potential barriers.

MEDIATREK

For a quick visual and verbal overview of the Trobriand Islands' Kula ring, go to MediaTrek 7.1 on the companion Web site or CD-ROM.

The Kula Ring

Because trade can be essential in the quest for survival and is often undertaken for the sake of luxury, people may go to great lengths to establish and maintain good trade relations. A classic example of this is the **Kula ring,** a form of balanced reciprocity that reinforces trade relations among a group of seafaring Melanesians inhabiting a large ring of islands in the southern Pacific off the eastern coast of Papua New Guinea. First described by Bronislaw Malinowski, who observed it during ethnographic research among Trobriand Islanders between 1915 and 1918, this centuries-old ceremonial exchange system involves thousands of men and continues to this day.[17]

Kula participants are men of influence who travel to islands within the Trobriand ring to exchange prestige items—red shell necklaces (*soulava*), which are circulated around the ring of islands in a clockwise direction, and white shell armbands (*mwali*), which are carried in the opposite direction (Figure 7.1). Each man in the Kula is linked to partners on the islands that neighbor his own. To a partner residing on an island in the clockwise direction, he offers a *soulava* and receives in return a *mwali*.

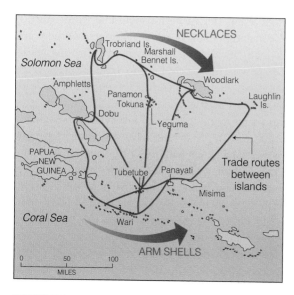

FIGURE 7.1

The ceremonial trading of shell necklaces and armbands in the Kula ring encourages trade throughout Melanesia.

He makes the reverse exchange of a *mwali* for a *soulava* to a partner living in the counterclockwise direction. Each of these trade partners eventually passes the object on to a Kula partner further along the chain of islands. Hand to hand, the objects make their way around the circle of islands. And so it is that men in the Kula ring may ultimately see necklaces and armbands return to them. By then, the objects have been exchanged many times, indirectly linking more than a dozen partners over hundreds of miles of ocean. For this reason, no one man keeps these valuables for very long. Holding on to an armband shell or necklace too long risks disrupting the path it must follow as it is passed from one partner to another. *Soulava* and *mwali* are ranked according to their size, their color, how finely they are polished, and their particular histories. Such is the fame of some that, when they appear in a village, they create a sensation.

Traditionally, men make their Kula journeys in elaborately carved dugout canoes, sailing and paddling these 20- to 25-foot long boats across open waters to shores some 60 miles or more away. The adventure is often dangerous and may take men away from their homes for several weeks, sometimes even months. Although men on Kula voyages may use the opportunity to trade for practical goods, acquiring such goods is not always the reason for such voyages—nor is Kula exchange a necessary part of regular trade expeditions. Perhaps the best way to view the Kula is as an indigenous insurance policy in an

---

[16]Coon, C. S. (1948). *A reader in general anthropology* (p. 594). New York: Holt, Rinehart and Winston.

[17]Weiner, pp. 139–157.

Kula ring A form of balanced reciprocity that reinforces trade relations among the seafaring Trobriand people who inhabit a large ring of islands in the southern Pacific off the eastern coast of Papua New Guinea, and other Melanesians.

economic order fraught with danger and uncertainty. It establishes and reinforces social partnerships between traders doing business on distant shores, ensuring a welcome reception from people who have similar vested interests. That said, this ceremonial exchange network does more than simply smooth or enhance the trade of foods and other goods essential for survival. Melanesians participating in the Kula ring have no doubt that their social position has to do with the company they keep, the circles in which they move. They derive their social prestige from the reputations of their partners and the valuables that they circulate. By giving and receiving armbands and necklaces that accumulate the histories of their travels and names of those who have possessed them, men proclaim their individual fame and talent, gaining considerable influence for themselves in the process. In Malinowski's own words,

> Each man has an enormous number of articles passing through his hands during his lifetime, of which he enjoys the temporary possession, and which he keeps in trust for a time. This possession hardly ever makes him use the articles, and he remains under the obligation soon again to hand them on to one of his partners. But the temporary ownership allows him to draw a great deal of renown, to exhibit his article, to tell how he obtained it, and to plan to whom he is going to give it. And all this forms one of the favourite subjects of tribal conversation and gossip, in which the feats and the glory in Kula of chiefs and commoners are constantly discussed and re-discussed.[18]

So it is that, like other forms of currency, *soulava* and *mwali* must flow from hand to hand; once they stop flowing, they may lose their value. A man who takes these valuables out of their inter-island circuit invites criticism. He may lose not only prestige, or "social capital" as a man of influence, but may become a target of sorcery for unraveling the cultural fabric that holds the islands together as a functioning social and economic order.

As an elaborate complex of ceremony, political relationships, economic exchange, travel, magic, and social integration, the Kula illustrates how inseparable economic matters are from the rest of culture. This is just as true in modern industrial societies as it is in traditional Trobriand society. For example, when the United States stopped trading with Cuba, Iran, and

A young Trobriand woman shows valuable Kula shells.

Estate of Annette B. Weiner

North Korea, it did so for political rather than economic reasons. Indeed, economic embargos have become popular as political weapons wielded by both governments and special interest groups. On a less political note, consider how retail activity in the United States peaks in December for a combination of religious and social reasons rather than purely economic ones.

Redistribution

Redistribution is a form of exchange in which goods flow into a central place where they are sorted, counted, and reallocated. Commonly, it involves an element of power. In societies with a sufficient surplus to support some sort of government, goods in the form of gifts, tribute, taxes, and the spoils of war are gathered into storehouses controlled by a chief or some other type of leader. From there they are handed out again. The leadership has three motives in redistributing this income: The first is to gain or maintain a position of superiority through a display of wealth and generosity; the second is to assure those who support the leadership an adequate standard of living by providing them with desired goods; and the third is to

---

[18]Malinowski, B. (1922). *Argonauts of the western Pacific* (p. 94). London: Routledge & Kegan Paul.

redistribution A form of exchange in which goods flow into a central place, where they are sorted, counted, and reallocated.

Many countries around the world have progressive income tax systems designed to redistribute wealth from those who have more to those who have less. In the United States the effectiveness of this system fluctuates due to periodic tax cut plans, such as those put forward by President George W. Bush, which critics claim favor the rich.

establish alliances with leaders of other groups by hosting them at lavish parties and giving them valuable goods.

The redistribution system of the ancient Inca empire in the Andean highlands of South America was one of the most efficient the world has ever known, both in the collection of tribute (obligatory contributions or gifts in the form of crops, goods, and services) and in its methods of administrative control.[19] Administrators kept inventories of resources and a census of the population, which at its peak reached 6 million. Each craft specialist had to produce a specific quota of goods from materials supplied by overseers. Required labor was used for some agricultural and mining work. Unpaid labor was also used in a program of public works that included a remarkable system of roads and bridges throughout the mountainous terrain, aqueducts that guaranteed a supply of water, temples for worship, and storehouses that held surplus food for times of famine. Careful accounts were kept of income and expenditures. A central administration, regulated by the Inca emperor and his relatives, had the responsibility for ensuring that production was maintained and that commodities were distributed. Holding power over this command economy, the ruling elite lived in great luxury, but sufficient goods were redistributed to the common people to ensure that no one would be left in dire need or face the indignity of pauperism.

Taxes, as imposed by central governments of countries all around the world today, are one form of redistribution—required payments typically based on a percentage of one's income and property value. People pay taxes to their government, some of which support the government itself while the rest are redistributed either in cash (such as welfare payments and government loans or subsidies to business) or in the form of services (such as military defense, law and order, food and drug inspection, highway construction, and the like). Tax codes vary greatly among countries. In many European countries, wealthy citizens pay considerably higher percentages of their incomes than those in the United States.

Spending Wealth to Gain Prestige

In societies where people devote most of their time to subsistence activities, gradations of wealth are small, kept that way through leveling mechanisms and systems of reciprocity that serve to spread quite fairly what little wealth exists. It is a different situation in ranked societies where substantial surpluses are produced, and the gap between the have-nots and the have-lots can be considerable. In these societies, showy display for social prestige—what economist Thorstein Veblen called **conspicuous consumption**—is a strong motivating force for the distribution of wealth. It has, of course, long been recognized that such excessive efforts to impress others with one's wealth or status also play a prominent role in industrial and postindustrial societies as individuals compete with one another for prestige. Indeed, many North Americans and Europeans spend much of their lives trying to impress others. This requires the display of items

---

[19]Mason, J. A. (1957). *The ancient civilizations of Peru.* Baltimore: Penguin.

conspicuous consumption A term coined by Thorstein Veblen to describe the display of wealth for social prestige.

© 1996 Steve Henrikson

The giving of gifts at a Kwakiutl potlatch on the Northwest Coast of North America. Among these Native Americans, one gains prestige by giving away valuables at the potlatch feast.

symbolic of prestigious positions in life—designer clothes, substantial jewelry, mansions, big cars, private planes. This all fits very neatly into an economy based on consumer wants:

> In an expanding economy based on consumer wants, every effort must be made to place the standard of living in the center of public and private consideration, and every effort must therefore be lent to remove material and psychological impediments to consumption. Hence, rather than feelings of restraint, feelings of letting-go must be in the ascendant, and the institutions supporting restraint must recede into the background and give way to their opposite.[20]

A form of conspicuous consumption also occurs in some crop-cultivating and foraging societies—as illustrated by lavish feasts hosted by "Big Men" in Papua New Guinea or potlatches given by the chiefs among the Kwakwaka'wakw, including the Kwakiutl, and neighboring indigenous groups living along North America's Northwest Coast. A **potlatch** is a ceremonial event in which a village chief publicly gives away stockpiled food and other goods that signify wealth. (The term comes

from the Chinook Indian word *patshatl,* which means "gift.") In extreme displays of wealth, chiefs even destroyed some of their precious possessions.

Outsiders are likely to see such grandiose displays as wasteful in the extreme, which is one reason why the Canadian government sought for many decades to suppress potlatches. However, these extravagant giveaway ceremonies have played an ecologically adaptive role in a coastal region where villages alternately faced periods of scarcity and abundance and relied upon alliances and trade relations with one another for long-term survival. Traditionally, a chief whose village had built up enough surplus to host such a feast for other villages in the region would give away large piles of sea otter furs, dried salmon, trade blankets, and other valuables while making boastful speeches about his generosity, greatness, and glorious ancestors. While other chiefs became indebted to him, he reaped the glory of successful and generous leadership and saw his prestige rise. In the future, his own village might face shortages, and he would find himself on the receiving end of a potlatch. Should that happen, he would have to listen to the self-serving and pompous speeches of rival chiefs. Obliged to receive, he would temporarily lose prestige and status.

MEDIATREK

To learn about potlatches among American Indian societies of the Pacific Northwest Coast and view an online exhibit, go to MediaTrek 7.2 on the companion Web site or CD-ROM.

The potlatch provided a ceremonial opportunity to strategically redistribute surplus food and goods among allied villages in response to periodic fluctuations in fortune. A strategy that features this sort of accumulation of surplus goods for the express purpose of displaying wealth and giving it away to raise one's status is known as a **pres-**

---

[20]Henry, J. (1974). A theory for an anthropological analysis of American culture. In J. G. Jorgensen & M. Truzzi (Eds.), *Anthropology and American life* (p. 14). Englewood Cliffs, NJ: Prentice-Hall.

potlatch A ceremonial event in which a village chief publicly gives away stockpiled food and other goods that signify wealth.
prestige economy Creation of a surplus for the express purpose of gaining prestige through a public display of wealth that is given away as gifts.

tige economy. In contrast to conspicuous consumption in industrial and postindustrial societies, the emphasis is not on amassing goods that then become unavailable to others. Instead, it is on gaining wealth in order to give it away for the sake of prestige and status. This serves as a leveling mechanism, preventing some individuals from obtaining and retaining excess wealth at the permanent expense of others, as shown in the following Original Study.

Original Study

Prestige Economics in Papua New Guinea

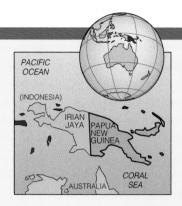

The average Enga patrilineage group [people who trace their descent back through men to a particular male ancestor] numbers about 33 and . . . [constitutes a] . . . close knit extended family. . . . At the next level, however, is the Enga subclan, a [larger order patrilineal descent] group numbering about 90 members that owns a sacred dance ground and a sacred grove of trees. Members of a subclan are required to pool wealth for bride payments whenever any of their members marry and in support of one of their members who is striving to become a Big Man. A subclan is in competition with other subclans for prestige, which affects its members' ability to obtain wives and their desirability as partners in regional alliances. An individual householder is motivated to contribute to his subclan's political and economic activities, therefore, because his immediate family's self-interest is intimately bound with that of the subclan.

The Enga subclan is a unit approximately the size of the largest corporate kin groups in societies occupying the less densely populated highland fringe of New Guinea, such as the Tsembaga [see Chapter 6]. But the Enga are organized into a still higher-level grouping [also based on patrilineal descent], the clan, which averages about 350 members and is the ultimate owner and defender of the territory of the clan, from which all clan members ultimately derive their subsistence. Clans own carefully defined territories and defend them both in battle and on ceremonial occasions. They are led by Big Men who speak for their clans in interclan relations and who work within their clans to mobilize the separate households for military, political, and ceremonial action.

Like the subclan, the clan is an arena for dramatic public activities. The clan owns a main dance ground and an ancestral cult house. At these ceremonial centers, public gatherings take place that emphasize the unity of the group as against other clans. Sackschewsky . . . sees this as an essential tactic to overcome the fierce independence of Enga households, where "each man makes his own decisions." Such familistic independence creates problems for Big Men, who encourage interfamily unity in the effort to enhance the strength of their own clans in a fiercely competitive and dangerous social environment.

Let us imagine the problems faced by the members of an Enga clan. They are trying to make an adequate subsistence from small amounts of intensely utilized land. Surrounding them is a world of enemies ready to drive them from their land and seize it at the first sign of weakness. They must attempt to neutralize this external threat by several means: (1) by maintaining a large, unified group, they show strength in numbers, making others afraid to attack them; (2) by collaborating in the accumulation of food and wealth to be generously given away at ceremonies, they make themselves attractive as feasting partners; and (3) by being strong and wealthy, they become attractive as allies for defensive purposes, turning their neighbors either into friends or into outnumbered enemies. These three goals can be achieved only if each member of a clan is willing to fight on behalf of other members, to avoid fighting within the clan (even though it is with his clan members that a man is most directly in competition for land, since they are his most immediate neigh-

bors), and to give up a share of his precious household accumulation of food and wealth objects in order that his Big Man may host an impressive feast.

This dependence of the household on the economic and political success of the clan is the basis of the Big Man's power. A Big Man is a local leader who motivates his followers to act in concert. He does not hold office and has no ultimate institutional power, so he must lead by pleading and bullyragging. His personal characteristics make him a leader. . . . : He is usually a good speaker, convincing to his listeners; he has an excellent memory for kinship relations and for past transactions in societies where there is no writing; he is a peacemaker whenever possible, arranging compensatory payments and fines in order to avoid direct violent retribution from groups who feel they have been injured; and, when all else fails, he leads his followers into battle.

Of great importance in this system is the exchange of brides between patrilineal groups, for which payments of food, especially pigs, and wealth objects are required. An individual's political position—which affects his access to land, pigs, and other necessities—depends on alliances formed via his own marriage and those of his close kin. A Big Man, skilled as a negotiator and extremely knowledgeable about the delicate web of alliances created across the generations by a myriad of previous marriages and wealth payments, can help a group to marry well and maintain its competitive edge. By arranging his own marriages, of course, the Big Man can not only increase the number of alliances in

[CONTINUED]

[CONTINUED]

which he is personally involved, but he can also bring more women, which is to say, more production of sweet potatoes and pigs, under his control. Hence, as he strengthens his group, he does not neglect his own personal power, as measured by his control of women, pigs, and wealth objects. His efforts both public and personal come together most visibly when he succeeds in hosting a feast.

Among the most dramatic economic institutions on earth, the Melanesian feasts have fascinated economic anthropologists. The Big Man works for months, painfully acquiring food and wealth from his reluctant followers, only to present them in spectacular accumulations—as *gifts* to his allies. But the generosity has an edge, as the Kawelka Big Man Ongka put it: "I have won. I have knocked you down by giving so much. . . . " And the Big Man expects that his turn will come to be hosted by his allies, when they will be morally bound to return his gift with an equivalent or larger one. The "conspicuous consumption" and underlying competitiveness of these displays of generosity have been regarded as so similar to philanthropy in our own economy as to seem to close the gap between "primitive" and "modern" economies.

But the Big Man feast must be understood in context. Similar to the famous potlatch of the northwest coast of North America, these feasts do not exist merely as arenas for grandiose men to flaunt their ambition. As analyzed for the northwest coast, the competitive feast is the most dramatic event in a complex of interactions that maintain what Newman . . . calls "the intergroup collectivity." We must remember that, beyond the Enga clan, there is no group that can guarantee the rights of the individual, in the sense that the modern state does for us. Beyond the clan are only allies, strangers, and enemies. Many of them covet the desirable lands of other clans, and, if they sense weakness, they will strike. Small groups—weak in numbers and vulnerable to attack—must seek to swell their numbers and to attract allies in other clans. Thus an individual family's access to the means of subsistence depends on the success of its clan in the political arena, ultimately in the size of fighting force that can be mounted from within the clan and recruited from allied clans.

In the absence of courts and constitutions regulating intergroup relations, the Big Men assume central importance. It is they who maintain and advertise their group's attractiveness as allies (hence the bragging and showmanship that accompany Big Man feasts), who mediate disputes to avoid the dangerous extremity of homicidal violence, who remember old alliances and initiate new ones. Despite the public competitiveness between Big Men as they attempt to humiliate one another with generosity, over time they develop relationships of a predictable, even trustworthy, nature with other Big Men, lending intergroup stability in an unstable world.

A good example of this stabilizing effect is seen in the *Te* cycle, a series of competitive exchanges that link many Central Enga clans. Starting at one end of the chain, initiatory gifts of pigs, salt, and other valuables are given as individual exchanges from one partner to the next down the chain of clans. Big Men do not have to be directly involved, since such individual exchanges follow personal lines of alliance. But because the gifts are flowing in one direction down the chain of clans, after a time the giving clans begin to demand repayment. As this signal passes through the system, individuals amass pigs for larger feasts at the opposite, or receiving end, of the chain. These larger interclan ceremonies are full of oratory and display that serve to advertise the size and wealth of individual clans. Over a period of months a series of large gifting ceremonies move back up the chain of clans toward the beginning. The emphasis on prestige in these ceremonies is certainly gratifying to the participants, but it serves larger purposes: to maintain peace by substituting competitive feasting for open warfare, to establish and reinforce alliances, and to advertise a clan's attractiveness as an ally and fearsomeness as an enemy.

The central points to note from this example are the following:

1. The high population density of the Enga . . . implies two related developments: First, there is little wild forest left and virtually no supply of wild foods for the diet; and, second, the best horticultural land is fully occupied and in permanent use. These two primary consequences of population growth have further implications.

2. One is an intensive mode of food production that does not rely so much on regeneration of natural soil fertility through fallowing as upon mounding and the addition of green manure to soils. Because of the Enga's reliance on pigs, these fields must support not only the human population but also that of the pigs, who consume as much garden produce as humans do. The labor costs of pigs therefore include both producing their food and building fences to control their predation of gardens. Although the Enga populations are able to provide their basic nutritional needs in this manner, other highland groups with similar economies do show some signs of malnutrition, suggesting that overall production is not much more than adequate.

3. Furthermore, with land scarce, warfare shows a clear emphasis on territorial expansion and displacement. In response to this basic threat to their livelihood, families participate, albeit somewhat reluctantly, in the political activities of the lineage and clan. Although these activities often appear belligerent and can lead to warfare by deflecting hostilities outside the clan or local alliance of clans, it remains true that they have the primary function of preventing violence and stabilizing access to land.

The three major paths for creating alliances are marriage exchanges, sharing of food at feasts (commensality), and an intricate web of debt and credit established through exchanges of food and wealth objects. All of these together constitute the prestige economies for which such groups are famous. Crucial junctures in the prestige economy are occupied by Big Men, who earn their status by personally managing the complex alliances that provide a degree of security to otherwise vulnerable groups of closely related kin. *(By A. Johnson. (1989). Horticulturists: Economic behavior in tribes. In S. Plattner (Ed.), Economic anthropology (pp. 63–67). Stanford, CA: Stanford University Press.)*

Market Exchange

To an economist, **market exchange** has to do with the buying and selling of goods and services, with prices set by rules of supply and demand. Personal loyalties and moral values are not supposed to play a role, but they often do. Since the actual location of the transaction is not always relevant in today's world, we must distinguish between the "marketplace" and "market exchange."

Typically, until well into the 20th century, market exchange was carried out in specific localities or *marketplaces*. This is still the case in much of the nonindustrial world and even in numerous centuries-old European and Asian towns and cities. In peasant or agrarian societies, marketplaces overseen by a centralized political authority provide the opportunity for farmers in the surrounding rural territories to exchange some of their livestock and produce for needed items manufactured in factories or in the workshops of craft specialists living (usually) in towns and cities. Thus, some sort of complex division of labor as well as centralized political organization is necessary for the appearance of markets. The traditional market is local, specific, and contained. Prices are typically set on the basis of face-to-face bargaining rather than by "market forces" wholly removed from the transaction itself. Notably, sales do not necessarily involve money; instead, goods may be directly exchanged through some form of barter among the specific individuals involved.

In industrial and postindustrial societies, some market transactions still take place in a specific identifiable location—much of the trade in cotton, for example, takes place in the New Orleans Cotton Exchange. But it is possible and increasingly common for people living in technologically wired parts of the world to buy and sell goods without ever being in the same city, let alone the same space, as those with whom they are doing busi-

In many societies, particularly in developing countries, the market is an important focus of social as well as economic activity, as typified by this market in Touboukro, Ivory Coast.

ness. When people talk about a market in today's industrial or postindustrial world, the particular geographical location where something is bought or sold is often not important at all. For example, think of the New York Stock Exchange or the Internet company eBay, where all buying and selling occurs electronically.

The faceless market exchanges that take place in industrial and postindustrial societies stand in stark contrast to experiences in the marketplaces of nonindustrial societies, which have much of the excitement of a fair. These traditional exchange centers are colorful places where one's senses are assaulted by a host of sights, sounds, and smells. In these markets social relationships and personal interactions are key elements, and noneconomic activities may even overshadow the economic. As anthropologist Stuart Plattner observes, the marketplace is where friendships are made, love

A packer working at an Amazon.com distribution center in Fernley, Nevada, prepares an order. With the advent of online shopping, people can buy and sell even though goods are not physically present.

market exchange The buying and selling of goods and services, with prices set by rules of supply and demand.

affairs begun, and marriages arranged.[21] Dancers and musicians may perform, and feasting and fighting may mark the end of the day. At the market, too, people gather to hear news. In ancient Mexico, among the Aztecs, people were required by law to go to market at specific intervals to keep informed about current events. Government officials held court and settled judicial disputes at the market. Thus, the market is a gathering place where people renew friendships, see relatives, gossip, and keep up with the world, while procuring needed goods they cannot produce for themselves. Over the last few decades many of the large urban and suburban malls built in the United States and other industrialized countries have tried to re-create, albeit in a more contrived manner, some of the interest and excitement of traditional marketplaces.

Although there have been marketplaces without money of any sort, money does facilitate trade. **Money** may be defined as something used to make payments for other goods and services as well as to measure their value. Its critical attributes are durability, portability, divisibility, recognizability, and fungibility (exchangeable or replaceable for any other monetary item of the same value, as when four quarters are substituted for a dollar bill). The wide range of things that have been used as money in one or another society includes salt, shells, stones, beads, feathers, fur, bones, teeth, and of course metals, from iron to gold and silver. Among the Aztecs of Mexico, both cacao beans and cotton cloaks served as money. The beans could be used to purchase merchandise and labor, though usually as a supplement to barter. If the value of the items exchanged was not equal, cacao beans could be used to make up the difference. Cotton cloaks represented a higher denomination in the monetary system, with one cloak being equivalent to 65 to 300 beans, depending on the cloak's quality. Cloaks could be used to obtain credit, to purchase land, as restitution for theft, and to ransom slaves, whose value in any case was measured in terms of cloaks. Interestingly, counterfeiting was not unknown to the Aztecs—unscrupulous people sometimes carefully peeled back the outer skin of cacao beans, removed the contents, and then substituted packed earth!

Copyright © The British Museum

Ancient Lydian money: the world's first coins. Lydia was located in Anatolia, which is now Turkey.

Among the Tiv of West Africa, brass rods might be exchanged for cattle, with the seller then using the rods to purchase slaves (the economic value of the cattle being converted into the rods and then reconverted into slaves). In both the Aztec and Tiv cases, the money in question is (or was) only used for special purposes. To a Tiv, the idea of exchanging a brass rod for subsistence foods is repugnant, and most market exchanges involve direct barter. Special-purpose monies usually have more moral restrictions on their use than do general-purpose monies, which can be used to purchase just about anything. Even the latter category, however, has limits. For example, in the United States it is considered immoral, as well as illegal, to exchange money for sexual and political favors, even though infractions of these constraints occur.

The United States, as part of a reaction to the increasingly impersonal nature of the modern economic system, is having something of a revival and proliferation of flea markets, where anyone, for a small fee, may display and sell handicrafts, secondhand items, farm produce, and paintings in a face-to-face setting. There is excitement in the search for bargains and an opportunity for haggling. A carnival atmosphere prevails, with eating, laughing, and conversation, and items even may be bartered without any cash passing hands. These flea markets, fairs, festivals, and farmers' markets are similar to the marketplaces of non-Western societies.

Flea markets also raise the issue of the distinction between the informal and formal sectors of the market economy. The **informal economy** may be defined as the system by which producers of goods and services provide marketable commodities that for various reasons escape government control (enumeration, regulation, or other types of public monitoring or auditing). Such enterprises

---

[21]Plattner, S. (1989). Markets and marketplaces. In S. Plattner (Ed.), *Economic anthropology* (p. 171). Stanford, CA: Stanford University Press.

money Anything used to make payments for other things (goods or labor) as well as to measure their value; may be special purpose or multipurpose.
informal economy The production of marketable commodities that for various reasons escape enumeration, regulation, or any other sort of public monitoring or auditing.

Kikuyu women picking tea in highland Kenya exemplify the fact that in Africa much of the farming is women's work. Failure to recognize this has led to the failure of many development schemes designed by outsiders and based on the assumption that men are the farmers.

© John Moss/Photo Researchers, Inc.

may encompass just about anything: gardening, house cleaning, child care, making and selling beer or other alcoholic beverages, doing repair or construction work, begging, selling things on the street, performing ritual services, lending money, dealing drugs, picking pockets, and gambling, to mention just a few. These sorts of "off-the-books" or black market activities have been known for a long time but generally have been dismissed by economists as marginal and therefore more of an annoyance than anything of importance. It is also difficult for them to track. Yet, in many countries of the world, the informal economy is, in fact, more important than the formal economy. In many places, large numbers of under- and unemployed people who have only limited access to the formal sector in effect improvise as best they can various means of "getting by" on scant resources. Meanwhile, more affluent members of society may evade various regulations in order to maximize returns and/or to vent their frustrations at their perceived loss of self-determination in the face of increasing government regulation.

ECONOMICS, CULTURE, AND THE WORLD OF BUSINESS

At the start of this chapter, we noted that anthropologists face the challenge of not falling prey to their own ethnocentric biases. Failing to overcome cultural biases can have serious consequences, especially in this era of globalization. For example, it has led prosperous countries to impose inappropriate development schemes in parts of the world that they regard as economically "underdeveloped" (which, in fact, is a problematic term). Typically, these schemes focus on increasing the target country's gross national product through large-scale production that all too often boosts the well-being of a few but results in poverty, poor health, discontent, and a host of other ills for many.

In northeastern Brazil, for example, development of large-scale plantations to grow sisal for export to the United States took over numerous small farms where peasants grew food in order to feed themselves. With this change, peasants were forced into the ranks of the unemployed or poorly paid wage laborers. Because they no longer had land for growing their own crops and did not earn enough to buy basic foodstuffs, they faced a dramatic increase in the incidence of malnutrition. Similarly, development projects in Africa, designed to bring about changes in local hydrology, vegetation, and settlement patterns—and even programs aimed at reducing certain diseases—have frequently led directly to *increased* disease rates.[22]

Such failures are tied to the fact that every culture is an integrated system (as illustrated by the barrel model) and that a shift in the infrastructure, or economic base, impacts interlinked elements of the society's social structure and superstructure. As the ethnographic examples of the potlatch and the Kula ring show, economic activities in

---

[22]Bodley, J. H. (1990). *Victims of progress* (3rd ed., p. 141). Mountain View, CA: Mayfield.

traditional cultures such as the Kwakiutl and the Trobrianders are intricately intertwined with social and political relations, and even involve spiritual elements. Development programs that do not take such complexities into consideration may have unintended negative consequences on a society. Fortunately, there is now a growing awareness on the part of development officials that future projects are unlikely to succeed without the expertise that anthropologically trained people can bring to bear.

MEDIATREK

To gain an understanding of the social, cultural, political, and economic implications of the global expansion of capitalism, go to MediaTrek 7.3 on the companion Web site or CD-ROM.

Achieving a cross-cultural understanding of the economic organizations of other peoples that is not distorted or limited by the logic, hopes, and expectations of one's own society has also become important for corporate executives in today's world. Recognizing how intertwined economic structures are with other aspects of a culture could help business corporations avoid problems of the sort experienced by Gerber, when it began selling baby foods in Africa. As in the United States, Gerber's labels featured a picture of a smiling baby. Only later did company officials learn that, in Africa, businesses routinely put pictures of the products themselves on the outside label, since many people cannot read. In a similar vein, Frank Perdue's line in ads for Perdue chickens, "It takes a strong man to make a tender chicken," was translated into Spanish as, "It takes an aroused man to make a chicken affectionate."[23] Anthropologists Edward and Mildred Hall describe another cross-cultural miscommunication:

> José Ybarra and Sir Edmund Jones are at the same party and it is important for them to establish a cordial relationship for business reasons. Each is trying to be warm and friendly, yet they will part with mutual distrust and their business transaction will probably fall through. José, in Latin fashion, moved closer and closer to Sir Edmund as they spoke, and this movement was miscommunicated as pushiness to Sir Edmund, who kept backing away from this intimacy, and this was miscommunicated to José as coldness.[24]

As globalization increases so does corporate awareness of the cost of such cross-cultural miscues. So it is

© 1998 Joel Gordon

Steve Barnett, who earned his Ph.D. in anthropology from the University of Chicago, was for many years head of a consulting firm that served several large corporations. He is now a vice president at Citibank in Long Island City, New York, where he studies long-term cultural trends in patterns of consumption worldwide.

not surprising that business recruiters on college campuses in North America and elsewhere are now on the lookout for job candidates with the kind of cross-cultural understanding of the world anthropology provides.

It is also of note that the business world has discovered that anthropological research methods are highly effective when it comes to identifying and analyzing what is and is not functioning within a particular corporate way of life. This has given rise to a career specialization known as business or corporate anthropology (see Anthropology Applied).

All of this said, it is important to note that powerful corporations headquartered in the so-called developed world, often with subsidiaries overseas, are in business to make a profit, not to protect the weak, benefit the poor, support the sick, favor small producers, or save the environment. Their agenda is universally promoted through slogans such as "free trade," "free markets," and "free enterprise." The commercial success of such multinationals does not come without a price, and all too often that price is paid by still surviving indigenous foragers, small farmers, herders and fishermen, local artisans such as weavers and carpenters, and so on. From the viewpoint of these structurally disadvantaged groups of people, such slogans of freedom have the ring of "savage capitalism," a term now often used in Latin America for a new world order in which the powerless feel condemned to dependency and poverty (see Chapter 16).

[23]Madison Avenue relevance. (1999). *Anthropology Newsletter, 40* (4), 32.

[24]Hall, E. T., & Hall, M. R. (1986). The sounds of silence. In E. Angeloni (Ed.), *Anthropology 86/87* (p. 65). Guilford, CT: Dushkin.

Anthropology Applied

Anthropology in the Corporate Jungle

For the first 15 years of my career as an anthropologist, I did what most people in the discipline had done for more than a century: I focused my research on the cultures of "exotic" peoples living in remote, nonindustrial corners of the world. For me it was the rainforests of Central America and the deserts of the Sahara. Then I decided to turn the lens on my own culture and use anthropology's methods to study businesses, non-profit organizations, and governmental and educational institutions. I became part of a growing wave of corporate anthropologists, so-called because we study corporate groups.

What makes corporate anthropology an interesting addition to our discipline's repertoire is that fieldwork takes place in a contemporary organization rather than in the jungles of Guatemala, New Guinea, or Samoa. And when you think about it, you don't have to go far away to find the exotic. Many of us live in jungles, whether concrete or green and leafy. The challenge for all of us, not just anthropologists, is to critically see the most familiar and mundane cultural practice as a view from afar, and in that shift of perspective to gain new insight about how we live. Looking through an anthropological lens, some of those practices can at times seem quite bizarre!

Imagine, for example, observing a typical office meeting from an anthropological perspective. There are the tribal elders milling around a huge polished wooden slab, shaking hands and pounding each other on the back. The men are all dressed in the same costumes, their "loin cloths" held up by suspenders or a belt, their feet encased in black polished footwear. On occasion a female voice is heard, only to be drowned out by the bleating of the males. And then there's the question of what to do when you are the anthropologist and all of your informants are too busy to talk with you? I resorted to stocking my office with exotic chocolates from all around the world and

sprinkling Hershey's Kisses, like breadcrumbs, down the hallways so that people could find me easily. I was never lonely after that.

There are moments when this work is entertaining. That said, my research is serious business. It has a practical side, a purpose. It provides corporations with insights about their operations that can lead to problem-solving solutions that increase productivity and profitability. Let me offer a specific example.

I served as visiting anthropologist with IBM for ten years from 1990–2000. During that time IBM was struggling to respond to new market demands as the computer industry morphed from mainframes to personal computers in the late 1980s. Their slow reaction prompted their executives to seek help, and I was called in. I was placed in charge of developing a methodology for changing their culture, and, if successful, IBM would apply the same methodology on its many customers and vendors around the world (the inception of the IBM Consulting Group, now a part of Global Services). I explained how I had developed rapid analysis software that could "x-ray" the company's culture—the human networks of its current work processes. This was possible thanks to a database I'd created of more than 200 examples of corporate networks from all around the world. Using my database, I could quickly diagnose and benchmark IBM's culture to determine

Courtesy of Karen Stephenson

the nature of any pathology. For the next several years, several divisions were analyzed, including their executive leadership. After a statistical analysis was performed, I developed a measure for cultural inertia (a resistance to change) and determined the sunk costs of operational inefficiencies. Fixing the problem was twofold:

1. Reorganizing the company by outsourcing divisions as independent companies partnering with IBM, reducing the overall employee population from 400,000 to 250,000.
2. Restructuring the pay and performance systems for the top executives so that they were rewarded for cooperating as a team rather than competing against neighboring divisions, perversely thwarting the overall organizational goals.

Both solutions were cultural in nature and difficult for those within the culture to detect. But with the help of my x-rays, IBMers saw for themselves how sometimes their best efforts were often misguided, hindering rather than helping. Accepting the findings and recommendations as objective and sound, they were willing to change their behaviors to improve productivity.

I also introduced another change at IBM: I was the first female executive to wear pants. When confronted with the news that I'd breached the fashion code, I just told them that females wearing pants was a more modest and conservative approach, totally in keeping with their cultural values. One vice president threw back his head and laughed: "I never thought of it that way!" *(By Karen Stephenson for this textbook. For more about Stephenson and her work, visit her company's Web site: www.netform.com.)* ■ ■ ■

Chapter Summary

■ An economic system is the means by which goods are produced, distributed, and consumed. Studying the economics of nonliterate, nonindustrial societies can be undertaken only in the context of the total culture of each society. Each society solves the problem of subsisting by allocating raw materials, land, labor, and technology and by distributing goods according to its own priorities.

■ Labor is a major productive resource, and the allotment of work is commonly governed by rules according to gender and age. Only a few broad generalizations can be made covering the kinds of work performed by men and women cross-culturally. Instead of looking for biological imperatives to explain the division of labor, a more productive strategy is to examine the kinds of work that men and women do in the context of specific societies to see how it relates to other cultural and historical factors. The cooperation of many people working together is a typical feature of both nonindustrial and industrial societies. Specialization of craft is important even in societies with very simple technologies.

■ All societies regulate the allocation of land and other valuable resources. In nonindustrial societies, individual ownership of land is rare; generally land is controlled by kinship groups, such as the lineage or band. The band provides flexibility of land use, since the size of the bands and their territories can be adjusted according to availability of resources in any particular place. The technology of a people, in the form of the tools they use and associated knowledge, is related to their mode of subsistence.

■ In food-foraging societies, codes of generosity promote free access to tools, even though individuals may have made these for their own use. Settled farming communities offer greater opportunities to accumulate material belongings, and inequalities of wealth may develop. In many such communities, though, a relatively egalitarian social order may be maintained through leveling mechanisms.

■ Nonindustrial peoples consume most of what they produce themselves, but they do exchange goods. The processes of distribution may be distinguished as reciprocity, redistribution, and market exchange. Reciprocity is a transaction between individuals or groups, involving the exchange of goods and services of roughly equivalent value. Usually it is prescribed by ritual and ceremony. Barter and trade take place between groups. Trading exchanges have elements of reciprocity but involve a greater calculation of the relative value of goods exchanged. Barter is one form of negative reciprocity, whereby scarce goods from one group are exchanged for desirable goods from another group. Silent trade, which need not involve face-to-face contact, is a specialized form of barter with no verbal communication. It allows control of the potential dangers of negative reciprocity. A classic example of exchange that partakes of both reciprocity and sharp trading is the Kula ring of the Trobriand Islanders.

■ Display for social prestige is a motivating force in societies that produce some surplus of goods. In the United States, goods accumulated for display generally remain in the hands of those who accumulated them, whereas in other societies they are generally given away; the prestige comes from publicly divesting oneself of valuables.

■ Strong, centralized political organization is necessary for redistribution to occur. The government assesses each citizen a tax or tribute, uses the proceeds to support the governmental and religious elite, and redistributes the rest, usually in the form of public services. The collection of taxes and delivery of government services and subsidies in the United States is a form of redistribution.

■ Exchange in the marketplace serves to distribute goods in a region. In nonindustrial societies, the marketplace is usually a specific site where produce, livestock, and material items the people produce are exchanged. It also functions as a social gathering place and a news medium. Although market exchanges may take place without money through bartering and other forms of reciprocity, some form of money at least for special transactions makes market exchange more efficient. In market economies, the informal sector may become more important than the formal sector as large numbers of under- and unemployed people with marginal access to the formal economy seek to survive. The informal economy consists of those economic activities that escape official scrutiny and regulation.

■ The anthropological approach to economics has taken on new importance in today's world of international development and commerce. Without it, development schemes for so-called underdeveloped countries are prone to failure, and international trade is handicapped as a result of cross-cultural misunderstandings.

Questions for Reflection

1. Imagine that you are a nomadic forager or pastoralist. How would that way of life challenge your social relations, your view of the natural environment, and your attitude toward possessions?

2. Consider the differences between reciprocity and market exchange. What role does each play in your own society?

3. As the potlatch ceremony shows, prestige may be gained by giving away wealth. Does such a prestige-building mechanism exist in your own society? If so, how does it work?

4. In the Kula ring, men of influence participate in a wide social network based on balanced reciprocity. Why would such a system not survive if individuals in this ring begin to operate on the basis of negative reciprocity?

5. As discussed in this chapter, economic relations in traditional cultures are usually wrapped up in social, political, and even spiritual issues. Can you think of any examples in your

own society in which the economic sphere is inextricably intertwined with other structures in the cultural system? Would tinkering with the economic sphere affect these other aspects of your culture?

Key Terms

Economic system	Kula ring
Technology	Redistribution
Leveling mechanism	Conspicuous consumption
Reciprocity	Potlatch
Generalized reciprocity	Prestige economy
Balanced reciprocity	Market exchange
Negative reciprocity	Money
Silent trade	Informal economy

Multimedia Review Tools

Companion Web Site

Visit **http://www.wadsworth.com/anthropology_d/** and click on the companion Web site for this textbook to access a wide range of material to aid your study of anthropology. Among the options for self-study in each chapter are learning objectives, flash cards, Internet activities, Web links, InfoTrac College Edition exercises, and practice tests that can be scored and emailed to your instructor.

CD-ROM

The *Doing Anthropology Today* CD-ROM supplied with your textbook provides unique and valuable information designed to enhance your learning experience. This interactive multimedia resource includes video clips, interviews with renowned anthropologists, map and timeline exercises, chapter study quizzes, and much more. *Doing Anthropology*

Today will not only help you in achieving your grade goals, but it will also make your learning experience fun and exciting!

Suggested Readings

Blumberg, R. L. (1991). *Gender, family and the economy: The triple overlap*. Newbury Park, CA: Sage.

A look at the interrelationship of gender, domestic life, and the economy.

Dalton, G. (1971). *Traditional tribal and peasant economies: An introductory survey of economic anthropology*. Reading, MA: Addison-Wesley.

This is just what the title says it is, by a major specialist in economic anthropology.

Halperin, R. H. (1994). *Cultural economies: Past and present*. Austin: University of Texas Press.

A cross-cultural approach to analyzing economic processes in cultural systems.

Plattner, S. (Ed.). (1989). *Economic anthropology*. Stanford, CA: Stanford University Press.

A collection of essays from twelve scholars in the field concerning a variety of issues ranging from economic behavior in foraging, horticultural, "preindustrial" state, peasant, and industrial societies; to gender roles, common property resources, informal economics in industrial societies, and mass marketing in urban areas.

Wilk, R. R. (1996). *Economics and cultures: An introduction to economic anthropology*. Boulder, CO: Westview Press.

This lively, up-to-date primer traces the history of the dialogue between anthropology and economics and identifies the subdiscipline's basic practical and theoretical problems.

© Kent Meireis/The Image Works

The Formation of Groups
The Challenge of Cooperation

PART 3

Introduction

One significant insight of anthropological study is how fundamental cooperation is to human survival. Acting together, humans handle even the most basic challenges of existence: the need for food and for protection, not just from the elements but from predatory animals and especially from one another. To some extent this is true for all primates. But what really sets human practices apart from those of other primates is the regularity of some form of cooperation among adults in subsistence activities.

Just as cooperation is basic to human survival, the social organization of groups is basic to cooperation. Humans form many kinds of groups, each geared toward meeting particular challenges that people encounter in their daily existence. Social groups are important to humans also because they give identity and support to their members. The basic building block in a culture's social structure is the household, where economic production, consumption, inheritance, child rearing, and shelter are commonly organized. Usually, the core of the household consists of some form of family: a group of relatives that stems from the parent–child bond and the interdependence of men and women, as illustrated in the opening photograph of a Tibetan family in the courtyard of their home between Lhasa and Gyangtse. Although it may be organized in many different ways, the family always provides for a measure of economic cooperation between men and women while furnishing the basic cultural framework required for child rearing.

Another challenge all human societies face is the need to regulate sexual activity—to balance sexual desires with the desire for stability and security. Marriage plays a key role in doing this. Given the inevitable connection between heterosexual activity and the production of children who require nurturing, a close interconnection among sexual reproductive practices, marriage, and family is to be expected. Many different marriage and family patterns exist the world over, but all societies have them in some form. The varied forms of family and marriage organization are to a large extent shaped by the specific kinds of challenges that people must solve in particular circumstances.

In almost every cultural system, solutions to many organizational challenges are beyond the scope of family and household. These include defense, allocation of resources, and labor for tasks too large for single households. Nonindustrial societies frequently meet these challenges through kinship groups. These large, cohesive groups of individuals base their loyalty to one another on descent from a common ancestor or on their relationship to a living individual. In cases where a great number of people

University of Pennsylvania Museum

are linked by kinship, these groups serve the important function of precisely defining the social roles of their members, including their rights and obligations toward one another. In this way they reduce the potential for tension that might arise from an individual's sudden and unexpected behavior. Kinship groups also provide members with material security and moral support through ritual activities.

Where kinship ties do not meet all of a society's organizational challenges, social groupings may be formed on the basis of gender and age divisions. Such is the case in many parts of the world, today and in the past. In many cases, too, social groups based on the common interests of their members serve a vital function.

Finally, groups based on social ranking—social classes—are characteristic of many cultural systems, past and present. Class structure involves inequalities among groups distinguished from one another by their economic, social, and political rankings. In this hierarchical form of social organization, one highly ranked group may try to dominate large numbers of lower-ranked people. To the extent that social class membership cuts across lines of kinship, residence, age, or other group membership, it may forge solidarity with other hierarchically organized groups, creating a vast network of social relations and thereby counteracting a society's tendency to fragment into special-interest groups. At the same time, however, class divisions systematically advantage higher-ranked groups while depriving others of access to important resources. Thus, class conflict has been a recurrent phenomenon in class-structured societies, despite the existence of political and religious institutions that serve to maintain the hierarchical social order.

CHAPTER 8

Sex and Marriage

© Richard T. Nowitz/Corbis

CHALLENGE ISSUE

ALL AROUND THE WORLD HUMANS FACE THE CHALLENGE OF MANAGING SEXUAL RELATIONS TO ESTABLISH STABLE SOCIAL ALLIANCES ESSENTIAL TO THE SURVIVAL OF INDIVIDUALS AND THEIR OFFSPRING. Marriage, in all of its many forms, provides a cultural structure that helps meet that challenge. The high value that many cultures place on the fundamental function of marriage is evident in spectacular wedding traditions, such as the one depicted in this photograph of a Yemenite Jewish bride and groom dressed in ceremonial clothes, posing along with their parents, at their ritual wedding feast in Southwest Asia.

1 What Is Marriage?

A nonethnocentric definition of marriage is a culturally sanctioned union between two or more people that establishes certain rights and obligations between the people, between them and their children, and between them and their in-laws. Although in many societies, spouses live together as members of the same household, this is not true in all societies. And although most marriages around the world involve unions between one woman and one man, numerous other arrangements exist. For example, many cultures not only permit but encourage marriage of one man to multiple wives.

2 What Is the Difference between Marriage and Mating?

All animals, including humans, mate—that is, form a sexual bond with other individuals. In some species, the bond lasts for life, but in others it lasts no longer than a single sex act. Thus, some animals mate with a single individual whereas others mate with several. Only marriage, however, is backed by economic, social, legal, and ideological forces. Consequently, although mating is biological, marriage is cultural.

3 Why Is Marriage Universal?

Marriage helps solve a universal human problem: the need to regulate sexual relations so that competition over sexual access and reproductive rights does not introduce a disruptive, combative influence into society. Because the problem marriage deals with is universal, it follows that the institution of marriage is universal. The specific form marriage takes is related to who has rights and obligations to offspring that may result from the marital union, as well as how property is distributed.

Among the Trobriand Islanders, whose yam exchanges and Kula voyages we examined in the previous chapter, children who have reached the age of 7 or 8 years begin playing erotic games and imitating adult seductive attitudes. Within another 4 or 5 years they begin to pursue sexual partners in earnest—changing partners often, experimenting sexually first with one and then another. By the time they are in their mid-teens, meetings between lovers take up most of the night, and affairs are apt to last for several months. Ultimately, lovers begin to meet the same partner again and again, rejecting the advances of others. When the couple is ready, they appear together one morning outside the young man's house as a way of announcing their intention to be married.

For young Trobrianders, attracting sexual partners is an important matter, and they spend a great deal of time making themselves look as attractive and seductive as possible. Youthful conversations during the day are loaded with sexual innuendoes, and magical spells as well as small gifts are employed to entice a prospective sex partner to the beach at night or to the house in which boys sleep apart from their parents. Because girls, too, sleep apart from their parents, youths and adolescents have considerable freedom in arranging their love affairs. Boys and girls play this game as equals, with neither having an advantage over the other.

As anthropologist Annette Weiner points out, all of this sexual activity is not a frivolous, adolescent pastime. Instead, she proposes that attracting lovers

is the first step toward entering the adult world of strategies, where the line between influencing others while not allowing others to gain control of oneself must be carefully learned. . . . Sexual liaisons give adolescents the time and occasion to experiment with all the possibilities and problems that adults face in creating relationships with those who are not relatives. Individual wills may clash, and the achievement of one's desire takes patience, hard work, and determination. The adolescent world of lovemaking has its own dangers and disillusionments. Young people, to the degree they are capable, must learn to be both careful and fearless.[1]

Until the latter part of the 20th century, the Trobriand attitude toward adolescent sexuality was in marked contrast to that of most Western cultures in Europe, North America, and elsewhere. In the United States, for example, individuals were not supposed to have sexual relations before or outside of marriage. Since then, practices in much of Europe and North America have converged toward those of the Trobriands, even though the traditional ideal of premarital abstinence has not been abandoned entirely.

---

[1]Weiner, A. B. (1988). *The Trobrianders of Papua New Guinea* (p. 71). New York: Holt, Rinehart and Winston.

VISUAL COUNTERPOINT
To attract lovers, young Trobriand Islanders must look as attractive and seductive as possible. The young men shown here have decorated themselves with Johnson's Baby Powder, while the young woman's beauty has been enhanced by decorations given by her father.

Estate of Annette B. Weiner

© Hideo Haga/HAGA/The Image Works

Unlike chimpanzees and other female apes that signal their fertility through highly visible swelling of their skin, the human female gives no such signal. Thus, human males do not know when females are fertile, an inducement for them to hang around for successful reproduction.

CONTROL OF SEXUAL RELATIONS

One important human characteristic is the ability for the human female, like the human male, to engage in sexual relations at any time she wants or whenever her culture deems it appropriate. Although this ability to perform at any time when provided with the appropriate cue is not unusual for male mammals in general, it is unusual for females. Among most primate species, females whose offspring are weaned but who have not yet become pregnant again are likely to engage in sexual activity around the time of ovulation (approximately once a month), at which time they advertise their availability through highly visible physical signs. Otherwise, they are little interested in such activity. Bonobos, one of the species most closely related to us, are an exception. Whereas among chimpanzees, female genital swelling indicates ovulation and signals readiness for sexual activity, female bonobos are in a constant state of genital swelling, so that sexual activity

may occur before, during, and after ovulation. Moreover, it may take place between individuals in virtually all combinations of ages and sex. Among humans, female fertility is not signaled by any visible display, but similar to bonobos they are likely to engage in sex at any time, even when the female is pregnant. In some human societies, intercourse during pregnancy is thought to promote the growth of the fetus. Among Trobriand Islanders, for example, a child's identity is thought to come from its mother, but it is the father's job to build up and nurture the child, which he begins to do before birth through frequent intercourse with its mother.

As for the homosexual behavior seen among bonobos, that, too, is not uncommon among humans. While such behavior is absolutely condemned in some societies, many others, as we saw in Chapter 5, are indifferent about such personal practices and openly tolerate individuals who engage in homosexual activities. Most languages do not even have a special term to distinguish such behavior as significant in its own right. In fact, in some cultures certain prescribed male-to-male sexual acts are part of male initiation rituals required of all boys to become respected adult men.[2] Certain New Guinea societies, for example, see the transmission of semen from older to younger boys, through oral sex, as vital for building up the strength needed to protect against the supposedly debilitating effects of adult heterosexual intercourse.[3] Even in the United States, with its long-standing obsession about and hostility toward homosexuality, the phenomenon is far from uncommon. Homosexuality is found in diverse contexts: from lifelong loving relationships to casual sexual

[2]Kirkpatrick, R. C. (2000). The evolution of human homosexual behavior. *Current Anthropology, 41*, 385.

[3]Herdt, G. H. (1993). Semen transactions in Sambia culture. In D. N. Suggs & A. W. Mirade (Eds.), *Culture and human sexuality* (pp. 298–327). Pacific Grove, CA: Brooks/Cole.

VISUAL COUNTERPOINT
Homosexuality is a widespread phenomenon in human societies. The United States is one of the few societies where it is generally condemned and where public displays of same-sex affection between men in particular are typically regarded as distasteful or even disgusting. One exception is the football field, where an extreme measure of rough-and-tumble masculine behavior makes it possible for players to pat one another on the behind or exchange celebratory hugs without bringing their manhood into question.

encounters to supposedly celibate clergy to inmate populations in both men's and women's prisons. During the past few decades, homosexuality has become an openly accepted part of the cosmopolitan lifestyle in urban cultural centers such as Amsterdam, London, and San Francisco. That said, the social rules and cultural meanings of *all* sexual behavior are subject to great variability from one society to another.

The ability of females as well as males to engage in sex at any time would have been advantageous to early humans and their ancestors to the extent that it acted, not alone but with other factors, to tie members of both sexes more firmly to the social groups so crucial to their survival. However, although sexual activity can reinforce group ties, it can also disrupt harmonious social relationships. The solution to this problem is to bring sexual activity under cultural control. Thus, just as a culture tells people what, when, and how they should eat, so does it tell them when, where, how, and with whom they should have sex.

Anthropology Applied   Anthropology and AIDS

An irony of human life is that sexual activity, necessary for perpetuation of the species as well as a source of pleasure and fulfillment, also can be a source of danger. The problem lies in sexually transmitted diseases, which in recent years have been spreading and increasing in variety. Among these is acquired immune deficiency syndrome, or AIDS, although intravenous drug use and blood transfusions also contribute to its spread. Recent reports specify that 16,000 new cases of AIDS arise in the world *every day* (see Figure 8.1). What follows is A. M. Williams' account of what she and other anthropologists have to contribute to our understanding and control of this disease.

After a decade and a half, it is clear that AIDS is a pandemic experienced in significant ways at local levels. The World Health Organization (WHO) estimates 36 million people are infected with HIV (the virus present in most people with AIDS) worldwide. While HIV and AIDS have hit areas of sub-Saharan Africa and Southeast Asia hardest, as of

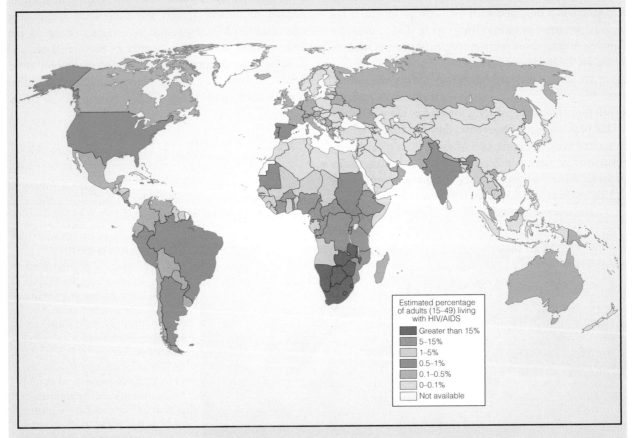

Estimated percentage of adults (15–49) living with HIV/AIDS

- Greater than 15%
- 5–15%
- 1–5%
- 0.5–1%
- 0.1–0.5%
- 0–0.1%
- Not available

FIGURE 8.1
HIV/AIDS around the world.

November 2000, there was a cumulative total of 920,000 AIDS cases in the United States. Where I work in San Francisco, California, a city of less than 800,000 people, there have been 24,509 AIDS cases and 16,838 deaths from AIDS reported since 1980. Of these cases, 22,161 are among gay and bisexual men in the city.[a]

To grasp the proportions of the pandemic, public health perspectives, epidemiological models, biomedical information, and psychological interpretations are used to help figure out who is infected, who will become infected, and where these infections are most likely to occur. However, anthropology takes a different approach, one that helps to clarify the dynamic relationship between people, who are infected or at risk for infection, and their social, cultural, political and economic surroundings. Such research is important because it can provide rich explanations of why people become infected or progress rapidly in HIV disease. This in turn can assist all manner of institutions in addressing a wide variety of local issues for those who need their services and support. Moreover, anthropological analyses often help describe the dynamic links between individual practices, social and cultural systems, and larger structural forces, all of which may combine in ways that encourage the problems of HIV.

Working alone or as part of teams to collect and analyze data, most anthropologists enter into an extended engagement with groups of people who are dealing with numerous aspects of HIV and AIDS. Since anthropology begins from the premise that circumstances and phenomena are complex within different populations, we employ a variety of methods and theoretical frameworks to reach our understandings. As a result, we do not develop monolithic models for explaining HIV and AIDS. For example, anthropologist Richard Parker's work in Brazil provided the formative research on sexual practices and their relationship to local systems of power and inequality needed to create more appropriate responses to the increasing spread of HIV/AIDS there. Others, like Paul Farmer, demonstrate how political economy and constructions of sickness among people in Haiti can negatively influence the quality of life of those

infected in ways that encourage the further spread of the virus. And some, like Emily Martin, show that within the relationships between science, clinical research, and people affected by HIV and AIDS there emerge new concepts of body and AIDS that can reveal dynamics about society and the authoritative role of experts in shaping public awareness.[b]

These anthropological studies and many others contribute to a very broad research and theoretical literature on HIV and AIDS, which can be drawn upon by community-based organizations, policy makers, and other researchers. However, some anthropologists like myself work more directly with groups and organizations on problems posed by primary prevention (preventing HIV transmission) and secondary prevention (slowing the disease's progression). Here anthropology is well-suited for both formative research and conducting evaluations of programs and services. As the anthropologist on a multidisciplinary research team at the Center for AIDS Prevention Studies, University of California San Francisco, I work directly with local gay male populations and such local AIDS organizations as the San Francisco AIDS Foundation and the STOP AIDS Project. While the team uses many strategies of inquiry, I specifically employ anthropological methods of investigation such as living and participating in the community, conducting a variety of in-depth interviews, and studying archival materials. I also rely on anthropological perspectives that require descriptions of the links between historical contexts, larger structural phenomena, and local practices and understandings.

Recently, by examining the relationship between HIV and drug use in two local groups of gay men who engage in unprotected sex, I was able to describe how groups of poorer gay male drug users in the city may be subjected to physical violence from their homophobic peers. This influences their ability to use condoms or openly seek HIV prevention education or support. At the same time, groups of more middle-class gay male drug users did not seek education or support because their social location and values encouraged them to believe that they did not need these resources because they had everything under control.[c] With a greater clarity regarding local social and

cultural barriers to HIV prevention, some local HIV prevention program designers rapidly developed more culturally appropriate prevention programs for these groups of men. Because HIV and AIDS are a dynamic part of lived experiences, learning about how people conceptualize and shape their ideas and practices around the virus, selfhood, sex practices, collective life, and institutions is important. And when these concepts become part of a foundation for HIV/AIDS programs, the services are better able to respond to people's needs since the programs make better sense within the contexts of people's lived realities.

As we move into the 21st century, biotechnology's advances are beginning to reconfigure the HIV/AIDS pandemic. While this is good news, it also means the meanings of HIV and AIDS become more complex and difficult to navigate. Moreover while new pharmaceutical therapies are providing hope for many enfranchised people in the West, infection rates climb and many more people remain unable to access these treatments. For most of us, culturally specific education and services will still be the most effective means to prevent infection or stem disease progression in many communities. In this light, the variety of perspectives offered by anthropology becomes even more crucial. This is because the foundations of these prevention efforts and services need to be developed with considerable understanding of how HIV and AIDS are constructed and shaped in a dynamic relationship with local complexities and concerns.

[a] *Centers for Disease Control semi-annual AIDS report (through June 1996).* (1997). Centers for Disease Control: Atlanta; *AIDS monthly surveillance summary (through July 1997).* (1997). San Francisco Department of Public Health AIDS Office, Seroepidemiology and Surveillance Branch: San Francisco. The earliest tracking of HIV and AIDS were problematic, and many people today still do not know their HIV status. Therefore, the cases reported in San Francisco or anywhere in the world must be understood to be undercounted.

[b] See, for example, Parker, R. (1991). *Bodies, pleasures, and passions: Sexual culture in contemporary Brazil;* Farmer, P. (1992). *AIDS and accusation: Haiti and the geography of blame;* and Martin, E. (1994). *Flexible bodies: Tracking immunity in American culture—From the days of polio to the age of AIDS.*

[c] See Williams, A. M. *Sex, drugs and HIV: A Sociocultural analysis of two groups of gay and bisexual male substance users who practice unprotected sex.* Unpublished manuscript.

Regulating Sexual Relations

All societies have cultural rules that seek to regulate sexual relations. In North America and Europe, the traditional ideal was that all sexual activity outside of marriage was taboo. Individuals were expected to establish a family through marriage, by which one gained an exclusive right of sexual access to another person. According to strict Judeo-Christian law, as prescribed in the book of Leviticus (20:10) in the Bible's Old Testament, adultery was punishable by death: "And the man that committeth adultery with another man's wife . . . , the adulterer and the adulteress shall surely be put to death." Deuteronomy adds: "Then ye shall bring them both out unto the gate of that city, and ye shall stone them with stones that they die; the damsel, because she cried not, being in the city; and the man, because he hath humbled his neighbor's wife: so thou shalt put away evil from among you."

Centuries later, among Christian colonists in 17th- and 18th-century New England, adultery by women remained a serious crime. While it did not lead to stoning, women so accused were shunned by the community and could even be imprisoned. As recounted in the famous novel *The Scarlet Letter*, by Nathaniel Hawthorne, the adulteress was forced to have the letter "A" stitched on her dress, publicly signifying her crime.

Such restrictions exist in many traditional Muslim societies in northern Africa and western Asia, where age-old "Shariah" law continues or has been reinstated to regulate social behavior in strict accordance with religious standards of morality. For instance, under Shariah law, women found guilty of having sexual relations outside marriage can be sentenced to death by stoning. In northern Nigeria, for example, a Muslim woman who had a child outside marriage was sentenced to death in 2002 for committing adultery. Her sentence was ultimately overturned by an Islamic appeals court, but it nonetheless drove home the rule of Shariah law. Turning legal transgressions into a public spectacle, authorities reinforce public awareness of the rules of social conduct.

One positive side effect of such restrictive rules of sexual behavior is that it could limit the spread of sexually transmitted diseases. For instance, the global epidemic of HIV/AIDS has had relatively little impact in sexually restrictive societies. Such societies, however, are a minority. In fact, most cultures in the world give greater reign to individual freedoms. They are much more relaxed about sexuality and do not sharply regulate personal practices. Indeed, a majority of all cultures are considered sexually permissive or semipermissive (the former having little or no restrictions on sexual experimentation before marriage, the latter allowing some experimentation but less openly). A minority of known societies—about 15 percent—have rules requiring that sexual involvement take place only within marriage.

The Nayar

The Nayar peoples of Southwest India, like the Trobriand Islanders noted above, are one of many examples of sexually permissive cultures.[4] A landowning warrior caste, their estates are held by corporations of sorts made up of kinsmen related in the female line. These blood relatives live together in a large household, with the eldest male serving as manager. Traditionally, Nayar boys began military training around the age of 7, and from this time through much of their young adulthood, they left home for significant stretches of time for military purposes.

Three traditional Nayar transactions are of interest in our discussion of sexual practices. The first occurred shortly before a girl experienced her first menstruation. It involved a ceremony that joined her with a "ritual husband" in a temporary union. This union, which did not necessarily involve sexual relations, lasted for a few days and then broke up. (Neither individual had any further obligation, although later, when the girl became a woman, she and her children typically participated in ritual mourning for the man when he died.) This temporary union established the girl as an adult ready for motherhood and eligible for sexual activity with men approved by her household.

The second transaction took place when a young Nayar woman entered into a continuing sexual liaison with a man approved by her family. This was a formal relationship that required the man to present her with gifts three times each year until the relationship was terminated. In return, the man could spend the nights with her. In spite of continuing sexual privileges, however, this "visiting husband" had no obligation to support his sex partner economically, nor was her home regarded as his home. In fact, she may have had such an arrangement with more than one man at the same time. Regardless of the number of men with whom she was involved, this second Nayar transaction, their version of marriage,

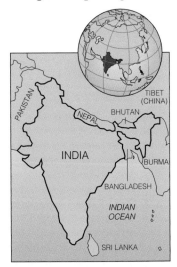

---

[4]Our interpretation of the Nayar follows W. H. Goodenough. (1970). *Description and comparison in cultural anthropology* (pp. 6–11). Chicago: Aldine.

Nayar girls and man in southwestern India, circa 1913.

clearly specified who had sexual rights to whom and included rules that deterred conflicts between the men.

This brings us to an anthropological definition of **marriage**—a culturally sanctioned union between two or more people that establishes certain rights and obligations between the people, between them and their children, and between them and their in-laws. Such marriage rights and obligations most often include, but are not limited to, sex, labor, property, child rearing, exchange, and status. Thus defined, marriage is universal. Notably, our definition of marriage refers to "people" rather than "a man and a woman" because in some societies, including Canada and the Netherlands, same-sex marriages are considered socially acceptable and allowed by law, even though opposite-sex marriages are far more common. We shall return to this point later in the chapter.

In the absence of effective birth control devices, the usual outcome of sexual activity between individuals of opposite sex is that, sooner or later, the woman becomes pregnant. When this happens among the Nayar, one of the men with whom she has a relationship (who may or may not be the biological father) must formally acknowledge paternity. He does this by making gifts to the woman and the midwife. This third transaction establishes the child's birth rights. In this sense, it is the counterpart of the registration of birth in North American and other modern industrial cultures, which clearly establishes motherhood and fatherhood.

Before we leave the Nayar, it is important to highlight some unusual features of Nayar marriage. Once a man has formally acknowledged fatherhood by gift giving, he may continue to take interest in the child, but he has no further obligations. Support and education for the child are the responsibility of the mother and her brothers with whom she and her offspring live. Indeed, unlike most other cultural groups in the world, the Nayar household includes only the mother, her children,

and her blood relatives, technically known as **consanguineal kin.** It does not include any of the "husbands" with whom she has shared the **conjugal bond** of marriage, including the man or men who fathered her children. Nor does it include any other people related through marriage, technically known as **affinal kin.** In other words, sisters and their offspring all live together with their brothers and their mother and her brothers. This arrangement answers the need for security in a cultural group where, traditionally, warfare repeatedly pulled young men away from their homes. Among the Nayar, sexual relations are forbidden between consanguineal relatives and thus are permitted only with individuals who live in other households. This brings us to another human universal: the incest taboo.

The Incest Taboo

Just as marriage in its various forms is found in all cultures, so is the **incest taboo**—the absolute forbiddance of sexual contact between certain close relatives. But, what is defined as close is not the same in all cultures. Moreover, such definitions may be subject to change over time. The scope and details of the taboo vary across cultures and time, but almost all societies past and present strongly forbid sexual relations at least between parents and children and nearly always between siblings. In some societies the taboo extends to other consanguineal relatives, such as uncles, aunts, first cousins, and even some affinal relatives linked through marriage. Anthropologists have long been fascinated by these taboos and have taken it as a challenge to explain its almost complete universality and cross-cultural variation.

Many explanations have been given. Of those that have gained some popularity at one time or another, the simplest and least satisfactory is based on "human nature"—that is, some instinctive horror of incest. It has been documented that human beings raised together have less sexual attraction for one another, but by itself

---

marriage A culturally sanctioned union between two or more people that establishes certain rights and obligations between the people, between them and their children, and between them and their in-laws. Such marriage rights and obligations most often include, but are not limited to, sex, labor, property, child rearing, exchange, and status.

consanguineal kin Relatives by birth; so-called blood relatives.

conjugal bond The bond between two individuals who are married.

affinal kin Relatives by marriage.

incest taboo The prohibition of sexual relations between specified individuals, usually parent–child and sibling relations at a minimum.

this "familiarity breeds contempt" argument may simply substitute the result for the cause. The incest taboo ensures that children and their parents, who are constantly in intimate contact, avoid regarding one another as sexual objects. Besides this, if an instinctive horror of incest exists, we would be hard-pressed to account for the far from rare violations of the incest taboo, such as occur in North American society (an estimated 10 to 14 percent of children under 18 years of age in the United States have been involved in incestuous relations[5]) or for cases of institutionalized incest, such as that requiring the god-king of the Inca empire in Peru to marry his own sister (in fact, she would have the same father, but rarely the same mother).

Various psychological explanations of the incest taboo have been advanced at one time or another. Sigmund Freud tried to account for it in his psychoanalytic theory of the unconscious. According to him, the son desires the mother, creating a rivalry with the father. (Freud called this the Oedipus complex.) The son must suppress these feelings or earn the wrath of the father, who is far more powerful than he. Similarly, the attraction of the daughter to the father (the Electra complex) places her in rivalry with her mother. From this, we might expect a same-sex bias in the case of intrafamily homicides—mother versus daughter or son versus father—but in fact no such bias exists.

Some psychologists have argued that young children can be emotionally scarred by sexual experiences, which they may interpret as violent and frightening acts of aggression. The incest taboo thus protects children against sexual advances by older members of the family. A closely related theory is that the incest taboo helps prevent girls who are socially and emotionally too young for motherhood from becoming pregnant.

Early students of genetics argued that the incest taboo prevents the harmful effects of inbreeding. While this is so, it is also true that, as with domestic animals, inbreeding can increase desired characteristics as well as detrimental ones. Furthermore, undesirable effects will show up sooner than without inbreeding, so whatever genes are responsible for them are quickly eliminated from the population. However, a preference for a genetically different mate does tend to maintain a higher level of genetic diversity within a population, and in evolution this generally works to a species' advantage. Without genetic diversity a species cannot adapt biologically to a changed environment when and if this becomes necessary.

A truly convincing explanation of the incest taboo has yet to be advanced. Certainly, there are persistent hints that it may be a cultural elaboration of an underlying biological tendency toward avoidance of inbreeding. Studies of animal behavior have shown such a tendency to be common among relatively large, long-lived, slow-to-mature, and intelligent species. Humans qualify for membership in this group on all counts. So do a number of other primates, including those most closely related to humans—bonobos and chimpanzees. Although they exhibit few sexual inhibitions, these apes do tend to avoid inbreeding between siblings and between females and their male offspring. This suggests that the tendency for human children to look for sexual partners outside the group in which they have been raised is not just the result of a cultural taboo. Studies that might seem to support this show that children raised together on an Israeli kibbutz (a communalistic rural village), although not required or even encouraged to do so, almost invariably marry outside their group. In this case, however, appearances seem to be deceiving. There is hardly a kibbutz, for example, without a report of sexual relationships between adolescents who have grown up together since infancy.[6] As for actual marriage, most Israeli youths leave the kibbutz in their late teens for obligatory service in the state's armed forces. This takes them away from the kibbutz precisely when they are most ready to consider marriage. Consequently, those most available as potential spouses are from other parts of the country.

An even greater challenge to the "biological avoidance" theory, however, is raised by detailed census records made in Roman Egypt about 2,000 years ago, demonstrating that brother–sister marriages were not uncommon among ordinary members of the farming class.[7] Moreover, anthropologist Nancy Thornhill found that, in a sample of 129 societies, only 57 had specific rules against parent–child or sibling incest (so much for the universality of the incest taboo!). Twice that number (114) had explicit rules to control activity with cousins, in-laws, or both.[8]

If indeed a biological basis for inbreeding avoidance exists among humans, it clearly is far from completely effective in its operation. Nor is its mechanism understood. Moreover, it still leaves us with questions: Why do some societies have an explicit taboo while others do not? And why do a handful of societies not only condone certain kinds of incest but even favor them for at least some of its members?

---

[5]Whelehan, P. (1985). Review of incest, a biosocial view. *American Anthropologist, 87*, 678.

[6]Leavitt, G. C. (1990). Sociobiological explanations of incest avoidance: A critical review of evidential claims. *American Anthropologist, 92*, 973.

[7]Leavitt, p. 982.

[8]Thornhill, N. (1993). Quoted in W. A. Haviland & R. J. Gordon (Eds), *Talking about people* (p. 127). Mountain View, CA: Mayfield.

Although children raised together on an Israeli kibbutz rarely marry one another, it is not because of any instinctive desire to avoid mating with people who are close. Rather, they marry outside their group because service in the military takes them out of their kibbutz, where they meet new people precisely when they are most likely to begin thinking about marriage.

Endogamy and Exogamy

Whatever its cause, the utility of the incest taboo can be seen by examining its effects on social structure. Closely related to prohibitions against incest are rules against **endogamy,** or marriage within a particular group of individuals (cousins and in-laws, for example). If the group is defined as one's immediate family alone, then societies generally prohibit or at least discourage endogamy, thereby promoting **exogamy,** or marriage outside the group. Yet, a society that practices exogamy at one level may practice endogamy at another. Among the Trobriand Islanders, for example, each individual has to marry outside of his or her own clan and lineage (exogamy). However, since eligible sex partners are to be found within one's own community, village endogamy, though not obligatory, is commonly practiced. Interestingly, a wide variety exists among societies as to which relatives are or are not covered by rules of exogamy. For example, the Catholic Church has long had a prohibition on marriages to first cousins, and such marriages are illegal in thirty of the United States; they are not illegal in the twenty other states nor in Europe. Furthermore, in numerous other societies, first cousins are preferred spouses. Despite myths to the contrary, there is no great risk to the children of first-cousin marriage.[9] (See a discussion of marriage prohibitions in the Biocultural Connection.)

In the 19th century, Sir Edward Tylor advanced the proposition that alternatives to inbreeding were either "marrying out or being killed out."[10] Our ancestors, he suggested, discovered the advantage of intermarriage to create bonds of friendship. French anthropologist Claude Lévi-Strauss elaborated on this idea. He saw exogamy as a form of exchange in which wife giving and wife taking created social alliances between distinct groups. By widening the human network, a larger number of people could pool natural resources and cultural information, including technology and other useful knowledge. (See Anthropologists of Note, p. 217.) Building on Lévi-Strauss's work, anthropologist Yehudi Cohen suggests that exogamy was an important means of promoting trade between groups, thereby ensuring access to needed goods and resources not otherwise available. Noting that incest taboos necessitating exogamy are generally most widely extended in the least complex of human societies but do not extend beyond parents and siblings in industrialized societies, he argues that as formal governments and other institutions have come to control trade, the need for extended taboos has been removed. Indeed, he suggests that this may have reached the point where the incest taboo is becoming obsolete altogether.

In a roundabout way, exogamy also helps to explain some exceptions to the incest taboo, such as that of

---

[9]Ottenheimer, M. (1996). *Forbidden relatives* (p.116–133). Champaign: University of Illinois Press.

---

[10]Quoted in Keesing, R. M. (1976). *Cultural anthropology: A contemporary perspective* (p. 286). New York: Holt, Rinehart and Winston.

endogamy Marriage within a particular group or category of individuals.
exogamy Marriage outside the group.

Biocultural Connection

Marriage Prohibitions in the United States

In the United States, every state has laws prohibiting some type of relatives from marrying each other. Today there is universal agreement when it comes to prohibiting mother–son marriage and preventing full siblings from marrying, but the laws vary when it comes to more distant relatives. Thirty states prohibit first cousins from marrying, while twenty do not. Furthermore, the prohibitions are not limited to people related by birth. A dozen states forbid some types of in-laws from intermarrying.

Despite the fact that the marriage prohibitions apply to people not related by birth, it is a common misconception among Americans that biological factors are the reason they exist. It is assumed that these prohibitions protect families from potential genetic defects in children of parents who are biologi-

cally "too close." The first-cousin prohibitions, in particular, are often defended for this reason. There are two major problems with this idea. First, the cousin prohibitions began to be enacted in the United States around the middle of the 19th century, long before the emergence of modern genetics. Second, modern genetic research has shown that first-cousin marriage does not present any great risk to offspring. Why then, do some Americans maintain this myth?

In 19th century United States, an evolutionary model of humans that included a notion about human progress depending upon outbreeding became widely accepted. Cousin marriage was thought to be characteristic of savagery, considered a form of degeneration based on inbreeding, believed to inhibit

the intellectual development of humans, and feared as a threat to civilized life. With the development of modern genetics, it was wrongly assumed that genetic data supported this now-discredited evolutionary dogma.

Human reproduction is a biological process situated in a cultural context. Each culture develops a particular understanding about the nature of reproduction. This can change over time. At present, the Western model of reproduction is undergoing a transformation stimulated by the recent discovery of mitochondrial DNA and the introduction of the new reproductive technologies. The process well illustrates that biological processes and culture are intimately intertwined, each affecting and being affected by the other. (By M. Ottenheimer for this textbook.)

obligatory brother and sister marriage within the royal families of ancient Egypt, the Inca empire, and Hawaii. Members of these royal families were considered semi-divine, and their very sacredness kept them from marrying mere mortals. The brother and sister married so as *not* to share their godliness, thereby maintaining the purity of the royal line, not to mention control of royal property. By the same token, in Roman Egypt, where women as well as men inherited property and where the relationship between land and people was particularly tight, brother–sister marriages among the farming class acted to prevent fragmentation of a family's holdings.

The Distinction between Marriage and Mating

Having defined marriage, in part, in terms of sexual access, we must make clear the distinction between marriage and mating. All animals, including humans, mate—some for life and some not, some with a single individual and some with several. Mates are secured and held solely

monogamy Marriage in which both partners have just one spouse.

through individual effort, as opposed to marriage, which is a right conferred by society. Only marriage is backed by legal, economic, and social forces that regulate sexual relations as well as reproductive rights and obligations. Even among the Nayar, where marriage seems to involve little other than a sexual relationship, a woman's husband is legally obligated to provide her with gifts at specified intervals. Nor may a Nayar woman legally have sex with a man to whom she is not married. Thus, while mating is biological, marriage is cultural.

The distinction between marriage and mating may be seen by looking, briefly, at practices in contemporary North American society, where **monogamy**—marriage in which both partners have just one spouse—is the only legally recognized form of marriage. Not only are other forms not legally sanctioned, but also systems of inheritance, whereby property and wealth are transferred from one generation to the next, are predicated upon the institution of monogamous marriage. Mating patterns, by contrast, are frequently *not* monogamous. Not only is adultery far from rare in Europe and North America, but it has become acceptable for individuals of the opposite sex—particularly young people who have not yet married—to live together outside of wedlock. None of these arrangements, however, are legally sanctioned. Frequently, even married couples who do not

Anthropologists of Note

Claude Lévi-Strauss (1908–)

© Brissaud-Figaro/Getty Images

Claude Lévi-Strauss is the leading exponent of French structuralism, which posits that the human mind imposes order by separating the perceived world into elementary bits of basic information. From this theoretical perspective, culture is viewed as the product of an underlying universal pattern of thought. Each culture is shaped and influenced by its unique physical and social environment as well as its history. Thus, cultures may vary considerably, even though the basic structure of the human thought processes responsible for them is the same for all people everywhere. The task of the anthropologist is to explain the fundamental principles by which humans accomplish this process and to uncover these underlying patterns.

According to Lévi-Strauss, human thought processes are structured into contrastive pairs of polar opposites, such as light versus dark, good versus evil, nature versus culture, dry versus wet, raw versus cooked, and male versus female. The ultimate contrastive pair is that of "self" versus "others," which is necessary for true symbolic communication to occur and upon which culture depends. Communication is a reciprocal exchange, which is extended to include goods and marital partners. Hence, the incest taboo stems from this fundamental contrastive pair of "self" versus "others." From this universal taboo are built the many and varied marriage rules ethnographers have described.

engage in sexual activity outside of wedlock mate with more than one individual as a consequence of death or divorce. For instance, more than 50 percent of first marriages in the United States end in divorce, and most divorced people ultimately remarry.

Among primates in general, monogamous mating patterns are not common. Although some smaller species of South American monkeys, a few island-dwelling populations of leaf-eating Old World monkeys, and all of the smaller apes (gibbons and siamangs) do mate for life with a single individual of the opposite sex, none of these is closely related to human beings. Nor do such "monogamous" primates ever display the degree of male–female body-size differences characteristic of our closest primate relatives and our own ancient ancestors. Thus, it is not likely that the human species began its evolutionary course with a monogamous mating pattern. Certainly, one cannot say the human species is, by nature, monogamous in its mating behavior, as some have tried to assert.

Although marriage need not involve establishment of a new family, it can easily serve this purpose, in addition to its important function of indicating who has continuing sexual access to whom. Consequently, new families are established through marriage in most human societies. We'll look at this family-making dimension of marriage more closely in the next chapter.

FORMS OF MARRIAGE

Monogamy is the form of marriage with which North Americans are most familiar. It is also the most common, but for economic rather than moral reasons. In many polygynous societies, a man must be fairly wealthy to be able to afford **polygyny,** or marriage to more than one wife. Among the Kapauku of western New Guinea, the ideal is to have as many wives as possible, and a woman actually urges her husband to spend money on acquiring additional wives.[11] She even has the legal right to divorce him if she can prove that he has money for bride-prices and refuses to take on additional wives. (Bride-price is explained on page 226.) As we saw in the earlier chapter on culture, in Kapauku society wives are desirable because they work in the gardens and care for pigs, by which wealth is measured, but not all men are wealthy enough to afford bride-prices for multiple wives.

Among the Turkana, a pastoral nomadic people of northern Kenya, the number of animals at a family's disposal is directly related to the number of adult women available to care for them. The more wives a man has, the more women there are to look after the livestock

---

[11]Pospisil, L. (1963). *The Kapauku Papuans of West New Guinea.* New York: Holt, Rinehart and Winston.

MEDIATREK

For engaging tutorials on sex and marriage provided by the Anthropology Program at Palomar College, go to MediaTrek 8.1 on the companion Web site or CD-ROM.

polygyny Marriage of a man to two or more women at the same time; a form of polygamy.

and the more substantial the family's holdings can be. Thus, it is not uncommon for a man's existing wife to actively search for another woman to marry her husband. Again, however, a substantial bride-price is involved in marriage, and only men of wealth and prominence can afford large numbers of wives.

Although monogamy may be the most common form of marriage around the world, it is not the most preferred. That distinction goes to polygyny, which is favored by about 80 to 85 percent of the world's societies. Commonly practiced in many parts of Asia and Africa, it also occurs in a few places in Europe and North America. In 1972, for example, English laws concerning marriage changed to accommodate immigrants who traditionally practiced polygyny. Since that time polygamous marriages have been legal in England for some specific religious minorities, including Muslims and Sephardic Jews. According to one family law specialist, the real impetus behind this law change was a growing concern that "destitute immigrant wives, abandoned by their husbands, [were] overburdening the welfare state."[12]

Even in the United States today, somewhere between 20,000 and 60,000 people in the Rocky Mountain states live in households made up of a man with two or more wives.[13] Most consider themselves Mormons, even though the official Mormon Church does not approve of the practice. A growing minority, however, call themselves "Christian polygamists," citing

the Old Testament of the Judeo-Christian Bible as justification.[14] Despite its illegality, regional law enforcement officials have adopted a "live and let live" attitude toward polygyny in their region. One woman—a lawyer and one of nine co-wives—expresses her attitude toward polygyny as follows:

> I see it as the ideal way for a woman to have a career and children. In our family, the women can help each other care for the children. Women in monogamous relationships don't have that luxury. As I see it, if this lifestyle didn't already exist, it would have to be invented to accommodate career women.[15]

Polygyny is particularly common in societies that support themselves by growing crops and where women do the bulk of the farm work. Under these conditions, women are valued both as workers and as child bearers. Because the labor of wives in polygynous households generates wealth and little support is required from husbands, the wives have a strong bargaining position within the household. Often, they have considerable freedom of movement and some economic independence from sale of crops. Commonly, each of the wives within the household lives with her children in her own dwelling, apart from the husband, who visits each but has a place of his

[12]Cretney, S. (2003). *Family law in the twentieth century: A history.* (pp. 72–73) New York: Oxford University Press.

[13]Egan, T. (1999, February 28). The persistence of polygamy. *New York Times Magazine,* 52.

[14]Wolfson, H. (2000, January 22). Polygamists make the Christian connection. *Burlington Free Press,* 2c.

[15]Johnson, D. (1996). Polygamists emerge from secrecy, seeking not just peace but respect. In W. A. Haviland & R. J. Gordon, (Eds.), *Talking about people* (2nd ed., pp. 129–131). Mountain View, CA: Mayfield.

VISUAL COUNTERPOINT A Christian polygamist poses with his three wives and children in front of their dormitory-style home in Utah, and a Baranarna man of Upper Guinea with his two wives and children.

own. Usually these dwellings are clustered together in some sort of larger household compound. In other words, the terms *dwelling* or *house* and *household* need not be synonymous. Because of this residential autonomy, fathers are less directly involved with their children, who grow up among women. As noted in Chapter 5, this is the sort of setting conducive to development of aggressiveness in adult males, who must prove their masculinity. As a consequence, polygynous societies with economies based on cultivation often place a high value on military glory. One reason for going to war in such societies is to capture women, who may become a warrior's co-wives, thus increasing his offspring and wealth. Wealth-increasing polygyny is found in its fullest elaboration in parts of sub-Saharan Africa, though it is known elsewhere as well (the Kapauku of western New Guinea are another case). Moreover, it is still intact in the world today, because its wealth-generating properties at the household level make it an economically productive system.[16]

In societies practicing wealth-generating polygyny, most men and women do enter into polygynous marriages, although some are able to do so earlier in life than others. This is made possible by a female-biased sex ratio and/or a mean age at marriage for females significantly below that for males. In fact, this marriage pattern is frequently found in societies where violence, including war, is common and where many young males lose their lives in fighting. Their high combat mortality results in a population where women outnumber men. By contrast, in societies where men are more heavily involved in productive work, generally only a small minority of marriages are polygynous. Under these circumstances, women are more dependent on men for support, so they are valued as child bearers more than for the work they do. This is commonly the case in pastoral nomadic societies where men are the primary owners and tenders of livestock. This makes women especially vulnerable if they prove incapable of bearing children, which is one reason a man may seek another wife. Another reason for a man to take on secondary wives is to demonstrate his high position in society. But where men do most of the productive work, they must work extremely hard to support more than one wife, and few actually do so. Usually, it is the exceptional hunter or male shaman ("medicine man") in a food-foraging society or a particularly wealthy man in an agricultural or pastoral society who is most apt to practice polygyny. When he does, it is usually of the *sororal* type, with the co-wives being sisters. Having lived their lives together before marriage, the sisters continue to do so with their husband, instead of occupying separate dwellings of their own.

Although monogamy and polygyny are the most common forms of marriage in the world today, other forms do occur, however rarely. **Polyandry,** the marriage of one woman to two or more men simultaneously, is known in only a few societies, perhaps in part because a man's life expectancy is usually shorter than a woman's, and male infant mortality is somewhat higher, so a surplus of men in a society is unlikely. Where sex ratios are balanced, many women are likely to remain unmarried. Another reason for polyandry's rarity is that it limits a man's descendants more than any other pattern. Among the Nayar, however, polyandry maximized female fertility, ensuring production of children for her descent group. Fewer than a dozen societies are known to have favored this form of marriage, but they involve people as widely separated from one another as the eastern Inuit (Eskimos), Marquesan Islanders of Polynesia, and Tibetans. In Tibet, where inheritance is in the male line and arable land is limited, the marriage of brothers to a single woman (*fraternal polyandry*) keeps the land together by preventing it from being repeatedly subdivided among sons from one generation to the next. Unlike monogamy, it also restrains population growth, thereby avoiding increased pressures on resources. Finally, among Tibetans who practice a mixed economy of farming, herding, and trading, fraternal polyandry provides the household with an adequate pool of male labor for all three subsistence activities.[17]

MEDIATREK

To click on a region of the world and find out about the wedding traditions there, go to MediaTrek 8.2 on the companion Web site or CD-ROM.

Group marriage, in which several men and women have sexual access to one another, also occurs but rarely. Among Eskimos in northern Alaska, for instance, sexual relations between unrelated individuals implied ties of mutual aid and support. In order to create or strengthen such ties, a man could lend his wife to another man for temporary sexual relationships:

> Thus in attracting and holding members of a hunting crew, an umialik [whaleboat headman] could lend his wife to a crew member and take his in turn. These men thereafter entered into a partnership relationship, one virtually as strong as kinship. The children of

[17]Levine, N. E., & Silk, J. B. (1997). Why polyandry fails. *Current Anthropology, 38,* 375–398.

polyandry Marriage of a woman to two or more men at one time; a form of polygamy.
group marriage Marriage in which several men and women have sexual access to one another.

[16]White, D. R. (1988). Rethinking polygyny: Co-wives, codes, and cultural systems. *Current Anthropology, 29,* 529–572.

such men, in fact, retained a recognized relationship to each other by virtue of the wife exchange of their parents.[18]

During the 1960s in North America and western Europe, people known as hippies began seeking alternatives to established cultural patterns in their own societies and experimented with group marriage. But, this seems to have been largely a transitory phenomenon, despite the sensationalist publicity it received.

The Levirate and the Sororate

In some societies, if a husband dies leaving a wife and children, it is customary that the wife marries a brother of the dead man. This custom, called the **levirate,** not only provides social security for the widow and her children but also is a way for the husband's family to maintain the established relationship with her family and their rights over her sexuality and her future children: It acts to preserve relationships previously established. When a man marries the sister of his dead wife, it is called the **sororate;** in essence, a family of "wife givers" supplies one of "wife takers" with another spouse to take the dead one's place. In societies that have the levirate and sororate, the established in-law relationship between the two families is maintained even after the spouse's death.

Serial Monogamy

A form of marriage increasingly common in North America today is **serial monogamy,** whereby the man or the woman marries a series of partners in succession. Currently, more than 50 percent of first marriages end in divorce, and some experts project that two-thirds of recent marriages will not last.[19] Upon dissolution of a marriage, the children more often than not remain with the mother. This pattern is similar to one sociologists

and anthropologists first described among Caribbean Islanders and low-income urban African Americans in the United States. Early in life, women begin to bear children by men who are not married to them. To support themselves and their children, the women must look for work outside of the household, but to do so they must seek help from other kin, most commonly their mothers. As a consequence, households are frequently headed by women (on average, about 32 percent are so headed in the Caribbean). After a number of years, however, an unmarried woman usually does marry a man, who may or may not be the father of some or all of her children. It is often increased economic hardship that drives women to seek this male support, owing to the difficulties of providing for themselves and their children while fulfilling their domestic obligations.

In the United States, with the rise of live-in premarital arrangements between couples, the increasing necessity for women to seek work outside the home, and rising divorce rates, a similar pattern is becoming more common among middle-class whites. In 90 per-

---

[18]Spencer, R. F. (1984). North Alaska Coast Eskimo. In D. Damas (Ed.), *Arctic, Vol. 5, Handbook of North American Indians* (pp. 320–337). Washington, DC: Smithsonian Institution.

[19]Stacey, J. (1990). *Brave new families* (pp. 15, 286, n. 46). New York: Basic Books.

levirate A marriage custom according to which a widow marries a brother of her dead husband (a man marries his dead brother's widow).
sororate A marriage custom according to which a widower marries his dead wife's sister (a woman marries her deceased sister's husband).
serial monogamy A marriage form in which a man or a woman marries or lives with a series of partners in succession.

© Uppa/Topham/The Image Works

Film celebrities Nicole Kidman and Tom Cruise. Their marriage, like 50 percent of those in the United States, ended in divorce. Even so, most divorced individuals remarry, making serial monogamy very common.

cent of divorce cases, women assume responsibility for any children. Furthermore, of all children born in the United States today, about a third are born out of wedlock. Frequently isolated from kin or other assistance, women in single-parent households commonly find it difficult to cope. Within a year following divorce, the standard of living for women drops some 73 percent whereas men's *increases* by about 42 percent.[20] To be sure, fathers are usually expected to provide child support, but in 50 percent of the cases of children born out of wedlock, paternity cannot be established. Furthermore, failure of fathers to live up to their obligations is far from rare. One solution for unmarried women is to marry (often, to remarry) to get the assistance of another adult.

In some countries, such as Norway and the Netherlands, a similar pattern has emerged for different reasons. In Norway, for example, over half of all children are born to unwed mothers. This is not a function of poverty but of wealth (from natural gas in the North Sea). In this very affluent society, the traditional eco-

nomic role of the husband as provider has been taken over by generous state support.

Choice of Spouse

The Western egalitarian ideal that an individual should be free to marry whomever he or she chooses is an unusual arrangement, certainly not universally embraced. However desirable such an ideal may be in the abstract, it is fraught with difficulties and certainly contributes to the apparent instability of marital relationships in modern North American and European society. Part of the problem is the great emphasis Western cultures place on the importance of youth and glamour—especially of women—for romantic love. Female youth and beauty are perhaps most glaringly exploited by the women's wear, cosmetics, and beauty salon industries, but movies, television, and the recorded-music business generally do not lag far behind, nor do advertisements for cigarettes, hard and soft drinks, beer, automobiles, and a host of other products that make liberal use of young, glamorous women. As anthropologist Jules Henry once observed, "even men's wear and toiletries could not be marketed as efficiently without an adoring, pretty woman (well under thirty-five years of age) looking at a man wearing a

---

[20]Weitzman, L. J. (1985). *The divorce revolution: The unexpected social and economic consequences for women and children in America* (p. 338). New York: Free Press.

The U.S. obsession with a particular ideal of feminine beauty is now spreading to other parts of the world, as illustrated by this photo of the 2003 Miss Universe beauty pageant.

VISUAL COUNTERPOINT Marriage is a means of creating alliances between groups of people. Since such alliances have important economic and political implications, the decision cannot be left in the hands of the two young and inexperienced people. At the left is shown an Indian couple, whose marriage has been arranged between their parents. The picture on the right was taken at the wedding of Prince Charles and Lady Diana in England. Their royal marriage later ended in a sensational divorce.

stylish shirt or sniffing at a man wearing a deodorant."[21] By no means are all individuals taken in by this, but it does tend to nudge people in such a way that marriages may all too easily be based on trivial and transient characteristics. In few other parts of the world are such chances taken with something as momentous as marriage.

In many societies, marriage and the establishment of a family are considered far too important to be left to the whims of young people. The marriage of two individuals who are expected to spend their whole lives together and raise their children together is incidental to the more serious matter of making allies of two families through the marriage bond. Marriage involves a transfer

[21]Henry, J. (1966). The metaphysic of youth, beauty, and romantic love. In S. Farber & R. Wilson (Eds.), *The challenge to women.* New York: Basic Books.

of rights between families, including rights to property and rights over children, as well as sexual rights. Thus, marriages tend to be arranged for the economic and political advantage of the family unit.

Arranged marriages, needless to say, are not commonplace in North American society, but they do occur. Among ethnic minorities, they may serve to preserve traditional values that people fear might otherwise be lost. Among families of wealth and power, marriages may be arranged by segregating their children in private schools and carefully steering them toward "proper" marriages. A careful reading of announced engagements in the society pages of the *New York Times* provides clear evidence of such family alliances. The following Original Study illustrates how marriages may be arranged in societies where such practices are commonplace.

Original Study

Arranging Marriage in India

Six years [after my first field trip] I returned to India to again do fieldwork, this time among the middle class in Bombay, a modern, sophisticated city. From the experience of my earlier visit, I decided to include a study of arranged marriages in my project. By this time I had met many Indian couples whose

marriages had been arranged and who seemed very happy. Particularly in contrast to the fate of many of my married friends in the United States who were already in the process of divorce, the positive aspects of arranged marriages appeared to me to outweigh the negatives. In fact, I thought I might even

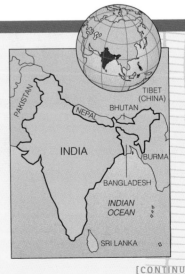

[CONTINUED]

participate in arranging a marriage myself. I had been fairly successful in the United States in "fixing up" many of my friends, and I was confident that my matchmaking skills could be easily applied to this new situation, once I learned the basic rules. "After all," I thought, "how complicated can it be? People want pretty much the same things in a marriage whether it is in India or America."

An opportunity presented itself almost immediately. A friend from my previous Indian trip was in the process of arranging for the marriage of her eldest son. In India there is a perceived shortage of "good boys," and since my friend's family was eminently respectable and the boy himself personable, well educated, and nice looking, I was sure that by the end of my year's fieldwork, we would have found a match.

The basic rule seems to be that a family's reputation is most important. It is understood that matches would be arranged only within the same caste and general social class, although some crossing of subcastes is permissible if the class positions of the bride's and groom's families are similar. Although dowry is now prohibited by law in India, extensive gift exchanges took place with every marriage. Even when the boy's family do not "make demands," every girl's family nevertheless feels the obligation to give the traditional gifts, to the girl, to the boy, and to the boy's family. Particularly when the couple would be living in the joint family—that is, with the boy's parents and his married brothers and their families, as well as with unmarried siblings—which is still very common even among the urban, upper-middle class in India, the girl's parents are anxious to establish smooth relations between their family and that of the boy. Offering the proper gifts, even when not called "dowry," is often an important factor in influencing the relationship between the bride's and groom's families and perhaps, also, the treatment of the bride in her new home.

In a society where divorce is still a scandal and where, in fact, the divorce rate is exceedingly low, an arranged marriage is the beginning of a lifetime relationship not just between the bride

and groom but between their families as well. Thus, while a girl's looks are important, her character is even more so, for she is being judged as a prospective daughter-in-law as much as a prospective bride. Where she would be living in a joint family, as was the case with my friend, the girl's ability to get along harmoniously in a family is perhaps the single most important quality in assessing her suitability.

My friend is a highly esteemed wife, mother, and daughter-in-law. She is religious, soft-spoken, modest, and deferential. She rarely gossips and never quarrels, two qualities highly desirable in a woman. A family that has the reputation for gossip and conflict among its womenfolk will not find it easy to get good wives for their sons. Parents will not want to send their daughter to a house in which there is conflict.

My friend's family were originally from North India. They had lived in Bombay, where her husband owned a business, for forty years. The family had delayed in seeking a match for their eldest son because he had been an Air Force pilot for several years, stationed in such remote places that it had seemed fruitless to try to find a girl who would be willing to accompany him. In their social class, a military career, despite its economic security, has little prestige and is considered a drawback in finding a suitable bride. Many families would not allow their daughters to marry a man in an occupation so potentially dangerous and which requires so much moving around.

The son had recently left the military and joined his father's business. Since he was a college graduate, modern, and well traveled, from such a good family, and, I thought, quite handsome, it seemed to me that he, or rather his family, was in a position to pick and choose. I said as much to my friend.

While she agreed that there were many advantages on their side, she also said, "We must keep in mind that my son is both short and dark; these are drawbacks in finding the right match." While the boy's height had not escaped my notice, "dark" seemed to me inaccurate; I would have called him "wheat" colored perhaps, and in any case, I did not realize that color would be a consideration. I discovered, however, that

while a boy's skin color is a less important consideration than a girl's, it is still a factor.

An important source of contacts in trying to arrange her son's marriage was my friend's social club in Bombay. Many of the women had daughters of the right age, and some had already expressed an interest in my friend's son. I was most enthusiastic about the possibilities of one particular family who had five daughters, all of whom were pretty, demure, and well educated. Their mother had told my friend, "You can have your pick for your son, whichever one of my daughters appeals to you most."

I saw a match in sight. "Surely," I said to my friend, "we will find one there. Let's go visit and make our choice." But my friend held back; she did not seem to share my enthusiasm, for reasons I could not then fathom.

When I kept pressing for an explanation of her reluctance, she admitted, "See, Serena, here is the problem. The family has so many daughters, how will they be able to provide nicely for any of them? We are not making any demands, but still, with so many daughters to marry off, one wonders whether she will even be able to make a proper wedding. Since this is our eldest son, it's best if we marry him to a girl who is the only daughter, then the wedding will truly be a gala affair." I argued that surely the quality of the girls themselves made up for any deficiency in the elaborateness of the wedding. My friend admitted this point but still seemed reluctant to proceed.

"Is there something else," I asked her, "some factor I have missed?" "Well," she finally said, "there is one other thing. They have one daughter already married and living in Bombay. The mother is always complaining to me that the girl's in-laws don't let her visit her own family often enough. So it makes me wonder, will she be that kind of mother who always wants her daughter at her own home? This will prevent the girl from adjusting to our house. It is not a good thing." And so, this family of five daughters was dropped as a possibility.

Somewhat disappointed, I nevertheless respected my friend's reasoning and geared up for the next prospect. This was also the daughter of a woman in

[CONTINUED]

[CONTINUED]

my friend's social club. There was clear interest in this family, and I could see why. The family's reputation was excellent; in fact, they came from a subcaste slightly higher than my friend's own. The girl, who was an only daughter, was pretty and well educated and had a brother studying in the United States. Yet, after expressing an interest to me in this family, all talk of them suddenly died down and the search began elsewhere.

"What happened to that girl as a prospect?" I asked one day. "You never mention her anymore. She is so pretty and so educated, what did you find wrong?"

"She is too educated. We've decided against it. My husband's father saw the girl on the bus the other day and thought her forward. A girl who 'roams about' the city by herself is not the girl for our family." My disappointment this time was even greater, as I thought the son would have liked the girl very much. But then I thought, my friend is right, a girl who is going to live in a joint family cannot be too independent or she will make life miserable for everyone. I also learned that if the family of the girl has even a slightly higher social status than the family of the boy, the bride may think herself too good for them, and this too will cause problems. Later my friend admitted to me that this had been an important factor in her decision not to pursue the match.

The next candidate was the daughter of a client of my friend's husband. When the client learned that the family was looking for a match for their son, he said, "Look no further, we have a daughter." This man then invited my friends to dinner to see the girl. He had already seen their son at the office and decided that "he liked the boy." We all went together for tea, rather than dinner—it was less of a commitment—and while we were there, the girl's mother showed us around the house. The girl was studying for her exams and was briefly introduced to us.

After we left, I was anxious to hear my friend's opinion. While her husband liked the family very much and was impressed with his client's business

accomplishments and reputation, the wife didn't like the girl's looks. "She is short, no doubt, which is an important plus point, but she is also fat and wears glasses." My friend obviously thought she could do better for her son and asked her husband to make his excuses to his client by saying that they had decided to postpone the boy's marriage indefinitely.

By this time almost six months had passed and I was becoming impatient. What I had thought would be an easy matter to arrange was turning out to be quite complicated. I began to believe that between my friend's desire for a girl who was modest enough to fit into her joint family, yet attractive and educated enough to be an acceptable partner for her son, she would not find anyone suitable. My friend laughed at my impatience: "Don't be so much in a hurry," she said. "You Americans want everything done so quickly. You get married quickly and then just as quickly get divorced. Here we take marriage more seriously. We must take all the factors into account. It is not enough for us to learn by our mistakes. This is too serious a business. If a mistake is made we have not only ruined the life of our son or daughter, but we have spoiled the reputation of our family as well. And that will make it much harder for their brothers and sisters to get married. So we must be very careful."

What she said was true and I promised myself to be more patient, though it was not easy. I had really hoped and expected that the match would be made before my year in India was up. But it was not to be. When I left India my friend seemed no further along in finding a suitable match for her son than when I had arrived.

Two years later, I returned to India and still my friend had not found a girl for her son. By this time, he was close to thirty, and I think she was a little worried. Since she knew I had friends all over India, and I was going to be there for a year, she asked me to "help her in this work" and keep an eye out for someone suitable. I was flattered that my judgment was respected, but knowing now how complicated the process was, I had lost my earlier confidence as

a matchmaker. Nevertheless, I promised that I would try.

It was almost at the end of my year's stay in India that I met a family with a marriageable daughter whom I felt might be a good possibility for my friend's son. The girl's father was related to a good friend of mine and by coincidence came from the same village as my friend's husband. This new family had a successful business in a medium-sized city in central India and were from the same subcaste as my friend. The daughter was pretty and chic; in fact, she had studied fashion design in college. Her parents would not allow her to go off by herself to any of the major cities in India where she could make a career, but they had compromised with her wish to work by allowing her to run a small dress-making boutique from their home. In spite of her desire to have a career, the daughter was both modest and home-loving and had had a traditional, sheltered upbringing. She had only one other sister, already married, and a brother who was in his father's business.

I mentioned the possibility of a match with my friend's son. The girl's parents were most interested. Although their daughter was not eager to marry just yet, the idea of living in Bombay—a sophisticated, extremely fashion-conscious city where she could continue her education in clothing design—was a great inducement. I gave the girl's father my friend's address and suggested that when they went to Bombay on some business or whatever, they look up the boy's family.

Returning to Bombay on my way to New York, I told my friend of this newly discovered possibility. She seemed to feel there was potential but, in spite of my urging, would not make any moves herself. She rather preferred to wait for the girl's family to call upon them. I hoped something would come of this introduction, though by now I had learned to rein in my optimism.

A year later I received a letter from my friend. The family had indeed come to visit Bombay, and their daughter and my friend's daughter, who were near in age, had become very good friends. During that year, the two girls had

[CONTINUED]

frequently visited each other. I thought things looked promising.

Last week I received an invitation to a wedding: My friend's son and the girl were getting married. Since I had found the match, my presence was particularly requested at the wedding. I was thrilled. Success at last! As I prepared to leave for India, I began thinking, "Now, my friend's younger son, who do I know who has a nice girl for him . . . ?" *(By S. Nanda, (1992). Arranging a marriage in India. In P. R. De Vita (Ed.). The naked anthropologist (pp. 139–143). Belmont, CA: Wadsworth.)*

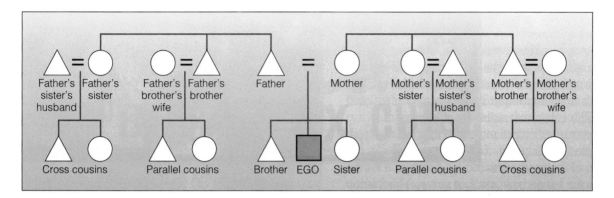

FIGURE 8.2

Anthropologists use diagrams of this sort to illustrate kinship relationships. Shown in this one is the distinction between cross and parallel cousins. In such diagrams, males are always shown as triangles, females as circles, marital ties by an =, sibling relationships as a horizontal line, and parent–child relationships as a vertical line. Terms are given from the perspective of the individual labeled *EGO*, who can be female or male.

Cousin Marriage

In some societies, preferred marriages are a man marrying his father's brother's daughter. This is known as **patrilateral parallel-cousin marriage** (Figure 8.2). A parallel cousin is the child of a father's brother or a mother's sister. Although not obligatory, such marriages have been favored historically among Arabs, the ancient Israelites, and also in ancient Greece. All of these societies are (or were) hierarchical in nature—that is, some people have more property than others—and although male dominance and descent are emphasized, property of interest to men is inherited by daughters as well as sons. Thus, when a man marries his father's brother's daughter (or, from the woman's point of view, she marries her father's brother's son), property is retained within the single male line of descent. In these societies, generally speaking, the greater the property, the more this form of parallel-cousin marriage is apt to occur.

Matrilateral cross-cousin marriage (Figure 8.2)—that is, of a man to his mother's brother's daughter, or a woman to her father's sister's son (a cross cousin is the child of a mother's brother or a father's sister)—is a preferred form of marriage in a variety of societies ranging from food foragers (the Aborigines of Australia, for example) to intensive agriculturists (such as various peo-ples of South India). Among food-foraging peoples, who inherit relatively little in the way of property, such marriages help establish and maintain ties of solidarity between social groups. In agricultural societies, however, the transmission of property is an important determinant. In societies that trace descent exclusively in the female line, for instance, property and other important rights usually pass from a man to his sister's son; under cross-cousin marriage, the sister's son is also the man's daughter's husband.

Marriage Exchanges

In the Trobriand Islands, when a young couple decides to get married, they sit in public on the veranda of the young man's adolescent retreat, where all may see them.

patrilateral parallel-cousin marriage Marriage of a man to his father's brother's daughter, or a woman to her father's brother's son (that is, to a parallel cousin on the paternal side).

matrilateral cross-cousin marriage Marriage of a woman to her father's sister's son, or a man to his mother's brother's daughter (her cross cousin on the paternal side, his cross cousin on the maternal side).

On the day her marriage is announced, the Trobriand bride must give up the provocative miniskirts she has worn until then in favor of longer skirts, the first of which the groom's sister provides. This announces that her days of sexual freedom are over.

In many African societies, bride-price takes the form of cattle, which are paid by the groom's family to the bride's family.

Here they remain until the bride's mother brings the couple cooked yams, which they then eat together, making their marriage official. A day later the bride is presented with three long skirts by the husband's sister, a symbol of the fact that the sexual freedom of adolescence is now over for the newly wed woman. This is followed by a large presentation of uncooked yams by the bride's father and her mother's brother, who represent both her father's and her own lineages.

Meanwhile, the groom's father and mother's brother—representing his father's and his own lineages—collect such valuables as stone axe blades, clay pots, money, and the occasional Kula shell (see Chapter 7) to present to the young wife's maternal kin and father. After the first year of the marriage, during which the

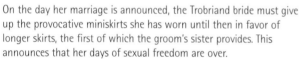

bride-price Compensation the groom or his family pays to the bride's family upon marriage. Also called "bride wealth."

bride's mother continues to provide the couple's meals of cooked yams, each of the young husband's relatives who provided valuables for his father and mother's brother to present to the bride's relatives will receive yams from her maternal relatives and father. All of this gift giving back and forth between the husband's and wife's lineages, as well as those of their fathers, serves to bind the four parties together in a way that makes people respect and honor the marriage and that creates obligations on the part of the woman's kin to take care of her husband in the future.

As among the Trobriand Islanders, marriages in many human societies are formalized by some sort of economic exchange. Among the Trobrianders, this takes the form of a gift exchange, as just described. Far more common is **bride-price**, sometimes called bride wealth. This involves payments of money or other valuables to a bride's parents or other close kin. This usually happens in societies where the bride will become a member of the household where her husband grew up; this house-

In some societies when a woman marries, she receives her share of the family inheritance (her dowry), which she brings to her new family (unlike bride-price, which passes from the groom's family to the bride's family). Shown here are Slovakian women carrying the objects of a woman's dowry.

In Europe, where both men and women inherit family wealth, the "marriage" of women to the Church as nuns passed wealth that might otherwise have gone to husbands and offspring to the Church instead.

hold will benefit from her labor as well as from the off-spring she produces. Thus, her family must be compensated for their loss.

Not only is bride-price *not* a simple "buying and selling" of women, but the bride's parents may use the money to purchase jewelry or household furnishings for her or to finance an elaborate and costly wedding celebration. It also contributes to the stability of the marriage, because it usually must be refunded if the couple separates. Other forms of compensation are an exchange of women between families—"My son will marry your daughter if your son will marry my daughter." Yet another is **bride service,** a period of time during which the groom works for the bride's family.

In a number of societies more or less restricted to the western, southern, and eastern margins of Eurasia, where the economy is based on intensive agriculture, women often bring a **dowry** with them at marriage. A form of dowry in the United States is the custom of the bride's family paying the wedding expenses. In effect, a dowry is a woman's share of parental property that, instead of passing to her upon her parents' death, is distributed to her at the time of her marriage. This does not mean that she retains control of this property after marriage. In a number of European countries, for example, a woman's property falls exclusively under her husband's

bride service A designated period of time after marriage when the groom works for the bride's family.
dowry Payment of a woman's inheritance at the time of her marriage, either to her or to her husband.

control. Having benefited by what she has brought to the marriage, however, he is obligated to look out for her future well-being, including her security after his death. Thus, one of the functions of dowry is to ensure a woman's support in widowhood (or after divorce), an important consideration in a society where men carry out the bulk of productive work and women are valued for their reproductive potential rather than for the work they do. In such societies, women incapable of bearing children are especially vulnerable, but the dowry they bring with them at marriage helps protect them against desertion. Another function of dowry is to reflect the economic status of the woman in societies where differences in wealth are important. Thus, the property that a woman brings with her at marriage demonstrates that the man is marrying a woman whose standing is on a par with his own. It also permits women, with the aid of their parents and kin, to compete through dowry for desirable (that is, wealthy) husbands.

Same-Sex Marriage

As noted earlier in this chapter, our definition of marriage refers to a union between "people" rather than "a man and a woman" because in some societies same-sex marriages are socially acceptable and allowed by law. Marriages between individuals of the same sex may provide a way of dealing with problems for which opposite-sex marriage offers no satisfactory solution. This is the case with woman–woman marriage, a practice sanctioned in many societies of sub-Saharan Africa, although in none does it involve more than a small minority of all women.

   Although details differ from one society to another, woman–woman marriages among the Nandi of western Kenya may be taken as reasonably representative of such practices in Africa.[22] The Nandi are a pastoral people who also do considerable farming. Control of most significant property and the primary means of production—livestock and land—is exclusively in the hands of men, and may only be transmitted to their male heirs, usually their sons. Since polygyny is the preferred form of marriage, a man's property is normally divided equally among his wives for their sons to inherit. Within the household, each wife has her own house in which she lives with her children, but all are under the authority of the woman's husband, who is a remote and aloof figure within the household. In such situations, the position of a woman who bears no sons is difficult; not only

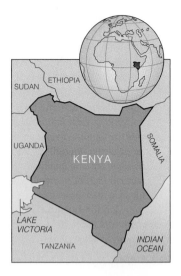

does she not help perpetuate her husband's male line—a major concern among the Nandi—but also she has no one to inherit the proper share of her husband's property.

   To get around these problems, a woman of advanced age who bore no sons may become a female husband by marrying a young woman. The purpose of this arrangement is for the young wife to provide the male heirs her female husband could not. To accomplish this, the woman's wife enters into a sexual relationship with a man other than her female husband's male husband; usually it is one of his male relatives. No other obligations exist between this woman and her male sex partner, and her female husband is recognized as the social and legal father of any children born under these conditions.

   In keeping with her role as female husband, this woman is expected to abandon her female gender identity and, ideally, dress and behave as a man. In practice, the ideal is not completely achieved, for the habits of a lifetime are difficult to reverse. Generally, it is in the context of domestic activities, which are most highly symbolic of female identity, that female husbands most completely assume a male identity.

   The individuals who are parties to woman–woman marriages enjoy several advantages. By assuming male identity, a barren or sonless woman raises her status considerably and even achieves near equality with men, who otherwise occupy a far more favored position in Nandi society than women. A woman who marries a female husband is usually one who is unable to make a good marriage, often because she (the female husband's wife) has lost face as a consequence of premarital pregnancy. By marrying a female husband, she too raises her status and also secures legitimacy for her children. Moreover, a female husband is usually less harsh and demanding, spends more time with her, and allows her a greater say in decision making than a male husband does. The one thing she may not do is engage in sexual activity with her marriage partner. In fact, female husbands are expected to abandon sexual activity altogether, even with their male husbands to whom they remain married even though the women now have their own wives.

   Recently, the issue of same-sex marriage has become a matter for debate in the United States. In sev-

---

[22]The following is based on Obler, R. S. (1982). Is the female husband a man? Woman/woman marriage among the Nandi of Kenya. *Ethnology, 19,* 69–88.

William Lippert, the only openly gay member of the Vermont House of Representatives, embraces his partner upon passage of a bill legalizing civil unions.

Lesbian "wedding" in Maine, where same-sex marriages are not legal. Lack of government approval has not kept gays or lesbians from making marriage commitments of the heart with their partners, usually in the presence of family and friends. The Massachusetts Supreme Judicial Court's 2003 ruling that same-sex marriage is a constitutional right in that state intensified public debate on this issue nationwide.

eral states, resolutions or laws have been passed forbidding such marriages. But in 2000 Vermont legalized "civil unions" between same-sex couples, granting same-sex partners some of the legal benefits of marriage. In 2003, the Massachusetts Supreme Judicial Court ruled that same-sex marriage is a constitutional right in that state, a decision that calls for full equal marriage rights for homosexual couples. The arguments most commonly marshaled by opponents of same-sex unions are, first, that marriage has always been between males and females, but as we have just seen, this is not true. Same-sex marriages have been documented not only for a number of societies in Africa but in other parts of the world as well. As among the Nandi, they provide acceptable positions in society for individuals who might otherwise be marginalized.

MEDIATREK

To get up-to-date information on the legal status of gay partnerships around the world, go to MediaTrek 8.3 on the companion Web site or CD-ROM.

A second argument against same-sex unions is that they legitimize marriages between gays and lesbians, whose sexual orientations have been widely regarded in the United States as unnatural. But again, as discussed in earlier chapters, neither cross-cultural studies nor studies of other species suggest that homosexual behavior is unnatural.

A third argument, that the function of marriage is to produce children, is also flawed. At best, it is a partial truth, as marriage involves economic, political, and legal considerations as well. Moreover, it is increasingly common for same-sex partners to have children through adoption or by turning to modern reproductive technologies. There is also the fact that in many societies, there is a separation between the sexual and reproductive attributes of women; two such cases are the Nandi and the Nayar.

DIVORCE

Like marriage, divorce in most societies is a matter of great concern to the couple's families. Since marriage is less often a religious than an economic matter, divorce arrangements can be made for a variety of reasons and with varying degrees of difficulty.

Among the Gusii farmers of western Kenya, sterility or impotence were grounds for a divorce. Among the Chenchu foragers inhabiting the thickly forested hills in central India and certain aboriginal peoples in northern Canada, divorce was discouraged after children were born; couples usually were urged by their families to adjust their differences. By contrast, in the southwestern United States, a Hopi Indian woman in Arizona could divorce her husband at any time merely by placing his belongings outside the door to indicate he was no longer welcome. Divorce was fairly common among the Yahgan, who lived at the southernmost tip of South America, and was seen as justified if the husband was considered cruel or failed as a provider. When divorce

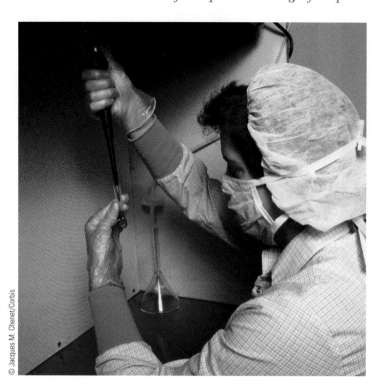

Shown here is a nurse creating a human embryo. No longer is biological sex the only way to beget children. New reproductive technologies have opened the way to a whole new industry and have helped transform children into consumer goods.

© Jacques M. Chenet/Corbis

occurred in these societies the children were cared for in one way or another. An adult unmarried woman is very rare in most non-Western societies, where a divorced woman usually soon remarries. In many societies, economic considerations are often the strongest motivation to marry. On the island of New Guinea, a man does not marry because of sexual needs, which he can readily satisfy out of wedlock, but because he needs a woman to make pots and cook his meals, to fabricate nets and weed his plantings. A man without a wife among the Aborigines of Australia is in an unsatisfactory position, since he has no one to supply him regularly with food or firewood. Likewise, women in communities whose security against outside enemies depends on males capable of fighting rely upon husbands who are raised to be able warriors as well as good hunters.

Although divorce rates may be high in various corners of the world (notably matrilineal societies such as the Hopi Indians in the southwestern United States), they have become so high in Western industrial and postindustrial societies that many worry about the future of what they view as traditional and familiar forms of marriage and the family. It is interesting to note that although divorce was next to impossible in Western societies between 1000 and 1800, few marriages lasted more than about 10 or 20 years, owing low life expectancy.[23]

With a lower rate of separation by death has come a higher rate by legal action.

Undoubtedly, the causes of divorce in the United States are many and varied. Among them are the trivial and transient characteristics we have already mentioned on which marriages may all too easily be based. Beyond this, marriage in the United States is supposed to involve an enduring, supportive, and intimate bond between a man and woman, full of affection and love. In this relationship, people are supposed to find escape from the pressures of the competitive workaday world, as well as from the legal and social constraints that so affect their behavior outside the family. Yet in a society where people are brought up to seek individual gratification, where this often is seen to come through competition at someone else's expense, and where women traditionally have been expected to be submissive to men, it should not come as a surprise that the reality of marriage does not always live up to the ideal. Harsh treatment and neglect of spouses—usually of wives by husbands—in the United States is neither new nor rare. But until recently people were more tolerant of violence directed against spouses and children than of violence against outsiders. Today people are less inclined toward moral censure of individuals—women especially—who seek escape from unsatisfactory marriages. No longer are people as willing to "stick it out at all costs" no matter how intolerable the situation may be. Thus, divorce is increasingly exercised as a sensible reaction to marriages that do not work.

[23]Stone, L. (1998). *Kinship and gender: An introduction* (p. 235). Boulder, CO: Westview Press.

Chapter Summary

■ Among primates, the human female is unusual in her ability to engage in sexual activity whenever she wants to or whenever her culture tells her it is appropriate, irrespective of whether she is fertile. Although such activity may reinforce social bonds between individuals, competition for sexual access can also be disruptive, so every society has rules that govern such access. The near universality of the incest taboo, which forbids sexual relations between parents and their children and usually between siblings, has interested generations of anthropologists, but a truly convincing explanation of the taboo has yet to be advanced. Related to incest are the practices of endogamy and exogamy. Endogamy is marriage within a group of individuals; exogamy is marriage outside the group. If the group is limited to the immediate family, almost all societies can be said to prohibit endogamy and practice exogamy. Likewise, societies that practice exogamy at one level may practice endogamy at another. Community endogamy, for example, is a relatively common practice. In a few societies, royal families are known to have practiced endogamy rather than exogamy among siblings to preserve the purity of the royal line and its property.

■ Although defined in terms of a continuing sexual relationship, marriage should not be confused with mating. Although mating occurs within marriage, it often occurs outside of it as well. Unlike mating, marriage is backed by social, legal, and economic forces. In some societies, new families are formed through marriage, but this is not true for all societies.

■ Although a majority of cultures are sexually permissive and do not sharply regulate personal sexual practices, others are restrictive and explicitly prohibit all sexual activity outside of marriage. Of these, a few punish adultery by imprisonment, social exclusion, or even death, as traditionally prescribed by orthodox Judeo-Christian and Muslim laws.

■ Monogamy, or the taking of a single spouse, is the most common form of marriage, primarily for economic reasons. A man must have a certain amount of wealth to be able to afford polygyny, or marriage to more than one wife at the same time. Yet in societies where women do most of the productive work, polygyny may serve as a means of generating wealth for a household. Although few marriages in a given society may be polygynous, it is regarded as an appropriate, and even preferred, form of marriage in the majority of the world's societies. Since few communities have a surplus of men, polyandry, or the custom of a woman having several husbands, is uncommon. Also rare is group marriage, in which several men and several women have sexual access to one another. The levirate ensures the security of a woman by providing that a widow marry her husband's brother; the sororate provides that a widower marry his wife's sister. Serial monogamy is a form of marriage in which a man or woman marries a series of partners. In recent decades, this pattern has become increasingly common among middle-class North Americans as individuals divorce and remarry.

■ In industrial and postindustrial countries of the West, marriages run the risk of being based on an ideal of romantic love that emphasizes youthful beauty. In no other parts of the world would marriages based on such trivial and transitory characteristics be expected to work. In non-Western societies economic considerations are of major concern in arranging marriages. Love follows, rather than precedes, marriage. The family arranges marriages in societies in which it is the most powerful social institution. Marriage serves to bind two families as allies.

■ Preferred marriage partners in many societies are particular cross cousins (mother's brother's daughter if a man; father's sister's son if a woman) or, less commonly, parallel cousins on the paternal side (father's brother's son or daughter). Cross-cousin marriage is a means of establishing and maintaining solidarity between groups. Marriage to a paternal parallel cousin serves to retain property and a woman's offspring within a single male line of descent.

■ In many human societies, marriages are formalized by some sort of economic exchange. Sometimes, this takes the form of reciprocal gift exchange between the bride's and groom's relatives. More common is bride-price, the payment of money or other valuables from the groom's to the bride's kin. This is characteristic of societies where the women both work and bear children for the husband's family. An alternative arrangement is for families to exchange daughters. Bride service occurs when the groom is expected to work for a period for the bride's family. A dowry is the payment of a woman's inheritance at the time of marriage to her or her husband. Its purpose is to ensure support for women in societies where men do most of the productive work, and women are valued for their reproductive potential alone.

■ In some societies, marriage arrangements exist between individuals of the same sex. An example is woman–woman marriage as practiced in many African societies. Such marriages provide a socially approved way to deal with problems for which marriages between individuals of opposite sex offer no satisfactory solution.

■ Divorce is possible in all societies, though reasons for divorce as well as its frequency vary widely from one society to another. In the United States, factors contributing to the breakup of marriages include the trivial and transitory characteristics upon which many marriages are based and the difficulty of establishing a supportive, intimate bond in a society in which people are brought up to seek individual gratification, often through competition at someone else's expense, and in which women have traditionally been expected to be submissive to men.

Questions for Reflection

1. Historically, most traditional societies were relatively isolated from other groups and, consequently, formed more or less closed communities. In the age of globalization, however, many have opened up to outside contact. Modern technologies not only make it possible for foreign ideas and com-

modities to quickly spread all around the world, but also provide similar opportunities for viruses and bacteria. In this context, consider the relative benefits and liabilities of sexual permissiveness. And how does this challenge individual rights and freedoms?

2. Although many people in North America and Europe choose to have children outside marriage, this institution fulfills an important social function. Considering some of the major functions of marriage, do you think there is a relationship between the type of society an individual belongs to and the choice to forgo the traditional benefits of marriage? Under which cultural conditions might the choice to remain unmarried turn into a serious problem?

3. Although most women in Europe and North America view polygyny as a marriage practice exclusively benefiting men, women in cultures where such marriages are traditional sometimes stress more positive sides of sharing a husband with several co-wives. Under which conditions do you think polygyny could be considered as relatively beneficial for women?

4. In nonindustrial communities of foragers, pastoralists, and farmers, people rarely act upon feelings of love as a basis for marriage. Considering the institution of marriage in such cultural systems, how does it relate to each of the barrel model's three major tiers (infrastructure, social structure, and superstructure)?

Key Terms

Marriage	Levirate
Consanguineal kin	Sororate
Conjugal bond	Serial monogamy
Affinal kin	Patrilateral parallel-cousin
Incest taboo	marriage
Endogamy	Matrilateral cross-cousin
Exogamy	marriage
Monogamy	Bride-price
Polygyny	Bride service
Polyandry	Dowry
Group marriage	

Multimedia Review Tools

Companion Web Site

Visit **http://www.wadsworth.com/anthropology_d/** and click on the companion Web site for this textbook to access a wide range of material to aid your study of anthropology. Among the options for self-study in each chapter are learning objectives, flash cards, Internet activities, Web links, InfoTrac College Edition exercises, and practice tests that can be scored and emailed to your instructor.

CD-ROM

The *Doing Anthropology Today* CD-ROM supplied with your textbook provides unique and valuable information designed to enhance your learning experience. This interactive multimedia resource includes video clips, interviews with renowned anthropologists, map and timeline exercises, chapter study quizzes, and much more. *Doing Anthropology Today* will not only help you in achieving your grade goals, but it will also make your learning experience fun and exciting!

Suggested Readings

DuToit, B. M. (1991). *Human sexuality: Cross-cultural readings.* New York: McGraw-Hill.

Of the numerous texts that deal with most aspects of human sexuality, this is one of the few that gives adequate recognition to the fact most peoples in the world do things differently from North Americans. This reader deals crossculturally with such topics as menstrual cycle, pair bonding, sexuality, pregnancy and childbirth, childhood, puberty, birth control, sexually transmitted diseases, sex roles, and the climacteric.

Goody, J. (1976). *Production and reproduction: A comparative study of the domestic domain.* Cambridge, England: Cambridge University Press.

This book is especially good in its discussion of the interrelationship between marriage, property, and inheritance. Although cross-cultural in its approach, readers will be fascinated by the many insights into the history of marriage in the Western world.

Ottenheimer, M. (1996). *Forbidden relatives.* Champaign: University of Illinois Press.

This book examines the laws against cousin marriage in the United States. It describes their distribution and explains why some states have such laws and others do not. It also contrasts these laws with the absence of such laws in any other country in the Western world and gives the reasons for this difference. Noting that there is no empirical evidence to support such anti-cousin marriage legislation, this book argues that it is based on a myth and analyzes the cultural historical context for the prohibition of such marriages by law.

Stone, L. (2000). *Kinship and gender: An introduction* (2nd ed.). Boulder, CO: Westview Press.

With a focus on gender, Stone considers all the cross-cultural variations in marriage practices in the broader context of kinship studies. A particular strength is the inclusion of specific case studies to illustrate general principles. The book ends with a thought-provoking discussion of new reproductive technologies and their repercussions for both kinship and gender.

Suggs, D. N., & Miracle, A. W. (Eds.). (1993). *Culture and human sexuality: A reader.* Pacific Grove, CA: Brooks/Cole.

This collection of articles covers a wide range of topics including evolution, gender, family, life cycle, incest, religion, sexual orientation, and disease-related issues. Illustrated are the variety of sexual expression around the world and the role of culture in the patterning of sexual ideas and activities.

CHAPTER 9

Family and Household

Photo by Todd Hoffman

A TUAREG FAMILY IN THEIR HOME IN MALI, WEST AFRICA. One of the basic functions of family is to meet the challenge of raising children. Because each upcoming generation will become responsible for maintaining a group's overall well-being and advancing its collective interests, children are an essential investment for a group's long-term survival. Each group has to work out the best possible and most effective arrangements to pass on the necessary cultural know-how and thus ensure enduring success. Adjusting to distinct environments and facing specific challenges, they work out their own arrangements in terms of child-rearing tasks, gender relations, household and family structures, and residence patterns. Changes in these conditions may produce constant social tensions and thus require adjustments.

1

What Is the Family?

Although the idea of *family* means different things to different people, in anthropological terms it is a group of two or more people related by blood, marriage, or adoption. The family may take many forms, ranging from a single parent with one or more children, to a married couple or polygamous spouses with offspring, to several generations of parents and their children. The particular form is related to particular social, historical, and ecological circumstances.

2

What Is the Difference between Family and Household?

Households are task-oriented residential units within which economic production, consumption, inheritance, child rearing, and shelter are organized and accomplished. In the vast majority of human societies, a household consists of a family or part of a family or their core members, even though some household members may not be relatives of the family around which it is built. In some societies, families may be less important in people's thinking than the households in which they live.

3

What Are Some of the Challenges of Family and Household Organization?

Although families and households exist to solve problems all peoples must deal with in various ways, the different forms they may take are accompanied by their own characteristic challenges. Where families and households are small and relatively independent, as they are in contemporary North American society, their members may be isolated from the aid and support of kin and must fend for themselves in many situations. By contrast, families that include several adults within the same large household must find ways to control tensions that invariably exist among their members.

The family, long regarded by North Americans as a critically necessary core social institution, today has become a matter of controversy and discussion. Women going outside the home to take income-producing jobs rather than staying home with children; couples, sometimes of the same sex, living together without the formality of marriage; high divorce rates; and increasing numbers of households headed by a single parent have raised questions about the functions of the husband-wife-children family unit in North American society and its ability to survive in a period of rapid social change. Evidence of widespread interest in these questions can be seen in the initial convening of the White House Conference on Families in 1980. Since then, scarcely a political campaign for national office has passed without frequent reference to what candidates like to call "traditional family values."

Historical and cross-cultural studies of the family offer as many different family patterns as the fertile human imagination can invent. Moreover, family patterns change over time. Thus, the definition of **family** noted in this chapter's opening pages is a broad one that encompasses in a nonethnocentric way the wide range of family forms recognized by societies around the world: Two or more people related by blood, marriage, or adoption. The family may take many forms, ranging from a single parent with one or more children, to a married couple or polygamous spouses with offspring, to several generations of parents and their children. This contrasts a widely used definition presented over 50 years ago by Yale University anthropologist George Murdock, founder of the Human Relations Area Files discussed in Chapter 2. He defined the family more narrowly as "a social group characterized by common residence, economic cooperation, and reproduction."[1]

The family form regarded as "normal" or "natural" by most Europeans and North Americans is the nuclear family consisting of a mother, father, and children (Figure 9.1). However, actual family patterns there have changed so much over the last few decades that a more current definition of this basic family unit seems necessary. (We offer one below, under the heading "Forms of the Family.") The point to be made here is that the nuclear family is no more normal or natural than any

---

[1]Murdock, G. P. (1949). *Social structure* (p. 2). New York: Macmillan.

---

family Two or more people related by blood, marriage, or adoption. The family may take many forms, ranging from a single parent with one or more children, to a married couple or polygamous spouses with offspring, to several generations of parents and their children.

© Bachman/Photo Researchers, Inc.

A nuclear family consisting of a married couple and dependent offspring is held up as the ideal in the United States.

other family structure and cannot be used as the standard for measuring other forms. In fact, the fully independent nuclear family that is so well known in North America and many European countries is not common in other societies, where smaller family units are typically embedded in larger familial groups. It emerged quite recently in human history in response to particular cultural conditions. We can trace its roots back to a series of regulations imposed by the Roman Catholic Church in the 4th century. The rules prohibited close marriages, discouraged adoption, and condemned polygyny, concubinage, divorce, and remarriage (all of which previously had been perfectly acceptable). In addition to strengthening the conjugal tie between one man and one woman, at the expense of consanguineal or "blood" ties, church prohibitions also ensured that large numbers of people

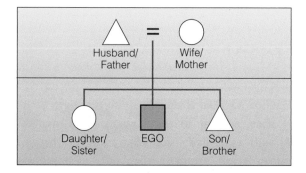

FIGURE 9.1

This diagram shows the relationships in an independent nuclear family form that is common but declining in North America and much of Europe.

The Holy Family of Christianity. Mary's husband, Joseph, was her father's brother's son and was himself the product of a leviratic marriage. Even though both kinds of marriage were considered proper in the early days of Christianity, they were not allowed by the Roman Catholic Church after the 4th century.

would be left with no male heirs. It is a biological fact that 20 percent of all couples will have only daughters, and another 20 percent will have no children at all. By eliminating polygyny, concubinage, divorce, and remarriage, and by discouraging adoption, the Church removed the means by which people increased their odds of having male heirs. In the absence of such heirs, property was commonly transferred from families to the Roman Catholic Church, which rapidly became the largest landowner in most European countries, a position it has retained to this day. By insinuating itself into the very fabric of domestic life—inheritance and marriage—the Church gained tremendous control over the grassroots of society, enriching itself in the process.[2]

With the industrialization of Europe and North America, the nuclear family became further isolated from other kin. One reason for this is that industrial economies require a mobile labor force; people must be prepared to move to where the jobs are, something that is most easily done without excess kin in tow. Another reason is that the family came to be seen as a kind of

refuge from a public world that people saw as threatening to their sense of privacy and self-determination.[3] Within the family, relationships were supposed to be enduring and unconditional, entailing love and affection, based upon cooperation, and governed by feeling and morality. Outside the family, where people sold their work and negotiated contracts, relationships were seen increasingly as competitive, temporary, and contingent upon performance, requiring buttressing by law and legal sanction. Such views were held most widely in the late 19th and early 20th centuries, and in the United States independent nuclear family households reached their highest frequency around 1950, when 60 percent of all households conformed to this model.[4] Since then, that number has dropped by more than half, and the number of households headed by divorced, separated, and never-married individuals has grown significantly.

This situation has arisen as ever-growing numbers of people find more intimacy and emotional support in relationships outside the family and are less inclined to tolerate the harsh treatment and neglect of children and spouses, especially wives, which occur all too commonly within families. In the United States, the number of violent domestic crimes against females declined 55 percent between 1993 and 2002. Nonetheless, half a million women were assaulted by an intimate partner in 2002. Death figures are not available for that year, but in the year 2000, nearly four women per day were killed by their bat-

[2]Goody, J. (1983). *The development of the family and marriage in Europe* (pp. 44–46). Cambridge, England: Cambridge University Press.

[3]Collier, J., Rosaldo, M. Z., & Yanagisako, S. (1982). Is there a family? New anthropological views. In B. Thorne & M. Yalom (Eds.), *Rethinking the family: Some feminist questions* (pp. 34–35). New York: Longman.

[4]Stacey, J. (1990). *Brave new families* (pp. 5, 10). New York: Basic Books.

In North America, families are widely believed to be places of refuge from the rough-and-tumble outside world. Yet, domestic violence is far from rare, and women and children are its usual victims.

terers—1,247 in all.[5] Reliable statistics are hard to come by, but it is clear that violence against women is present in every country around the world. For example, a United Nations report released in 2000 included statistics garnered since 1993 from every continent. A small sampling of these: 29 percent of women in Canada have been physically assaulted by a current or former partner; 45 percent of married men in India's state of Uttar Pradesh acknowledged physically abusing their wives; 32 percent of Arab women in Israel reported at least one episode of physical abuse by their partner; 41 percent of women surveyed in two districts in Uganda, Africa, reported being beaten or physically harmed by a partner; 19 percent of women surveyed in Colombia, South America, said they have been physically assaulted by their partner; and the list goes on.[6]

FAMILY AND SOCIETY

Although many people think of families as standing in opposition to the rest of society, the truth is that they are affected by, and in turn affect, the values and structure of the society in which they are embedded. Because there is a continuum of family arrangements, from the smallest domestic unit of immediate relatives to ever larger groups related by blood and marriage, anthropologists distinguish among different types of families, as discussed a few pages ahead in the section about family forms.

The family, as it has emerged in all corners of the world, is the product of particular historical and social circumstances. As part of a cultural system (as illustrated by the three-tiered barrel model presented in Chapter 2), family forms are intricately interconnected to other features in a society's infrastructure, social structure, and superstructure. Not only do they differ among societies that have contrasting structural features, but they change within each society as it experiences shifts in any of its structural layers. Thus, how men and women in other societies live together must be studied not as bizarre and exotic forms of human behavior but as logical outcomes of people's experience living in particular times, places, and social situations. This chapter's Original Study offers a closer look at the relationship between family and society.

---

[5]U.S. Department of Justice, Bureau of Justice Statistics, *www.ojp.usdoj.gov/bjx.*

[6]Domestic violence against women and girls. (2000, June). *Innocenti Digest, 6*, 4, Florence: United Nations Children's Fund, Innocenti Research Center.

MEDIATREK
To explore a range of familial topics concerning women throughout the world, from a cross-cultural look at the legal status of abortion to the issue of domestic violence, go to MediaTrek 9.1 on the companion Web site or CD-ROM.

Original Study

The Ever-Changing Family in North America

In colonial North America during the 17th and 18th centuries, people lived in farming households, each typically consisting of a nuclear family; wealthier households contained servants as well. In addition, many less wealthy families sent their children to more prosperous households to work as servants or to learn a trade, a practice also common in Europe. Thus many households contained large numbers of people who were not kin to one another. It was these households, rather than their own biological families as such, that were important in people's daily lives. Biological children were treated much like servants, especially if they were of similar age.

The households themselves did not contain separate, private spaces for married couples or for parents and their children. As Stephanie Coontz (in her book on the history of American families) writes: "The central room or hall was where work, meals, play, religious instruction, and often sleep took place. . . . Even genteel families put several people to a room and several people to a bed. . . . There was thus little concept of a private family set apart from the world of work, servants, and neighbors." Households were closely linked to one another and highly interdependent on one another for cooperation and economic exchanges. What we would consider very private

business today was then considered the business of neighbors, church officials, and the whole community.

This point is strikingly illustrated by Coontz, who uses Nancy Cott's study of colonial divorce records to show how "neighbors nonchalantly entered what modern people would consider the most private areas of life. Mary Angel and Abagail Galloway, for example, testified that they had caught sight through an open window of Adam Air 'in the Act of Copulation' with Pamela Brichford. They walked into the house 'and after observing them some time . . . asked him if he was not Ashamed to act so when he had a Wife at home.'"

[CONTINUED]

Also in contrast to later North America, in colonial times "the home" was not seen as a retreat from the strain of the outside world. Indeed, since the colonial household was a center of economic production (in terms of, for example, agriculture and farm management, cloth production, and trade), there was little division between the public and domestic spheres of life.

In the household, both women and men played active roles in production. Each household was under the authority of its male property owner. Wives were under the authority of husbands, but so were children, servants, apprentices, and anyone else attached to the man's household. In fact, colonial society itself was altogether hierarchical, such that lower-ranking males were subservient to higher ones to the same extent that wives were to husbands. This was a society that viewed its parts as interdependent and so required a hierarchy for its organization. Women were clearly subordinate, but a colonial woman's subordination was viewed as a social necessity—one of many unequal relations required by society—not as a unique female condition related to her biology.

Many of us associate colonial society with rather strict rules governing sexual activity. Indeed, there were laws against fornication and adultery in all the colonies. Adultery (defined as sex between a man and a married woman) was often severely punished, with public flogging or even death. Dancing and certain forms of dress were also widely forbidden. Still, sex was frankly discussed, offenses were openly described and punished, and sexual matters were not hidden away from children. Moreover, wives were expected to be affectionate companions to husbands.

The patriarchal colonial family faded away as population expansion, migration, new waves of immigrants, urbanization, and other economic and political changes occurred in North America. There was a trend toward increasing privacy of the nuclear family. However, this trend took hold much more slowly in rural and working-class families; and among all classes families maintained important ties with wider kin for support and help, especially during periods of war, economic disruption, and urbanization over the next few centuries.

Important changes in family life and gender relationships correlated with industrialization in the late 18th and early 19th centuries. New industries needed workers and managers, often at work sites away from the home. Whereas the household had formerly been a unit of production and consumption, it was now a unit of consumption only. Hence the split between the home (private, domestic) and the workplace (public, productive) was born. Among poor and working-class people, both women and men went out to work, though women were pushed into lower-paying jobs with less hope of advancement—as is still common for North American women today. Among the middle and upper classes, industrialization meant the withdrawal of women from production. Their roles became confined to the home, to child rearing, to domesticity. Indeed, among the middle classes, a nonworking wife was important for the social image and self-esteem of males, who believed it was their duty to provide for and protect wives and children. Removed from production, wives became economically dependent on husbands and in this condition were easily subordinated to them. Now, however, women's subordination to men was not seen as a societal necessity, but rather as rooted in nature, reflecting natural or biological differences between women and men. Women's natural "place" was in the home.

By the end of World War II, some North Americans embarked on what many look back to as the Golden Age of the American family, sometimes called the 1950s "Leave It to Beaver" family. A thoroughly middle-class phenomenon, this was a nuclear family that had moved to the suburbs, where it eventually owned its own home. The father-husband went off to work and functioned as the "breadwinner." The full-time wife-mother stayed at home, absorbed in domestic efficiency, child rearing, and being a companion to her husband. According to this particular ideal, the father, though busy at work, had an active family life too. This ideal family was very private, and its members spent quality time together; all were happy and had a lot of good, clean middle-class fun.

But Coontz suggests that this 1950s family is largely a myth; it represents nostalgia for a recreated past, not a solid American tradition. For one thing, she contends, this ideal family was never a reality for the majority of North Americans and certainly not for groups such as black people and the poor. Some families maintained a facade of this ideal on the outside, but inside were wracked by alcoholic parents and abusive relationships. And women of this time were excluded from so many fields and suffered so many financial restrictions (for example, not being allowed to take out credit cards in their own names) that, in Coontz's words, "there were not many permissible alternatives to baking brownies [or] experimenting with new canned soups." Even so, many women were discontent with their isolated, domestic roles and their full economic dependence on their husbands.

Even for those few North Americans who had anything like the ideal 1950s family, this outcome, according to Coontz, was an historical fluke. It is true that, with the end of the war and relief at its end, the age of marriage dropped, fertility rose, divorce declined, and the middle class moved to the suburbs. But the 1950s family with its nonworking wives and affordable homes emerged only because of North America's brief postwar prosperity. Within a short span of time, the American dream was no longer affordable, and middle-class women went out to work.

Women's participation in the labor force increased and has been increasing ever since. Today a majority of working-age women and a majority of women with young children are in the workforce. This increase among working women was as much a function of economic necessity as a response to the doldrums of housework.

Alongside women's greater participation in the workforce, the later decades of the 20th century saw a dramatic increase in divorce and remarriage. As a result, many families today are headed by single parents, most often single women, or they may be "blended" families, consisting of a married couple with children from the spouses' previous unions. By this same process, many children feel they belong

[CONTINUED]

[CONTINUED]

to two families, each containing a divorced parent, with possibly one or both of these families including a step-parent and stepsiblings.

Thus today's North American families are more diverse than ever before, with parenthood being defined more in social and legal terms and less by reproduction. When we add to these family changes other recent developments, such as movements for recognition of gay and lesbian marriage/parenthood and the new reproductive technologies (such as surrogate motherhood and in vitro fertilization), we see even greater diversity and flexibility in North American cultural definitions of "family" and kin relationships. The most promi-nent trend today is that family and kin-ship are more and more a matter of per-sonal choice and self-determination and less a matter of biological connection. *(Adapted from L. Stone. (1998). Kinship and gender: An introduction (pp. 248–250, 255–256). Boulder, CO: Westview Press. Updated by Stone for this textbook, 2003.)*

FUNCTIONS OF THE FAMILY

Among humans, reliance on group living for survival is a basic characteristic. They have inherited this from their primate ancestors, though they have developed it in their own distinctively human ways. Even among monkeys and apes, group living requires the participation of adults of both sexes. Among primate species that, like us, have taken up life on the ground, as well as among species most closely related to us, adult males are normally much larger and stronger than females and their teeth are usually more efficient for fighting. Thus, they are essential for the group's defense. Moreover, the close and prolonged relationship between infants and their mothers, without which the infants cannot survive, renders the adult primate female less well suited than the male to handle defense.

Nurturing of Children

Taking care of the young is primarily the job of the adult primate female. Primate babies are born relatively helpless and remain dependent upon their mothers for a longer time than other animals (a chimpanzee, for example, cannot survive without its mother until it reaches age 4 or even 5). Not only is this dependence for food and physical care, but also, as numerous studies have shown, primate infants deprived of maternal atten-tion will not grow and develop normally, if they survive at all. The protective presence of adult males shields the mothers from both danger and harassment from other group members, allowing them to give their infants the attention they require.

Among humans, the division of labor by gender has been developed beyond the sexual division of other pri-mates. Until the recent advent of substitutes for human breast milk, human females more often than not were occupied much of their adult lives with child rearing. And human infants need no less active "mothering" than do the young of other primates. For one thing, they are even more helpless at birth, and for another, the period of infant dependency is longer in humans. Besides all this, studies have shown that human infants, no less than other primates, need more than just food and physical care if they are to develop normally. But among humans, unlike other primates, the infant's biological mother does not have to provide all this "mothering." Not only may other

Photo by Todd Hoffman

A Tuareg father and his child in their tented home on the edge of Africa's Sahara Desert, near Timbuktu, Mali. In many societies chil-dren are handled as much by men as by women.

One alternative to the family as a child-rearing unit is the Israeli kibbutz, a communal agricultural settlement. Here, children of a kibbutz are shown in a supervised session of creative play.

women provide the child with much of the attention it needs, but so may men. In many societies children are cared for as much by men as by women, and in some societies men are more nurturing to children than are women.

Economic Cooperation

In all human societies, even though women may be the primary providers of child care, women have other responsibilities as well. Although several of the economic activities they have engaged in traditionally have been compatible with their child-rearing role and have not placed their offspring at risk, this cannot be said of all their activities. Consider how the common combination of child care with food preparation, especially if cooking is done over an open fire, creates a potentially hazardous situation for children. With the mother (or other caregiver) distracted by some other task, the child may all too easily receive a severe burn or bad cut, with serious consequences. What can be said is that the economic activities of women generally have complemented those of men, even though, in some societies, individuals may perform tasks normally assigned to the opposite gender, as occasion dictates. Thus, men and women could share the results of their labors on a regular basis, as discussed in Chapters 6 and 7.

An effective way to facilitate economic cooperation between men and women and simultaneously provide for a close bond between mother and child is through the establishment of residential groups that include adults of both sexes. The differing nature of male and female roles, as defined by different cultures, requires a child to have an adult of the same sex available to serve as a proper model for the appropriate adult role. The presence of adult men

and women in the same residential group provides for this. For cross-cultural analytical purposes, anthropologists distinguish between the **family of orientation,** which is the family into which someone is born or adopted and raised, and the **family of procreation,** which refers to the family that is formed when someone becomes a parent and raises one or more children.

Well suited though the family may be for these tasks, we should not suppose it is the only unit capable of providing such conditions, or even the best one. In fact, other arrangements that are no less effective are possible, one example being the Israeli kibbutz, a communal agricultural settlement where paired teams of male and female specialists raise groups of children. In many food-foraging societies (the Ju/'hoansi and Mbuti, discussed in earlier chapters, are good examples), all adult members of a community share in the responsibilities of child care. Thus, when parents go off to hunt or to

family of orientation The family into which someone is born or adopted and raised.
family of procreation The family that is formed when someone becomes a parent and raises one or more children.

A celebration at the palace in the Yoruba city of Oyo, Nigeria. As is usual in societies where royal households are found, that of the Yoruba includes many individuals not related to the ruler, as well as the royal family.

collect plants and herbs, they may leave their children behind, secure in the knowledge they will be looked after by whatever adults remain in the camp. Yet another domestic arrangement may be seen among the Mundurucu, a horticultural people living in the center of Brazil's Amazon rainforest. In Mundurucu villages boys live in houses with their mothers and sisters, separate from all men until the age of 13. At that point the boys move into the men's house. Their sisters, on the other hand, continue to live with their mothers and the younger boys in two or three houses grouped around the men's house. As among the Nayar, married men and women are members of separate households, meeting periodically for sexual activity.

FAMILY AND HOUSEHOLD

Just as there is a continuum of social arrangements among relatives, from nuclear to extended families, there exists a continuum of domestic arrangements involving the household. For purposes of cross-cultural comparison, anthropologists define the **household** as the basic residential unit where economic production, consumption, inheritance, child rearing, and shelter are organized and carried out. Given this broad definition, the house-

> *household* The basic residential unit where economic production, consumption, inheritance, child rearing, and shelter are organized and carried out.
> *conjugal family* A family formed on the basis of marital ties.
> *consanguineal family* Related women, their brothers, and the women's offspring.

hold is considered universally present and comes in many forms. In the vast majority of human societies, most households are made up of families. Often, a household may consist of one nuclear family along with some other relatives. But there are many other arrangements. For instance, among the Mundurucu, just noted, the men's house constitutes one household inhabited by adult males and their sexually mature sons, and the women's houses, inhabited by adult women and prepubescent boys and girls, constitute others. In other situations, co-residents of a household may be unrelated, such as the service personnel in an elaborate royal household, apprentices in the household of craft specialists, or low-status clients in the household of rich and powerful patrons.

FORMS OF THE FAMILY

To discuss the various forms families take in response to particular social, historical, and ecological circumstances, we must, at the outset, make a distinction between a **conjugal family** (in Latin *conjugere* means "to join together"), which is formed on the basis of marital ties, and a **consanguineal family** (based on the Latin word *consanguineous*, literally meaning "of the same blood"), which consists of related women, their brothers, and the women's offspring. Consanguineal families are not common, but there are more examples than the classic case of the Nayar described in the previous chapter. Among these are the Musuo of southwestern China and the Tory Islanders, a Roman Catholic, Gaelic-speaking fisherfolk living off the coast of Ireland. The Tory Islanders, who do not marry until they are in their late 20s or early 30s, look at it this way: "Oh well, you get married at that age, it's too late to break up arrangements that you have already known for a long time. . . . You know, I have my sisters and brothers to look after, why should I leave home to go live with a husband? After all, he's got his sisters and his brothers looking after him."[7] Because the community numbers but a few hundred people, husbands and wives are within easy commuting distance of each other.

According to a cross-cultural survey of family types in 192 cultures around the world, the extended family is most common, present in 48 percent of those cultures, compared to the nuclear family at 25 percent, and polygamous at 22 percent.[8] Each of these is discussed below. Also of note is the **blended family**—comprised of a married couple raising children together from their previous unions. In recent years the already complex landscape of family forms has become even more varied. This is due not only to rising divorce rates but also to **new reproductive technologies** (NRTs), such as in vitro fertilization, as well as open adoption, which make it possible for a child to have a relationship with both the biological and adoptive parents.

The Nuclear Family

The smallest conjugal domestic unit is known as the nuclear family. Long applied to the mother, father, and child(ren) unit, over the last few decades the term has come to embrace family units consisting of single parents with child(ren), as well as same-sex couples with child(ren). Anthropologist Robin Fox moved the definition in this direction in the late 1960s, referring to the nuclear family as "derivative" and the mother-child unit as "basic."[9] Accordingly, a definition of **nuclear family** (from the Latin word *nucleus*, which means "kernel," or more literally "little nut") that more adequately covers the social reality of several types of small parent-child units is this: a group consisting of one or more parents and dependent offspring, which may include a stepparent, stepsiblings, and adopted children.

In the early 1970s, nuclear families comprised 45 percent of all households in the United States, compared to only 24 percent today.[10] Despite its decline, this particular family form is still widely regarded as the ideal in

One alternative to the traditional nuclear family is the gay or lesbian family, which, through adoption or new reproductive technologies, may include children.

various parts of the world, including western Europe and North America. In such places it is not generally considered desirable for young people to live with their parents beyond a certain age, nor is it considered a moral responsibility for a couple to take their aged parents into their home when the old people can no longer care for themselves. Retirement communities and nursing homes provide these services, and to take aged parents into one's home is commonly regarded as not only an economic burden but also a threat to the household's privacy and independence—and sometimes to that of the elderly themselves.

The two-parent nuclear family is also likely to be prominent in societies such as the Inuit, who live in the harsh Arctic environments of Canada and Greenland. In the winter the traditional Inuit husband and wife, with their children, roam the vast snowscape in their quest for food. The husband hunts and makes shelters. The wife cooks, is responsible for the children, and makes the clothing and keeps it in good repair. One of her chores is to chew her husband's boots to soften the leather for the next day so that he can resume his quest for game. The wife and her children could not survive without the husband, and life for a man is unimaginable without a wife.

---

[7]Fox, R. (1981, December 3). [Interview]. Coast Telecourses, Inc., Los Angeles.

---

[8]Winick, C. (Ed.). (1970). *Dictionary of anthropology* (p. 202). Totowa, NJ: Littlefield, Adams, & Co.

---

[9]Fox, R. (1967). *Kinship and marriage* (p. 39). Baltimore: Penguin.

---

[10]Irvine, M. (1999, November 24). Mom-and-Pop houses grow rare. *Burlington Free Press;* Current Population Survey. (2002). U.S. Census Bureau.

---

blended family A married couple raising children together from their previous unions.
new reproductive technologies Known as NRTs, this term refers to alternative means of reproduction such as surrogate motherhood and in vitro fertilization.
nuclear family A group consisting of one or more parents and dependent offspring, which may include a stepparent, stepsiblings, and adopted children.

© John Eastcott/Eva Momatiuki

Among the Inuit, nuclear families such as the one shown here are typical, although they are not as isolated from other kin as are nuclear families in the United States.

Certain parallels can be drawn between the nuclear family in industrial societies and families living under especially harsh environmental conditions. In both cases, the family is an independent unit that must be prepared to fend for itself. This creates for individual members a strong dependence on one another. Minimal help is available from outside in the event of emergencies or catastrophes. When their usefulness ends, the elderly are cared for only if it is feasible. In the event of the mother or father's death, life becomes precarious for the child. Yet this form of family is well adapted to a life that requires a high degree of geographical mobility. For the Inuit, this mobility permits the hunt for food; for other North Americans, the hunt for jobs and improved social status requires a mobile form of family unit.

Not even among the Inuit, however, is the nuclear family as independent from other kin as it has become among most non-native North Americans. When Inuit families are off by themselves, it is regarded as a matter of temporary expediency; most of the time, they are found in groups of at least a few families together, with members of one family having relatives in all of the others.[11] Thus families cooperate with one another on a daily basis, sharing food and other resources, looking out for one another's children, and sometimes even eating together. The sense of shared responsibility for one another's children and for the general welfare in Inuit multifamily groups contrasts with families in the United States, which

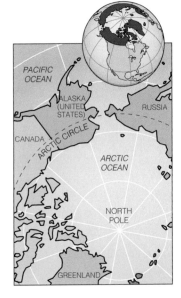

are basically "on their own." Here the states assign an individual sole responsibility to family for child care and the welfare of family members, with relatively little assistance from outside.[12] To be sure, families can and often do help one another out, but they are under no obligation to do so. In fact, once children reach the age of majority (18), parents have no further legal obligation to them, nor do the children to their parents. When families do have difficulty fulfilling their assigned functions—as is increasingly the case—even though it be through no fault of their own, less support is available to them from the community at large than in most of the world's "stateless" societies, including that of the Inuit.

The Extended Family

When two or more closely related nuclear families cluster together into a large domestic group, they form a unit known as the **extended family.** In part conjugal and in part consanguineal, this larger family unit typically consists of siblings with their spouses and offspring, and often

---

[11]Graburn, N. H. H. (1969). *Eskimos without igloos: Social and economic development in Sugluk* (pp. 56–58). Boston: Little, Brown.

extended family Several closely related nuclear families clustered together into a large domestic group.

---

[12]Collier, Rosaldo, & Yanagisako, pp. 34–35.

their parents. In North America, nuclear families have not always had the degree of independence that they came to have with the rise of industrialism. In an earlier, more agrarian era, the small nuclear family was sometimes part of a larger extended family. All of these people, some related "by blood" and some by marriage, lived and worked together. Because members of the younger generation brought their spouses (husbands or wives) to live in the family, extended families, like consanguineal families, had continuity through time. As older members died off, new members were born into the family.

In the United States, extended families can still be found on many American Indian reservations. They also exist in some non-Indian communities, for example along the Maine coast,[13] where they developed in response to a unique economy featuring a mix of farming and seafaring, coupled with an ideal of self-sufficiency. Because family farms were incapable of providing self-sufficiency, sea-faring was taken up as an economic alternative. Sea-going commerce, however, was periodically afflicted by depression, so family farming remained important as a cushion against economic hard times. The need for a sufficient labor pool to tend the farm, while at the same time furnish officers, crew, or (frequently) both for locally owned vessels, was satisfied by the practice of a newly married couple settling on the farm of either the bride's or the groom's parents. Thus, most people spent their lives cooperating on a day-to-day basis in economic activities with close relatives, all of whom lived together (even if in separate houses) on the same farm.

The Maya of Guatemala, Belize, and southern Mexico also continue to live in extended family households.[14] In many of their communities, sons bring their wives to live in houses built on the edges of a small open plaza, on one edge of which their father's house already stands (Figure 9.2). Numerous household activities are

---

[13]Haviland, W. A. (1973). Farming, seafaring and bilocal residence on the coast of Maine. *Man in the Northeast, 6,* 31–44.

[14]Vogt, E. Z. (1990). *The Zinacantecos of Mexico, A modern Maya way of life* (2nd ed., pp. 30–34). Fort Worth: Holt, Rinehart and Winston.

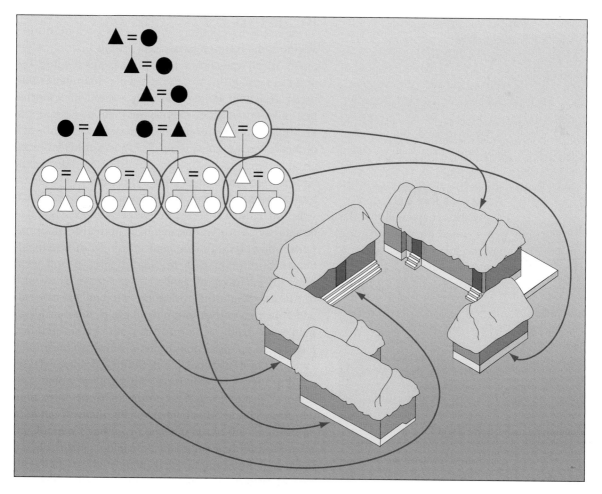

FIGURE 9.2

This diagram shows the living arrangements and relationships in a patrilocal extended family. Deceased household members are blacked out.

Members of modern Maya extended families carry out various activities on the household plaza; here, for example, women weave, while other family members engage in other activities.

carried out on this plaza; here women may weave, men may receive guests, and children play together. The head of the family is the sons' father, who makes most of the important decisions. All members of the family work together for the common good and deal with outsiders as a single unit.

Extended families living together in single households were and often still are important social units among the Hopi Indians of Arizona.[15] Ideally, the head of the household is an old woman; her married daughters, their husbands, and their children live with her. Together, the women perform household tasks, such as processing food or making pottery. They own land, but the men (usually their husbands) till it. When extra help is needed during the harvest, other male relatives or friends, or people designated by local religious organizations form work groups and turn the hard work into a festive occasion.

As briefly noted in the previous chapter, during the 1960s and 1970s young people in western Europe and North America tried to reinvent a form of extended family living. Their "families" (often called communes) consisted of unrelated nuclear families that held property in

---

[15]Forde, C. D. (1950). *Habitat, economy and society* (pp. 225–245). New York: Dutton.

---

polygamous family One individual with multiple spouses and all of their children.
polygynous family A type of polygamous family involving a man with multiple wives and their children.
polyandrous family A type of polygamous family involving a woman with multiple husbands and their children.
patrilocal residence A residence pattern in which a married couple lives in the locality associated with the husband's father's relatives.
matrilocal residence A residence pattern in which a married couple lives in the locality associated with the wife's parents.

---

common and lived together. The lifestyle of these modern extended families often emphasized the kinds of cooperative ties found in the rural North American extended family of old, which provided a labor pool for the many tasks required for economic survival. In some of them the members even reverted to traditional gender roles; the women took care of child rearing and household chores, while the men handled tasks outside of the household itself.

The Polygamous Family

The **polygamous family** (*poly* means "many" in Greek and *gamos* is "marriage"), consisting of one individual with multiple spouses and all of their children, comes in two forms. The **polygynous** version includes a man, his multiple wives, and their collective offspring. The **polyandrous** version, which is extremely rare, includes a woman, her husbands, and their offspring. More details about such families appear in the upcoming section about the challenges polygamous families face.

RESIDENCE PATTERNS

Where some form of conjugal or extended family is the norm, family exogamy requires that either the husband or wife, if not both, must move to a new household upon marriage. There are five common patterns of residence that a newly married couple may adopt—the prime determinant being ecological circumstances, although other factors enter in as well. Thus, postmarital residence arrangements, far from being arbitrary, are adaptive in nature. One option is **patrilocal residence,** in which a woman goes to live with her husband in the household in which he grew up—a pattern followed by the Maya just described. This arrangement is favorable in situations where men play a predominant role in subsistence, particularly if they own property that can be accumulated, if polygyny is customary, if warfare is prominent enough to make cooperation among men especially important, and if an elaborate political organization exists in which men wield authority. These conditions are most often found together in societies that rely on animal husbandry and/or intensive agriculture for their subsistence. Where patrilocal residence is customary, the bride often must move to a different band or community. In such cases, her parents' family is not only losing the services of a useful family member, but they are losing her potential offspring as well. Hence, some kind of compensation to her family, most commonly bride-price, is usual.

Matrilocal residence, where the man leaves the family he grew up in to go live with his wife in her parents' household, is a likely result if ecological circumstances make the role of the woman predominate for sub-

This old photo shows members of a Hopi Indian matrilocal extended family in front of their house. Traditionally, women who were sisters and daughters lived with their husbands in adjacent rooms of a single building.

sistence. It is found most often in horticultural societies, where political organization is relatively uncentralized and where cooperation among women is important. The Hopi Indians provide one example. Although it is the Hopi men who do the farming, the women control access to land and "own" the harvest. Indeed, men are not even allowed in the granaries. Under matrilocal residence, men usually do not move very far from the family in which they were raised so they are available to help out there from time to time. Therefore, marriage usually does not involve compensation to the groom's family.

Ambilocal residence (*ambi* in Latin means "both"), a pattern in which a married couple may choose either matrilocal or patrilocal residence, is adaptive in situations where economic cooperation of more people than are available in the nuclear family is needed but where

resources are limited in some way. Because the couple can join either the bride's or the groom's family, family membership is flexible, and the two can live where the resources look best or where their labor is most needed. This was once the situation on the peninsulas and islands along the coast of Maine, where, as already noted, extended family households were based upon ambilocal residence. The same residential pattern is particularly common among food-foraging peoples, as among the Mbuti Pygmies of Africa's Ituri forest. Typically, a Mbuti marries someone from another band, so that one spouse always has in-laws who live elsewhere. Thus, if foraging is bad in their part of the tropical rainforest, the couple has somewhere else to go where food may be more readily available. Ambilocality greatly enhances the Mbutis' opportunity to find food. It also provides a place to go if a dispute breaks out with someone in the band where the couple is currently living. Consequently, Mbuti camps are constantly changing their composition as people split off to go live with their in-laws, while others are joining from other groups. For a people like food foragers, who find their food in nature and who maintain an egalitarian social order, ambilocal residence can be a crucial factor in both survival and conflict resolution.

Under **neolocal residence,** a married couple forms a household in a separate location. This occurs where the independence of the nuclear family is emphasized. In industrial societies such as the United States, where most economic activity occurs outside rather than inside the family and where it is important for individuals to be able to move where jobs can be found, neolocal residence is better suited than any of the other patterns.

ambilocal residence A pattern in which a married couple may choose either matrilocal or patrilocal residence.
neolocal residence A pattern in which a married couple may establish their household in a location apart from either the husband's or the wife's relatives.

Although Hopi society is matrilocal, it is men's labor that produces the crops grown for food. In the past, however, it is probable that women were the farmers, with men taking over the task as irrigation became more important.

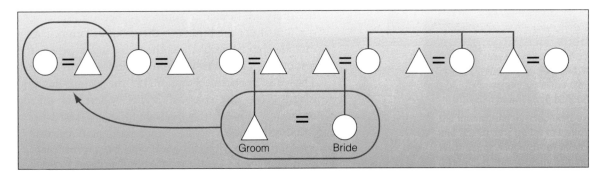

FIGURE 9.3

Under avunculocal residence, a newly married couple goes to live with the husband's mother's brother.

Avunculocal residence (*avunculus* in Latin refers to "maternal uncle"), in which a married couple goes to live with the groom's mother's brother (Figure 9.3), is favored by the same factors that promote patrilocal residence but only in societies where descent through women is deemed crucial for the transmission of important rights and property. Such is the case among the people of the Trobriand Islands, where each individual is a member from birth of a group of relatives who trace their descent back through their mother, their mother's mother, and so on to the one woman all others are descended from. Each of these descent groups holds property, consisting of hamlet sites, bush and garden lands, and, in some cases, beach fronts, to which members have rights of access. These properties are controlled each generation by a male chief or other leader who inherits these rights and obligations, but because descent is traced exclusively through women, a man cannot inherit these from his father. Thus, succession to positions of leadership passes from a man to his sister's son. For this reason, a man who is in line to take control of his descent group's assets will take his wife to live with the one he will succeed—his mother's brother. This enables him to observe how the older man takes care of his hamlet's affairs, as well as to learn the oral traditions and magic he will need to be an effective leader.

Although Trobriand leaders and chiefs live avunculocally, most married couples in this society live patrilocally. This allows sons to fulfill their obligations to their fathers, who helped build up and nurture them when they were small. In return, the sons will inherit personal property from their fathers—property that traditionally included such items as clay pots and valuable stone axe blades. This residence pattern also gives men access to land controlled by their fathers' descent groups in addition to their own land, enabling them to improve their own economic and political position in Trobriand society. In short, here, as in any human society, practical considerations play a central role in determining where people will live following marriage.

MEDIATREK

For interactive tutorials on marriage systems and residence rules, plus an intriguing array of ethnographic examples from far-flung corners of the world, go to MediaTrek 9.2 on the companion Website or CD-ROM.

Estate of Annette B. Weiner

This Trobriand Island chief, shown in front of his house, will be succeeded by his sister's son. Hence, men who will become chiefs live avunculocally.

avunculocal residence Residence of a married couple with the husband's mother's brother.

CHALLENGES OF FAMILY AND HOUSEHOLD ORGANIZATION

Effective as the family may be at organizing economic production, consumption, inheritance, and child rearing, at the household level relationships within the family inevitably involve a certain amount of conflict and tension. This does not mean that they may not also involve a great deal of support and affection. Nevertheless, at least the potential for conflict is always there and must be dealt with lest families become dysfunctional. Different forms of families are associated with different sorts of tensions, and the means employed to manage these tensions differ accordingly.

Polygamous Family Challenges

A major source of tension within polygamous families is the potential for conflict that exists among a person's multiple spouses. One practice that offers a possible solution to such conflicts is **sororal polygyny,** the marriage of one man to women who are sisters. Presumably, women who have grown up together can get along as co-wives of a man more easily than can women who grew up in different households and have never had to live together before. Another mechanism is to provide each wife with a separate apartment or dwelling within a family compound and perhaps require the husband to adhere to a system of rotation for sleeping purposes. The latter at least prevents the husband from playing obvious favorites among his wives. Although polygyny can be difficult for the women involved, this is not always the case (recall the appreciative comments of the women in polygynous marriages in the Rocky Mountains discussed in the previous chapter). In some polygynous societies, women enjoy considerable economic autonomy, and in societies where women's work is hard or tedious, polygyny allows sharing of the workload and alleviating boredom through sociability.

In polyandrous families in which a wife has more than one husband, two distinctive structural characteristics may cause difficulty. One is that a woman's older husbands are apt to dominate the younger ones. The other is that, under conditions of **fraternal polyandry** in which a woman is married to several brothers (the most common kind of polyandry), youngest brothers are likely to be considerably younger than their wives, whose reproductive years are limited. Hence, a young husband's chances of reproducing successfully are reduced, compared to those of the older husbands. Not surprisingly, when polyandrous families in Tibet break up, it is usually the younger husbands who depart.[16]

---

[16]Levine, N. E., & Silk, J. B. (1997). Why polyandry fails. *Current Anthropology, 38,* 385–387.

A Bakhtiari man, his wives, and his children. In polygamous families, tensions may arise among co-wives (in the case of polygyny) or co-husbands (in the case of polyandry), not to mention between them and their shared spouse.

Extended Family Challenges

Extended families too, no matter how well they may work, have their own potential areas of stress. Decision making in such families usually rests with an older individual, and other family members must defer to the elder's decisions. Among a group of siblings, an older one usually has the authority. Other difficulties confront in-marrying spouses, who must adjust their ways to conform to the expectations of the family they have joined. To combat these problems, cultures rely on various techniques to promote harmony, including such things as dependence training and the concept of "face" or "honor." Dependence training, discussed in Chapter 5, is typically associated with extended family organization and raises people who are more inclined to be compliant and accept their lot in life than are individuals raised to be independent. One of the many problems faced by young people in North American society who have experimented with extended family living is that they generally have been raised to be independent, making it hard to defer to others' wishes when they disagree.

The concept of saving face or maintaining dignity may constitute a particularly potent check on the power

---

sororal polygyny Marriage of one man to women who are sisters.
fraternal polyandry Marriage of one woman to men who are brothers.

of senior members of extended families. Among pastoral nomads of North Africa, for example, young men can escape from ill treatment by a father or older brother by leaving the patrilocal extended family to join the family of his maternal relatives, in-laws, or even an unrelated family willing to take him in.[17] Because men lose face if their sons or brothers flee in this way, they are generally at pains to control their behavior in order to prevent this from happening. Women, who are the in-marrying spouses, also may return to their birth families if they are mistreated in their husband's family. A woman who does this exposes her husband and his family to scolding by her kin, again causing loss of face.

Effective as such techniques may be in societies that stress the importance of the group over the individual and where loss of face is to be avoided at almost any cost, not all conflict may be avoided. When all else fails to restore

harmony, siblings may be forced to demand their share of family assets in order to set up separate households, and in this way new families arise. Divorce, too, may be possible, although how easily this may be accomplished varies considerably from one society to another. In societies that practice matrilocal residence, divorce rates tend to be high, reflecting the ease with which unsatisfactory marriages may be terminated. In some (not all) societies with patrilocal residence, by contrast, divorce may be all but impossible, at least for women (the in-marrying spouses). This was the case in traditional China, for example, where women were raised to be cast out of their families.[18] When they married, they exchanged their dependence on fathers and brothers for absolute dependence on husbands and, later in life, sons. Without divorce as an option to protect themselves against ill treatment, women went to great lengths to develop the strongest bond possible between themselves and their sons so that the latter would rise to their mother's defense when necessary. So single-minded were many women toward developing such relationships with their sons that they often made life miserable for their daughters-in-law, who were seen as competitors for their sons' affections.

Nuclear Family Challenges

Just as extended families have built into them particular sources of stress and tension, so too do nuclear families, especially in modern industrial and postindustrial societies where two-parent nuclear family households have lost one of their chief reasons for being: their economic function as basic units of production. Instead of staying within the fold, working with and for each other, one or both adults must seek work for wages outside of the family. Furthermore, that work may keep them away for prolonged periods. If both spouses are employed outside the home (as is increasingly the case, since couples find it ever more difficult to maintain their desired standard of living on one income, and many workplaces offer few options for part-time work beyond minimum wage jobs), the requirement for workers to go where their jobs take them may pull the husband and wife in different directions.

On top of all this, neolocal residence tends to isolate husbands and wives from both sets of kin. Because clearly established patterns of responsibility no longer exist between husbands and wives, couples must work these out for themselves. Two factors make this difficult. The first is women's traditional dependence on men that for so long has been a feature of middle- and upper-class societies in Europe and North America. The second factor is the great emphasis North American society places

---

[17]Abu-Lughod, L. (1988). *Veiled sentiments: Honor and poetry in a Bedouin society* (pp. 99–103). Berkeley: University of California Press.

Some young North Americans have attempted to re-create the extended family in the formation of communes. These attempts sometimes run into trouble as members cope with stress associated with extended family organization for which they are unprepared.

[18]Wolf, M. (1972). *Women and the family in rural Taiwan* (pp. 32–35). Stanford, CA: Stanford University Press.

on the pursuit of individual gratification through competition, often at someone else's expense. The problem is especially acute if the husband and wife grew up in households with widely divergent outlooks on life and ways of doing things. Furthermore, their separation from kin means no one is on hand to help stabilize the new marriage; for that matter, intervention of kin is commonly regarded as interference.

Separation from other relatives also means that a young mother-to-be must face pregnancy and childbirth without the direct aid and support of female kin with whom she already has a relationship and who have been through pregnancy and childbirth themselves. Instead, for advice and guidance she must turn to physicians (who are more often men than women), books, the Internet, and friends and neighbors who themselves are often inexperienced. The problem continues through motherhood, in the absence of experienced women within the family as well as a clear model for child rearing. So reliance on physicians, books, and mostly inexperienced friends for advice and support continues. The problems are exacerbated because families differ widely in how they deal with their children. In the competitive society of the United States, the children themselves recognize this and often use such differences against their parents to their own ends.

Women who have devoted themselves entirely to raising children confront a further problem: What to do when the children are gone? One answer to this, of course, is to pursue an outside career, but this, too, may present problems. She may have a husband with traditional values who thinks "a woman's place is in the home." Or it may be difficult to begin a career in middle age. To begin a career earlier, though, may involve difficult choices: Should she have her career at the expense of having children, or should she have both simultaneously? If the latter, she is not likely to find kin available to look after the children, as would be possible in an extended family, so arrangements must be made with people who are not kin. And, of course, all of these thorny decisions must be made without the aid and support of kin.

The impermanence of the nuclear family itself may constitute a problem in the form of anxieties over old age. Once the children are gone, who will care for the parents in their old age? In North American society, no requirement exists for their children to do so. The problem does not arise in an extended family, where one is cared for from womb to tomb.

Gender Issues and Other Challenges of Nontraditional Families

In North America and parts of Europe, increasing numbers of people live in nonfamily households, either alone or with non-relatives (Figure 9.4). In fact, some 32 percent of households in the United States fall into this category.[19] Many others live as members of what are often called *nontraditional families*. These include single-parent households. Such households are often the result of

---

[19]Current Population Survey. (2002). U.S. Census Bureau.

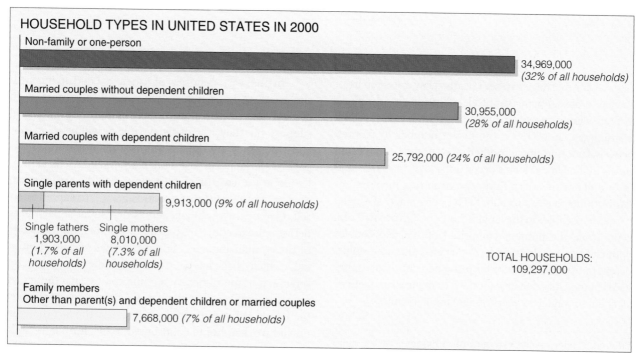

FIGURE 9.4

Household types in the United States, based on U.S. Census Bureau figures for 2000.

Anthropology Applied   Dealing with Infant Mortality

In 1979 Dr. Margaret Boone, an anthropologist who now works as a social science analyst with the Program Evaluation and Methodology Division of the U.S. government's General Accounting Office, began a residency on the staff of Washington D.C.'s only public hospital. Her task was to gain an understanding of the sociocultural basis of poor maternal and infant health among inner-city blacks—something about which little was known at the time—and to communicate that understanding to the relevant public and private agencies, as well as to a wider public. As Dr. Boone put it:

"The problem was death—the highest infant death rate in the United States. In Washington, D.C., babies were dying in their first years of life at the highest rate for any large American city, and nobody could figure out why."[a]

In Washington, as in the rest of the United States, infant mortality has become a major health problem for African Americans because of the large and increasing number of disadvantaged black women. Their infants die at almost twice the rate of white infants. In the hospital in which Boone worked, the population served was overwhelmingly poor and African American.

For the next year and a half, Boone worked intensively reviewing medical, birth, and death records; carrying out statistical analyses; and interviewing women whose infants had died, as well as nurses, physicians, social workers, and administrators. As she herself points out, no matter how important the records review and statistical analyses were (and they were important), her basic understanding of reproduction in the inner-city black community came from the daily experience working in the "community center for birth and death," which was the hospital—classic anthropological participant observation.

What Boone found out was that infant death and miscarriage are associated with absence of prenatal care, smoking, the consumption of alcohol, psychological distress during pregnancy and hospitalization, evidence of violence, ineffective contraception, rapid childbearing in the teens (average age at first pregnancy was 18), and the use of several harmful drugs together (contrary to everyone's expectations, heroin abuse was less important a factor than alcohol abuse, and drug abuse in general was no higher among women whose infants died than among those whose infants did not). Cultural factors found to be impor-

tant include a belief in a birth for every death, a high value placed on children, a value on gestation without necessarily any causal or sequential understanding of the children it will produce, a lack of planning ability, distrust of both men and women, and a separation of men's roles from the process of family formation (indeed, three-quarters of the women in Boone's study were unmarried at the time of delivery). Of course, some of these factors were already known to be related to infant mortality, but many were not.

As a consequence of Boone's work, there have been important changes in policies and programs relating to infant mortality. It is now widely recognized that the problem goes beyond mere medicine and that medical solutions have gone about as far as they can go. Only by dealing with the social and cultural factors connected to poor health of inner-city African Americans will further progress be made, and new service delivery systems are slowly emerging to reflect this fact. ■ ■ ■

[a]Boone, E. S. (1987). Practicing sociomedicine: Redefining the problem of infant mortality in Washington, D.C. In R. M. Wulff & S. J. Fiske (Eds.), *Anthropological praxis: Translating knowledge into action* (p. 56). Boulder, CO: Westview Press.

---

divorce or a marriage partner's death. They also stem from increased sexual activity outside of wedlock, combined with declining marriage rates among women of childbearing age, as well as a rise in the number of women actively choosing single motherhood. About a third of all births in the United States occur outside of marriage, and in several northwestern European countries, the nonmarital birthrate is close to half.[20] The percentage of single-parent households in the United States has grown to 9 percent, while the number comprised of married couples with children has dropped to 24 percent. Although single-parent households account for just 9 percent of all households in the United States, they are home to 28 percent of all children (under 18 years of age) in the country.[21]

In the vast majority of cases, a child living in a single-parent household is with his or her mother. In divorce cases, fathers are usually required to pay child support, but they are not always able or willing to do this, and when they are the amount is often not sufficient to pay for all the necessary food, clothes, and medical care, let alone the cost of child care so that the woman can seek or continue income-producing work to support herself. One of the problems here is that support payments determined in court are based not so much on the needs of the woman and her children as on her "earning potential," which, if she has been true to middle-class values by staying at home rather than going out to earn money, is seen as low given that she has not brought income into the family. What is ignored, of course, is the fact that her unpaid work at home contributed to her husband's ability to pursue a financially rewarding career, but since she is not paid for her work at home, no value is set on it. Notably, single fathers in the United States are three

---

[20]Recent Demographic Developments in Europe—2000. Council of Europe.

[21]Current Population Survey. (2002). U.S. Census Bureau.

© Andy Levin/Photo Researchers

In the United States, single mothers who are heads of households are often placed in no-win situations. If they work to support the household, they are seen as unfit mothers. If they stay home with the children, they are labeled "deadbeats."

times more likely to have a cohabiting partner in the home than are single mothers.[22] Going at it alone, single mothers are far more likely to face poverty.

As also in the case of working women who remain with their husbands, kin may not be available to look after the single mother's children, so outside help must be sought and (usually) paid for, thereupon making it even more difficult for the mother to support herself adequately. To compound the problem, women frequently lack the skills necessary to secure more than menial and low-paying jobs, not having acquired such skills earlier in order to raise children. Even when they do have skills, it is still a fact women are not paid as much as are men who hold the same jobs.

Not surprisingly, as the number of female-headed households has increased, so has the number of women (and, of course, their children) who live below the poverty line. More than one-third of all female-headed households in the United States now fall into this category, and one-quarter of all children are poor. Moreover, these women and children are the ones most severely affected by cutbacks in social welfare programs made since 1980. Even before then, the purchasing power of

women was declining, and ever since, the programs that most assisted women and children have suffered the deepest cuts.

One reason for this is a flawed assumption that is nonetheless entrenched in public policy: that the poverty seen in so many female-headed households is caused by the supposedly deviant nature of such households. This deviation is allegedly caused in part by women wanting to go outside the home to earn money instead of finding husbands to support them so that they can stay home and bring up the children, as women are "supposed" to do. In fact, women have participated in the labor force throughout U.S. history, whereas only a limited proportion of the population ever possessed the resources to be "proper," nonworking "ladies."[23] Far from deviant, female-headed households are in fact a rational response to economic constraints in a society that defines gender roles in such a way as to put women at a disadvantage.

Single-parent households headed by women are neither new nor restricted to industrialized societies such as the United States. They have been known and studied for a long time in the countries of the Caribbean Sea, where men historically have been exploited as a cheap source of labor on sugar and coffee or banana plantations. Under such seasonal work conditions, men are absent from their families for many months each year, have no social or political power and few economic rewards. Hence they are tenuously attached at best to any particular household. These are held together by women, who as producers of subsistence foods provide the means of economic survival for households. Similar female-headed households are becoming increasingly common in other "underdeveloped" countries, too, as development projects restrict the ability of women to earn a living wage (reasons for this are discussed in later chapters).

For a complex range of historical reasons, some of which are pointed out in this book, women constitute the majority of the poor, the underprivileged, and the economically and socially disadvantaged in most of the world's societies, just as is becoming true in Europe and North America. In "underdeveloped" countries, the situation has been made worse by economic and social policies that the International Monetary Fund (IMF) requires them to follow in order to renegotiate payment of foreign debts. Cutbacks in government education, health, and social programs for debt service have their most direct (and negative) impact on women and children, while further development designed to increase foreign exchange (for debt repayment and the financing of further industrialization) also comes at the expense of

---

[22]Current Population Survey. (2002). U.S. Census Bureau.

[23]Mullings, L. (1989). Gender and the application of anthropological knowledge to public policy in the United States. In S. Morgen (Ed.). *Gender and anthropology* (pp. 362–365). Washington: American Anthropological Association.

women and children. Meanwhile, the prices people must pay for basic necessities of life increase (to cut down on unfavorable trade balances). If a woman is lucky, the wage she earns to buy bread for herself and her children remains constant, even if low, while the price she must pay for that bread continues to rise.

At the start of this chapter we posed a number of questions relating to the effectiveness of industrial society's nuclear families in meeting human needs. From what we have just discussed, it is obvious that the nuclear family form can impose considerable anxiety and stress upon its members. Deprived of the security and multiplicity of emotional ties found in polygamous, extended, or consanguineal families, these nuclear families find that if something goes wrong, it is potentially more devastat-

ing to the individuals involved. Yet it is also obvious that alternative forms of family and household organization come complete with their distinctive stresses and strains. To the question of which alternative is preferable, we must answer that it depends on what problems one wishes to overcome and what price one is willing to pay.

In the United States, it is clear that the conditions that gave rise to its nuclear families have changed. However, so far, no single family structure or ideology has arisen to supplant the nuclear family, nor can we predict which (if any) of the alternatives will gain preeminence in the future. The only certainty is that the family and household arrangements, not just in North America but throughout the world, will continue to evolve, as they always have, as the conditions to which they are sensitive change.

Chapter Summary

■ Dependence on group living for survival is a basic human characteristic. Traditionally nurturing children has been the adult female's job, although men also may play a role, and in some societies men are even more involved with their children than are women. In addition to at least some child care, women also carry out other economic tasks that complement those of men. The presence of adults of both sexes in a residential group is advantageous, in that it provides the child with adult models of the same sex, from whom they can learn the gender-appropriate roles as defined in that society.

■ A nonethnocentric definition of the family is two or more people related by blood, marriage, or adoption. The family may take many forms, ranging from a single parent with one or more children, to a married couple or polygamous spouses with offspring, to several generations of parents and their children. Anthropologists distinguish between the family of orientation, which is the family into which someone is born or adopted and raised, and the family of procreation, which refers to the family that is formed when someone becomes a parent and raises one or more children.

■ A family is distinct from a household, which is the basic residential unit where economic production, consumption, inheritance, child rearing, and shelter are organized and carried out. In the vast majority of human societies, most households are made up of families or parts of families, but there are many other household arrangements.

■ Far from being stable, unchanging entities, families and households may take any one of a number of forms in response to particular social, historical, and ecological circumstances. Conjugal families are those formed on the basis of marital ties. The smallest conjugal unit is the nuclear family, traditionally defined by anthropologists as a mother, father, and their dependent children, but defined in this text as a group consisting of one or more parents and dependent offspring,

which may also include a stepparent, stepsiblings, and adopted children. Contrasting with the conjugal is the consanguineal family, consisting of related women, their brothers, and the women's dependent children. The nuclear family, which is common in the industrial countries of North America and Europe, is also found in societies that live in harsh environments, as do the Inuit. The nuclear family must be able to look after itself. The result is that individual members are strongly dependent on very few people. This form of family is well suited to the mobility required both in food-foraging groups and in industrial societies where job changes are frequent. Among food foragers, however, the nuclear family is not as isolated from other kin as it is in modern industrial society.

■ Characteristic of many nonindustrial societies is the large extended, or conjugal-consanguineal, family, in which some members are related by blood, and others are related by marriage. Extended family members all live together in a single household, typically working together as well. Conjugal or extended families follow one of five basic residence patterns: patrilocal, matrilocal, ambilocal, neolocal, and avunculocal.

■ Polygamous families come in two forms: polygynous ones consisting of one man and his several wives and their children, and the extremely rare polyandrous form, consisting of one woman with multiple husbands and her children.

■ Different forms of family organization are accompanied by their distinctive problems. Polygamous families have the potential for conflict among the several spouses of the individual to whom they are married. One way to resolve this problem is through sororal polygyny or fraternal polyandry. Under fraternal polyandry, an added difficulty for younger husbands is reduced opportunity for reproduction. In extended families, the allocation of authority may be a source of stress, as decisions are made by an older individual whose views may not coincide with those of the younger family members. Inmarrying spouses in particular may have trouble complying with the demands of the family in which they must now live.

- In neolocal nuclear families, individuals are removed from the direct aid and support of kin, so husbands and wives must work out their own solutions to the problems of living together and having children. The problems are especially difficult in North American society, owing to the inequality that still persists between men and women, the great emphasis placed on individualism and competition, and an absence of clearly understood patterns of responsibility between husbands and wives, as well as a clear model for child rearing.

- In North America, the percentage of single-parent households has grown significantly over the past three decades, constituting a new form of nuclear family, while that of the mother-father-child(ren) nuclear family has declined. The vast majority of single-parent households are headed by a woman. Female-headed households are also common in underdeveloped countries. Because the women in such households are hard-pressed to provide adequately for themselves as well as for their children, more women than ever in the United States and abroad find themselves sinking deeper into poverty.

Questions for Reflection

1. Raising children is a challenge not only for parents but also for the larger community in which they are born and are expected to become productive members. Why do you think your own culture has developed the kind of family and household organization most familiar to you? Why do you think those particular organizational forms came into being? Can you imagine under which circumstances these arrangements may become inadequate and have to change?

2. Single motherhood in North America has typically been seen as something tied to poverty or low incomes, yet it is becoming increasingly common among women across the economic spectrum. What do you consider to be the reasons for this, based on the barrel model of culture with its three tiers of infrastructure, social structure, and superstructure?

3. Imagine yourself living in a consanguineal family such as the Nayar, consisting of a group of related women, their brothers, and women's children, but excluding spouses and the men's offspring. What might be the advantages and disadvantages of this arrangement?

4. What residence patterns do you see in your own family? Are they typical of the society in which you live? What are the benefits and challenges of the pattern(s) with which you are familiar?

Key Terms

Family	Blended family
Family of orientation	New reproductive technologies
Family of procreation	Nuclear family
Household	Extended family
Conjugal family	Polygamous family
Consanguineal family	Polygynous family
Polyandrous family	Neolocal residence
Patrilocal residence	Avunculocal residence
Matrilocal residence	Sororal polygyny
Ambilocal residence	Fraternal polyandry

Multimedia Review Tools

Companion Web Site

Visit **http://www.wadsworth.com/anthropology_d/** and click on the companion Web site for this textbook to access a wide range of material to aid your study of anthropology. Among the options for self-study in each chapter are learning objectives, flash cards, Internet activities, Web links, InfoTrac College Edition exercises, and practice tests that can be scored and emailed to your instructor.

CD-ROM

The *Doing Anthropology Today* CD-ROM supplied with your textbook provides unique and valuable information designed to enhance your learning experience. This interactive multimedia resource includes video clips, interviews with renowned anthropologists, map and timeline exercises, chapter study quizzes, and much more. *Doing Anthropology Today* will not only help you in achieving your grade goals, but it will also make your learning experience fun and exciting!

Suggested Readings

Cigno, A. (1994). *Economics of the family*. New York: Oxford University Press.

An economic explanation of changes in family organization.

Edwards, J. (Ed.). (1999). *Technologies of procreation: Kinship in the age of assisted conception*. New York: Routledge (Distributed by St. Martin's Press).

British anthropologists discuss how assisted conception techniques create the potential for a redefinition of relationships. Based on data and ideas from ethnographic studies, household interviews, and debates in Parliament and among clinicians.

Goody, J. (1983). *Development of the family and marriage in Europe*. Cambridge, England: Cambridge University Press.

This historical study shows how the nature of the family changed in Europe in response to regulations the Catholic Church introduced to weaken the power of kin groups and gain access to property. It explains how European patterns of kinship and marriage came to differ from those of the ancient Mediterranean world and from those that succeeded them in the Middle East and North Africa.

Modell, J. (1994). *Kinship with strangers: Adoption and interpretations of kinship in American culture*. Berkeley: University of California Press.

The author, an adopter and an anthropologist, analyzes the "core symbols" of kinship in American culture—birth, biology, and blood—and examines their impact on people who experience the "fictive" kinship of adoption.

Netting, R. M., Wilk, R. R., & Arnold, E. J. (Eds.). (1984). *Households: Comparative and historical studies of the domestic group.* Berkeley: University of California Press.

This collection of essays by twenty anthropologists and historians focuses on how and why households vary within and between societies and over time within single societies.

Skolnick, A., & Skolnick, J. (Eds.). (2002). *Family in transition* (12th ed.). Boston: Allyn & Bacon.

This reader features accessible articles that place current trends in historical context, revealing how family life is intertwined with the social, economic, and ideological circumstances of particular times and places.

Stacey, J. (1990). *Brave new families: Stories of domestic conflict in late twentieth century America.* New York: Basic Books.

Written by a sociologist, this book takes an anthropological approach to understanding the changes affecting family structure in the United States. Her conclusion is that "the family" is *not* here to stay, nor should we wish otherwise. For all the difficulties attendant on the family's demise, alternative arrangements offer hopeful possibilities for the future.

CHAPTER 10

Kinship and Descent

© Wally Turnbull

CHALLENGE ISSUE

ALL HUMANS FACE THE CHALLENGE OF CREATING AND MAINTAINING A SOCIAL NETWORK THAT REACHES BEYOND THE CAPABILITIES OF THEIR IMMEDIATE FAMILY OR HOUSEHOLD TO PROVIDE SUPPORT AND SECURITY. On a very basic level, that network is arranged by means of kinship. In the highlands of Scotland, as among many traditional peoples around the world, large kinship groups known as clans have been important units of social organization. Now dispersed all over the world, clan members gather and express their sense of kinship with one another by wearing a tartan skirt, or kilt, with a distinct plaid pattern and color identifying clan membership. Shown here is a Turnbull clan gathering in Stone Mountain, Georgia.

1 What Is Kinship?

Kinship is a network of relatives within which individuals possess certain mutual rights and obligations. One's place in this network, or kinship status, determines what these rights and obligations are. Providing groups of relatives with a social structure, kinship helps shield them from the dangers of disorganization and fracture. Kinship is especially important in societies where other institutions such as a centralized government, a professional military, or financial banks are absent or do not function well. In such societies, individuals must depend on a wide network of relatives for support and protection.

2 What Are Descent Groups?

A descent group is a kind of kinship group in which being in the direct line of descent from a particular real or mythical ancestor is a criterion of membership. Descent may be reckoned exclusively through men or women, or through either at the discretion of the individual. Two different means of reckoning descent may be used at the same time to assign individuals to different groups for different purposes. In societies without descent groups, such as many food-foraging and industrial societies, people rely instead on the kindred, a group of people related by birth with a living blood relative in common. The kindred, however, does not endure beyond a single generation, nor is its membership as clearly and explicitly defined. Hence, it is generally a weaker unit than the descent group.

3 What Functions Do Descent Groups Serve?

Descent groups of various kinds, such as lineages and clans, are convenient devices for solving a number of specific challenges that commonly confront human societies: maintaining the integrity of resources that cannot be divided without being destroyed; providing work forces for tasks that require a labor pool larger than households can provide; and allowing members of one independent local group to claim support and protection from members of another. Descent groups arise from extended family organization. With the passage of time, first to develop are localized lineages, followed by larger, dispersed groups such as clans. Kinship terminology is affected by and adjusts to the kinds of descent or other kinship groups that are important in a society.

All societies have found some form of family and/or household organization a convenient way to deal with the challenges humans face: how to facilitate economic cooperation between the sexes, how to provide a proper setting for child rearing, and how to regulate sexual activity. As efficient and flexible as family and household organization may be for facing such challenges, the fact is that many societies confront problems that are beyond the coping ability of family and household organization. For one, members of one self-governing local group often need some means of interacting with other groups, of claiming support and protection from individuals in another group. This can be important for defense against natural or human-made disasters. If people have the right of entry into local groups other than their own, they can secure protection or critical resources when their own group cannot provide them. Also, a group frequently needs to share rights to some means of production that cannot be divided without destroying it. This is often the case in horticultural societies, where division of land is impractical beyond a certain point. The problem can be avoided if land ownership is vested in a corporate group that exists in perpetuity. Finally, people often need some means of providing cooperative work forces for tasks that require more participants than households alone can provide.

Many ways to deal with these sorts of problems exist. One is through a formal political system, with personnel to make and enforce laws, keep the peace, allocate resources, and perform other regulatory and societal functions. A more common way in nonindustrial societies—especially horticultural and pastoral societies—is by means of **kinship,** a network of relatives within which individuals possess certain mutual rights and obligations.

---

kinship A network of relatives within which individuals possess certain mutual rights and obligations.

descent group Any publicly recognized social entity requiring lineal descent from a particular real or mythical ancestor for membership.

lineage A corporate descent group—a unified body or corps of consanguineal relatives who trace their genealogical links to a common ancestor and associate with one another for a shared purpose.

clan Typically consisting of several lineages, a clan is noncorporate descent group whose members assume descent from a common ancestor (real or fictive) without actually knowing the genealogical links to that ancestor.

unilineal descent Descent that establishes group membership exclusively through either the male or female line.

DESCENT GROUPS

A common way of organizing a society along kinship lines is by creating what anthropologists call descent groups. A **descent group** is any publicly recognized social entity requiring being in the direct line of descent from a particular real or mythical ancestor for membership. Members of a descent group trace their connections back to a common ancestor through a chain of parent–child links. This feature may explain why descent groups are found in so many human societies. They appear to stem from the parent–child bond, which is built upon as the basis for a structured social group. The addition of a few culturally meaningful obligations and taboos acts as a kind of glue to help hold the group together.

The two fundamental forms of a descent group are lineages and clans. A **lineage** is a corporate descent group—a unified body or corps of consanguineal relatives who trace their genealogical links to a common ancestor and associate with one another for a shared purpose. Typically consisting of several lineages, a **clan** is a noncorporate descent group whose members assume descent from a common ancestor (real or fictive) without actually knowing the precise genealogical links to that distant ancestor.

Descent group membership must be sharply defined in order to operate effectively. If membership is allowed to overlap, it will not be clear where someone's primary loyalty belongs. Membership can be restricted in a number of ways. It can be based on where people live. For example, if someone's parents live patrilocally, affiliation with one's father's descent group might be automatic. Another way is through choice; each individual might be presented with a number of options. This, however, introduces a possibility of dispute and conflict as groups compete for members. The most common way to restrict membership is by making gender a critically distinguishing feature. Instead of tracing membership back to the common ancestor, sometimes through male and sometimes through female parents, one does it exclusively through one gender. In this way, each individual is automatically assigned from the moment of birth to his or her mother's or father's group and to that group only.

Unilineal Descent

Unilineal descent (sometimes called *unilateral descent*) establishes descent group membership exclusively through the male or the female line. In non-Western societies, unilineal descent groups are quite common. The individual is assigned at birth to membership in a specific descent group, which may be traced either by

On this altar, King Yax-Pac of the ancient Maya city of Copan portrays himself and his predecessors, thereby tracing his descent back to the founder of the dynasty. In many human societies, such genealogical connections are used to define each individual's rights, privileges, and obligations.

matrilineal descent, through the female line, or by **patrilineal descent,** through the male line, depending on the culture. In patrilineal societies the males are far more important than the females, for they are considered responsible for the group's continued existence. In matrilineal societies, this responsibility falls on the female members of the group, whose importance is thereby enhanced.

There seems to be a close relationship between the descent system and a cultural system's infrastructure. Generally, patrilineal descent predominates where male labor is considered of prime importance, as among pastoralists and intensive agriculturalists. Matrilineal descent predominates mainly among horticulturists in societies where female work in subsistence is especially important. Numerous matrilineal societies are found in southern Asia, one of the cradles of food production in the Old World. These include societies in India, Sri Lanka, Indonesia, Tibet, and South China. They are also prominent in parts of indigenous North America, South America's tropical lowlands, and parts of Africa.

No matter which form of descent predominates, the kin of both mother and father are important components of the social structure in all societies. Just because descent may be reckoned patrilineally, for example, does not mean that matrilineal relatives are necessarily unimportant. It simply means that, for purposes of *group membership,* the mother's relatives are excluded. Similarly, under matrilineal descent, the father's relatives are excluded for purposes of group membership. By way of example, we have already seen in the two preceding chapters how important paternal relatives are

among the matrilineal Trobriand Islanders. Although children belong to their mother's descent groups, fathers play an important role in nurturing and building them up. Upon marriage, the bride's and groom's paternal relatives contribute to the exchange of gifts, and, throughout life, a man may expect his paternal kin to help him improve his economic and political position in society. Eventually, sons may expect to inherit personal property from their fathers.

Patrilineal Descent and Organization

Patrilineal descent (sometimes called agnatic or male descent) is the more widespread of the two systems of unilineal descent. The male members of a patrilineal descent group trace through other males their descent from a common ancestor (Figure 10.1). Brothers and sisters belong to the descent group of their father's father, their father, their father's siblings, and their father's brother's children. A man's son and daughter also trace their descent back through the male line to their common ancestor. In the typical patrilineal group, authority over the children rests with the father or his elder brother. A woman belongs to the same descent group as her father and his brothers, but her children cannot trace their descent through them. A person's paternal aunt's children, for example, trace their descent through the patrilineal group of her husband.

matrilineal descent Descent traced exclusively through the female line to establish group membership.
patrilineal descent Descent traced exclusively through the male line to establish group membership.

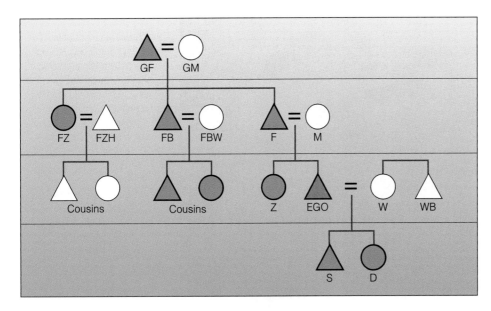

FIGURE 10.1

How patrilineal descent is traced. Only the individuals symbolized by a filled-in circle or triangle are in the same descent group as EGO. The abbreviation F stands for father, B for brother, H for husband, S for son, M for mother, Z for sister, D for daughter, and W for wife.

Traditional China: A Patrilineal Society

Until the communist takeover in 1949, rural Chinese society was strongly patrilineal. Since then, considerable changes have occurred, although vestiges of the old system persist to varying degrees in different regions. Traditionally, the basic unit for economic cooperation was the large extended family, typically including aged parents and their sons, their sons' wives, and their sons' children.[1]

Residence, therefore, was patrilocal, as defined in the previous chapter. As in most patrilocal societies, children grew up in a household dominated by their father and his male relatives. The father was a source of discipline from whom a child would maintain a respectful social distance. Often, the father's brother and his sons were members of the same household. Thus, one's paternal uncle was rather like a second father and was treated with obedience and respect, while his sons were like one's brothers. Accordingly, the kinship term applied to one's own father was extended to the father's brother, as the term for a brother was extended to the father's brother's sons. When families became too large and unwieldy, as frequently happened, one or more sons would move elsewhere to establish separate households.

When a son did so, however, the tie to the household in which he was born remained strong.

While family membership was important for each individual, the primary social unit was the lineage, or the *tsu*, as it is known in China. Each *tsu* consisted of men who traced their ancestry back through the male line to a common ancestor, usually within about five generations. Although a woman belonged to her father's *tsu*, for all practical purposes she was absorbed by the *tsu* of her husband, with whom she lived after marriage. Nonetheless, members of her natal (birth) *tsu* retained some interest in her after her departure. Her mother, for example, would assist her in the birth of her children, and her brother or some other male relative would look after her interests, perhaps even intervening if her husband or other members of his family treated her badly.

The function of the *tsu* was to assist its members economically and to gather on ceremonial occasions such as weddings and funerals or to make offerings to the ancestors. Recently deceased ancestors, up to about three generations back, were given offerings of food and paper money on the anniversaries of their births and deaths, while more distant ancestors were collectively worshipped five times a year. Each *tsu* maintained its own shrine for storage of ancestral tablets on which the names of all members were recorded. In addition to its economic and ritual functions, the *tsu* also functioned as a legal body, passing judgment on misbehaving members.

Just as families periodically split up into new ones, so would the larger descent groups periodically splinter along the lines of their main family branches. Causes included disputes among brothers over management of landholdings and suspicion of unfair division of profits. When such fissioning occurred, a representative of the new *tsu* would return periodically to the ancestral tem-

---

[1]Most of the following is from Hsiaotung, F. (1939). *Peasant life in China*. London: Kegan, Paul, Trench and Truber.

Culver Pictures

© Bettmann/Corbis

VISUAL COUNTERPOINT
In patrilineal and other societies that promote the dominance of men over women, this condition sometimes goes to the extreme of inflicting physical, as well as social, disabilities on women. In the 19th century, Chinese women had their feet tightly bound, while in North America women often were tightly corseted. Both practices caused physical deformity and impairment.

ple in order to pay respect to the ancestors and record recent births and deaths in the official genealogy. Ultimately, though the lineage tie to the old *tsu* still would be recognized, a copy of the old genealogy would be made and brought home to the younger *tsu,* and then only its births and deaths would be recorded. In this way, over many centuries, a whole hierarchy of descent groups developed, with all persons having the same surname considering themselves to be members of a great patrilineal clan. With this went surname exogamy, meaning that none of the many bearing the same clan name could marry anyone else within that large group. This marriage rule is still widely practiced today even though clan members no longer carry on ceremonial activities together.

The patrilineal system permeated all of rural Chinese social relations. Children owed obedience and respect to their fathers and older patrilineal relatives in life and had to marry whomever their parents chose for them. It was the duty of sons to care for their parents when they became old and helpless, and even after death sons had ceremonial obligations to them. Inheritance passed from fathers to sons, with an extra share going to the eldest, since he ordinarily made the greatest contribution to the household and had the greatest responsibility toward his parents after their death. Women, by contrast, had no claims on their families' heritable property. Once married, a woman was in effect cast off by her own patrilineal kin (even though they might continue to take an interest in her) in order to produce children for her husband's family and *tsu.*

As the preceding suggests, a patrilineal society is very much a man's world. No matter how valued women may be, they inevitably find themselves in a difficult position. Far from resigning themselves to a subordinate position, however, they actively manipulate the system to their own advantage as best they can. The following Original Study about rural women in a traditional Chinese society in Taiwan offers one example of how they go about this.

Original Study

Coping as a Woman in a Man's World

Women in rural Taiwan do not live their lives in the walled courtyards of their husbands' households. If they did, they might be as powerless as their stereotype. It is in their relations in the outside world (and for women in rural Taiwan that world consists almost entirely of the village) that women develop sufficient backing to maintain some independence under their powerful mothers-in-law. A successful venture into the men's world is no small feat when one recalls that the men of a village were born there and are often

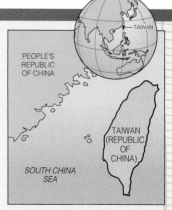

related to one another, whereas the women are unlikely to have either the

[CONTINUED]

[CONTINUED]

ties of childhood or the ties of kinship to unite them. All the same, shared interests and common problems of women are reflected in every village in a loosely knit society that can when needed be called on to exercise considerable influence.

Women carry on as many of their activities as possible outside the house. They wash clothes on the riverbank, clean and pare vegetables at a communal pump, mend under a tree that is a known meeting place, and stop to rest on a bench or group of stones with other women. There is a continual moving back and forth between kitchens, and conversations are carried on from open doorways through the long, hot afternoons of summer. The shy young girl who enters the village as a bride is examined as frankly and suspiciously by the women as an animal that is up for sale. If she is deferential to her elders, does not criticize or compare her new world unfavorably with the one she has left, the older residents will gradually accept her presence on the edge of their conversations and stop changing the topic to general subjects when she brings the family laundry to scrub on the rocks near them. As the young bride meets other girls in her position, she makes allies for the future, but she must also develop relationships with the older women. She learns to use considerable discretion in making and receiving confidences, for a girl who gossips freely about the affairs of her husband's household may find herself always on the outside of the group, or worse yet, accused of snobbery.

I described in *The House of Lim* the plight of Lim Chui-ieng, who had little village backing in her troubles with her husband and his family as a result of her arrogance toward the women's community. In Peihotien the young wife of the storekeeper's son suffered a similar lack of support. Warned by her husband's parents not to be too "easy" with the other villagers lest they try to buy things on credit, she obeyed to the point of being considered unfriendly by the women of the village. When she began to have serious troubles with her husband and eventually his family, there

was no one in the village she could turn to for solace, advice, and most important, peacemaking.

Once a young bride has established herself as a member of the women's community, she has also established for herself a certain amount of protection. If the members of her husband's family step beyond the limits of propriety in their treatment of her—such as refusing to allow her to return to her natal home for her brother's wedding or beating her without serious justification—she can complain to a woman friend, preferably older, while they are washing vegetables at the communal pump. The story will quickly spread to the other women, and one of them will take it upon herself to check the facts with another member of the girl's household. For a few days the matter will be thoroughly discussed whenever a few women gather. In a young wife's first few years in the community, she can expect to have her mother-in-law's side of any disagreement given fuller weight than her own—her mother-in-law has, after all, been a part of the community a lot longer. However, the discussion itself will serve to curb many offenses. Even if the older woman knows that public opinion is falling to her side, she will be somewhat more judicious about refusing her daughter-in-law's next request. Still, the daughter-in-law who hopes to make use of the village forum to depose her mother-in-law or at least gain herself special privilege will discover just how important the prerogatives of age and length of residence are. Although the women can serve as a powerful protective force for their defenseless younger members, they are also a very conservative force in the village.

Taiwanese women can and do make use of their collective power to lose face for their menfolk in order to influence decisions that are ostensibly not theirs to make. Although young women may have little or no influence over their husbands and would not dare express an unsolicited opinion (and perhaps not even a solicited one) to their fathers-in-law, older women who have raised their sons properly retain considerable influence over their sons' actions,

even in activities exclusive to men. Further, older women who have displayed years of good judgment are regularly consulted by their husbands about major as well as minor economic and social projects. But even men who think themselves free to ignore the opinions of their women are never free of their own concept, face. It is much easier to lose face than to have face. We once asked a male friend in Peihotien just what "having face" amounted to. He replied, "When no one is talking about a family, you can say it has face." This is precisely where women wield their power. When a man behaves in a way that they consider wrong, they talk about him—not only among themselves, but to their sons and husbands. No one "tells him how to mind his own business," but it becomes abundantly clear that he is losing face and by continuing in this manner may bring shame to the family of his ancestors and descendants. Few men will risk that.

The rules that a Taiwanese man must learn and obey to be a successful member of his society are well developed, clear, and relatively easy to stay within. A Taiwanese woman must also learn the rules, but if she is to be a successful woman, she must learn not to stay within them, but to appear to stay within them; to manipulate them, but not to appear to be manipulating them; to teach them to her children, but not to depend on her children for her protection. A truly successful Taiwanese woman is a rugged individualist who has learned to depend largely on herself while appearing to lean on her father, her husband, and her son. The contrast between the terrified young bride and the loud, confident, often lewd old woman who has outlived her mother-in-law and her husband reflects the tests met and passed by not strictly following the rules and by making purposeful use of those who must. The Chinese male's conception of women as "narrow-hearted" and socially inept may well be his vague recognition of this facet of women's power and technique. *(By M. Wolf. (1972). Women and the family in rural Taiwan (pp. 37–41). Stanford, CA: Stanford University Press.)*

Matrilineal Descent and Organization

In one respect, matrilineal descent is the opposite of patrilineal. It is reckoned through the female line (Figure 10.2). The matrilineal pattern differs from the patrilineal, however, in that descent does not automatically confer authority. Thus, although patrilineal societies are patriarchal, matrilineal societies are not necessarily matriarchal. Although descent passes through the female line and women may have considerable power, they do not hold exclusive authority in the descent group. They share it with men. These are the brothers, rather than the husbands, of the women through whom descent is reckoned. Apparently, the adaptive purpose of matrilineal systems is to provide continuous female solidarity within the female work group. Matrilineal systems are usually found in horticultural societies in which women perform much of the productive work. In part because women's labor as crop cultivators is regarded as so important to the society, matrilineal descent prevails.

In a matrilineal system, brothers and sisters belong to the descent group of the mother, the mother's mother, the mother's siblings, and the mother's sisters' children. Males belong to the same descent group as their mother and sister, but their children cannot trace their descent through them. For example, the children of a man's maternal uncle are considered members of the uncle's wife's matrilineal descent group. Similarly, a man's children belong to his wife's, but not his, descent group.

Although not true of all matrilineal systems, a common feature is the weakness of the tie between wife and husband. The wife's brother, and not the husband-father, distributes goods, organizes work, settles disputes, administers inheritance and succession rules, and supervises rituals. The husband does not have accepted authority in the household of which he forms part, but

The Masuo of Southwest China are strongly matrilineal. The women in the family shown here are blood relatives of one another, and the men are their brothers. As among the Nayar, discussed in Chapter 8, Masuo husbands live apart from their wives, in the households of their sisters.

in that of his own sister. Furthermore, his property and status are inherited by his sister's son rather than his son. Thus, brothers and sisters maintain lifelong ties with one another, whereas marital ties are easily severed. In matrilineal societies, unsatisfactory marriages are more easily ended than in patrilineal societies.

The Hopi: A Matrilineal Society

In northeastern Arizona are the villages, or *pueblos,* of the Hopi Indians, a farming people whose ancestors have lived in the region for thousands of years. Their society is divided into a number of named clans based strictly on matrilineal descent.[2] (A discussion on clans

---

[2]Most of the following is from Connelly, J. C. (1979). Hopi social organization. In A. Ortiz (Ed.), *Handbook of North American Indians, Vol. 9, Southwest* (pp. 539–553). Washington: Smithsonian Institution.

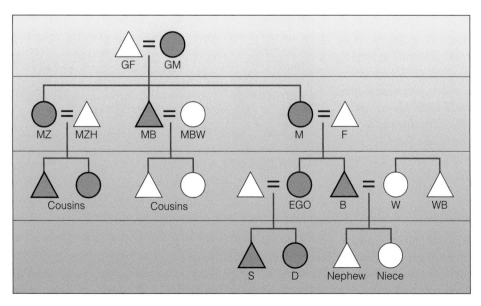

Gai Ming-sheng/HK China Tourism Press

FIGURE 10.2

This diagram, which traces descent matrilineally, can be compared with that in Figure 10.1, showing patrilineal descent. The two patterns are virtually mirror images. Note that a man cannot transmit descent to his own children.

GF = GM

MZ = MZH   MB = MBW   M = F

Cousins   Cousins   EGO   B = W   WB

S   D   Nephew   Niece

comes up a bit later in this chapter. For now it is sufficient to know that a clan is a set of relatives whose members believe they descend from a distant common ancestor.) At birth, every Hopi is assigned to his or her mother's clan. This affiliation is so important that, in a very real sense, a person has no identity apart from it. Two or more clans together constitute larger supraclan units, or phratries, of which nine exist in Hopi society. Within each phratry, member clans are expected to support one another and to observe strict exogamy. Because members of all nine phratries can be found living in any given Hopi village, marriage partners usually can be found in one's home community. This same dispersal of membership provides individuals with rights of entry into villages other than their own. (Phratries are discussed in more detail later in this chapter.)

Although phratries and clans are the major kinship units in Hopi culture, the actual functional units consist

of lineages, and there are several in each village. Each Hopi lineage is headed by a senior woman—usually the eldest, although it is her brother or mother's brother who keeps the sacred "medicine bundle" (objects of spiritual power considered essential for people's well-being) and plays an active role in running lineage affairs. The woman, however, is no mere figurehead. She may act as mediator to help resolve disputes among group members. Also, although her brother or mother's brother have the right to offer her advice and criticism, they are equally obligated to listen to what she has to say, and she does not yield her authority to them. Most female authority, however, is exerted within the household, which is the smallest distinct unit of Hopi society, and here men clearly take second place. These households consist of the women of the lineage with their husbands and unmarried sons, all of whom used to live in sets of adjacent rooms in single large buildings. Nowadays, nuclear families often live (frequently with a maternal relative or two) in separate houses, but pickup trucks enable related households to maintain close contacts and to cooperate as before.

Hopi lineages function as landholding corporations, allocating land for the support of member households. These lands are farmed by "outsiders," the husbands of the women whose lineage owns the land, and

the harvest belongs to these women. Thus, Hopi men spend their lives laboring for their wives' lineages, and in return they are given food and shelter. Although sons learn from their fathers how to farm, a man has no real authority over his son. This is because a man's own children belong to his wife's lineage while his sister's children form part of his. Thus, when parents have difficulty with an unruly child, the mother's brother is called upon to mete out discipline. A man's loyalties are therefore divided between his wife's household on the one hand and his sisters' on the other. If, at any time, a man is perceived as being an unsatisfactory husband, his wife merely has to place his personal belongings outside the door, and the marriage is over.

In addition to their economic and legal functions, lineages play a role in Hopi ceremonial activities. Although membership in the associations that actually perform ceremonies is open to all who have the proper qualifications, clans own and manage all the associations, and in each village, a leading lineage acts as its clan's representative. This lineage owns a special house where the clan's religious paraphernalia are stored and cared for by the "clan mother." Together with her brother, the clan's "Big Uncle," she helps manage ceremonial activity. Although men control most of the associations that do the actual performing, women still have

Arizona State Museum, University of Arizona, Helga Teiwes, Photographer

Many of the things that Hopi women do are done in the company of other women; thus, they have ample opportunity to discuss issues of importance to them.

vital roles to play. For example, they provide the corn-meal, symbolic of natural and spiritual life that is a necessary ingredient in virtually all ceremonies.

Traditionally, each Hopi village was politically autonomous, with its own chief and village council. Here again, however, descent group organization made itself felt, for the council was made up of men who inherited their positions through their clans. Moreover, the powers of the chief and his council were limited; the chief's major job was to maintain harmony between his village and the spiritual world, and whatever authority he and his council wielded was directed at coordination of community effort, not enforcement of official decrees. Decisions were made on a consensual basis, and women's views had to be considered, as well as those of men. Once again, although men held positions of authority, women had considerable control over their decisions in a behind-the-scenes way. These men, after all, lived in households women controlled, and their position within them depended largely on how well they got along with the senior women. Outside the household, women's refusal to play their part in the performance of ceremonies gave them veto power. Small wonder, then, that Hopi men readily admit that "women usually get their way."[3]

Double Descent

Double descent, or double unilineal descent, whereby descent is reckoned both patrilineally and matrilineally at the same time, is very rare. In this system descent is matrilineal for some purposes and patrilineal for others. Generally, where double descent is reckoned, the matrilineal and patrilineal groups take action in different spheres of society.

For example, among the Yakö of eastern Nigeria, property is divided into both patrilineal possessions and matrilineal possessions.[4] The patrilineage owns perpetual productive resources, such as land, whereas the matrilineage owns consumable property, such as livestock. The legally weaker matriline is somewhat more important in religious matters than the patriline. Through double descent, a Yakö might inherit grazing lands from the father's patrilineal group and certain ritual privileges from the mother's matrilineal group.

Ambilineal Descent

As previously noted, unilineal descent does not mean that relatives outside one's own descent line are ignored or forgotten. As a consequence, some tension or conflict may exist between descent group interests on the one hand and other kinship-based sentiments on the other.[5] Still, unilineal descent does provide an easy way of restricting descent group membership so as to minimize problems of divided loyalty and the like.

A number of societies, many of them in the Pacific and in Southeast Asia, accomplish the same thing in other ways, though perhaps not quite so neatly. The resultant descent groups are known as ambilineal or cognatic. **Ambilineal descent** provides a measure of flexibility not normally found under unilineal descent; each individual has the option of affiliating with either the mother's or the father's descent group. In many of these societies, an individual is allowed to belong to only one group at any one time, regardless of how many groups he or she may be eligible to join. Thus, the society may be divided into the same sorts of separate kin groups as in a patrilineal or matrilineal society. Other ambilineal societies, however, such as the Samoans of the South Pacific or some of those of the Pacific Northwest Coast of North America, allow overlapping membership in a number of descent groups. However, too great a range of individual choice interferes with the orderly functioning of any kin-ordered society: An individual's plural membership almost inevitably turns into one primary affiliation, which is strongly motivated by residence, and one or more secondary memberships in which participation in descent group affairs is only partial or occasional.[6]

Ambilineal Descent among New York City Jews
For an example of ambilineal organization we might easily turn to a traditional non-Western society, as we have for patrilineal and matrilineal organization. Instead, we shall turn to contemporary North American society to dispel the common (but false) notion that descent groups are not compatible in structure and function with the demands of

[3]Schlegel, A. (1977). Male and female in Hopi thought and action. In A. Schlegel (Ed.), *Sexual stratification* (p. 254). New York: Columbia University Press.

[4]Forde, C. D. (1968). Double descent among the Yakö. In P. Bohannan & J. Middleton (Eds.), *Kinship and social organization* (pp. 179–191). Garden City, NY: Natural History Press.

[5]Stone, L. (1998). *Kinship and gender* (p. 73). Boulder, CO: Westview Press.

[6]Murdock, G. P. (1960). Cognatic forms of social organization. In G. P. Murdock, *Social structure in Southeast Asia* (p. 11). Chicago: Quadrangle Books.

double descent A system tracing descent matrilineally for some purposes and patrilineally for others.
ambilineal descent Descent in which the individual may affiliate with either the mother's or the father's descent group.

Close family ties have always been important in eastern European Jewish culture. To maintain such ties in the United States, the descendants of eastern European Jews developed ambilineal descent groups.

modern industrial or postindustrial society. In fact, large corporate descent groups that hold assets in common and exist with some permanence are to be found in New York City, as well as in every large city in the United States where a substantial Jewish population of eastern European background is to be found.[7]

Moreover, these descent groups are not survivals of an old eastern European descent-based organization. Rather, they represent a social innovation designed to restructure and preserve the traditionally close family ties of the old eastern European Jewish culture following immigration to the United States. The earliest of these descent groups did not develop until the end of the first decade of the 1900s, some 40 years after the immigration of eastern European Jews began in earnest. Although some groups have disbanded, they generally have remained alive and vital right down to the present day.

FORMS AND FUNCTIONS OF DESCENT GROUPS

Descent groups with restricted membership, regardless of how descent is reckoned, are usually more than mere groups of relatives providing emotional support and a sense of belonging; in nonindustrial societies they are tightly organized working units providing

security and services in what can be a difficult, uncertain life. The tasks descent groups perform are manifold. Besides acting as economic units providing mutual aid to their members, they may act to support the aged and infirm and help with marriages and deaths. Often, they play a role in determining who an individual may or may not marry. The descent group also may act as a repository of religious traditions. Ancestor worship, for example, is often a powerful force acting to reinforce group solidarity.

Lineage

As defined above, a lineage (such as the Hopi lineage or the Chinese *tsu*) is a corporate descent group composed of blood relatives who trace descent genealogically through known links back to a common ancestor. The term is usually employed where a form of unilineal descent is the rule.

The lineage is ancestor oriented; membership in the group is recognized only if relationship to a common ancestor can be traced and proved. In many societies an individual has no legal or political status except as a lineage member. Since "citizenship" is derived from lineage membership and legal status depends on it, political and religious power is derived from it as well. Important religious and magical powers, such as those associated with the cults of gods and ancestors, may also be bound to the lineage.

In some cultures, lineages facing exceptional challenges to their survival may choose to ritually adopt individuals not related by birth. Such was the case among Iroquois Indians in Northeast America, for instance. In the 17th and 18th centuries, they often incorporated specially selected war captives and other valued strangers, including some Dutch, French, English, and other non-Indians, into their lineages in order to make up for population losses due to warfare

---

[7]Mitchell, W. E. (1978). *Mishpokhe: A study of New York City Jewish family clubs.* The Hague: Mouton.

and diseases. As soon as these newcomers were ceremonially naturalized, they acquired essentially the same birthright status as those actually born into the lineage.

Because a lineage is a corporate body (operating as a collective entity) that endures after the deaths of members with new members continually born into it, it has a continuing existence that enables it to act like a corporation, as in owning property, organizing productive activities, distributing goods and labor power, assigning status, and regulating relations with other groups. Thus it is a strong, effective base of social organization.

A common feature of lineages is exogamy. This means that lineage members must find their marriage partners in other lineages. One advantage of lineage exogamy is that potential sexual competition within the group is curbed, promoting the group's solidarity. Lineage exogamy also means that each marriage is more than a union between two individuals; it amounts as well to a new alliance between lineages. This helps to maintain them as components of larger social systems. Finally, lineage exogamy maintains open communication within a society, promoting the diffusion of knowledge from one lineage to another.

In contemporary North American Indian communities, genealogy plays an essential role in tribal membership—as illustrated in this chapter's Anthropology Applied.

Clan

In the course of time, as generation succeeds generation and new members are born into the lineage, its membership may become too large to be manageable, or too much for the lineage's resources to support. When this happens, as we have seen with the Chinese *tsu,* **fission** occurs; that is, the original lineage splits into new, smaller lineages. Usually the members of the new lineages continue to recognize their original relationship to one another. The result of this process is the appearance of a larger kind of descent group, the clan. The term *clan* has been used differently by different anthropologists, and a certain amount of confusion exists about its precise meaning. As noted early on in this chapter, the clan is now generally defined as a noncorporate descent group whose members assume descent from a common ancestor (who may be real or fictive) but are unable to trace the precise genealogical links back to that ancestor.

fission The splitting of a descent group into two or more new descent groups.
totemism The belief that people are related to particular animals, plants, or natural objects by virtue of descent from common ancestral spirits.

This stems from the great genealogical depth of the clan, whose founding ancestor lived so far in the past that the links must be assumed rather than known in detail. A clan differs from a lineage in another respect: It lacks the residential unity generally—although not invariably—characteristic of a lineage's core members. As with the lineage, descent may be patrilineal, matrilineal, or ambilineal.

Because clan membership is dispersed rather than localized, it usually does not hold tangible property corporately. Instead, it tends to be more a unit for ceremonial and political matters. Only on special occasions will the membership gather together for specific purposes. Clans, however, may handle important integrative functions. Like lineages, they may regulate marriage through exogamy. Because of their dispersed membership, they give individuals the right of entry into local groups other than their own. Members usually are expected to give protection and hospitality to others in the clan. Hence, these can be expected in any local group that includes people who belong to a single clan.

Clans, lacking the residential unity of lineages, frequently depend on symbols—of animals, plants, natural forces, colors and special objects—to provide members with solidarity and a ready means of identification. These symbols, called *totems,* often are associated with the clan's mythical origin and reinforce for clan members an awareness of their common descent. The word *totem* comes from the Ojibwa American Indian word *ototeman,* meaning "he is a relative of mine." **Totemism** was defined by the British anthropologist A. R. Radcliffe-Brown as a set of "customs and beliefs by which there is set up a special system of relations between the society and the plants, animals, and other natural objects that are important in the social life."[8] Hopi Indian matriclans, for example, bear such totemic names as Bear, Bluebird, Butterfly, Lizard, Spider, and Snake.

Totemism is a changing concept that varies among cultures. A kind of watered-down totemism may be found even in modern North American society, where baseball and football teams are given the names of such powerful wild animals as bears, tigers, and wildcats. This extends to the Democratic Party's donkey and the Republican Party's elephant, to the Elks, the Lions, and other fraternal and social organizations. These animal emblems, or mascots, however, do not involve notions of biological descent and strong sense of kinship that they have for clans, nor are they linked with the various ritual observances associated with clan totems.

[8]Radcliffe-Brown, A. R. (1931) Social organization of Australian tribes. *Oceana Monographs, 1,* 29.

Anthropology Applied

Resolving a Native American Tribal Membership Dispute

In autumn 1998, I received a call from the tribal chief of the Aroostook Band of Micmacs in Northern Maine asking for help in resolving a bitter tribal membership dispute. The conflict centered on the fact that several hundred individuals had become tribal members without proper certification of their Micmac kinship status. Traditionalists in the community argued that their tribe's organization was being taken over by "non-Indians." With the formal status of so many members in question, the tribal administration could not properly determine who was entitled to benefit from the available health, housing, and education programs. After some hostile confrontations between the factions, tribal elders requested a formal inquiry into the membership controversy, and I was called in as a neutral party with a long history of working with the Band.

My involvement as an advocacy anthropologist began in 1981, when these Micmacs (also spelled Mi'kmaq) first employed me (with Bunny McBride) as co-Director of Research and Development. At the time, they formed a poor and landless community not yet officially recognized as a tribe. During that decade, we helped the band define its political strategies, which focused on petitioning for federal recognition of their Indian status, claiming traditional rights to hunt, trap, and fish, and even demanding return of lost ancestral lands. To generate popular support for the effort, I co-produced a film about the community (*Our Lives in Our Hands*, 1986). Most important, we gathered oral histories and detailed archival documentation to address kinship issues and other government criteria for tribal recognition. The latter included important genealogical records showing that most Micmac adults in the region were at least "half-blood" (having two of their grandparents officially recorded as Indians). Furthermore, research demonstrated that the loosely structured Micmac community, with its informal

system of political leadership, matched that of traditional hunting bands in their ancestral homeland. It also showed that Northern Maine fell within the aboriginal range of the band's ancestors.

Based on this evidence, we effectively argued that Aroostook Micmacs could claim aboriginal title to lands in the region and convinced politicians in Washington, D.C., to introduce a special bill to acknowledge their tribal status and settle their land claims. When formal hearings were held in 1990, I testified in the U.S. Senate as expert witness for the Micmacs. The following year, the Aroostook Band of Micmacs Settlement

The Sanipass-Lafford family cluster in Chapman, Maine, represents a traditional Mi'kmaq residential kin group. Such extended families typically include grandchildren and bilaterally related family members such as in-laws, uncles, and aunts. Taken from the Sanipass family album, this picture shows a handful of members in the mid-1980s: Marline Sanipass Morey with two of her nephews and uncles.

Act became federal law. This made the band eligible for the financial assistance (health, housing, education and child welfare) and economic development loans available to all federally recognized tribes in the United States. Moreover, it provided the band with funding to buy a 5,000-acre territorial base in Maine.

Flush with federal funding and rapidly expanding its activities, the 500-member band became overwhelmed by complex bureaucratic regulations now governing their existence. Without formally established ground rules determining who could apply for tribal membership, and

overlooking federally imposed regulations, hundreds of new names were rather casually added to its tribal rolls. Many of them were Micmacs hailing from across the Canadian border, even though U.S. federal law stipulates that only U.S. citizens may be added. Others never provided documentary evidence of their Micmac ancestry or could not prove their ties to the region. Most importantly, however, the successive tribal administrations had lost sight of the federal law stipulating that new members had to be officially approved by the U.S. Secretary of Interior, who controls the Bureau of Indian Affairs.

By 1997, the Aroostook Band population had ballooned to almost 1,200 members, and Micmac traditionalists were questioning the legitimacy of many whose names had been added to the band roll. With mounting tension threatening to destroy the band, the tribal chief invited me to evaluate critically the membership claims of more than half the tribe. In early 1999, I reviewed kinship records submitted by hundreds of individuals whose membership on the tribal rolls was in question. Several months later, I offered my final report to the Micmac community. After traditional prayers, sweetgrass burning, drumming, and a traditional meal of salmon and moose, I formally presented my findings: Based on the official criteria, about 100 lineal descendants of the original members and just over 150 newcomers met the minimum required qualifications for membership; several hundred would have to be stripped from the tribal rolls. After singing, drumming, and closing prayers, the Micmac gathering dispersed. Today, the band numbers about 850 members and is doing well. It has purchased several tracts of land (collectively over 600 acres), including a small residential reservation near Presque Isle, now home to about 200 Micmacs. Also located here are new tribal administration offices, a health clinic, and a cultural center. *(By Harald Prins, co-author of this textbook, 2004.)* ■ ■ ■

Anthropologist Peggy Reeves Sanday with members of a matrilineal clan among the Minangkabau of Sumatra gathered for a house-raising ceremony. The one adult male is the brother of the senior female leader (the woman on Sanday's left); he is the clan's male leader. Absence of other men on this special occasion reflects the predominance of women in this society.

Courtesy of Peggy Reeves Sanday

In addition to the earlier mentioned matriclans, there are also patriclans tracing descent exclusively through men from a founding ancestor. Historically, a few dozen of such clans existed in the Scottish highlands, often identified with the prefix "Mac" or "Mc" (from an old Celtic word meaning "son of"). During the past few hundred years, large Scottish clans such as McGregor and Mackenzie broke apart as many members moved away in search of economic opportunity. Today, their descendents live dispersed all across the globe, especially in countries such as Australia, Canada, England, New Zealand, and the United States. During the past few decades, widely scattered descendants have sought to re-establish their kinship ties to ancestral clans, and many travel from afar to attend the annual gathering of their clan, preferably in their traditional ancient homeland in the highlands of Scotland. As this chapter's opening photograph illustrates, these clan members like to express their bonds of kinship with one another by wearing woolen shawls, kilts, or other pieces of clothing made of their clan tartan—a distinct plaid pattern and color identifying their particular clan membership. Although each Scottish clan has its own traditional tartan, the patterns themselves are not very ancient. In fact, almost all of them were designed since the early 1800s. Their popularity today, however, is based on the fact that they are a colorful symbol of a shared heritage among very distant relatives living very far apart.[9]

---

[9]Trevor-Roper, H. (1992). Invention of tradition: The highland tradition of Scotland. In E. Hobsbawm & T. Ranger (Eds.), *The invention of tradition* (ch. 2). Cambridge, England: Cambridge University Press.

Phratries and Moieties

Larger kinds of descent groups are phratries and moieties (Figure 10.3). We touched briefly on phratries a few pages back in our discussion about Hopi Indians. A **phratry** (after the Greek word for "brother") is a unilineal descent group composed of at least two clans that supposedly share a common ancestry, whether or not they really do. Like individuals in the clan, phratry members cannot trace precisely their descent links to a common ancestor, although they firmly believe such an ancestor existed.

If the entire society is divided into only two major descent groups, whether they are equivalent to clans or

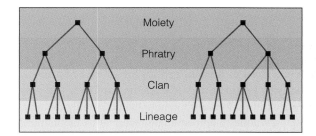

FIGURE 10.3

This diagram shows how lineages, clans, phratries, and moieties form an organizational hierarchy. Each moiety is subdivided into phratries, each phratry is subdivided into clans, and each clan is subdivided into lineages.

phratry A unilineal descent group composed of two or more clans that assume they share a common ancestry but do not know the precise genealogical links of that ancestry. If only two such groups exist, each is a moiety.

phratries, each group is called a **moiety** (after the French word for "half"). Members of the moiety believe themselves to share a common ancestor but cannot prove it through definite genealogical links. As a rule, the feelings of kinship among members of lineages and clans are stronger than those of members of phratries and moieties. This may be due to the much larger size and more diffuse nature of the latter groups.

Like lineages and clans, phratries and moieties are often exogamous and so are bound together by marriages between their members. And like clans, they provide members rights of access to other communities, as among the Hopi. In a community that does not include one's clan members, one's phratry members are still there to turn to for hospitality. Finally, moieties may perform reciprocal services for one another. Among them, individuals turn to members of the opposite "half" in their community for the necessary mourning rituals when a member of their own moiety dies. Such interdependence between moieties, again, serves to maintain the cohesion of the entire society. The kin-ordered social structure of the Winnebago Indian nation offers an interesting ethnographic example of the moiety system. Organized in twelve patrilineal clans, they were divided between "those who are above" (Sky) and "those who are below" (Earth). The Sky moiety included the Eagle, Hawk, Pigeon, and Thunder clans, whereas those belonging to the Earth "half" consisted of the Bear, Buffalo, Deer, Elk, Fish, Snake, Water Spirit, and Wolf clans. These exogamous moieties not only regulated marriage and leadership positions among the Winnebago, but even structured their settlement patterns, with Sky clans inhabiting the southwest half of each village and those of the Earth moiety the northeast.[10]

Bilateral Kinship and the Kindred

Important though descent groups are in many societies, they are not found in all societies, nor are they the only kinds of extended kinship groups to be found. Bilateral kinship (sometimes erroneously referred to as bilateral

descent), a characteristic of Western society as well as a number of food-foraging societies, affiliates a person with close "blood" relatives (but not in-laws) through both sexes. In other words, the individual traces descent through both parents, all four grandparents, and so forth, recognizing multiple ancestors. Theoretically, one is associated equally with all consanguineal relatives on both the mother's and father's sides of the family. Thus, this principle relates an individual lineally to all eight great-grandparents and laterally to all third and fourth cousins. Since such a huge group is too big to be socially practical, it is usually reduced to a small circle of paternal and maternal relatives, called the **kindred.** The kindred may be defined as an individual's close consanguineal relatives on the maternal and paternal side of his or her family. Since the kindred is laterally rather than lineally organized—that is, ego, or the focal person from whom the degree of each relationship is reckoned, is the center of the group (Figure 10.4)—it is not a true descent group.

North Americans are all familiar with the kindred; those who belong are simply called relatives. It includes those consanguineal relatives on both sides of the family who are seen on important occasions, such as family weddings, reunions, and funerals. Most people in the United States can identify the members of their kindred up to grandparents and first, if not always second, cousins. The limits of the kindred, however, are variable and indefinite. No one ever can be absolutely certain which relatives to invite to every important function and which to exclude. Inevitably, situations arise that require some debate about whether or not to invite particular, usually distant, relatives. Kindreds are thus not clearly bounded and lack the distinctiveness of the unilineal or ambilineal descent group. (They are also temporary, lasting only as long as the functions for which they are assembled.)

Because of its bilateral structure, a kindred is never the same for any two people except siblings (brothers and sisters). Thus, no two people other than siblings belong to the same kindred. The kindred of ego's first cousin on the father's side, for example, includes not only the father's sister (or brother), as does ego's, but the father's sister's (or brother's) spouse, as well as consanguineal relatives of the latter. As for the kindreds of ego's parents, these will range lineally to grandparents and laterally to cousins too distant for ego to know, and the same is true of ego's aunts and uncles. Thus, the kindred is not composed of people with an ancestor in common but with a living relative in common—ego. Furthermore, as ego goes through life, the kindreds he or she is affiliated with will change. When young, individuals belong to the kindreds of

---

[10]Radin, P. (1923). The Winnebago tribe. In *37th annual report of the Bureau of American Ethnology, 1915–1916* (pp. 33–550). Washington, DC: Government Printing Office.

moiety Each group that results from a division of a society into two halves on the basis of descent.
kindred An individual's close relatives on the maternal and paternal sides of his or her family.

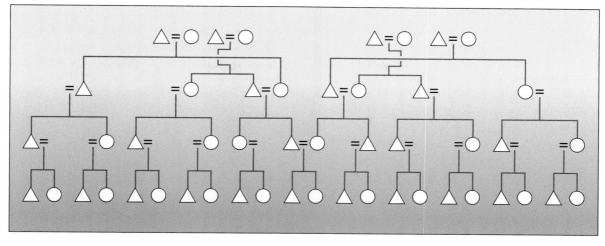

FIGURE 10.4

The kinship pattern of the kindred. These people are related not to a common ancestor but, rather, to a living relative—here, the sister and brother shown at the center of the bottom row.

their parents. Ultimately, they belong to the kindreds of their sons and daughters as well as their nieces and nephews.

Because of its vagueness, temporary nature, and changing affiliation, the kindred cannot function as a group except in relation to ego. Unlike descent groups, it is not self-perpetuating—it ceases with ego's death. It has no constant leader, nor can it easily hold, administer, or pass on property. In most cases, it cannot organize work, nor can it easily administer justice or assign status. It can, however, be turned to for aid. In non-Western societies, for example, raiding or trading parties may be composed of kindreds. The group comes together to perform some particular function, shares the results, and then disbands. It also can act as a ceremonial group

for rites of passage: initiation ceremonies and the like. In traditional European societies, kindreds acted to raise bail, compensate a victim's family, or take revenge for the murder or injury of someone in one's own kindred. Finally, kindreds also can regulate marriage through exogamy.

Kindreds are frequently found in industrial and postindustrial societies such as that of the United States, where mobility weakens contact with relatives. Individuality is emphasized in such societies, and strong kinship organization is usually not as important as it is among non-Western peoples. Even so, bilateral kindreds also may be found in societies where kinship ties are important, and in some instances, they even occur alongside descent groups.

Members of the groom's personal kindred shown here are his father, mother, two brothers, aunt, and niece.

© Anita de Laguna Haviland

Cultural Evolution of the Descent Group

Just as different types of families occur in different societies, so do different kinds of nonfamilial kin groups. Descent groups, for example, are not a common feature of food-foraging societies, where marriage acts as the social mechanism for integrating individuals within communities. In horticultural, pastoral, or many intensive agricultural societies, however, the descent group usually provides the structural framework upon which the fabric of the society rests.

It is generally agreed that lineages arise from extended family organization, so long as organizational problems exist that such groups help solve. All that is required, really, is that as members of existing extended families find it necessary to split off and establish new households elsewhere, they not move too far away; that the core members of such related families (men in patrilocal, women in matrilocal, members of both sexes in ambilocal extended families) explicitly acknowledge their descent from a common ancestor; and that they continue to participate in common activities in an organized way. As this process proceeds, lineages will develop, and these may with time give rise to clans and ultimately phratries.

Another way that clans may arise is as legal fictions to integrate otherwise autonomous units. The six Iroquois Indian nations of what now is New York State, for example, developed clans by simply behaving as if lineages of the same name in different villages were related. Thus, their members became fictitious "brothers" and "sisters." By this device, members of, say, a Bear clan in a Mohawk village could travel to a nearby Oneida village, or more distant Onondaga, Cayuga, Tuscarora, or even Seneca villages some 200 miles west of their homeland, and be welcomed in and hosted in any of these Iroquois settlements by members of local Bear clans. In this way, the "Six Nations" achieved a wider unity than had previously existed.

As larger, dispersed descent groups develop, the conditions that gave rise to extended families and lineages may change. For example, economic diversity and the availability of alternative occupations for individuals may conflict with the residential unity of extended families and (usually) lineages. Or, lineages may lose their economic bases if developing political institutions take control of resources. In such circumstances, lineages would be expected to disappear as important organizational units. Clans, however, might survive, if they continue to provide an important integrative function. Such is the case with the Scottish clans discussed earlier. This helps explain their continued strength and vitality even

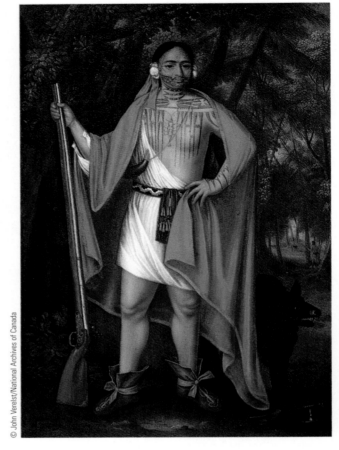

© John Verelst/National Archives of Canada

Clans among the "Six Nations" of the Iroquois confederacy in New York State are a kinship construct that allowed people to freely travel among multiple member villages. This portrait, done in 1710, shows Sa Ga Yeath Qua Pieth Tow, a chief of the Mohawk Nation. Behind him stands a bear, which represents his clan.

far outside Scotland today. They perform an integrative function among kin who are geographically dispersed as well as socially diverse but in a way that does not conflict with the mobility characteristic of industrial or postindustrial societies.

In societies where small domestic units—nuclear families or single-parent households—are of primary importance, bilateral kinship and kindred organization are likely to result. This can be seen in modern industrial and postindustrial societies, in newly emerging societies in the "underdeveloped" world, and in still-existing food-foraging societies throughout the world.

MEDIATREK

For an overview of kinship terminology and descent, plus an interactive kinship tutorial, go to MediaTrek 10.1 on the companion Web site or CD-ROM.

Anthropologists of Note

Lewis Henry Morgan (1818–1881)

© Bettmann/Corbis

This major theoretician of 19th-century North American anthropology has been regarded as the founder of kinship studies. In *Systems of Consanguinity and Affinity of the Human Family* (1871), he classified and compared the kinship systems of peoples around the world in an attempt to prove the Asiatic origin of American Indians. In doing so, he developed the ethnocentric idea that the human family evolved through a series of stages, from primitive promiscuity on the one hand to the monogamous, patriarchal family on the other. Although subsequent work showed Morgan to be wrong about this and a number of other things, his work showed the potential value of studying the distribution of different kinship systems in order to frame hypotheses of a developmental or historical nature. And, by noting the connection between terminology and behavior, his work showed the value of kinship for sociological study. Besides his contributions to kinship and evolutionary studies, he produced an ethnography of the Iroquois, which still stands as a major source of information.

KINSHIP TERMINOLOGY AND KINSHIP GROUPS

Any system of organizing people who are relatives into different kinds of groups, whether descent based or EGO oriented, is bound to have an important effect upon the ways in which relatives are labeled in any given society. The fact is, the kinship terminologies of other peoples reflect the positions individuals occupy within their cultural system. In particular, kinship terminology is affected by, and adjusts to, the kinds of kinship groups that exist in a society. However, other factors also are at work in each system of kinship terminology that help differentiate one relative from another. Factors include gender, generational differences, or genealogical differences. In the various systems of kinship terminology, any one of these factors may be emphasized at the expense of others. And sometimes they are qualified by distinguishing younger from older individuals in a particular category or by emphasizing the gender of the person referring to a particular relative.

Regardless of the factors emphasized, all kinship terminologies accomplish two important tasks. First, they classify similar kinds of individuals into single specific categories; second, they separate different kinds of individuals into distinct categories. Generally, two or more kin are merged under the same term when the individuals have more or less the same rights and obligations with respect to the person referring to them as such. Such is the case among most English-speaking North Americans, for instance, when someone refers to a mother's sister and father's sister both as an "aunt." As far as the speaker is concerned, both relatives possess a similar status.

Several different systems of kinship terminology result from the application of the above principles just mentioned, including the Eskimo, Hawaiian, Iroquois, Crow, Omaha, Sudanese, Kariera, and Aranda systems, each named after the ethnographic example best described by anthropologists. Some of these systems, especially the last three, are fascinating in their complexity and are found among only a few of the world's societies. However, in order to illustrate some of the basic principles involved, we will focus our attention on the first four systems only.

Eskimo System

The **Eskimo system,** comparatively rare among all the world's systems, is the one used by Euroamericans, as well as by a number of food-foraging peoples (including the Inuit and other Eskimos; hence the name). The Eskimo or lineal system emphasizes the nuclear family by specifically identifying mother, father, brother, and sister while lumping together all other relatives into a few large categories (Figure 10.5). For example, the father is distinguished from the father's brother (uncle); but the father's brother is not distinguished from the mother's brother (both are called "uncle"). The mother's sister and father's sister are treated similarly, both called "aunt." In addition, all the sons and daughters of aunts

Eskimo system System of kinship terminology, also called lineal system, which emphasizes the nuclear family by specifically identifying the mother, father, brother, and sister, while lumping together all other relatives into broad categories such as uncle, aunt, and cousin.

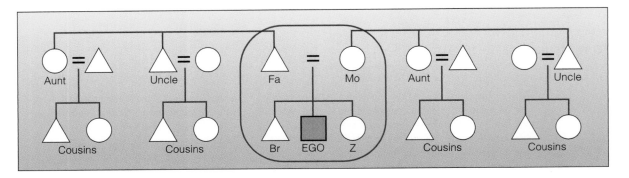

FIGURE 10.5

The Eskimo system of kinship terminology emphasizes the nuclear family (surrounded by the red line). Ego's father and mother are distinguished from ego's aunts and uncles, and siblings from cousins.

and uncles are called "cousin," thereby making a generational distinction but without indicating the side of the family to which they belong or even their gender.

Unlike other terminologies, the Eskimo system provides separate and distinct terms for the nuclear family members. This is probably because the Eskimo system is generally found in bilateral societies where the dominant kin group is the kindred, in which only immediate family members are important in day-to-day affairs. This is especially true of modern North American society, where the family is independent, living apart from, and not directly involved with, other kin except on ceremonial occasions. Thus, English-speaking North Americans (and others) generally distinguish between their closest kin (parents and siblings) but lump together (as aunts, uncles, cousins) other kin on both sides of the family.

Hawaiian System

The **Hawaiian system** of kinship terminology, common (as its name implies) in Hawaii and other Malayo-Polynesian-speaking areas but found elsewhere as well, is the least complex system, in that it uses the fewest terms. The Hawaiian system is also called the generational system, since all relatives of the same generation and sex are referred to by the same term

Hawaiian system Kinship reckoning in which all relatives of the same sex and generation are referred to by the same term.

Iroquois system Kinship terminology wherein a father and father's brother are referred to by a single term, as are a mother and mother's sister, but a father's sister and mother's brother are given separate terms. Parallel cousins are classified with brothers and sisters, while cross cousins are classified separately, but (unlike Crow and Omaha kinship) not equated with relatives of some other generation.

(Figure 10.6). For example, in one's parents' generation, the term used to refer to one's father is used as well for the father's brother and mother's brother. Similarly, one's mother, her sister, and one's father's sister are all lumped together under a single term. In ego's generation, male and female cousins are distinguished by gender and are equated with brothers and sisters.

The Hawaiian system reflects the absence of strong unilineal descent and is usually associated with ambilineal descent. Because ambilineal rules allow individuals the option of tracing their ancestry back through either side of the family, and members on both the father's and the mother's side are viewed as more or less equal, a certain degree of similarity is created among the father's and the mother's siblings. Thus, they are all simultaneously recognized as being similar relations and are merged together under a single term appropriate for their gender. In like manner, the children of the mother's and father's siblings are related to ego in the same way brother and sister are. Thus, they are ruled out as potential marriage partners.

Iroquois System

In the **Iroquois system** of kinship terminology, the father and father's brother are referred to by a single term, as are the mother and mother's sister; however, the father's sister and mother's brother are given separate terms (Figure 10.7). In one's own generation, brothers, sisters, and parallel cousins (offspring of parental siblings of the same sex, that is, the children of the mother's sister or father's brother) of the same sex are referred to by the same terms, which is logical enough considering that they are the offspring of people who are classified in the same category as EGO's actual mother and father. Cross cousins (offspring of parental siblings of opposite sex, that is, the children of

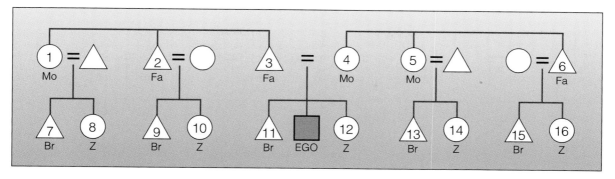

FIGURE 10.6

The Hawaiian kinship system. The men numbered 2 and 6 are called by the same term as father (3) by EGO; the women numbered 1 and 5 are called by the same term as mother (4). All cousins of EGO's own generation (7–16) are considered brothers (Br) and sisters (Z).

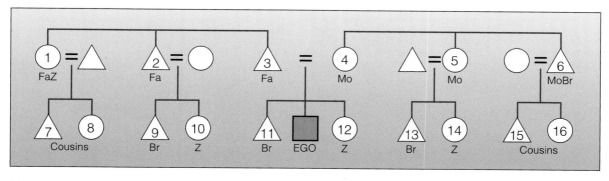

FIGURE 10.7

According to the Iroquois system of kinship terminology, the father's brother (2) is called by the same term as the father (3); the mother's sister (5) is called by the same term as the mother (4); but the people numbered 1 and 6 have separate terms for themselves. Those people numbered 9 to 14 are all considered siblings, but 7, 8, 15, and 16 are considered cousins.

the mother's brother or father's sister) are distinguished by terms that set them apart from all other kin. In fact, cross cousins are often preferred as spouses, for marriage to them reaffirms alliances between related lineages or clans.

Iroquois terminology, named for the Iroquoian Indians of northeastern North America, is in fact very widespread and is usually found with unilineal descent groups. It was, for example, the terminology in use until recently in rural Chinese society.

Crow System

In the preceding systems of terminology some relatives were grouped under common terms, while others of the same generation were separated and given different labels or terms. In the Crow system, another variable enters the picture. The system ignores the distinction that occurs between generations among certain kin.

The **Crow system** (named for the Crow Indians, also known as the Apsaroke, of the northern Great Plains, Montana), found in many parts of the world,

happens to be the one used by the Hopi Indians, who were discussed earlier in this chapter. Associated with strong matrilineal descent organization, it groups differently the relations on the father's side and mother's side (Figure 10.8). Cross cousins on the father's side are equated with relatives in the parental generation while those on the mother's side are equated with ego's children's generation. Otherwise, the system is much like Iroquois terminology.

To those unfamiliar with it, the Crow system seems terribly complex and illogical. Why does it exist? In societies such as that of the Hopi, where individual identity is dependent on descent group affiliation and descent is matrilineal, it makes sense to merge the

Crow system Kinship classification usually associated with matrilineal descent in which a father's sister and father's sister's daughter are called by the same term, a mother and mother's sister are merged under another, and a father and father's brother are lumped in a third. Parallel cousins are equated with brothers and sisters.

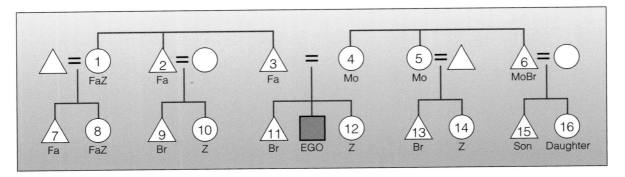

FIGURE 10.8

The Crow system. Those numbered 4 and 5 are merged under a single term, as are 2 and 3. EGO's parallel cousins (9, 10, 13, 14) are considered siblings, while the mother's brother's children are equated with the children of a male EGO and his brother.

In matrilineal societies with the Crow kinship system, sisters remain close to one another throughout their lives. So it was among the Hopi of Arizona, in whose traditional housing sisters lived in adjacent rooms. There is little in such living circumstances that differentiates a mother from her sister or her children from her sister's children. The mother's brother and his children, however, live elsewhere.

father's sister, her daughter, and even her mother together under a single term, regardless of generation. These are women whose descent is traced through the lineage that sired EGO, just as a male EGO's children, along with those of his mother's brother, were sired by men of EGO's lineage. Thus, it is perfectly logical for EGO to equate his maternal cross cousins with his own children's generation.

MEDIATREK

To see how anthropologists record and analyze kinship data from all around the world, go to MediaTrek 10.2 on the companion Web site or CD-ROM.

Kin Term Challenges in the Age of New Reproductive Technologies

If systems of kinship reckoning other than one's own seem strange and complex, consider the implications of an event that took place in 1978: the production of the world's first test-tube baby, in a petri dish outside the womb, without sexual intercourse. Since then, thousands of babies have been created in this way, and all sorts of new technologies have become part of the reproductive repertoire. It is now possible, for example, for a woman to give birth to her genetic uncle; does that make her his niece or his mother? If a child is conceived from a donor egg, implanted in another woman's womb

© PhotoEdit

Here, the pregnancy of a woman in whom another woman's egg has been implanted is monitored. The development of new reproductive technologies has profound implications for notions of kinship, at the same time allowing the commodification of children.

to be raised by yet another woman, who is its mother? To complicate matters even further, the egg may have been fertilized by sperm from a donor not married to, or in a sexual relationship with, any of these women. Indeed, it has been suggested that we need at least ten different terms to cover the concepts of "mother" and "father" in today's changing societies:[11]

1. Genetic mother
2. Carrying mother
3. Nurturing mother
4. Complete mother
5. Genetic/carrying mother
6. Genetic/nurturing mother
7. Carrying/nurturing mother
8. Genetic father
9. Nurturing father
10. Complete father

While we cannot predict what the future will bring, it seems evident that the new reproductive technologies will have an important impact on traditional notions of gender and kinship. Today, growing numbers of anthropologists focus on kinship in the context of these artificial reproductive technologies.[12] Beyond transforming our sense of being human, these technologies force us to redefine traditional ideas about the status of relatives—challenging us to rethink what being "related" to others is about and, specifically, what our rights and obligations are toward such unfamiliar categories of kinfolk around us.

---

[11]Stone, L. (1998). *Kinship and gender* (p. 272). Boulder, CO: Westview Press.

[12]Edwards, J., Franklin, S., Hirsch, E., Price F., & Strathern, M. (Eds.). (1999). *Technologies of procreation: Kinship in the age of assisted conception* (2nd ed.). London: Routledge; Edwards, J. (2000). *Born and bred: Idioms of kinship and new reproductive technologies in England.* Oxford: Oxford University Press.

Chapter Summary

■ In nonindustrial societies, kinship groups commonly deal with challenges that families and households cannot handle alone—challenges involving defense, allocation of property, and the pooling of other resources. As societies become larger and more complex, formal political systems take over many of these matters. A common form of kinship group is the descent group, which has as its criterion of membership descent from a common ancestor through a series of parent–child links. Unilineal descent establishes kin group membership exclusively through the male or female line. Matrilineal descent is traced through the female line; patrilineal, through the male.

■ The descent system is closely tied to a society's economic base. Generally, patrilineal descent predominates where males do the majority of the primary productive work and matrilineal where females do it. Anthropologists recognize that in all societies the kin of both mother and father are important elements in the social structure, regardless of how descent group membership is defined.

■ The male members of a patrilineage trace their descent from a common male ancestor. In a patrilineage a female belongs to the same descent group as her father and his brother, but her children cannot trace their descent through them. Typically, authority over the children lies with the father or his elder brother. The requirement for younger men to defer to older men and for women to defer to men, as well as to the women of a household they marry into, are common sources of tension in a patrilineal society.

■ In one respect, matrilineal descent is the opposite of patrilineal, with descent being traced through the female line. Unlike the patrilineal pattern, which confers authority on men, matrilineal descent does not necessarily confer public authority on women, although they usually have more say in decision making than they do in patrilineal societies. The matrilineal system is common in societies where women perform much of the productive work. This system may be a source of family tension, since the husband's authority lies not in his own household but in that of his sister. This, and the ease with which unsatisfactory marriages may be ended, often result in higher divorce rates in matrilineal than in patrilineal societies. Double descent is matrilineal for some purposes and patrilineal for others. Ambilineal descent provides a measure of flexibility in that an individual has the option of affiliating with either the mother's or father's descent group.

■ Descent groups are often highly structured economic units that function to provide aid and security to their members. They also may be repositories of religious tradition, with group solidarity enhanced by worship of a common ancestor. A lineage is a corporate descent group made up of consanguineal kin who can trace their genealogical links to a common ancestor. Since lineages are commonly exogamous; sexual competition within the group is largely avoided. In addition, marriage of a group member represents an alliance of two lineages. Lineage exogamy also serves to maintain open communication within a society and fosters the exchange of information among lineages.

■ Fission is the splitting of a large lineage group into new, smaller ones, with the original lineage becoming a clan. Clan members claim descent from a common ancestor but without actually knowing the precise genealogical links to that ancestor. Unlike lineages, clan residence is usually dispersed rather than localized. In the absence of residential unity, clan identification is often reinforced by totems, usually symbols from nature that remind members of their common ancestry. A phratry is a unilineal descent group of two or more clans that supposedly share a common ancestry. When a society is divided into two halves, each half consisting of one or more clans, these two major descent groups are called moieties.

■ In bilateral societies, such as industrial, postindustrial, and many food-foraging societies, individuals are affiliated equally with all relatives on both the mother's and father's sides. Such a large group is socially impractical and is usually reduced to a small circle of paternal and maternal relatives called the kindred. A kindred is never the same for any two people except siblings. Different types of descent systems appear in different societies. In those where the nuclear family predominates, bilateral kinship and kindred organization are likely to prevail.

■ In any society cultural rules dictate the way kinship relationships are defined. Factors such as gender and generational or genealogical differences help distinguish one kin from another. The Hawaiian system is the simplest system of kinship terminology. All relatives of the same generation and gender are referred to by the same term. The Eskimo system, also used by English-speaking North Americans and many others, emphasizes the nuclear family and merges all other relatives in a given generation into a few large, generally undifferentiated categories. In the Iroquois system, a single term is used for father and his brother and another for a mother and her sister. Parallel cousins are equated with brothers and sisters but distinguished from cross cousins. The same is true in the Crow system, except they equate cross cousins with relatives of other generations.

■ With the advent of new reproductive technologies that separate conception from birth and eggs from wombs, traditional notions of kinship and gender are being challenged, and new social categories are emerging.

Questions for Reflection

1. Suppose that for reasons of support and security, you were forced to create and maintain a social network of relatives beyond your immediate family or household. How would you meet that challenge?

2. People growing up in modern industrial and postindustrial societies generally treasure ideas of personal freedom, individuality, and privacy as essential in their pursuit of happiness. Considering the social functions of kinship relations in traditional non-state societies, why do you think that such ideas may be considered unsociable and even dangerously selfish?

3. In some North American Indian languages, the English word for "loneliness" is translated as "I have no relatives." What does that tell you about the importance of kinship in those Native cultures?

4. One major reason anthropologists are so interested in getting a handle on a culture's kinship terminology system is that it offers them a quick but crucially important insight into a group's social structure. Why do you think this is especially true for traditional communities of foragers, herders, and farmers, but is less so for urban neighborhoods in industrial and postindustrial societies?

5. Why do you think that one of the most simple kinship terminology systems imaginable, namely the Eskimo system, is functionally adequate for most Europeans, North Americans, and others living in complex modern societies?

Key Terms

Kinship	Fission
Descent group	Totemism
Lineage	Phratry
Clan	Moiety
Unilineal descent	Kindred
Matrilineal descent	Eskimo system
Patrilineal descent	Hawaiian system
Double descent	Iroquois system
Ambilineal descent	Crow system

Multimedia Review Tools

Companion Web Site

Visit **http://www.wadsworth.com/anthropology_d/** and click on the companion Web site for this textbook to access a wide range of material to aid your study of anthropology. Among the options for self-study in each chapter are learning objectives, flash cards, Internet activities, Web links, InfoTrac College Edition exercises, and practice tests that can be scored and emailed to your instructor.

CD-ROM

The *Doing Anthropology Today* CD-ROM supplied with your textbook provides unique and valuable information designed to enhance your learning experience. This interactive multimedia resource includes video clips, interviews with renowned anthropologists, map and timeline exercises, chapter study quizzes, and much more. *Doing Anthropology Today* will not only help you in achieving your grade goals, but it will also make your learning experience fun and exciting!

Suggested Readings

Carsten, J. (Ed.). (2000). *Cultures of relatedness: New approaches to the study of kinship.* Cambridge, England: Cambridge University Press.

A cross-cultural examination of what it means to be a "relative" at a time when established ideas about kinship are being transformed by radical changes in marriage arrangements and gender relations, as well as new reproductive technologies.

Finkler, K. (2000). *Experiencing the new genetics: Family and kinship on the medical frontier.* Philadelphia: University of Pennsylvania Press.

An exploration of medical and genetic aspects of kinship and debates concerning the social impact of modern medical/genetic knowledge and practices.

Fox, R. (1968). *Kinship and marriage in an anthropological perspective.* Baltimore: Penguin.

An excellent introduction to the concepts of kinship and marriage, this book outlines some of the methods of analysis used in the anthropological treatment of kinship and marriage. It updates Radcliffe-Brown's *African Systems of Kinship and Marriage* and features a perspective focused on kinship groups and social organization.

Parkin, R. (1997). *Kinship: An introduction to basic concepts.* Cambridge, MA: Blackwell.

A solid, useful, readable text on the basics of kinship study.

Schusky, E. L. (1983). *Manual for kinship analysis* (2nd ed.). Lanham, MD: University Press of America.

This useful book discusses the elements of kinship, diagramming, systems classification, and descent with specific examples.

Stone, L. (2000). *Kinship and gender: An introduction* (2nd ed.). Boulder, CO: Westview Press.

Anthropological interest in kinship languished somewhat in the 1980s but has since undergone a strong revival. Part of this renewed interest relates to new reproductive technologies and their implications for kinship. This book provides coverage of the field of kinship at the introductory level, while exploring the repercussions of the new reproductive technologies on both kinship and gender.

Grouping by Gender, Age, Common Interest, and Class

© David Young-Wolff/PhotoEdit

CHALLENGE ISSUE

INDIVIDUALS BORN AND RAISED WITHIN LARGE-SCALE SOCIETIES FACE THE CHALLENGE OF SUCCEEDING WITHIN A COMPLEX SOCIAL STRUCTURE THAT EXTENDS WELL BEYOND KINSHIP. These Asian American female teenagers in California with their violins in hand exemplify the phenomenon of grouping by age, gender, ethnicity, and common interest, some of the means by which people may be organized into groups without recourse to kinship or descent.

What Principles Do People Use to Organize Societies?

Besides kinship and marriage, people group themselves by gender, age, common interest, and rank (including class) within a society to deal with problems not conveniently handled by marriage, the family and/or household, descent group, or kindred.

2 What Is Age Grading?

Age grading—the formation of groups on an age basis—is a widely used means of organizing people in societies, including those of Europe and North America. In addition to age grades, some societies feature age sets—formally established groups of people born during a certain time span who move through the series of age grade categories together.

3 What Are Common-Interest Associations?

Common-interest associations are formed to deal with specific problems or opportunities. Membership may be voluntary to compulsory. Common-interest associations have been a feature of human societies since the appearance of the first farming villages several thousand years ago, but have become especially prominent in modern industrial or industrializing societies.

4 What Is Social Stratification?

Stratification is the division of society into two or more social classes of people who do not share equally in basic resources, power, or prestige. Such a hierarchical social structure is characteristic of all of the world's societies having large and heterogeneous populations with centralized political control. Among others, these include ancient kingdoms and empires, but also modern republics. Social classes can be relatively open, as in North America where membership is based primarily on personal achievement or wealth. They can also be closed, as in India, where membership in hierarchically ranked groups known as castes is determined by birth and remains fixed for life.

Social organization based on kinship and marriage has received considerable attention from anthropologists. There are several reasons for this: In one way or another, kinship and marriage operate as organizing principles in all societies, and in the small stateless societies so often studied by anthropologists, they are usually the most important organizational principles. There is, too, a certain fascination in the almost mathematical way kinship systems at least appear to work. To the unwary, all this attention to kinship and marriage may give the impression that these are the only principles of social organization that really matter. Yet it is obvious from analyzing modern industrial societies that other principles of social organization not only exist but also may be quite important. These include grouping by gender, age, common interest, and social rank—each of which we will examine in this chapter.

GROUPING BY GENDER

As shown in preceding chapters, division of labor along gender lines occurs in all human societies. In some societies—the previously discussed Ju/'hoansi for example—many tasks that men and women undertake may be shared. People may perform work normally assigned to the opposite sex without loss of face. In others, however, men and women are rigidly segregated in what they do. For instance, among the Mohawk, Oneida, Onondaga, Cayuga, Seneca, and Tuscarora Indians of New York—the famous Six Nations of the Iroquois—society was divided into two parts consisting of sedentary women on the one hand and highly mobile men on the other.

Women who were "blood" relatives to one another lived in the same village and shared the job of growing the corn, beans, and squash that all Iroquois relied upon for subsistence. Although men built the houses and the wooden palisades that protected villages and also helped women clear fields for cultivation, they did their most important work some distance away from the villages. This consisted of hunting, fishing, trading, warring, and diplomacy. As a consequence, men were mostly transients in the villages, being present for only brief periods.

Traditionally, Iroquois viewed women's activities as less prestigious than those of men, but they explicitly acknowledged women as the sustainers of life. Moreover, women headed the longhouses (dwellings occupied by matrilocal extended families), descent and inheritance passed through women, and ceremonial life centered on women's activities. Although men held all leadership positions outside households—sitting on the councils of the villages, tribes, and the league of Six Nations—the women of their clans were the ones who nominated them for these positions and held veto power over them. Thus, Iroquois male leadership was balanced by female authority.

Overall, the phrase "separate but equal" accurately describes relations between the sexes in Six Nations Iroquois society, with members of neither sex being dominant nor submissive to the other. Related to this seems to have been a low incidence of rape, for outside observers in the 19th century widely commented upon its apparent absence within Iroquois communities. Even in warfare, sexual violation of female captives was virtually unheard of—as noted in this back-handed compliment made by U.S. Brigadier General James Clinton in 1779: "Bad as the savages are,

VISUAL COUNTERPOINT Among the Iroquois of New York, society was divided into sedentary women and highly mobile men, whose work was carried out away from the village. Many still follow this pattern today, as men leave their villages for extended periods to do much of the high steel work in the cities of North America.

In North America, women were long expected to submit to male authority, but in recent decades, there has been a major effort to achieve egalitarian gender relations. Among numerous examples where this has not yet been achieved is the Southern Baptist Convention's official policy that women should submit gracefully to men.

they never violate the chastity of any women of their prisoners."[1]

Although Iroquoian men were absent from the village often, when present they ate and slept with women. This contrasts the habits of the Mundurucu Indians of the Amazon rainforest in Brazil, discussed briefly in Chapter 9. Mundurucu men not only work apart from women but also eat and sleep separately. From age 13 onward males live together in one large house, while women, girls, and preteen boys occupy two or three houses grouped around the men's house. For all intents and purposes, men associate with men, and women with women. The relation between the sexes is not harmonious but rather one of opposition. According to Mundurucu belief, sex roles were once reversed: Women ruled over men and controlled the sacred trumpets that are the symbols of power and represent the reproductive capacities of women. But because women could not hunt, they could not supply the meat demanded by the ancient spirits contained within the trumpets, enabling the men to take the trumpets from the women, establishing their dominance in the process. Ever since, the trumpets have been carefully guarded and hidden in the men's house, and no woman can see them under penalty of gang rape. Thus, Mundurucu men express fear and envy toward women and seek to control them by force. For their part, the women neither like nor accept a submissive status, and even though men occupy all formal positions of political and religious leadership, women are autonomous in the economic realm.

Alongside notable differences, there are also interesting similarities between Mundurucu beliefs and those of traditional European and Euroamerican cultures. For example, many 19th-century European and Euroamerican intellectuals held to the idea that patriarchy (rule by men) had replaced an earlier state of matriarchy (rule by women). Moreover, the idea that men may use force to control women is deeply embedded in both Judaic and Christian traditions (and even today, despite changing attitudes, one out of three women in the United States is sexually assaulted at some time in her life). A major difference between Mundurucu and traditional European societies is that, in the latter, women often have not had control over their own economic activities. This has changed significantly over the past few decades, but women in North America and other Western countries still have some distance to go before they achieve economic parity with men.

GROUPING BY AGE

Age grouping is so familiar and so important that it and sex have been called the only universal factors that determine a person's positions in society. In North America today, a child's first friends are usually children of his or her own age. They begin preschool or kindergarten with age mates and typically move through a dozen or more years in the educational system together. At specified ages they are allowed to see certain movies, drive a car, and do things reserved for adults, such as voting, drinking alcoholic beverages, and serving in the military. Ultimately, North Americans retire from their jobs at a specified age and, more and more, spend the final

---

[1]Littlewood, R. (1997). Military rape. *Anthropology Today, 13*(2), 14.

Age grading in modern North America is exemplified by the educational system, which specifies that children should begin kindergarten at about 5 years of age.

years of their lives in retirement communities, segregated from the rest of society. As North Americans age, they are labeled "teenagers," "middle-aged," and "senior citizens," whether they like it or not and for no other reason than the number of years they have lived.

Age classification also plays a significant role in non-Western societies, which, at a minimum, make a distinction between immature, mature, and older people whose physical powers are waning. In these societies old age often has profound significance, bringing with it the period of greatest respect (for women it may mean the first social equality with men). Rarely are the elderly shunted aside or abandoned. Even the Inuit, who are often cited as a people who literally abandon their aged relatives, do so only in truly desperate circumstances, when the group's physical survival is at stake. In all nonliterate societies, elders are the repositories of accumulated wisdom for their people. Recognized as such and no longer expected to carry out many subsistence activities, they play a major role in passing on cultural traditions to their grandchildren. For a nonliterate society to cast them aside would be analogous to closing down all the schools, archives, and libraries in a modern industrial state.

In the United States people rely on the written word, rather than on their elders, for long-term memory. Moreover, people have become so accustomed to rapid change that they tend to assume that the experiences of their grandparents and others of their generation are hardly relevant to them in "today's world." Indeed, retirement from earning a living is often con-

strued as a sign that one has nothing further to offer society and should stay out of the way of those who are younger. "The symbolism of the traditional gold watch (once a customary retirement gift) is all too plain: you should have made your money by now, and your time has run out. The watch will merely tick off the hours that remain between the end of adulthood and death."[2]

Elder status in North America is becoming even more problematic because senior citizens 65 years and older now constitute nearly 13 percent of the overall population, and experts predict their numbers will swell to about 70 million (20 percent of the overall population) by 2030.[3] With more and more people living longer, achieving old age seems less of an accomplishment than it once did and so commands less respect. An increasingly common view of the elderly is that they are unproductive and, even worse, a serious economic burden. The ultimate irony is that in the United States all of the ingenuity of modern science is used to keep alive the bodies of individuals who, in virtually every other way, society pushes aside.

In the institutionalization of age, cultural rather than biological factors are of prime importance in determining social status. All human societies recognize a number of life stages; precisely how they are defined varies from one culture to another. Out of this recognition they establish patterns of activity, attitudes, prohibitions, and obligations. In some instances, these are designed to help the transition from one age to another, to teach needed skills, or to lend economic assistance. Often they are taken as the basis for the formation of organized groups.

Institutions of Age Grouping

An organized category of people with membership on the basis of age is known as an **age grade.** Theoretically speaking, membership in an age grade ought to be automatic: One reaches the appropriate age and so is included, without question, in the particular age grade. Just such situations exist, for example, among the East African Tiriki, whose system we will examine shortly. Sometimes, though, individuals must buy their way into the age grade for which they are eligible. This was the case among some of the Indians of North America's plains, who required boys to purchase the appropriate costumes, dances, and songs for age-grade membership. In societies where entrance fees are expensive, not all people eligible for membership in a particular age grade may actually be able to join.

age grade An organized category of people based on age; every individual passes through a series of such categories over his or her lifetime.

---

[2]Turnbull, C. M. (1983). *The human cycle* (p. 229). New York: Simon & Schuster.

---

[3]U.S. Department of Commerce, Census Bureau, January 2000.

Entry into and transfer out of age grades may be accomplished individually, either by a biological distinction, such as puberty, or by a socially recognized status, such as marriage or childbirth. Whereas age-grade members may have much in common, may engage in similar activities, may cooperate with one another, and may share the same orientation and aspirations, their membership may not be entirely parallel with physiological age. A specific time is often ritually established for moving from a younger to an older grade. An example of this is the traditional Jewish ceremony of the bar mitzvah (a Hebrew term meaning "son of the commandment"), marking that a 13-year-old boy has reached the age of religious duty and responsibility.

Although members of senior groups commonly expect deference from and acknowledge certain responsibilities to their juniors, this does not necessarily mean that one grade is seen as better, or worse, or even more important than another. There can be standardized competition (opposition) between age grades, such as that traditionally between first-year students and sophomores on U.S. college campuses. Individuals can, comparably, accept the realities of being a teenager without feeling the need to prove anything. In addition to age grades, some societies feature *age sets* (sometimes referred to as *age classes*). An **age set** is a formally established group of people born during a certain time span who move through the series of age-grade categories together. Age sets, unlike age grades, do not cease to exist after a specified number of years; the members of an age set usually remain closely associated throughout their lives.

There has been some argument among anthropologists over the relative strength, cohesiveness, and stability that go into an age grouping. The age-set notion implies strong feelings of loyalty and mutual support. Because such groups may possess property, songs, shield designs, and rituals and are internally organized for collective decision making and leadership, a distinction is

called for between them and simple age grades. One also may distinguish between transitory age grades—which initially concern younger men (sometimes women too) but become less important and disintegrate as the members grow older—and the comprehensive systems that affect people through the whole of their lives.

Age Grouping in African Societies

Although age is a criterion for group membership in many parts of the world, its most varied and elaborate use is found in Africa, south of the Sahara. An example may be seen among the Tiriki, one of several pastoral nomadic groups living in Kenya.[4] In this society, each boy born within a 15-year period becomes a member of a particular age set then open for membership. Seven such named age sets exist, only one of which is open for membership at a time; when membership in one is closed, the next one is open for a 15-year period, and so on, until the

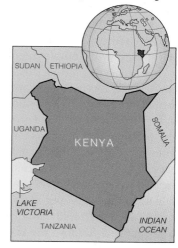

---

[4]Sangree, W. H. (1965). The Bantu Tiriki of Western Kenya. In J. L. Gibbs, Jr. (Ed.), *Peoples of Africa* (pp. 69–72). New York: Holt, Rinehart and Winston.

age set A formally established group of people born during a certain time span who move through the series of age grade categories together.

In many societies it is common for children of the same age to play, eat, and learn together, such as these East African Maasai boys, who are gathering for the first time to receive instruction for their initiation into an age grade. As members of the same age set, they will move together through a series of age grades in the course of their lives.

© Bruce Davidson/Earth Scenes

passage of 105 years (7 times 15), when the first set once again takes in new "recruits."

Members of Tiriki age sets remain together for life as they move through four age grades: Advancement occurs at 15-year intervals at the same time one age set closes and another opens for membership. Each age grade has its particular duties and responsibilities. Traditionally, the first, or "Warrior" age grade, served as guardians of the country, and members gained renown through fighting. Since colonial times, however, this traditional function has fallen by the wayside with the cessation of warfare, and members of this age grade now find excitement and adventure by leaving their community for extended employment or study elsewhere.

The next age grade, the "Elder Warriors," had few specialized tasks in earlier days beyond learning skills they would need later on by assuming an increasing share of administrative activities. For example, they would chair the postfuneral gatherings held to settle property claims after someone's death. Traditionally, Elder Warriors also served as envoys between elders of different communities. Nowadays, they hold nearly all of the administrative and executive roles opened up by the creation and growth of a centralized Tiriki administrative bureaucracy.

"Judicial Elders," the third age grade, traditionally handled most tasks connected with the administration and settlement of local disputes. Today, they still serve as the local judiciary body. Members of the "Ritual Elders," the senior age grade, used to preside over the priestly functions of ancestral shrine observances on the household level, at subclan meetings, at semiannual community appeals, and at rites of initiation into the various age grades. They also were credited with access to special magical powers. With the decline of ancestor worship over the past several decades, many of these traditional functions have been lost, and no new ones have arisen to take their places. Nonetheless, Ritual Elders continue to hold the most important positions in the initiation ceremonies, and their power as sorcerers and expungers of witchcraft are still recognized.

GROUPING BY COMMON INTEREST

The rise of urban, industrialized societies in which individuals are commonly separated from their kin has led to a proliferation of **common-interest associations**—associations that result from an act of joining and are based on sharing particular activities, objectives, values, or beliefs. As anthropologist Meredith Small observes,

> We often imprint lines of kinship on friends and colleagues, transferring familial expectations onto those with whom we share time but not blood or genes or vows, so that we can have the experience of an extended family. Young people join gangs, older people join clubs, and even babies are put into play groups. Pushed by a culture that favors independence and self-reliance, the social animal in us nonetheless seeks connections, even if they are bloodless and fragile.[5]

Moreover, common-interest associations help with such problems as learning to cope with life in a new and bewildering environment, or learning a new language or mannerisms necessary for the change from village to city, or one country to another. Because common-interest associations are by nature flexible, they have

common-interest associations Associations that result from an act of joining based on sharing particular activities, objectives, values, or beliefs.

---

[5]Small, M. F. (2000). Kinship envy. *Natural History, 109*(2), 88.

VISUAL COUNTERPOINT The diversity of common-interest associations is astounding, as these two photos suggest.

often been turned to, both in cities and in traditional villages, as a way of filling these needs. Common-interest associations are not, however, restricted to modernizing societies alone. They also are found in many traditional societies, and there is reason to believe they arose with the emergence of the first horticultural villages. Furthermore, associations in traditional societies may be just as complex and highly organized as those of countries such as the United States and Canada.

Common-interest associations have often been referred to in the anthropological literature as *voluntary associations,* but this term is misleading. The act of joining may range from fully voluntary to one required by law. For example, in the United States, under the draft laws individuals often became members of the armed forces without choosing to join. It is not really compulsory to join a labor union, but unless one does, one cannot work in a union shop. What the term *voluntary association* really refers to are those associations not based on sex, age, kinship, marriage, or territory that result from an act of joining. The act often may be voluntary, but it does not have to be.

Kinds of Common-Interest Associations

The variety of common-interest associations is astonishing. In the United States, they include such diverse entities as women's clubs of all sorts, street gangs, private militias, sport and service clubs, Parent Teacher Associations, churches and other religious organizations, political parties, labor unions, environmental organizations, human rights organizations such as Amnesty International—the list could go on and on. Their goals may include the pursuit of friendship, recreation, and

promotion of certain values, as well as governing and the pursuit or defense of economic interests. Associations also have served to preserve traditional songs, history, language, and moral beliefs among various ethnic minorities; the Tribal Unions of West Africa, for example, continue to serve this purpose. Similar organizations, often operating secretly, have kept traditions alive among North American Indians, who are undergoing a resurgence of ethnic pride despite generations of schooling designed to stamp out their cultural identity.

Another significant force in the formation of associations may be a supernatural experience common to all members. The Crow Indian Tobacco Society, the secret associations of the Kwakiutl Indians of British Columbia with cycles of rituals known only to initiates, and the Kachina associations of the Hopi Indians are well-known examples. Among other traditional forms of association are military, occupational, political, and entertainment groups that parallel such familiar organizations as the American Legion, labor unions, block associations, college fraternities and sororities, not to mention co-ops of every kind.

In nonindustrial societies, such organizations are frequently exclusive, but a prevailing characteristic is their concern for the general well-being of an entire village or group of villages. The rain that falls as a result of the work of Hopi rainmakers nourishes the crops of members and nonmembers alike.

MEDIATREK

To gain access to a vast range of service and common-interest groups, go to MediaTrek 11.1 on the companion Web site or CD-ROM.

Courtesy of International Indian Treaty Council

Nongovernmental organizations such as the International Indian Treaty Council are common-interest associations that have arisen to promote the rights of indigenous peoples. Shown here are Antonio Gonzales of the Council and Chief Gideon James of Venetie, Alaska, testifying at the 54th session of the UN Commission on Human Rights at Geneva in 1998.

Men's and Women's Associations

In some societies women have not established formal common-interest associations to the extent men have because they live in male-dominated cultures that restrict them or because women are absorbed on the domestic front with the constant and often unpredictable demands of rearing children. Moreover, some functions of men's associations—such as military duties—often are culturally defined as purely for men or repugnant to women. In a number of the world's traditional societies, however, the opportunities for female sociability are so great that there may be little need for structured women's associations. A historical example of this can be found among the Indians of northeastern North America (including the Six Nations Iroquois discussed earlier). In these societies men spent extended periods off in the woods hunting, either by themselves or with a single companion. The women, by contrast, spent most of their time in their village and working in the nearby gardens in close everyday contact with all the other women of the community. Not only did they have many people to talk to, but they always had someone available to help with whatever tasks required assistance.

Still, as cross-cultural research makes clear, women often play important roles in associations of their own as well as in those in which men predominate. Among the Crow (Apsaroke) Indians, women participated in the secret Tobacco Society, in addition to their own exclusive groups. Throughout Africa women's social clubs complement the men's and are concerned with educating women, with crafts, and with charitable activities. In Sierra Leone, where once-simple dancing societies have developed under urban conditions into complex organizations with a set of new objectives, the dancing *compin* is made up of young women as well as men who together perform plays based on traditional music and dancing and raise money for various mutual-benefit causes.

Women's rights organizations, consciousness-raising groups, and professional organizations for women are examples of some of the associations arising directly or indirectly out of today's social climate. These groups cover the entire range of association formation, from simple friendship and support groups to associations centered on politics, sports, the arts, spirituality, charity, and economic endeavors—on a national and even international scale. If an unresolved point does exist in the matter of women's participation, it is in determining why women are excluded from associations in some societies, while in others their participation is essentially equal to that of men.

Associations in the Postindustrial World

In spite of the recent diversity and vitality of common-interest associations, some have noted a recent decline in participation in all sorts of these groups, at least in North America. Those who have observed this trend see it is part of a more general drop in civic participation. People are spending less time socializing with others in bars, at dinner parties, having friends over, and so on. One can only speculate on the causes, but they likely include further isolation of individuals as they spend more and more of their free time with home entertainment. For example, in the United States, adults spend an average of 4 hours each day watching television. Then, too, the frequency with which people move interferes with their ability to establish more than superficial friendship with others. Add to this the fact that North Americans work longer hours on

Increasingly common among women around the world are common-interest groups centered on sports, as seen in this photo of the Swedish national women's soccer team.

© Chris Trotman/New Sport/Corbis

average than people in almost all industrialized countries, leaving less time for socialization. In this connection, some have noted a 10 percent drop in civic participation for every 10 minutes of commuting time.

Finally, there is the rise of the Internet; as people spend more and more time online, they can stay in touch without having to leave home. The cyberworld has seen an explosion of what are, in effect, virtual common-interest associations, all of which have their own particular rules on matters such as what members may or may not post and how they should behave online. In short, common-interest associations may not be showing a decline so much as a transformation. As an example of this transformation, the following Original Study explores the use of the Internet by Native Americans and other indigenous peoples.

With new computer technology has come the rise of virtual online common-interest associations having to do with everything from ethnicity to hobbies to special education needs. This deaf Hopi woman can learn sign language and participate in chat rooms with other Native Americans as well as other deaf individuals.

Original Study

Digital Revolution: Indigenous Peoples in Cyberia

The current digital revolution is changing the world we all live in, and many indigenous communities are taking active part in this global transformation. Linking even the most remote corners of the world by fiberoptic cables, radio, and communication satellites orbiting the planet, modern cybertechnology enables anyone with access to Internet-connected computers to instantly communicate and exchange information. Lured by the promises and opportunities of the World Wide Web (www), hundreds of North American Indian communities (or First Nations) have already put up their own Web sites. With the help of powerful search engines, it is not difficult to navigate through cyberspace and discover the virtual home of one or another indigenous communities in Canada, the United States, New Zealand, or elsewhere in the world.

The idea of the Internet started in 1962. Initially developed for U.S. military purposes during the Cold War, it quickly expanded to academic institutions. As soon as a special networking protocol was developed 10 years later, widely dispersed computer networks were "inter-

netted." From then on, electronically linked machines could instantly communicate and exchange information. Soon, commercial services began to offer access to the Internet, resulting in an explosive growth rate in cyberspace development. Essential graphical browser software to design and put up Web sites was developed in 1992. Precisely 500 years after Columbus' "discovery" of the Americas, another "New World" had emerged—the www.

Immediately, technologically more advanced institutions, media organizations, and commercial companies rushed to post their own sites on the www. Within the first year, the Web expanded from a handful to several thousand sites. With the growth rate doubling every six months, there are now millions. Although most Internet users reside in wealthy industrialized countries, hundreds of millions across the globe now participate in this electronic communication revolution.

Allowing instant gathering and spreading of almost unlimited information, the Internet renders it difficult for governments and corporate print and

broadcast media to be gatekeepers of information. Widely recognized as an effective collaboration tool for local, regional, national, and global political organizations, cultural institutions, businesses, and so on, the Internet has also been adopted as an effective communications medium by many indigenous communities. Quickly recognizing its strategic potential for global networking, information sharing, marketing, and political action, as well as other functions, a myriad of indigenous organizations and enterprises have become active on the Internet and have posted their own Web sites.

As early as May 1994, even before the U.S. President's Office in the White House made its presence known on the WWW, the Oneida Indian Nation, one of the six Iroquois nations still residing in upstate New York, had posted its own Web site, *oneida-nation.net*. Emblazoned on its home page is its official seal, depicting the Iroquois Confederacy wampum belt superimposed on a green pine tree with an eagle perched atop, all on a field of red. The site reports news and events and offers basic information

[CONTINUED]

[CONTINUED]

about Iroquois cultural history, clans, wampum belts, and treaties. In addition to Web pages devoted to the Oneida cultural center, it contains links to pages dealing with the controversial Oneida Indian land claim (including an email address for comments and questions). There are links to Oneida-owned business enterprises, government resources, and other indigenous Web sites; the site also hosts a special communication section for a number of smaller Indian communities in the region that do not yet have their own Internet capabilities.

In Canada, the first indigenous group to launch its own Web site was the Blackfoot Confederacy in Alberta, organized as the Treaty 7 First Nation Reserves Interband Council (in September 1995). These Blackfoot Indians mark their virtual headquarters (*www.treaty7.org*) with a logo of its own "coat of arms"—a shield with five eagle feathers dangling down, a stylized thunderbird doubling as a mountain range, a yellow sun at the top, and a crossed spear and stone tomahawk at the center. The Blackfoot also took the initiative to establish Canada's first Native Internet server, which provides links to a host of other Indian Web sites. Capitalizing on their modern electronic communications skills, they also offer multimedia development services through a special computing and Internet services department. These services include video digitizing, editing, and titling, as well as photo/document scanning and editing, video,

audio, graphics design and animation production in 2D and 3D, as well as CD-ROM production.

Today, taking an excursion through virtual "Indian Country," one may even opt for a guided cybertour, choosing from a dozen or so indigenous "Web rings." For instance, the Seminole Tribe in Florida runs the Indian Web ring, while the Lac d'Oreille Ojibway own the Native People's Ring. One of the most heavily trafficked indigenous Web rings is The Native Trail, which interconnects about 600 Canadian Native and Native-related sites. Some of these Web rings offer cybermaps to a wide range of clearly marked and hyperlinked indigenous Web sites. These sites are not only of value to widely dispersed members of indigenous communities but, for various reasons, must also appeal to outside visitors. Typically identifiable as "Indian," these sites are often beautifully designed with stereotypical images such as eagles, buffalo skulls, feathers, calumets (ceremonial pipes), tipis, war bonnets, petroglyphs (rock etchings), or wild animal tracks.

Especially since 1997, the Internet has made deep inroads on other indigenous peoples scattered throughout the world. Tens of thousands, often living far away from their home villages, log on frequently to stay in touch with one another, trying to stay informed about their relatives and friends and letting one another know about gossip, political news, and special celebrations. Through

the Internet, they seek to maintain a sense of cultural belonging in spite of the enormous geographic distances that may separate them from their native homes.

Although indigenous peoples are proportionally underrepresented in cyberspace—for obvious reasons such as economic poverty, technological inexperience, linguistic isolation, political repression, and/or cultural resistance—the Internet has vastly extended traditional networks of information and communication. Greatly enhancing the visibility of otherwise marginal communities and individuals, the information superhighway enables even very small and isolated indigenous communities to expand their sphere of influence and mobilize political support in their struggles for cultural survival. In addition to maintaining contact with their own communities, indigenous peoples also use the Internet to connect with other such widely dispersed groups in the world. Today, it is not unusual for a Mi'kmaq in Newfoundland to go on the Internet and communicate with individuals belonging to other remote groups such as the Maori in New Zealand, Saami in Norway, Kuna in Panama, or Navajo in Arizona. Together with the rest of us, they have pioneered across the new cultural frontier and are now surfing daily through Cyberia. *(By H. E. L. Prins. (2000). Digital revolution: Indigenous peoples in Cyberia. Manuscript © by author, Department of Anthropology, Kansas State University.)*

GROUPING BY SOCIAL RANK IN STRATIFIED SOCIETIES

The study of social class and other categories of social stratification involves the examination of distinctions that, when we think about them, strike us as unfair and even outrageous. Yet social stratification is a common and powerful phenomenon in some of the world's societies. Especially urban civilizations with their large and heterogeneous populations, are invariably stratified.

stratified societies Societies in which people are divided or ranked into social tiers and do not share equally in the basic resources that support life, influence, and prestige.

Basically, **stratified societies** are those in which people are hierarchically divided or ranked into social strata, or layers, and do not share equally in basic resources that support survival, influence, and prestige. Members of low-ranked strata typically have fewer privileges and less power than those in higher ranked strata. In addition, the restrictions and obligations they face are usually more oppressive, and they must work harder for less reward. In short, social stratification amounts to institutionalized inequality. Without ranking—high versus low—no stratification exists; social differences without this do not constitute stratification. In the United States, Hispanic, African American, and American Indian groups are among those who have struggled with their positions in the low-ranked strata. As profiled in this

Anthropology Applied

Anthropologists and Social Impact Assessment

A kind of policy research anthropologists frequently do is a social impact assessment, which entails collection of data about a community or neighborhood for planners of development projects. Such an assessment seeks to determine a project's effect by determining how and upon whom its impact will fall and whether the impact is likely to be positive or negative. In the United States, any project requiring a federal permit or license, or using federal funds, by law must be preceded by a social impact assessment as part of the environmental review process. Examples of such projects include highway construction, urban renewal, water diversion schemes, and land reclamation. Often, projects of these sorts are sited so that their impact falls most heavily on neighborhoods or communities inhabited by people in low socioeconomic strata, sometimes because the projects are seen as ways of improving the lives of poor people and sometimes because the poor people are seen as having less political power to block proposals that others conceive as (sometimes rightly, sometimes wrongly) in "the public interest."

As an illustration of this kind of work, anthropologist Sue Ellen Jacobs was hired to do a social impact assessment of a water diversion project in New Mexico planned by the Bureau of Land Reclamation in cooperation with the Bureau of Indian Affairs. This project proposed construction of a diversion

dam and an extensive canal system for irrigation on the Rio Grande. Affected by this would be twenty-two communities inhabited primarily by Spanish Americans, as well as two Indian Pueblos. In the region, unemployment was high and the project was seen as a way to promote a perceived trend to urbanism (which theoretically would be associated with industrial development), while bringing new land into production for intensive agriculture.

What the planners failed to take into account was that both the Hispanic and Indian populations were heavily committed to farming for household consumption, with some surpluses raised for the market, using a system of irrigation canals established as long as 300 years ago. These canals are maintained by elected supervisors who know the communities as well as the requirements of the land and crops, water laws, and ditch management skills. Such individuals can allocate water equitably in times of scarcity and can prevent and resolve conflict in the realm of water and land use, as well as in community life beyond the ditches. Under the proposed project, this system was to be given up in favor of one in which fewer people would control larger tracts of land, and water allocation would be in the hands of a government technocrat. One of the strongest measures of local government would be lost.

Not surprisingly, Jacobs discovered widespread community opposition to this project, and her report helped convince Congress that any positive impact was far outweighed by negative effects. One of the major objections to the construction of the project was that it would result in the obliteration of the 3 hundred-year-old irrigation system structures. Project planners did not seem to recognize the antiquity and cultural significance of the traditional irrigation system. These were referred to as "temporary diversion structures." The fact that the old dams associated with the ditches were attached to local descent groups was simply not recognized by the official documents.[a]

Other negative effects of the project, besides loss of local control, would be problems associated with population growth and relocation, loss of fishing and other river-related resources, and new health hazards, including increased threat of drowning, insect breeding, and airborne dust. Finally, physical transformation of the communities' life space was likely to result in changes in the context of the informal processes of enculturation that take place within the communities. ■ ■ ■

[a] Van Willigen, J. (1986). *Applied anthropology* (p. 169). South Hadley, MA: Bergin and Garvey.

---

chapter's Anthropology Applied, their needs are often ignored in development efforts.

Stratified societies stand in sharp contrast to **egalitarian societies,** in which everyone has about equal access to and power over basic resources. As we saw in Chapter 6, foraging societies are characteristically egalitarian, although there are some exceptions. Such societies have as many valued positions as people capable of filling them. Hence, individuals depend mostly on their own abilities for their positions in society. A poor hunter may become a good hunter if he has the ability; he is not excluded from such a prestigious position because he comes from a group of poor hunters. Poor hunters do not constitute a social stratum. Furthermore, they have as much right to their society's resources as any other of

its members. No one can deny a poor hunter a fair share of food, the right to be heard when important decisions are to be made, or anything else to which a man is entitled.

Social Class and Caste

A **social class** may be defined as a category of individuals of equal or nearly equal prestige according to the system of evaluation. The qualification "nearly equal" is

> *egalitarian societies* Societies in which everyone has about equal access to and power over basic resources.
> *social class* A category of individuals who enjoy equal or nearly equal prestige according to the system of evaluation.

Despite their close association, the clothing worn by these two individuals and the way they interact clearly indicate they are of different social classes.

important, for a certain amount of inequality may occur even within a given class. If this is so, to an outside observer low-ranking individuals in an upper class may not seem much different from the highest ranking members of a lower class. Yet marked differences exist when the classes are compared as wholes with one another. The point here is that class distinctions are not clear-cut and obvious in societies such as those of North America that have a continuous range of differential privileges, for example, from virtually none to many. Such a continuum can be divided into classes in a variety of ways. If fine distinctions are made, then many classes may be recognized. If, however, only a few major distinctions are made, then only a few classes will be recognized. Thus, some speak of North American society as divided into three classes: lower, middle, and upper. Others speak of several classes: lower lower, middle lower, upper lower, lower middle, and so forth.

A **caste** is a closed social class in which membership is not based on personal achievement or wealth but

caste A closed social class in which membership is determined by birth and fixed for life.

determined by birth and fixed for life. The opposite of the principle that all humans are born equal, the caste system is based on the principle that humans neither are nor can be equal. Castes are strongly endogamous, and offspring are automatically members of their parents' caste. The classic ethnographic example is the traditional Hindu caste system of India. Perhaps the world's longest surviving social hierarchy, it encompasses a complex ranking of social groups on the basis of "ritual purity." Each of the numerous different castes considers itself as a distinct community higher or lower than other castes, although their particular ranking varies among geographic regions and over time. The different castes are associated with specific occupations and customs, such as food habits and styles of dress, along with rituals involving notions of purity and pollution. Differences in status are traditionally justified by the religious doctrine of karma, a belief that one's place in life is determined by one's deeds in previous lifetimes.

All these more than 2,000 castes, or *jatis,* are organized into four basic orders or *varnas* (literally meaning "colors"), distinguished partly by occupation and ranked in order of descending religious status of purity. The religious foundation for this social hierarchy is found in a sacred text known as the Laws of Manu, an ancient work about 2,000 years old

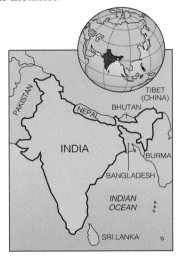

and considered by traditional Hindus as the highest authority on their cultural institutions. It defines the *Brahmans* as the purest and therefore highest varna. As priests and lawgivers, Brahmans represent the world of religion and learning. Next comes the order of fighters and rulers, known as the *Kshatriyas.* Below them are the *Vaisyas* (merchants and traders), who are engaged in commercial, agricultural, and pastoral pursuits. At the bottom are the *Shudras* (artisans and laborers), an order required to serve the other three varnas and who also make a living by handicrafts. Falling outside the varna system is a fifth category of degraded individuals known as "untouchables" or *Dalits.* Considered the most impure of all people, these outcasts can own neither land nor the tools of their trade. Untouchables constitute a large pool of cheap labor at the beck and call of those controlling economic and political affairs. In an effort to bestow some dignity on these poverty-stricken victims of the caste system, Hindu nationalist leader Mahatma Gandhi renamed them *harijan* or "children of God."

Although India's national constitution of 1950 sought to abolish caste discrimination and the practice of untouchability, the caste system remains deeply entrenched in Hindu culture and is still widespread throughout southern Asia, especially in rural India. In what has been called India's "hidden apartheid," entire villages in many Indian states remain completely segregated by caste. Representing about 15 percent of India's population—or some 160 million people—the widely scattered Dalits endure near complete social isolation, humiliation, and discrimination based exclusively on their birth status. Even a Dalit's shadow is believed to pollute the upper castes. They may not cross the line dividing their part of the village from that occupied by higher castes, drink water from public wells, or visit the same temples as the higher castes. Dalit children are still often made to sit at the back of classrooms.

MEDIATREK

For an audio-visual report on India's caste system presented by National Public Radio (including links to other sites on the subject, such as Human Rights Watch 2001 report on caste discrimination), go to MediaTrek 11.2 on the companion Web site or CD-ROM.

Although some argue that the term *caste* should be restricted to the Indian situation, others find this much too narrow a usage, since castelike situations are known elsewhere in the world. In Bolivia, Ecuador, and several other South and Central American countries, for example, the wealthy upper class is almost exclusively white and rarely intermarries with people of non-European descent. In contrast, the lower class of working poor in those countries is primarily made up of American Indian laborers and peasants. Racial segregation also existed in the United States, where the nation's upper class was made up exclusively of individuals of white European descent. After the American Revolution, several states in New England joined Virginia and other southern states and made it illegal for whites to marry blacks or American Indians. After the U.S. federal government officially abolished slavery in 1863, these anti-miscegenation laws remained in force in many states from Maine to Florida for several decades. In 1924, Virginia's General Assembly passed the Racial Integrity Act to prevent light-skinned individuals with some African ancestry from "passing" as whites. Known as the "one-drop" rule, it codified the idea of white racial purity by classifying individuals as black if just one of their multiple ancestors was of African origin ("one drop of Negro blood"). However light-skinned, they were subject to a wide range of discriminatory practices not applicable to whites. Such institutionalized racial discrimination continued for a century after slavery was abolished, and today self-segregation exists in many parts of the United States. Despite U.S. civil rights laws passed in the 1960s (prohibiting discrimination in accommodations, schools, employment, and voting for reasons of color, race, religion, or national origin), ethnic inequality persists in which the typical African American household has 54 cents of income and 12 cents of wealth for every corresponding dollar in the typical white American household.[6]

Another castelike social system based on skin color and wealth exists in South Africa where a white minority created a political regime known as apartheid ("aparthood"), which relegated indigenous black Africans to a low-ranking stratum in a racially divided society. Although the foundations for the policy of strict racial segregation were laid earlier, apartheid became national law in 1948. During the next few decades, the white minority in control of the South African government issued a series of racist laws and regulations creating a social order privileging whites and discriminating against blacks. From then on, the government policy of racial segregation affected every level of social existence. It not only prohibited racially mixed marriages, but laws also stipulated where blacks were allowed to live, work, and play. Invading private lives, apartheid laws even made interracial sexual relations a crime. In the early 1960s, South Africa's apartheid regime declared that territories historically inhabited by South Africa's indigenous nations such as the Swazi, Xhosa, and Zulu were to become semi-independent countries known as homelands. According to the apartheid regime, blacks were allowed to own property in these black homelands, but could not own land in vast areas exclusively reserved for white settlement. Internationally isolated and facing growing problems within the country, the South African government finally agreed to abolish the apartheid system in 1993. A year later, following the deeply divided country's first all-race multiparty elections, Nelson Mandela became South Africa's first non-white president. Today, more than a decade after the abolition of apartheid, the white minority no longer controls the government, and racial policies are no longer in effect. In daily practice, however, segregation still exists; few whites can be found in South Africa's vast underclass of have-nots, who are almost all black.

All of this brings to mind the concepts of ritual purity and pollution so basic to the Indian caste system. In South Africa, whites feared pollution of their purity through improper contact with blacks. In India and South Africa, untouchables and blacks comprised categories of landless or near-landless people who served as a body of mobile laborers always available for exploitation by those in political control. A similar mobile labor force of landless men at the state's disposal emerged in China as many as 2,200 years ago.

Paradoxically, at the very same time that South Africa has changed its system, a new castelike underclass has

[6]Boshara, R. (2003, January/February). Wealth inequality: The $6,000 solution. *Atlantic Monthly*.

Biocultural Connection

African Burial Ground Project

In 1991, construction workers in lower Manhattan unearthed what turned out to be New York City's African Burial Ground, the final resting place of some 10,000 enslaved African captives brought to New York in the 17th and 18th centuries to build the city and provide the labor for its thriving economy. The discovery sparked controversy as the African American public held protests and prayer vigils to stop the part of a federal building project that nearly destroyed the site. A research team led by biological anthropologist Michael Blakey, then at Howard University, worked together with the descendant African American community to develop a plan that included both extensive biocultural research and the humane retention of the sacred nature of the site ultimately through reburial and the creation of a fitting memorial. The research also involved archaeological and historical studies that used a broad African diaspora context for understanding the lifetime experiences of these people who were enslaved and buried in New York.

Studying a sample population of 419 individuals from the burial ground, Blakey and his team used an exhaustive range of skeletal biological methods, producing a database containing more than 200,000 observations of genetics, morphology, age, sex, growth and development, muscle development, trauma, nutrition, and disease. The bones revealed an unmistakable biocultural connection: physical wear and tear of an entire community brought on by the social institution of slavery. We now know, based on this study, that life for Africans in colonial New York was characterized by poor nutrition, grueling physical labor that enlarged and often tore muscles, and death rates that were unusually high for 15- to 25-year old people. Many of these young adults died soon after arriving on slaving ships. Few Africans lived past 40 years of age, and less than 2 percent lived beyond 55. Church records show strikingly different mortality trends for the Europeans of New York: About eight times as many English as Africans lived past 55 years of age, and mortality in adolescence and the early 20s was relatively low.

Skeletal research also showed that those Africans who died as children and were most likely to have been born in New York exhibited stunted and disrupted growth and exposure to high levels of lead pollution—unlike those with evidence of having been born in Africa (filed teeth). Fertility was very low among enslaved women in New York, and infant mortality was high. In these respects, this northern colonial city was very similar to South Carolina and the Caribbean to which its economy was tied—regions where conditions for African captives were among the harshest.

Individuals in this deeply troubling burial ground came from warring African states including Calibar, Asante, Benin, Dahomey, Congo, Madagascar, and many others—states that wrestled with the European demand for human chattel. They resisted their enslavement through rebellion, and they resisted their dehumanization by carefully burying their dead and preserving what they could of their cultures. *(By Michael Blakey. (2003). African burial ground project. Manuscript © by author, Department of Anthropology, College of William & Mary.)* ■ ■ ■

---

emerged in the United States, as automation has reduced the need for unskilled workers, and downsizing has taken place. This underclass accounts for about 20 percent of the total U.S. population, and its members consist of unemployed, unemployable, or drastically underemployed people who own little, if any, property and who live "out on the streets" or—at best—in urban or rural slums. Lacking both economic and political power, they have no access to the kinds of educational facilities that would enable them or their children to improve their lot. Under conditions of significant unemployment, this new underclass has served the economy by ensuring a significant incidence of permanent unemployment, thereby making the employed feel less secure in their jobs. As a consequence, the employed were apt to be less demanding of wages and benefits from their employers. Now, with outright unemployment at historically low levels, the underclass (as in China, India, and South Africa) provides a pool of cheap labor.

India, South Africa, China, and the United States—all very different countries, in different parts of the world and with different ideologies—have produced a similar phenomenon. Is there something about the structure of socially stratified states that sooner or later produces some sort of exploitable, impoverished outcast group? The answer to this is up for debate. Certainly the issue has caught the attention of anthropologists and other social scientists.

The basis of social class structure is role differentiation. Some role differentiation, of course, exists in any society, at least along the lines of gender and age. Furthermore, any necessary role will always be valued to some degree. In a food-foraging society, the role of "good hunter" will be valued. The fact that one man may already play that role does not, however, prevent another man from playing it, too, in an egalitarian society. Therefore, role differentiation by itself is not sufficient for stratification. Two more ingredients are necessary: formalized evaluation of roles involving attitudes such as like/dislike or admiration/revulsion and restricted access to the more highly valued roles. Obviously, the greater the diversity of roles in a society, the more complex evaluation and restriction can become. Since great role diversity is most charac-

VISUAL COUNTERPOINT Homeless men sleeping on sidewalks—one in India, one in the United States. Outcast groups such as India's untouchables are a common feature of stratified societies. In the United States, 20 to 23 percent of the population is trapped in poverty. A disproportionate number in this underclass are African Americans, many still victimized by discrimination that is a remnant of slavery.

teristic of civilizations, centrally organized state societies in which large numbers of people live in cities, it is not surprising they provide the greatest opportunities for stratification. Furthermore, the large size and heterogeneity of populations in civilizations create a need for classifying people into a manageable number of social categories. Small wonder, then, that social stratification is one of the defining characteristics of an urban civilization.

Social classes are manifest in several ways. One is through **verbal evaluation**—what people say about others in their own society. For this, anything can be singled out for attention and spoken of favorably or unfavorably: political, military, religious, economic, or professional roles; wealth and property; kinship; physical qualities (skin color, for example); community activity; linguistic dialect; and a host of other traits. Cultures do this differently, and what may be spoken of favorably in one may be spoken of unfavorably in another and ignored in a third. Furthermore, cultural values may change, so that something regarded favorably at one time may not be at another. This is one reason why a researcher may be misled by verbal evaluation, for what people say may not correspond completely with social reality. As an example, the official language of Egypt is Classical Arabic, the language of the Koran (the holiest of Islamic texts). Though it is highly valued, no one in Egypt uses this language in daily interaction; rather, it is for official documents or on formal occasions. Those most proficient in it are not of the upper class but, rather, of the lower middle classes. These are the people educated in the public schools (where Classical Arabic is the language of schooling) and who hold jobs in the government bureaucracy (which requires the most use of Classical Arabic). Upper-class Egyptians, by contrast, go to private schools, where they learn the foreign languages essential for success in diplomacy and (in the global economy) business and industry.[7]

Social classes also are manifest through patterns of association—not just who interacts with whom but how and in what context. In Western society, informal, friendly relations take place mostly within one's own class. Relations with members of other classes tend to be less informal and occur in the context of specific situations. For example, a corporate executive and a janitor normally are members of different social classes. They may have frequent contact with each other, but it occurs in the setting of the corporate offices and usually requires certain stereotyped behavior patterns.

A third way social classes are manifest is through **symbolic indicators.** Included here are activities and possessions indicative of class. For example, in North American society, occupation (a garbage collector has different class status than a physician); wealth (rich people—see Figure 11.1—generally are in a higher social class than poor people); dress (we have all heard the expression "white collar" versus "blue collar"); form of recreation (upper-class people are expected to play golf rather than shoot pool down at the pool hall—but they can shoot pool at home or in a club); residential location (upper-class people do not ordinarily live in slums); kind of car; and so on. The fact is all sorts of status symbols are indicative of class position, including measures such as how many bathrooms a person's house has. At the same time, symbolic

---

[7]Haeri, N. (1997). The reproduction of symbolic capital: Language, state, and class in Egypt. *Current Anthropology, 38*, 795–816.

verbal evaluation What people in a stratified society say about others in their society.
symbolic indicators In a stratified society, activities and possessions indicative of social class.

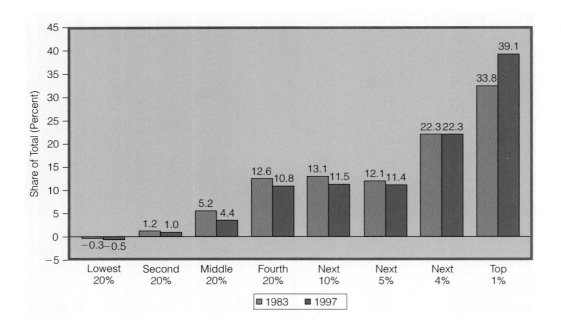

FIGURE 11.1

Wealth inequality has grown in the 1990s. As of 1997 (the latest year for available data), the top 1 percent of U.S. households controlled 39.1 percent of all wealth. When comparing the changes in wealth distribution over the 1983–1997 period, the large shift in wealth primarily benefited the top 1 percent (rising from 33.8 percent to 39.1 percent of all wealth). In comparison, the bottom 95 percent of the wealth distribution experienced falling growth in wealth over the same period.

indicators may be cruder reflections of class position than verbal indicators or patterns of association. One reason is that access to wealth may not be wholly restricted to upper classes, enabling individuals to buy symbols suggestive of upper-class status whether or not this really is their status. To take an extreme example, the head of an organized crime ring may display more of the symbols of high-class status (such as gold jewelry, tailor-made suits, and luxury cars) than may some members of old, established upper-class families. For that matter, someone from an upper class deliberately may choose a simpler lifestyle than is customary. Instead of driving a slick Mercedes SUV, he or she may drive a beat-up Volvo station wagon.

Symbolic indicators involve factors of lifestyle, but differences in life chances may also signal differences in class standing. Life is apt to be less hard for members of an upper class as opposed to a lower class. This shows up in a tendency for lower infant mortality and longer life expectancy for the upper class. There is also a tendency for greater physical stature and robustness among upper-class people, the result of better diet and protection from serious illness in their juvenile years.

social mobility The ability to change one's class position.
closed-class societies Stratified societies that severely restrict social mobility.

Social Mobility

All stratified societies offer at least some **social mobility,** and this helps to ease the strains inherent in any system of inequality. Even the Indian caste system, with its guiding ideology that all hierarchical social arrangements within it are fixed, has a degree of flexibility and mobility, not all of it associated with the recent changes modernization has brought to India. As a rather dramatic case in point, in the Indian state of Rajasthan, those who own and control the most land and who are wealthy and politically powerful are not of the warrior caste, as one would expect, but of the lowest caste. Their tenants and laborers, by contrast, are Brahmans. Thus, the group that is ritually superior to all others finds itself in the same social position as untouchables, whereas the landowners who are the Brahmans' ritual inferiors are superior in all other ways. Meanwhile, a group of leatherworkers in the untouchable category, who have gained political power in India's new democracy, are trying to better their position by claiming they are Brahmans who were tricked in the past into doing defiling work. Although individuals cannot move up or down the caste hierarchy, whole groups can do so depending on claims they can make for higher status and on how well they can manipulate others into acknowledging their claims.

With their limited mobility, caste-structured societies exemplify **closed-class societies.** Those that permit

© A. Ramey/PhotoEdit

© 1997 Joel Gordon

VISUAL COUNTERPOINT Symbolic indicators of class or caste include factors of lifestyle, such as the size and style of housing in which one lives.

a great deal of mobility are referred to as **open-class societies.** Yet even in these, mobility is apt to be more limited than one might suppose. In the United States, despite its rags-to-riches ideology, most mobility involves a move up or down only a notch, although if this continues in a family over several generations, it may add up to a major change. Nonetheless, U.S. society makes much of relatively rare examples of great upward mobility consistent with its cultural values and does its best to ignore, or at least downplay, the numerous cases of little or no upward, not to mention downward, mobility.

The degree of mobility in a stratified society is related to the prevailing kind of family organization. In societies where the extended family is the usual form, mobility is apt to be difficult, because each individual is strongly tied to the large family group. Hence, for a person to move up to a higher social class, his or her family must move up as well. Mobility is easier for independent nuclear families where the individual is closely tied to

fewer people. Moreover, under neolocal residence, individuals normally leave their family of birth. So it is, then, that through careful marriage, occupational success, and disassociation from the lower-class family in which they grew up, all of which are made possible by residential mobility, individuals can more easily "move up" in society.

Gender Stratification

Closely associated with class and caste stratification is the related phenomenon of gender stratification. For instance, in our earlier discussion of sex as an organizing principle, we saw that in some (but not all) societies, men and women may be regarded as unequal, with the for-

open-class societies Stratified societies that permit a great deal of social mobility.

© Beryl Goldberg

In industrial and postindustrial societies such as the United States, the ability to move up in the system of stratification is increasingly dependent upon access to higher education.

mer outranking the latter. Generally speaking, gender inequality is characteristic of societies stratified in other ways as well; thus women have historically occupied a position of inferiority to men in the class-structured societies of the Western world. Nevertheless, gender inequality sometimes may be seen in societies not otherwise stratified; in such instances, men and women are always physically as well as conceptually separated from each other. Yet, as the Iroquoian case cited earlier in this chapter demonstrates, not all societies in which men and women are separated exhibit gender stratification.

The rise of gender stratification often seems to be associated with the development of strongly centralized states. For example, among the Maya of Mesoamerica the basic social unit in the past as today was the complementary gender pair. On the household level, men raise the crops and bring in the other raw materials, which the women transform into food, textiles, and other cultural objects. The same complementarity existed in public ritual and politics, but about 2,100 years ago at the Maya city of Tikal, things began to change. With the development of strong dynastic rule by men, women began to be excluded from favored places for burial, their graves were not as richly stocked with material items as were those of

This carved stone lintel from the Maya city of Yaxchilan features a king with one of his wives. To the knowing eye it illustrates gender inequality, for the woman is shown only because of her relation to men: her husband the king, and her son who succeeded to kingship.

important men, they all but disappeared from public art, and they were rarely mentioned in inscriptions. When women were portrayed or mentioned, it was because of their relationship to a particular male ruler. Clearly, women came to hold a lesser place in Maya society than did men, although gender stratification was not nearly as marked at the grass roots of society as it was among the elite. When the Tikal state collapsed, as it did in the 9th century, the relationship of equality between men and women returned to what it had been 900 years before.[8]

Development of Stratification

Because social stratification of any kind generally makes life oppressive for large segments of a population, the lower classes are usually placated through religion, which promises them a better existence in the hereafter. If they have this to look forward to, they are more likely to accept an existing disadvantaged position. In India, for example, belief in reincarnation and the existence of an incorruptible supernatural power that assigns people to a particular caste position as a reward or punishment for the deeds and misdeeds of past lives justifies one's position in this life. If, however, individuals perform the duties appropriate to their caste in this lifetime, then they can expect to be reborn into a higher caste in a future existence. Truly exemplary performance of their duties may even release them from the cycle of rebirth, to be reunited with the divinity from which all existence springs. In the minds of orthodox Hindus, then, one's caste position is something earned (an achieved status) rather than the accident of birth (ascribed) as it appears to outside observers. Thus, although the caste system explicitly recognizes (and accepts as legitimate) inequality among people, it is underlain by an implicit assumption of ultimate equality. This contrasts with the situation in the United States, where the equality of all people is proclaimed even while various groups clearly are treated as unequal.

When considering the origin of social stratification, we must reckon with such common tendencies as the desire for prestige, either for oneself or one's group. Although the impulse need not result inevitably in the ranking of individuals or groups relative to one another, it sometimes may. For example, among the Iroquois and Hopi Indians of North America, the Sherente Indians of South America, and Ugandan peoples of East Africa, the superiority of some kinship lineages over others is recognized in electing chiefs, performing sacred rituals, and other special tasks, whether or not membership entails any economic advantages.

---

[8]Haviland, W. A. (1997). The rise and fall of sexual inequality: Death and gender at Tikal, Guatemala. *Ancient Mesoamerica, 8,* 1–12.

The high status of the two Maya kings shown in this painting from a pottery vessel is revealed by their jewelry, elaborate headdress, and the fact they sit on thrones. Among these people, stratification arose as certain lineages monopolized important offices.

This sort of situation could easily develop into full-fledged stratification. Just such a development may have taken place among the Maya of Mesoamerica.[9] These people began as horticulturists with a relatively egalitarian, kinship-based organization. By 2,600 years ago elaborate rituals had developed for dealing with the very serious problems of agriculture, such as uncertain rains, vulnerability of crops to a variety of pests, and periodic devastation from hurricanes. As this development took place, a full-time priesthood arose, along with some craft specialization in the service of religion. Out of the priesthood developed the hereditary ruling dynasties mentioned earlier. In this developmental process, certain lineages seem to have monopolized the important civic and ceremonial positions, and so came to be ranked above other lineages, forming the basis of an upper class.

Just as lineages may come to be ranked differentially relative to one another, so may ethnic groups. In South Africa, for example, Europeans came as conquerors, establishing a social order by which they could maintain their favored position. In the United States, as noted above, the importation of African slaves produced a severely disadvantaged castelike group at the bottom of the social order. Even without conquest and/or slavery, ethnic differences often are a factor in the definition of social classes and castes, as not only African Americans but also members of other North American minorities have experienced through the racial stereotyping that leads to social and economic disadvantages.

Although the cost is great—social classes do, after all, make life oppressive for large numbers of people—classes may nevertheless perform an integrative function in society. By cutting across some or all lines of kinship, residence, occupation, and age group, depending on the particular society, they counteract potential tendencies for society to fragment into discrete entities. In India, diverse national groups were incorporated into the larger society by certification of their leaders as warriors and by marriage of their

---

[9]Haviland, W. A. (2003). Tikal, Guatemala: A Maya way to urbanism. 3rd INAH Pennsylvania State University Conference on MesoAmerican Urbanism. Unpublished manuscript; Haviland, W. A. (1975). The ancient Maya and the evolution of urban society. *University of Colorado Museum of Anthropology Miscellaneous Series, 37;* and Haviland, W. A., & Moholy-Nagy, H. (1992). Distinguishing the high and mighty from the hoi polloi at Tikal, Guatemala. In A. F. Chase & D. Z. Chase (Eds.), *Mesoamerican elites: An archaeological assessment.* Norman: University of Oklahoma Press.

VISUAL COUNTERPOINT Although the caste system has been outlawed for some 50 years in India, huge, caste-based gaps in wealth, prestige, and power continue, as evidenced in these photos contrasting the palace of the Maharajas in Jaipur and the street shanties inhabited by low caste families in Bombay.

© Joel Gordon

In the United States, racial profiling is one of the means by which those who control society try to keep others "in their place."

women to Brahmans. The problem is that stratification, by its very nature, provides a means by which one, usually small, group of people may dominate and make life miserable for large numbers of others, as in South Africa where 4.5 million whites dominated 25 million non-whites. In India a succession of conquerors was able to move into the caste hierarchy near its top as warriors.

In any system of stratification, those who dominate proclaim their supposedly superior status, which they try to convert into respect, or at least acquiescence on the part of the lower classes. As anthropologist Laura Nader points out, "Systems of thought develop over time and reflect the interests of certain classes or groups in the society who manage to universalize their beliefs and values."[10] One sees this, for example, in religious ideologies that assert that the social order is divinely fixed and therefore not to be questioned. Thus, they hope that members of the lower classes will thereby "know their place" and not contest their domination by the "chosen elite." If, however, this domination is contested, the elite usually control the power of the state, which they use to protect their privileged position.

---

[10]Nader, L. (1997). Controlling processes: Tracing the dynamic components of power. *Current Anthropology, 38,* 271.

Chapter Summary

■ Grouping by gender separates men and women to varying degrees in different societies; in some, they may be together much of the time, while in others they may spend much of their time apart, even to the extreme of eating and sleeping separately. Although men in some sexually segregated societies perceive women to be their inferiors, in other societies men perceive women as equals.

■ Age grouping is another form of association that may augment or replace kinship grouping. An age grade is a category of people organized by age. Some societies have not only age grades, but also age sets, comprised of individuals who are initiated into an age grade at the same time and move together through a series of life stages. A specific time is often ritually established for moving from a younger to an older age grade. The most varied use of age grouping is found in African societies south of the Sahara. Among the Tiriki of East Africa, for example, seven named age sets pass through four successive age grades. Each age set embraces a 15-year span and so opens to accept new initiates every 105 years. In principle, the system resembles our college classes, where, say, the Class of 2004 (an age set) will move through the four age grades: first year, sophomore, junior, senior.

■ Common-interest associations are linked with rapid social change and urbanization. They have increasingly assumed the roles formerly played by kinship or age groups. In urban areas they help new arrivals cope with the changes demanded by the move. Common-interest associations also are seen in traditional societies, and their roots may be found in the first horticultural villages. Membership may range from voluntary to legally compulsory. Women are barred from associations in some societies while in others they participate on an equal basis with men. Recently, participation in conventional common-interest associations has shown a decline, as many individuals have less time for civic participation and spend more of their free time in their homes. Compensating for this is the rise of the Internet and virtual (online) associations.

■ A stratified society is divided into two or more categories of people who do not share equally in basic resources, influence, or prestige. This form contrasts with the egalitarian society, which has as many valued positions as people capable of filling them. Societies may be stratified by gender, age, social class, or caste. Members of a class enjoy equal or nearly equal access to basic resources and prestige (according to the way the latter is defined). Class differences are not always clear-cut and obvious. Where fine distinctions are made in privileges, the result is a multiplicity of classes. In societies where only major distinctions are made, only a few social classes may be recognized. Caste is a closed form of social class in which membership is determined by birth and fixed for life. Endogamy is particularly marked within castes, and children automatically belong to their parents' caste.

■ Social class is based on role differentiation, although this by itself is not sufficient for stratification. Also necessary are formalized positive and negative attitudes toward roles and restricted access to the more valued ones. Social classes are given expression in several ways. One is through verbal evaluation, or what people say about other people in their society.

Another is through patterns of association—who interacts with whom, how, and in what context. Social classes are also manifest through symbolic indicators: activities and possessions indicative of class position. Finally, they are reflected by differences in life chances, as high-status people generally live longer and in better health than people of low status.

■ Mobility is present to a greater or lesser extent in all stratified societies. Open-class societies are those with the easiest mobility. In most cases, however, the move is limited to one rung up or down the social ladder. The degree of mobility is related to factors such as access to higher education or the type of family organization that prevails in a society. Where the extended family is the norm, mobility tends to be severely limited. The independent nuclear family makes mobility easier.

Questions for Reflection

1. When teenagers leave their parental home to go to college or find employment in a distant part of the country, they face the challenge of establishing social relationships that are not based on kinship but on common interest. To which common interest associations do you belong and why?

2. At what point do you think kinship ceases to be the major organizational principle in a social structure?

3. Why do you think that members of an upper class or caste in a socially stratified system have a greater vested interest in the idea of "law and order" than those forced to exist on the bottom of such societies?

4. Slavery in the United States was officially abolished in 1863, caste-based discrimination of untouchables became constitutionally outlawed in India in 1950, and race-based segregation in South Africa officially ended with the abolition of apartheid in 1993. Considering these important political changes, do you think that social repression against traditionally inferior groups in these three societies has now ended for good?

Key Terms

Age grade	Caste
Age set	Verbal evaluation
Common-interest associations	Symbolic indicators
Stratified societies	Social mobility
Egalitarian societies	Closed-class societies
Social class	Open-class societies

Multimedia Review Tools

Companion Web Site

Visit **http://www.wadsworth.com/anthropology_d/** and click on the companion Web site for this textbook to access a wide range of material to aid your study of anthropology. Among the options for self-study in each chapter are learning objectives, flash cards, Internet activities, Web links, InfoTrac College Edition exercises, and practice tests that can be scored and emailed to your instructor.

CD-ROM

The *Doing Anthropology Today* CD-ROM supplied with your textbook provides unique and valuable information designed to enhance your learning experience. This interactive multimedia resource includes video clips, interviews with renowned anthropologists, map and timeline exercises, chapter study quizzes, and much more. *Doing Anthropology Today* will not only help you in achieving your grade goals, but it will also make your learning experience fun and exciting!

Suggested Readings

Bernardi, B. (1985). *Age class systems: Social institutions and policies based on age.* New York: Cambridge University Press.

This is a cross-cultural analysis of age as a device for organizing society and seeing to the distribution and rotation of power.

Bradfield, R. M. (1998). *A natural history of associations.* New York: International Universities Press.

First published in 1973, this major anthropological study of common-interest associations attempts to provide a comprehensive theory of the origin of associations and their role in kin-based societies.

De Mott, B. (1990). *The imperial middle: Why Americans can't think straight about class.* New York: Morrow.

This critical commentary on the "myth" that the United States is a classless society demonstrates the great social and political costs of buying into that idea.

Hammond, D. (1972). *Associations.* Reading, MA: Addison-Wesley Modular Publications, 14.

This is a brief, first-rate review of anthropological thinking and of the literature on common-interest associations and age groups.

Lenski, G. E. (1984). *Power and privilege: A theory of social stratification.* New York: McGraw-Hill.

In this classic text, the author uses a historical and broadly comparative approach to analyze how stratification develops in societies.

Price, T. D., & Feinman, G. M. (Eds.). (1995). *Foundations of social inequality.* New York: Plenum.

This book is a collection of essays by various contributors that examines the emergence of social inequality.

Sanday, P. R. (1981). *Female power and male dominance: On the origins of sexual inequality.* Cambridge, England: Cambridge University Press.

In this cross-cultural study, Sanday reveals the various ways that male–female relations are organized in human societies and demonstrates that male dominance is not inherent in those relations. Rather, it appears to emerge in situations of stress as a result of chronic food shortages, migration, and colonial domination.

© Reuters/Corbis

Search for Order
The Challenge of Disorder

Introduction

An irony of human life is that something as fundamental to our existence as cooperation should contain within it the seeds of its own destruction. It is nonetheless true that the groups that people form to fulfill important organizational needs do not just facilitate cooperation among the members of those groups, but they also create conditions that may lead to the disruption of society. We see this in a wide range of situations: in riots among fans rooting for different soccer teams, in the gang violence that takes place in many North American cities, and all the more seriously in bloody conflicts between neighboring ethnic groups such as Serbs and Albanians in southern Europe and Tutsi and Hutu in East Africa. The attitude that "my group is better than your group" is not confined to any one of the world's cultures, and it not infrequently takes the form of rivalry between groups: descent group against descent group, men against women, age grade against age grade, social class against social class, and so forth. This does not mean that such rivalry has to be disruptive; indeed, it may function to ensure that the members of groups perform their jobs well so as not to "lose face" or be subject to ridicule. Rivalry, however, can become a serious problem if it erupts into violence.

The fact is, social living inevitably entails a certain amount of friction—not just between groups but between individual members of groups as well. Thus, any society can count on a degree of disruptive behavior by some of its members at one time or another. Yet, no one can know precisely when such outbursts will occur or what form they will take. Not only does this uncertainty go against the predictability social life demands, but it also goes against the deep-seated psychological need each individual has for structure and certainty, which we discussed in Chapter 5. Therefore, every society must have means by which conflicts can be resolved and breakdown of the social order prevented. Chapter 12 investigates this, focusing on politics, power, and management of the social order.

Religion and politics may seem like strange bedfellows, but both fulfill the same goal: to protect society against the unexpected and unwanted. Effective though a culture may be in equipping, organizing, and controlling a society to provide for its members' needs, certain problems always defy existing technological or organizational solutions. The response of every culture is to devise a set of concepts and beliefs about the ultimate shape and substance of reality (including the invisible and eternal), along with a set of rituals to express them. Some

© Chris Lisle/Corbis

of these rituals aim to address and perhaps even solve problems through the manipulation of supernatural beings and powers. In short, what we think of as religion and magic serve to transform the uncertainties of life into certainties. In addition, they may serve as powerful integrative forces through commonly held values, beliefs, and practices. Also important is rationalization of the existing social order in such a way that it becomes a moral order as well. Thus, there is a link between religion and magic on the one hand and political organization and social control on the other. Culture and the supernatural, then, is an appropriate subject for discussion in Chapter 13.

Like religion and magic, the arts also contribute to human well-being and help give shape and significance to life. Indeed, the relationship between art and religion goes deeper than this, for much of what we call art has been created in the service of religion: myths to explain ritual practices, objects to portray important deities, music and dances for ceremonial use, pictorial art to record supernatural experiences and/or to serve as objects of supernatural power in their own right. In a very real sense, music, dance, or any other form of art, like magic, exploits psychological susceptibilities so as to enchant others and cause them to perceive social reality in a way favorable to the interests of the enchanter. And, like religion, art of any kind expresses the human search for order, in that the artist gives form to some essentially formless raw material. Accordingly, Chapter 14 concerns the arts, concluding this section.

CHAPTER 12

Politics, Power, and Violence

AP Photo/Santiago Andrade

CHALLENGE ISSUE

I N ALL SOCIETIES, FROM THE LARGEST TO THE SMALLEST, PEOPLE MUST DECIDE WHO GETS WHAT, WHEN, WHERE, AND HOW. This is the basic challenge of politics. Political organization takes many forms, of which the state is just one. Often, states are controlled by members of one nationality who use power to repress (or even exterminate) other nationalities within the state. Here, Quechna Indians burn an effigy of Equador's president, in protest against government policies that they feel enrich the wealthy at the expense of poor indigenous communities.

1
How Are Power and Political Organization Different?

All social relations involve power, which essentially refers to the ability of individuals or groups to impose their will upon others and make them do things even against their own wants or wishes. Power also operates on the level of entire societies. The ability to impose or maintain order and to resolve conflicts requires political organization, which refers to the means by which a society maintains order internally and manages its affairs with other societies externally. It may be relatively uncentralized and informal, as in bands and tribes, or more centralized and formal, as in chiefdoms and states.

2
How Are Social and Political Order Formed and Maintained?

Social controls may be internalized—in cultural values that are "built into" individuals—or externalized, in the form of sanctions. Positive sanctions encourage approved behavior, while negative sanctions discourage unacceptable behavior. Negative sanctions are called laws if they are formalized and enforced by an authorized political agency. Force may be employed to impose or maintain order within a society or between groups. Although states and chiefdoms frequently practice warfare as a means of achieving political objectives, some groups avoid such organized violence.

3
How Do Political Systems Obtain Popular Support?

In uncentralized systems people give loyalty and cooperation freely because everyone participates in making most decisions. Centralized systems, by contrast, rely more heavily on power, even coercion, although in the long run these may lessen the system's effectiveness. To a greater or lesser extent, political organizations all over the world seek to legitimize their power through recourse to supernatural ideas.

Louis XIV proclaimed, "I am the state." With this sweeping declaration, the 17th-century French king claimed absolute rule over his vast domain and its millions of inhabitants. Answerable only to God, he held himself to be the law, the lawmaker, the court, the judge, the jailer, and the executioner—in short, the embodiment of all political power in France.

This absolutist ruler took tremendous responsibility on his royal shoulders; had he actually performed each of these functions, he would have done the work of thousands of people, the number required to keep the machinery of a large political organization such as a state running at full steam. As a form of political organization, the French kingdom was not much different from states today. All large states require elaborate centralized structures, with hierarchies of executives, legislators, and judges who initiate, pass, and enforce laws that affect many people.

Such complex structures first began to emerge about 5,000 years ago. Commonly unstable, many have disappeared in the course of history, some temporarily and others forever. Some were annexed by other states, and others collapsed or fragmented into small political units. Although some present-day states are very old—such as Japan, which has endured as a state for almost 1,500 years—most are not much older than the United States of America. Despite the predominance of state societies today, there are still societies where political organization consists of flexible and informal kinship systems whose leaders lack real **power**—defined as the ability of individuals or groups to impose their will upon others and make them do things even against their own wants or wishes. Between these two polarities of kin-ordered and state-organized political organization lies a world of variety.

KINDS OF POLITICAL SYSTEMS

The term **political organization** refers to the way power is distributed and embedded in society, whether in organizing a giraffe hunt, managing irrigated farmlands, or raising an army. In short, it is the means through which a society creates and maintains social

> *power* The ability of individuals or groups to impose their will upon others and make them do things even against their own wants or wishes.
> *political organization* The way power is distributed and embedded in society; the means through which a society creates and maintains social order and reduces social disorder.
> *band* A relatively small and loosely organized kin-ordered group that inhabits a specific territory and that may split periodically into smaller extended family groups that are politically independent.

order and reduces social disorder. It assumes a variety of forms among the peoples of the world, but anthropologists have simplified this complex subject by identifying four basic kinds of political systems: bands, tribes, chiefdoms, and states (Figure 12.1). The first two are uncentralized systems; the latter two are centralized.

Uncentralized Political Systems

Until recently, many non-Western peoples have had neither chiefs with established rights and duties nor any fixed form of government, as those who live in modern states understand the term. Instead, marriage and kinship have formed their principal means of social organization. The economies of these societies are primarily of a subsistence type, and populations are typically small. Leaders do not have real power to force compliance with the society's customs or rules, but if individuals do not conform, they may become targets of scorn and gossip or even be banished. Important decisions are usually made in a collective manner by agreement among adults. Dissenting members may decide to act with the majority, or they may choose to adopt some other course of action, including leaving the group. This egalitarian form of political organization provides great flexibility, which in many situations offers an adaptive advantage. Since power in these kin-ordered communities is shared, with nobody exercising exclusive control over collective resources or public affairs, individuals typically enjoy much more freedom than those who form part of larger and more complex political systems.

Band Organization

The **band** is a relatively small and loosely organized kin-ordered group that inhabits a specific territory and that may split periodically into smaller extended family groups that are politically independent. Typically, bands are found among food foragers and other nomadic societies where people organize into politically autonomous extended-family groups that usually camp together, although the members of such families may periodically break up into smaller groups to forage for food or visit other relatives. Thus, bands are kin groups, composed of men and/or women who are related (or are assumed to be) with their spouses and unmarried children. Bands may be characterized as associations of related families who occupy a common (often loosely defined) territory and who live there together as long as environmental and subsistence circumstances are favorable. The band is probably the oldest form of political organization, since all humans were once food foragers and remained so until the development of farming and pastoralism over the past 10,000 years.

TYPES OF POLITICAL ORGANIZATION

The symbol ➝ indicates that the attribute varies between less and more complex societies of that type.

	BAND	TRIBE	CHIEFDOM	STATE
MEMBERSHIP				
Number of people	Dozens and up	Hundreds and up	Thousands and up	Tens of thousands and up
Settlement pattern	Mobile	Mobile or fixed: 1 or more villages	Fixed: 2 or more villages	Fixed: Many villages and cities
Basis of relationships	Kin	Kin, descent groups	Kin, rank, and residence	Class and residence
Ethnicities and languages	1	1	1	1 or more
GOVERNMENT				
Decision making, leadership	"Egalitarian"	"Egalitarian" or Big-Man	Centralized, hereditary	Centralized
Bureaucracy	None	None	None, or 1 or 2 levels	Many levels
Monopoly of force and information	No	No	No ➝ Yes	Yes
Conflict resolution	Informal	Informal	Centralized	Laws, judges
Hierarchy of settlement	No	No	No ➝ Paramount village or head town	Capital
ECONOMY				
Food production	No	No ➝ Yes	Yes ➝ Intensive	Intensive
Labor specialization	No	No	No ➝ Yes	Yes
Exchanges	Reciprocal	Reciprocal	Redistributive ("tribute")	Redistributive ("taxes")
Control of land	Band	Descent group	Chief	Various
SOCIETY				
Stratified	No	No	Yes, ranked by kin	Yes, by class or caste
Slavery	No	No	Some, small-scale	Some, large-scale
Luxury goods for elite	No	No	Yes	Yes
Public architecture	No	No	No ➝ Yes	Yes
Indigenous literacy	No	No	No ➝ Some	Often

FIGURE 12.1
Four kinds of political systems.

Since bands are egalitarian and small, numbering at most a few hundred people, no real need exists for formal, centralized political systems. Since everyone is related to—and knows on a personal basis—everyone else with whom dealings are required, there is high value placed on "getting along." Conflicts that do arise are usually settled informally through gossip, ridicule, direct negotiation, or mediation. When negotiation or mediation are used, the emphasis is on achieving a solution considered just by the concerned parties, rather than on conforming to some abstract law or rule. Where all else fails, disgruntled individuals have the option of leaving the band to go live in another where they may have relatives or try to establish a new community of their own.

Decisions affecting a band are made with the participation of all its adult members, with an emphasis on achieving consensus—a collective agreement—rather than a simple majority. Leaders become such by virtue of their abilities and serve in that capacity only as long as they retain the confidence of the community. They have no real power to force people to abide by their decisions. A leader who exceeds what people are willing to accept quickly loses followers.

An example of the informal nature of band leadership is found among the Ju/'hoansi Bushmen of the Kalahari Desert mentioned in earlier chapters. Each Ju/'hoansi band is composed of a group of families that live together, linked through kinship to one another and to the headman (or, less often, headwoman). Although each band has rights to the territory it occupies and the resources within it, two or more bands may range over the same land. The head, called the *kxau,* or "owner," is the focal point for the band's claims on the territory. He or she does not personally own the land or resources but symbolically represents the rights of band members to

Documentary Educational Resources

Toma, a Ju/'hoansi headman is known to many people worldwide through the ethnographic film *The Hunters*.

them. If the head leaves the area to live elsewhere, people turn to someone else to lead them.

The head coordinates band migration when resources are no longer adequate for subsistence in a particular territory. This leader's major duty is to plan when and where the group will move, and when the move begins his or her position is at the head of the line. The leader selects the site for the new settlement and has the first choice of a spot for his or her own fire. There are few other material rewards or duties. For example, a Ju/'hoansi head is not a judge and does not punish other band members. Wrongdoers are judged and held accountable by public opinion, usually expressed by gossip. A prime technique for resolving disputes, or even avoiding them in the first place, is mobility. Those unable to get along with others of their group simply move to another group where kinship ties may give them rights of entry.

Tribal Organization

The second type of uncentralized authority system is the *tribe*. This term is problematic because it has many meanings. The English term is derived from the Latin word *tribus*, which referred to each of the three original divisions of the Roman people more than 2,500 years ago. Even after the number of Roman tribes increased to thirty-five, this term stuck, still referring to a major subdivision of a nation. When the Biblical texts were translated from Hebrew into Latin, and much later into

English, the term *tribe* was also applied to the twelve subdivisions of Israel. Over time, it came to be widely used as a label for any people not organized into states.

In the past few centuries, when the English and other Europeans expanded their powerful reach across the globe, the term gained popularity as a way to contrast people whom they regarded as inferior to their own supposedly superior civilization. The term was even applied to non-Western peoples who in fact had strongly centralized states (the Aztecs, for example). The word *tribe* is still often used in a negative or degrading way. For instance, political unrest in many parts of the world is often blamed on "tribalism," when in fact the strife is usually the direct consequence of the creation of states that make it possible for a governing elite of one ethnic group or nationality to exploit others for their own benefit.[1]

To complicate matters, the term *tribe* also has a distinct legal meaning in some countries, including the United States. For instance, lumping together for administrative purposes a variety of groups historically organized as bands, tribes, or chiefdoms, U.S. law defines *tribe* as "any Indian tribe, band, nation, or other organized group or community . . . recognized as eligible for the special programs and services provided by the United States to Indians because of their status as Indians."[2]

In anthropology, this problematic term **tribe** refers to a wide range of kin-ordered groups that are politically

tribe In anthropology, refers to a range of kin-ordered groups that are politically integrated by some unifying factor and whose members share a common ancestry, identity, culture, language, and territory.

[1]Whitehead, N. L., & Ferguson, R. B. (1993, November 10). Deceptive stereotypes about tribal warfare (p. A48). *Chronicle of Higher Education;* Van Den Berghe, P. L. (1992). The modern state: Nation builder or nation killer? *International Journal of Group Tensions, 92*(3), 199–200.

[2]25 U.S. Code, par.450–450n.

Ray Baldwin Louis

Shown here is a meeting of the Navajo Tribal Council, a nontraditional governing body created in response to requirements set by the U.S. government in order for the Navajo to exercise national sovereignty.

integrated by some unifying factor and whose members share a common ancestry, identity, culture, language, and territory. In these larger political entities, people sacrifice a degree of household autonomy in return for greater security against such perils as enemy attacks or starvation. Typically, though not invariably, a tribe has an economy based on some form of crop cultivation or herding. Since these subsistence methods usually yield more food than those of the food-foraging band, tribal membership is usually larger than band membership. While band population densities are usually less than one person per square mile, tribal population densities generally exceed that and may be as high as 250 per square mile. Greater population density brings a new set of problems to be solved as opportunities for bickering, begging, adultery, and theft increase markedly, especially among people living in permanent villages.

Each tribe consists of one or more self-supporting and self-governing local communities that may then form alliances with others for various purposes. As in the band, political organization in the tribe is informal and temporary. Whenever a situation requiring political integration of all or several groups within the tribe arises—perhaps for defense, to carry out a raid, to pool resources in times of scarcity, or to capitalize on a windfall that must be distributed quickly lest it spoil—groups join to deal with the situation in a cooperative manner. When the problem is satisfactorily solved, each group then returns to its autonomous state.

Leadership among tribes is also relatively informal. The Navajo Indians in the southwestern United States, for example, did not think of government as something fixed and all-powerful, and leadership was not vested in

a central authority. A local leader was a man respected for his age, integrity, and wisdom. His advice therefore was sought frequently, but he had no formal means of control and could not force any decision on those who asked for his help. Group decisions were made by public consensus, although the most influential man usually played a key role in reaching a decision. Social mechanisms that induced members to abide by group decisions included gossip, criticism, withdrawal of cooperation, and the belief that antisocial actions caused sickness and other misfortune.

MEDIATREK

For links to resources concerning issues related to legal anthropology—from indigenous rights to forced labor to genocide, go to MediaTrek 12.1 on the companion Web site or CD-ROM.

Another example of tribal leadership is the Big Man. Common in the southern Pacific, such men are leaders of localized descent groups or of a territorial group. The Big Man combines a small amount of interest in his tribe's welfare with a great deal of cunning and calculation for his own personal gain. His authority is personal; he does not come to office in any formal sense, nor is he elected. His status is the result of acts that raise him above most other tribe members and attract to him a number of loyal followers.

The Kapauku of western New Guinea typify this form of political organization. Among them, the Big Man is called the *tonowi,* or "rich one." To achieve this status, one must be male, wealthy, generous, and eloquent. Physical bravery and an ability to deal with the

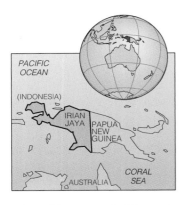

supernatural are also common *tonowi* characteristics, but they are not essential. The *tonowi* functions as the headman of the village unit.

Because Kapauku culture places a high value on wealth, a wealthy man is considered successful and admirable—provided he is also generous when it comes to making loans. Those who refuse to lend money to other villagers may be ostracized, ridiculed, and, in extreme cases, actually executed by a group of warriors. This social pressure ensures that economic wealth is distributed throughout the group.

The *tonowi* acquires political power through his loans. Other villagers comply with his requests because they are in his debt (often interest-free), and they do not want to have to repay their loans. Those who have not yet borrowed from him may wish to do so in the future, so they, too, want to keep his goodwill.

The *tonowi* gains further support by taking into his household young male apprentices who receive business training along with food and shelter. He also gives them a loan that enables them to marry when the apprenticeship ends. In return, they act as messengers and bodyguards. After leaving, they remain tied to the *tonowi* by bonds of affection and gratitude. Political support also comes from the *tonowi's* kinsmen, whose relationship brings with it varying obligations.

The *tonowi* functions as a leader in a wide variety of situations. He represents his group in dealing with outsiders and other villages and acts as negotiator and/or judge when disputes break out among his followers. As discussed in an earlier chapter, the *tonowi's* wealth comes from his success at breeding pigs—the focus of the entire Kapauku economy. It is not uncommon for a *tonowi* to lose his fortune rapidly due to bad management or bad luck with his pigs. Thus the Kapauku political structure shifts frequently; as one man loses wealth and consequently power, another gains it and becomes a *tonowi*. These changes confer a degree of flexibility on the political organization and prevent any one *tonowi* from holding political power for too long.

Although it is far more common for tribal chiefs to be men, in some cultures women serve in such leadership positions. For instance, several Algonquian Indian communities in southern New England historically recognized female chiefs. The Saconnet who inhabited what is now Rhode Island were represented by a charismatic woman named Awashunkes. She was an impor-

George Holton/Photo Researchers, Inc.

This Big Man from New Guinea is wearing his "official" regalia.

tant chief, or *sachem,* who represented her tribe in a 1671 peace treaty and subsequent dealings with English colonists.[3]

Kinship Organization

In many tribal societies the organizing unit and seat of political authority is the clan, comprised of people who consider themselves descended from a common ancestor. Within the clan, elders or headmen and/or headwomen regulate members' affairs and represent their clan in relations with other clans. As a group, the elders of all the clans may form a council that acts within the community or for the community in dealings with outsiders. Because clan members usually do not all live together in a single community, clan organization facilitates joint action with members of related communities when necessary.

---

[3]Plane, A. M. (1996). Putting a face on colonization: Factionalism and gender politics in the life history of Awashunkes, the "squaw sachem" of Saconnet." In R. S. Grumet (Ed.), *Northeastern Indian lives, 1632–1816* (pp.140–175). Amherst: University of Massachusetts Press.

Another form of tribal kinship bond that provides political organization is the **segmentary lineage system.** Usually found in societies in which people trace their ancestry in the male line to the same founding ancestor, this system refers to a relatively rare form of kin-ordered organization in which a tribal group is segmented, or split, into several branches made up of clans or major lineages, each of which is further divided into minor lineages, which, in turn, can be split into minimal lineages. Well-known examples include East African tribal groups such as the Dinka and Nuer, neighboring and often feuding cattle herders of the Sudan. Unlike other East African pastoralists (the Maasai, for example), these pastoral nomads lack the age-grading organization that cuts across descent group membership.

The economy of the segmentary tribe is generally just above subsistence level. Production is small scale, and the labor pool is just large enough to provide necessities. Since each lineage in the tribe produces the same goods, none depends on another for goods or services. Political organization among segmentary lineage societies is usually informal: They have neither political offices nor chiefs, although older tribal members may exercise some personal authority. In his classic study of segmentary lineage organization, Marshall Sahlins[4] writes that segmentation is the social means of temporary unification of a fragmented tribal society to join in a particular action. He describes how this works among

Nuer pastoralists living in the swampland and savannah of the southern Sudan. With a population of about 200,000, the Nuer comprise at least twenty clans. Each is patrilineal and segmented ("sawed up") into maximal lineages; each of these is in turn segmented into major lineages, which are segmented into minor lineages, which in turn are segmented into minimal lineages. The minimal lineage is a group descended from one great-grandfather or great-great-grandfather (Figure 12.2).

The lineage segments, or sections, among the Nuer are all equal, and no real leadership or political organization at all exists above the level of the autonomous minimal or primary segments. The entire superstructure of the lineage is nothing more than an alliance, active only during conflicts between any of the minimal segments. In any serious dispute between members of different minimal lineage segments, members of all other segments take the side of the contestant to whom

---

[4]Sahlins, M. (1961). The segmentary lineage: An organization of predatory expansion. *American Anthropologist, 63,* 322–343.

> **segmentary lineage system** A rare form of kin-ordered organization in which a tribal group is split into several branches made up of clans or major lineages, each of which is further divided into minor lineages and minimal lineages.

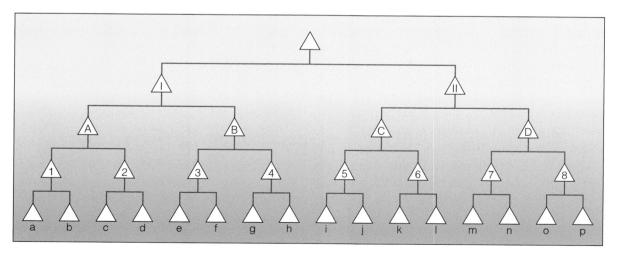

FIGURE 12.2

Segmentary lineage organization: **a** and **b** represent minimal lineages of **1; 1** and **2** represent minor lineages of **A; A** and **B** represent major lineages of **I;** and **I** and **II** represent maximal lineages of a single clan. In a serious dispute between, say, **a** and **e,** members of **b, c,** and **d** will join forces against **e** because they are more closely related to **a** than they are to **e.**

Among the Nuer, the leopard-skin chief tries to settle disputes between lineages.

they are most closely related, and the issue is then joined between the higher-order lineages involved. Such a system of political organization is known as *complementary* or *balanced opposition*.

Disputes among the Nuer are frequent, as they are among others with similar organization, and under the segmentary lineage system, they can lead to widespread feuds. This possible source of social disruption is minimized by the actions of the "leopard-skin chief," not really a chief but a holder of a ritual office of conciliation. The leopard-skin chief has no political power and is viewed as standing outside the lineage network. All he can do is try to persuade feuding lineages to accept payment in "blood cattle" rather than taking another life. His mediation gives each side the chance to back down gracefully before too many people are killed; but if the participants are for some reason unwilling to compromise, the leopard-skin chief has no authority to enforce a settlement.

Political Integration beyond the Kin Group

As discussed in the previous chapter, age grades and age sets provide tribal societies such as the Tiriki herders of East Africa with a means of political inte-

gration beyond the kin. Cutting across territorial and kin groupings, these organizations link members from different lineages and clans. Among the Tiriki, for example, the Warrior age grade guards the village and grazing lands, while Judicial Elders resolve disputes. The oldest age grade, the Ritual Elders, advise on matters involving the well-being of all the Tiriki people. With the tribe's political affairs in the hands of the various age grades and their officers, this type of organization enables the largely independent kin groups to solve conflicts and sometimes even avoid feuding between the lineages.

Another system of political integration found among tribes in many parts of the world is the common-interest association, also discussed in the previous chapter. For example, among many Indian nations inhabiting North America's Great Plains in the 19th century, the band comprised the basic territorial and political unit. In addition, however, there existed a number of military societies or warrior clubs. Among the Cheyenne, for instance, there were seven of these groups. A boy might be invited to join one of these societies when he achieved warrior status, whereupon he became familiar with the society's particular insignia, songs, and rituals. In addition to their military functions, the warrior societies also had ceremonial and social functions.

The Cheyenne warriors' daily tasks consisted of overseeing movements in the camp, protecting a moving column, and enforcing rules against individual hunting when the whole tribe was on a buffalo hunt. In addition, each warrior society had its own repertoire of dances, which its members performed on special ceremonial occasions. Since each Cheyenne band had identical military societies bearing identical names, the societies served to integrate the entire tribe for military and political purposes.[5]

MEDIATREK
To learn the basics about the Association for Political and Legal Anthropology, go to MediaTrek 12.2 on the companion Web site or CD-ROM.

Centralized Political Systems

In bands and tribes, political authority is uncentralized, and each group is economically and politically autonomous. Political organization is vested in kinship, age, and common-interest groups. Populations are small and relatively homogeneous, with people engaged for the most part in the same sorts of activities

---

[5]Hoebel, E. A. (1960). *The Cheyennes: Indians of the Great Plains.* New York: Holt, Rinehart and Winston.

A Kpelle town chief settles a dispute.

throughout their lives. As a society's social life becomes more complex, however—as population rises and technology becomes more complex and as specialization of labor and trade networks produce surplus goods—the opportunity increases for some individuals or groups to exercise control at the expense of others. In such societies, political authority and power are concentrated in a single individual, the chief, or in a body of individuals, the state.

Chiefdoms

A **chiefdom** is a regional polity in which two or more local groups are organized under a single ruling individual—the chief—who is at the head of a ranked hierarchy of people. An individual's status in such a polity is determined by the closeness of his or her relationship to the chief. Those closest are officially superior and receive deferential treatment from those in lower ranks.

The office of the chief is usually for life and often hereditary. Typically, it passes from a man to his son or his sister's son, depending on whether descent is reckoned patrilineally or matrilineally. Unlike the headmen or headwomen in bands and tribes, the leader of a chiefdom is generally a true authority figure, whose authority serves to unite members in all affairs and at all times. For example, a chief can distribute land among community members and recruit people into military service. Chiefdoms have a recognized hierarchy consisting of major and minor authorities who control major and minor subdivisions. Such an arrangement is, in effect, a chain of command, linking leaders at every level. It serves to bind groups in the heartland to the chief's

headquarters, be it a mud and dung hut or a marble palace. Although leaders of chiefdoms are almost always men, in some cultures a politically astute wife, sister, or single daughter of a deceased male chief could inherit such a powerful position as well. One historical example is Aimata, who succeeded her deceased half-brother Pomare III as leader of the Polynesian chiefdom of Tahiti in 1827, ruling as Queen Pomare IV until her death 50 years later.

Chiefs usually control the economic activities of those who fall under their political rule. Typically, chiefdoms involve redistributive systems, and the chief has control over surplus goods and perhaps even over the community's labor force. Thus, he (and sometimes she) may demand a quota of rice from farmers, which will then be redistributed to the entire community. Similarly, laborers may be recruited to build irrigation works, a palace, or a temple.

The chief may also amass a great amount of personal wealth and pass it on to offspring. Land, cattle, and luxury goods produced by specialists can be collected by the chief and become part of the power base. Moreover, high-ranking families of the chiefdom may engage in the same practice and use their possessions as evidence of noble status.

An example of this form of political organization may be seen among the Kpelle of Liberia in West

chiefdom A regional polity in which two or more local groups are organized under a single chief, who is at the head of a ranked hierarchy of people.

Africa.[6] Among them is a class of paramount chiefs, each of whom presides over one of the Kpelle chiefdoms (each of which is now a district of the Liberian state). The paramount chiefs' traditional tasks are hearing disputes, preserving order, seeing to the upkeep of trails, and maintaining "medicines." In addition, they are now salaried officials of the Liberian government, mediating between it and their own people. Also, a paramount chief receives government commissions on taxes and court fees collected within his chiefdom, plus a commission for furnishing the rubber plantations with laborers. Moreover, he gets a stipulated amount of rice from each household, and gifts from people who come to request favors and intercessions. In keeping with his exalted station in life, a paramount chief has at his disposal uniformed messengers, a literate clerk, and the symbols of wealth: many wives, embroidered gowns, and freedom from manual labor.

In a ranked hierarchy beneath each Kpelle paramount chief are several lesser chiefs: one for each district within the chiefdom, one for each town within a district, and one for each quarter of all but the smallest towns. Each acts as a kind of lieutenant for his chief of the next higher rank and also serves as a liaison between him and those of lower rank. Unlike paramount or district chiefs, who are comparatively remote, town and quarter chiefs are readily accessible to people at the local level.

Traditionally, chiefdoms in all parts of the world have been highly unstable, with lesser chiefs trying to take power from higher ranking chiefs or paramount chiefs vying with one another for supreme power. In precolonial Hawaii, for example, war was the way to gain territory and maintain power; great chiefs set out to conquer one another in an effort to become paramount chief of all the islands. When one chief conquered another, the loser and all his nobles were dispossessed of

all property and were lucky if they escaped alive. The new chief then appointed his own supporters to positions of political power. As a consequence, there was very little continuity of governmental or religious administration.

State Systems

The **state,** the most formal of political organizations, is one of the hallmarks of what is commonly referred to as civilization. It is a centralized political system involving large numbers of people within a defined territory who are organized and directed by a formal government that has the capacity and authority to make laws, and use force to defend the social order. From the perspective of the political elite in control of the state, its formation and endurance are typically represented as something favorable—as progress. This view is not necessarily shared by those who exist on the political underside and do not possess much personal freedom to say and do as they please. As anthropologist Bruce Knauft observes,

> It is likely . . . that coercion and violence as systematic means of organizational constraint developed especially with the increasing socioeconomic complexity and potential for political hierarchy afforded by substantial food surplus and food production.[7]

A large population requires increased food production. Together, these lead to a transformation of the landscape by way of irrigation and terracing, carefully managed crop rotation cycles, intensive competition for clearly demarcated lands, and rural populations big enough to support market systems and a specialized urban sector. Under such conditions, corporate groups that stress exclusive membership proliferate, ethnic differentiation and ethnocentrism become more pronounced, and the potential for social conflict increases dramatically. Given these circumstances, state institutions, which minimally involve a bureaucracy, a military, and (usually) an official religion, provide a means for numerous and diverse groups to function together as an integrated whole.

Although their guiding ideology is that they are permanent and stable, the truth is, since their first appearance some 5,000 years ago, states have been anything but permanent. Whatever stability they have achieved has been short term at best; over the long term, they show a clear tendency toward instability and transience. Nowhere have states even begun to show the staying power exhibited by more uncentralized political

---

[6]Gibbs, J. L., Jr. (1965). The Kpelle of Liberia. In J. L. Gibbs, Jr. (Ed.), *Peoples of Africa* (pp. 216–218). New York: Holt, Rinehart and Winston.

state In anthropology, a centralized political system that has the capacity and authority to make laws, and use force to maintain social order.

---

[7]Knauft, B. M. (1991). Violence and sociality in human evolution. *Current Anthropology, 32,* 391.

systems, the longest lasting social forms invented by humans.

An important distinction to make at this point is between state and nation. As noted in Chapter 1, a **nation** is a people who share a collective identity based on a common culture, language, territorial base, and history.[8] Today, there are roughly 200 internationally recognized states in the world, most of which did not exist before the end of World War II (1945). By contrast, there are about 5,000 nations, many of which have existed since "time immemorial." Rarely do state and nation coincide, as they do, for example, in Iceland, Japan, and Swaziland.

About 73 percent of the world's states are pluralistic societies, having within their boundaries peoples of more than one nation.[9] Often, smaller nations and other groups find themselves at the mercy of one or more dominant nations or ethnic groups controlling the state. Frequently facing discrimination, even repression, some minority nations seek to improve their political position by founding an independent state. In the process, they usually encounter stiff opposition, even violent confrontations. So it is with the Kurdish people inhabiting the borderlands of Iran, Iraq, and Turkey (Figure 12.3), the Palestinians whose lands have been occupied by Israel, the Chechens in the Russian federation, and the Aceh in Indonesia, to cite a few examples. While the outcome of armed struggle may be the formation of a new state (such as Bosnia's recent split from Serb-dominated Yugoslavia or East Timor's successful struggle for independence from Indonesia), some nations have forged their own states without open violence. Such was the case, for instance, with Suriname, a former Dutch colony on the northeast coast of South America.

An important aspect of the state is its delegation of authority to maintain order within and outside its borders. Police, foreign ministries, war ministries, and other bureaucracies function to control and punish disruptive acts of crime, terror, and rebellion. By such agencies the state asserts authority impersonally and in a consistent, predictable manner.

Western forms of government, like that of the United States (in reality, a superstate), of course, are state governments, and their organization and workings are undoubtedly familiar to most everyone. An example of a not-so-familiar state is that of the Swazi of Swaziland (one of the world's few true nation-states), a

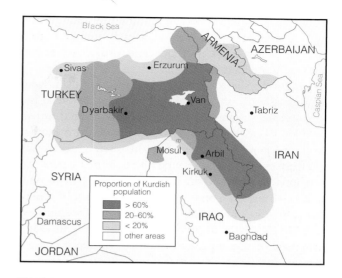

FIGURE 12.3

The Kurds, most of whom live in Iran, Iraq, and Turkey, are an example of a nation without a state.

Bantu-speaking people who live in Southeast Africa.[10] They are primarily farmers, but cattle raising there is more highly valued than farming: The ritual, wealth, and power of their authority system are all intricately linked with cattle. In addition to farming and cattle raising, there is some specialization of labor; certain people become specialists in ritual, smithing, wood carving, and pottery. Their goods and services are traded, although the Swazi do not have elaborate markets.

The traditional Swazi authority system was characterized by a highly developed dual monarchy (now a thing of the past), a hereditary aristocracy, and elaborate kinship rituals, as well as by statewide age sets. The king and his mother were the central figures of all national activity, linking all the people of the Swazi state: They

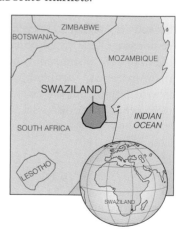

---

[8]Clay, J. W. (1996). What's a nation? In W. A. Haviland & R. J. Gordon (Eds.), *Talking about people* (2nd ed., p. 188). Mountain View, CA: Mayfield.

[9]Van Den Berghe, P. L. (1992). The modern state: Nation builder or nation killer? *International Journal of Group Tensions, 92*(3), 193.

---

[10]Kuper, H. (1965). The Swazi of Swaziland. In J. L. Gibbs, Jr. (Ed.), *Peoples of Africa* (pp. 475–512). New York: Holt, Rinehart and Winston.

nation A people who share a collective identity based on a common culture, language, territorial base, and history.

presided over higher courts, summoned national gatherings, controlled age classes, allocated land, disbursed national wealth, took precedence in ritual, and helped organize important social events.

Advising the king were the senior princes, who were usually his uncles and half-brothers. Between the king and the princes were two specially created *tinsila,* or "blood brothers," who were chosen from certain common clans. These men were his shields, protecting him from evildoers and serving him in intimate personal situations. In addition, the king was guided by two *tindvuna,* or counselors, one civil and one military. The people of the state made their opinions known through two councils: the *liqoqo,* or privy council (dissolved in 1986), composed of senior princes, and the *libanda,* or council of state, composed of chiefs and headmen and open to all adult males of the state. The *liqoqo* could advise the king, make decisions, and carry them out. For example, they could rule on questions about land, education, traditional ritual, court procedure, and transport.

Swazi government extended from the smallest local unit—the homestead—upward to the central administration. The head of a homestead had legal and administrative powers; he was responsible for the crimes of those under him, controlled their property, and spoke for them before his superiors. On the district level, political organization was similar to that of the central government. The relationship between a district chief, however, and his subjects was personal and familiar; he knew all the families in his district. The main check on any autocratic tendencies he might have exhibited rested in his subjects' ability to transfer their allegiance to a more responsive chief. Swazi officials held their positions for life and were dismissed only for treason or witchcraft. Incompetence, drunkenness, and stupidity were frowned upon, but they were not considered to be sufficient grounds for dismissal.

POLITICAL LEADERSHIP AND GENDER

Irrespective of cultural configuration or type of political organization, women hold important positions of political leadership far less often than men. Furthermore, when they do occupy publicly recognized offices, their power and authority rarely exceed those of men. Nevertheless, significant exceptions occur. Historically, one might cite the already mentioned female Indian *sachems* in southern New England, as well as powerful queens such as Candace of the ancient Nubian monarchy of Cush (Ethiopia) in the Upper Nile Valley, Isabella I ("the Catholic") of Castile in Spain, Elizabeth I ("the Virgin Queen") of England, or Catherine ("the Great")

of Russia. Perhaps most notable is Queen Victoria, the long-reigning queen of England, Scotland, Wales, and Ireland. Also recognized as monarch in a host of colonies all over the world, Victoria even acquired the title Empress of India. Ruling the British empire from 1837 until 1901, she was perhaps the most powerful leader in the entire world.

Also of note is the Dutch Queen Wilhelmina. During the last decade of her reign, she ruled over a vast domain that included not only the Netherlands but also many overseas colonies, especially the East Indies (which became independent as Indonesia in 1948). According to the constitution of the Netherlands, the title to the royal throne is hereditary and does not discriminate on the basis of gender. It passes on by succession to the monarch's legitimate descendants in order of seniority. When the last male king died in 1890, his only surviving child Wilhelmina succeeded him, becoming queen in 1890 and reigning until 1948. She was succeeded as queen by her daughter Juliana, who, in turn, was succeeded by her daughter Beatrix, the currently reigning queen of the Netherlands. One could say, in other words, that the Dutch throne has been occupied by a royal matrilineage for more than a century.

In addition to inheriting high positions of political leadership, growing numbers of women have also been elected as presidents or prime ministers. Countries with female heads of state now or in recent years include Indonesia, Pakistan, Ireland, Sri Lanka, Norway, India, Turkey, and the Philippines, to mention just a few. While such high profile female leadership is still relatively rare, women regularly enjoy as much political power as men in a number of societies. In band societies, for example, it is common for females to have as much of a say in public affairs as males, even though more often than not the latter are the nominal leaders of their groups. Among the Iroquois nations of New York State (discussed in the last chapter), all leadership positions above the household and clan level were, without exception, filled by men. Thus men held all positions on the village and tribal councils, as well as on the great council of the Iroquois Confederacy. However, they were completely beholden to women, for only women could nominate men to high office. Moreover, women actively lobbied the men on the councils and could have someone removed from office whenever it suited them.

As this case makes clear, lower visibility in politics does not necessarily indicate that women lack power in political affairs. And just as there are various ways in which women play a role behind the scenes, so it is when they have more visible roles, as in the dual-sex system of the Igbo in Nigeria, West Africa. Among the Igbo, each political unit has separate political institutions for men and women, so that both have an autonomous

© Gianni Dagli Orti/Corbis

Although worldwide women hold important positions of political leadership far less often than men, there have been and continue to be significant exceptions. Among them is Queen Victoria, who reigned over the British empire from 1837 until 1901. She may have been the most powerful leader in the world in her day.

sphere of authority, as well as an area of shared responsibility.[11] At the head of each political unit was a male *obi,* considered the head of government although in fact he presided over the male community, and a female *omu,* the acknowledged mother of the whole community but in practice concerned with the female section of the community. Unlike a queen (though both she and the *obi* were

crowned), the *omu* was neither the *obi's* wife nor the previous *obi's* daughter.

Just as the *obi* had a council of dignitaries to advise him and act as a check against any arbitrary exercise of power, the *omu* was served by a council of women in equal number to the *obi's* male councilors. The duties of the *omu* and her councilors involved such tasks as establishing rules and regulations for the community market (marketing was a woman's activity) and hearing cases involving women brought to her from throughout the town or village. If such cases also involved men, then she and her council would cooperate with the *obi* and his council. Widows also went to the *omu* for the final rites required to end their period of mourning for dead husbands. Since the *omu* represented all women, she had to be responsive to her constituency and would seek their approval and cooperation in all major decisions.

In addition to the *omu* and her council, the Igbo women's government included a representative body of women chosen from each quarter or section of the village or town. Moreover, political pressure groups of

---

[11]Okonjo, K. (1976). The dual-sex political system in operation: Igbo women and community politics in midwestern Nigeria. In N. Hafkin & E. Bay (Eds.), *Women in Africa.* Stanford, CA: Stanford University Press.

women acted at the village or lineage level to stop quarrels and prevent wars. These pressure groups included women born into a community (most of whom lived elsewhere since villages were exogamous and residence was patrilocal) and women who had married into the community. Their duties included helping companion wives in times of illness and stress and meting out discipline to lazy or recalcitrant husbands.

In the Igbo system, then, women managed their own affairs, and their interests were represented at all levels of government. Moreover, they had the right to enforce their decisions and rules with sanctions similar to those employed by men, including strikes, boycotts, and "sitting on a man" or woman. Political scientist Judith Van Allen describes the latter:

> To "sit on" or "make war on" a man involved gathering at his compound, sometimes late at night, dancing, singing scurrilous songs which detailed the women's grievances against him and often called his manhood into question, banging on his hut with the pestles women used for pounding yams, and perhaps demolishing his hut or plastering it with mud and roughing him up a bit. A man might be sanctioned in this way for mistreating his wife, for violating the women's market rules, or for letting his cows eat the women's crops. The women would stay at his hut throughout the day, and late into the night if necessary, until he repented and promised to mend his ways.[12]

Given the high visibility of women in the Igbo political system, it may come as a surprise to learn that when the British imposed colonial rule upon these people in the late 1800s, they failed to recognize the autonomy and power of the women. One reason is that the British were blinded by their own cultural values, reflecting a male-dominated society in which the domestic sphere was seen as the ideal place for women. This is ironic because the long-reigning and powerful head of the British empire at the time was, as mentioned earlier, Queen Victoria. Nevertheless, unable to imagine that Igbo women might play important roles in politics, the British introduced "reforms" that destroyed traditional forms of female autonomy and power without providing alternative forms in exchange. As a result, Igbo women lost much of their traditional equality and became subordinate to men.

POLITICAL ORGANIZATION AND THE MAINTENANCE OF ORDER

Whatever form a society's political organization may take, it always involves maintaining social order. Always it seeks to ensure that people behave in acceptable ways and defines the proper action to take when they do not. In chiefdoms and states, some sort of authority has the power to regulate the affairs of society. In bands and tribes, however, people behave generally as they are expected to, without the direct intervention of any centralized political authority. To a large degree, gossip, criticism, fear of supernatural forces, and the like serve as effective deterrents to antisocial behavior.

As an example of how such seemingly informal considerations serve to keep people in line, we may look at the Wape people of Papua New Guinea, who believe the spirits of deceased ancestors roam lineage lands, protecting them from trespassers and helping their hunting descendants by driving game their way.[13] These ancestral spirits also punish those who have wronged them or their descendants by preventing hunters from finding game or causing them to miss their shots, thereby depriving people of much needed meat. Nowadays, the Wape hunt with shotguns, which the community purchases for the use of one man, whose job it is to hunt for all the others. The cartridges used in the hunt, however, are invariably supplied by individual community members. Thus, if the gunman shoots and misses, it is not viewed as his failing. Rather, it is because the owner of the fired shell, or some close relative, has quarreled or wronged another person whose deceased relative is securing revenge by causing the hunter to miss. Or, if the gunman cannot even find game, it is because vengeful ancestors have chased the animals away. As a proxy hunter for the villagers, the gunman is potentially subject to sanctions by ancestral spirits in response to collective wrongs by those for whom he hunts.

For the Wape, then, successful hunting depends upon avoiding quarrels and maintaining tranquility within the community so as not to antagonize anybody's deceased ancestor. Unfortunately, complete harmony is impossible to achieve in any human community, and the Wape are no exception. Thus, when hunting is poor, the gunman must discover what quarrels and wrongs have occurred within his village to identify the proper ancestral spirits to appeal to for renewed success. Usually, this is done in a special meeting where confessions of wrongdoing may be forthcoming. If not, ques-

---

[12]Van Allen, J. (1979). Sitting on a man: Colonialism and the lost political institutions of Igbo women. In S. Tiffany (Ed.), *Women in society* (p. 169). St. Albans, VT: Eden Press.

[13]Mitchell, W. E. (1973, December). A new weapon stirs up old ghosts. *Natural History Magazine*, 77–84.

tioning accusations are bandied about until resolution occurs, but even with no resolution, the meeting must end amicably to prevent new antagonisms. Thus, everyone's behavior comes under public scrutiny, reminding all of what is expected of them and encouraging all to avoid acts that will cast them in an unfavorable light.

Internalized Controls

The Wape concern about ancestral spirits is a good example of internalized, or cultural, controls—beliefs that are so thoroughly ingrained that each person becomes personally responsible for his or her own conduct. **Cultural control** may be thought of as control through beliefs and values deeply internalized in the minds of individuals, as opposed to **social control,** which involves external enforcement through open coercion. Examples of cultural control can also be found in North American society. For instance, people refrain from committing incest not so much from fear of legal punishment as from a sense of deep disgust at the thought of the act or the shame they would feel in performing it. Obviously, not all members of North American society have these feelings, for if they did, there would not be the high incidence of incest that occurs, especially between fathers and daughters. But, then, no deterrent to misbehavior is ever 100 percent effective. Cultural controls are embedded in our consciousness and rely on deterrents such as fear of supernatural punishment—ancestral spirits sabotaging the hunting, for example—and magical retaliation. Like the devout Christian who avoids sinning for fear of hell, the individual expects some sort of punishment, even though no one in the community may be aware of the wrongdoing.

Externalized Controls

Because internalized controls are not wholly sufficient even in bands and tribes, every society develops externalized social controls known as **sanctions** and designed to encourage conformity to social norms. Operating within social groups of all sizes and involving a mix of cultural and social controls, sanctions may vary significantly within a given society, but they fall into one of two categories: positive or negative. Positive sanctions consist of incentives to conformity such as awards, titles, and recognition by one's neighbors. Negative sanctions consist of threats such as imprisonment, fines, corporal punishment, or ostracism from the community for violation of social norms. For sanctions to be effective, they cannot be arbitrary. They must be applied consistently,

© Michael Leckel/Reuters/Corbis

Shirin Ebadi of Iran won the Nobel Peace Prize in 2003 for efforts for democracy and human rights. Such awards are examples of positive sanctions, by which societies promote approved behavior.

and they must be generally known among members of the society. If some individuals are not convinced of the advantages of social conformity, they are still more likely to obey society's rules than to accept the consequences of not doing so.

Sanctions may also be categorized as either formal or informal, depending on whether or not a legal statute is involved. In the United States, the man who goes shirtless in shorts to a church service may be subject to a variety of informal sanctions, ranging from disapproving glances from the clergy to the chuckling of other parishioners. If, however, he were to show up without any clothing at all, he would be subject to the formal negative sanction of arrest for indecent exposure. Only in the second instance would he have been guilty of breaking the law.

cultural control Control through beliefs and values deeply internalized in the minds of individuals.
social control External control through open coercion.
sanctions Externalized social controls designed to encourage conformity to social norms.

Negative sanctions may involve some form of regulated combat, seen here as armed dancers near Mount Hagen in New Guinea demand redress for murder.

Formal sanctions, such as laws, are always organized, because they attempt to precisely and explicitly regulate people's behavior. Other examples of organized sanctions include, on the positive side, military decorations and monetary rewards. On the negative side are loss of face, exclusion from social life and its privileges, seizure of property, imprisonment, and even bodily mutilation or death. Informal sanctions emphasize cultural control and are diffuse in nature, involving spontaneous expressions of approval or disapproval by members of the group or community. They are, nonetheless, very effective in enforcing a large number of seemingly unimportant customs. Because most people want to be accepted, they are willing to acquiesce to the rules that govern dress, eating, and conversation, even in the absence of actual laws.

To show how informal sanctions work, we will examine them in the context of power relationships among the Bedouins of Egypt's western desert. This example, featured in the following Original Study, is especially interesting, for it shows how sanctions not only act to control people's behavior but also act to keep individuals in their place in a hierarchical society.

Original Study

Limits on Power in Bedouin Society

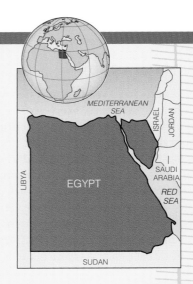

Where individuals value their independence and believe in equality, those who exercise authority over others enjoy a precarious status. In Bedouin society, social precedence or power depends not on force but on demonstration of the moral virtues that win respect from others. Persons in positions of power are said to have social standing (*gíma*), which is recognized by the respect paid them. To win the respect of others, in particular dependents, such persons must adhere to the ideals of honor, provide for and protect their dependents, and be fair, taking no undue advantage of their positions. They must assert their authority gingerly lest it so compromise their dependents' autonomy that it provokes rebellion and be exposed as a sham.

Because those in authority are expected to treat their dependents, even children, with some respect, they must draw as little attention as possible to the inequality of their relationships. Euphemisms that obscure the nature of such relationships abound. For example,

[CONTINUED]

Sa`ádi [free tribes] individuals do not like to call Mrábit [client tribes] associates Mrábtín in their presence. My host corrected me once when I referred to his shepherds by the technical word for shepherd, saying, "We prefer to call them 'people of the sheep' [*hal il-ghanam*]. It sounds nicer." The use of fictive kin terms serves the same function of masking relations of inequality, as for example in the case of patrons and clients.

Those in authority are also expected to respect their dependents' dignity by minimizing open assertion of their power over them. Because the provider's position requires dependents, he risks losing his power base if he alienates them. When a superior publicly orders, insults, or beats a dependent, he invites the rebellion that would undermine his position. Such moments are fraught with tension, as the dependent might feel the need to respond to a public humiliation to preserve his dignity or honor. Indeed, refusal to comply with an unreasonable order, or an order given in a compromising way, reflects well on the dependent and undercuts the authority of the person who gave it.

Tyranny is never tolerated for long. Most dependents wield sanctions that check the power of their providers. Anyone can appeal to a mediator to intervene on his or her behalf, and more radical solutions are open to all but young children. Clients can simply leave an unreasonable patron and attach themselves to a new one. Young men can always escape the tyranny of a father or paternal uncle by leaving to join maternal relatives or, if they have them, affines, or even to become clients to some other family. For the last twenty years or so, young men could go to Libya to find work.

Younger brothers commonly get out from under difficult elder brothers by splitting off from them, demanding their share of the patrimony and setting up separate households. The dynamic is clear in the case of four brothers who constituted the core of the camp in which I lived. Two had split off and lived in separate households. Another two still shared property, herds, and expenses. While I was there, tensions began to

develop. Although the elder brother was more important in the community at large, and the younger brother was slightly irresponsible and less intelligent, for the most part they worked various enterprises jointly and without friction. The younger brother deferred to his older brother and usually executed his decisions.

But one day the tensions surfaced. The elder brother came home at midday in a bad mood only to find that no one had prepared him lunch. He went to one of his wives and scolded her for not having prepared any lunch, asserting that his children had complained that they were hungry. He accused her of trying to starve his children and threatened to beat her. His younger brother tried to intervene, but the elder brother then turned on him, calling him names. Accusing him of being lazy (because he had failed to follow through on a promise involving the care of the sheep that day), he then asked why the younger brother let his wife get away with sitting in her room when there was plenty of work to be done around the household. Then he went off toward his other wife carrying a big stick and yelling.

The younger brother was furious and set off to get their mother. The matriarch, accompanied by another of her sons, arrived and conferred at length with the quarreling men. The younger son wished to split off from his elder brother's household; the other brother scolded him for being so sensitive about a few words, reminding him that this was his elder brother, from whom even a beating should not matter. His mother disapproved of splitting up the households. Eventually everyone calmed down. But it is likely that a few more incidents such as that will eventually lead the younger brother to demand a separate household.

Even a woman can resist a tyrannical husband by leaving for her natal home "angry" (*mughtáóa*). This is the approved response to abuse, and it forces the husband or his representatives to face the scolding of the woman's kin and, sometimes, to appease her with gifts. Women have less recourse against tyrannical fathers or guardians, but various informal means

to resist the imposition of unwanted decisions do exist. As a last resort there is always suicide, and I heard of a number of both young men and women who committed suicide in desperate resistance to their fathers' decisions, especially regarding marriage. One old woman's tale illustrates the extent to which force can be resisted, even by women. Náfla reminisced:

My first marriage was to my paternal cousin [*ibn 'amm*]. He was from the same camp. One day the men came over to our tent. I saw the tent full of men and wondered why. I heard they were coming to ask for my hand [*yukhultú fiyya*]. I went and stood at the edge of the tent and called out, "If you're planning to do anything, stop. I don't want it." Well, they went ahead anyway, and every day I would cry and say that I did not want to marry him. I was young, perhaps fourteen. When they began drumming and singing, everyone assured me that it was in celebration of another cousin's wedding, so I sang and danced along with them. This went on for days. Then on the day of the wedding my aunt and another relative caught me in the tent and suddenly closed it and took out the washbasin. They wanted to bathe me. I screamed. I screamed and screamed; every time they held a pitcher of water to wash me with, I knocked it out of their hands.

His relatives came with camels and dragged me into the litter and took me to his tent. I screamed and screamed when he came into the tent in the afternoon [for the defloration]. Then at night, I hid among the blankets. Look as they might, they couldn't find me. My father was furious. After a few days he insisted I had to stay in my tent with my husband. As soon as he left, I ran off and hid behind the tent in which the groom's sister stayed. I made her promise not to tell anyone I was there and slept there.

But they made me go back. That night, my father stood guard nearby with his gun. Every time I started to leave the tent, he would take a puff

[CONTINUED]

[CONTINUED]

on his cigarette so I could see that he was still there. Finally I rolled myself up in the straw mat. When the groom came, he looked and looked but could not find me.

Finally I went back to my family's household. I pretended to be possessed. I tensed my body, rolled my eyes, and everyone rushed about, brought me incense and prayed for me. They brought the healer [or holyman, *fg'ih*], who blamed the unwanted marriage. Then they decided that perhaps I was too young and that I should not be forced to return to my husband. I came out of the seizure, and they were so grateful that they forced my husband's family to grant a divorce.

My family returned the bride-price, and I stayed at home.

Náfla could not oppose her father's decision directly, but she was nevertheless able to resist his will through indirect means. Like other options for resistance by dependents unfairly treated, abused, or humiliated publicly, her rebellion served as a check on her father's and, perhaps, more important, her paternal uncle's power.

Supernatural sanctions, which seem to be associated with the weak and with dependents, provide the final check on abuse of authority. Supernatural retribution is believed to follow when the saintly lineages of Mrábtín are mistreated, their curses causing death or the

downfall of the offender's lineage. In one Bedouin tale, when a woman denied food to two young girls, she fell ill, and blood appeared on food she cooked—a punishment for mistreating the helpless. Possession, as Náfla's tale illustrates, may also be a form of resistance. . . .

All these sanctions serve to check the abuse of power by eminent persons who have the resources to be autonomous and to control those who are dependent upon them. At the same time, moreover, figures of authority are vulnerable to their dependents because their positions rest on the respect these people are willing to give them. *(By L. Abu-Lughod. (1986). Veiled sentiments: Honor and poetry in a Bedouin society (pp. 99–103). Berkeley: University of California Press.)*

SOCIAL CONTROL THROUGH WITCHCRAFT

Another agent of control in societies, with or without centralized political systems, is witchcraft. An individual will think twice before offending a neighbor if convinced that the neighbor could retaliate by resorting to black magic. Similarly, individuals may not wish to be accused of practicing witchcraft, and so they behave with greater circumspection. Among the Azande of the Sudan, people who think they have been bewitched may consult an oracle, who, after performing the appropriate mystical rites, then may establish or confirm the identity of the offending witch.[14] Confronted with this evidence, the "witch" will usually agree to cooperate in order to avoid any additional trouble. Should the victim die, the relatives of the deceased may choose to make magic against the witch, ultimately accepting the death of some villager both as evidence of guilt and of the efficacy of their magic. For the Azande, witchcraft provides not only a sanction against antisocial behavior but also a means of dealing with natural hostilities and death. No one wishes to be thought of as a witch, and surely no one wishes to be victimized by one. By institutionalizing their emotional responses, the Azande successfully maintain social order. (For more on witchcraft, see Chapter 13.)

SOCIAL CONTROL THROUGH LAW

Among the Inuit of northern Canada, all offenses are considered to involve disputes between individuals; thus, they must be settled between the disputants themselves. One way they may do so is through a song duel, in which they heap insults upon one another in songs specially composed for the occasion. Although society does not intervene, its interests are represented by spectators, whose applause determines the outcome. If, however, social harmony cannot be restored—and that is the goal, rather than assigning and punishing guilt—one or the other disputant may move to another band. Ultimately, there is no binding legal authority.

In Western society, by contrast, someone who commits an offense against another person may become subject to a series of complex legal proceedings. In criminal cases the primary concern is to assign and punish guilt rather than to help out the victim. The offender will be arrested by the police; tried before a judge and, perhaps, a jury; and, depending on the severity of the crime, may be fined, imprisoned, or even executed. Rarely does the victim receive restitution or compensation. Throughout this chain of events, the accused party is dealt with by police, judges, jurors, and jailers, who may have no personal acquaintance whatsoever with the plaintiff or the defendant. How strange this all seems from the standpoint of traditional Inuit culture! Clearly, the two systems operate under distinctly different assumptions.

[14]Evans-Pritchard, E. E. (1937). *Witchcraft, oracles and magic among the Azande.* London: Oxford University Press.

Definition of Law

Once two Inuit settle a dispute by engaging in a song contest, the affair is considered closed; no further action is expected. Would we choose to describe the outcome of such a contest as a legal decision? If every law is a sanction but not every sanction is a law, how are we to distinguish between social sanctions in general and those to which we apply the label "law"?

The definition of law has been a lively point of contention among anthropologists in the 20th century. In 1926, Bronislaw Malinowski argued that the rules of law are distinguished from the rules of custom in that "they are regarded as the obligation of one person and the rightful claim of another, sanctioned not by mere psychological motive, but by a definite social machinery of binding force based . . . upon mutual dependence."[15] In other words, laws exemplify social control because they employ overt coercion.

An example of one rule of custom in contemporary North American society might be the dictate that guests at a dinner party should repay the person who gave the party with entertainment in the future. A host or hostess who does not receive a return invitation may feel cheated out of something thought to be owed but has no legal claim against the ungrateful guest for the $30 spent on food and drinks. If, however, an individual was cheated out of the same sum by the grocer when shopping, the law could be invoked. Although Malinowski's definition introduced several important elements of law, his failure to distinguish adequately between legal and nonlegal sanctions left the problem of formulating a workable definition of law in the hands of later anthropologists.

According to E. Adamson Hoebel, an important pioneer in the anthropological study of law, "A social norm is legal if its neglect or infraction is regularly met, in threat or in fact, by the application of physical force by an individual or group possessing the socially recognized privilege of so acting."[16] In stressing the legitimate use of physical coercion, Hoebel de-emphasized the traditional association of law with a centralized court system. Although rules enacted by an authorized legislative body and enforced by the judicial mechanisms of the state are fundamental features of Western jurisprudence, they are not the universal backbone of human law. Can any concept of law be applied to societies for whom the notion

Having a song duel is the traditional approach to dispute resolution among the Inuit of northern Canada.

of a centralized judiciary is virtually meaningless? How shall we categorize duels, song contests, and other socially condoned forms of self-help that seem to meet some but not all of the criteria of law?

Ultimately, it is always of greatest value to consider each case within its cultural context. After all, law reflects a society's basic postulates, so to understand any society's laws, one must understand the underlying values and assumptions. Nonetheless, a working definition of law is useful for purposes of discussion and cross-cultural comparison, and for this, **law** is adequately characterized as formal negative sanctions.

Functions of Law

In Hoebel's 1954 book, *The Law of Primitive Man,* he wrote of a time when the idea that private property should be generously shared was a fundamental principle in traditional Cheyenne Indian culture. Subsequently, however, some men assumed the privilege of borrowing other men's horses without bothering to obtain permission. When Wolf Lies Down complained of such unauthorized borrowing to the members of the Elk Soldier Society, the Elk Soldiers not only had his horse returned to him but also secured an award for damages from the offender. The Elk Soldiers then announced that, to avoid such difficulties in the future, horses no longer could be borrowed without permission. Furthermore, they declared their intention to retrieve any such property and whip anyone who resisted the return of improperly borrowed goods.

This case illustrates three basic functions of law. First, it defines relationships among society's members and marks out proper behavior under specified circumstances.

---

[15]Malinowski, B. (1951). *Crime and custom in savage society* (p. 55). London: Routledge.

[16]Hoebel, E. A. (1954). *The law of primitive man: A study in comparative legal dynamics* (p. 28). Cambridge, MA: Harvard University Press.

law Formal negative sanctions.

Knowledge of the law permits each person to know his or her rights and duties with respect to every other member of society. Second, law allocates the authority to employ coercion in the enforcement of sanctions. In societies with centralized political systems, such authority is generally vested in the government and its judiciary system. In societies that lack centralized political control, the authority to employ force may be allocated directly to the injured party. Third, law functions to redefine social relations and to ensure social flexibility. As new situations arise, law must determine whether old rules and assumptions retain their validity and to what extent they must be altered. Law, if it is to operate efficiently, must allow room for change.

In practice, law is never as neat as a written description about it. In any given society, people are usually members of various subgroups—and fall under the varied dictates of these diverse groups. For example, among the Kapauku discussed earlier in this chapter, each individual is simultaneously a member of a family, a household, a sublineage, and a confederacy and is subject to all the rules and regulations of each. In some cases, as noted by anthropologist Leopold Pospisil, it may be impossible for an individual to submit to contradictory legal indications:

> In one of the confederacy's lineages, incestuous relations between members of the same clan were punished by execution of the culprits, and in another by severe beating, in the third constituent lineage such a relationship was not punishable and . . . was not regarded as incest at all. In one of the sublineages, it became even a preferred type of marriage.[17]

Furthermore, the power to employ sanctions may vary from level to level within a given society. The head of a Kapauku household may punish a household member by slapping or beating, but the authority to confiscate property is vested exclusively in the headman of the lineage. Analogous distinctions exist in the United States among municipal, state, and federal jurisdictions. The complexity of legal jurisdiction within each society makes any easy generalization about law difficult.

---

[17]Pospisil, L. (1971). *Anthropology of law: A comparative theory* (p. 36). New York: Harper & Row.

---

negotiation The use of direct argument and compromise by the parties to a dispute to arrive voluntarily at a mutually satisfactory agreement.
mediation Settlement of a dispute through negotiation assisted by an unbiased third party.
adjudication Mediation with an unbiased third party making the ultimate decision.

Crime

As we have observed, an important function of negative sanctions, legal or otherwise, is to discourage the breach of social norms. A person contemplating theft is aware of the possibility of being caught and punished. Yet, even in the face of severe sanctions, individuals in every society sometimes violate the norms and subject themselves to the consequences of their behavior.

In Western societies a clear distinction is made between offenses against the state and offenses against an individual. However, in non-state societies such as bands and tribes, all offenses are viewed as transgressions against individuals or kin-groups (families, lineages, clans, and so on). Disputes between individuals or kin-groups may seriously disrupt the social order, especially in small groups where the number of disputants, though small in absolute numbers, may be a large percentage of the total population. For example, although the Inuit traditionally have no effective domestic or economic unit beyond the family, a dispute between two people will interfere with the ability of members of separate families to come to one another's aid when necessary and is consequently a matter of wider social concern. The goal of judicial proceedings in such instances is restoring social harmony rather than punishing an offender. When distinguishing between offenses of concern to the community as a whole and those of concern only to a few individuals, we may refer to them as collective or personal.

Basically, disputes are settled in either of two ways. First, disputing parties may, through argument and compromise, voluntarily arrive at a mutually satisfactory agreement. This form of settlement is referred to as **negotiation** or, if it involves the assistance of an unbiased third party, **mediation.** In bands and tribes a third-party mediator has no coercive power and thus cannot force disputants to abide by such a decision, but as a person who commands great personal respect, the mediator frequently may effect a settlement.

MEDIATREK
For a comprehensive gateway to conflict resolution resources, including key ongoing conflicts around the world and the cultural background information needed to understand them, go to MediaTrek 12.3 on the companion Web site or CD-ROM.

Second, in chiefdoms and states, an authorized third party may issue a binding decision the disputing parties will be compelled to respect. This process is referred to as **adjudication.** The difference between mediation and adjudication is basically a difference in authorization. In a dispute settled by adjudication, the disputing parties pres-

Canada's recently revised Criminal Code opened the door for new justice processes drawing on Native American traditions, such as the Talking Circle.

© Martin Neptune

ent their positions as compellingly as they can, but they do not participate in the ultimate decision making.

Although the adjudication process is not universally characteristic, every society employs some form of negotiation to settle disputes. Often negotiation acts as a prerequisite or an alternative to adjudication. For example, in the resolution of U.S. labor disputes, striking workers may first negotiate with management, often with the mediation of a third party. If the state decides the strike constitutes a threat to the public welfare, the disputing parties may be forced to submit to adjudication. In this case, the responsibility for resolving the dispute is transferred to a presumably impartial judge.

The judge's work is difficult and complex. Not only must the evidence presented be sifted through, but also the judge must consider a wide range of norms, values, and earlier rulings to arrive at a decision intended to be considered just not only by the disputing parties but by the public and other judges as well.

Punitive justice, such as imprisonment, may be the most common approach to justice in North America, but has not proven to be an effective way of changing criminal behavior—certainly not among Native Americans. For a number of years, Native American communities in Canada pressed their federal government to reform justice services to make them more consistent with aboriginal values and traditions. In 1999 Canada's Supreme Court amended sentencing law in the country's Criminal Code to include the following principle: "All available sanctions other than imprisonment that are reasonable in the circumstances should be considered for all offenders, with particular attention to the circumstances of aboriginal offenders."[18] Native communities have pressed especially for restorative justice

techniques such as the Talking Circle, traditionally used by Native American groups. For this, parties involved in a conflict come together in a circle with equal opportunity to express their views—one at a time, free of interruption. Usually, a "talking stick" (or eagle feather or some other symbolic tool) is held by whoever is speaking to signal that she or he has the right to talk at that moment and others have the responsibility to listen.

In the United States, over the past three decades there has been significant movement away from the courts in favor of outside negotiation and mediation to resolve a wide variety of disputes. Many jurists see this as a means to clear overloaded court dockets so as to concentrate on more important cases. A correlate of this move is a change in ideology, elevating order and harmony to positive values and replacing open coercion (seen as undemocratic) with control through persuasion.

In the abstract, this seems like a good idea and suggests a return to a system of cultural control characteristic of band and tribal societies. However, a crucial difference exists. In tribal and band societies, agreement is less likely to be coercive because all concerned individuals can negotiate and mediate on relatively equal terms. The United States, by contrast, has great disparities in power, and evidence indicates that it is the stronger parties that prefer mediation and negotiation. As anthropologist Laura Nader points out, there is now less emphasis on justice and concern with causes of disputes than on smoothing things over in ways that tend to be pacifying and restrictive—an emphasis that produces order of a repressive sort.[19] That said, leaders in the field of dispute resolution in the United States and other parts of the industrial and postindustrial world are finding effective

---

[18]Criminal Code of Canada, s.718.2(e).

[19]Nader, L. (1997). Controlling processes: Tracing the dynamic components of power. *Current Anthropology, 38,* 714–715.

© Dr. James Gribbs, Anthropology Department, Stanford University

© Hans Halberstadt/Photo Researchers, Inc.

VISUAL COUNTERPOINT

Two means of psychological stress evaluation: a Kpelle "trial by ordeal" and a Western polygraph ("lie detector").

ways to bring about balanced solutions to conflict. An example of this appears in Anthropology Applied.

In many politically centralized societies, incorruptible supernatural, or at least nonhuman, powers are thought to make judgments through a "trial by ordeal." Among the Kpelle of Liberia, for example, when guilt is in doubt an "ordeal operator" licensed by the government may apply a hot knife to a suspect's leg. If the leg is burned, the suspect is guilty; if not, innocence is assumed. But the operator does not merely heat the knife and apply it. After massaging the suspect's legs and determining the knife is hot enough, the operator then strokes his own leg with it without being burned, demonstrating that the innocent will escape injury. The knife is then applied to the suspect. Up to this point—consciously or unconsciously—the operator has read the suspect's nonverbal cues: gestures, the degree of muscular tension, amount of perspiration, and so forth. From this the operator can judge whether or not the accused is showing so much anxiety as to indicate probable guilt; in effect, a psychological stress evaluation has been made. As the knife is applied, it is manipulated to either burn or not burn the suspect, once this judgment has been made. The operator does this manipulation easily by controlling how long the knife is in the fire, as well as the pressure and angle at which it is pressed against the leg.[20]

Similar to this is the use of the lie detector (polygraph) in the United States, although the guiding ideology is scientific rather than supernaturalistic. Nevertheless, an incorruptible nonhuman agency is thought to establish who is lying and who is not, whereas in reality the polygraph operator cannot just "read" the needles of the machine. He or she must judge whether or not they are registering a high level of anxiety brought on by the testing situation, as opposed to the stress of guilt. Thus, the polygraph operator has much in common with the Kpelle ordeal operator.

---

[20]Gibbs, J. L., Jr. (1983). [Interview]. *Faces of culture: Program 18.* Fountain Valley, CA: Coast Telecourses.

POLITICAL ORGANIZATION AND EXTERNAL AFFAIRS

Although the regulation of internal affairs is an important function of any political system, it is by no means the sole function. Another is the management of external affairs—relations not just among different states but among different bands, lineages, clans, or whatever the largest autonomous political unit may be. And just as the threatened or actual use of force may be used to maintain order within a society, it also may be used in the conduct of external affairs.

War

Our species has a horrific track record when it comes to violence. Far more lethal than spontaneous and individual outbursts of aggression, organized violence in the form of war is responsible for enormous suffering and deliberate destruction of life and property. In the past 5,000 years or so, some 14,000 wars have been fought, resulting in many hundreds of millions of casualties.

Generally, we may distinguish among different motives, objectives, methods, and scales of warfare as organized violence. For instance, some societies engage in defensive wars only and avoid armed confrontations with others unless seriously threatened or actually attacked. Others initiate aggressive wars to pursue particular strategic objectives, including material benefits in the form of precious resources such as slaves, gold, or oil, as well as territorial expansion or control over trade routes. In some cultures, aggressive wars are waged for ideological reasons, such as spreading one's own worldview or religion and defeating "evil" ideas or heresies elsewhere. The scale of warfare ranges from local armed conflicts to far-reaching wars fought on a global scale. In addition, we may distinguish among various civil wars (in which armies from different geographical sections, ethnic or religious groups, or political parties within the same state are

Anthropology Applied

Dispute Resolution and the Anthropologist

In an era when the consequences of violent approaches to dispute resolution are more far-reaching than ever, conflict management is of growing importance. A world leader in this profession is William L. Ury, an independent negotiations specialist who earned his Ph.D. in anthropology at Harvard University. Asked why he was drawn to study anthropology, Ury says: "I was attracted by the focus on understanding human beings—who we are in all our rich diversity, where we've come from, and where we're going—as viewed through a multifaceted, holistic perspective."[a]

In his first year at graduate school, Ury began looking for a way to apply anthropology to practical problems, including conflicts of all dimensions. He wrote a paper about the role of anthropology in peacemaking, and on a whim sent it to Roger Fisher, a law professor noted for his work in negotiation and world affairs. Fisher, in turn, invited the young graduate student to co-author a kind of how-to book for international mediators. The book they researched and wrote together turned out to have a far wider audience, for it presented basic principles of negotiation that could be applied to household spats, management–employee conflicts, or international crises. Titled *Getting to Yes: Negotiating Agreement without Giving In* (1981), it sold millions of copies, was translated into twenty-one languages, and earned the nickname "negotiator's bible."

While working on the book, Ury and Fisher co-founded the Program on Negotiation (PON) at Harvard Law School, pulling together an interdisciplinary group of academics interested in new approaches to and applications of the negotiation process. Today this applied research center is a multi-

university consortium that trains mediators, businesspeople, and government officials in negotiation skills. It has four keys goals: (1) design, implement, and evaluate better dispute resolution practices; (2) promote collaboration among practitioners and scholars; (3) develop education programs and materials for instruction in negotiation and dispute resolution; (4) increase public awareness and understanding of successful conflict resolution efforts.

In 1982, Ury earned his Ph.D. with a dissertation titled *Talk Out or Walk Out: The Role and Control of Conflict in a*

© Jay Dickman

Kentucky Coal Mine. Afterward, he taught for several years while maintaining a leadership role at PON. In particular, he devoted himself to PON's Global Negotiation Project (initially known as the Project on Avoiding War). Today, having left his teaching post at Harvard, Ury continues to serve as director of the Global Negotiation Project, writing, consulting, and running regular workshops

on dealing with difficult people and situations. Utilizing a cross-cultural perspective sharpened through years of anthropological research, he specializes in ethnic and secessionist disputes, including those between white and black South Africans, Serbs and Croats, Turks and Kurds, Catholics and Protestants in Northern Ireland, Russians and Chechens in the former Soviet Union.

Among the most effective tools in Ury's applied anthropology work are his books on dispute resolution. In 1993 he wrote *Getting Past No: Negotiating Your Way from Confrontation,* which explores ways to reach out to hostile parties who are not interested in negotiation. His 1999 book, *Getting to Peace: Transforming Conflict at Home, at Work, and in the World,* examines what he calls the "third side," which is the role that the surrounding community can play in preventing, resolving, and containing destructive conflict between two parties.[b] His 2002 edited volume *Must We Fight?* challenges entrenched ideas that violence and war are inevitable and presents convincing evidence that human beings have as much inherent potential for cooperation and coexistence as they do for violent conflict. The key point in this book is that violence is a choice. In Ury's words, "Conflict is not going to end, but violence can."[c] What Ury and others in this field are doing is helping create a culture of negotiation in a world where adversarial, win-lose attitudes are out of step with the increasingly interdependent relations between people. ■ ■ ■

[a] Personal communication. (2003, November 9).
[b] Pease, T. (2000). Taking the third side. *Andover Bulletin,* spring.
[c] Ury, W. (2002). A global immune system. *Andover Bulletin,* winter; see also www.PON.harvard.edu and www.thirdside.org.

VISUAL COUNTERPOINT Public displays of human skulls may serve to commemorate victory over enemies slain in battle or sacrificed as war captives—as depicted on this stone wall in the ancient Maya city of Chichen Itza in southeastern Mexico. Such displays may also serve as a gruesome monument of organized violence as in this Cambodian map made of skulls belonging to victims of the ruthless Red Khmer regime that claimed the lives of some 1.7 million innocent Cambodians in the 1970s.

pitted against each other), formally declared international wars fought by professional armed forces, and low-intensity guerilla warfare involving small-scale hit-and-run tactical operations instead of pitched battles.

Why do wars occur? Some argue that humans are naturally aggressive. As evidence of this they point to aggressive group behavior exhibited by chimpanzees in Tanzania where researchers observed one group systematically destroy another and take over their territory. Also, they cite the behavior of people such as the Yanomami Indians who range on either side of the border between Brazil and Venezuela. These tropical gardeners and foragers have been described as living in a chronic state of war, and some scientists suggest this exemplifies the way all humans once behaved.

Critics of these arguments point out that "warlike" behavior among chimpanzees and their close relatives, bonobos, has not been widely observed.[21] In fact bonobos are noted for their ability to resolve disputes peacefully. As for the Yanomami, not all agree that they are as fierce as portrayed, nor can we assume that all people once lived the way they do. Like all people, the Yanomami have a history, and their present activities undoubtedly reflect a particular historical context—one that, since the mid-20th century, has included increasing levels of disruption and violence due to pressures created by outsiders penetrating and exploiting Yanomami territory.[22]

In other words, warfare among humans, as well as aggressive group behavior among apes, may be situation specific rather than an unavoidable expression of some sort of biological predisposition. This is not to say that violence was unknown among ancient humans, as some have argued. The occasional discovery of stone spear points embedded in human skeletons, such as that of a more than 9,000-year-old man found in Kennewick in the northwestern United States or even older ones from the Grimaldi caves in Italy prove otherwise. Nevertheless, it is clear that war is not a universal phenomenon, for in various parts of the world there are societies that do not practice warfare as we know it. Examples include people as diverse as the Bushmen of southern Africa, the Arapesh of New Guinea, and the Jain of India. Among societies that do practice warfare, levels of violence may differ dramatically. Anthropologist Robert Gordon, for example, compares the "indiscriminate killing" of modern warfare with warfare in New Guinea. The latter, he writes, is

> slightly more "civilized" than the violence of warfare which we [of the industrialized world] practice insofar as it's strictly between two groups. And as an outsider, you can go up and interview people and talk to them while they're fighting and the arrows will miss you. It's quite safe and you can take photographs.[23]

We have ample reason to suppose that war has become a problem only in the last 10,000 years, since the invention of food-production techniques and especially since the formation of centralized states 5,000 years ago. It has reached crisis proportions in the past 200 years, with the invention of modern weaponry and increased direction of violence against civilian populations. In con-

---

[21]Power, M. G. (1995). Gombe revisited: Are chimpanzees violent and hierarchical in the "free" state? *General Anthropology, 2*(1), 5–9.

---

[22]Mann, C. C. (2000). Misconduct alleged in Yanomami studies. *Science, 289*, 2,253.

---

[23]Gordon, R. J. (1981, December). [Interview]. Los Angeles: Coast Telecourses.

Often depicted as "warlike by nature," the Yanomami may be no such thing; rather, Yanomami warfare is likely a recent phenomenon related to outside pressures originating in the Brazilian and Venezuelan states.

temporary warfare, we have reached the point where casualties not just of civilians but also of *children* far outnumber those of soldiers. Thus, war is not so much an age-old problem as it is a relatively recent one.

Among food foragers, with their uncentralized political systems, violence may erupt sporadically, but warfare was all but unknown until recent times. There are several reasons for this. First of all, since territorial boundaries and membership among food-foraging bands are usually fluid and loosely defined, a man who hunts with one band today may hunt with a neighboring band next month. This renders warfare impractical. So, too, does the systematic interchange of marriage partners among food-foraging groups, which makes it likely that someone in each band will have a sister, a brother, or a cousin in a neighboring band. Moreover, the absence of a food surplus among foragers makes prolonged combat difficult. Finally, a worldview in which people perceive themselves as part of the natural world rather than superior to it tends to work against exploitation of other people. In sum, where populations are small and see themselves as part of the natural world, where food surpluses are absent, property ownership minimal, and no state organization exists, the likelihood of organized violence by one group against another is small.[24]

Despite the traditional view of the gardener or farmer as a gentle tiller of the soil, it is among such people, along with pastoralists, that warfare becomes prominent. One reason may be that food-producing peoples have a more exploitative worldview than do food foragers. Another is that they are far more prone to population growth than are food foragers, whose numbers are generally maintained well below carrying capacity. This population growth, if unchecked, can lead to resource depletion, one solution to which may be seizure of some other people's resources. In addition, the commitment to a fixed piece of land inherent in farming makes such societies somewhat less fluid in their membership than those of food foragers. Instead of marrying distantly, farmers marry locally, depriving them of long-distance kin networks. In rigidly matrilocal or patrilocal societies, each new generation is bound to the same territory, no matter how small it may be or how large the group trying to live within it.

The availability of unoccupied lands may not serve as a sufficient detriment to the outbreak of war. Among swidden farmers, for example, competition for land cleared of old growth forest frequently leads to hostility and armed conflict. The centralization of political control and the possession of valuable property among farming people provide many more stimuli for warfare. It is among such peoples, especially those organized into states, where the violence of warfare is most apt to result in indiscriminate killing. This development has reached its peak in modern states. Indeed, much (but not all) of the warfare that has been observed in recent stateless societies (so-called tribal warfare) has been induced by states as a reaction to colonial expansion.[25]

_____

[24]Knauft, pp. 391–409.

[25]Whitehead, N. L., & Ferguson, R. B. (1993, November). Deceptive stereotypes about tribal warfare. *Chronicle of Higher Education*, A48.

Although warfare was certainly present in northeastern America before the arrival of Europeans, intergroup conflicts began to increase and intensify in the 16th century as a direct consequence of dispossession of Indian lands and the huge demand in Europe for precious furs, especially beaver ("soft gold"). Competition over game-rich territories, intensified by the availability of muskets and other deadly European weapons, led to violence. Alcohol introduced by Europeans as a trade commodity no doubt fueled the aggression, and each killing called for revenge. All of this triggered a cycle of bloody warfare commonly referred to as the Beaver Wars, involving virtually all native groups—food foragers and horticulturalists alike—from Cape Breton Island down to Chesapeake Bay and as far inland as the Great Lakes. These wars—periodic vicious outbursts—continued throughout much of the 17th century. [26]

Among the many American Indian groups involved in the Beaver Wars were the Iroquoian nations—Mohawk, Oneida, Onondaga, Cayuga, and Seneca. Before Europeans landed on their shores, these neighboring groups had resolved to end warfare among themselves by creating an alliance and directing their aggressive activities against outsiders. In this way the famous Iroquois Confederacy came into being. Warring frequently against their immediate and more distant neighbors, members of the confederacy gained dominance and forced their victims to acknowledge Iroquoian superiority. The relation between victim and victor, however, was not outright subordination. Imposed payment of tribute purchased "protection" from the Iroquois. The price of protection went further than this, though; it included constant and public ceremonial deference to the Iroquois, free passage for their war parties through the subordinate group's country, and the contribution of young men to Iroquoian war parties.

An instructive comparison can be made between the Iroquois nations and European Christians. In the year 1095 the Roman Catholic Pope Urban II launched the first crusade ("War of the Cross"), with a speech urging the Christian nobles of Europe to end their ceaseless wars against each other by directing their hostilities toward Muslim Turks and Arabs in the Middle East, who Europeans saw as infidels. In the same speech the pope also alluded to the economic benefits to be realized by seizing the resources of the "infidels." Although it is clear that the Crusades were motivated by more than religious ideology, they were justified as a holy war to liberate Jerusalem and the Holy Land from Muslims. Their success was limited, and 20 years after the ninth

and final crusade of 1271 to 1272, the last Christian stronghold in Palestine surrendered to a Muslim army.

Within the next few centuries, however, Europe's Christian powers turned their attention to state building and colonial expansion in other parts of the world. Proceeding in concert with this growth and outward expansion was the development of the technology and organization of warfare. With the emergence of states (not just in Europe but in other parts of the world as well) has come a dramatic increase in the scale of warfare. Perhaps this is not surprising, given the state's acceptance of force as a legitimate tool for regulating human affairs and its ability to organize large numbers of people.

Consider, for example, the Aztec state in the central Mexican highlands, which engaged in continuous warfare from the mid-1400s until its demise in the early 1520s. By way of battle, the state collected tribute and achieved regional dominance. Moreover, by waging war against their neighbors, Aztecs obtained prisoners to use as offerings for gods that they believed required human sacrifice to maintain the cosmic order: "The warrior slated for sacrifice was a *teomiqui*, 'he who dies in godlike fashion,' and would feed the sun so that it might shine upon the world and keep it in motion."[27] Among Aztecs, this worldview justified, even sanctified, perpetual aggression. In fact, according to the noted anthropologist Eric Wolf, priests bearing the images of the Aztec war god Huitilopochtli and other deities walked ahead of the army and gave the signal to commence combat by lighting a fire and blowing on shell trumpets. The victory that followed, Wolf wrote, "always had the same results: long lines of captives, wooden collars about their necks, made the long journey to Tenochtitlán to be offered upon the altars of the gods."[28] Several thousand captives could be sacrificed after a military campaign, and within a single year as many as 20,000 may have been offered to the gods in that capital city of the Aztec state.

This Aztec example, as well as that of the Christian Crusades, shows that ideological motivations and justifications for war are embedded in a society's worldview—the collective body of ideas that members of a culture generally share concerning the ultimate shape and substance of their reality. We will discuss other aspects of worldview in the following chapter, which focuses on religion and the supernatural.

Currently, there are several dozen wars going on in the world, often resulting in massive killing fields

[26]Prins, H. E. L. (1996). *The Mi'kmaq: Resistance, accommodation, and cultural survival* (p. 106). Orlando: Harcourt Brace.

[27]Keen, B. (1971). *The Aztec image in Western thought* (p. 13). New Brunswick, NJ: Rutgers University Press.

[28]Wolf, E. R. (1999). *Envisioning power: Ideologies of dominance and crisis* (p. 263). Berkeley: University of California Press.

Many armies around the world recruit children. Today, there are more than 300,000 child soldiers, many as young as 12 years old. Among them are these boys training to be guerillas in Sahel, Eritrea.

(Figure 12.4). Most of the victims of war today are noncombatants, including elders, women, and children. And many contemporary wars are not between states but often occur within countries where the government is either corrupt, ineffective, or without popular support. The following examples offer some specific data. Between 1975 and 1979, Khmer Rouge soldiers in Cambodia murdered 1.7 million fellow citizens, or 20 percent of that country's population. In the 1990s, between 2 and 3 million died due to warfare in the southern Sudan. Another 5 million died in the recent war in Congo (1998–2003), which involved armies from a handful of neighboring states as well. Add to these the war the Russian army is now waging against Chechen separatists who want an independent homeland, the Indonesian army fighting against the Aceh in northern Sumatra who want the same, the U.S. army against guerillas in Afghanistan and Iraq, the ongoing combat operations in Colombia, and so on. Moreover, there are hundreds of violent flashpoints or hot spots such as Palestine, Liberia, Kosovo, and northern Ireland. And not all the combatants are adult males. Many armies, including the U.S. military, also have women serving in combat operations. Moreover, many armies around the world also recruit children. Today, there are more than 300,000 child soldiers, many as young as 12 years old.

As the above examples show, the causes of warfare are complex, involving economic, political, and ideological factors. The challenge of eliminating human warfare has never been greater than it is in today's world—nor has the cost of *not* finding a way to do so.

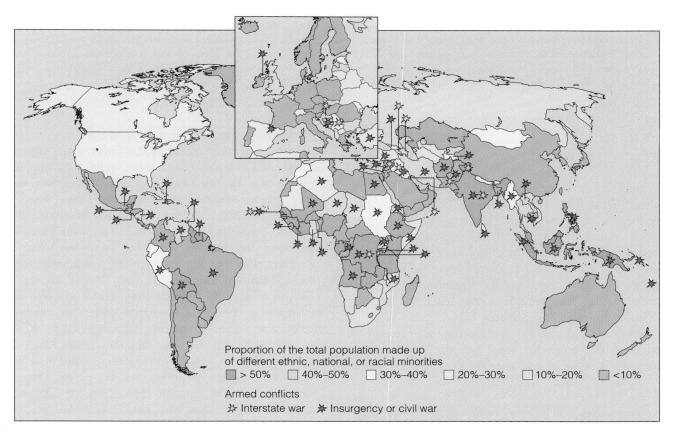

Proportion of the total population made up of different ethnic, national, or racial minorities

> 50% 40%–50% 30%–40% 20%–30% 10%–20% <10%

Armed conflicts

Interstate war   Insurgency or civil war

FIGURE 12.4

In multinational states, warfare is common as one nationality suppresses others within the country.

Anthropologists of Note

Laura Nader (1930–)

Courtesy of Dr. Laura Nader

Laura Nader has stood out among her peers from the start of her career in 1960, when she became the first woman faculty member in the anthropology department at the University of California, Berkeley.

Nader and her three siblings grew up in Winsted, Connecticut, children of immigrants from Lebanon. As she recalls, "My dad left Lebanon for political reasons, and when he came to the land of the free, he took it seriously. So we were raised to believe that you should be involved in public issues." They were also taught to question assumptions. Both Nader and her younger brother Ralph have made careers of doing this. She is an anthropologist noted for her cross-cultural research on law, justice, and social control and their connection to power structures. He is a consumer advocate and former U.S. presidential candidate who is a watchdog on issues

of public health and the safety and quality of life.

Laura Nader's undergraduate studies included a study-abroad year in Mexico. Later, while earning her Ph.D. in anthropology at Radcliffe College, she returned to Mexico to do fieldwork in a Zapotec Indian peasant village in the Sierra Madre Mountains of Oaxaca. Reflecting on this and subsequent research, she says, "In the 1950s, when I went to southern Mexico, I was studying how the Zapotec organize their lives, what they do with their problems, what they do when they go to court. And when I came back to this country, I started looking at American equivalents, at how Americans solve their consumer and service complaints."

Nader's first decade of teaching at Berkeley coincided with the Vietnam War, an era when the campus was in a perpetual state of turmoil with students demonstrating for peace and civil rights. Turning into a scholar-activist, she called upon colleagues to "study up" and do research on the world's power elite. "The study of man," she wrote in 1972, "is confronted with an unprecedented situation: Never before

have a few, by their actions and inactions, had the power of life and death over so many members of the species . . ." To date, the results of Nader's own research have appeared in over 100 publications. Among these are her numerous books, including *Naked Science—Anthropological Inquiry into Boundaries, Power, and Knowledge* (1996), and *The Life of the Law: Anthropological Projects* (2002).

Playing a leading role in the development of the anthropology of law, Nader has taken on specialists in the fields of law, children's issues, nuclear energy, and science (including her own profession), critically questioning the basic assumptions ("central dogmas") under which these experts operate. She presses her students to do the same—to think critically, question authority, and break free from the "controlling processes" of the power elite. In 2000, Nader accepted one of the highest honors of the American Anthropological Association—an invitation to give the distinguished lecture at its annual gathering. *(Adapted from Interview with Laura Nader.* California Monthly. *November 2000.)*

POLITICAL SYSTEMS AND THE QUESTION OF LEGITIMACY

Whatever form a society's political system may take, it always must find some way to obtain and retain the people's allegiance. In uncentralized systems, where every adult participates in all decision making, loyalty and cooperation are freely given, since each person is considered a part of the political system. As the group grows larger, however, and the organization becomes more formal, the problem of obtaining and keeping public support becomes greater.

Centralized political systems may also rely upon coercion as a means of social control. This, however, carries a measure of risk since the personnel needed to

legitimacy The right of political leaders to govern—to hold, use, and allocate power—based on the values a particular society holds.

apply force often must be numerous and may grow to be a political power. Also, the emphasis on force may create resentment and lessen cooperation. Thus, police states are generally short-lived; most societies choose less extreme forms of social coercion. In the United States, this is reflected in the increasing emphasis placed on cultural, as opposed to social, control. Laura Nader (see Anthropologists of Note) is well known for her anthropological research concerning issues of power, including social and cultural control.

Also basic to the political process is the concept of **legitimacy,** or the right of political leaders to govern. Like force, legitimacy is a form of support for a political system; unlike force, legitimacy is based on the values a particular society holds. For example, among the Kapauku the legitimacy of the *tonowi's* power comes from his wealth; the kings of Hawaii, and of England and France before their revolutions, were thought to have a divine right to rule; and the head of the Dahomey state of West Africa acquired legitimacy through his age, as he was always the oldest living male.

© Reuters/Corbis

© K. Prouse/Pressnet/Topham/The Image Works

VISUAL COUNTERPOINT In contrast to countries such as the United States, where religion and state are constitutionally separated, others such as Iran and Great Britain permit a much closer relationship between political and religious affairs. For instance, Shiite Muslim religious leader Ayatollah Khamenei is not only Iran's supreme spiritual leader but also his country's highest political authority. In England, Queen Elizabeth is not only her country's nominal head of state but also head of the Anglican Church.

Legitimacy grants the right to hold, use, and allocate power. Power based on legitimacy results in authority. It is distinct from power based solely on force: Obedience to authority results from the belief that obedience is "right"; compliance to power based on force results from fear of being deprived of liberty, physical well-being, life, or material property. Thus, power based on legitimacy is symbolic and depends upon the positive expectations of those who recognize and accept it. If the expectations are not met regularly (if the head of state fails to deliver economic prosperity or the leader is continuously unsuccessful in preventing or dealing with calamities), the legitimacy of the recognized power figure erodes or may collapse altogether.

RELIGION AND POLITICS

As already suggested by the examples of Aztec warfare and the Crusades, religion is often intricately connected with politics. Religious beliefs may influence laws: Acts that people believe to be sinful, such as incest, are often illegal as well. Frequently it is religion that legitimizes the political order.

In both industrial and nonindustrial societies, belief in the supernatural is important and is reflected in people's governments. One place where the effect of religion on politics was well exemplified was in medieval Europe: Holy wars were fought over the smallest matter; labor was mobilized to build immense cathedrals in honor of the Virgin and other saints; kings and queens ruled by "divine right" and (in the West) pledged allegiance to the pope and asked his blessing in all important ventures, were they marital or martial.

In the pre-Columbian Americas the Aztec state was a religious state, with a divine king, that thrived in spite of more-or-less constant warfare carried out to procure captives for human sacrifices to assuage or please the gods. In Peru the Inca emperor proclaimed absolute authority based on the proposition that he was descended from the sun god. Modern Iran was proclaimed an "Islamic republic" and its first head of state was the most holy of all Shiite Muslim holy men. In the United States the Declaration of Independence, which is an expression of the country's social and political values, stresses a belief in a supreme being. The document states that "all men are created [by God] equal," a tenet that gave rise to American democracy because it implied that all people should participate in governing themselves. The fact that the president of the United States takes the oath of office by swearing on the Bible is another instance of the use of religion to legitimize political power, as is the phrase "one nation, under God" in the Pledge of Allegiance. On U.S. coins is the phrase "In God We Trust," many meetings of government bodies begin with a prayer or invocation, and the phrase "so help me God" is routinely used in legal proceedings. In spite of an official separation of church and state, religious legitimization of government lingers on.

Chapter Summary

- Through political organization, societies impose and maintain social order, manage public affairs, and reduce social disorder. No group can function without persuading or coercing its members to conform to agreed-upon rules of conduct.
- Four basic types of political systems may be identified, ranging from uncentralized bands and tribes to centralized chiefdoms and states. The band is a relatively small and loosely organized kin-ordered group that inhabits a specific territory and that may split into smaller extended family groups that are politically independent. Political organization in bands is

democratic, and informal control is exerted by public opinion in the form of gossip and ridicule. Band leaders are usually older men whose personal authority lasts only as long as members believe they are leading well and making the right decisions.

■ In anthropology, *tribe* refers to a range of kin-ordered groups that are politically integrated by some unifying factor and whose members share a common ancestry, identity, culture, language, and territory. With an economy usually based on crop cultivation or herding, the tribe's population is larger than that of the band, although family units within the tribe are still relatively autonomous and egalitarian. As in the band, political organization is transitory, and leaders have no coercive means of maintaining authority.

■ One variant of authority in tribes is the Big Man, who builds up his wealth and political power until he must be reckoned with as a leader. In many tribal societies the organizing political unit is the clan, comprised of people who consider themselves descended from a common ancestor. A group of elders or headmen or headwomen regulate the affairs of members and represent their group in relations with other clans. The segmentary lineage system, usually found in societies in which people trace their ancestry in the male line to the same founding ancestor, is a relatively rare form of kin-ordered organization. Tribal age-grade systems cut across territorial and kin groupings. Leadership is vested in men in the group who were initiated into the age grade at the same time and passed as a set from one age grade to another until reaching the proper age to become elders. Common-interest associations wield political authority in some tribes.

■ As societies include larger numbers of people and become more heterogeneous socially, politically, and economically, leadership becomes more centralized. A chiefdom is a regional polity in which two or more local kin-ordered groups are organized under a chief. An individual's status is determined by his or her position in a descent group and distance of relationship to the chief, whose role is to unite his community in all matters. The chief may accumulate great personal wealth, which enhances his power base and which he may pass on to his heirs.

■ The most centralized of political organizations is the state—a complex political institution involving large numbers of people within a defined territory. Its members are organized and directed by a formal government that has the capacity and authority to make laws and use force to maintain the social order. The state is found in diverse, stratified societies, with unequal distribution of wealth and power. States are inherently unstable and transitory and differ from nations, which are communities of people who share a collective identity based on a common culture, language, territorial base, and history.

■ Research shows that far fewer women than men have held important positions of political leadership. Nonetheless, in a number of societies, women have enjoyed political equality with men, as among the Iroquoian peoples in northeastern North America. Under centralized political systems, women are most likely to be subordinate to men.

■ Two kinds of control exist: internalized and externalized. Internalized controls are self-imposed by enculturated individuals. They rely on personal shame, fear of divine punishment, and magical retaliation. Externalized controls, called sanctions, mix cultural and social control. Positive sanctions are rewards or recognition by others, whereas negative sanctions include threat of imprisonment, fines, corporal punishment, or loss of face. Sanctions are either formal, including actual laws, or informal, involving norms. Other important agents of social control are witchcraft beliefs and religious sanctions. Sanctions serve to assure conformity to group norms, including actual law, and to maintain the place of each social faction in a community. Law, formal negative sanctions, defines relationships and prescribes and prohibits behavior among a society's members and allocates authority to enforce sanctions. In centralized political systems, this authority rests with the government and court system, whereas uncentralized societies give this authority directly to the injured party.

■ In contrast to bands, tribes, and chiefdoms, state societies distinguish between crimes (offenses against the state) and offenses against an individual. A dispute may be settled in two ways: negotiation and adjudication. All societies use negotiation to settle individual disputes. In negotiation the parties to the dispute reach an agreement themselves, with or without the help of a third party. In adjudication, an authorized third party issues a binding decision. Political systems also attempt to regulate external affairs, or relations between politically autonomous units. In doing so they may resort to the threat or use of force.

■ War is not a universal phenomenon. In contrast to non-state organized societies with a naturalistic worldview, centralized political systems have to obtain and maintain loyalty and support. Reliance on force and coercion eventually lessens a political system's effectiveness. Legitimacy, or the right of political leaders to exercise power, is required to govern with authority. Legitimate government may be distinguished from rule based on intimidation or force. To a greater or lesser extent, most governments the world over use ideology, including religion to legitimize political power.

Questions for Reflection

1. The basic challenge for people in all societies is to decide who gets what, when, where, and how. In many states, political power is concentrated in the hands of an elite few belonging to a dominant nationality or ethnic group. Imagine you belong to a repressed group such as the Quechna of Ecuador, depicted in the chapter's opening photograph. What would you do if you were systematically frustrated in the exercise of your human rights in a political system that discriminates against your ethnic group?

2. Given the basic definition of politics presented in the beginning of this chapter, why do you think that power in egalitarian societies plays a relatively insignificant role?

3. If political organization functions to impose or maintain order and to resolve conflicts, why do you think that a government in a country such as your own is so interested in legit-

imizing its power? What happens when a government loses such legitimacy?

4. Which nationalities or ethnic groups do you know that are dominant, and which can you identify that are in a minority position or are repressed? What is the basis for this inequality?

5. When your own government declares war against another country, on which basis does it seek to justify its decision to send soldiers into battle? Do you know the death ratio of non-combatants to soldiers in your country's most recent war?

Key Terms

Power	Cultural control
Political organization	Social control
Band	Sanctions
Tribe	Law
Segmentary lineage system	Negotiation
Chiefdom	Mediation
State	Adjudication
Nation	Legitimacy

Multimedia Review Tools

Companion Web Site

Visit **http://www.wadsworth.com/anthropology_d/** and click on the companion Web site for this textbook to access a wide range of material to aid your study of anthropology. Among the options for self-study in each chapter are learning objectives, flash cards, Internet activities, Web links, InfoTrac College Edition exercises, and practice tests that can be scored and emailed to your instructor.

CD-ROM

The *Doing Anthropology Today* CD-ROM supplied with your textbook provides unique and valuable information designed to enhance your learning experience. This interactive multimedia resource includes video clips, interviews with renowned anthropologists, map and timeline exercises, chapter study quizzes, and much more. *Doing Anthropology Today* will not only help you in achieving your grade goals, it will also make your learning experience fun and exciting!

Suggested Readings

Gledhill, J. (2000). *Power and its disguises: Anthropological perspectives on politics* (2nd ed.). Boulder, CO: Pluto Press.

Exploring the power relations that shape the global order, the author discusses the politics of agrarian civilizations and societies without indigenous states and then turns to the politics of domination and resistance within the colonial context, followed by an examination of contemporary politics of Africa, Asia, and Latin America.

Gordon, R. J., & Meggitt, M. J. (1985). *Law and order in the New Guinea highlands.* Hanover, NH: University Press of New England.

This ethnographic study of the resurgence of tribal fighting among the Mae-Enga addresses two issues of major importance in today's world: the changing nature of law and order in "underdeveloped" countries and the nature of violence in human societies.

Johnson, A. W., & Earle, T. (1987). *The evolution of human societies, from foraging group to agrarian state.* Stanford, CA: Stanford University Press.

Although written as a synthesis of economic and ecological anthropology, this is also a book on the evolution of political organization in human societies. Proceeding from family-level organization up through state organization, the authors discuss nine levels, illustrating each with specific case studies and specifying the conditions that give rise to each level.

Kurtz, D. V. (2001) *Political anthropology: Paradigms and power.* Boulder, CO: Westview Press.

This contemporary overview covers political power/leaders/authority from kinship to the state and paradigms from political evolution to postmodernism.

Nader, L., & Todd, H. F., Jr. (1978). *The disputing process: Law in ten societies.* New York: Columbia University Press.

A revealing, cross-cultural look at dispute resolution.

Ury, W. (Ed.). (2002). *Must we fight? From the battlefield to the schoolyard—A new perspective on violent conflict and its prevention.* Hoboken, NJ: Jossey-Bass.

This fresh exploration of the question of whether violence and war are inevitable presents evidence from leading anthropologists and others that human beings have as much inherent potential for cooperation and coexistence as they do for violent conflict.

Whitehead, N., & Ferguson, R. B. (Eds.) (1992). *War in the tribal zone.* Santa Fe: School of American Research Press.

The central point of this book is that the transformation and intensification of war, as well as the formation of tribes, result from complex interaction in the "tribal zone" that begins where centralized authority makes contact with stateless people it does not rule. In such zones, newly introduced plants, animals, diseases, and technologies often spread widely, even before colonizers appear. These and other changes disrupt existing social and political relationships, fostering new alliances and creating conflicts.

CHAPTER 13

Spirituality, Religion, and the Supernatural

Photographer: Hester & Hardaway Photographers. The Menil Collection, Houston.

CHALLENGE ISSUE

AS SELF-CONSCIOUS AND SELF-REFLECTING BEINGS, HUMANS FACE CHALLENGES BEYOND BIOLOGICAL SURVIVAL; THEY FACE MENTAL ONES BORN OF THE NEED TO MAKE MEANINGFUL SENSE OF THEIR EXISTENCE. Among other concerns, they wrestle with questions about human origin and destiny. Most cultures have origin-of-life stories that are passed on from one generation to the next, helping to define the individual and the group's place in the world. For example, the Jains, a Hindu sect in India, believe that all life springs from a cosmic being that has existed since the beginning of time, such as the one pictured here.

1 What Is Religion?

Religion forms part of a cultural system's superstructure, which comprises a society's worldview. It is an organized system of ideas about spiritual reality, or the supernatural, along with associated beliefs and ceremonial practices. Religion (as well as less formalized spiritual beliefs and practices) guides humans in their attempts to give meaning to the world and their place in it and to deal with problems that defy ordinary explanation or solution through direct means. To overcome these challenges, people appeal to, or seek to influence and even manipulate, spiritual or supernatural beings and powers.

2 What Are Religion's Identifying Features?

Religion consists of various beliefs and rituals—prayers, songs, dances, offerings, and sacrifices—that people use to interpret, appeal to, and manipulate supernatural beings and powers to their advantage. These beings and powers may consist of gods and goddesses, ancestral and other spirits, or impersonal powers, either by themselves or in various combinations. In all societies certain individuals are especially skilled at dealing with these beings and powers and assist other members of society in their ritual activities. A body of myths rationalizes or "explains" the system in a manner consistent with people's experience in the world in which they live.

3 What Functions Does Religion Serve?

Whether or not a particular religion accomplishes what people believe it does, all religions serve a number of important psychological and social functions. They reduce anxiety by explaining the unknown and provide comfort with the belief that supernatural aid is available in times of crisis. They provide notions of right and wrong, setting precedents for acceptable behavior and transferring the burden of decision making from individuals to supernatural powers. Through ritual, religion may be used to enhance the learning of oral traditions. Finally, religion plays an important role in maintaining social solidarity.

According to their creation story, the Tewa-speaking Pueblo Indians in the southwestern United States emerged from a lake far north of where they now live. Once on dry land, they divided into two groups, the Summer People and the Winter People, and migrated south along the Rio Grande River. During their travels they made twelve stops before finally reuniting into a single community in what is now called New Mexico.

For the Tewa Indians all existence is divided into six categories, three human and three spiritual or supernatural. Each of the human categories, which are arranged in a hierarchy, is matched by a spiritual category so that when people die, they immediately pass into their proper spiritual role. The supernatural categories also correspond to divisions in the natural world. This, in essence, comprises the Tewa **worldview**—the collective body of ideas that members of a culture generally share concerning the ultimate shape and substance of their reality.

To those with different worldviews, such spiritual beliefs may seem, at best, irrational and arbitrary, but in fact they are neither. The late Alfonso Ortiz, an anthropologist and a member of the Tewa Pueblo, showed that his culture's traditional worldview is not only coherent and spiritually meaningful, but also socially functional. In fact, it forms part of this indigenous cultural system's superstructure, as it represents the very model of Tewa community.[1] These Indians have a social organization that divides their *pueblo* (Spanish for "people" as well as "village" or "town") into two independent moieties, each with its own resources, social organization, ceremonies, and authority. Individuals are introduced into one of these moieties, and their membership is regularly reinforced through a series of life-cycle rituals that correspond to the twelve stops made on the mythical journey down the Rio Grande River. The ceremonial rites of birth and death are shared by the whole community; other rites differ between the two moieties. The highest

status of the human hierarchy belongs to the priests, who help to integrate this divided village community by mediating between the human and spiritual world, as well as between the two moieties.

Tewa worldview is intricately intertwined with religious beliefs and practices, and both are part of virtually every aspect of Tewa life and society. Their worldview is the basis of the simultaneously dualistic and unified sense of self, pueblo community, and the larger world held by each Tewa. And their religion provides numerous points of mediation so that the two moieties can continue to exist together as a single community. It sanctifies the community by linking its origin with the domain of the supernatural, and it offers divine sanction to ceremonial rituals that help individuals deal with life's major transitions as members of their community. Also, by providing a coherent idea of an afterworld that is the mirror image of human society, it answers the question of death in a manner that reinforces social structure. In short, Tewa religion, by weaving all elements of Tewa experience into a single pattern, gives a solid foundation to the cultural stability and continuity of Tewa society.

Among the Tewa, as among people in all cultures, particular spiritual or religious beliefs and practices fulfill numerous social and psychological needs, such as the need to confront and explain death. Religion gives meaning to individual and group life, drawing power from spiritual forces or beings and offering continuity of existence beyond death. It can provide the path by which people transcend their burdensome and mortal existence and attain, if only momentarily, spiritual hope and relief. The social functions of religion are no less important than the psychological ones. A traditional religion reinforces group norms, provides moral sanctions for individual conduct, and furnishes the underlayer of common purpose and values upon which the well-being of the community rests. Religion appears to be universal, perhaps because it fulfills these and other social and psychological needs common to humans across cultures. Indeed, we know of no group of people anywhere on the face of the earth who, at any time over the past 100,000 years, has been without spirituality or religion. Not even in Albania and the Soviet Union, where atheism was the communist state dogma during much of the 20th century, did religion entirely disappear.

In the 19th century, the European intellectual tradition gave rise to the idea that modern science would ultimately replace religion by showing people the irrationality of their spiritual beliefs and practices. The expectation was that as valid scientific explanations became available, people would abandon their religious beliefs and rituals as superstitious myths and false worship. But to date, that has not occurred. In fact, in many places, the opposite trend seems to prevail. Although traditional, mainline Christian religions have shown some decline, nondenominational spirituality is on the rise. Also on the rise

---

[1]Ortiz, A. (1969). *The Tewa world* (p. 43). Chicago: University of Chicago Press.

---

worldview The collective body of ideas that members of a culture generally share concerning the ultimate shape and substance of their reality.

are fundamentalist religions, which often take a strong antiscience position. Examples include Islamic fundamentalism in countries such as Afghanistan, Algeria, and Iran; Jewish fundamentalism in Israel and the United States; and Hindu fundamentalism in India. Christian fundamentalism is represented in the dramatic growth of evangelical denominations in the United States, Central America, and sub-Saharan Africa. Within the United States, non-Christian religions are also growing in popularity: Islam (5–7 million followers—up from 527,000 in 1990), Buddhism (1.1 million—up from 401,000 in 1990), Hinduism (800,000—up from 227,000 in 1990), not to mention various "New Age" options such as Wicca (a modern, nature-oriented religion based upon ancient western European and pre-Christian beliefs and now counting about 310,000 adherents).[2] Notably, just 14 percent of the adult population throughout the world claims to be nonreligious (Figure 13.1).

MEDIATREK

To explore contemporary efforts to identify common ground between science and religion, including spirituality and health issues, go to MediaTrek 13.1 on the companion Web site or CD-ROM.

Beyond noting that science has not destroyed spiritual beliefs or religion, one could even say that it has actually fostered the fundamentalist religious boom, for it has removed many traditional psychological props while creating, in its technological applications, a host of new problems. These include nuclear catastrophe, threats of chemical or biological terrorism, health hazards from pollution, unease about the consequences of new developments in biotechnology such as the cloning of animals, production of new strains of genetically engineered organisms, ability to store human sperm and

---

[2]U.S. Census 2000; *Adherents.com.*

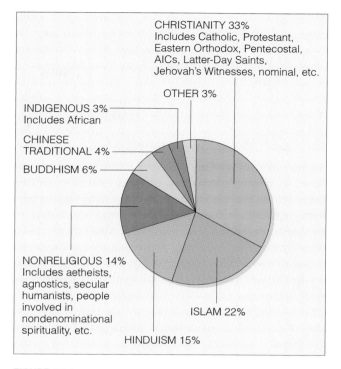

FIGURE 13.1

Major religions of the world and their percentage of all believers, 2002.

CHRISTIANITY 33%
Includes Catholic, Protestant, Eastern Orthodox, Pentecostal, AICs, Latter-Day Saints, Jehovah's Witnesses, nominal, etc.

OTHER 3%

INDIGENOUS 3%
Includes African

CHINESE TRADITIONAL 4%

BUDDHISM 6%

NONRELIGIOUS 14%
Includes aetheists, agnostics, secular humanists, people involved in nondenominational spirituality, etc.

HINDUISM 15%

ISLAM 22%

eggs for future fertilization, and manipulation of human DNA. On top of these, many people face emotional turmoil and psychological upheaval brought on by the breakup of traditional communities due to globalization, plus invasions of foreign ideas and values through mass media controlled by unfamiliar powers. These are but a few of many modern-day issues confronting the human species. In the face of these new anxieties, religion offers social and psychological support.

The continuing strength of religion in the face of Western scientific rationalism clearly reveals that it remains a dominant and dynamic force in society.

VISUAL COUNTERPOINT Far from causing religion's death, the growth of scientific knowledge may have contributed to the continuing practice of religion in modern life by producing new anxieties and raising new questions about human existence. North Americans continue to participate in traditional religions, such as Judaism (left), as well as imported sects, such as the new Vrindaban (middle) and evangelism (right).

Although anthropologists are not qualified to pass judgment on the metaphysical truth of any particular religion or spiritual belief, they can show how each embodies a number of revealing facts about humans and society.

THE ANTHROPOLOGICAL APPROACH TO RELIGION

Anthropologist Anthony F. C. Wallace defined religion as "a set of rituals, rationalized by myth, which mobilizes supernatural powers for the purpose of achieving or preventing transformations of state in man and nature."[3] Behind his definition lies a recognition that people, when they cannot "fix" through technological or organizational means serious problems that cause them anxiety, try to do so through manipulation of supernatural or spiritual beings and powers. This requires ritual, or "religion in action," which can be seen as the primary expression of religion. Its major functions are to reduce anxiety and boost confidence, thereby helping people cope with reality. It is this that gives religion survival value.

With these aspects in mind, we offer a somewhat simpler definition of **religion:** an organized system of ideas about spiritual reality, or the supernatural, along with associated beliefs and ceremonial practices by which people try to interpret and control aspects of the universe otherwise beyond their control. Similar to religion, **spirituality** is also concerned with the sacred, as distinguished from material matters, but it is often individual rather than collective and does not require a distinctive format or traditional organization.

Since no known culture, including those of modern industrial societies, has achieved complete certainty in controlling existing or future conditions and circumstances, spirituality and/or religion play a role in all known cultures. However, considerable variability exists here. At one end of the human spectrum are food-foraging peoples, whose technological ability to manipulate their environment is limited and who tend to see themselves more as part, rather than masters, of nature.

---

[3]Wallace, A. F. C. (1966). *Religion: An anthropological view.* New York: Random House.

religion An organized system of ideas about spiritual reality, or the supernatural, along with associated beliefs and ceremonial practices by which people try to interpret and control aspects of the universe otherwise beyond their control.
spirituality Concern with the sacred, as distinguished from material matters. In contrast to religion, spirituality is often individual rather than collective and does not require a distinctive format or traditional organization.

© AP/Wide World Photos

Pope John Paul II presiding over the ceremony in which the Albanian Christian Missionary known as Mother Teresa was made a saint. Roman Catholicism, with its hierarchy of supernatural beings—God, Christ, angels, and saints or holy people—reflects and confirms the stratified nature of the society in which it is embedded. (Note the portrait of Mother Teresa behind the Pope.)

This is what we referred to in the last chapter as a naturalistic worldview. Among food foragers religion is likely to be inseparable from the rest of daily life. It also mirrors and confirms the egalitarian nature of social relations in their societies, in that individuals do not plead for aid to high-ranking deities the way members of stratified societies do. At the other end of the human spectrum is Western civilization, with its ideological commitment to overcoming problems through technological and organizational skills. Here religion is less a part of daily activities and is restricted to more specific occasions. Moreover, with its hierarchy of supernatural beings—for instance, God, and (in some religions) the angels, saints or holy people—it reflects and confirms the stratified nature of the society in which it is embedded.

Even so, there is variation within a complex and stratified social order. Religious activity may be less prominent in the lives of social elites, who may see themselves as more in control of their own destinies, than it is in the lives of peasants or members of lower classes. Among the latter, religion may afford some compensation for a dependent position in society. Yet religion is still important to elite members of society, in that it rationalizes the system in such a way that less advantaged people are not as likely to question the existing social order as they might otherwise be. With hope for a better existence after death, one may be more willing to put up with a disadvantaged position in life. Thus, religious beliefs serve to influence and perpetuate conceptions, if not actual relations, between different classes of people.

MEDIATREK

For a global introduction to the study of religion, including an overview of a half dozen of the major religions in the world, go to MediaTrek 13.2 on the companion Web site or CD-ROM.

THE PRACTICE OF RELIGION

Much of religion's value comes from the activities called for by its prescriptions and rules. Participation in religious ceremonies may bring a sense of personal lift—a wave of reassurance, security, and even ecstasy—or a feeling of closeness to fellow participants. Although the beliefs and ceremonial practices of religions vary considerably, even rituals that seem bizarre to outsiders can be shown to serve the same basic social and psychological functions as their own rituals.

Supernatural Beings and Powers

A hallmark of religion is belief in spiritual beings and forces. In attempting to control by religious means what cannot be controlled in other ways, humans turn to prayer, sacrifice, and other religious or spiritual rituals. These presuppose existence of spiritual forces that can be tapped into, or spiritual beings interested in human affairs and available for aid. For convenience we may divide these beings into three categories: major deities (gods and goddesses), ancestral spirits, and other sorts of spirit beings. Although the variety of deities and spirits recognized by the world's cultures is tremendous, it is possible to make certain generalizations about them.

Gods and Goddesses

Gods and goddesses are the great and more remote beings. They are usually seen as controlling the universe. If more than one is recognized (known as **polytheism**), each has charge of a particular part of the universe. Such was the case with the gods and goddesses of ancient Greece: Zeus was lord of the sky, Poseidon was ruler of the sea, and Hades was lord of the underworld and ruler of the dead.

In addition to these three brothers, Greek mythology features a host of other deities, female as well as male, each similarly concerned with specific aspects of life and the universe. A **pantheon,** or the collection of gods and goddesses such as those of the Greeks, is common in non-Western states as well. Since states commonly have grown through conquest, often their pantheons have expanded as local deities of conquered peoples were incorporated into the official state pantheon. Another frequent though not invariable feature of pantheons is the presence of a supreme deity, who may be all but totally ignored by humans. The Aztecs of the Mexican highlands, for instance, recognized a supreme pair to whom they paid little attention. After all, being so remote, this divine duo was unlikely to be interested in human affairs. The sensible practice, then, was to focus attention on less remote deities who therefore were more directly concerned with human affairs.

Whether or not a people recognize gods, goddesses, or both has to do with how men and women relate to each other in everyday life. Generally speaking, societies that subordinate women to men define the supreme deity in masculine terms. In preindustrial parts of the world, such societies are mainly those with economies based upon the herding of animals or intensive agriculture carried out or controlled by men, who are dominating figures to their children.

Goddesses, by contrast, are likely to be most prominent in societies where women play a significant role in the economy, where women enjoy relative equality with men, and where men are less controlling figures to their wives and children. Such societies are most often those that depend upon crop cultivation carried out solely or mostly by women. As an illustration, the early Israelites, like other pastoral nomadic tribes of the Middle East, described their god in masculine, authoritarian terms. By contrast, goddesses played central roles in religious ritual and in the popular imagination of the region's farming peoples. Associated with these goddesses were concepts of light, love, fertility, and procreation. About 3,200 years ago, the Israelite tribes crossed the Jordan River and entered the land of Canaan (Palestine) where they began to till the soil and grow crops, requiring them to establish a new kind of relationship with the land. As they settled down and became sedentary, dependent upon rainfall and concerned about seasonal cycles and soil fertility (as the region's Canaanites already were), they adopted many of the region's already established Canaanite goddess cults.

polytheism Belief in several gods and/or goddesses (as contrasted with monotheism—belief in one god or goddess).
pantheon The several gods and goddesses of a people.

The patriarchal nature of Western society is expressed in its theology, in which a masculine god gives life to the first man, as depicted here on the ceiling of the Sistine Chapel in Rome. Only later is the first woman created from the first man.

© Scala/Art Resource

Although diametrically opposed to the original Israelite cult, worship of these Canaanite female deities appealed to the farming people's desire for security by seeking to control the forces of fertility in the interest of people's well-being.

Later on, when the Israelite tribes sought national unity in the face of a military threat by neighboring nations and when they ethnocentrically strengthened their own identity as a supernaturally "chosen people," the goddess cults lost out to followers of the old masculine tribal god. This ancient masculine-authoritarian concept of god has been perpetuated down to the present, not just in the Judaic tradition but also by most Christians and Muslims, whose religions stem from the old Israelite religion. As a consequence, this masculine-authoritarian model has played an important role in perpetuating a relationship between men and women in which the latter traditionally have been expected to submit to the rule of men at every level of Jewish, Christian, and Islamic society.

Ancestral Spirits

A belief in ancestral spirits is consistent with the widespread notion that human beings are made up of two closely intertwined parts, a physical body and some mental component or spiritual self. For example, traditional belief of the Penobscot Indians in Maine holds that each person has a vital spirit capable of traveling apart from the body. Given such a concept, the idea of the spirit being freed from the body in trance and dreams or by death, and having an existence thereafter, seems quite reasonable. Frequently, where a belief in ancestral spirits exists, these beings are seen as retaining an active interest and even membership in society. In the previous chapter, for instance, we discussed how the Wape Papuans in New Guinea believe that ancestral spirits act to provide or withhold meat from their living descendants. Like living persons, such spirit beings are viewed as benevolent or malevolent, but no one is ever quite sure what their behavior will be. The same feeling of uncertainty—"How will they react to what I have done?"—may be displayed toward ancestral spirits as it often is toward people of an older generation who hold authority over individuals. Beyond this, ancestral spirits closely resemble living humans in their appetites, feelings, emotions, and behavior. Thus, they reflect and reinforce social reality.

A belief in ancestral spirits of one sort or another is found in many parts of the world, especially among people with unilineal descent systems. In several such African societies, the concept is highly elaborate. Here one frequently finds ancestral spirits behaving just like humans. They are able to feel hot, cold, and pain, and they may be capable of dying a second death by drowning or burning. They even may participate in family and lineage affairs, and seats will be provided for them, even though the spirits are invisible. If they are annoyed, they may send sickness or death. Eventually, they are reborn as new members of their lineage, and, in societies that hold such beliefs, adults need to observe infants closely to determine just who has been reborn.

Ancestor spirits played an important role in the patrilineal society of traditional China. For the gift of life, a boy was forever indebted to his parents, owing them obedience, deference, and a comfortable old age. Even after their death, he had to provide for them in the spirit world,

Anthropologists of Note

Sir Edward B. Tylor (1873–1917)

British scholar Sir Edward B. Tylor is credited with bringing the concept of animism to the attention of anthropologists. Though not university educated, Tylor was the first person to hold a chair in anthropology at a British university, with his appointment first as lecturer, then reader, and finally (in 1895) as professor at Oxford. His interest in anthropology developed from travels that took him as a young man to the United States (where he visited an Indian pueblo), Cuba, and Mexico, where he was especially impressed by the achievements of the ancient Aztec and the more recent blend of Indian and Spanish culture.

Tylor's numerous publications ranged over such diverse topics as the possible historical connection between the games of pachisi and patolli (played in India and ancient Mexico); the origin of games of cat's cradle; and the structural connections between postmarital residence, descent, and certain other customs such as in-law avoidance and the *couvade* (the confinement of a child's father following birth). Tylor also formulated the first widely accepted definition of culture (see Chapter 2). The considerable attention he paid to religious concepts and practices in his writings stemmed from a lifelong commitment to combat the idea, still widely held in his time, that so-called savage people had degenerated more than civilized people from an original state of grace. To Tylor, who was raised a Quaker, "savages" were intellectuals just like anyone else, grappling with their problems but handicapped (as was Tylor in his intellectual life) by limited information.

offering them food, money, and incense on the anniversaries of their births and deaths. In addition, people collectively worshiped all lineage ancestors periodically throughout the year. Giving birth to sons was regarded as an obligation to the ancestors, because boys inherited their father's ancestral duties. To fulfill his ancestors' needs for descendants (and his own need to be respectable in a culture that demanded satisfying the needs of one's ancestors), a man would go so far as to marry a girl who had been adopted into his family as an infant so she could be raised as a dutiful wife for him, even when this arrangement went against the wishes of both parties. Furthermore, a father readily would force his daughter to marry a man against her will. In fact, a female child was raised to be cast out by her natal family yet might not find acceptance in her husband's family for years. Not until after death, when her vital spirit was carried in a tablet and placed in the shrine of her husband's family, was she an official member of it. As a consequence, once a son was born to her, a woman worked long and hard to establish the strongest possible tie between herself and her son to ensure she would be looked after in life.

Strong beliefs in ancestral spirits are particularly appropriate in a society of descent-based groups with their associated ancestor orientation. More than this, though, these beliefs provide a strong sense of continuity that links the past, present, and future.

Animism

One of the most widespread beliefs about supernatural beings is **animism,** a belief that nature is animated (enlivened or energized) by distinct personalized spirit beings separable from bodies. Spirits such as souls and ghosts are thought to dwell in humans and animals, but also in human-made artifacts, plants, stones, mountains, wells, and other natural features. So too the woods may be full of a variety of unattached or free-ranging spirits. The various spirits involved are a highly diverse lot. Generally speaking, though, they are less remote from people than gods and goddesses and are more involved in daily affairs. They may be benevolent, malevolent, or just plain neutral. They also may be awesome, terrifying, lovable, or even mischievous. Since they may be pleased or irritated by human actions, people are obliged to be concerned about them.

Animism is typical of those who see themselves as being a part of nature rather than superior to it. This includes most food foragers, as well as those food-producing peoples who acknowledge little qualitative difference between a human life and that of any living entity from turtles to trees, or even rivers and mountains. In such societies, gods and goddesses are relatively unimportant, but the woods are full of spirits. Gods and goddesses, if they exist at all, may be seen as having created the world and perhaps making it fit to live in; but it is spirits that individuals turn to for healing or even curing, who help or hinder the shaman, and whom the ordinary hunter may meet when off in the woods.

> **animism** A belief that nature is enlivened or energized by distinct personalized spirit beings separable from bodies.

Native Americans carved these faces into a rock along the Connecticut River to depict spirit beings they saw here while in states of trance.

© William A. Haviland

Animatism

Although supernatural power is often thought of as being vested in supernatural beings, it does not have to be. The Melanesians, for example, think of *mana* as a force inherent in all objects. It is not in itself physical, but it can reveal itself physically. A warrior's success in fighting is not attributed to his own strength but to the mana contained in an amulet that hangs around his neck. Similarly, a farmer may know a great deal about horticulture, soil conditioning, and the correct time for sowing and harvesting, but nevertheless may depend upon mana for a successful crop, often building a simple altar to this power at one end of the field. If the crop is good, it is a sign that the farmer has in some way appropriated the necessary mana. Far from being a personalized force, mana is abstract in the extreme, a power or potency lying always just beyond reach of the senses. As R. H. Codrington described it, "Virtue, prestige, authority, good fortune, influence, sanctity, luck are all words which, under certain conditions, give something near the meaning. . . . *Mana* sometimes means a more than natural virtue or power attaching to some person or thing."[4] This concept of impersonal potency, or energy, also was widespread among North American Indians. The Iroquois called it *orenda;* to the Sioux it was *wakonda;* to the Algonquians, *manitou.* Nevertheless, though found on every continent, the concept is not necessarily universal.

R. R. Marett referred to this concept of nature being enlivened or energized by an impersonal spiritual power or supernatural potency as **animatism.** The two concepts—animatism (which lacks particular substance or individual form) and animism (a belief in distinct spirit beings)—are not mutually exclusive. They are often found in the same culture, as in Melanesia and also in the North American Indian societies just mentioned.

People trying to comprehend beliefs in the supernatural beings and powers that others recognize frequently ask how such beliefs are maintained. In part, the answer is through manifestations of power. Given a belief in animatism and/or the powers of supernatural beings, one is predisposed to see what appear to be results of the application of such powers. For example, if a Melanesian warrior is convinced of his power because he possesses the necessary mana and he is successful, he is likely to interpret this success as proof of the power of mana. "After all, I would have lost had I not possessed it, wouldn't I?" Beyond this, because of his confidence in his mana, he may be willing to take more chances in his fighting, and this indeed could mean the difference between success or failure.

Failures, of course, do occur, but they can be explained. Perhaps one's prayer was not answered because a deity or spirit was still angry about some past insult. Or perhaps the Melanesian warrior lost his battle—the obvious explanation is that he was not as successful in bringing mana to bear as he thought, or else his opponent had more of it. In any case, humans generally emphasize successes over failures, and long after many of the latter have been forgotten, tales probably still will be told of striking cases of the workings of supernatural powers.

Another feature that tends to perpetuate beliefs in supernatural beings is that the beings have attributes with which people are familiar. Allowing for the fact that supernatural beings are in a sense larger than life, they generally are conceived of as living the way people do and as having the same sorts of interests. For example, the Penobscot Indians believed in a quasi-human culture hero, a giant

---

[4]Quoted by Lienhardt, G. (1960). Religion. In H. Shapiro (Ed.), *Man, culture, and society* (p. 368). London: Oxford University Press.

animatism A belief that nature is enlivened or energized by an impersonal spiritual power or supernatural potency.

magician called Gluskabe. Like ordinary mortals, Gluskabe traveled about in a canoe, used snowshoes, lived in a wigwam, and made stone arrowheads. He possessed all the familiar human lusts and jealousies. Such characteristics serve to make supernatural beings believable.

The role of mythology in maintaining beliefs should not be overlooked. Myths, which are discussed in some detail in the next chapter, are explanatory narratives that rationalize religious beliefs and practices. To many Euroamericans, the word *myth* immediately conjures up the idea of an invented story about imaginary events, something that did not factually happen; but the people for whom a particular myth comprises part of their worldview usually do not see it that way. To them myths are sacred and true stories, not unlike historical documents in contemporary European or North American culture. Even so, myths exist even in literate societies, as in the case of the two Judaic and Christian accounts of creation contained in the Bible's Book of Genesis. Invariably, myths are full of accounts about the doings of various supernatural beings and thus serve to reinforce beliefs in them.

Religious Specialists

Priests and Priestesses

All human societies include individuals who guide and supplement the religious practices of others. Such individuals are seen to be highly skilled at contacting and influencing supernatural beings and manipulating supernatural forces. Often their qualification for this is that they have undergone special training. In addition, they may display certain distinctive personality traits that make them particularly well suited to perform these tasks.

Societies with the resources to support full-time occupational specialists give the role of guiding religious practices and influencing the supernatural to the **priest** or **priestess.** He or she is the socially initiated, ceremonially inducted member of a recognized religious organization, with a rank and function that belong to him or her as the holder of a position others have held before. The sources of power are the society and the institution within which the priest or priestess functions. The priest, if not the priestess, is a familiar figure in Western societies; he is the priest, minister, pastor, rector, rabbi, or whatever the official title may be in an organized religion. With their god defined historically in masculine, authoritarian terms, it is not surprising that, in the Judaic, Christian, and Islamic religions, the most important positions traditionally have been filled by men. Female religious specialists are likely to be found only in societies where women make a major publicly recognized contribution to the economy and where gods and goddesses are both recognized.

Shamans

Societies that lack full-time occupational specialization have existed far longer than those with such specialization, and the former have always included individuals with special powers and skills that enable them to contact, tap into, and manipulate supernatural beings and

priest or priestess A full-time religious specialist formally recognized for his or her role in guiding the religious practices of others and for contacting and influencing supernatural powers.

VISUAL COUNTERPOINT
Traditional Mapuche shaman in Chile and New Age shaman in North America. Shamanism is by no means absent in modern industrial societies.

© Topham/The Image Works

© Dan Budnick/Woodfin Camp & Associates

forces. These powers and skills have come to them through some personal experience, usually in solitude. In an altered state of consciousness, they receive a vision that empowers them to heal the sick, change the weather, control the movements of animals, and foretell the future. As they perfect these and related skills, they assume the role of shaman.

The word *shaman* originally referred to medical-religious specialists, or spiritual guides, among the Tungus and other Siberian seminomads with animist beliefs. By means of various techniques such as fasting, drumming, chanting, or dancing, as well as hallucinogenic mushrooms, these Siberian shamans enter into a trance, or altered state of consciousness. While in this waking dream state, they experience visions of an alternate reality inhabited by spirit beings such as guardian animal spirits who may assist in the healing.

Cross-cultural research of shamanism shows that similar medical-religious healing practices also exist in traditional cultures outside Siberia. For that reason, the term *shaman* has also been applied to a variety of part-time spiritual leaders and traditional healers ("medicine men") active in North and South American indigenous communities and beyond. As defined by anthropologist Michael Harner, one of the world's foremost experts in shamanism, a **shaman** is

> a man or woman who enters an altered state of consciousness—at will—to contact and utilize an ordinarily hidden reality in order to acquire knowledge, power, and to help other persons. The shaman has at least one, and usually more, "spirits" in his personal service.[5]

The term *shaman* has become so popular in recent decades that any non-Western local priest, healer, or diviner is often indiscriminately referred to as one.[6]

In the United States millions of people learned something about shamans through the popular autobiography of Black Elk, a traditional Lakota Indian Holy Man, and Carlos Castañeda's largely fictional accounts of his experiences with Don Juan, the Yaqui Indian shaman. Numerous books and other publications on shamanism have appeared over the past four decades, and some

Euroamericans have gone into practice as shamans, a development that has triggered considerable resentment among some Native Americans ("They stole our land, now they are stealing our religion."). In addition to so-called New Age enthusiasts, among whom shamanism is particularly popular, the faith healers and many other evangelists among fundamentalist Christians share many of the characteristics of shamanism.

Typically, one becomes a shaman by passing through stages of learning and practical experience, often involving psychological and emotional ordeals brought about by isolation, fasting, physical torture, sensory deprivation, and/or hallucinations. These hallucinations (derived from the Latin word for "mental wandering") occur when the shaman is in a trance, which may occur spontaneously but can also be induced by consuming mind-altering drugs such as psychoactive vines or mushrooms.

Among the Penobscot Indians in northern New England, for example, any person could become a shaman, since no formal institution provided rules and regulations to guide religious consciousness. The search for shamanic visions was pursued by most adult Penobscot males, who would go off alone and, through meditation, sensory deprivation, and hyperventilation, induce an altered state of consciousness in which they hoped to receive a vision. Not all were successful, but failure did not result in social disgrace. Those who did achieve success experienced a sense of being freed from their bodily existence in which they established a special relationship with a particular animal spirit that appeared in their trance state. This became the shaman's animal helper—a common element in shamanism—who thereafter would assist the shaman in performing his tasks.

MEDIATREK
For a huge compilation of information on numerous religions around the world, as well as myth, magic, witchcraft, shamanism, voodoo, and more, go to MediaTrek 13.3 on the companion Web site or CD-ROM.

Because shamanism is rooted in altered states of consciousness, and because the human nervous system that produces these trance states is a human universal, those involved in shamanism experience similarly structured visual, auditory, somatic (touch), olfactory (smell), and gustatory (taste) hallucinations. The widespread occurrence of shamanism and the remarkable similarities among shamanic traditions everywhere are consequences of this universal neurological inheritance. At the same time, the meanings ascribed to sensations experienced in altered states and made of their content are culturally determined; hence, despite their overall similarities, local traditions always vary in their details.

---

[5]Harner, M. (1980). *The way of the shaman: A guide to power and healing* (p. 20). San Francisco: Harper & Row.

---

[6]Kehoe, A. (2000). *Shamans and religion: An anthropological exploration in critical thinking.* Prospect Heights, IL: Waveland Press.

---

shaman A person who enters an altered state of consciousness—at will—to contact and utilize an ordinarily hidden reality in order to acquire knowledge, power, and to help others.

The shaman is essentially a religious go-between who acts on behalf of some human client, often to bring about healing or to foretell some future event. To do so, the shaman intervenes to influence or impose his or her will on supernatural powers. The shaman can be contrasted with the priest or priestess, whose "clients" are the deities. Priests and priestesses frequently tell people what to do; the shaman tells supernaturals what to do. In return for services rendered, the shaman may collect a fee—fresh meat, yams, or a favorite possession. In some cases, the added prestige, authority, and social power attached to the shaman's status are reward enough.

When a shaman acts on behalf of a client, he or she may put on something of a show—one that heightens the basic drama with a sense of danger. Typically, the shaman enters a trance state, in which he or she experiences the sensation of traveling to the alternate world and seeing and interacting with spirit beings. The shaman tries to impose his or her will upon these spirits, an inherently dangerous contest, considering the superhuman powers spirits usually are thought to possess. One example of this is afforded by the trance dances of the Ju/'hoansi Bushmen of Africa's Kalahari Desert. Among these people shamans constitute, on average, about half the men and a third of the older women in any group. The most common reasons for their going into trance are to bring rain, control animals, and—as in the following Original Study—to heal the sick (always an important activity of shamans, wherever they are found).

Original Study

Healing among the Ju/'hoansi of the Kalahari

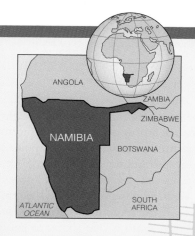

Ju/'hoansi healers, when entering trance, are assisted by others among the trance dancers.

One way the spirits affect humans is by shooting them with invisible arrows carrying disease, death, or misfortune. If the arrows can be warded off, illness will not take hold. If illness has already penetrated, the arrows must be removed to enable the sick person to recover. An ancestral spirit may exercise this power against the living if a person is not being treated well by others. If people argue with her frequently, if her husband shows how little he values her by carrying on blatant affairs, or if people refuse to cooperate or share with her, the spirit may conclude that no one cares whether or not she remains alive and may "take her into the sky."

Interceding with the spirits and drawing out their invisible arrows is the task of [Ju/'hoansi] healers, men and women who possess the powerful healing force called *n/um* [the Ju/'hoansi equivalent of mana]. *N/um* generally remains dormant in a healer until an effort is made to activate it. Although an occasional healer can accomplish this through solo singing or instrumental playing, the usual way of activating *n/um* is through the medicinal curing ceremony or trance dance. To the sound of undulating melodies sung by women, healers dance around and around the fire, sometimes for hours. The music, the strenuous dancing, the smoke, the heat of the fire, and the healers' intense concentration cause their *n/um* to heat up. When it comes to a boil, trance is achieved.

At this moment the *n/um* becomes available as a powerful healing force, to serve the entire community. In trance, a healer lays hands on and ritually cures everyone sitting around the fire. His hands flutter lightly beside each person's head or chest or wherever illness is evident; his body trembles; his breathing becomes deep and coarse; and he becomes coated with a thick sweat— also considered to be imbued with power. Whatever "badness" is discovered in the person is drawn into the healer's own body and met by the *n/um* coursing up his spinal column. The healer gives a mounting cry that culminates in a soul-wrenching shriek as the illness is catapulted out of his body and into the air.

[CONTINUED]

[CONTINUED]

While in trance, many healers see various gods and spirits sitting just outside the circle of firelight, enjoying the spectacle of the dance. Sometimes the spirits are recognizable—departed relatives and friends—at other times they are "just people." Whoever these beings are, healers in trance usually blame them for whatever misfortune is being experienced by the community. They are barraged by hurled objects, shouted at, and aggressively warned not to take any of the living back with them to the village of the spirits.

To cure a very serious illness, the most experienced healers may be called upon, for only they have enough knowledge to undertake the dangerous spiritual exploration that may be necessary to effect a cure. When they are in a trance, their souls or vital spirits are said to leave their bodies and to travel to the spirit world to discover the cause of the illness or the problem. An ancestral spirit or a god is usually found responsible and asked to reconsider. If the healer is persuasive and the spirit agrees, the sick person recovers. If the spirit is elusive or unsympathetic, a cure is not achieved. The healer may go to the principal god, but even this does not always work. As one healer put it, "Sometimes, when you speak with God, he says, 'I want this person to die and won't help you make him better.' At other times, God helps; the next morning, someone who has been lying on the ground, seriously ill, gets up and walks again."

These journeys are considered dangerous because while the healer's soul is absent his body is in half-death. Akin to loss of consciousness, this state has been observed and verified by medical and scientific investigators. The power of other healers' *n/um* is all that is thought to protect the healer in this state from actual death. He receives lavish attention and care—his body is vigorously massaged, his skin is rubbed with sweat, and hands are laid on him. Only when consciousness returns—the signal that his soul has been reunited with his body—do the other healers cease their efforts. *(Excerpted from M. Shostak. (1983).* Nisa: The life and words of a !Kung woman *(pp. 291–293). New York: Vintage.)*

In many human societies, sleight-of-hand tricks and ventriloquism occur at the same time as trancing. Among Arctic peoples, for example, a shaman may summon spirits in the dark and produce all sorts of flapping noises and strange voices to impress the audiences. Some Western observers regard this kind of trickery as evidence of the fraudulent nature of shamanism, but is this so? The truth is that shamans know perfectly well that they are manipulating people with their tricks. Yet virtually everyone who has studied them agrees that shamans really believe in their power to deal with supernatural forces and spirit beings. Their power, verified by the trance experience, gives them the right as well as the ability to manipulate people in minor technical matters. In short, the shaman regards his or her ability to perform extraordinary tricks as further proof of superior powers.

The importance of shamanism in a society should not be underestimated. For individual members, it promotes, through the drama of performance, a feeling of ecstasy and release of tension. It provides psychological assurance, through prevailing upon supernatural powers and spirits otherwise beyond human control, for such things as invulnerability from attack, success at love, or the return of health. In fact, a frequent reason for a shamanic performance is poor health—a concept that is difficult to define effectively in cross-cultural terms. Not only do people in diverse cultures recognize and experience different types of illnesses, they may also view and explain them in different terms. The culturally defined diagnosis of an illness, in turn, determines how the patient will be treated according to the beliefs of the culture, in order to achieve a healing.

Although the shamanic treatment may not be physiologically effective, the psychological state of mind induced in the patient is often critical to his or her recovery. From an anthropological perspective, shamanic healings can be understood by means of a three-cornered model we call the *shamanic complex* (Figure 13.2). This triangle is created by the relationships among the shaman and the patient and the community to which both belong. For a healing to take place, the shaman needs to be convinced of the effectiveness of his or her spiritual powers and techniques. Likewise, the patient must see the shaman as a genuine healing master using appropriate techniques. Finally, to close the triangle's "magic field," the community within which the shaman operates on the patient must view the healing ceremony and its practitioner as potentially effective and beneficial. Such dynamics are not unique to shamanic healing ceremonies, for similar social psychological processes are involved in Western medical treatments as well.

What shamanism provides for society is a focal point of attention. This places the shaman in a precarious position. In the eyes of the community, someone with so much skill and power has the ability to work evil as well as good and so is potentially dangerous. The group may interpret a shaman's failures as evidence of malpractice and may drive out or even kill him or her.

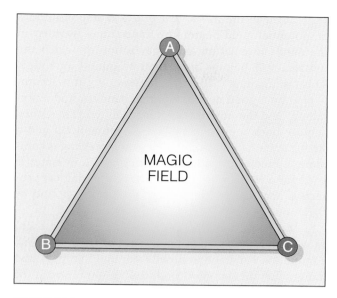

FIGURE 13.2

The Shamanic Complex. Shamanic healing takes place within a "magic field" created when the shaman (A) and patient (B), as well as their community (C), are all convinced that the shaman is a genuine healing master using appropriate techniques that are effective and beneficial.

Likewise, the shaman may help maintain social control through an ability to detect and punish evildoers.

The benefits of shamanism for the shaman are that it provides prestige and perhaps even wealth. In that respect, they are not unlike medical doctors in Western societies, who also enjoy considerable prestige and reap economic benefits from their profession. Shamanism may also be therapeutic for the shaman, in that it provides an approved outlet for the outbreaks of what otherwise might seem an unstable personality. An individual who is psychologically unstable (and not all shamans are) may get better by becoming intensely involved with the problems of others. In this respect, shamanism is a bit like self-analysis. As such, individuals likely to become shamans in an indigenous culture would perhaps choose to become a psychologist or psychiatrist if they were born in a Western society. Finally, shamanism is a good outlet for the theatrical self-expression of those who might be described as having an artistic temperament. Although opportunities for artistic self-expression also exist in Western societies, shamanism is unique in that it combines the theatrical and medical, the psychological and spiritual.

Rituals and Ceremonies

Not all rituals are religious in nature (consider, for example, college graduation ceremonies in North America), but those that are play a crucial role in religious activity. Religious ritual is the means through which people relate to the supernatural; it is religion in action. Ritual serves to relieve social tensions and reinforce a group's collective bonds. More than this, it provides a means of marking many important events and lessening the social disruption and individual suffering of crises, such as death. Anthropologists have classified several different types of ritual. These include rites of passage and rites of intensification, both discussed in detail below.

Rites of Passage

Rites of passage are rituals that mark important stages in an individual's life cycle. In one of anthropology's classic works, French folklorist Arnold van Gennep analyzed the rites of passage that help individuals through the crucial crises or major social transitions in their lives, such as birth, puberty, marriage, parenthood, advancement to a higher class, occupational specialization, and death.[7] He found it useful to divide ceremonies for all of these life crises into three stages: **separation, transition,** and **incorporation**—first ritual removal of the individual from everyday society, followed by a period of isolation, and, finally, formal return and readmission back into society in his or her new status.

Van Gennep described the male initiation rites of the Aborigines of Australia. When the elders decide the time for initiation, the boys are taken from the village (separation), while the women cry and make a ritual show of resistance. At a place distant from the camp, groups of men from many villages gather.

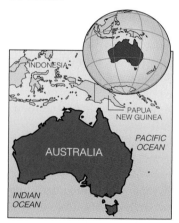

The elders sing and dance, while the initiates act as though they are dead. The climax of this part of the ritual

---

[7]Van Gennep, A. (1960). *The rites of passage.* Chicago: University of Chicago Press.

rites of passage Rituals that mark important stages in an individual's life cycle, such as birth, marriage, and death.
separation In rites of passage, the ritual removal of the individual from society.
transition In rites of passage, isolation of the individual following separation and prior to incorporation into society.
incorporation In rites of passage, reincorporation of the individual into society in his or her new status.

is a bodily operation, such as circumcision or the knocking out of a tooth. Anthropologist A. P. Elkin comments:

> This is partly a continuation of the drama of death. The tooth-knocking, circumcision or other symbolical act "killed" the novice; after this he does not return to the general camp and normally may not be seen by any woman. He is dead to the ordinary life of the tribe.[8]

In this transitional stage, the novice may be shown secret ceremonies and receive some instruction, but the most significant element is his complete removal from society. In the course of these Australian puberty rites, the initiate must learn the lore that all adult men are expected to know; he is given, in effect, a "cram course." The trauma of the occasion is a pedagogical technique that ensures he will learn and remember everything; in a nonliterate society the perpetuation of cultural traditions requires no less, and so effective teaching methods are necessary.

On his return to society (incorporation) the novice is welcomed with ceremonies, as though he had returned from the dead. This alerts the society at large to the individual's new status—that people can expect him to act in certain ways, and in return they must act in the appropriate ways toward him. The individual's new rights and duties are thus clearly defined. He is spared, for example, the problems of a teenager in North America, a time when an individual is neither adult nor child, a person whose status is ill defined.

In the Australian case just cited, boys are prepared not just for adulthood but also for *manhood*. In their society, for example, courage and endurance are considered important masculine virtues, and the pain of tooth-knocking and circumcision help instill these in initiates. In a similar way, female initiation rites help prepare Mende girls in West Africa for womanhood. After they have begun to menstruate, the girls are removed from society to spend weeks, or even months, in seclusion. There they discard the clothes of childhood, smear their bodies with white clay, and dress in short skirts and many strands of beads. Shortly after entering this transitional stage, they undergo clitoridectomy—surgery that excises part of the female genitals (clitoris and small labia), something they believe enhances their reproductive potential. Until their incorporation back into society, they

are trained in the moral and practical responsibilities of potential child bearers by experienced women in the Sande association, an organization to which the initiates will belong once their training has ended. This training is not all harsh, however, for it is accompanied by a good deal of singing, dancing, and storytelling, and the initiates are very well fed. Thus, they acquire both a positive image of womanhood and a strong sense of sisterhood. Once their training is complete, a medicine made by brewing leaves in water is used for a ritual washing, removing the magical protection that has shielded them during the period of their confinement.

Mende women emerge from their initiation, then, as women in knowledgeable control of their sexuality, eligible for marriage and childbearing. The pain and danger of the surgery, endured in the context of intense social support from other women, serves as a metaphor for childbirth, which may well take place in the same place of seclusion, again with the support of women in the Sande association. It also has been suggested that, symbolically, the clitoridectomy (excision of the clitoris, the feminine version of the penis) removes sexual ambiguity.[9] Once it is done, a woman knows she is "all woman." Thus we have symbolic expression of gender as something important in people's cultural lives.

In the case just cited, the anthropological commitment to cultural relativism permits an understanding of the practice of clitoridectomy in the Mende female initiation rites. But as discussed early on in this book, cultural relativism does not preclude the anthropologist from criticizing a given practice. In this case, removal of the clitoris (like male circumcision) is a form of genital mutilation, and a particularly dangerous one at that. An estimated 100 to 140 million women in the world have undergone some form of female genital mutilation (fgm), ranging from removal of the clitoris to removal of the entire external female genitalia, including the partial closing of the vaginal opening (surgically opened, or even torn open, for intercourse and closed again after giving birth until the male again desires intercourse). And it is estimated that an additional 2 million girls per year may undergo such surgery. The practice is particularly widespread in Africa, where it occurs in twenty-eight countries. The custom is found also among some groups outside Africa: in Oman, Yemen, the United Arab Emirates (but not Iran, Iraq, Jordan, Libya, or Saudi Arabia);

---

[8]Elkin, A. P. (1964). *The Australian Aborigines*. Garden City, NY: Doubleday/Anchor Books.

[9]MacCormack, C. P. (1977). Biological events and cultural control. *Signs, 3,* 98.

among some Muslims in Indonesia and southern Malaysia; and an estimated 27,000 women in New York State.[10] As this list suggests, female genital mutilation is not required by Islamic religion; neither the Koran nor the Bible makes any mention of cutting women to please God. Where the custom is practiced by Muslims (as well as the occasional Christian and Jewish group), it functions as a means for men to control women's sexuality (unlike among the Mende).

The consequences for women are extreme. One Somali woman who underwent the procedure as a child poses these questions:

> What about the girl back in the bush, walking miles and miles to water her goats, while she's in such pain from her period that she can barely stand up straight? Or the wife who will be sewn back up with a needle and thread like a piece of cloth as soon as she gives birth, so her vagina will remain tight for her husband? Or the woman nine months pregnant hunting for food to feed her other eleven starving children? Or what happens to the new wife whose first baby is to be born?[11]

Apart from the pain and the effect of the operation on a woman's future sexual satisfaction, significant numbers of young women die from excessive bleeding, shock, infection, damage to the urethra or anus, tetanus, bladder infections, septicemia, HIV, hepatitis B, or (later on) when giving birth as scar tissue tears. Not surprisingly, the practice has been widely condemned as a human rights violation in recent years, and committees to end such practices have been set up in twenty-two African countries.

Rites of Intensification

Rites of intensification are rituals that take place during a crisis in the life of the group and serve to bind individuals together. Whatever the precise nature of the crisis—a drought that threatens crops, the sudden appearance of an enemy war party, the onset of an epidemic—mass ceremonies are performed to ease the sense of danger. This unites people in a common effort so that fear and confusion yield to collective

AP/Wide World Photos

Waris Dirie, a Somali woman who underwent genital mutilation at age 6, holds the book in which she recounts her experience.

action and a degree of optimism. The balance in the relations of all concerned is restored to normal, and the community's values are celebrated and affirmed.

While an individual's death might be regarded as the ultimate crisis in that person's life, it is, as well, a crisis for the entire group, particularly if the group is small. A member of the community has been removed, so its composition has been seriously altered. The survivors, therefore, must readjust and restore balance. They also need to reconcile themselves to the loss of someone to whom they were emotionally tied. Funerary ceremonies, then, can be regarded as rites of intensification that permit the living to express in nondisruptive ways their upset over the death while providing for social readjustment. A frequent feature of such ceremonies is ambivalence toward the dead person. For example, one part of the funerary rites of certain Melanesians was the eating of the dead person's flesh. This ritual cannibalism, witnessed by anthropologist Malinowski, was performed with "extreme repugnance and dread and usually followed by a violent vomiting fit. At the same time

---

[10]Female genital mutilation. (2000). Fact Sheet No. 241. World Health Organization; Dirie, W., & Miller, C. (1998). *Desert flower: The extraordinary journey of a desert nomad* (pp. 218, 219). New York: William Morrow.

[11]Dirie & Miller, p. 213.

rites of intensification Rituals that take place during a crisis in the life of the group and serve to bind individuals together.

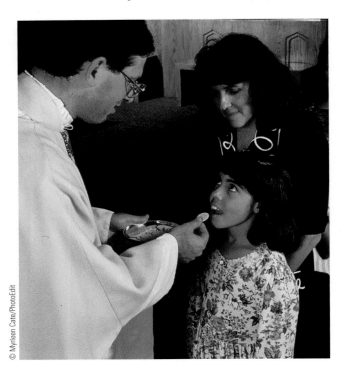

Ritual cannibalism appears in various societies in diverse forms. In Christianity, it is symbolic rather than actual, although some Christians believe the communion wafer actually becomes the body of Christ.

it is felt to be a supreme act of reverence, love, and devotion."[12] This custom and the emotions accompanying it clearly reveal an ambiguous attitude toward death: On the one hand, there is the survivors' desire to maintain the tie to the dead person, and, on the other hand, they feel disgust and fear at the transformation wrought by death. According to Malinowski, funeral ceremonies provide an approved collective means for individuals to express these feelings while maintaining social cohesiveness and preventing disruption of society.

The performance of rites of intensification does not have to be limited to times of overt crisis. In regions where the seasons differ enough that human activities must change accordingly, they will take the form of annual ceremonies. These are particularly common among horticultural and agricultural people, with their planting, first fruit, and harvest ceremonies. These are critical times in the lives of people in such societies, and the ceremonies express a reverent attitude toward nature's forces of generation and fertility upon which people's very existence depends. If all

goes well, as it often does at such times, participation in a festive situation reinforces group involvement. It also serves as a kind of dress rehearsal for serious crisis situations; it promotes a habit of reliance on supernatural forces through ritual activity, which can be activated easily under stressful circumstances when it is important not to give way to fear and despair.

RELIGION, MAGIC, AND WITCHCRAFT

Among the most fascinating of ritual practices is application of the belief that supernatural powers can be compelled to act in certain ways for good or evil purposes by recourse to certain specified formulas. This is a classical anthropological notion of magic. Many societies have magical rituals to ensure good crops, the replenishment of game, the fertility of domestic animals, and the avoidance or healing of illness in humans.

Although many Western peoples today, seeking to objectify and demythologize their world, have often tried to suppress the existence of magic mysteries in their own consciousness, they continue to be fascinated by them. Not only are books and films about demonic possession and witchcraft avidly devoured and discussed, but horoscope columns are a regular feature of daily newspapers in the United States. While it may raise few eyebrows that Abraham Lincoln's wife invited psychics to the White House, it caused a considerable stir when it was learned that President Reagan's wife regularly consulted an astrologer. As for psychics or spirit mediums, they are consulted by growing numbers of people in the United States today. A 1996 Gallup poll found that 20 percent of the respondents believed the dead could contact the living, and another 22 percent thought it might be possible. Anthropologist Lauren Kendall notes,

> Many witches, wizards, druids, Cabalists, and shamans . . . practice modern magic in contemporary England and the United States, where their ranks are comfortably reckoned in the tens of thousands. . . . The usual magician is ordinary, generally middle class, and often highly intelligent—a noticeable number of them have something to do with computers.[13]

Although it is certainly true that non-Western and peasant peoples tend to endow their world quite freely with magical properties, so do many academically educated Western peoples.

---

[12]Malinowski, B. (1954). *Magic, science and religion* (p. 50). Garden City, NY: Doubleday.

[13]Kendall, L. (1990, October). In the company of witches. *Natural History*, 92.

Nancy Reagan, whose advice was important to her husband when he served as president of United States in the 1980s, consulted regularly with an astrologer during their years in the White House.

In the 19th century Sir James George Frazer, author of one of the most widely read anthropological books of all time, *The Golden Bough,* made a strong distinction between religion and magic. Religion he saw as "a propitiation or conciliation of powers superior to man which are believed to direct and control the course of nature and human life."[14] Magic, by contrast, he saw as an attempt to manipulate certain perceived laws of nature. The magician never doubts the same causes always will produce the same effects. Thus, Frazer saw magic as a sort of pseudoscience, differing from modern science only in its misconception of the nature of the particular laws that govern the succession of events.

Useful though Frazer's characterization of magic has been, anthropologists no longer accept his distinction between it and religion. Far from being separate, magical procedures are frequently part of religious rituals, and both magic and religion deal directly with the supernatural. In fact, Frazer's distinction seems to be no more than a bias of Western culture, which regards magic as separate from religion.

Frazer did make a useful distinction between two fundamental principles of magic. The first principle, that "like produces like," he named **imitative magic** (sometimes called *sympathetic magic*). In Burma (Myanmar) in Southeast Asia, for example, a rejected lover might

[14]Frazer, J. G. (1931). Magic and religion. In V. F. Calverton (Ed.), *The making of man: An outline of anthropology* (p. 693). New York: Modern Library.

imitative magic Magic based on the principle that like produces like; sometimes called sympathetic magic.

VISUAL COUNTERPOINT What these two pictures have in common is that both are examples of institutionalized magical responses to concerns many harbor in their societies. In death penalty states, executing criminals does no more to deter violent crimes than Aztec human sacrifices did to keep the sun in the sky.

The treasuring of objects once touched or owned by famous people is well represented in Western cultures. Here we see Princess Diana's evening gown being auctioned at Christie's in New York City in June 1997.

AP/Wide World Photos

engage a sorcerer to make an image of his would-be love. If this image were tossed into water, to the accompaniment of certain charms, it was expected that the hapless girl would go mad. Thus, the girl would suffer a fate similar to that of her image.

Frazer's second principle was called **contagious magic**—the idea that things or persons once in contact can influence each other after the contact is broken. The most common example of contagious magic is the permanent relationship between an individual and any part of his or her body, such as hair, fingernails, or teeth. Frazer cites the Basutos of Lesotho in southern Africa, who were careful to conceal their extracted teeth, because these might fall into the hands of certain mythical beings who could harm the owners of the teeth by working magic on them. Related to this is the custom, in Western societies, of treasuring things that have been touched by special people. Such things range from a saint's relics to possessions of other admired or idolized individuals, such as the singer Elvis Presley or England's Princess Diana.

contagious magic Magic based on the principle that things once in contact can influence each other after the contact is broken.
witchcraft An explanation of events based on the belief that certain individuals possess an innate psychic power capable of causing harm, including sickness and death.

Witchcraft

In Salem, Massachusetts, 200 suspected witches were arrested in 1692; of these, nineteen were hanged and one was hounded to death. Despite the awarding of damages to descendants of some of the victims 19 years later, not until 1957 were the last of the Salem witches exonerated by the Massachusetts legislature. **Witchcraft** is an explanation of events based on the belief that certain individuals possess an innate psychic power capable of causing harm, including sickness and death.

Although many North Americans suppose it to be something that belongs to a less enlightened past, witchcraft is alive and well in the United States today. Indeed, starting in the 1960s, witchcraft began to undergo something of a boom in this country. North Americans are by no means alone in this; for example, as the Ibibio of Nigeria have become increasingly exposed to modern education and scientific training, their reliance on witchcraft as an explanation for misfortune has increased.[15] Furthermore, it is often the younger, more educated members of Ibibio society who accuse others of bewitching them. Frequently, the accused are older, more traditional members of society;

[15]Offiong, D. (1985). Witchcraft among the Ibibio of Nigeria. In A. C. Lehmann & J. E. Myers (Eds.), *Magic, witchcraft, and religion* (pp. 152–165). Palo Alto, CA: Mayfield.

thus, we have an expression of the intergenerational hostility that often exists in fast-changing traditional societies.

Ibibio Witchcraft

Among the Ibibio of Nigeria, as among most traditional peoples of sub-Saharan Africa, witchcraft beliefs are highly developed and long-standing. A rat that eats up a person's crops is not really a rat but a witch that changed into one; if a young and enterprising man cannot get a job or fails an exam, he has been bewitched; if someone's money is wasted or if the person becomes sick, is bitten by a snake, or is struck by lightning, the reason is always the same—witchcraft. Indeed, virtually all misfortune, illness, or death is attributed to the malevolent activity of witches. The modern Ibibio's knowledge of such facts as the role microorganisms play in disease has little impact; after all, it says nothing about why these were sent to the afflicted individual. Although Ibibio religious beliefs provide alternative explanations for misfortune, they carry negative connotations and do not elicit nearly as much sympathy from others. Thus, if evil befalls a person, witchcraft is a far more satisfying explanation than something such as offspring disobedience or violation of a taboo.

Who are these Ibibio witches? They are thought to be men or women who have within them a special substance acquired from another established witch. From swallowing this substance—made up of needles, colored threads, and other ingredients—one is believed to become endowed with a special power that causes injury, even death, to others regardless of whether its possessor intends harm or not. The power is purely psychic, and witches do not perform rites or make use of "bad medicine." It is believed to give them the ability to transform into animals and travel any distance at incredible speed to get at their unsuspecting victims, whom they may torture or kill by transferring the victim's soul or vital spirit into an animal, which is then eaten.

To identify a witch, an Ibibio looks for any person living in the region whose behavior is considered odd, out of the ordinary, immoral, or unsocial. Any combination of the following may cause someone to be labeled a witch: not being fond of greeting people; living alone in a place apart from others; charging too high a price for something; enjoying adultery or committing incest; walking about at night; not showing sufficient grief upon the death of a relative or other member of the community; taking improper care of one's parents, children, or wives; and hard-heartedness. Witches are apt to look and act mean and to be socially disruptive people in the sense that their behavior exceeds the range of variance considered acceptable.

Neither the Ibibio in particular nor Africans in general are alone in attributing most harmful happenings to witchcraft. Similar beliefs can be found in any human society. As among the Ibibio, the powers (however they may be gained) are generally looked upon as innate and uncontrollable; they result in activities that are the antithesis of proper behavior, and persons displaying undesirable personality characteristics (however these may be defined) are generally the ones accused of being witches.

The Ibibio make a distinction between sorcerers, whose acts are especially diabolical and destructive, and benign witches, whose witchcraft is relatively harmless, even though their powers are thought to be greater than those of their malevolent counterparts. This exemplifies a common distinction between what British anthropologist Lucy Mair has dubbed "nightmare witches" and "everyday witches."[16] The nightmare witch is the very embodiment of a society's conception of evil, a being that flouts the rules of sexual behavior and disregards every other standard of decency. Nightmare witches, being almost literally the product of dreams and repressed fantasies, have much in common wherever they appear: The modern Navajo and the ancient Roman, for example, like the Ibibio, conceived of witches that could "shape change," that is, turn themselves into animals and gather to feast on their victims. Everyday witches are often the community's nonconformists: Typically, they are morose, arrogant, and unfriendly people who keep to themselves but otherwise cause little disturbance. Such witches are thought to be dangerous when offended—likely to retaliate by causing sickness, death, crop failure, cattle disease, or any number of lesser ills. This given, it is not surprising that people viewed as witches are usually treated with considerable caution and respect.

The Functions of Witchcraft

Why witchcraft? We might better ask, why not? As Mair aptly observed, in a world where there are few proven

---

[16]Mair, L. (1969). *Witchcraft* (p. 37). New York: McGraw-Hill.

© The Cover Story/Corbis

In North America, interest in and practice of witchcraft have grown significantly over the past 30 years, often among highly educated segments of society. Contrary to popular belief, witchcraft is *not* concerned exclusively, or even primarily, with working evil.

techniques for dealing with everyday crises, especially sickness, a belief in witches is not foolish; it is indispensable. No one wants to resign oneself to illness, and if the malady is caused by a witch's curse, then magical countermeasures should cure it. Not only does the idea of personalized evil answer the problem of unmerited suffering, but it also provides an explanation for many happenings for which no cause can be discovered. Witchcraft, then, cannot be refuted. Even if we could convince a person that his or her illness was due to natural causes, the victim would still ask, as the Ibibio do, Why me? Why now? Such a view leaves no room for pure chance; everything must be assigned a cause or meaning. Witchcraft offers an explanation and, in so doing, also provides both the basis and the means for taking counteraction.

Nor is witchcraft always harmful; even during the Spanish Inquisition, church officials recognized a benev-

---

divination A magical procedure or spiritual ritual designed to find out about what is not knowable by ordinary means, such as foretelling the future by interpreting omens.

---

olent variety. The positive functions of even malevolent witchcraft may be seen in many African societies where people believe sickness and death are caused by witches. The ensuing search for the perpetrator of the misfortune becomes, in effect, a communal probe into social behavior.

A witch-hunt is, in fact, a systematic investigation, through a public hearing, into all social relationships involving the victim of the sickness or death. Was a husband or wife unfaithful or a son lacking in the performance of his duties? Were an individual's friends uncooperative, or was the victim guilty of any of these wrongs? Accusations are reciprocal, and before long just about every unsocial or hostile act that has occurred in that society since the last outbreak of witchcraft (as manifested in sickness, death, or some other misfortune) is brought into the open.[17]

Through such periodic public scrutiny of everyone's behavior, people are reminded of what their society regards as both strengths and weaknesses of character. This encourages individuals to suppress as best they can those personality traits that are looked upon with disapproval, for if they do not, they at some time may be accused of being a witch. A belief in witchcraft thus serves a function of social control.

Psychological Functions of Witchcraft among the Navajo

Widely known among American Indians are the Navajo of the southwestern United States, who possess a highly developed concept of witchcraft. Several types of witchcraft are distinguished. *Witchery* encompasses the practices of witches, who are said to meet at night to practice cannibalism and kill people at a distance. *Sorcery* is distinguished from witchery only by the methods used by the sorcerer, who casts spells on individuals using the victim's fingernails, hair, or discarded clothing. *Wizardry* is not distinguished so much by its effects as by its manner of working: Wizards kill by injecting a cursed substance, such as a tooth from a corpse, into the victim's body.

Whether or not a particular illness results from Navajo witchcraft is determined by **divination**—a magical procedure or spiritual ritual designed to find out about what is not knowable by ordinary means. Once a person is charged with witchcraft, he or she is publicly interrogated—in the past, possibly even tortured until there is a confession. It is believed the witch's own curse

---

[17]Turnbull, C. M. (1983). *The human cycle* (p. 181). New York: Simon & Schuster.

will turn against the witch once this happens, so it is expected that the witch will die within a year. Some confessed witches have been allowed to live in exile.

According to Clyde Kluckhohn, Navajo witchcraft serves to channel anxieties, tensions, and frustrations caused by the pressures from Euroamericans.[18] The rigid rules of proper behavior among the Navajo allow little means for expression of hostility, except through accusations of witchcraft. Such accusations funnel pent-up negative emotions against individuals without upsetting the wider society. Another function of witchcraft accusations is that they permit direct expression of hostile feelings against people toward whom one ordinarily would be unable to express anger or enmity. On a more positive note, individuals strive to behave in ways that will prevent them from being accused of witchcraft. Since excessive wealth is believed to result from witchcraft, individuals are encouraged to redistribute their assets among friends and relatives, thereby leveling economic differences. Similarly, because Navajos believe elders, if neglected, will turn into witches, people are strongly motivated to take care of aged relatives. And because leaders are thought to be witches, people are understandably reluctant to go against their wishes, less they suffer supernatural retribution.

Analyses such as these demonstrate that witchcraft, in spite of its often negative image, frequently functions in a very positive way to manage tensions within a society. Nonetheless, events may get out of hand, particularly in crisis situations, when widespread accusations may cause great suffering. This certainly was the case in the Salem witch trials, but even those pale in comparison to the half a million individuals executed as witches in Europe from the 15th through the 17th centuries. This was a time of profound change in European society, marked by a good deal of political and religious conflict. At such times, it is all too easy to search out scapegoats on whom to place the blame for what people believe are undesirable changes.

THE FUNCTIONS OF RELIGION

Just as belief in witchcraft may serve a variety of psychological and social functions, so too do religious beliefs and practices in general. Here we may summarize these functions in a somewhat more systematic way. One psychological function is to provide an orderly model of the universe, which plays a key role in establishing orderly human behavior. Beyond this, by explaining the unknown and making it understandable, religion reduces the fears and anxieties of individuals. As we have seen, the explanations typically assume the existence of various sorts of supernatural beings and powers, which people may potentially appeal to or manipulate. This being so, a means is provided for dealing with crises: Divine aid is, theoretically, available when all else fails.

A social function of religion is to prompt reflection concerning conduct. In this context, religion plays a role in social control, which, as we saw in the last chapter, does not rely on law alone. This is done through notions of right and wrong, good and evil. Right actions earn the approval of whatever supernatural powers are recognized by a particular culture. Wrong actions may cause revenge or punishment through supernatural agencies. In short, by deliberately *raising* people's feelings of guilt and anxiety about their actions, religion helps keep them in line.

Religion does more than this, though; it sets guidelines for acceptable behavior. We have noted already the connection between myths and religion. Usually, myths feature tales of extraordinary or supernatural beings that in various ways illustrate the society's ethical code in action. So it is that Gluskabe, the Penobscot Indian culture hero, is portrayed in that society's traditions as tricking and punishing those who lie, mock others, express greed, overreact, or engage in other behaviors deemed inappropriate in Penobscot culture. Moreover, the specific situations relayed in myths serve as guidelines for human behavior in similar circumstances. The Old and New Testaments of the Bible are rich in the same sort of material, as is the Koran. Related to this, by the models religion presents and the morals it espouses, religion serves to justify and perpetuate a particular social order. Thus, in the Jewish, Christian, and Islamic traditions, a masculine-authoritarian godhead along with a creation story that portrays a woman as responsible for a fall from grace serve to justify a social order in which men exercise control over women.

A psychological function also is tied up in this. A society's moral code, since it is considered to be divinely ordained, lifts the burden of responsibility for conduct from the shoulders of the society's individual members, at least in important situations. It can be a tremendous relief to individuals to know that the responsibility for the way things are rests with the gods or spirit forces rather than with themselves.

Another social function of religion is its role in the maintenance of social solidarity. In our discussion of

---

[18]Kluckhohn, C. (1944). Navajo witchcraft. *Papers of the Peabody Museum of American Archaeology and Ethnology, 22*(2).

Anthropology Applied

Reconciling Modern Medicine with Traditional Beliefs in Swaziland

Although the biomedical germ theory is generally accepted in Western societies today, this is not the case in many other societies around the world. In southern Africa's Swaziland, for example, many illnesses are generally thought to be caused by sorcery or by loss of ancestral protection. (Sexually transmitted diseases—STDs—and other contagious diseases are exceptions to these beliefs.) Even where the effectiveness of Western medicine is recognized, the ultimate question remains: Why did a disease come to a particular person in the first place? Thus, for the treatment of disease, the Swazi have traditionally relied upon herbalists, diviner mediums through whom ancestor spirits are thought to work, and (more recently) Christian faith healers. Unfortunately, such individuals have usually been regarded as quacks and charlatans by the medical establishment, even though the herbal medicines used by traditional healers are effective in several ways, and the reassurance provided patient and family alike through rituals that reduce stress and anxiety plays an important role in the patient's recovery. In a country where there is 1 traditional healer for every 110 people, but only 1 physician for every 10,000, the potential benefit of cooperation between physicians and healers seems self-evident. Nevertheless, it was largely unrecognized until proposed by anthropologist Edward C. Green.

Green, a senior researcher at the Harvard School of Public Health, went to Swaziland in 1981 as a researcher for the Rural Water-Borne Disease Control Project, funded by the United States Agency for International Development. Assigned the task of finding out about knowledge, attitudes, and practices related to water and sanitation, and aware of the serious deficiencies of conventional surveys that rely on precoded questionnaires (see Chapter 1), Green used instead the traditional anthropological techniques of open-ended interviews with key informants, along with participant observation. The key informants were traditional healers, their patients, and rural health motivators (individual communities chose to receive 8 weeks of training in preventive health care in regional clinics). Without such anthropological research, Green would have found it impossible to design and interpret a reliable survey instrument, but the added payoff was that Green learned a great deal about Swazi theories of illness and its treatment.

Disposed at the outset to recognize the positive value of many traditional practices, Green could also see how cooperation with physicians might be achieved. For example, traditional healers already recognized the utility of Western medicines for treatment of diseases considered not indigenous to Africa, and traditional medicines were routinely given to children through inhalation and a kind of vaccination. Thus, nontraditional medicines and vaccinations might be accepted, if presented in traditional terms.

Realizing the suspicion existing on both sides, Green and his Swazi associate Lydia Makhubu (a chemist who had studied the properties of native medicines) recommended to the minister of health a cooperative project focused on a problem of concern to health professionals and native healers alike: infant diarrheal diseases. These had recently become a health problem of high concern to the general public; healers wanted a means to prevent such diseases, and a means of treatment existed—oral rehydration therapy—that was compatible with traditional treatments for diarrhea (herbal preparations taken orally over a period of time). Packets of oral rehydration salts, along with instructions, were provided to healers in a pilot project, with positive results. This helped convince health professionals of the benefits of cooperation, while the healers saw the distribution of packets to them as a gesture of trust and cooperation on the part of their government.

Since then, further steps toward cooperation have been taken, such as work in prevention of AIDS, STDs and TB. All of this demonstrates the importance of finding how to work in ways compatible with existing belief systems. Directly challenging traditional beliefs, as all too often happens, does little more than create stress, confusion and resentment among people. *(Adapted from E. C. Green. (1987). The planning of health education strategies in Swaziland, and the integration of modern and traditional health sectors in Swaziland. In R. M. Wulff & S. J. Fiske (Eds.), Anthropological praxis: Translating knowledge into action (pp. 15–25, 87–97). Boulder, CO: Westview Press. 2003 update by authors based on personal communication with Green.)* ▪ ▪ ▪

shamans, we saw how such individuals provide focal points of interest, thus supplying one ingredient of assistance for maintaining group unity. In addition, common participation in rituals, coupled with a basic uniformity of beliefs, helps to bind people together and reinforce their identification with their group. Particularly effective may be their joint participation in rituals, when the atmosphere is charged with emotion. The ecstatic feelings people may experience in such circumstances serve as a positive reinforcement in that they feel good as a result. Here, once again, we find religion providing psychological assurance while fulfilling the needs of society.

One other area in which religion serves a social function is education. In our discussion of rites of passage, we noted that puberty rituals of Aborigines in Australia served as a kind of cram course in traditional lore. By providing a memorable occasion, initiation rites can serve to enhance learning and so help ensure the perpetuation of a nonliterate culture. And as we saw in the female initiation rites among the Mende, they can serve to ensure that individuals have the knowledge they will need to fulfill their adult roles in society. Education also may be served by rites of intensification. Frequently, such rites involve dramas that portray matters of cultural importance. For example, among a food-foraging people, dances may imitate the movement of game and techniques of hunting. Among farmers a fixed round of ceremonies may emphasize the steps necessary for good crops. All of this helps preserve knowledge important to a people's material well-being, gives expression to their worldview, and thereby reinforces their collective self understanding. In addition to all of the above, people often turn to religion in the hope of reaching a specific goal, such as the healing of physical, emotional, or social ills—as illustrated in this chapter's Original Study and the Anthropology Applied features.

RELIGION AND CULTURAL CHANGE

Revitalization Movements

Although the subject of culture change is taken up in a later chapter, no anthropological consideration of religion is complete without some mention of **revitalization movements**—movements for radical cultural reform in response to widespread social disruption and collective feelings of anxiety and despair. One of many examples of this took place in 1931 at Buka, in the Solomon Islands (in the Pacific Ocean). A native religious movement suddenly emerged there when prophets predicted that a deluge would soon engulf all whites, and a ship would then arrive filled with Western industrial commodities. The prophets told their followers to construct a storehouse for the goods and to prepare themselves to repulse the colonial police. They also spread word that the ship would come only after the natives had used up all their own supplies, and because of this believers ceased working in the fields. Although the leaders of the movement were arrested, the cult continued for some years.

This was not an isolated event. Such **cargo cults**—and many other spiritual movements promising resurrection of deceased relatives, destruction or enslavement of whites, and the magical arrival of utopian riches—have sporadically appeared through-

© Ken Schles Inc. All rights reserved.

Shown here are members of the Unarius Academy of Science, a New Age revitalization movement founded in 1954 on the idea that wise space beings would come to earth and inspire a new spiritual awareness in human beings. Unarius is an acronym for Universal Articulate Interdimensional Understanding of Science.

out the southern Pacific ever since the region's Melanesian cultures were radically disrupted following sudden contact with Western capitalist powers in the beginning of the 20th century. Since these cults are widely separated in space and time, their similarities are apparently the result of similarities in social conditions. In these areas the traditional cultures of the indigenous peoples have been uprooted. Europeans, or European-influenced natives, hold all political and economic power. Natives are employed in unloading and distributing Western-made goods but have no practical knowledge of how to attain these goods.

revitalization movements Movements for radical cultural reform in response to widespread social disruption and collective feelings of anxiety and despair.
cargo cults Spiritual movements in Melanesia in reaction to disruptive contact with Western capitalism promising resurrection of deceased relatives, destruction or enslavement of white foreigners, and the magical arrival of utopian riches.

VISUAL COUNTERPOINT In the United States, Mormonism is an example of a revitalization movement that has been enormously successful at gaining acceptance in the wider society. By contrast, the Branch Davidians so antagonized elements of mainstream society that a violent confrontation occurred, culminating in the mass burning of many cult members at the movement's headquarters in Waco, Texas.

When cold reality offers no hope from the daily frustrations of cultural deterioration and economic deprivation, religion offers the solution.

As deliberate efforts to construct a more satisfying culture, revitalization movements aim to reform not just the religious sphere of activity but an entire cultural system. Such drastic measures are taken when a group's anxiety and frustration have become so intense that the only way to reduce the stress is to overturn the entire social system and replace it with a new one. From the cargo cults of Melanesia to the 1890 Ghost Dance of many North American Indians to the Mau Mau of the Kikuyu in Kenya in the 1950s, extreme and sometimes violent religious reactions to European domination are so common that anthropologists have sought to formulate their underlying causes and general characteristics.

Revitalization movements are by no means restricted to the colonial world, and in the United States alone hundreds of them have sprung up. Among the more widely known in that part of the world are Mormonism, which began in the 19th century; the more recent Unification Church of the Reverend Sun Myung Moon; the Branch Davidians whose Seventh Day Adventist "prophet" was David Koresh; and the Heaven's Gate cult led by Marshall Herf Applewhite and Bonnie Lu Trousdale Nettles. As these four examples suggest, revitalization movements show a great deal of diversity, and some have been more successful than others.

Anthropologist Anthony Wallace outlined a sequence common to all expressions of the revitalization process.[19] First is the normal state of society, in which stress is not too great, and sufficient cultural means exist to satisfy needs. Under certain conditions, such as domination by a more powerful group or severe economic depression, stress and frustration are steadily amplified; this ushers in the second phase, or period of increased individual stress. If there are no significant adaptive changes, a period of cultural distortion follows, in which stress becomes so chronic that socially approved methods of releasing tension begin to break down. This steady deterioration of the culture may be checked by a period of revitalization, during which a dynamic cult or religious movement grips a sizable portion of the population. Often the movement will be so out of touch with existing circumstances that it is doomed to failure from the beginning. This was the case with the Heaven's Gate cult, which mixed bits and pieces of apocalyptic Christian beliefs predicting destruction of the world at the end of the millennium with folk myths of contemporary North American culture, in particular those having to do with UFOs (alien spaceships). Its followers committed mass suicide out of a conviction that their spiritual essences would reunite with higher extraterrestrial beings in a spaceship that

[19]Wallace, A. F. C. (1970). *Culture and personality* (2nd ed., pp. 191–196). New York: Random House.

awaited them behind the tail of the Hale-Bopp comet, ready to take them "home." A similar case of self-destruction took place among the Branch Davidians, whose hostility toward government authorities prompted an official assault on the cult's compound in Waco, Texas. In reaction, cult members set fire to their own headquarters, sending their movement and their lives up in flames.

More rarely, a movement may tap long-dormant adaptive forces underlying a culture, and an enduring religion may result. Such was the case with Mormonism. Though heavily persecuted at first and hounded from place to place, Mormons adapted to the point that their religion thrives in the United States today. Indeed, revitalization movements lie at the root of all known religions—Judaism, Christianity, and Islam included. We will return to revitalization movements in Chapter 15.

MEDIATREK

For vivid images of sacred sites all around the world and links to various other sites concerning pilgrimage places, go to MediaTrek 13.4 on the companion Web site or CD-ROM.

From the ongoing need to make meaningful sense of their existence, humans continue to explore metaphysically or spiritually as well as scientifically. All around the globe we see indications of the effort, not only in buildings and other structures created for religious purposes, but in natural places that people have designated as sacred sites. The search is also evident in many works of art, as discussed in the next chapter.

Chapter Summary

■ Religion, an organized system of ideas about spiritual reality, or the supernatural, is a key part of every culture's worldview. It consists of beliefs and practices by which people try to interpret and control aspects of the universe otherwise beyond their control. Among food-foraging peoples, religion is intertwined in everyday life. As societies become more complex, religion may be restricted to particular occasions.

■ Religion is characterized by a belief in supernatural beings and forces, which can be appealed to for aid through prayer, sacrifice, and other rituals. Supernatural beings may be grouped into three categories: major deities (gods and goddesses), ancestral spirits, and other sorts of spirit beings. Gods and goddesses are great but remote beings that control the universe or a specific part of it. Whether people recognize gods, goddesses, or both has to do with how men and women relate to each other in everyday life. Belief in ancestral spirits is based on the idea that human beings are made up of a body and a soul or vital spirit. Freed from the body at death, the spirit continues to participate in human affairs. It is characteristic of descent-based groups with their associated ancestor orientation.

■ Animism, common among peoples who see themselves as part of nature, is a belief that nature is animated or energized by distinct personalized spirit beings separable from bodies. Closer to humans than gods and goddesses, these spirit beings are intimately concerned with human activities. Animatism, sometimes found alongside animism, is a belief that nature is animated or energized by an impersonal spiritual power, which may make itself manifest in any object.

■ Belief in supernatural beings and powers is maintained through what people perceive as manifestations of power. Belief is also fueled by the fact that supernatural beings seem real because they possess certain attributes that are familiar to people. Finally, they are explained and reinforced by myths.

■ All human societies have specialists—priests and priestesses and/or shamans—to guide religious practices and to intervene with the supernatural world. Shamans are individuals skilled at contacting and manipulating supernatural beings and powers through altered states of consciousness. Their performances promote a release of tension among individuals in a society, and the shaman can help to maintain social control. The benefits of shamanism for the shaman are prestige, sometimes wealth, and an outlet for artistic self-expression.

■ Religious rituals are religion in action. Through ritual acts, social bonds are reinforced. Rituals carried out to mark important stages in an individual's life cycle are rites of passage and include three stages: separation, transition, and incorporation. Rites of intensification are rituals that mark occasions of crisis in the life of the group rather than the individual. They serve to unite people, quiet fear, and prompt collective action. They include ceremonies tied to a range of significant events in the community—from death to life-sustaining activities such as planting and harvesting. Magic, which can be viewed as a ritual practice that makes supernatural powers act in certain ways, can be differentiated into imitative magic and contagious magic.

■ Witchcraft functions as an effective way for people to explain away personal misfortune without having to shoulder any personal blame. Even malevolent witchcraft may function positively in the realm of social control. It may also provide an outlet for feelings of hostility and frustration without disturbing the norms of the larger group.

■ Religion (including magic and witchcraft) serves several important social functions. First, it sanctions a wide range of conduct by providing notions of right and wrong. Second, it sets standards for acceptable behavior and helps perpetuate an existing social order. Third, it lifts the burden of decision making from individuals and places responsibility with the gods. Fourth, it plays a large role in maintaining social solidarity. Fifth, it enhances the learning of traditional lore and thus ensures continuation of a nonliterate culture. Finally, religion is employed in the hope of reaching a specific goal, such as the healing of physical, emotional, or social ills.

■ Revitalization movements occur when people seek radical cultural reform in response to widespread social disruption and collective feelings of anxiety and despair. They can happen in any culture. Among Melanesian islanders radically disturbed by Western colonization and capitalism, these movements have often taken the form of cargo cults, which have appeared spontaneously at different times since the beginning of the 20th century. No matter where they occur, revitalization movements follow a common sequence, and all religions stem from such movements.

Questions for Reflection

1. Beyond biological survival, humans face mental challenges born of the need to make meaningful sense of their existence. Do you ever ponder questions such as the meaning of your life and big issues such as the origin or destiny of the human species? How does your culture, including your religion or spiritual beliefs, offer you guidance in finding meaningful answers to such big questions?

2. You have read about female genital mutilation as a rite of passage in some cultures. Do you know of any genital mutilation practices in your society? What is the reason so many boys in the United States are immediately circumcised after their birth?

3. Do the basic dynamics of the shamanic complex also apply to preachers or priests in modern churches and medical doctors working in modern hospitals? Can you think of some similarities among the shaman, preacher, and medical doctor in terms of their respective fields of operation?

4. Revitalization movements occur in reaction against the upheavals caused by rapid colonization and modernization. Do you think that the rise of Christian fundamentalism in the North American Bible Belt today is a response to such upheavals as well?

5. In postindustrial societies such as western Europe, the United States, and Canada, there is growing interest in shamanism and alternative healing techniques. Is there any relationship between globalization and this phenomenon?

Key Terms

Worldview	Separation
Religion	Transition
Spirituality	Incorporation
Polytheism	Rites of intensification
Pantheon	Imitative magic
Animism	Contagious magic
Animatism	Witchcraft
Priest or Priestess	Divination
Shaman	Revitalization movements
Rites of passage	Cargo cults

Multimedia Review Tools

Companion Web Site

Visit **http://www.wadsworth.com/anthropology_d/** and click on the companion Web site for this textbook to access a wide range of material to aid your study of anthropology. Among the options for self-study in each chapter are learning objectives, flash cards, Internet activities, Web links, InfoTrac College Edition exercises, and practice tests that can be scored and emailed to your instructor.

CD-ROM

The *Doing Anthropology Today* CD-ROM supplied with your textbook provides unique and valuable information designed to enhance your learning experience. This interactive multimedia resource includes video clips, interviews with renowned anthropologists, map and timeline exercises, chapter study quizzes, and much more. *Doing Anthropology Today* will not only help you in achieving your grade goals, it will also make your learning experience fun and exciting!

Suggested Readings

Guthrie, S. (1993). *Faces in the clouds: A new theory of religion.* New York: Oxford University Press.

An accessible, thought-provoking exploration of anthropomorphism in religion.

Kalwet, H. (1988). *Dreamtime and inner space: The world of the shaman.* New York: Random House.

This book surveys the practices and paranormal experiences of healers and shamans from Africa, the Americas, Asia, and Australia.

Kehoe, A. (1989). *The ghost dance: Ethnohistory and revitalization.* Fort Worth: Holt, Rinehart and Winston.

A description and analysis of the 1890 Ghost Dance movement among Plains Indians, including its influence on present-day Native American cultures and religious beliefs and practices.

Klass, M. (1995). *Ordered universes: Approaches to the anthropology of religion.* Boulder, CO: Westview Press.

An introductory text offering an accessible and broad overview of key issues in the anthropology of religion and religious diversity.

Klass, M., & Weisgrau, M. (Eds.). (1999). *Across the boundaries of belief: Contemporary issues in the anthropology of religion.* Boulder, CO: Westview Press.

A thought-provoking collection of up-to-date articles.

Lehmann, A. C., & Myers, J. E. (Eds.). (2000). *Magic, witchcraft, and religion: An anthropological study of the supernatural* (5th ed.). Mountain View, CA: Mayfield.

This anthology of readings is cross-cultural in scope, covering traditional as well as nontraditional themes. Well represented are both "tribal" and modern religions. It is a good source for discovering the relevance and vitality of anthropological approaches to the supernatural.

Pandian, J. (1998). *Culture, religion, and the sacred self: A critical introduction to the anthropological study of religion.* Englewood Cliffs, NJ: Prentice-Hall.

With an eye on religious symbolism and its relationship to the cultural formulations of the self, the author summarizes relevant anthropological studies on myth, ritual, shamanism, and religious movements.

Rappaport, R. A. (1999). *Holiness and humanity: Ritual in the making of religious life.* New York: Cambridge University Press.

This last work by one of anthropology's most innovative thinkers on the subject investigates the nature, meaning, and functions of ritual in religion.

Scupin, R. (Ed.). (2000). *Religion and culture: An anthropological focus.* Upper Saddle River, NJ: Prentice-Hall.

A collection of essays about the major religious traditions of the world.

Wallace, A. F. C. (1966). *Religion: An anthropological view.* New York: Random House.

This is a classic textbook treatment of religion by an anthropologist who has specialized in the study of revitalization movements.

CHAPTER 14

The Arts

© Vince Hemingson

CHALLENGE ISSUE

Humans in all cultures throughout time face the challenge of creatively articulating their feelings and ideas about themselves and the world around them. Although not all societies distinguish "art" as a special cultural domain, people everywhere have developed aesthetic forms—visual, verbal, musical, movement, and so on—to symbolically express, appreciate, and share experiences of beauty in all its variety. One of these many art forms involves tattooing—puncturing and coloring human skin with symbolic designs—as practiced by humans for thousands of years.

1 What Is Art?

Although difficult to define, art may be understood as the creative use of the human imagination to interpret, express, and enjoy life. Although many contemporary Western peoples consider art as purely aesthetic, serving no practical purpose, most societies past and present have used art to symbolically express almost every part of their culture, including ideas about religion, kinship, and ethnic identity. In fact, almost anything humans can lay their hands on can become an object of artistic creativity— skin, hair, dress, dwellings, vehicles, weapons, utensils, and so on.

2 Why Do Anthropologists Study Art?

Anthropologists have found that art often reflects a society's collective ideas, values, and concerns. This is especially true of the verbal, musical, and visual arts—myths, songs, paintings, carvings, and so on. From these, anthropologists may learn how a people imagine their reality and understand themselves and other beings around them. Through the cross-cultural study of art and creativity, we discover much about different worldviews, religious beliefs, political ideas, social values, kinship structures, economic relations, and historical memory as well.

3 What Are the Functions of Art?

Aside from adding beauty and pleasure to everyday life, art serves a number of functions. Myths, for example, may offer basic explanations about the world and set cultural standards for right behavior, and the verbal arts generally transmit and preserve a culture's customs and values. Songs, too, may do this within the structures imposed by musical form. And any art form, to the degree that it is characteristic of a particular society, may contribute to the cohesiveness or solidarity of that society. Yet, art may also express political themes and influence events to create social change. Often it is created for religious purposes, to honor or beseech the aid of a divine power, a sacred being, an ancestral spirit, or an animal spirit.

In North America, the arts often are seen as a luxury, something to be engaged in apart from more productive pursuits—for personal enjoyment, to provide pleasure for others, or both. This attitude becomes apparent whenever public funds are in short supply. On the local level, for example, in battles over school budgets, art programs are often the first to be cut. Unlike sports, which most adults in North America believe nurture skills vital for success in a competitive world, the arts are seen as nonessential—pleasurable and worthwhile but expensive and having little practical payoff. On the national level, fiscal conservatives seek to cut back funds for the arts on the premise that they lack the practical importance of defense, economic, or other governmental activities. Indeed, a significant portion of the society views artists and their supporters as an elite group subsidized at the expense of hard-working "practical" people. Yet one might ask, why are museum exhibits, theater performances, or even movies so often

the center of hot political controversy? If art really carries so little weight and only serves to entertain us, why do governments, politicians, and religious leaders so often devote great time and energy to bitter fights to control the kind of art that is accessible to the public?

Artistic expression is far from unimportant and is as basic to human beings as talking. Just as speech is used to communicate feelings and to make statements, so too is artistic expression. As defined in the chapter preview, **art** is the creative use of the human imagination to interpret, express, and enjoy life. It is not merely a special category of people called "artists" who do this. For example, all human beings adorn their bodies in certain ways and by doing so make a statement about who they are, both as individuals and as members of society. Similarly, people in all cultures tell stories in which they express their values, hopes, and concerns, and in the process reveal much about themselves and the nature of the world as they see it. In short, all peoples engage in artistic expression as they use their imaginations creatively to interpret, understand, celebrate, and enjoy life. What's more, they have been doing this for some 40,000 years. Far from being a luxury to be afforded or appreciated by a minority of sophisticated experts or frivolous lovers of art, creativity is a necessary activity in which everyone participates in one way or another.

The idea of art serving purely aesthetic but nonpractical purposes seems firmly entrenched in the thinking of many contemporary Western peoples. Today, for example, the objects from the ancient tomb of the young Egyptian king Tutankhamen are on display in a museum, where they may be seen and admired as the exquisite

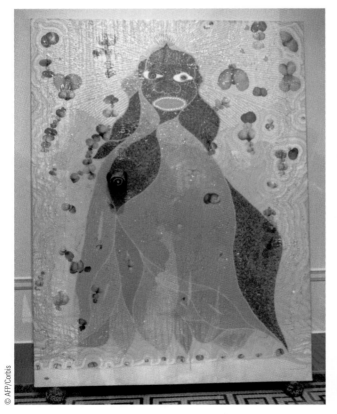

The power of art is illustrated by the public uproar against the exhibition of Chris Ofilis' *The Holy Virgin Mary* in New York's Brooklyn Museum in 1999. The artist had scattered elephant dung on the painting, and the city's mayor was so outraged he tried to withdraw funding from the museum.

art The creative use of the human imagination to interpret, express, and enjoy life.

This picture of a child not yet 1 year of age sitting at a piano suggests the importance of music for developing brains; studies show that exposure to music early in life significantly enhances learning.

works of art that they are. They were made, however, not for human eyes but to guarantee the eternal life of the king and protect him from evil forces that might enter his body and gain control over it. Similarly, we may listen to the singing of a sea chantey purely for aesthetic pleasure, as a form of entertainment. But, in fact, in the days of sailing by wind power alone, sea chanteys served very useful and practical purposes. They set the appropriate rhythm for the performance of specific shipboard tasks such as hoisting or reefing sails, and the same qualities that make them pleasurable to listen to today served to coordinate joint tasks or relieve the boredom of those jobs.

Such links between art and other aspects of everyday life are common in human societies around the world. This can also be seen in the way that art has commonly been incorporated into everyday, functional objects—from pottery and baskets used to carry or store food to carpets and mats woven by herders to cover the ground inside their dwellings. Designs painted on or woven or carved into such objects typically express ideas, values, and things that have meaning to an entire community. Only in the West—and only recently at that—has *fine art* become established as a distinct category of art for art's sake, less accessible to members of the society at large than to wealthy collectors who commission and purchase artworks for personal enjoyment in the privacy of their homes. Yet, folk art continues to thrive. Because art, like any aspect of culture, is inextricably intertwined with everything else people do, it affords us glimpses into other aspects of people's lives, including their values and worldview.

To people today, the making of exquisite objects of gold and precious stones to be buried in a grave might seem like throwing them away. Yet, something similar happens when a Navajo Indian traditional healer or "Singer" creates an intricate sand painting—symbolic designs made with colored powders of ground sandstone, ocher, charcoal, clay, and dried vegetable matter composed on a surface of clean sand—as part of a ritual healing act, only to destroy it once the ceremony is over.

Whether a particular work of art is intended to be appreciated purely for beauty or to serve some practical

© Syndey Byrd

Courtesy of the National Museum of the American Indian, Smithsonian Institution

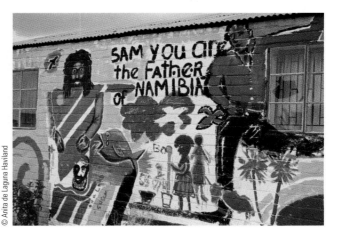

© Anita de Laguna Haviland

VISUAL COUNTERPOINT Much of the world's art is created for functional as well as aesthetic purposes. Shown here, counterclockwise, are examples of art used to cure sickness (a Navajo sand painting), to express cultural identity (the Mardi Gras costume of one of New Orleans' "Black Indians"), and to make a political statement (graffiti from Katatura, Namibia, Southwest Africa).

purpose, it will in every case require the same special combination of the symbolic representation of form and the expression of feeling that constitute the creative imagination. Since the creative use of the human ability to symbolize is universal and both expresses and is shaped by cultural values and concerns, it is an important subject for anthropological study.

As an activity or behavior that contributes to human well-being and that helps give shape and significance to life, art is related to, yet distinct from, religion. As British anthropologist Raymond Firth observed: "Religion is an art of making sense out of experience, and like any other art, say, poetry, it must be taken symbolically, not literally."[1] Nor is it easy to say, for example, precisely where art stops and religion begins in an elaborate ceremony involving ornamentation, masks, costumes, songs, dances, and effigies. Furthermore music, dance, and other arts may be used, like magic, to "enchant"—to take advantage of the emotional or psychological predispositions of another person or group so as to cause them to perceive reality in a way favorable to the interests of the "enchanter." Indeed, the arts may be used to manipulate a seemingly inexhaustible list of human passions, including desire, terror, wonder, cupidity, fantasy, and vanity.[2] Marketing specialists, of course, are well aware of this, which is why they routinely employ certain music and images in their advertising.

THE ANTHROPOLOGICAL STUDY OF ART

In approaching art as a cultural phenomenon, anthropologists have the pleasant task of cataloguing, photographing, recording, and describing all possible forms of imaginative activity in any particular culture. An enormous variety of forms and modes of artistic expression exists in the world. Because people everywhere continue to create and develop in ever-new ways, there is no end in sight to the interesting process of collecting and describing the world's ornaments, body decorations, clothing variations, blanket and rug designs, pottery and basket styles, architectural embellishments, monuments, ceremonial masks, legends, work songs, dances, and other art forms. Eventually, however, the collecting

© Jeff Becom/Photo 20-20

The effectiveness of this Coca-Cola ad in southern Mexico lies in the use of these particular colors. To the region's Maya Indians, red is the color of sacred blood and symbolizes the dawn and birth; green, the color of jade, symbolizes life-giving rain and the heavens, precious water, and fertility.

process must lead to some kind of analysis and generalizations about relationships between art and the rest of culture.

A good way to begin a study of the relationships between art and the rest of culture is to examine critically some of the generalizations that have already been made about specific arts. Since it is impossible to cover all art forms in the space of a single chapter, we shall concentrate on just a few: visual, verbal, and musical, in that order.

Visual Art

For many people, the first thing that springs to mind in connection with the word *art* is some sort of visual image, be it a painting, drawing, sketch, or whatever. And indeed, in many parts of the world, people have been making pictures in one way or another for a very long time—etching in bone, engraving in rock, painting on cave walls and rock surfaces, carving and painting on wood, gourds, and clay pots, or painting on textiles, bark cloth, animal hide, or even their own bodies. Some form of visual art is a part of every historically known human culture.

As a type of symbolic expression, visual art may be representational (imitating closely the forms of nature) or abstract (drawing from natural forms but representing only their basic patterns or arrange-

---

[1]Quoted in Herdt, G. H. (1993). Semen transactions in Sambia culture. In D. N. Suggs & A. D. Mirade (Eds.), *Culture and human sexuality* (p. 319). Pacific Grove, CA: Brooks/Cole.

---

[2]Gell, A. (1988). Technology and magic. *Anthropology Today, 4*(2), 7; Lewis-Williams, J. D. (1997). Agency, art and altered consciousness: A motif in French (Quercy) upper Paleolithic parietal art. *Antiquity, 71,* 810–830.

This stylized painting on a ceremonial shirt represents a bear. Though the art of the Indians in southern Alaska and British Columbia often portrays actual animals, they are not depicted in a naturalistic style. To identify them, one must be familiar with the symbolic use of this indigenous art.

The two rows of diagrams at the top show the stylized human figures that are the basic "bricks" used in the construction of genealogical patterns. Each figure is designed to be joined limb-and-limb with adjacent figures to illustrate descent or other kin relationships. The diagrams just below show how these basic figures are linked arm-and-leg with diagonally adjacent figures to depict descent. For thousands of years people all over the world have linked such figures together, creating the familiar geometrical patterns that we see in countless art forms, from pottery to sculpture to weaving—patterns that informed eyes recognize as genealogical.

ments). Actually, the two categories are not mutually exclusive, for even the most naturalistic portrayal is partly abstract to the extent it generalizes from nature and abstracts patterns of ideal beauty, ugliness, or typical expressions of emotion. But between the most naturalistic and the most schematic or symbolic abstract art lies a continuum. In some of the Indian art of North America's Northwest Coast, for example, animal figures may be so highly stylized as to be difficult for an outsider to identify. Although the art appears abstract, the artist has created it based on nature, even though he or she has exaggerated and deliberately transformed various shapes to express a particular feeling toward the animals. Because artists do these exaggerations and transformations according to the aesthetic principles of Northwest Coast Indian culture, their meanings are understood not just by the artist but by other members of the community as well.

This collective understanding of symbols is a hallmark in traditional art. Unlike modern Western art, which is judged in large part on its creative originality and the unique vision of an individual artist, traditional art is all about community and shared symbolism. As discussed in several earlier chapters, hunter–gatherers, nomadic herders, swidden farmers, and others living in small-scale traditional societies are profoundly interested in kinship relations—who is related to whom and how. In such societies, concerns about kinship may be symbolically expressed in stylized motifs and colorful designs. As described by North American art historian Carl Schuster and anthropologist Edmund Carpenter, cross-cultural and historical comparisons of certain widespread and recurrent geometric motifs—etched or painted on human skin, animal hides or bones, clay pottery, wood, rocks, or almost any other surface imaginable—indicate that many designs that we perceive as purely decorative, ornamental, or abstract are actually symbolic. This symbolism, they show, can often be decoded in terms of a genealogical iconography primarily illustrating social relations of marriage and descent.[3]

Shared symbolism has also been fundamental to the traditional art of tattooing—although that is changing in some parts of the world, as discussed in the following Original Study.

MEDIATREK

For a virtual tour of an amazing body art exhibition rich with photographs and information, go to MediaTrek 14.1 on the companion Web site or CD-ROM.

[3]Schuster, C., & Carpenter, E. (1996). *Patterns that connect: Social symbolism in ancient and tribal art*. New York: Abrams; see also Prins, H. E. L. (1998). Book review of Schuster, C., & Carpenter, E. *American Anthropologist, 100*(3), 841.

Original Study

The Modern Tattoo Community

As an anthropology graduate student in the early 1990s, I had no idea what (or, more accurately, whom) to study for my field research. Because of my work as an animal advocate, I had a house full of rabbits, cats, dogs, birds, and assorted farm animals to care for, which left me in no position to do much long-term travel. This effectively eliminated most "traditional" cultures as potential study subjects.

Then one of my professors suggested a topic that was literally under my nose—tattooing. Although I myself had several tattoos and spent quite a bit of time with other tattooed people, including my husband, who had just become a professional tattooist, I had never thought about this as a research topic. Part of my everyday life, it didn't seem "exotic" enough. My professor assured me I was wrong, and I began my research assuming that it would not be difficult since I was already accustomed to attending tattoo conventions, getting tattooed, and hanging around tattoo studios.

As it turned out I had unanticipated obstacles to overcome. Early on in my research, I, along with my husband, strove to find a way to "join" what is known as the "tattoo community," finding that it was not as friendly and open as we had imagined it to be. As a tattooed person, married to a fledgling tattooist, I often felt excluded. But as an anthropologist I came to see that what I was experiencing was the lower rungs of a highly stratified social group,

One of several tattoos inscribed on Dr. Margo DeMello, author of this study.

in which an artist's status is based on such features as class, geography, and professional and artistic credentials, and a "fan" might be judged on the type and extent of his or her tattoos, the artist(s) who created them, the level of media coverage achieved, and more. It was my personal experiences as both insider (tattooed person) and outsider (anthropologist) with this community that in fact led to one of the major focuses of my work: how class and status increasingly came to define this once working-class art form.

Ultimately, I spent almost 5 years studying and writing about tattooing, finding my "community" wherever tattooed people talked about themselves and each other—within the pages of tattoo magazines and mainstream newspapers, on Internet newsgroups, and at tattoo-oriented events across the country. I spent countless hours in tattoo shops watching the artists work; I collected what I call "tattoo narratives," which are often elaborate, some-

[CONTINUED]

times spiritual, stories that people tell about their tattoos; and I followed the careers of seminal artists. I even learned to tattoo a bit myself, placing a few particularly ugly images on my patient husband's body.

Tattoos are created by inserting ink or some other pigment through the epidermis (outer skin) into the dermis (the second layer of skin) through the use of needles. Like many other forms of what might be called folk art, they usually serve both aesthetic and functional purposes. They may be beautiful as designs in and of themselves, but they can also express a multitude of meanings about the wearer and his or her place within the social group. Whether used in an overt punitive fashion (as in the tattooing of slaves or prisoners) or to mark clan or cult membership, religious or tribal affiliation, social status, or marital position, tattoos have historically been a social sign. They have long been one of the simplest ways of establishing humans as social beings—or, to use the language of French anthropologist Claude Lévi-Strauss, transforming them from "raw" animals, into "cooked" cultural beings. In fact, tattooing is one of the most persistent and universal forms of body art and may date back as far as the Upper Paleolithic era (10,000–35,000 years ago). The earliest firm evidence of it is Ötzi "the Iceman." Discovered by mountain hikers on the Italian-Austrian border, this 5,300-year-old mummified body has fifty-seven bluish-black tattoos.

Tattoos as signs derive their communicative power from more than a simple sign-to-meaning correspondence: They also communicate through color, style, manner of execution, and location on the body. Traditionally inscribed on easily viewable parts of the body, tattoos were designed to be "read" by others. Today, however—at least in Western parts of the world such as the United States—tattoos have increasingly moved from the functional to the artistic, from the literal to the abstract, losing much of their traditional communicative power in the process. Tattoos for many middle-class North Americans have become a way to express personal rather than collective identity, as well as a more "sophisticated"

artistic sensibility. For many, tattoos are now more about private statement than public sign, and these individuals, especially women, tend to favor smaller tattoos in private spots.

The process by which tattooing has expanded in the United States from a working-class folk art into a more widespread and often refined aesthetic practice is related to a number of shifts in North American culture that occurred during the 1970s and 1980s. This would include the development of various transformational social movements such as the women's, environmental, New Age, gay and lesbian, and men's movements, all of which provided a symbolic and discursive context for the changes occurring within tattooing. In addition, this time period saw the introduction of finely trained artists into tattooing, bringing with them radically different backgrounds and artistic sensibilities to draw from. Finally, more and more middle-class men and women began getting tattooed, attracted by the expanded artistic choices and the new, more spiritual context of body decoration.

Within this context, tattoos have been partially transformed into fine art by a process of redefinition and framing based on formal qualities (that is, the skill of the artist, the iconic content of the tattoo, the style in which the tattoo is executed, and so on) and ideological qualities (the discourses that surround "artistic" tattoos, discourses that point to some higher reality on which the tattoo is based). When it is judged that a tattoo has certain formal artistic qualities as well as expresses a higher, often spiritual, reality, then it is seen as art. Moreover, certain tattoos, like those that mimic the styles of Japan, Micronesia, or Melanesia, are seen as paradigmatic—as the fine art tattoos against which all others are compared, and which, in fact, define the genre for many Americans.

While it may seem as though tattoos are not good candidates to be defined as art, due to their lack of permanence (the body, after all, ages and dies) and their seeming inability to be displayed within a gallery setting, modern tattoo art shows get around these problems by photographing tattoos and displaying them in a way that showcases the "art" and often

minimizes the body. By both literally and figuratively "framing" tattoos in a museum or gallery setting, or within an art book, the tattoo is removed from its social function and remade into art.

The basic working-class American tattoo designs (such as "Mother" or "Donna" inscribed alongside a heart) have been relegated to the bottom rung of today's tattoo hierarchy in the United States. Such tattoos are now seen by middle-class artists and fans as too literal, too transparently obvious, and too grounded in everyday experience and social life to qualify as art. The modern, artistic tattoos that have increasingly gained favor are less "readable" and no longer have an easily recognizable function. Often derived from foreign (or "exotic") cultures and custom-drawn for the wearer, they tend to eliminate the social aspect in favor of the highly individualistic. These artistic tattoos are no longer part of a collectively understood system of inscription in which people communicate information about themselves to others. Some are purely decorative, and those that are intended to signify meaning often do so only for the individual or those in his or her intimate circle.

Tattoos in the United States have traveled a long way from the tattoo of old: brought to North America by way of Captain James Cook's 18th-century explorations of the Pacific, moving, over time, from a mark of affiliation to a highly individual statement of personal identity, losing and regaining function, meaning, and content along the way. In our increasingly global world, tattoo designs and motifs move swiftly and easily across cultural boundaries. As this happens, their original, communal meanings are often lost—but they are not meaningless. An animal crest tattoo traditionally worn by Indians on the Northwest Coast of North America to signify clan membership may now be worn by a non-Native in Boston as an artful, often private, sign of rebellion against Western "coat and tie" consumer culture. *(By Margo DeMello. (2003). The modern tattoo community. Ms. © by author. Department of Anthropology, San Francisco State University. Dr. DeMello is author of* Bodies of inscription: A cultural history of the modern tattoo community. *(2000). Durham: Duke University Press.)*

Southern African Rock Art

The rock art of the Bushmen in southern Africa, which has been researched in considerable detail, is a rich non-Western tradition that helps illustrate different ways of approaching the study of art. One of the world's oldest traditions, it was practiced continually from at least 27,000 years ago until the beginning of the 20th century, when European colonization led to the demise of the Bushman societies responsible for creating it. Ju/'hoansi and other Bushman groups that have survived in places such as Namibia and Botswana did not themselves produce rock art but do share the same general belief system the rock art expresses.

Bushman rock art consists of both paintings and engravings on the faces of rock outcrops as well as on the walls of rock shelters. It depicts a variety of animals as well as humans in highly sophisticated ways, sometimes in static poses but often in highly animated scenes. Associated with these figures are a variety of what appear to be abstract signs including dots, zigzags, nested curves, and the like. Until fairly recently, the significance of these abstract features was not understood by non-Bushmen. Equally enigmatic was the frequent presence of new pictures painted or engraved directly over existing ones.

Despite its puzzling aspects, southern African rock art has long been considered worthy of being viewed and admired. The paintings, especially, are generally seen as beautiful and pleasurable to look at. Consequently, it is not surprising that the specialists who first studied this art took the aesthetic approach, analyzing *how* things were depicted. Investigating the pigments, they found that the Bushmen had used charcoal and specularite for black; silica, china clay, and gypsum for white; and ferric oxide for red and reddish-brown

hues—and that they had mixed the colors with fat, blood, and perhaps water. The paint had been applied to the rough rock with great skill. Indeed, the effectiveness of line and the way shading was used to suggest the contours of the animals' bodies elicits admiration, as does the rendering of realistic details. Very often Bushman artists painted the eland. They depicted this large ox-like antelope with considerable detail, including the tuft of red hair on its forehead, the black line running along its back, the darkening of its snout, its cloven hoofs, the folds of skin on its shoulders, and the twist of its horns.

Bushman rock art often shows details of human anatomy, along with particulars of dress, headgear, and body ornamentation, including leather bands and ostrich eggshell beads. However, the human forms look more like caricatures than literal depictions. Features such as fatness and thinness may be exaggerated, and the figures are sometimes elongated, often in positions suggestive of flying across the rock face. Sometimes, too, the feet take on the appearance of a swallowtail or a fish's tail. Even more puzzling are figures that appear to be part human–part animal (therianthropes).

In addition to the aesthetic approach of analyzing *how* Bushman rock paintings and engravings are created, specialists also study the art as "narrative," investigating *what* it depicts. Certainly, aspects of Bushman life are shown, as in several hunting scenes of men with bows, arrows, quivers, and hunting bags. Some depictions show hunting nets and also fish traps. Women are also portrayed—identifiable by their visible sexual characteristics and the stone-weighted digging sticks they carry. Curiously, they are rarely shown gathering food. Considering the importance of food gathered by women in the Bushman diet, this seems odd. Of course,

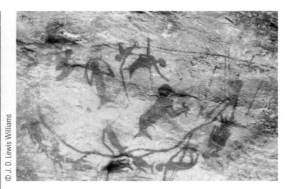

Bushman rock paintings and engravings from southern Africa often depict animals thought to possess great supernatural powers. Shamans appear as well: In the painted example at the right, we see rain shamans with swallowtails acting in the spirit realm to protect people from the dangers of storms. Like modern Bushman shamans, several of these hold paired dance sticks. The idea of shamans transforming into birds, as well as being greatly elongated (note one figure's long, undulating body above the lower row of shamans), is based on sensations experienced in trance.

it might merely reflect the importance Bushmen attach to the hunt, but the fact is that hunting scenes are not at all common, either. Furthermore, the animals that appear most often in the art (such as the eland) are *not* representative of the meat most commonly eaten by Bushmen. Thus, a narrative approach can lead to a distorted view of Bushman life.

Other scenes portrayed in the art relate to the trance dance, still the most important ritual among Bushmen today (see the Original Study in the previous chapter). This is clearly indicated by several features: the numbers of people shown and the arrangement of hand-clapping women surrounding dancing men whose bodies are bent forward (in the distinctive posture caused by the cramping of abdominal muscles as they go into trance), whose noses are bleeding (common today when Bushmen trance), whose arms are stretched behind their backs (present-day Bushmen do this to gather more of the supernatural potency—*n/um*), and who are wearing dance rattles and carrying fly whisks (used to extract invisible arrows of sickness). Here we have a significant clue as to what the art is really all about, although we cannot discern this from the narrative and aesthetic approaches alone. For this we need the third, or *interpretive,* approach.

The distinction between the aesthetic, narrative, and interpretive approaches becomes clear if we pause for a moment to consider a famous work of Western art, Leonardo da Vinci's painting *The Last Supper*.[4] A non-Christian viewing this late 15th-century mural in Italy will see thirteen people at a table, apparently enjoying a meal. Although one of the men clutches a bag of money

and appears a bit clumsy, knocking over the salt, nothing else here indicates the scene to be anything out of the ordinary. Aesthetically, our non-Christian observer may admire the way the composition fits the space available, the way the attitudes of the men are depicted, and the way the artist conveys a sense of movement. As narrative, the painting may be seen as a record of customs, table manners, dress, and architecture. But to know the real meaning of this picture, the viewer must be aware that, in Western culture, spilling the salt is a symbol of impending disaster and that money symbolizes the root of all evil. But even this is not enough; for a full understanding of this work of art, one must know something of the beliefs of Christianity. To move to the interpretive level, then, requires knowledge of the symbols and beliefs of the people responsible for the art.

Applying the interpretive approach to southern African rock art requires knowledge of two things: Bushman ethnography and the nature of trance. With respect to the latter, a clear understanding comes from a combination of ethnographic data and data gained experimentally in laboratories. Because all human beings have essentially the same nervous system, whether they are urban dwellers from the United States, food foragers from southern Africa, or horticulturalists from the Amazon forest, they all progress through the same three stages when going into trance. In the first stage, the nervous system generates a variety of luminous, pulsating, revolving, and constantly shifting geometric patterns known as **entoptic phenomena** (anyone who has suffered from migraine headaches is familiar with these). Typical imagery includes

---

[4]This example is drawn from Lewis-Williams, J. D. (1990). *Discovering southern African rock art* (p. 9). Cape Town and Johannesburg: David Philip.

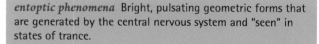

entoptic phenomena Bright, pulsating geometric forms that are generated by the central nervous system and "seen" in states of trance.

Leonardo da Vinci's *The Last Supper*. To really understand this painting, one must know something about Christianity and about the general cultural symbols and beliefs of the famous Italian artist (1452–1519) in his own place and time.

© Scala/Art Resource, NY

The curves and zigzags in two of these pictures, drawn by migraine sufferers, are classic entoptic phenomena seen in early stages of trance. The "tunnel" with lattice walls in the lower right picture is representative of those seen when passing from the second to third stage of trance.

grids, parallel lines, zigzags, dots, nested curves, and filigrees, often in a spiral pattern.

As one goes into deeper trance, the brain tries to make sense of these abstract forms, just as it does of sensations received when in an unaltered state of consciousness. This process is known as *construal,* and here differences in culture and experience come into play. Commonly, a Bushman in trance will construe a grid pattern as markings on the skin of a giraffe, nested curves as a honeycomb (honey is a Bushman delicacy, and the auditory sensation of buzzing that often accompanies trance promotes the illusion), and dots as *nu/m,* the potency seen only by shamans in trance. Obviously, we would not expect an Inuit or someone from Los Angeles to construe these patterns in the same way.

In the third and deepest trance stage, subjects cease to be observers of their visions but seem to become part of them. As this happens, they feel themselves passing

iconic images Visions of people, animals, and monsters seen in the deepest stage of trance.

into a rotating tunnel or vortex with latticelike sides and on which appear images of animals, humans, and monsters of various sorts. In the process, the entoptic forms of the earlier stages become integrated into these **iconic images,** as they are called. The entoptics may be hard to discern apart from the main image, although sometimes they appear as a kind of background. Iconic images are culture specific; individuals see what their culture disposes them to see; often, these images are things having high emotional content. In the case of Bushmen, they often see the eland, an animal thought to be imbued with especially strong potency, particularly for rainmaking. Given this, one of the things shamans try to do in trance is to "capture" elands—"rain animals"—for purposes of making rain.

All of this helps us understand why elands are so prominent in the rock art. Moreover, it reveals the significance of the zigzags, dots, grids, and so forth that are so often a part of the compositions. It also leads to an understanding of other puzzling features of the art. For example, the third trance stage includes such sensations as being stretched out or elongated, weightless-

This late Stone Age painting from the Peche-Merle cave in France incorporates dot entoptics over and near the body of a bull, one indication the artist was painting something seen in a state of trance. An association of rock art with trance experience has been noted in many parts of the world.

ness as in flight or in the water, and difficulty breathing as when under water. Hence we find depictions in the art of humans who appear to be abnormally long, as well as individuals who appear to be swimming or flying. Another well-documented trance phenomenon is the sense of being transformed into some sort of animal. Such sensations are triggered in the deepest stage of trance if the individual sees or thinks of an animal, and the sensation accounts for the part human–part animal therianthropes in the art. Finally, the superpositioning of one work of art over another becomes comprehensible; not only are the visions seen in trance commonly superimposed on one another as they rotate and move, but if the trancer stares at a painting or engraving of an earlier vision, the new one will appear as if projected on the old.

The interpretive approach makes clear, then, that the rock art of southern Africa—even in the case of compositions that otherwise might appear to be scenes of everyday life—is intimately connected with the practices and beliefs of shamanism. After shamans came out of trance and reflected on their visions, they proceeded to paint or engrave their recollections on the rock faces. But these were more than records of important visions; they had their own innate power, owing to their supposed supernatural origin. This being so, when the need arose for a new trance experience, it might be held where the old vision was recorded to draw power from it.

MEDIATREK

For a virtual visit to Lascaux Cave in southwestern France, famous for the ancient paintings on its walls, go to MediaTrek 14.2 on the companion Web site or CD-ROM.

Verbal Art

The term **folklore** is a 19th-century term first used to denote the unwritten stories, sayings, beliefs, and customs of the European peasants (as opposed to the traditions of the literate elite) and later extended to those traditions preserved orally in all societies. The subsequent study of folklore, **folkloristics,** has become a discipline allied to but somewhat independent of anthropology, working on cross-cultural comparisons of themes, motifs, genres, and structures from a literary as well as ethnological point of view. Many linguists and anthropologists prefer to speak of a culture's oral traditions and verbal arts rather than its folklore and folktales, recognizing that creative verbal expression takes many forms and that the implied distinction between folk and fine art is a projection imposed by European (and European-derived) elites onto creative expressions traditionally produced and appreciated by rural peoples.

The verbal arts include narratives, dramas, poetry, incantations, proverbs, riddles, word games, and even naming procedures, compliments, and insults, when these take structured and special forms. Narrative seems to be one of the easiest kinds of the verbal arts to record or collect. Perhaps because they also are the most publishable, with popular appeal in North American culture,

folklore A 19th-century term first used to denote the unwritten stories, sayings, beliefs, and customs of the European peasants (as opposed to the traditions of the literate elite) and later extended to those traditions preserved orally in all societies.
folkloristics The study of folklore (as linguistics is the study of language).

they have received the most study and attention. Generally, narratives have been divided into three basic and recurring categories: myth, legend, and tale.

Myth

Derived from the Greek word *mythos,* meaning "speech" or "story," a **myth** is a sacred narrative that explains the fundamentals of human existence (where we and everything in our world came from, why we are here, and where we are going). Beyond this explanatory function, a myth provides a rationale for religious beliefs and practices and sets cultural standards for "right" behavior. A typical creation or origin myth, traditional with the western Abenaki of northwestern New England and southern Quebec, goes as follows:

> In the beginning, *Tabaldak,* "The Owner," created all living things but one—the spirit being who was to accomplish the final transformation of the earth. Man and woman *Tabaldak* made out of a piece of stone, but he didn't like the result, their hearts being cold and hard. This being so, he broke them up, and their remains today can be seen in the many stones that litter the landscape of the Abenaki homeland. But *Tabaldak* tried again, this time using living wood, and from this came all later Abenakis. Like the trees from which the wood came, these people were rooted in the earth and (like trees when blown by the wind) could dance gracefully. The one living thing not created by *Tabaldak* was *Odzihózo,* "He Makes Himself from Something." This being seems to have created himself out of dust, but since he was a transformer, rather than creator, he wasn't able to accomplish it all at once. At first, he managed only his head, body, and arms; the legs came later, growing slowly as legs do on a tadpole. Not waiting until his legs were grown, he set out to transform the shape of the earth. He dragged his body about with his hands, gouging channels that became the rivers. To make the mountains, he piled dirt up with his hands. Once his legs grew, *Odzihózo's* task was made easier; by merely extending his legs, he made the tributaries of the main streams.

> *Odzihózo,* then, was the Abenaki transformer who laid out the river channels and

lake basins and shaped the hills and mountains. Just how long he took is a subject which Abenakis have discussed for as long as any can remember. Once he was finished, he surveyed his handiwork and found it was good. The last work he made was Lake Champlain, and this he found especially good. He liked it so well that he climbed onto a rock in Burlington Bay and changed himself into stone so that he could sit there and enjoy his masterpiece through the ages. He still likes it, because he is still there and he is still given offerings of tobacco as Abenakis pass this way. The Abenaki call the rock *Odzihózo,* since it is the Transformer himself.[5]

Such a myth, insofar as it is believed, accepted, and perpetuated in a culture, may be said to express a part of the traditional worldview of a people. (As noted in earlier chapters, *worldview* is the collective body of ideas that members of a culture generally share concerning the ultimate shape and substance of their reality.) Extrapolating from the details of this particular Abenaki myth, we might arrive at the conclusion that these people recognize a kinship among all living things; after all, they were all part of the same creation, and humans even were made from living wood. Moreover, an attempt to make them of nonliving stone was not satisfactory. This idea of a closeness among all living things led the Abenaki to show special respect to the animals they hunted in order to sustain their own lives. For example, after killing a beaver, muskrat, or waterfowl, one could not unceremoniously toss its bones into the nearest garbage pit. Proper respect required that the bones be returned to the water, with a request to continue its kind. Similarly, before eating meat, the Abenaki placed an offering of grease on the fire to thank *Tabaldak.* More generally, waste was to be avoided so as not to offend the animals. Failure to respect their rights would result in an unwillingness to sacrifice their lives that people might live.

By transforming himself into stone in order to enjoy his work for all eternity, *Odzihózo* may be seen as setting an example for people; they should see the beauty in things as they are and not seek to alter what is already good. To question the goodness of existing reality would be to call into question the judgment of a powerful deity. A characteristic of explanatory myths, such as this one, is that the unknown is simplified and explained in terms of the known. This myth, in terms of

---

myth A sacred narrative that explains the fundamentals of human existence (where we and everything in our world came from, why we are here, and where we are going).

---

[5]Haviland, W. A., & Power, M. W. (1994). *The original Vermonters: Native inhabitants, past and present* (rev. and exp. ed., p. 193). Hanover, NH: University Press of New England.

To the Abenaki, these rocks in a northern New England blueberry field are the remains of the first man and woman, who were broken up by the Creator because their hearts were cold and hard. The large rock pictured in the second photo is known as *Odzihózo* among the Abenaki, named for the mythical transformer who laid out the river channels and lake basins in northeastern North America. It is located in Burlington Bay, Lake Champlain, Vermont.

human experience, accounts for the existence of rivers, mountains, lakes, and other features of the landscape, as well as of humans and all other living things. It also sanctions particular attitudes and behaviors. It is a product of creative imagination, and it is a work of art, as well as a potentially religious statement.

One aspect of mythology that has attracted a good deal of interest over the years is the similarity of certain themes in the stories of peoples living in separate parts of the world. One of these themes is the myth of matriarchy, or one-time rule by women. In a number of societies, stories tell about a time when women ruled over men. Eventually, so these stories go, men were forced to rise up and assert their dominance over women to combat their tyranny or incompetence (or both). In the 19th century, a number of European scholars interpreted such myths as evidence for an early stage of matriarchy in the evolution of human culture—an idea recently revisited by some feminists. Although anthropologists have identified societies in which the two sexes relate to each other as equals (Western Abenaki society was one), they have never found one where women control or dominate men. The interesting thing about myths of matriarchy is that generally they are found in societies where men dominate women, even though the latter have considerable autonomy.[6] Under such conditions, male dominance is insecure, and a rationale is needed to justify it. Thus, myths of men overthrowing women and taking control reflect an existing paradoxical relationship between the two sexes.

The analysis of myths has been carried to great lengths, becoming a field of study almost unto itself. Myth making is an extremely significant kind of human creativity, and studying the myth-making process and its results can give valuable clues to the way people perceive and think about their world. The problems of interpretation, however, are great, as evidenced in these questions: Are myths literally believed or perhaps accepted symbolically or emotionally as a different kind of truth? To what extent do myths actually determine or reflect human behavior? Can an outsider discover the meaning that a myth has in its own culture? How do we account for contradictory myths (such as the two accounts of creation in the Bible's Book of Genesis) in the same culture? New myths arise and old ones die. Is it then the myth's content or the structure that is important? All of these questions deserve, and are currently receiving, serious consideration.

Legend

Less problematic but perhaps more complex than myth is the legend. A **legend** is a story about a memorable event or figure handed down by tradition and told as true but without historical evidence. An example of a modern "urban legend" in the United States is one that was often told by Ronald Reagan when he was president, about an African American woman on welfare in Chicago. Supposedly, her ability to collect something like 103 welfare checks under different names enabled

---

[6]Sanday, P. R. (1981). *Female power and male dominance: On the origins of sexual inequality* (p. 181). Cambridge, England: Cambridge University Press.

legend A story about a memorable event or figure handed down by tradition and told as true but without historical evidence.

her to live lavishly. Although proven to be false, the story was told as if true (by the president even after he was informed that it was not true) as legends are. This particular legend illustrates a number of features all such narratives share: They cannot be attributed to any known author; they always exist in multiple versions, but, in spite of variation, they are told with sufficient detail to be plausible; and they tell us something about the cultures in which they are found. In this case, we learn something about popular anger against wasteful government spending of taxpayer dollars ("big government" policies to help the poor), mainstream society's views on self-reliant individualism and hard work (distrust, if not dislike of the poor), and last but not least, enduring racism in U.S. society (the story is told by whites, who identify the woman as African American).

As this illustration shows, legends (no more than myths) are not confined to nonliterate, nonindustrialized societies. Commonly, legends consist of pseudo-historical narratives that account for the deeds of heroes, the movements of peoples, and the establishment of local customs, typically with a mixture of realism and the supernatural or extraordinary. As stories, they are not necessarily believed or disbelieved, but they usually serve to entertain as well as to instruct and to inspire or bolster pride in family, community, or nation.

To a degree, in literate societies, the function of legends has been taken over by history. Yet much of what passes for history, to paraphrase one historian, consists of the legends we develop to make ourselves feel better about who we are.[7] The trouble is that history does not always tell people what they want to hear about themselves, or, conversely, it tells them things that they would prefer not to hear. By projecting their culture's hopes and expectations onto the record of the past, they seize upon and even exaggerate some past events while ignoring or giving scant attention to others. Although this often takes place unconsciously, so strong is the motivation to transform history into legend that states often have gone as far as to deliberately rewrite it, as when the Aztecs in the reign of their 15th-century King Itzcoatl rewrote their history in a way more flattering to their position of dominance in ancient Mexico.

There are countless examples of the fact that different groups often recall and recount the same historical event in highly contrasting ways. For instance, white

Part of an ancient Mexican Indian manuscript. During the reign of King Itzcoatl ("Obsidian Snake") in the mid-1400s, the Aztecs rewrote their history in a way that glorified their ancestral past. In politically centralized states, such revisions of what really happened are not uncommon and often include deliberate inventions and falsifications of the historical record.

colonists and their descendants who settled in New England portrayed the region's 17th-century Indian rebellion led by Chief Metacomet (better known in American history books as "King Philip") as a treacherous uprising and described his defeat as a divinely guided military victory over heathen savages. In this violent conflict, thousands on both sides lost their lives. Although many Indian survivors found refuge among neighboring indigenous nations, hundreds of Indian captives were sold as slaves and died in foreign lands. Unable to resist English colonial land grabs and repression, Indians who were allowed to remain in their homeland were confined to small reservations where they came under the administrative control of white agents. In public commemorations and written historical accounts, the Indian side of this conflict remains largely unvoiced and unknown to the general public.[8] For this reason, American Indians sometimes joke bitterly about such one-sided versions of the past as *"his* story," and scholars attempting to separate historical fact from fiction frequently incur the wrath of people who refuse to abandon what they wish to believe is true, whether or not it really is.

A long legend—sometimes in poetry, rhythmic prose, or even basic melody—is known as an **epic.** In parts of western and central Africa, people hold remark-

© Werner Forman/Art Resource, NY

---

[7]Stoler, M. (1982). To tell the truth. *Vermont Visions, 82*(3), 3.

epic A long oral narrative, sometimes in poetry or rhythmic prose, recounting the glorious events in the life of a real or legendary person.

---

[8]Calloway, C. (1997). Introduction: Surviving the dark ages. In C. G. Calloway (Ed.), *After King Philip's war: Presence and persistence in Indian New England* (pp. 1–28). Hanover, NH: University Press of New England.

ably elaborate and formalized recitations of extremely long legends, lasting several hours and even days. These long narratives have been described as veritable encyclopedias of a culture's most diverse aspects, with direct and indirect statements about history, institutions, relationships, values, and ideas. Epics are typically found in nonliterate societies with some form of state political organization; they serve to transmit and preserve a culture's legal and political precedents and practices.

Legends may incorporate mythological details, especially when they make an appeal to the supernatural, and are therefore not always clearly distinct from myth. We see this in the Mwindo epic told by the Nyanga people living in the mountainous rainforests in central Africa. This legend follows the hero Mwindo through the earth, the atmosphere, the underworld, and the remote sky and gives a comprehensive picture of the Nyanga people's view of the organization and limits of their world. While relaying Mwindo's adventures and his emergence as a wise, generous, and benevolent ruler, it provides an overview of Nyanga culture, including kinship and marriage customs, political structures, ceremonies, behavior patterns, values, and material objects. The narrative is punctuated with songs and also features dancing and drumming. Legends may also incorporate proverbs and incidental tales and thus be related to other forms of verbal art as well. For example, a recitation of the Kambili epic of the Mende people who we discussed in the previous chapter has been said to include as many as 150 proverbs.

For the anthropologist, a major significance of the secular and apparently realistic portions of legends, whether long or short, is the clues they provide to what constitutes a culture's approved or ideal ethical behavior. The subject matter of legends is essentially problem solving and mentoring, and the content is likely to include combat, warfare, confrontations, and physical and psychological trials of many kinds. Certain questions may be answered explicitly or implicitly. In what circumstances, if any, does the culture permit homicide? What kinds of behavior are considered brave or cowardly? What is the etiquette of combat or warfare? Does the culture honor or recognize a concept of altruism or self-sacrifice? Here again, however, there are pitfalls in the process of interpreting art in relation to life. It is always possible that certain kinds of behavior are acceptable or even admirable, with the distance or objectivity afforded by art, but are not at all so approved in daily life. In Euroamerican culture, murderers, charlatans, and rascals sometimes have become popular heroes and the subjects of legends; North Americans would object, however, to an outsider's inference that they necessarily approved or wanted to emulate the morality of the notorious 19th-century Wild West outlaws Billy the Kid or Jesse James.

Tale

The **tale** is a nonspecific label for a third category of creative narratives—purely secular, nonhistorical, and recognized as fiction for entertainment, although they may draw a moral or teach a practical lesson as well. Consider this brief summary of a tale from Ghana in West Africa, known as "Father, Son, and Donkey":

> A father and his son farmed their corn, sold it, and spent part of the profit on a donkey. When the hot season came, they harvested their yams and prepared to take them to storage, using their donkey. The father mounted the donkey and they all three proceeded on their way until they met some people. "What? You lazy man!" the people said to the father. "You let your young son walk barefoot on this hot ground while you ride on a donkey? For shame!" The father yielded his place to the son, and they proceeded until they came to an old woman. "What? You useless boy!" said the old woman. "You ride on the donkey and let your poor father walk barefoot on this hot ground? For shame!" The son dismounted, and both father and son walked on the road, leading the donkey behind them until they came to an old man. "What? You foolish people!" said the old man. "You have a donkey and you walk barefoot on the hot ground instead of riding?" And so it goes. Listen: when you are doing something and other people come along, just keep on doing what you like.

This is precisely the kind of tale that is of special interest in traditional folklore studies. It is an internationally popular "numbskull" tale. Versions of it have been recorded in India, Southwest Asia, southern and western Europe, and North America, as well as in West Africa. It is classified or catalogued as exhibiting a basic **motif** or story situation—father and son trying to please everyone—one of the many thousands that have been found to recur in world folktales. Despite variations in detail, every version follows the same basic structure in the sequence of events, sometimes called the *syntax* of the tale: A peasant father and son work together, a beast of burden is purchased, the three set out on a short excursion, the father rides and is criticized, the son rides and is criticized, both walk and are criticized, and a conclusion is drawn.

Tales of this sort (not to mention myths and legends) that are found to have wide geographical distribution raise

tale A creative narrative recognized as fiction for entertainment.
motif A story situation in a folktale.

A scene such as this may bring to mind the internationally popular "Father, Son, and Donkey" tale. Told in different versions featuring localized draft animals, this tale conveys a basic motif or story situation—father and son trying in vain to please everyone.

the question: Where did they originate? Did the story arise only once and then pass from one culture to another (*diffusion*)? Or did the stories arise independently (*independent invention*) in response to like causes in similar settings, or perhaps as a consequence of inherited mental preferences and images deeply embedded in the evolutionary construction of the human brain? Or is it merely that there are logical limits to the structure of stories, so that, by coincidence, different cultures are bound to come up with similar motifs and syntax?[9] A surprisingly large number of motifs in European and African tales are traceable to ancient sources in India, evidence of diffusion of tales. Of course, purely local tales also exist. Within any particular culture, anthropologists usually can categorize local types of tales: animal, human experience, trickster, dilemma, ghost, moral, scatological, nonsense tales, and so on. In West Africa, for example, there is a remarkable prevalence of stories with animal protagonists. Many were carried to the slaveholding areas of the Americas; the Uncle Remus stories about Brer Rabbit and Brer Fox may be part of this tradition.

---

[9]Gould, S. J. (2000). The narthex of San Marco and the pangenetic paradigm. *Natural History, 109*(6), 29.

The significance of tales for the anthropologist rests partly in this matter of their distribution. They provide evidence of either cultural contacts or cultural isolation and of limits of influence and cultural cohesion. Debated for decades now, for example, has been the extent to which the cultures of West Africa were transmitted to the historical slaveholding regions in the southeastern United States. As far as folktales are concerned, one school of folklorists always has found and insisted on European origins; another school, somewhat more recently, points to African prototypes. Anthropologists are interested, however, in more than these questions of distribution. Like legends, tales very often illustrate local solutions to universal human ethical problems, and in some sense they state a moral philosophy. Anthropologists see that whether the tale of the father, the son, and the donkey originated in West Africa or arrived there from Europe or the Middle East, the very fact it is told in West Africa suggests that it states something valid for that culture. The tale's lesson of a necessary degree of self-confidence in the face of arbitrary social criticism is therefore something that can be read into the culture's values and beliefs.

Other Verbal Arts

Myths, legends, and tales, prominent as they are in anthropological studies, in many cultures turn out to be no more important than the other verbal arts. In the culture of the Awlad 'Ali Bedouins of Egypt's western desert, for example, poetry is a lively and active verbal art, especially as a vehicle for personal expression and private communication. These people use two forms of poetry. One is the elaborately structured and heroic poems men chant or recite only on ceremonial occasions and in specific public contexts. The other is the *ghinnáwas* or "little songs" that punctuate everyday conversations. Simple in structure, these deal with personal matters and feelings more appropriate to informal social situations, and older men regard them as the unimportant productions of women and youths. Despite this official devaluation in the male-dominated Bedouin society, however, they play a vital part in people's daily lives. In their "little songs" individuals are shielded from the consequences of making statements and expressing sentiments that contravene the moral system. Paradoxically, by sharing these "immoral" sentiments only with intimates and veiling them in impersonal traditional formulas, those who recite them demonstrate that they have a certain control, which actually enhances their moral standing.

As is often true of folklore in general, the "little songs" of the Awlad 'Ali provide a culturally appropriate outlet for otherwise taboo thoughts or opinions. Disaster jokes are an example of this in contemporary North American society. As anthropologist Lila Abu-Lughod points out:

The *ghinnáwas* or "little songs" of the Awlad 'Ali Bedouins punctuate conversations carried out while the people perform everyday chores, such as making bread, as these young women are doing. Through these "little songs," they can express what otherwise are taboo topics.

What may be peculiar to Awlad 'Ali is that their discourse of rebellion is both culturally elaborated and sanctioned. Although poetry refers to personal life, it is not individual, spontaneous, idiosyncratic, or unofficial but public, conventional, and formulaic—a highly developed art. More important, this poetic discourse of defiance is not condemned, or even just tolerated, as well it might be given all the constraints of time and place and form that bind it. Poetry is a privileged discourse in Awlad 'Ali society. Like other Arabs, and perhaps like many oral cultures, the Bedouins cherish poetry and other verbal arts. . . . They are drawn to *ghinnáwas,* and at the same time they consider them risqué, against religion, and slightly improper. . . . This ambivalence about poetry is significant, and it makes sense only in terms of the cultural meaning of opposition. Because ordinary discourse is informed by the values of honor and modesty, the moral correlates of the ideology that upholds the Awlad 'Ali social and political system, we would expect the antistructural poetic discourse with its contradictory messages, to be informed by an opposing set of values. This is not the case. Poetry as a discourse of defiance of the system symbolizes freedom—the ultimate value of the system and the essential entailment of the honor code.[10]

In all cultures the words of songs constitute a kind of poetry. Poetry and stories recited with gesture, movement, and props become drama. Drama combined with dance, music, and spectacle becomes a public celebration. The more we look at the individual arts, the clearer

it becomes that they often are interrelated and interdependent. The verbal arts are, in fact, simply differing manifestations of the same creative imagination that produces music and the other arts.

Musical Art

The study of music in specific cultural settings, beginning in the 19th century with the collection of folksongs, has developed into a specialized field, called **ethnomusicology.** Like the study of folktales for their own sake, ethnomusicology is both related to and somewhat independent of anthropology. Nevertheless, it is possible to sort out several concerns that are of interest to the general discipline of anthropology.

To begin, we may ask, How does a culture conceive of music? What is considered of primary importance when distinguishing music from other modes of expression? Music to one person may be merely noise to another. Music is a form of communication that includes a nonverbal component. The information transmitted is often abstract emotion rather than concrete ideas, and is experienced in a variety of ways by different listeners. This, and music's communication of something that is verbally incommunicable, make it very difficult to discuss music. In fact, not even a single definition of music can be agreed upon, because different peoples may include or exclude different ideas within that category. Ethnomusicologists must often rely upon a working definition as the basis for their investigations and often distinguish between "music" and that which is "musical." The way to approach an unfamiliar kind of musical expression is to define it either in indigenous terms or in orthodox musicological terms such as melody, rhythm, and form.

---

[10]Abu-Lughod, L. (1986). *Veiled sentiments* (p. 252). Berkeley: University of California Press.

ethnomusicology The study of a society's music in terms of its cultural setting.

Much of the historical development of ethnomusicology has been based upon musicology, which is primarily the study of European music. One problem has been the tendency to discuss music in terms of elements considered important in European music (tonality, rhythm, melody, and so on), when these may be of little importance to the practitioner. European music is defined, primarily, in terms of the presence of melody and rhythm. Melody is a function of tonality, and rhythm is an organizing concept involving tempo, stress, and measured repetition. Although these can be addressed in non-European music, they may not be the defining characteristics of a performance.

Early investigators of non-European song were struck by the apparent simplicity of *pentatonic* (five-tone) scales and a seemingly endless repetition of phrases. They often did not give sufficient credit to the formal function of repetition in such music, confusing repetition with lack of invention. A great deal of complex, sophisticated, non-European music was dismissed as "primitive" and formless and typically treated as trivial. Repetition, nevertheless, is a fact of music, including European music, and a basic formal principle.

In general, human music is said to differ from natural music—the songs of birds, wolves, and whales, for example—by being almost everywhere perceived in terms of a repertory of tones at fixed or regular intervals: in other words, a scale. Scale systems and their modifications comprise what is known as **tonality** in music. Humans make closed systems out of a formless range of possible sounds by dividing the distance between a tone and its first *overtone* or sympathetic vibration (which always has exactly twice as many vibrations as the basic tone) into a series of measured steps. In the Western or European system, the distance between the basic tone and the first overtone is called the *octave;* it consists of seven steps—five *whole* tones and two *semitones.* The whole tones are further divided into semitones for a total working scale of twelve tones. Interestingly, some birds pitch their songs to the same scale as Western music,[11] perhaps influencing the way these people developed their scale. Ambient sound is a central component of natural habitats, and it has been observed that this is similar to a modern orchestra. The voice of each creature has its own frequency, amplitude, timbre, and duration and occupies a unique niche among the other "musicians." This "animal orchestra," which sends a clear acoustic message, represents a unique sound grouping for any given biome.[12] Perhaps this is one reason why something that sounds natural to one people sounds unnatural to another. In any event, Western people learn at an early age to recognize and imitate the arbitrary twelve-tone scale and its conventions, and it begins to sound natural. Yet the overtone series, on which it is partially based, is the only part of it that can be considered a wholly natural phenomenon.

One of the most common alternatives to the semitonal system is the pentatonic system, which, as noted, divides the scale into five nearly equidistant tones. Such scales may be found all over the world, including in much European folk music. On the Indonesian island of Java people use scales of both five and seven equal steps, which have no relation to the intervals Europeans and Euroamericans hear as "natural." Arabic and Persian music have smaller units of a third of a tone with scales of seventeen and twenty-four steps in the octave. Even quarter-tone scales are used in India with subtleties of shading that are nearly indistinguishable to a Western ear. Small wonder, then, that even when Westerners can hear what sounds like melody and rhythm in these systems, the total result may sound peculiar to them, or "out of tune." Anthropologists need a practiced ear to learn to appreciate some of the music they hear, and only some of the most skilled folksong collectors have attempted to notate and analyze the music that is not semitonal.

As another organizing factor in music, whether regular or irregular, rhythm may be more important than tonality. One reason for this may be our constant exposure to natural rhythms, such as our own heartbeat and rhythms of breathing and walking, not to mention surrounding rhythms such as dripping water or lapping waves. Even before we are born, we are exposed to our mother's heartbeat and rhythms of her movements, and as infants we experience rhythmic touching, petting, stroking, and rocking.[13]

Traditional European music is most often measured into recurrent patterns of two, three, and four beats, with combinations of weak and strong beats to mark the division and form patterns. Non-European music is likely to move in patterns of five, seven, or eleven beats, with complex arrangements of internal beats and sometimes polyrhythms: one instrument or singer going in a pattern of three beats, for example, while another is in a pattern of five or seven. Polyrhythms are frequent in the drum music of West Africa, which shows remarkable precision in the overlapping of rhythmic lines. Non-European music also may contain shifting rhythms: a pattern of three beats, for example, followed by a pattern of two or five beats with little or no regular recurrence or repeti-

---

[11]Gray, P. M., Krause, B., Atema, J., Payne, R., Krumhansl, C., & Baptista, L. (2001). The music of nature and the nature of music. *Science, 291,* 52.

tonality In music, scale systems and their modifications.

---

[12]Gray et al., p. 53.

---

[13]Dissanayake, E. (2000). Birth of the arts. *Natural History, 109*(10), 89.

Even among food-foraging peoples, music plays an important role. Shown here is an Australian Aborigine playing a digeridoo.

tion of any one pattern, although the patterns are fixed and identifiable as units.

Although anthropologists do not necessarily have to untangle these complicated technical matters, they need to know enough to be aware of the degree of skill involved in a performance. This means understanding the extent to which people in a culture have learned to practice and respond to this creative activity. Moreover, the distribution of musical forms and instruments can reveal much about cultural contact or isolation.

FUNCTIONS OF ART

Art in all its many forms has countless functions beyond providing aesthetic pleasure, some of which have been touched upon or hinted at in the preceding paragraphs. For anthropologists and others seeking to understand cultures beyond their own, art offers insights into a culture's worldview, giving clues about everything from gender and kinship relations to religious beliefs, political ideas, historical memory, and so on.

For those within a society, art may serve to display social status, spiritual identity, and political power. An example of this can be seen in the totem poles of Indians living along America's Northwest Coast. Erected in front of the homes of chiefs, these poles are inscribed with symbols that are visual reminders of the social hierarchy. Similarly, art is used to mark kinship ties, as seen in Scottish tartans designed to identify clan affiliation. It can also affirm group solidarity and identity beyond kinship lines, as evidenced in national emblems such as the dragon (Bhutan), bald eagle (United States), maple leaf (Canada), crescent moon (Turkey), or cedar tree (Lebanon) that typically appear on coins, government buildings, and so on. Sometimes art is employed to express political themes and influence events, as in the counter-culture rock and folk

music of the 1960s in the United States. Other times it is used to transmit traditional culture and ancestral ties, as in epic poems passed down from generation to generation. Often it is created for religious purposes, to honor or beseech the aid of a deity, an ancestral spirit, or an animal spirit. Perhaps the best way to convey the many functions of art is to focus on one of its forms: music.

Even without concern for technical matters, anthropologists can productively investigate the function of music in a society. First, music making seems to be a part of all cultures. Bone flutes and whistles that date back some 40,000 years and resemble today's recorders have been found by archaeologists. And historically known food-foraging peoples were not without music. In the Kalahari Desert, for example, a Ju/'hoansi hunter off by himself would play a tune on his bow simply to help while away the time (long before anyone thought of beating swords into plowshares, some genius discovered that bows could be used not just to kill but to make music as well). In northern New England Abenaki shamans used cedar flutes to call game, lure enemies, and attract women. In addition, a drum over which two rawhide strings were stretched to produce a buzzing sound, thought to represent singing, gave the shaman the power to communicate with the spirit world.

Music is also a powerful identifier. Many marginalized groups have used music for purposes of self-identification, bringing the group together and in many cases contraposing their own forms against the onslaught of a dominant culture or voicing social and political commentary. Examples of this range from ethnic groups sponsoring music festivals to rock bands such as Britain's Rolling Stones and Cold Play to North American rap artists such as Outkast, Eminem, and Puff Daddy. Potlatches and powwows, among other occasions, allow

A widespread technique used by shamans is persistent drumming, as rhythmic and audio driving are effective ways to induce trance.

various Native American groups to reaffirm and celebrate their ethnic identity, among other functions. Music plays an important part at these gatherings, thus becoming closely bound to the group identity, both from without and from within the group. It should be understood, too, that these associations of music with groups are not dependent upon words alone but also upon particular tonal, rhythmic, and instrumental conventions. For example, Scottish gatherings would not be "Scottish" without the sound of the Highland bagpipes and the fiddle.

This power of music to shape identity has been recognized everywhere, with varying consequences. The English recognized the power of the bagpipes for creating a strong sense of identity among the Highland regiments of the British army and encouraged it within certain bounds, even while suppressing piping in Scotland itself under the Disarming Act. Over time, the British military piping tradition was assimilated into the Scottish piping tradition and so was accepted and spread by Scottish pipers. As a result, much of the supposedly Scottish piping one hears today consists of marches written within the conventions of the musical tradition of England, though shaped to fit the physical constraints of the instrument. Less often heard is the "classical" music known as

Although much music performed by Scottish pipers is of English origin, it has been so thoroughly absorbed that most people think of it as an ancient and authentic art form of the Scottish Highlands.

pibroch, or *ceol mor*. The latter, however, has been undergoing a series of revivals over the past century and is now often associated with rising nationalist sentiments.

The English adoption of the highland bagpipe into Scottish regiments is an instance of those in authority employing music to further a political agenda. So too in Spain, former dictator Francisco Franco (who came to power in the 1930s) established community choruses in even the smallest towns to promote the singing of patriotic songs. Similarly, in Ireland *Comhaltas Ceoltoiri Eireann* has promoted the collection and performance of traditional Irish music, and in Brittany and Galicia music is playing an important role in attempts to revive the spirits of the indigenous Celtic cultures in these regions of France and Spain. But however played, or for whatever reason, music (like all art) is a creative skill that one can cultivate and be proud of, whether from a sense of accomplishment or the sheer pleasure of performing; and it is a form of social behavior through which there is a communication or sharing of feelings and life experience with other humans. Still, because each human's creativity is constrained by the traditions of his or her particular culture, each society's art is distinctive and helps to define its members' sense of identity.

The social function of music is perhaps most obvious in song, since these contain verbal text. This is probably why many earlier studies concentrated upon them. Songs, like other verbal forms, often express a group's values, beliefs, and concerns, but they do so with an increased formalism resulting from adherence to the restrictions of systematic rules or conventions of pitch, rhythm, timbre, and musical genre. For this reason, music, like other arts, plays an important part in the cultural preservation and revitalization efforts of indigenous peoples around the world whose traditions were repressed or nearly exterminated through colonialism. Examples of this are featured in this chapter's Anthropologists of Note and Anthropology Applied boxes.

Songs serve many purposes, entertainment being only one of these. Work songs long have played an important part in manual labor, serving to coordinate efforts in heavy or dangerous labor, such as weighing anchor and furling sail aboard ships, to coordinate axe or hammer strokes, and to pass time and relieve tedium—as with oyster-shucking songs. Songs also have been used to soothe babies to sleep, to charm animals into giving more milk, to keep witchcraft at bay, and to advertise goods. Songs may also serve social and political purposes, spreading particular ideas swiftly and effectively by giving them a special form involving poetic language and rhythm and by attaching a pleasing and appropriate tune, be it solemn or light.

In the United States numerous examples exist of marginalized social and ethnic groups attempting to gain a larger audience and more compassion for their

Anthropologists of Note

Frederica de Laguna (1906–)

A concern with the arts of non-Western people has always been an important part of anthropology, as illustrated by the work of anthropologist Frederica de Laguna. Educated at Bryn Mawr College and Columbia University, where she earned her Ph.D., she made her first trip into the field with a Danish expedition to Greenland in 1929. A year later, she began work in southeastern Alaska, a region to which she has returned repeatedly. Her first research there was archaeological, and she was a pioneer in southeastern Alaskan prehistory. But as her interest in native peoples

grew, she became increasingly involved with ethnographic work as well. She found out that to understand the past, one had to know what it led to, just as to understand the present native people, one had to know their past.

In 1949, after many seasons of work in different localities, de Laguna began a project to trace the roots of the lifeways of the Tlingit Indians of Yakutat through combining archaeological and ethnographic research. This resulted in a monumental three-volume work published in 1972, *Under Mount St. Elias*. Considerable space in this trilogy is devoted to transcriptions of Tlingit songs and stories just as they were related and performed by elders now long dead. Beyond its scientific anthropological value, this work has come to be of enormous importance to the Tlingit themselves.

When "Freddy" de Laguna began to work at Yakutat, Tlingit children were being sent to government boarding schools, where they were told nothing of their own culture and were harshly punished for even speaking their own language. The aim was to stamp out native culture to facilitate assimilation into mainstream American culture. Thus, as the elders died out, many traditions were being lost. But with the publication of de Laguna's trilogy, the community has been able to revitalize much that they were in danger of losing. As de Laguna says, songs and stories are for giving back, and so it was that in 1997 the Tlingit of Yakutat honored her for what she gave back to them. They readily acknowledge that their renewed cultural vigor and pride in who they are owes much to their "Grandmother Freddy's" work.

---

plight through song. Perhaps no better example exists than African Americans, whose ancestors were captured and carried across the Atlantic Ocean to be sold as slaves. Out of their experience emerged spirituals and, ultimately gospel, jazz, blues, rock and roll, and rap. These forms all found their way into the North American mainstream, and white performers such as Elvis Presley and Benny Goodman (the latter with integrated bands—unusual in the 1930s) presented their own versions of this music to white audiences. Even composers of so-called serious music ranging from Leonard Bernstein to George Gershwin to Antonin Dvořák to Francis Poulenc

were influenced by the music of African Americans. In short, music of a marginalized group of former slaves eventually captivated the entire world, even while the descendants of those slaves have had to struggle continually to escape their subordinate status.

In the 1950s and 1960s performers such as Pete Seeger and Joan Baez gained great visibility when supporting civil and human rights causes in the United States. Indeed, both performers' celebrity status led to the broader dissemination of their social and political beliefs. Such celebrity status comes from skill in performing and communicating with the intended audience. So powerful a force was music in the civil rights and peace movements of the time that Seeger was targeted by right-wing Senator Joseph McCarthy's anti-Communist crusade, which aimed to discredit the political left as anti-American and unpatriotic. Seeger became one of many performers blacklisted by the entertainment industry due to this political witch-hunt.

In Australia, traditional songs of the Aborigines have taken on a new legal function, as they are being introduced into court as evidence of early settlement patterns. This helps the native peoples to claim more extensive land ownership, thus allowing them greater authority to use the land, as well as to negotiate and profit from the sale of natural resources. This had been impossible before. The British, upon their annexation of Australia, declared the land ownerless (*Terra Nullius*). Although the Aborigines

Laborers in Mali, West Africa, working to the beat of a drum, which serves to set the pace of work, unify the workforce, and relieve boredom.

© 2000 Bob Livingston

Like other art forms, music is often culturally distinct, yet foreign influences can lead to creative innovations or mixtures—as shown in this photo of North American cowboy singer Bob Livingston playing with Arab musicians in Kuwait on a worldwide tour.

had preserved their records of ownership in song and story, these were not admissible in the British courts. In the early 1970s, however, the Aborigines exposed the injustice of the situation, and the Australian government began responding in a more favorable, if still limited, fashion, granting the claims of traditional ownership to groups in the Northern Territory. In 1992 the legitimacy of the concept of *Terra Nullius* was overturned, and native claims are now being presented in the other territories as well. These newer claimants are granted equal partnership with developers and others. Sacred sites are being recognized, and profits are being shared with the traditional owners. Proof of native ownership includes recordings of Aboriginal songs indicative of traditional patterns of settlement, travel, and land use.[14]

Music gives a concrete form, made memorable and attractive with melody and rhythm, to basic human ideas. Whether a song's content is didactic, satirical, inspirational, religious, political, or purely emotional, the formless has been given form, and feelings hard to express in words alone are communicated in a symbolic and memorable way that can be repeated and shared. The group is consequently united and has the sense that their shared experience, whatever it may be, has shape and meaning. This, in turn, shapes and gives meaning to the community.

MEDIATREK

For many indigenous peoples, art is a key to cultural survival. To visit an e-store where you'll find images and information about indigenous art, artists, and their cultures, go to MediaTrek 14.3 on the companion Web site or CD-ROM.

---

[14]Koch, G. (1997). Songs, land rights, and archives in Australia. *Cultural Survival Quarterly, 20*(4).

ART, GLOBALIZATION, AND CULTURAL SURVIVAL

Clearly, there is more to art than meets the eye or ear (not to mention the nose and tongue—consider how burning incense or tobacco are part of the artfulness of sacred ceremonies, and imagine the cross-cultural array of smells and tastes in the cooking arts). In fact, art is such a significant part of any culture that many indigenous groups around the world whose lifeways have been threatened—first by colonialism and now by globalization—are using aesthetic expressions as part of a cultural survival strategy. They are finding that a traditional art form—a carpet, a basket, a carving, or anything that is distinctly beautiful and well made or performed—can serve as a powerful symbol that conveys the vital message, "We're still here, and we're still a culturally distinct people with our own particular beliefs and values."

Art can and does play a role in indigenous rights efforts. For example, consider the native rights case of the Aroostook Band of Micmac Indians in northern Maine, described in detail in the Anthropology Applied box in Chapter 10. Building support for this particular case involved making a documentary film to inform politicians and the general public about the band's cultural identity and tribulations.[15] At the time, only a dozen or so families in this band still practiced traditional wood-splint basketry. However, it had been a common livelihood for many generations, and almost every band member had parents or grandparents who had made baskets. Emblematic of Micmac identity, including their stubborn desire for self-determination, basketry became a focal point of the film, which ultimately played a key role in the success of the band's native rights case. More than this, the film helped create a wider market for Micmac baskets, and by conveying the diligence and real skill involved in making them, it justified raising the prices of the baskets to levels that make the craft a viable livelihood. This, in turn, has prompted young people to take up basketry and strengthened their relationships with Micmac elders, who are now passing the age-old art on to a new generation.

Similar examples of the link between art and cultural survival can be found all around the world. One is featured in the following Anthropology Applied, which brings this chapter to a close.

---

[15]Prins, H. E. L., & Carter, K. (1986). *Our lives in our hands*. Video and 16mm. Color. 50 min. Distributed by Watertown, MA: Documentary Educational Resources and Bucksport, ME: Northeast Historic Film; see also Prins, H. E. L. (2002). Visual media and the primitivist perplex: Colonial fantasies, indigenous imagination, and advocacy in North America. In F. D. Ginsburg et al., *Media worlds: Anthropology on new terrain* (pp. 58–74). Berkeley: University of California Press.

Anthropology Applied

Protecting Cultural Heritages

The time is long past when the anthropologist could go out and describe small band and tribal groups in out-of-the-way places that (supposedly) had not been "contaminated" by contact with Western people. Not only do few such groups exist in the world today, but those that do remain face strong pressures to abandon their traditional ways in the name of "progress." All too often, band and tribal peoples are made to forfeit their indigenous identity and are pressed into a mold that allows them neither the opportunity nor the motivation to rise above the lowest rung of the social ladder. From an autonomous people able to provide for their own needs, with pride and a strong sense of their own identity as a people, they are transformed into a deprived underclass with neither pride nor a sense of their own identity, often despised by more fortunate members of some multinational state in which they live.

The basic rights of groups of people to be themselves and not to be deprived of their own distinctive cultural identities is a primary consideration in anthropology. However, anthropologists have additional reasons to be concerned about the disappearance of the societies and cultures they have studied traditionally. For one thing, the need to acquire information about them has become increasingly urgent. If we are ever to have a realistic understanding of that elusive thing called human nature, we need reliable data on all humans. More is involved than this, though; once a traditional society is gone, it is lost to humanity, unless an adequate record of it exists. When this happens we are all poorer for the loss. Hence, anthropologists have in a sense rescued many such societies from oblivion. This not only helps to preserve the human heritage, but it also may be important to an ethnic group that, having

become Westernized, wishes to rediscover and reassert its traditional cultural identity. Better yet, of course, is to find ways to prevent the loss of cultural traditions in the first place.

To the Pomo Indians of California, the art of basketry has been important for their sense of who they are since long before the coming of European settlers. Employing seven different types of weaving and using various reeds and sedges, they created everything from boats to buildings (constructing their homes out of woven mats). They wove exquisite utilitarian containers of many shapes and sizes, including baskets so tightly fashioned that they could be used to carry water. Notably, even though

© Inga Spence/Tom Stack & Associates

they lived as hunter–gatherers, they practiced agriculture for basketry—cultivating sedge to ensure its availability for this all-important craft. Recognized for their skilled techniques and aesthetic artistry, Pomo baskets—some of the finest in the world—are prized by museums and private collectors alike. Nevertheless, the art of Pomo basketry was threatened in the 1970s by the impending construction of the Warm Springs Dam–Lake Sonoma Project to the north of San Francisco. The effect of this project would be to wipe out the best habitat in one important valley for the particular species of sedge essential for the weaving of Pomo baskets.

Accordingly, a coalition of archaeologists, Native Americans, and others with objections to the project brought suit in federal district court. As it happened, the U.S. Army Corps of Engineers had recently hired anthropologist Richard N. Lerner for its San Francisco District Office to advise on sociocultural factors associated with water resources programs in northwestern California. One of Lerner's first tasks, therefore, was to undertake studies of the problem and to find ways to overcome it.

After comprehensive archaeological, ethnographic, and other studies were completed in 1976, Lerner succeeded in having the Pomo basketry materials recognized by the National Register of Historic Places as "historic property," requiring the Corps of Engineers to find ways to mitigate the adverse impact dam construction would have. The result was a complex ethnobotanical project developed and implemented by Lerner. Working in concert with Pomo Indians as well as botanists, Lerner coordinated relocating 48,000 sedge plants onto nearly 3 acres of suitable lands downstream from the dam. By fall 1983, the sedge was doing well enough to be harvested and proved to be of excellent quality. Since this initial harvest, groups of weavers have returned each year. As of this writing they continue to gather sedge material at this location, helping to ensure the survival of the art of Pomo Indian basketry. *(Adapted from Richard N. Lerner. (1987). Preserving plants for Pomos. In R. M. Wulff & S. J. Fiske (Eds.), Anthropological praxis: Translating knowledge into action (pp. 212–222). Boulder, CO: Westview Press. With additional and updated information provided by Lerner through personal communication, November 2003.)* ■ ■ ■

Chapter Summary

- Although hard to explain, art can be regarded as the creative use of the human imagination to interpret, express, and enjoy life. It stems from the uniquely human ability to use symbols to give shape and significance to the physical world for more than just a utilitarian purpose. Anthropologists are concerned with art as a reflection of the cultural values and concerns of people. Not all societies distinguish "art" as a special category, but people everywhere have developed aesthetic forms to symbolically express, appreciate, and share experiences of beauty in all its variety.

- Visual art may be regarded as either representational or abstract, although in truth these categories represent polar ends of a continuum. The rock art of southern Africa illustrates three ways the study of art may be approached. The aesthetic and narrative approaches focus on *how* and *what* things are depicted. By themselves they reveal little about what the art is all about, and they may convey a distorted view of the people responsible for it. Only the interpretive approach can reveal the *meaning* of another people's art. This approach requires a rich body of ethnography and often other sets of data to draw on, and it may reveal the art to be far more complex than expected. Applied to southern African rock art, it shows how paintings and engravings are intimately connected with the practices and beliefs of shamanism.

- Oral traditions denote a culture's unwritten stories, beliefs, and customs. Verbal arts include narrative, drama, poetry, incantations, proverbs, riddles, and word games. Narratives, which have received the most study, have been divided into three categories: myths, legends, and tales. Myths are sacred narratives that explain how the world came to be as it is. By describing an orderly universe, myths function to set standards for orderly behavior. Legends are stories told as if true that often recount the exploits of heroes, the movements of people, and the establishment of local customs. Epics, which are long legends in poetry or prose, typically are found in nonliterate societies that have some form of state political organization. They serve to transmit and preserve a culture's legal and political practices. In literate states, history has taken over these functions to one degree or another. Anthropologists are interested in legends because they provide clues about what constitutes model ethical behavior in a culture. Tales are fictional, secular, and nonhistorical narratives that instruct as they entertain, and their distribution provides evidence of cultural contacts or isolation.

- The study of music in specific cultural settings has developed into the specialized field of ethnomusicology. Almost everywhere human music is perceived in terms of a scale. Scale systems and their modifications vary across cultures and comprise tonality in music. Tonality determines the possibilities and limits of melody and harmony. Rhythm, which also varies across cultures, is an organizing factor in music.

- Aside from adding beauty and pleasure to everyday life, art serves a wide and varied a number of functions. Myths, for example, set standards for orderly behavior, and the verbal arts—including words put to music—generally transmit and preserve a culture's customs, values, and concerns. To the degree that art is characteristic of a particular society, it may contribute to the cohesiveness or solidarity of that society. Yet, it may also be used to express political themes and influence events to create social change. Often it is created for religious purposes, to honor or beseech the aid of a deity, an ancestral spirit, or an animal spirit. Moreover, it offers insights into a culture's worldview and is often used to indicate a person or group's kinship ties, social status, political position, and spiritual or religious identity.

- Because art is so fundamental to a culture's identity, it is often part of the cultural survival efforts of non-Western peoples struggling to hold on to their particular cultural beliefs, values, and traditions in the floodtide of globalization.

Questions for Reflection

1. Since the beginning of our species as culture-bearing animals, humans everywhere have tried to creatively articulate their feelings and ideas about themselves and the world around them. Considering the range of possible art forms available to them, how have people in your own home community met this particular challenge? Can you identify some specific examples in music, dance, images, or sculptures that are not only beautiful but also meaningful?

2. In many parts of the world, especially in Polynesian cultures, tattooing is a traditional form of skin art. Among Polynesian nations such as the Maori, tattoo designs are typically based on significant cultural symbols, the meanings of which are understood by all members in the community. Are the tattoo designs that you or others in your group have based on traditional motifs from your own culture, and do they have a symbolic meaning?

3. Kinship relations are important in small-scale traditional societies. Ideas about marriage and descent are often symbolically represented in artistic designs and motifs. What are some of the major concerns in your own society, and are these concerns reflected or represented in any of your own culture's art forms?

4. You have read that in some cultures art is produced not to be preserved and enjoyed by the living, but to be buried. In fact, in some cultures highly valued art objects may also be burned or otherwise destroyed. If such an attitude toward art does not reflect a lack of appreciation for beauty, can you think of any reasons for such seemingly irrational cultural practices?

5. Many museums and private collectors in Europe and North America are interested in so-called tribal art such as African statues or American Indian masks originally used in or made for sacred rituals. Do you know of any sacred objects such as paintings or carvings that have a place in your own religion that might also be collected, bought, or sold as art?

Key Terms

Art

Entoptic phenomena

Iconic images

Folklore

Folkloristics

Myth

Legend

Epic

Tale

Motif

Ethnomusicology

Tonality

Multimedia Review Tools

Companion Web Site

Visit **http://www.wadsworth.com/anthropology_d/** and click on the companion Web site for this textbook to access a wide range of material to aid your study of anthropology. Among the options for self-study in each chapter are learning objectives, flash cards, Internet activities, Web links, InfoTrac College Edition exercises, and practice tests that can be scored and emailed to your instructor.

CD-ROM

The *Doing Anthropology Today* CD-ROM supplied with your textbook provides unique and valuable information designed to enhance your learning experience. This interactive multimedia resource includes video clips, interviews with renowned anthropologists, map and timeline exercises, chapter study quizzes, and much more. *Doing Anthropology Today* will not only help you in achieving your grade goals, it will also make your learning experience fun and exciting!

Suggested Readings

Caton, S. C. (1999). *Lawrence of Arabia: A film's anthropology.* Berkeley: University of California Press.

This visual anthropological study focuses on David Lean's 1962 epic Hollywood drama *Lawrence of Arabia.* Building on an anthropological tradition of cross-cultural film analysis pioneered by Gregory Bateson, Margaret Mead, and Hortense Powdermaker in the mid-1900s, Caton demonstrates that feature film can reveal essential elements about the culture in which it is produced.

DeMello, M. (2000). *Bodies of inscription: A cultural history of the modern tattoo community.* Durham, NC: Duke University Press.

An authentic look at tattoos by an anthropologist who is tattooed and married to a tattooist. The author identifies and describes a range of tattoo communities—from gangs to bikers to middle-class baby-boomers to Gen-Xers—and analyzes tattoos as socioeconomic indicators.

Dundes, A. (1980). *Interpreting folklore.* Bloomington: Indiana University Press.

A collection of articles that assesses the materials folklorists have amassed and classified, this book seeks to broaden and refine traditional assumptions about the proper subject matter and methods of folklore.

Hannah, J. L. (1988). *Dance, sex, and gender.* Chicago: University of Chicago Press.

Like other art forms, dances are social acts that contribute to the continuation and emergence of culture. One of the oldest—if not the oldest—art forms, dance shares the same instrument, the human body, with sexuality. This book, written for a broad nonspecialist audience, explicitly examines sexuality and the construction of gender identities as they are played out in the production and visual imagery of dance.

Hatcher, E. P. (1985). *Art as culture: An Introduction to the anthropology of art.* New York: University Press of America.

This handy, clearly written book does a nice job of relating the visual arts to other aspects of culture. Numerous line drawings help the reader understand the varied forms of art in non-Western societies.

Layton, R. (1991). *The anthropology of art* (2nd ed.). Cambridge, England: Cambridge University Press.

This readable introduction to the diversity of non-Western art deals with questions of aesthetic appreciation, the use of art, and the big question: What *is* art?

Merriam, A. P. (1964). *The anthropology of music.* Chicago: Northwestern University Press.

This book focuses upon music as a complex of behavior that resonates throughout all of culture: social organization, aesthetic activity, economics, and religion.

Otten, C. M. (1971). *Anthropology and art: Readings in cross-cultural aesthetics.* Garden City, NY: Natural History Press.

This is a collection of articles by anthropologists and art historians with emphasis on the functional relationships between art and culture.

Randy Olson/National Geographic Image Collection

Change and the Future
The Challenge of Globalization

PART 5

Chapter 15
Processes of Change

Chapter 16
Global Challenges, Local Responses, and the Role of Anthropology

Introduction

Understanding the processes of cultural change, the subject of Chapter 15, is one of the most fundamental and significant of anthropological goals. It is a challenging task, in part due to ethnocentric perceptions about change. Typically, people in wealthy industrial and post-industrial societies equate change with "progress." And more often than not they think of progress as a technologically propelled movement toward a better collective future, according to a predetermined global process in which the rest of humanity will follow their admirable example. This deeply ingrained notion leads many Europeans and North Americans to characterize different cultures in other parts of the world as misguided, backward, outdated, or underdeveloped. Of course, such conclusions are ill founded, for as we saw in Chapter 6, cultures are often highly developed in distinctively different ways, and no culture or cultural feature that effectively meets the needs of its members is outdated. For instance, when it comes to desert travel, the dromedary pictured here in a traffic jam in South Asia is far more reliable than motorized vehicles.

Belief in progress and its inevitability has important implications for the world's peoples, whether they form part of wealthy and powerful states or inhabit countries that are relatively poor in resources and technology. For many North Americans, for example, it means that change is almost by definition something good and desirable and that whatever is old, by virtue of that simple fact alone, is something to be cast aside as outdated and unsatisfactory, no matter how well it seems to be working. North Americans who accept this idea on the home front are likely to assume that entire societies branded as "old," "traditional," or just "primitive" must somehow be stuck in the past in humanity's great march forward. This ethnocentric and false reasoning amounts to a global charter for massive intervention into the lives of peoples with traditional cultures—no matter how well adapted those cultures may be to particular circumstances.

A conscious attempt to identify and critique the cultural biases in wealthy industrial and postindustrial societies enables us to understand the processes of change in a very different way. It allows us to recognize that although people can intentionally change their ways in response to particular forces or problems, much change occurs accidentally. The fact is that the historical record is quirky and full of random events. And although it is true that without the capacity for change cultures could never adapt to altered conditions, we also must recognize that sweeping changes generated or imposed by powerful outside forces may place entire peoples and their cultures in jeopardy. These changes may conflict with the social need for predictability, discussed in Chapter 2; the individual's need for regularity and structure, discussed in Chapter 5; and a population's collective need for an adaptive fit with its environment, discussed in Chapter 6.

The more anthropologists study change and learn about the various ways people solve their problems of existence, the more aware they become of a great paradox of culture. The basic function of culture is to solve problems but doing so almost inevitably creates new difficulties that also demand solutions. Perhaps it is for this reason that humans spend considerable time reflecting on change and the events that cause it. We do this in numerous ways, including art. For instance, on a remote hill in the heartland of a car-obsessed country stands a Native American memorial comprised of old vehicles. The artist created it to honor a Pima Indian and his fellow Marines who were famously photographed raising an American flag at Iwo Jima Island in the Pacific Ocean after a ferocious battle at the end of the Second World War.

Harald E. L. Prins

When we see the numerous global challenges confronting the human species today (Chapter 16), most of them the result of technological inventions and cultural practices, we may wonder if we have passed some critical threshold where our capacities are no longer adequate to deal with rapidly growing problems. This does not necessarily mean the future has to be bleak for the generations to come, but it is irresponsible to project a rosy future as foreordained, at least on the basis of current evidence.

To help bring about a future in which humans live in harmony with one another and the nature that sustains us all, and where strife and suffering are limited or even eliminated, we are pressed to critically assess the hard facts of the human condition today. We must work not only to create new opportunities but also to eliminate or correct a host of unjust, wasteful, and ultimately destructive ideas and behaviors that threaten serious long-term damage to our own species—and that have already annihilated so many other life forms. Many parts of the world are dangerously overpopulated, and almost everywhere there are unbearably sharp differences in access to essential basic resources. These problems carry with them a range of other potentially catastrophic ills—from poverty and starvation to environmental pollution to the culture of discontent, hopelessness, and bitterness that arises from the ever-widening economic gap between the have-lots and the have-nots.

CHAPTER 15

Processes of Change

Harald Prins

CHALLENGE ISSUE

THE ABILITY TO CHANGE HAS ALWAYS BEEN VITAL TO HUMAN CULTURES, FOR ADAPTING TO DIF-FERENT ENVIRONMENTS, SHIFTING CIR-CUMSTANCES, AND NEW CONDITIONS IS A REQUIREMENT FOR LONG-TERM SUR-VIVAL. Today billions of humans are engulfed in a sea of technological and other major changes that radically challenge us to adjust at an ever-faster pace. These challenges are all the more unsettling for traditional peoples around the world, for whom changes are often imposed by powerful outside forces undermining their customary ways of life and creating new realities not of their own choosing. Nambikwara Indians, pictured here in their traditional homeland in southern Brazil, are threatened by hordes of illegal loggers destroying their forests, as well as gold miners and farmers who are polluting their streams and rivers. Here, two Nambikwara point to dangerous pesticides and insecticides dumped on their lands by non-Indian soybean farmers, who have encroached on their territory in order to produce cheap crops for export to European markets.

1
Why Do Cultures Change?

All cultures change at one time or another for a variety of reasons. Although people may deliberately alter their ways in response to problems or challenges, much change is unforeseen, unplanned, and undirected. Changes in existing values and behavior may also come about due to contact with other peoples who introduce new ideas or tools. This may even involve the massive imposition of foreign ideas and practices through conquest of one group by another. Through cultural change, societies can adapt to altered conditions; however, not all change is positive or adaptive.

2
How Do Cultures Change?

The mechanisms of cultural change include innovation, diffusion, cultural loss, and acculturation. Innovation is the discovery or creation of something that is then accepted by fellow members in a society. Diffusion is the borrowing of something from another group, and cultural loss is the abandonment of an existing practice or trait, with or without replacement. Acculturation is a massive change that comes about in a group due to intensive first-hand contact with another, usually more powerful, group. Typically, it occurs when dominant societies forcefully expand their activities beyond their borders, pressuring other societies to abandon their traditional cultures in favor of the foreign.

3
What Is Modernization?

Modernization is a problematic term referring to a process of change by which traditional, nonindustrial societies acquire characteristics of technologically complex societies. Accelerated modernization interconnecting all parts of the world is known as globalization. Although commonly assumed to be a good thing, modernization has led to a new "culture of discontent" in which expectations far exceed the limits of local resources and opportunities. It has also led to the destruction of treasured customs and values.

Culture has become the primary medium through which the human species adapts to changes and solves the problems of existence. Various cultural institutions—such as religion, kinship and marriage, and political and economic organization—mesh to form an integrated cultural system. Because systems generally work to maintain stability, cultures are often fairly stable and remain so unless there is a change in the conditions to which they are adapted or in human perceptions of those conditions. Archaeological studies reveal how elements of a culture may persist for long periods. For example, in Chapter 6 we saw how the culture of the indigenous inhabitants of northeastern America remained relatively consistent over thousands of years.

Although stability may be a striking feature of many traditional cultures, all cultures are capable of adapting to changing conditions—climatic, economic, political, or ideological. Adaptation is a consequence of change that happens to work favorably for a population. However, not all change is positive or adaptive, and not all cultures are equally well equipped for making the necessary adjustments in a timely fashion. In a stable society, change may occur gently and gradually, without altering in any fundamental way the culture's underlying structures. Sometimes, though, the pace of change may increase dramatically, to the point of destabilizing or even wrecking a cultural system. The modern world is full of examples of such radical changes, from the disintegration of the Soviet Union to the utter devastation of many indigenous communities in the Amazon caused by state efforts to develop Indian homelands and capitalize on the vast rainforest's natural resources.

The causes of change are many, including accidental discoveries, deliberate attempts to solve a perceived problem, and interaction with other people who introduce—or force—new ideas or tools or ways of life. Sometimes change is caused by the unexpected outcome of particular actions or events. Among countless examples is the establishment of European colonies in the homelands of Algonquian-speaking natives in northeastern America nearly 500 years ago. Many people today assume this came about because the culture of the newcomers was better or more advanced than that of the region's original inhabitants. However, one could just as well argue that it was the reverse, for at the time, these Indians had higher quality diets, enjoyed better health, and experienced less violence in their lives than did most Europeans.[1]

A deeper look at American history shows that the colonial settlements in New England were actually the outcome of a series of unrelated historical events that happened to coincide at a critical time. In the 1500s, economic and political developments in England drove large numbers of small farmers off the land during a period of population growth, thereby forcing an outward migration. By pure chance, this took place shortly after the European discovery of the Americas. Seeing the New World as an answer to its overpopulation, the English attempted to establish overseas colonies in lands they claimed and renamed New England. Early efforts failed, until an epidemic of unprecedented scope resulted in the sudden death of 75 to 90 percent of the indigenous inhabitants. This devastating epidemic occurred because the region's native communities were exposed to a host of foreign diseases through contact with European fishermen and traders. It left the weakened remnants of indigenous survivors with few defenses against aggressive colonizers, many of whom had become immune to the diseases. (For centuries, Europeans had been living under conditions that were ideal for the incubation and spread of infectious diseases, which periodically killed off up to 80 percent of local populations. Since those who survived had a higher resistance to the diseases than those who succumbed, such resistance became more common in European populations over time. Indians at the time of the European invasion, by contrast, lacked all resistance to these diseases.)

Although the crucial issue of immunity played a huge role in England's North American colonization efforts, it is unlikely the English could have dispossessed the surviving indigenous peoples from their land were it not for one other important factor: They crossed the Atlantic Ocean equipped with the political and military techniques for dominating other peoples—tactics previously used to impose rule over the Scots, Irish, and Welsh. In addition, they came with the ideology of "just war," which they believed justified dispossessing America's indigenous peoples who fought back in defense.

MEDIATREK

For an exploration of the processes and consequences of culture change, go to MediaTrek 15.1 on the companion Web site or CD-ROM.

Change imposed upon one group by another continues in much of the world today as culture contact intensifies between societies unequal in power. Among those who have the power to drive and direct change in their favor, it is typically referred to as "progress." But progress (defined in chapter 6) is a relative term that implies improvement *as defined* by the people who profit or otherwise benefit from the changes set into motion. In other words, progress is in the eye of the beholder.

---

[1]Stannard, D. E. (1992). *American holocaust* (pp. 57–67). Oxford: Oxford University Press.

MECHANISMS OF CHANGE

Innovation

The ultimate source of all cultural change is innovation: any new idea, method, or device that gains widespread acceptance in society. **Primary innovation** is the creation, invention, or discovery, by chance, of a completely new idea, method, or device. A **secondary innovation** is a deliberate application or modification of an existing idea, method, or device.

An example of a primary innovation is the discovery that the firing of clay makes it permanently hard. Presumably, accidental firing of clay occurred frequently in ancient cooking fires—but a chance occurrence is of no account unless someone perceives an application of it. This perception first took place about 25,000 years ago, when people began making figurines of fired clay. However, it was not until some time between 9,000 and 8,500 years ago that people recognized a highly practical application of fired clay and began using it to make pottery containers and cooking vessels.

As nearly as we can reconstruct it, the development of the earliest known pottery vessels came about in the following way:[2] Nine thousand years ago, people in Southwest Asia still relied upon stone bowls, baskets, and animal-hide bags for containers. However, they were familiar with the working of clay, using it to build houses, line storage pits, and model figurines. In addition, their cooking areas included clay-lined basins built into the floor and clay ovens and hearths, making the accidental firing of clay inevitable. Once the significance of fired clay—the primary innovation—was understood, then the application of known techniques to it—secondary innovation—became possible. Clay could be modeled in the familiar way but now into the known shapes of existing containers. It could then be fired, either in an open fire or in the same facilities used for cooking food. The earliest known southwestern Asian pottery imitates leather and stone containers, but over time potters developed shapes and decorative techniques specifically suited to the new technology.

Since men are rarely the potters in traditional societies (unless the craft has become something of a commercial specialization), women probably made the first pottery. The clay vessels that they produced were initially handmade, and the earliest furnaces or kilns were the same ovens used for cooking. As people became more adept at making pottery, they refined the technology. To aid in production, the clay could be modeled on a mat or other surface that could be turned as work progressed. Hence, the potter could sit in one place while she worked, without having to get up to move around the clay. A further refinement was to mount the movable

---

[2]Amiran, R. (1965). The beginnings of pottery-making in the Near East. In F. R. Matson (Ed.), *Ceramics and man* (pp. 240–247). Viking Fund Publications in Anthropology, 41.

primary innovation The creation, invention, or chance discovery of a completely new idea, method, or device.
secondary innovation A new and deliberate application or modification of an existing idea, method, or device.

A Hopi woman firing pottery vessels. The discovery that firing clay vessels makes them more durable probably came about when clay-lined basins next to cooking fires in the Middle East were accidentally fired.

© Stephen Trimble

surface on a vertical rotating shaft—an application of a known principle used for drills—creating the potter's wheel and permitting mass production. Kilns, too, were modified for better heat circulation by separating the firing chamber from the fire itself. By chance, these improved kilns produced enough heat to smelt metal ores such as copper, tin, gold, silver, and lead. Presumably, this discovery was made by accident—another primary innovation—and set the stage for the eventual development of the forced-draft furnace out of the earlier pottery kiln.

The accidents responsible for primary innovations are not generated by environmental change or some other need, nor are they necessarily adaptive (see Figure 15.1). They are, however, given structure by the cultural context. Thus, the outcome of the discovery of fired clay by migratory food foragers 25,000 years ago was very different from what it was when discovered later by more sedentary farmers in Southwest Asia, where it set off a cultural chain reaction as one invention led to another. Indeed, given particular sets of cultural goals, values, and knowledge, certain innovations are nearly inevitable.

Although a culture's internal dynamics may encourage certain innovative tendencies, they may discourage or remain neutral about others. Indeed, Polish astronomer Nicolaus Copernicus' discovery of the rotation of the planets around the sun and the European botanist Gregor Mendel's discovery of the basic laws of heredity are instances of genuine creative insights out of step with the established needs, values, and goals of their times and places. In fact, Mendel's work remained obscure until 16 years after his death, when three scien-

Things invented for one particular purpose may come to serve other, quite unrelated purposes. In England researchers from the University of Liverpool found men using their mobile phones as display pieces to advertise to women their status and desirability as potential mates.

tists working independently rediscovered, all in the same year (1900), the same laws of heredity. Thus, in the context of turn-of-the-century Western culture, Mendel's laws were bound to be discovered, even if Mendel's experiments had not revealed them earlier.

Although an innovation must be reasonably consistent with a society's needs, values, and goals in order to gain acceptance, it takes more than this. Force of custom or habit tends to obstruct ready acceptance of the new or unfamiliar, for people typically stick with what they are used to rather than adopt something strange that requires adjustment on their part. An example of this can be seen in the continued use of the QWERTY keyboard, named for the lineup of the top row of letters and familiar to all who use English language keyboards today. Devised in 1874, the QWERTY system's overall arrangement of letters minimized jamming. This, combined with other desirable mechanical features, helped it to become the first commercially successful typewriter. Yet, the QWERTY keyboard has a number of serious drawbacks. The more typing one can do in the "home row" (second from bottom) of keys, the faster one can type, with the fewest errors and least strain on the fingers. But with QWERTY, only 32 percent of strokes are done on the home row, versus 52 percent on the upper row and 16 percent on the (hardest) bottom row. What's more, it requires overuse of the weaker (left) hand and the weakest (fifth) finger.

In 1932, after extensive study, U.S. education professor August Dvorak developed a keyboard that avoids

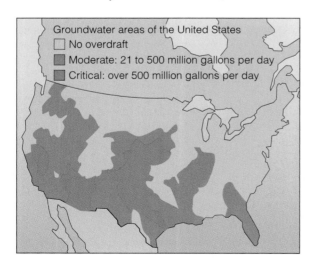

FIGURE 15.1

Human practices may or may not be adaptive. In the United States, for example, it is not adaptive over the long run to deplete groundwater in regions of fast-growing populations, yet this does not stop people from doing this.

FIGURE 15.2
Dvorak and QWERTY keyboards, compared. Although superior to the latter in virtually every way, Dvorak has not been adopted owing to the head start enjoyed by QWERTY.

the defects of QWERTY (Figure 15.2). Consistently, tests have shown that the Dvorak keyboard can be learned in one-third the time it takes to master QWERTY. Moreover, once learned, the Dvorak system is less fatiguing and increases the average keyboard operator's accuracy by 68 percent and speed by 74 percent. So why has not Dvorak replaced QWERTY? The answer is commitment. Because QWERTY had a head start, by the time Dvorak came along manufacturers, typists, teachers, salespeople, and office managers were committed to the old keyboard. It was what they were used to—and it remains the standard on English language keyboards to this day.[3]

---

[3]Diamond, J. (1997). The curse of QWERTY. *Discover, 18*(4), 34–42.

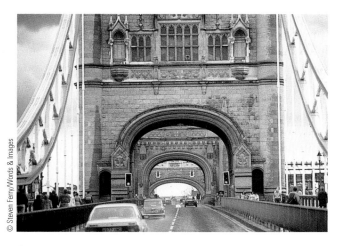

Once one's reflexes become adjusted to doing something one way, it becomes difficult to do it differently. Thus, when a North American goes to Great Britain, or vice versa, learning to drive on the "wrong" side of the road is difficult.

Obviously, an innovation is not assured of acceptance simply because it is notably better than the thing, method, or idea it might replace. Much may depend on the prestige of the innovator and potential adopters. If the innovator's prestige is high, this will help gain more general acceptance for the innovation. If it is low, acceptance is less likely, unless the innovator can attract a sponsor who has high prestige.

Diffusion

When the Pilgrims established their colony of New Plymouth in North America, they very likely would have starved to death had the Indians not showed them how to grow the crop native to North America: corn. The spread of certain ideas, customs, or practices from one culture to another is known as **diffusion.** So common is cross-cultural borrowing that the late Ralph Linton, a North American anthropologist, suggested that it accounts for as much as 90 percent of any culture's content. People are creative about their borrowing, however, picking and choosing from multiple possibilities and sources. Usually their selections are limited to those compatible with the existing culture. In Guatemala in the 1960s, for example, Maya Indians, who then (as now) made up more than half of that country's population, would adopt Western ways if the practical advantage of what they adopted was self-evident and did not conflict with deeply rooted traditional values and

diffusion The spread of certain ideas, customs, or practices from one culture to another.

© 1995 Karen Tranberg Hansen

The way people creatively shape things borrowed from other cultures to make them distinctively their own is illustrated by the way these teenage boys in the African country, Zambia, reconfigure used clothing imported from the United States.

customs. The use of metal hoes, shovels, and machetes became standard early on, for they are superior to stone tools and yet compatible with the cultivation of corn in the traditional way by men using hand tools.

Yet, certain other modern practices that might seem advantageous to the Maya were resisted if they were perceived to be in conflict with Indian tradition. Pursuing these practices could make one a social outcast. This happened to a young farmer who tried his hand at growing vegetables to sell, using chemical fertilizers and pesticides to grow cash crops not eaten by the Maya and having market value only in the city. Following this line of work, he found he could not secure a "good" woman for a wife—a "good" woman being one who has never had sex with another man and is hard-working, skilled at domestic chores, and willing to attend to her husband's needs. However, after abandoning his unorthodox ways, he gained acceptance in his community as a "real" man—one who provides for his household by working steadily at farming and making charcoal in the traditional ways. No longer conspicuous as someone different from other local men, he married well within a short time.[4]

The tendency toward cultural borrowing is so great that it prompted anthropologist Robert Lowie to comment that culture is a thing of shreds and patches. That said, borrowed traits usually undergo sufficient modifications to make this wry comment more colorful than accurate. Moreover, existing cultural traits may be modified to fit better with a borrowed one. An awareness of the extent of cultural borrowing can be eye opening. Take, for example, the numerous things that people all around the globe have borrowed from American Indians. Domestic plants developed ("invented") by the Indians— potatoes, avocados, beans, squash, tomatoes, peanuts, manioc, chili peppers, chocolate, sweet potatoes, and last but not least corn or maize, to name a few—furnish a major portion of the world's food supply. In fact, American Indians are recognized as primary contributors to the world's varied cuisine and credited with developing the largest array of nutritious foods.[5]

As for drugs and stimulants introduced by Indians, tobacco is the best known (Figure 15.3), but others include the coca in cocaine, ephedra in ephedrine, datura in pain relievers, and cascara in laxatives. Early on, Europeans discovered that Indians had a most sophisticated pharmacy. For instance, Spanish Jesuit missionaries in Peru and Ecuador in the 17th century learned from indigenous healers about the medicinal properties of the bitter tree bark of which quinine is extracted to treat malaria. All told, 200 plants and herbs used by Native Americans for medicinal purposes have at one time or another been included in the *Pharmacopeia of the United States* or in the *National Formulary*. On top of this, varieties of cotton developed by Indians supply much of the world's clothing needs, while the woolen poncho, the parka, and moccasins are universally familiar items. These borrowings are so thoroughly integrated into contemporary societies across the globe that few people are aware of their source.

Despite the obvious importance of diffusion, an innovation from another culture probably faces more obstacles when it comes to being accepted than does one that is "homegrown" simply because it is foreign. In the United States, for example, this is one reason why people have been so reluctant to abandon completely the awkward and cumbersome old English system of weights and measures for the far more logical metric system. While all other countries in the world have essentially converted to metric, in the United States the switchover is still less than about 50 percent. Hence, ethnocentrism may act as a barrier to cultural borrowing.

[4]Reina, R. E. (1966). *The law of the saints* (pp. 65–68). Indianapolis: Bobbs-Merrill.

[5]Weatherford, J. (1988). *Indian givers: How the Indians of the Americas transformed the New World* (p. 115). New York: Ballantine.

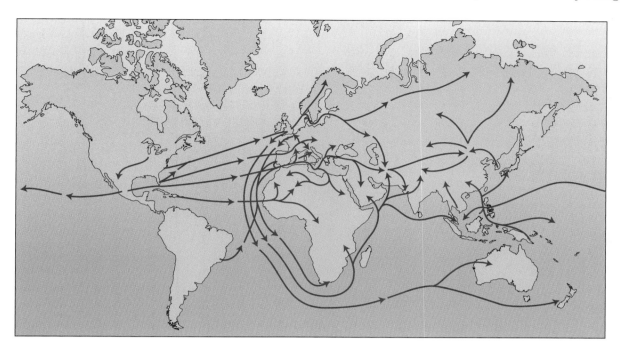

FIGURE 15.3

The diffusion of tobacco. Having spread from the tropics of the Western Hemisphere to much of the rest of North and South America, it spread rapidly to the rest of the world after explorer Christopher Columbus crossed the Atlantic in 1492.

While cultural change may have unanticipated consequences, so may resistance to change. The U.S. reluctance to adopt the metric system led to a spacecraft crash on Mars. One set of engineers was using the metric system, while another used the old English system.

Cultural Loss

Most often people look at cultural change as an accumulation of innovations. A little reflection, however, leads to the realization that frequently the acceptance of a new innovation results in **cultural loss**—the abandonment of an existing practice or trait. For example, in ancient times chariots and carts were used widely in northern Africa and southwestern Asia, but wheeled vehicles virtually disappeared from Morocco to Afghanistan about 1,500 years ago. They were replaced by camels, not because of some reversion to the past but because camels used as pack animals worked better. The old Roman Empire roads had deteriorated, and these sturdy animals traveled well with or without roads. Their endurance, longevity, and ability to ford rivers and traverse rough ground made pack camels admirably suited for the region. Plus, they were economical in terms of labor: A wagon required a man for every two draft animals, but a single person could manage up to six pack camels. Reflecting on this, biologist Stephen Jay Gould commented that this surprises most Westerners because:

cultural loss The abandonment of an existing practice or trait.

New inventions may result in unexpected cultural change, as microwave ovens have contributed to the demise of family meals in the United States.

© Dion Ogust/The Image Works

Wheels have come to symbolize in our culture . . . intelligent exploitation and technological progress. . . . The success of camels reemphasizes a fundamental theme. . . . Adaptation, be it biological or cultural, represents a better fit to specific, local environments, not an inevitable stage in a ladder of progress. Wheels were a formidable invention, and their uses are manifold (potters and millers did not abandon them, even when cartwrights were eclipsed). But camels may work better in some circumstances. Wheels, like wings, fins, and brains, are exquisite devices for certain purposes, not signs of intrinsic superiority.[6]

Often overlooked is another facet of losing apparently useful traits: loss without replacement. An example of this is the historical absence of boats among the indigenous inhabitants of the Canary Islands, a group of small islands isolated off North Africa's Atlantic coast. The ancestors of these people must have had boats, for without them they could never have transported themselves and their domestic livestock to the islands in the first place. Later, without boats, they had no way to communicate between islands or with the mainland. This loss of

something useful came about due to the islands' lack of stone suitable for making polished stone axes, which in turn limited the islanders' carpentry.[7]

REPRESSIVE CHANGE

Innovation, diffusion, and cultural loss all may take place among peoples who are free to decide for themselves what changes they will or will not accept. Not always, however, do people have the liberty to make their own choices. Frequently, changes they would not willingly make themselves have been forced upon them by some other group, usually in the course of conquest and colonialism. A direct outcome in many cases is a phenomenon anthropologists call acculturation.

Acculturation

Acculturation is the massive cultural change that occurs in a society when it experiences intensive firsthand contact with a more powerful society. It always involves an element of force, either directly, as in conquests, or indirectly, as in the implicit or explicit threat that force will be used if people refuse to make the demanded changes. Other variables include degree of cultural difference; circumstances, intensity, frequency, and hostility of contact; relative status of the agents of contact; who is dominant and who is submissive; and whether the nature of the flow is reciprocal or nonre-

---

[6]Gould, S. J. (1983). *Hens' teeth and horses' toes* (p. 159). New York: Norton.

acculturation Massive cultural changes that people are forced to make as a consequence of intensive firsthand contact between their own group and another, often more powerful, society.

---

[7]Coon, C. S. (1954). *The story of man* (p. 174). New York: Knopf.

ciprocal. *Acculturation* and *diffusion* are not equivalent terms; one culture can borrow from another without being in the least acculturated.

In the course of cultural contact, any one of a number of things may happen. Merger or fusion occurs when two cultures lose their separate identities and form a single culture, as historically expressed by the melting pot ideology of English-speaking Protestant Euroamerican culture in the United States. Sometimes, though, one of the cultures loses its autonomy but retains its identity as a subculture in the form of a caste, class, or ethnic group. This is typical of conquest or slavery situations, and the United States has examples of this in spite of its melting pot ideology—we need look no further than the nearest American Indian reservation. In virtually all parts of the world today, people are faced with the tragedy of forced removal from their traditional homelands, as entire communities are uprooted to make way for hydroelectric projects, grazing lands for cattle, mining operations, or highway construction. In Brazil's rush to develop the vast Amazon rainforest, for instance, entire indigenous communities have been relocated to "national parks," where resources are inadequate for the number of people and where former enemies are often forced to live in close proximity.

Cultural extinction typically occurs when so many carriers of a culture die that those who manage to survive become refugees, living among peoples of different cultures. Examples of this may be seen in many parts of the world today (Figure 15.4). A particularly well-documented case occurred in Brazil's Amazon basin in 1968, when developers hired killers to wipe out several Indian groups, using arsenic, dynamite, and machine guns from light planes. Violence continues to be used in Brazil as a means of dealing with indigenous peoples (see Original Study, page 418). For example, according to conservative estimates, at least 1,500 Yanomami died in the 1980s, many the victims of deliberate massacres, as cattle ranchers and gold miners poured into northern Brazil. By 1990, 70 percent of Yanomami land in Brazil had been illegally expropriated; fish supplies were poisoned by mercury contamination of rivers; and malaria, venereal disease, and tuberculosis were running rampant. The Yanomami were dying at the rate of 10 percent a year, and their fertility had dropped to near zero. Many villages were left with no children or old

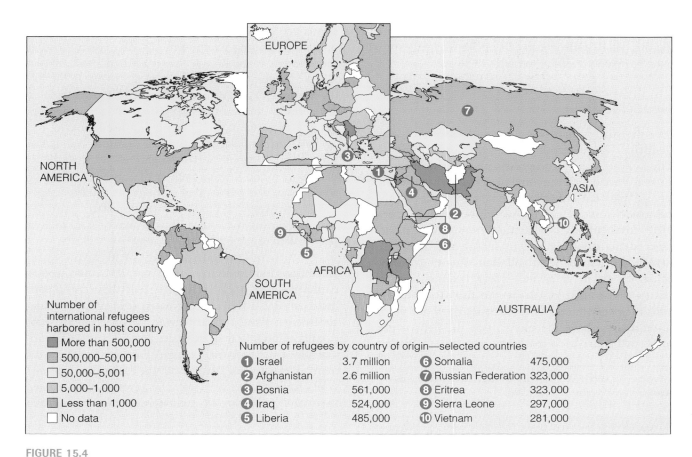

FIGURE 15.4

Increasing refugee populations, a consequence of conflict between nationalities living in multinational states, have become a burden and source of instability in the states to which they have fled.

people, and the survivors awaited their fate with a profound terror of extinction.[8]

The typical attitude of Brazilians toward such situations is illustrated by their government's reaction to a diplomatic journey that two Kayapó Indians and an anthropologist made to the United States. They ventured north to speak with World Bank authorities and various government officials in the U.S. Congress and State Department concerning the destruction of their land and way of life caused by internationally financed development projects. All three were charged with violating Brazil's Foreign Sedition Act. This charge and other relevant atrocities provoked international outrage, which in turn prompted Brazilian authorities to recommend policy changes that could favorably impact the country's indigenous peoples. However, whether their recommendations will be sufficient to effect positive change, or will even be acted upon fully, remains to be seen.

Genocide

The Brazilian Indian case just cited raises the issue of **genocide**—the extermination of one people by another, often in the name of progress, either as a deliberate act or as the accidental outcome of activities carried out by one people with little regard for their impact on others. Genocide is not new in the world. In North America in 1637, for example, a deliberate attempt was made to destroy the Pequot Indians by setting afire their village at Mystic, Connecticut, and then shooting down all those—primarily unarmed elders, women, and children—who sought to escape the fire. To ensure that even their very memory would be stamped out, colonial authorities forbade the mention of the Pequot name.

---

[8]Turner, T. (1991). Major shift in Brazilian Yanomami policy. *Anthropology Newsletter, 32*(5), 1, 46.

> **genocide** The extermination of one people by another, often in the name of progress, either as a deliberate act or as the accidental outcome of activities carried out by one people with little regard for their impact on others.

Several other massacres of Indian peoples occurred thereafter, up until the last one at Wounded Knee, South Dakota, in 1890.

Of course, such acts were by no means restricted to North America. One of the most famous 19th-century acts of genocide was the extermination of the indigenous inhabitants of Tasmania, a large island just south of Australia. In this case, the use of military force failed to achieve the complete elimination of the Tasmanians, but what the military could not achieve, an English Protestant missionary could. George Augustus Robinson managed to round up the surviving natives and bring them to his mission station. Once there, the deadly combination of psychological depression and European diseases brought about the demise of the last full-blooded Tasmanians in time for Robinson to retire to England a moderately wealthy man.

The most widely known act of genocide in recent history was the attempt of the Nazi Germans during World War II to wipe out European Jews and Roma (gypsies) in the name of racial superiority and "improvement" of the human species. Unfortunately, the common practice of referring to this as *"the* Holocaust"—as if it were something unique, or at least exceptional—tends to blind us to the fact that this thoroughly monstrous act is one example of an all-too-common phenomenon. Among many examples of mass murder in more recent years, Khmer Rouge soldiers in Cambodia killed 1.7 million fellow citizens in the 1970s. In the following decade, government-sponsored terrorism against indigenous communities in Guatemala reached its height, and the Iraqi government used poison gas against Kurdish villagers. In the 1990s, more than half a million Tutsi people were slaughtered by their Hutu neighbors in the African country of Rwanda, and today the Russian army is waging war against Chechen separatists who want an independent homeland. Estimates vary, but during the 20th century, as many as 83 million people died of genocide and tyranny.[9]

If such ugly practices are ever to end, we must gain a better understanding of what is behind them. Anthropologists are actively engaged in this, carrying out cross-cultural as well as specific case studies. One finding to emerge is the regularity with which religious, economic, and political interests are allied in cases of genocide. In Tasmania, for example, British wool growers wanted indigenous peoples off the island so that they could have it for their sheep. The government advanced their interests through its military campaigns against the

---

[9]White, M. (2001). *Historical atlas of the twentieth century.* http://users.erols.com/mwhite28/20centry.htm; see also Van Den Berghe, P. (1992). The modern state: Nation builder or nation killer? *International Journal of Group Tensions, 22*(3), 198.

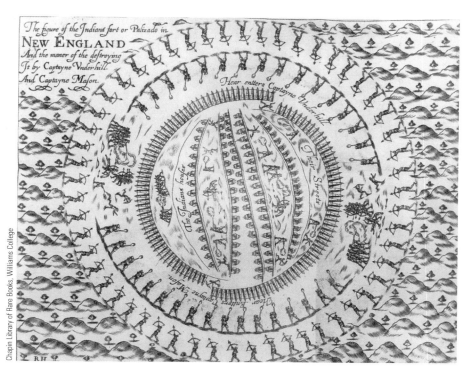

Genocide is not new in the world; this 1638 illustration shows English colonists with their Narragansett allies (the outer ring of bowmen) shooting down Pequot Indian women, children, and unarmed men attempting to flee their burning homes.

VISUAL COUNTERPOINT Two of many examples of attempted genocide in the 20th century: Hitler's Germany against Jews and gypsies in the 1930s and the 1940s; and Hutus against Tutsis in Rwanda, as in this 1994 massacre.

In Namibia, Bushmen from the Kalahari Desert were collected in settlements like Tsumkwe, shown here. Deprived of the means to secure their own necessities in life, such people commonly lapse into apathy and depression.

natives, but it was Robinson's missionary work that finally secured Tasmania for the commercial wool interests.

In another part of the world during the 1960s and 1970s, the Ju/'hoansi bushmen of Namibia in southern Africa found themselves in a situation remarkably similar to that experienced by the Tasmanians. Victimized by a combination of religious (Dutch Reformed Church), political (Namibia's Department of Nature Conservation), and economic (agricultural/pastoral and tourism) interests, the Ju/'hoansi were forced into confinement on a reserve where disease and apathy caused death rates to outstrip birthrates. Other such cases might be cited, but the latter one is important, for it illustrates that genocide is not always a deliberate act. It can occur as the unforeseen outcome of activities carried out with little regard for their impact on other peoples. For the people whose lives are snuffed out, however, it makes no difference whether or not the genocide is intentional, for either way they face the same deadly outcome.

Directed Change

The most extreme cases of acculturation occur as a result of military conquest or massive invasion and breaking up of traditional political structures by dominant newcomers who know or care nothing about the culture they control. The indigenous people, unable to resist effec-

tively changes imposed on them and obstructed in carrying out many of their traditional social, religious, and economic activities, may be forced into new practices that tend to isolate individuals and destroy the integrity of their societies. So it was with the Ju/'hoansi of Namibia, noted above. Rounded up in the early 1960s, these Bushmen were confined to a reservation in Tsumkwe where they could not possibly provide for their own needs. The government provided them with rations, but these were insufficient to meet basic nutritional needs. In poor health and prevented from developing meaningful alternatives to traditional activities, the Ju/'hoansi became argumentative and depressed, and, as already noted, their death rate came to exceed birthrates. After a visit to the reserve in 1980, Namibian anthropologist Robert J. Gordon commented: "I had never been in a place where one could literally smell death and decay, as in Tsumkwe."[10] Within the next few years, however, surviving Ju/'hoansi began to take matters into their own hands. They returned to water holes in their traditional homeland, where, assisted by anthropologists and others concerned with their welfare, they are trying to sustain themselves by raising livestock. Whether this will succeed or not remains to be seen, as there are still many obstacles to success.

MEDIATREK

For up-to-date news concerning directed change efforts in the areas of peace building, antiracism, women's rights, and environmental protection, go to MediaTrek 15.2 on the companion Web site or CD-ROM.

---

[10]Gordon, R. J. (1992). *The Bushman myth: The making of a Namibian underclass* (p. 3). Boulder, CO: Westview Press.

One by-product of colonial dealings with indigenous peoples has been the growth of *applied anthropology*, defined in Chapter 1 as the use of anthropological techniques and knowledge for the purpose of solving practical problems. For example, in the United States, the Bureau of American Ethnology was founded in 1876 to gather reliable data the government might use to formulate Indian policies. At the time, anthropologists were convinced of the practicality of their discipline, and many who did ethnographic work among Indians devoted a great deal of time, energy, and even money to assisting their informants, whose interests were frequently threatened from outside.

In the 20th century, the scope and intent of applied anthropology as a form of social engineering broadened. In the first part of that century, the applied work of Franz Boas—who almost single-handedly trained a generation of anthropologists in the United States—proved instrumental in reforming the country's immigration policies. With impressive statistical data based on comparative skull measurements, this German Jewish immigrant challenged popular race theories of the day. He demonstrated that theories privileging non-Jewish immigrants from western Europe and discriminating against Jews and others deemed undesirable as newcomers in the United States were based not on fact but on deeply rooted racial prejudice. In the 1930s, anthropologists with clearly pragmatic objectives did a number of studies in industrial and other institutional settings in the United States. With World War II came increased involvement at colonial administration beyond U.S. borders, especially in the Pacific, by American officers trained in anthropology. The rapid postwar recovery of Japan was due in no small measure to the influence of anthropologists in structuring the U.S. occupation. Anthropologists continue to play an active role today in administering U.S. trust territories in the Pacific.

All too often, however, states and other powerful institutions directly meddling in the affairs of different ethnic groups or foreign societies fail to seek professional advice from anthropologists who possess relevant cross-cultural expertise and deeper insights. Such failures have contributed to a host of avoidable errors in planning and executing nation-building programs in ethnically divided countries such as Iraq and Afghanistan, both of which are now devastated by war and violence.

MEDIATREK

To learn about international efforts toward sustainable development, go to MediaTrek 15.3 on the companion Web site or CD-ROM.

Today, applied anthropologists are in growing demand in the field of international development because of their specialized knowledge of social structure, value systems, and the functional interrelatedness of cultures targeted for development. Development anthropologists face a particular challenge: As anthropologists, they are bound to respect other peoples' dignity and cultural integrity, yet they are asked for advice on how to change certain aspects of those cultures. If the request comes from the people themselves, that is one thing, but more often than not, it comes from outsiders. Supposedly, the proposed change is for the good of the targeted population, yet members of that community do not always see it that way. Just how far applied anthropologists should go in advising outsiders how to manipulate people—especially those without the power to resist—to embrace changes proposed for them is a serious ethical question.

In direct response to such critical questions concerning the application and benefits of anthropological research, an alternative type of practical anthropology has emerged during the last half century. Known by a variety of names—including action anthropology and committed, engaged, involved, and advocacy anthropology—this involves community-based research and action in collaboration and solidarity with indigenous societies, ethnic minorities, and other besieged or repressed groups.

In sum, the practical application of anthropology is thriving today as never before. As the Anthropology Applied features throughout this book illustrate, anthropologists now practice their profession in many different nonacademic settings, both at home and abroad.

REACTIONS TO REPRESSIVE CHANGE

The reactions of indigenous peoples to the changes outsiders have thrust upon them have varied considerably. Some have responded by moving to the nearest available forest, desert, or other remote places in hopes of being left alone. In Brazil, a number of communities once located near the coast took this option a few hundred years ago and were successful until the great push to develop the Amazon forest began in the 1960s. Others, like many Indians of North America, took up arms to fight back but were ultimately forced to sign treaties and surrender much of their ancestral lands, after which they were reduced to an impoverished underclass in their own land. Today, they continue to fight to retain their identities as distinct peoples through nonmilitary means and seek to regain control over natural resources on their lands.

Anthropology Applied

Development Anthropology and Dams

Over a 35-year career in scholarly and applied work, Michael M. Horowitz, president and executive director of the Institute for Development Anthropology (IDA) and Distinguished Professor of Anthropology at the State University of New York at Binghamton, has made pioneering contributions to applied anthropology. His work has focused on achieving equitable economic growth, environmental sustainability, conflict resolution, and participatory government in the former colonial world.

Since co-founding IDA in 1976, Horowitz has been its principal leader. He has played a key role in bringing anthropology forward as an applied science in international development organizations such as the World Bank, the United Nations Food and Agriculture Organization, the UN Fund for Women, and the US Agency for International Development (USAID), as well as nongovernmental organizations (NGOs) such as Oxfam and the International Union for the Conservation of Nature. He has mentored several generations of young scholars and professionals—paying particular attention to those from developing countries—encouraging the application of anthropology's comparative and holistic methodologies and theories to empower low-income majorities in the so-called underdeveloped world.

Local woman eats her breakfast overlooking the ship locks of China's Three Gorges hydroelectric dam on the Yangtze River. Under construction since 1992 and due for completion in 2009, the dam has been controversial since its inception, raising concerns among environmentalists around the world, not to mention among peasant farmers living downstream. If completed, the dam will result in the largest forced displacement of people in the world's history. Close to two million people must be relocated to make way for its 365-mile-long reservoir, and bitter complaints abound among those who have already been moved. *Unlike* the dam described in this Anthropology Applied box, not one social scientist was consulted in the planning and assessment phase of Three Gorges Dam.

Horowitz's work with pastoralists and floodplain dwellers has had substantial positive impact on the well-being of small producers and small landholders in developing countries. A clear example of this is the impact of his work on the lives and livelihoods of people living downstream of a hydropower dam in West Africa. Beginning in the 1980s, he and his IDA team carried out rigorous anthropological research along the Senegal River, which flows through Mali, Senegal, and Mauritania. Their study showed that traditional, pre-dam,

flood-recession farming yielded better results than irrigated agriculture and was better for the environment. This finding influenced decisions made by these countries and affiliated NGOs to manage the system with a controlled release from the Manatali Dam in Mali in order to reproduce as much as possible the pre-dam flow system. Horowitz's long-term field research demonstrated that seasonal flooding would provide economic, environmental, and sociocultural benefits for nearly a million small producers.

Recognized by national governments, NGOs, and development funding agencies, the work of Horowitz and his IDA colleagues on the Senegal River Basin Monitoring Activity (SRBMA) was a breakthrough in the concepts of resettlement and river management, and it continues to influence development policy. Prior to IDA's work in West Africa, no hydropower dam had ever been managed with a controlled flood. Since then, IDA has been asked to help apply the SRMBA model to other parts of the world, including the lower Zambezi River in Mozambique and the Mekong River in Laos, Cambodia, and Vietnam. *(Adapted from W. Young. (Ed.). (2000). Kimball Award winner. Anthropology News, 41(8), 29, with update based on personal communication with IDA, November 2003.)* ■ ■ ■

When people are able to hold on to some of their traditions in the face of powerful outside domination, the result may be **syncretism**—a blending of indigenous and foreign traits to form a new system. A fine illustration of

this is the game of cricket as played by the Trobriand Islanders of Melanesia, some of whose practices we looked at in earlier chapters. When Trobrianders were under British rule, missionaries introduced them to this rather quiet and composed British game to replace the erotic dancing and open sexuality that normally followed the yam harvests. Traditionally, this was the season when chiefs sought to spread their fame by hosting nights of

syncretism In acculturation, the blending of indigenous and foreign traits to form a new system.

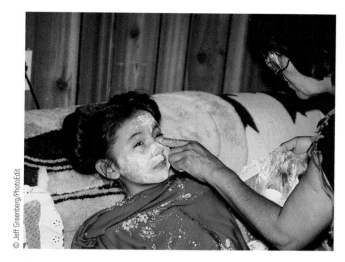

An example of syncretism. Although the Hopi Indians have adopted a number of items from Euroamericans (note the glasses and electrical outlet), such "borrowed" things are combined with traditional ones, as in the ritual use of cornmeal, here being applied to a young girl as required by ancient tradition.

dancing, providing food for the hundreds of young married people who participated. For several months, there would be night after night of provocative dancing, accompanied by chanting and shouting full of sexual innuendo, each night ending as couples disappeared into the bush together. Since no chief wished to be outdone by any other (being outdone brought into question the strength of one's magic), the dancing had a strong competitive element, and fighting sometimes erupted. To the British Protestant missionaries, cricket seemed a good way to end all of this in a way that would encourage conformity to "civilized" comportment in dress, religion, and sportsmanship. The Trobrianders, however, were determined to

"rubbish" (throw out) the British rules of the game. They did this by turning it into the same kind of distinctly Trobriand event that their thrilling dance competitions had once been.

Making cricket their own, Trobrianders added battle dress and battle magic and incorporated erotic dancing into the festivities. Instead of inviting dancers each night, chiefs now arrange games of cricket. Pitching has been modified from the British style to one closer to their old way of throwing a spear. Following the game, they hold massive feasts, where wealth is displayed to enhance their prestige. Cricket, in its altered form, has been made to serve traditional systems of prestige and exchange. Neither primitive nor passively accepted in its original form, Trobriand cricket was thoughtfully and creatively adapted into a sophisticated activity reflecting the importance of basic indigenous cultural premises. Exuberance and pride are displayed by everyone associated with the game, and the players are as much concerned with conveying the full meaning of who they are as with scoring well. From the sensual dressing in preparation for the game to the team chanting of songs full of sexual metaphors to erotic chorus-line dancing between the innings, it is clear that each participant is playing for his own importance, for the fame of his team, and for the hundreds of attractive young women who usually watch the game.

Revitalization Movements

Another common reaction to repressive change is revitalization. As noted in Chapter 13, revitalization movements are efforts toward radical cultural reforms in response to widespread social disruption and collective feelings of anxiety and despair. When primary ties of culture, social

Indigenous peoples have reacted to colonialism in many different ways. When British missionaries pressed Trobriand Islanders of Melanesia to celebrate yam harvests with a game of cricket rather than traditional erotic dances, Trobrianders responded by transforming the staid British sport into an exuberant event that featured sexual chants and dances between innings.

relationships, and activities are broken and meaningless activity is imposed by outside forces, individuals and groups characteristically react with a rejection of newly introduced cultural elements, reclamation of historical roots and traditional identity, as well as spiritual imagination. Some of these revitalization movements take on a revolutionary character, as did the Taliban in Afghanistan.

In the United States, revitalization movements have occurred often—whenever significant segments of the population have found their conditions in life to be at odds with the values of the American Dream. For example, in the 19th century, periodic depression and the disillusionment that lingered for decades after the Civil War produced a host of revitalization movements, the most successful being that of the Mormons. In the 20th century, movements sprang up repeatedly in the slums of major cities, as well as in depressed rural areas such as Appalachia. By the 1960s, a number of movements were becoming less inward looking and more activist, a good example being the rise of the Black Muslim movement. The 1960s also saw the rise of revitalization movements among the young of middle-class and even upper-class families. In their case, the professed cultural values of peace, equality, and individual freedom were seen to be at odds with the realities of persistent war, poverty, and constraints on individual action imposed by a variety of impersonal institutions. Youths countered these realities by advocating free love, joining hippie communes, celebrating new forms of rock and folk music, using mind-altering drugs, challenging authority, growing their hair long, and wearing unconventional clothes.

By the 1980s revitalization movements were becoming prominent even among older, more affluent segments of society, as in the rise of the so-called religious right. In these cases, the reaction is not so much against a perceived failure of the American Dream as it is against perceived threats to that dream by dissenters and activists within their society, by foreign governments, by new ideas that challenge other ideas they prefer to believe, and by the sheer complexity of modern life.

Clearly, when value systems get out of step with existing realities, for whatever reason, a condition of cultural crisis is likely to build up that may breed some forms of reactive movement. Not all suppressed, conquered, or colonized people eventually rebel against established authority, although why they do not is still a debated issue. When they do, however, cultural resistance may take one of several forms, all of which are varieties of revitalization movements. A culture may seek to speed up the acculturation process to share more fully in the supposed benefits of the dominant cultures.

> **rebellion** Organized armed resistance to an established government or authority in power.

© Bettmann/Corbis

Revitalization movements that attempt to revive traditional ways of the past are not restricted to "underdeveloped" countries; in the United States, the Reverend Pat Robertson is a leader in such a movement.

Melanesian cargo cults of the post–World War II era generally have been of this sort, although earlier ones stressed a revival of traditional ways. Sometimes, a movement tries to reconstitute a destroyed but not yet forgotten way of life, as did many Plains Indians with the Ghost Dance in the late 19th century and as do movements of the religious right today. Sometimes, a suppressed pariah group, which has long suffered in an inferior social standing and which has its own special subcultural ideology, attempts to create a new social order; the most familiar examples of this to Western peoples are prophetic Judaism and early Christianity.

REBELLION AND REVOLUTION

When the scale of discontent within a society reaches a certain level, the possibilities are high for **rebellion**— organized armed resistance to an established government or authority in power. For instance, there have been many peasant rebellions around the world in the course of history. Often, such rebellions are triggered by repressive regimes imposing new taxes on the already struggling small farmers unable to feed their families under such unacceptable levels of exploitation. One example is the ongoing Zapatista Maya Indian uprising in southern Mexico. This rebellion involves thousands of small Indian farmers whose livelihoods have been threatened by the changes imposed on them and whose rights under the Mexican constitution have never been fully implemented.

In contrast to rebellions, which have rather limited objectives, revolutions involve a more radical turnover. When the level of discontent is very high, it may lead to **revolution**—a radical change in a society or culture. In the political arena, revolution refers to the forced overthrow of an old government and the establishment of a completely new one. Such was the case when Muslim fundamentalists in Iran toppled the imperial regime of the shah in 1979 and replaced him with Ayatollah Khomeini, a high-ranking Shiite Muslim religious leader who returned to his homeland from exile and became Iran's new leader.

The question of why revolutions erupt, as well as why they frequently fail to live up to the expectations of the people initiating them, is unsolved. It is clear, however, that the colonial policies of countries such as Britain, France, Spain, Portugal, and the United States during the 19th and early 20th centuries have created a worldwide situation in which revolution is nearly inevitable. Despite the political independence most colonies have gained since World War II, more powerful countries continue to exploit many of these "underdeveloped" countries for their natural resources and cheap labor, causing a deep resentment of rulers beholden to foreign powers. Further discontent has been caused as governing elites in newly independent states try to assert their control over peoples living within their boundaries. By virtue of a common ancestry, possession of distinct cultures, persistent occupation of their own territories, and traditions of self-determination, the peoples they aim to control identify themselves as distinct nations and refuse to recognize the legitimacy of what they regard as a foreign government.

Thus, in many a former colony, large numbers of people have taken up arms to resist annexation and absorption by imposed state governments run by people of other nationalities. As they attempt to make their multi-ethnic states into unified countries, ruling elites of one nationality set about stripping the peoples of other nations within their states of their lands, resources, and particular cultural identities. The phenomenon is so common that it led anthropologist Pierre Van Den Berghe to label what modern states refer to as "nation building" as, in fact, "nation killing."[11] One of the most

© Jose Guterres/Getty Images

In many countries of the world, governments directed by people of one nation frequently use repression to control people of other nations within the state. This frequently results in internal warfare as in the case of East Timor, whose people recently gained their independence from Indonesia.

important facts of our time is that the vast majority of the distinct peoples of the world have never consented to rule by the governments of states within which they find themselves living.[12] In many a newly emerged country, such peoples feel they have no other option than to fight.

From an examination of various revolutions of the past, the following conditions have been offered as causes of rebellion and revolution:

1. Loss of prestige of established authority, often from the failure of foreign policy, financial difficulties, dismissals of popular ministers, or alteration of popular policies.

2. Threat to recent economic improvement. In France and Russia, sections of the population (professional classes and urban workers) whose economic fortunes previously had taken an upward swing were radicalized by unexpected setbacks, such as steeply rising food prices and unemployment.

3. Government indecisiveness, as exemplified by a lack of consistent policy. Such governments appear to be controlled by, rather than in control of, events.

---

[11]Van Den Berghe, P. (1992). The modern state: Nation builder or nation killer? *International Journal of Group Tensions, 22*(3), 191–207.

[12]Nietschmann, B. (1987). The third world war. *Cultural Survival Quarterly, 11*(3), 3.

revolution Radical change in a society or culture. In the political arena, it refers to the forced overthrow of an old government and establishment of a completely new one.

© Reuters/Corbis

Slobodan Milosovic, deposed president of the Yugoslav Republic on trial for war crimes in the International Court of Justice in The Hague, Netherlands. This Serbian strongman is accused of ethnic cleansing and mass murder of ethnic Bosnians, Croatians, and Kosovo Albanians seeking independence.

4. Loss of support from the intellectual class. Such a loss deprived the prerevolutionary governments of France and Russia of philosophical support and popularity among the literate public.

5. A leader or group of leaders with enough charisma, or popular appeal, to mobilize a substantial part of the population against the establishment.

Apart from resistance to internal authority, such as in the Chinese, French, and Russian revolutions, many revolutions in modern times have been struggles against an authority imposed by outsiders. Such resistance usually takes the form of independence movements that wage campaigns of armed defiance against colonial powers. The Algerian struggle for independence from France is a relevant example. Of the hundreds of armed conflicts in the world today, almost all are in the economically poor countries of Africa, Asia, Central and South America, many of which were at one time under European colonial domination (Figure 15.5). Of these wars, the majority are between the state and one or more nations or ethnic groups within the state's borders who are seeking to maintain or regain control of their personal lives, communities, lands, and resources in the face of what they regard as repression or subjugation by a foreign power.[13]

Not all revolts are truly revolutionary in their consequences. According to South African anthropologist Max Gluckman, rebellions

"throw the rascals out" and substitute another set, but there is no attempt to alter either the cultural ideology or the form of the social structure. In political revolution, attempts are made to seize the offices of power in order to change

social structure, belief systems, and their symbolic representations. Political revolutions are usually turbulent, violent, and not long-lasting. A successful revolution soon moves to re-establish a stable, though changed, social structure; yet it has far-reaching political, social and sometimes economic and cultural consequences.[14]

Revolutions do not always accomplish what they set out to do. One of the stated goals of the Chinese communist revolution in the late 1940s, for example, was to liberate women from the oppression of a strongly patriarchal society in which a woman owed lifelong obedience to some male relative—first her father, later her husband and, after his death, her oldest son. Although changes were made, the transformation overall has been frustrated by the cultural lens through which the revolutionaries viewed their work. A tradition of deeply rooted patriarchy extending back at least 22 centuries is not easily overcome and has unconsciously influenced many of the decisions made by communist China's leaders since 1949. In rural China today, as in the past, a woman's life is still usually determined by her relationship to a man, be it her father, husband, or son, rather than by her own efforts or failures. What's more, women are being told more and more that their primary roles are as wives and mothers. When they do work outside the house, it is generally at jobs with low pay, low status, and no benefits. Indeed, the 1990s saw a major outbreak of the abduction and sale of women from rural areas as brides and workers. Their no-wage labor for their husbands' household or low-wage labor outside (which goes

[13]Nietschmann, p. 7.

[14]Quoted in Hoebel, E. A. (1972). *Anthropology: The study of man* (4th ed., p. 667). New York: McGraw-Hill.

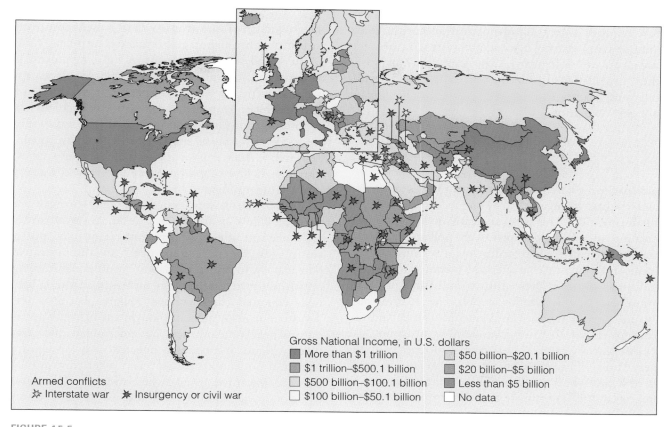

Gross National Income, in U.S. dollars
- More than $1 trillion
- $1 trillion–$500.1 billion
- $500 billion–$100.1 billion
- $100 billion–$50.1 billion
- $50 billion–$20.1 billion
- $20 billion–$5 billion
- Less than $5 billion
- No data

Armed conflicts
- ✻ Interstate war
- ✺ Insurgency or civil war

FIGURE 15.5

Armed conflict in the 1990s was concentrated among the world's poor countries, as it is today.

back to the household) has been essential to China's economic expansion, which relies on the allocation of labor by the heads of patrilineal households.[15] Thus, despite whatever freedom women may achieve for a while, they become totally dependent in their old age on their sons.

---

[15]Gates, H. (1996). Buying brides in China—again. *Anthropology Today, 12*(4), 10.

This situation shows that the undermining of revolutionary goals, if it occurs, is not necessarily by political opponents. Rather, it may be a consequence of the revolutionaries' own cultural background. In rural China, as long as women marry out and their labor is controlled by male heads of families, women always will be seen as something of a commodity.

It should be understood that revolution is a relatively recent phenomenon, occurring only during the

In China, women's labor has become critical to economic expansion. Much of this labor is controlled by male heads of families, who act as agents of the state in allocating labor.

© A. Ramey/PhotoEdit

past 5,000 years or so. The reason is that political rebellion requires a centralized political authority (chiefdom or state) to rebel against, and states (if not chiefdoms) did not exist before 5,000 years ago. Obviously, then, in societies organized as tribes and bands, without central authority, there could be no rebellion or political revolution.

MODERNIZATION

One of the most frequently used terms to describe social and cultural changes as they are occurring today is **modernization.** This is most clearly defined as an all-encompassing and global process of political and socioeconomic change, whereby developing societies acquire some of the cultural characteristics common to Western industrial societies. Derived from the Latin word *modo* ("just now"), modernization literally refers to something "in the present time." The dominant idea behind this concept is that "becoming modern" is becoming like North American and other industrial societies, with the very clear implication that not to do so is to be stuck in the past—backward, inferior, and needing to be improved. It is unfortunate that the term *modernization* continues to be so widely used. Since we seem to be stuck with it, the best we can do at the moment is to recognize its problematic one-sidedness, even as we continue to use it.

The process of modernization may be best understood as consisting of four subprocesses, of which one is *technological development.* In the course of modernization, traditional knowledge and techniques give way to the application of scientific knowledge and techniques borrowed mainly from the industrialized West. Another subprocess is *agricultural development,* represented by a shift in emphasis from subsistence farming to commercial farming. Instead of raising crops and livestock for their own use, people turn with growing frequency to the production of cash crops, with increased reliance on a cash economy and on global markets for selling farm products and purchasing goods. A third subprocess is *industrialization,* with a greater emphasis placed on material forms of energy—especially fossil fuels—to drive machines. Human and animal power becomes less important, as do handicrafts in general. The fourth subprocess is *urbanization,* marked particularly by population movements from rural settlements into cities. Although all four subprocesses are interrelated, there is no fixed order of appearance.

As modernization proceeds, other changes are likely to follow. In the political realm, political parties and some sort of electoral apparatus frequently appear, along with the development of an administrative bureaucracy. In formal education, institutional learning opportunities expand, literacy increases, and an indigenous educated elite develops. Religion becomes less important in many areas of thought and behavior as traditional beliefs and practices are undermined. Many traditional rights and duties connected with kinship are altered, if not eliminated, especially where distant relatives are concerned. Finally, where social stratification is a factor, social mobility increases as ascribed status becomes less important and personal achievement counts for more.

Two other features of modernization go hand in hand with those already noted. One, **structural differentiation,** is the division of single traditional roles that embrace two or more functions (for example, political, economic, and religious) into two or more separate roles, each with one particular specialized function. This represents a kind of fragmentation of society, which must be counteracted by new **integrative mechanisms** if the society is not to fall apart into a number of discrete units. These new mechanisms include formal governmental structures, official state ideologies, political parties, legal codes, labor and trade unions, as well as other common-interest associations. All of these crosscut other societal divisions and thus serve to oppose differentiating forces. These two forces, however, are not the only ones in opposition in a situation of modernization. To them must be added a third, the force of **tradition**—customary ideas and practices passed on from generation to generation, which in a modernizing society may form an obstacle to new ways of doing things. Yet, the conflict does not have to be total. Traditional ways on occasion may facilitate modernization. For example, traditional kinship ties may assist rural people as they move into cities if they have relatives already there to turn to for aid. One's relatives, too, may provide the financing necessary for business success.

modernization The process of political and socioeconomic change, whereby developing societies acquire some of the cultural characteristics of Western industrialized societies.
structural differentiation The division of single traditional roles that embrace two or more functions (for example, political, economic, and religious) into two or more roles, each with a single specialized function.
integrative mechanisms Cultural mechanisms that oppose forces for differentiation in a society; in modernizing societies, they include formal governmental structures, official state ideologies, political parties, legal codes, labor and trade unions, and other common-interest associations.
tradition Customary ideas and practices passed on from generation to generation, which in a modernizing society may form an obstacle to new ways of doing things.

VISUAL COUNTERPOINT Structural differentiation. Whereas most items for daily use were once made at home, such as butter (*left*), almost everything we use today is the product of specialized production, as are the dairy products we buy in the food store.

One aspect of modernization, the technological explosion, has made it possible to transport human beings and ideas from one place to another with astounding speed and in great numbers. Formerly independent cultural systems have been brought into contact with others. Cultural differences between New York and Pukapuka are declining, while differences between fisherfolk and physicists are increasing. No one knows whether this implies a net gain or net loss in cultural diversity, but the worldwide spread of anything—whether it is DDT (an insecticide banned in the United States as too toxic) or a new idea—should be viewed with at least caution. That human beings and human cultural systems are different is the most exciting thing about them, yet the destruction of diversity is implicit in the worldwide spread of blue jeans, Coca-Cola, rock and roll, socialism, capitalism, or anything else. When a song is forgotten or a ceremony ceases to be performed, a part of the human heritage is destroyed forever.

A closer examination of traditional cultures that have felt the impact of modernization or other cultural changes will help to pinpoint some of the problems such cultures have met. We will focus here on the Shuar Indians of Ecuador and the Skolt Lapps, one of several groups of Saami people living in the Arctic regions of Norway, Sweden, Finland, and Russia.

Skolt Lapps and the Snowmobile Revolution

The Skolt Lapps, whose homeland is in northern Finland, traditionally supported themselves by fishing and reindeer herding.[16] Although they depended on the outside world for certain material goods, the resources crucial for their socioeconomic system were present locally and were available to all. No one was denied access to critical resources, and little social and economic differentiation existed among the people. Theirs was basically an egalitarian society.

As with most Saami people, reindeer herding has played such an important role in the lives of Skolt Lapps that it is central to their definition of themselves as a people. For generations reindeer supplied meat for home consumption or for sale to procure outside goods. They also provided hides for shoes and clothes, sinew for sewing, and antlers and bones for making various objects. Furthermore, reindeer were used to pull sleds in the winter and as pack animals when there was no snow on the ground. Understandably, these animals were the objects of much attention. The herds were not large, but nonetheless

[16]Pelto, P. J. (1973). *The snowmobile revolution: Technology and social change in the Arctic.* Menlo Park, CA: Cummings.

they required considerable care and time, especially during the long winter months. Men tended the animals, moving about on skis and associating closely with the herds—intensively from November to January and periodically from January to April.

In the early 1960s snowmobiles came on the market, and Skolt reindeer herders speedily adopted them, convinced that the new machines would make herding physically easier and economically more advantageous. The first snowmobile arrived in Finland in 1962. By 1971 there were seventy operating machines owned by the Skolt Lapps and others in the area. A small number of Lapps continued herding activity on skis but lost considerable prestige doing so. And reindeer sleds all but disappeared as regular means of transportation. As early as 1967 only

four people were still using sleds for winter travel, and most no longer kept reindeer to serve as draft animals. Herders that had not converted to snowmobiles felt disadvantaged compared to the rest.

The consequences of this mechanization have been extraordinary and far-reaching. As snowmobile technology replaced traditional skills, the ability of the Lapps to creatively survive on their own disappeared, and their dependency on the outside world grew enormously. Given the high cost of buying snowmobiles (several thousand dollars in the Arctic), as well as the expense of maintaining and fueling them, Lapps faced a sharp rise in their need for cash. To obtain money, men began going outside their communities for wage work more than just occasionally, as had previously been the case. And, with unprecedented dependency, they looked for help to external sources such as government pensions or welfare.

The argument may be made that dependency and the need for cash are prices worth paying for an improved system of reindeer herding. But has it actually improved? In truth, snowmobiles contributed in a significant way to a disastrous decline in reindeer herding. By 1971 the average size of the family herd had dropped from fifty to twelve. Herds this small are not economically viable.

A Saami man, standing beside his family's base tent in Scandinavia's arctic tundra, searches for his reindeer herd. Engaged in an age-old occupation, he uses modern snowmobiles to herd the animals.

Moreover, they are all but impossible to maintain because most of the time reindeer range freely, and animals in such small herds will take the first opportunity to run off to join another larger one. The old close, prolonged, and largely peaceful relationship between herder and beast has changed into a noisy, traumatic one. Nowadays, the people that reindeer encounter come speeding out of the woods on snarling, smelly machines that invariably chase the animals, often for long distances. Instead of helping the animals in their winter food quest, aiding female reindeer with their calves, and protecting the herd from predators, men appear either to slaughter or castrate them. Naturally enough, the reindeer have become wary of people. The result has been actual de-domestication, with reindeer scattering and running off to more inaccessible areas, given the slightest chance. Moreover, there are indications that snowmobile harassment has adversely affected the number of viable calves added to the herds. This is a classic illustration of the fact change is not always adaptive.

The cost of mechanized herding—and the decline of the herds—have led many Skolt Lapps to abandon herding altogether. Now, the majority of males are no longer herders at all. This constitutes a serious economic problem, since few economic alternatives are available. The problem is compounded by the fact that participation in a cash-credit economy means that most people, employed or not, have payments to make. This is more than just an economic problem, for in the Lapps' traditional culture, being a reindeer herder is the very essence of manhood. Hence, today's nonherders are not only poor in a way that they could not have been in previous times, but there is a sense that they are not quite the men they used to be.

This economic differentiation with its reevaluation of roles has led to the development of a stratified society out of the older egalitarian one. Differences have arisen in terms of wealth and, with this, lifestyles. It is difficult to break into reindeer herding now, for one needs a substantial cash outlay. And herding now requires skills and knowledge that were not a part of traditional culture. Not everyone has these, and those without them are dependent on others if they are to participate. Hence, access to critical resources is now restricted, where once it had been open to all.

The Shuar Solution

Although the Skolt Lapps have not escaped many negative aspects of modernization, the choice to modernize or not was essentially theirs. By contrast, the Shuar Indians (historically better known as Jivaro) deliberately avoided modernization until they felt that they had no other option if they were to fend off the same outside forces that elsewhere in the Amazon Basin have

destroyed whole societies. In 1964, threatened with the loss of their land base as more and more Ecuadoran colonists intruded into their territory, the Shuar founded a fully independent corporate body, the Shuar Federation, to take control over their own future. Recognized by Ecuador's government, albeit grudgingly, the federation is officially dedicated to promotion of the social, economic, and moral advancement of its members and to coordination of development with official governmental agencies. Since its founding, the federation has secured title to more than 96,000 hectares of communal land; established a cattle herd of more than 15,000 head as the people's primary source of income; taken control of their own education, using their own language and mostly Shuar teachers; and established their own bilingual broadcasting station and a bilingual newspaper. Obviously, all of this has transformed daily life among the Shuar, but they have been able to maintain a variety of distinctive cultural markers, including their language, communal land tenure, cooperative production and distribution, a basically egalitarian economy, and kin-based communities that retain maximum autonomy. Thus, for all the changes, they feel they are still Shuar and distinct from other Ecuadorans.[17]

The Shuar case shows that Amazonian Indian nations are capable of taking control of their own destinies even in the face of intense outside pressures, *if* allowed to do so. Unfortunately, until recently, few have had that option. Prior to European invasions of the Amazonian rainforest, more than 700 distinct indigenous nations inhabited this vast region. By 1900 in Brazil, the number was down to 270, and today something like 180 remain.[18] Many of these survivors find themselves in situations not unlike that of the Yanomami, described earlier in this chapter. Nevertheless, some are showing a new resourcefulness in resisting the outside forces of destruction arrayed against them. In the following Original Study, an anthropologist who lives in Brazil and has done fieldwork in the Amazon since 1976 illustrates just how formidable these forces are.

---

[17]Bodley, J. H. (1990). *Victims of progress* (3rd ed., pp. 160–162). Mountain View, CA: Mayfield.

---

[18]*Cultural Survival Quarterly,* (1991), *15*(4), 38.

Original Study

Violence against Indians in Brazil

The last thirty years have brought about the political victories and "conquests" by the indigenous movement in Brazil, as demonstrated in an exemplary fashion by the Federation of Indigenous Organizations of the Rio Negro in the Northwest Amazon. With the demarcation of a large and continuous land reserve and the participation of indigenous leadership in key positions of municipal government, these victories mark significant advances for the approximately 20,000 Indians of various linguistic families in the region. I intended to focus on this area because it is where I have conducted anthropological and historical research since 1976, and I have been in contact with the Federation over the past 12 years since I returned to live in Brazil. A remarkable situation has changed from complete subordination and dependence on external agents of contact (the missionaries and military, principally) 20 years ago, to an effervescence of local indigenous political associations (over 20), coordinated by a regionwide indigenous confederation. Cultural traditions long suppressed by the missionaries to the point where indigenous people were "embarrassed" with their identity have evolved in the form of a brilliant leader, Baniwa Gersen Luciano Santos, whose intellectual contribution to the indigenous movement in Amazonia in general will surely have long-term consequences.

The Northwest Amazon has become a critical testing ground in Brazil for important questions revolving around sustainable development and how these models are to be translated into practice. Are such models viable alternatives in the Northwest Amazon context, or is there still an enormous distance between NGOs [nongovernment organizations] and academic discourses about such models and the specific and imme-

diate needs of native peoples? What are the effects of NGO involvement in local-level politics on Indian/white relations and the indigenous cultural revitalization movement in general in this area? The immediate problem is not the new models, but the old problems and the old wounds that have never had sufficient time to heal. Racism and impunity, the two principal villains, constantly tear away at the heart of victories. [For this reason, it is important to chronicle not only the victories but also the setbacks in the ongoing struggle for indigenous rights in Brazil.]

Every year the Indigenous Missionary Council (a branch of the Brazilian Catholic Church most directly involved in indigenous affairs) publishes a report on

Statue "celebrating" gold miner in the main square of Boa Vista in Brazil. Gold miners and others who have invaded Indian lands have caused massive death and devastation. In 1993, when a group of Indians succeeded in evicting a rancher from their land, a man phoned one radio show, identified himself as a professional "hit man," and offered to kill the local bishop (who supported the Indians), cut off his head, and display it in the miner's pan.

violence against the indigenous population in Brazil. The statistics show that not only is there an increase in violence year by year, but also in the kinds of aggression committed against indigenous peoples: murders of leaders, massacres, epi-

demic diseases caused by neglect of official health agencies, illegal detentions, and police brutality. One can only be shocked by the repeated acts of violence against Indians throughout the country. Yet how are these cases represented and reported in the national media and how are they dealt with by authorities? Are there patterns in the violence that characterize Indian/white relations?

Violence against Indigenous People in Brazil

The most common pattern characterizing violence against indigenous people in Brazil is impunity. Violence against the indigenous people in Brazil is horrible and lamentable, but it is ultimately beyond control. In case after case, the same scenario is revealed in which violent acts against Indians are never brought to justice. Conflicts and tensions, particularly over land and resource rights, build up over the years, and coupled with the inertia of FUNAI [Brazil's Indian service] explode in traumatic massacres or murders. Investigations are immediately initiated and the accused are apprehended; in this initial phase, international pressure has played an important role. The second phase includes a long period of procrastination, which takes the steam out of the initial urgency of the case. Next, the accused stall for time to manipulate the proceedings while the investigations drag on. When, or if the case is finally brought to the courts, there is never sufficient evidence to incriminate the accused who are then absolved or given light sentences. The consequence of this scenario is the reproduction of violence in interethnic relations.

For example, a well-known Guaraní leader, Marçal Tupã-y, was murdered in 1983 by the hired gunmen of a local rancher that disputed the lands of Marçal's people. An entire decade passed before the perpetrator of the crime—known to everyone in the region—was brought to trial in a local court. In the end, the rancher was absolved of the crime for "lack of evidence." Another example is the 1988 massacre of Ticuna Indians of the upper Solimões that left fourteen dead, twenty-three wounded, and ten "disappeared." The massacre was perpetrated by fourteen gunmen hired by a local lumber businessman in order to "settle" a land claim. This claim had dragged on for years because both federal authorities and local interests wished to suppress the movement. Despite the immediate national and international attention, today, nearly a decade later, news of the process has virtually disappeared from the press, and the process of judicial procrastination has not gotten further than determining the jurisdiction for the trial—if there is to be one.

There is yet another scenario in which, through the manipulation of discourse about violence by the mass media, actual victims are transformed into perpetrators of violence against themselves or "blaming the victim," in which actual physical violence is compounded with symbolic violence against the victims. The case of the Yanomami [Indians] in Brazil and Venezuela is certainly the most dramatic instance of this process.

In this case, structural amnesia and impunity have not been worse because

the eyes of the world have focused on the Yanomami situation for so long. This has not immunized the Yanomami from physical violence (the 1993 massacre of seventeen Yanomami of the village of Haxlmu), or from racist attacks such as those that characterized the articles published by Janer Cristaldo, an unknown journalist, in the Folha de São Paulo, 2 years ago. Cristaldo, in his initial article titled "Behind the Scenes of the Lano-Bluff," not only questioned the evidence of the massacre, but also systematically diverted the focus of the issue by claiming that numerous aggressions by indigenous peoples against the white man had never been brought to justice. Basing his characterization of the Yanomami on the "Fierce People" image popularized by Napoleon Chagnon, Cristaldo argued that Yanomami culture is itself "marked by violence" and that the international outrage over the Haxlmu massacre was nothing more than a conspiracy organized by anthropologists and indigenous defense organizations. He characterized the Yanomami as fodder for a supposed campaign to internationalize Amazonia "[e]ither the Armed Forces beware of this conspiracy by anthropologists," he warned, "or soon we will have the blue helmets [referring to UN intervention] in Amazonia." In this discourse, Brazilians are the victims while the Yanomami and their supporters are the aggressors.

"Sensationalizing" Violence

Numerous other cases could be analyzed to illustrate the kinds of structural violence that characterize Indian/white relations in Brazil today and the ways mass media has represented interethnic violence. In many cases, it is clear that

media discourse serves the interests of local, regional, and national power structures. It is also clear that the explanation of such violence is not sufficient to account for the incidents of brutality against individuals or whole groups of people. Indigenous peoples have shown that they are able to resist, adapt, and change, often in extraordinarily creative ways, to demands imposed on them from outside. Brazilian society, however, has repeatedly demonstrated that it is incapable of overcoming two of its deepest internal conflicts: racism and impunity. Governments continue to demonstrate their inability to implement viable political and economic models that could enable ethnic and social minorities to co-exist and live in dignity in a plural society. The seriousness of this problem came to the fore yet again in 1997, when a Pataxó Indian leader was brutally murdered after "Indian Day" festivities in Brazil's capital city—set afire by five youths from upper-middle-class families.

... On Indian Day in Brazil, a kind of macabre ritual [always] takes place. The mass media talk about the "inevitable extinction" of indigenous peoples as if they were a disappearing species. Ecologists and anthropologists reaffirm the vitality of socio-diversity and the necessity of indigenous peoples for the future survival of the planet. Brazilian consciousness, in relation to Indians and minorities in general, needs to change, not the Indians who have shown that they are not merely "survivors" or "remnants" of a once great past, but fully capable of forging viable models for their future. (Adapted from R. M. Wright. (1997). Violence on Indian Day in Brazil 1997: Symbol of the past and future. Cultural Survival Quarterly, 21(2), 47–49.)

Globalization and the "Underdeveloped" World

The examples just examined show how modernization has affected indigenous peoples surviving within contemporary state societies. Throughout the so-called underdeveloped world, in Africa, Asia, South and Central America, and elsewhere, whole countries are in the throes of radical political and economic change and overall cultural transformation. In fact, new inventions

and major advances in industrial production, mass transportation, and communication and information technologies are transforming societies in Europe and North America as well. This worldwide process of accelerated modernization in which all parts of the earth are becoming interconnected in one vast interrelated and all-encompassing system is known as globalization—as defined in Chapter 1.

All around the globe we are witnessing the removal of economic activities—or at least their control—from

Anthropologists of Note

Eric R. Wolf (1923–1999)

Courtesy of Eric Wolf

The tribulations of the 20th century, including two world wars, are reflected in the life history of Eric Wolf. Having personally experienced state-sponsored violence, he turned to anthropology to sort through issues of power. Viewing anthropology as the most scientific of the humanities and the most humane of the sciences, he became famous for his comparative historical studies on peasants, power, and the transforming impact of capitalism on traditional nations.

Eric Wolf's life began in Austria shortly after the first world war. During that terrible conflict, his Austrian father had been a prisoner of war in Siberia, where he met Wolf's mother, a Russian exile. When peace returned, the couple married and settled in Vienna, where Eric was born in 1923. Growing up in Austria's capital and then (because of his father's job) in Sudetenland in what is now the Czech Republic, young Eric enjoyed a life of relative ease. He relished summers spent in the Alps among local peasants in exotic costumes, and he drank in his mother's tales about

her father's adventures with Siberian nomads.

Life changed for Eric in 1938 when Adolf Hitler grabbed power in Germany, annexed Austria and Sudetenland, and threatened Jews like the Wolfs. Seeking security for their 15-year-old son, Eric's parents sent him to high school in England. In 1940, a year after World War II broke out, British authorities believed invasion was imminent and ordered aliens, including Eric, into an internment camp. There he met other refugees from Nazi-occupied Europe and had his first exposure to Marxist theories. Soon, he left England for New York City and enrolled at Queens College, where Professor Hortense Powdermaker, a former student of Malinowski, introduced him to anthropology.

In 1943, the 20-year-old refugee enlisted in the U.S. Army's 10th Mountain Division. Fighting in the mountains of Tuscany, Italy, he won a Silver Star for combat bravery. At the war's end, Wolf returned to the United States, completed his B.A., and went on to graduate school at Columbia University, studying under Julian Steward and Ruth Benedict. After earning his Ph.D. in 1951, based on fieldwork in Puerto Rico, he did extensive research on Mexican peasants.

Following short stints at various U.S. universities, he became a professor at the University of Michigan in 1961. A prolific writer, Wolf gained tremendous recognition for his fourth book, *Peasant Wars of the Twentieth Century*, published in 1969 during the height of the Vietnam War. Against that war, he headed a newly founded ethics committee in the American Anthropological Association and helped expose counter-insurgency uses of anthropological research in Southeast Asia.

Wolf left Michigan in 1971, accepting a distinguished professorship at Lehman College in the Bronx, New York. There his classes were filled with working-class students of all ethnic backgrounds, including many who took the courses he taught in Spanish. In addition, he taught anthropology at the Graduate School of the City University of New York. After many more publications, Wolf wrote his award-winning book, *Europe and the People without History* (1982). In 1990, he received a MacArthur "genius" prize. Shortly before his death of cancer in 1999, he published *Envisioning Power: Ideologies of Dominance and Crisis*, which explores how ideas and power are connected though the medium of culture.

---

the family/community setting. And we are seeing the altered structure of the family in the face of the changing labor market: the increased reliance of young children on parents alone for affection, instead of on the extended family; the decline of general parental authority; schools replacing the family as the primary educational unit; old people spending their last days in nursing homes rather than with family members; and many other changes. The difficulty is that it all happens so fast that traditional societies are unable to deal with it gradually. Changes that took generations to accomplish in Europe and North America are attempted within the span of a single generation in developing countries. In the process they frequently face the erosion of a number

of dearly held values they had no intention of giving up. Anthropologists doing fieldwork in distant communities throughout the world have witnessed how these traditional cultures have been affected, and often destroyed, by the powerful global forces. One of the first and most prominent anthropologists to focus on these worldwide transformations was Eric Wolf, who personally experienced the global havoc and upheaval of the 20th century (see Anthropologists of Note).

Commonly, the burden of modernization falls most heavily on women. For example, the commercialization of agriculture often involves land reforms that overlook or ignore women's traditional land rights. This reduces their control of and access to resources at the same time that mechanization of food production and processing drastically reduces their opportunities for employment. As a consequence, women are confined more and more to traditional domestic tasks, which, as commercial production becomes peoples' dominant concern, are increasingly downgraded in value. Moreover, the domestic workload tends to increase, because men are less available to help out, while tasks such as fuel gathering and water collection are made more difficult as common land and resources come to be privately owned and as woodlands are reserved for commercial exploitation. To top it all off, the growing of nonfood crops such as cotton and sisal or luxury crops such as tea, coffee, and cacao (source of chocolate) for the world market makes households vulnerable to wide price fluctuations. As a result, people cannot afford the high-quality diet subsistence farming provided and become malnourished. In short, with modernization, women frequently find themselves in an increasingly inferior position. As their workload increases, the value assigned the work they do declines, as does their relative educational status, not to mention their health and nutrition.

Globalization: Must It Be Painful?

Most anthropologists see the change that is affecting traditional non-Western peoples caught up in the modern technological world as an ordeal. Yet, the more common attitude in the industrial West has been that modernization is both inevitable and good—that however disagreeable the "medicine" may be, it is worth it for the

"backward" people to become just like people in the West. This view has little to do with the cold political and economic realities of the contemporary world. It overlooks the stark fact that the standard of middle- and upper-class living in the Western world is based on a rate of consumption of nonrenewable resources whereby a small fraction of the world's population uses the vast majority of these precious resources. By the early 1970s, for example, the people of the United States comprised less than 5 percent of the world's population but were consuming over 50 percent of all of the world's resources. The imbalance continues, suggesting that it is impossible for most peoples of the world to achieve a material standard of living at all comparable to that of many people in Western countries in the near future. At the very least, the peoples of the industrial and postindustrial West would have to cut drastically their unrelenting and often wasteful consumption of resources. So far, few have shown a willingness to seriously adjust their standard of living in order to do this.

Countless people around the world today aspire to a material standard of living like that enjoyed by the middle class and well-to-do in many in industrialized and postindustrialized countries, even as the gap between the rich and the poor continues to widen. Every year, many millions of people slide below the poverty level.[19] This has led to the development of what anthropologist Paul Magnarella called a new "culture of discontent" in which aspirations far exceed the bounds of local opportunities.

_____

[19]Kurth, P. (1998, October 14). Capitol crimes. *Seven Days, 7.*

An urban slum near Juarez, Mexico. All over the world, millions of people are fleeing to the cities for a better life, all too often only to experience disease, poverty, and early death in such slums.

© Paul Conklin/PhotoEdit

No longer satisfied with traditional values and often unable to sustain themselves in the rural backlands, people all over the world are moving to the large cities to find a better life. All too often they live out their days in poor, congested, and diseased slums while attempting to achieve what is usually beyond their reach. Unfortunately, despite rosy predictions about a better future, hundreds of millions of people in our world remain trapped in this wretched reality, struggling against poverty, hunger, poor health, and other dangers.

Chapter Summary

■ Although cultures may be remarkably stable, culture change is characteristic of all cultures to a greater or lesser degree. Change is often caused by accidents, including the unexpected outcome of particular actions or events. Another cause is people's deliberate attempt to solve some perceived problem. Finally, change may be forced upon one group in the course of especially intense contact between two societies. Adaptation and progress are consequences rather than causes of change, although not all changes are necessarily adaptive. *Progress* is a relative term, meaning different things to different cultural groups.

■ The mechanisms involved in cultural change are innovation, diffusion, cultural loss, and acculturation. The ultimate source of cultural change is innovation: any new idea, method, or device that gains widespread acceptance in society. A primary innovation is the creation, invention, or discovery of a new idea, method, or device—such as the discovery that firing clay makes it permanently hard. A secondary innovation is a new application or modification of an existing idea, method, or device—for example, modeling clay into familiar forms to be fired by known techniques. Primary innovations may prompt rapid culture change and stimulate other inventions. An innovation's chance of being accepted depends partly, but not entirely, on its perceived superiority to the method or object it replaces. Its acceptance is also connected with the prestige of the innovator. Diffusion is the borrowing of a cultural element from one society by another. Cultural loss involves the abandonment of some trait or practice with or without replacement. Anthropologists have given considerable attention to acculturation: massive culture changes that people are forced to make as a consequence of intensive, first-hand contact between their own group and a more powerful society.

■ Applied anthropology—the application of anthropological insights and methods to solving practical problems—arose as anthropologists sought to provide colonial administrators with a better understanding of native cultures, often to control them better, sometimes to avoid serious disruption of them. An alternative type of practical anthropology has emerged during the last half century. Known under a variety of different names, including action anthropology, it involves community-based research and action in collaboration and solidarity with indigenous societies, ethnic minorities, and other besieged or repressed groups. A serious ethical issue for applied anthropologists is how far they should go in trying to change the ways of other peoples.

■ Reactions of indigenous peoples to imposed changes vary considerably. Some have retreated to inaccessible places in hopes of being left alone, while some others have lapsed into apathy. Some, like the Trobriand Islanders, have reasserted their traditional culture's values by modifying foreign practices to conform to indigenous values, a phenomenon known as syncretism. If a culture's values get widely out of step with reality, the situation may give rise to revitalization movements—collective efforts for radical cultural reform in response to widespread social disruption and collective feelings of anxiety and despair. Some revitalization movements try to speed up the acculturation process to get more of the benefits expected from the dominant culture. Others try to reconstitute a bygone but still remembered way of life. In other cases, a repressed group may try to introduce a new social order based on its ideology. When the scale of discontent within a society reaches a certain level, the possibilities are high for rebellion—organized armed resistance to an established government or authority in power. And if the level of dissatisfaction rises even higher, it may lead to revolution—a radical change in a society or culture. In the political arena, revolution refers to the forced overthrow of an old government and the establishment of a new one.

■ Modernization refers to an all-encompassing and global process of political and socioeconomic change, whereby developing societies acquire some of the cultural characteristics common to Western industrial societies. The process consists of four subprocesses: technological development, agricultural development, industrialization, and urbanization. Other changes follow in the areas of political organization, education, religion, and social organization. Two other accompaniments of modernization are structural differentiation and new forces of social integration. An example of modernization is found in the Skolt Lapps of Finland, whose traditional reindeer-herding economy was all but destroyed when snowmobiles were adopted to make herding easier. In Ecuador, the Shuar Indians modernized to escape the destruction visited upon many other Amazonian peoples. So far they have been successful, and others are mobilizing their resources in attempts to achieve similar success. Nevertheless, formidable forces are still arrayed against such cultures, and on a worldwide basis, it is probably fair to say that modernization has led to deterioration rather than improvement of peoples' quality of life.

Questions for Reflection

1. As you have read in this chapter, a people's ability to change their culture has always been a key requirement for long-term human survival. However, globalization radically challenges all of us to adjust at an ever-faster pace. Considering your own situation, can you identify any powerful outside force such as a government agency or large corporation that has had caused changes for your own family, community, or neighborhood? Do you feel that these changes are good for everyone?

2. What are some of the driving forces of culture change in the world today? Which groups are benefiting the most from free markets all across the globe?

3. On a regular basis, the news media are reporting about violent uprisings or rebellion and armed conflicts that result in death and destruction. Why do you think many people feel the need to fight?

4. When societies become involved in the modernizing process, all levels of their cultural systems are affected by these changes. Do you think that people are always aware of the long-term consequences of the changes they themselves may have welcomed? Can you come up with any examples of unforeseen changes in your own community or neighborhood?

Key Terms

Primary innovation	Rebellion
Secondary innovation	Revolution
Diffusion	Modernization
Cultural loss	Structural differentiation
Acculturation	Integrative mechanisms
Genocide	Tradition
Syncretism	

Multimedia Review Tools

Companion Web Site

Visit **http://www.wadsworth.com/anthropology_d/** and click on the companion Web site for this textbook to access a wide range of material to aid your study of anthropology. Among the options for self-study in each chapter are learning objectives, flash cards, Internet activities, Web links, InfoTrac College Edition exercises, and practice tests that can be scored and emailed to your instructor.

CD-ROM

The *Doing Anthropology Today* CD-ROM supplied with your textbook provides unique and valuable information designed to enhance your learning experience. This interactive multimedia resource includes video clips, interviews with renowned anthropologists, map and timeline exercises, chapter study quizzes, and much more. *Doing Anthropology Today* will not only help you in achieving your grade goals, it will also make your learning experience fun and exciting!

Suggested Readings

Barnett, H. G. (1953). *Innovation: The basis of cultural change.* New York: McGraw-Hill.

This is the standard work on the subject, widely quoted by virtually everyone who writes about change.

Bodley, J. H. (1998). *Victims of progress* (4th ed.). New York: McGraw-Hill.

Few North Americans are aware of the devastation unleashed upon indigenous peoples in the name of progress, nor are they aware this continues on an unprecedented scale today and the extent of their own society's contributions to it. For most, this book will be a real eye-opener.

Gordon, R. J. (1992). *The Bushman myth: The making of a Namibian underclass.* Boulder, CO: Westview Press.

An enlightening study of how both Bushman culture and European myths about the Bushman have changed over the past 150 years.

Inda, J. X., & Renato, R. (Eds.). (2001). *The anthropology of globalization: A reader.* Malden, MA, and Oxford: Blackwell.

This wide-ranging reader focuses simultaneously on the large-scale processes through which various cultures are becoming increasingly interconnected and on the ways that people around the world—from Africa and Asia to the Caribbean and North America—mediate these processes in culturally specific ways.

Maybury-Lewis, D. (2001). *Indigenous peoples, ethnic groups, and the state* (2nd ed.). Boston: Allyn & Bacon.

The author, who founded the organization Cultural Survival, summarizes modernization's effect on "tribalism and ethnic parochialism." Revealing the peculiar situation of indigenous peoples as ethnic minorities alien to the states in which they live, he describes the worldwide proliferation of ethnic conflicts and the growing demands for indigenous rights. The book stands on its own, while serving as introduction to a series of individual ethnographies on indigenous peoples and their struggles.

Prins, H. E. L. (1996). *The Mi'kmaq: Resistance, accommodation, and cultural survival.* Belmont, CA: Wadsworth.

This slim but content-rich case study spans 500 years of history, chronicling the endurance of a tribal nation—its ordeals in the face of colonialism and its current struggle for self-determination and cultural revitalization. Rare for its multivocality.

Stannard, D. E. (1992). *American holocaust.* Oxford: Oxford University Press.

Stannard deals with 500 years of culture change in the Americas arising from contact between European and native cultures. In doing so, he focuses on genocide, relates it to the Holocaust of World War II, and demonstrates how deeply rooted the phenomenon is in Western culture and Christianity.

Global Challenges, Local Responses, and the Role of Anthropology

© Luis Marden/NGS Image Collection

CHALLENGE ISSUE

THROUGHOUT TODAY'S WORLD, COUNTRIES AND COMMUNITIES FACE THE CHALLENGE OF FINDING WAYS TO DEAL WITH A FLOOD OF ECONOMIC AND POLITICAL REFUGEES FLEEING FOR SURVIVAL. **One major driving force is poverty and the ever-widening economic gap** between destitute and otherwise troubled countries and wealthy states primarily in western Europe and North America. Another force is fear—the desperate need to escape from political turmoil and violent repression in states controlled by a dominant ethnic or religious group trampling the human rights of minorities who are trying to retain their own natural resources, national identities, and cultural traditions.

1

What Can Anthropologists Tell Us of the Future?

Although anthropologists cannot accurately predict future cultural forms, they can identify certain patterns and trends and foresee some of the consequences these might have if they continue. Moreover, they can shed light on already identified problems by showing how they relate to each other and to cultural features and structures that are often below the radar of experts in other disciplines. This ability to systematically consider cultural facts and their underlying structures in a wider context and from a comparative perspective is a recognized anthropological specialty.

2

What Are Today's Cultural Trends?

One major cultural trend is globalization, including world-wide adoption of the products, technologies, ideas, and cultural practices of powerful Western countries. This move toward a homogenized, global culture is countered by an opposite trend of ethnic and religious groups all over the world to reassert their distinctive cultural identities and emphasize their unique historical traditions. A third trend is the emerging sense, shared by many, that rising populations, spiraling energy use, and growing consumption are devastating our natural resources, overwhelming us with waste, and poisoning our environment.

3

What Problems Must Be Solved for Humans to Have a Viable Future?

Creative, effective, and responsible solutions need to be found to deal with a host of serious problems posed by demographic shifts, unequal distribution of wealth, vanishing natural resources, environmental destruction, ever-more powerful technologies, and explosive population growth. One difficulty is that most people fail to recognize that many problems facing us are interconnected. Anthropology provides us with a critical and realistic understanding of the emergence of a global cultural system and its radical impact on local communities. Its cross-cultural and historically informed perspective is essential for solving problems and ensuring a future in which all peoples enjoy basic human rights.

Anthropology is often described by those who know little about it as an exotic discipline interested mainly in what happened long ago and far away. The most common stereotype is that anthropologists devote all of their attention to digging up the past and describing the last surviving tribal peoples with traditional ways of life. Yet, as detailed in numerous examples in this book, neither archaeologists nor paleoanthropologists (the anthropologists most devoted to looking into the past) limit their interests to ancient times, nor are ethnographers (who focus on contemporary cultures) uninterested in the ways and workings of industrial and even postindustrial societies. Indeed, anthropologists are interested in the entire range of human cultures—in their similarities and differences and in the multiple ways they influence one another.

Moreover, anthropologists have a special concern with the future and the changes it may bring. Many wonder what today's globalizing processes will create and what they will transform, disrupt, or damage beyond repair. As we saw in the preceding chapter, when traditional peoples are exposed to intense contact with technologically empowered Western peoples, their cultures typically change with unprecedented speed, often for the worse, becoming both less supportive and less adaptive. Since globalization seems unstoppable, we are compelled to ask: How can the thousands of different cultures, developed in the course of centuries if not millennia, deal successfully with the multiple challenges hurled at them?

THE CULTURAL FUTURE OF HUMANITY

To comprehend anthropology's role in understanding and solving problems in times to come, we must look at flaws frequently seen in literature and planning efforts concerning the future. First of all, rarely do futurist writers or planners look more than about 50 years ahead, and more often than not the trends they project are those of recent history. This predisposes people to think that a trend that seems obvious today will always be so. The danger of this assumption is neatly captured in anthropologist George Cowgill's comment: "It is worth recalling the story of the person who leaped from a very tall building and on being asked how things were going as he passed the 20th floor replied 'Fine, so far.'"[1]

A second flaw typical in futurist projections is a tendency to treat subjects in isolation, without reference to pertinent trends outside an expert's field of competence. For example, agricultural planning is often based on the

assumption that a certain amount of water is available for irrigation, whether or not urban planners or others have designs upon that same water. Thus, people may be counting on natural resources in the future that will not, in fact, be available. This brings us to a third flaw common among futurists: A tendency to project the hopes and expectations of one's own social group or culture into the future interferes with the scientific objectivity necessary to see and address emerging problems.

Against this background, anthropology's contribution to our understanding of the future is clear. With their holistic and integrative perspective, anthropologists are specialists at seeing how parts fit together into a larger whole. With their comparative and long-term historical perspective, they can place short-term trends in deeper and wider perspective. With more than 100 years of cross-cultural research behind them—based on ancient archaeological finds, linguistic information, biological data, as well as participant observation within living cultures—anthropologists can recognize culture-bound assertions when they encounter them. Last but not least, they are familiar with alternative ways of dealing with a wide variety of problems.

Global Culture

Human populations have always been on the move. But today, more people travel faster and farther than ever before due to modern means of transportation (Figure 16.1). Moreover, revolutions in communication technology—from print media to telegraph and telephone to radio, television, satellites, and the Internet—make it possible to exchange more information with more people more swiftly and over greater distances. Obviously, the global flow of humans—their products and their ideas—plays a major role in cultural change.

A popular belief since the mid-1900s has been that the future world will see the development of a single homogeneous world culture. This idea is based largely on the observation that, due to technological developments in communication, transportation, and trade, peoples of the world are increasingly watching the same television programs, reading the same newspapers, eating the same foods, wearing the same types of clothes, and communicating via satellites and the Internet. Also of note, at least 175 million people (2.5 percent of the world's population) now live outside their countries of birth—not as refugees, but as migrants who earn their living in one country while being citizens in another. The continuation of such trends, so this thinking goes, should lead North Americans who travel in the year 2100 to Afghanistan, Botswana, Colombia, or Denmark to find the local inhabitants living in a manner identical or similar to theirs. Yet, looking at ethnic conflicts around the world, we must ask, Is this so?

---

[1]Cowgill, G. L. (1980). Letter, *Science, 210*, 1,305.

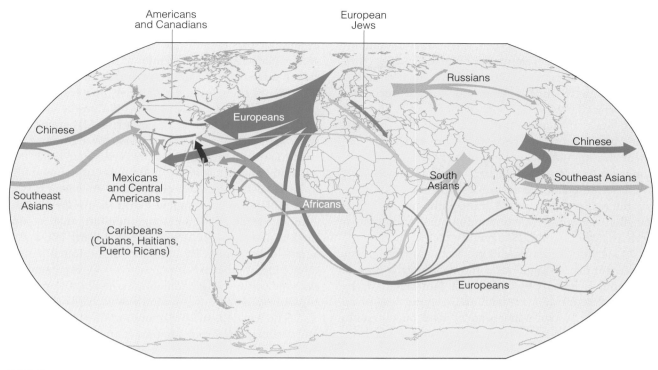

FIGURE 16.1

World migrations. Migration has had and continues to have a significant effect on world geography, contributing to culture change and development, to the diffusion of ideas and innovations, and to the complex mixture of people and cultures found in the world today. *Internal migration* occurs within the boundaries of a country; *external migration* is movement from one country or region to another. Over the last 50 years, the most important migrations in the world have been internal, largely the rural-to-urban migration that has been responsible for the recent rise of global urbanization. Prior to the mid-20th century, three types of external migration were most important: *voluntary,* most often in search of better conditions and opportunities; *involuntary* or *forced,* involving people who have been driven from their homelands by war, political unrest, or environmental disasters, or transported as slaves or prisoners; and *imposed,* not entirely forced but made advisable by circumstances. (From Allen, J. L., & Shalinsky, A. C., Student Atlas of Anthropology, p. 73. Copyright © 2004 McGraw-Hill, Inc. A division of the McGraw-Hill Companies.)

The worldwide spread of such products as Pepsi is taken by some as a sign that a homogeneous world is developing.

Is the World Coming Together or Coming Apart?

Certainly it is striking, the extent to which such items as Western-style clothing, bicycles, cars, cameras, computers, and soft drinks have spread to virtually all parts of the world. And many countries—Japan, for example—appear to have gone a long way toward becoming "Westernized." Moreover, looking back over the past 5,000 years of human history, we see that political units have tended to become larger and more all-encompassing—and fewer in number. The logical outcome of this trend would be a further reduction of autonomous political units into a single one encompassing the entire globe. In fact, some anthropologists predict that the world will become politically integrated, perhaps as early as the 23rd century.[2]

One problem with such a prediction is that it ignores something that all large states throughout time have in common: a tendency to come apart. Not only have the great empires of the past, without exception, broken up into numbers of smaller independent states, but also states in virtually all parts of the world today show this same tendency to fragment, usually along major geographic and ethnic divisions. The threat of political collapse is ever-present in multi-ethnic states without a strong government, especially when these countries are large, difficult to travel in, and lack major unifying cultural forces such as a common national language. Such is the case, for instance, with Afghanistan. This vast, mountainous country is inhabited by several major ethnic groups, including the Pashtun who live mainly in the south, and Tajik, Uzbek, Hazara, and Turkmen who live mainly in the north. Although the Pashtun are greatest in number and most dominant in the past two centuries, they were never able to successfully impose their political will on the other ethnic groups who maintain a great deal of independence, nor did they succeed in making their own native tongue, Pashto, the country's national language.

The tendency of multi-ethnic states to break apart has been especially noteworthy since the end of the Cold War between the United States and the former Soviet Union around 1990. For example, 1991 saw the dramatic breakup of the Soviet Union into about a dozen independent republics—Russia, Armenia, Kazakhstan, Ukraine, and several others. In 1992 Czechoslovakia split into the Czech and the Slovak republics. That same year the Republic of Yugoslavia began splintering into what are now five independent states in the Balkan Mountains. The splintering tendency of multi-ethnic states can also be seen in separatist movements such as that of French-speaking peoples in Canada; Basques in Spain; Tibetans in China;

the Karen in Burma (Myanmar); Aceh in Indonesia; Kurds in Turkey, Iran, and Iraq, and so on—this list is far from exhaustive. Nor is the United States immune, as can be seen in Native American attempts to secure greater political self-determination on their reservations.

All of these examples involve peoples who see themselves as members of distinct nations by virtue of birth and cultural and territorial heritage—nations over whom peoples of some other ethnic background have tried to assert political control. An estimated 5,000 such national groups exist in the world today, as opposed to a mere 191 states formally admitted as members of the United Nations (up from fewer than fifty in the 1940s).[3] Although some of these ethnic groups are small in population and area—100 or so people living on a few acres—many others are quite large. The Karen people inhabiting southern Burma (Myanmar), for example, number some 4.5 to 5 million, exceeding the populations of nearly half of the countries in the world.

The reactions of such groups to forced annexation and domination by state regimes controlled by people of other nations range all the way from the nonviolence of Scottish and Welsh nationalism to bloody fights for national independence by the Irish, Algerians, or Vietnamese. Many struggles for independence have been going on for years.

Today, about 35 million people in almost half of the world's countries are either internally displaced or have crossed international borders as refugees. (See Figure 15.4 on page 403.) Some 12 million of these unfortunates have been forced outside their countries, most of them suffering in makeshift camps where they cannot make a living. In some cases, a large proportion of an ethnic group's entire population finds itself forced to abandon their homes and flee for their lives. For instance, although hardly ever mentioned in the Western media, some 4 million Dinka, Nuer, and dozens of other African peoples in central and southern Sudan are currently either internally displaced or refugees.

It is just possible that we are reaching a point where the old tendency for political units to increase in size while decreasing in number is being canceled out by the tendency for such units to fragment into a greater number of smaller ones. Despite these examples, there are also a few instances of reunification. Best known among these is the 1990 reunification of the German nation, divided since the end of World War II as East and West Germany, into one large federal republic. Another notable exception is the recent integration of European countries into the European Community—however hindered by mutual distrusts.

---

[2]Ember, C. R., & Ember, M. (1985). *Cultural anthropology* (4th ed., p. 230). Englewood Cliffs, NJ: Prentice-Hall.

[3]*Cultural Survival Quarterly* (1991), *15*(4), 38.

Almost 50 years ago, when the Chinese communist government in Beijing annexed Tibet and imposed its rule over the Buddhist people in this Himalayan region, tens of thousands of Tibetans were forced to flee to neighboring Nepal and India, where they found safety in refugee camps. Among the many refugees is the Dalai Lama (left), Tibet's spiritual leader, who escaped his homeland across the freezing cold and snow-covered mountains in 1959 and still lives in exile.

MEDIATREK

For extensive up-to-date information about conflict and ethnicity specific to particular countries and regions, go to MediaTrek 16.1 on the companion Web site or CD-ROM.

Global Culture: A Good Idea or Not?

The idea of a shared global culture may have a degree of popular appeal, in that it might diminish chances for the kinds of misunderstandings and conflicting viewpoints that so often in the past few hundred years have led to violent clashes and even full-scale wars. Anthropologists greet this prognosis with skepticism, though, suspecting that distinctive worldviews will persist as they have for hundreds of years, even in the face of massive changes. Indeed, one might argue that the chance for conflicting viewpoints actually increases, as evidenced in the sharply divided opinions within European states long allied to the United States concerning its decision to invade and occupy Iraq in 2003.

Some have argued that perhaps a generalized world culture would be desirable in the future, because some traditional cultures may be too specialized to adjust to a changed environment. For instance, when Amazonian Indians pursuing a traditional way of life well adapted to South America's tropical rainforest are confronted with sudden, radical changes brought on by foreign invaders, their long-established culture often collapses. The reason for this, it is argued, is that the forest dwellers' traditions and political and social organizations are not at all

adapted to modern ways, and that they are naturally destined to give way to the new. A problem with this argument is that, far from being unable to adapt, such traditional societies have been robbed repeatedly of the opportunity to work out their own adaptations based on their own agendas. Their demise is caused not by laws of nature but rather by the political and economic choices of the powerful, fueled by arrogance, intolerance, and greed, along with a willingness to invade and exploit lands already inhabited by indigenous people.

The possibility of Amazonian Indians adapting to the changing realities, if allowed to do so, without losing their distinctive ethnic and cultural identity, is demonstrated by the Shuar case in Ecuador, noted in the preceding chapter. However, the pressures to "develop" the Amazon rainforest in Brazil are so great that whole indigenous communities are dispossessed, swept aside, or even destroyed so that global timber, energy, and mining corporations and agribusinesses are free to pursue their unrestrained profit-making activities. People do not have much chance to work out their own adaptations to the globalizing world if they are driven from their homelands and abruptly deprived of their means of survival so that more acreage can be devoted to the raising of beef cattle. Much of this meat is refrigerated and shipped directly to Europe. And much of the profits also leave the country since the major ranches are owned and operated by foreign corporations. Although large tracts of land have been set aside as Indian reservations since the mid-1990s, the devastation process continues.

A key point to be made here is that in the globalization process economically and technologically empowered people have defined others—indeed, whole societies—as inferior, subservient, irrelevant, and not entitled to human rights, including self-determination.

Ethnic Resurgence

Despite the worldwide adoption of such products as blue jeans, sunglasses, Coca-Cola, and the Big Mac, and despite ever-growing pressures on traditional cultures to disappear, it is clear that cultural differences are still very much with us in the world today. In fact, resistance to many aspects of globalization is growing in many parts of the world. We see evidence of this in examples already noted, including repeated public protests around the globe against policies of the Geneva-based World Trade Organization. In addition, Greenpeace and a host of less radical environmental groups can be found demonstrating worldwide against such practices as French nuclear testing in the Pacific or Japanese commercial whaling. Other examples include symbolic attacks by small farmers in France against corporate control, genetically modified crops, industrial agriculture, and the McDonald's fast-food outlets. Resistance to globalization is also evident in revolutionary movements in Peru and Colombia, as well as Muslim fundamentalist movements in Algeria and Egypt. The remarkable recent revival of shamanism in former communist Mongolia is yet another example, as is the increasing political activism of many other indigenous peoples from every corner of the world.

During the 1970s the world's indigenous peoples began to organize self-determination movements, culminating in the formation of the World Council of Indigenous Peoples in 1975. This group now has official status as a nongovernmental organization of the United Nations, which allows it to present the cases of indigenous peoples before the world community. Leaders of this movement see their own societies as community based, egalitarian, and close to nature, and they are intent upon keeping them that way. In 1993, representatives of some 124 indigenous groups and organizations agreed to a draft Declaration of the Rights of Indigenous Peoples that had taken a decade to produce. Presented to the UN General Assembly, it contains some 150 articles urging respect for indigenous cultural heritages, calling for recognition of indigenous land titles and rights of self-determination, and demanding an end to all forms of oppression and discrimination as a principle of international law. So far, this drafted document is largely symbolic. It remains under consideration by the UN, which to date has agreed upon only a handful of its articles. Whether it will be adopted remains to be seen.

Euroamericans often have difficulty adjusting to the fact that not everyone wants to be just like they are. In the United States, children are taught to believe that the American way of life is one to which all other peoples aspire. Although it is true that many peoples from poor countries across the world seek to improve their living conditions and enjoy the fruits of freedom, such aspirations should not be confused with wanting to become "American." Moreover, in the globalizing world dominated by the United States, Japan, and a handful of European capitalist states today, whole countries that once valued Western ways are now drawing the line or even turning against Western ideas, trends, and practices. One striking case of such a cultural reaction is that of a group of Muslim religious fundamentalists in

Jean-Philippe Ksiazek/AFP/Getty Images

Increasingly, indigenous peoples around the world are organizing to defend their own interests against both developers and governments. Here we see several delegates from the United Nations Permanent Forum on Indigenous Issues at a world summit gathering in Geneva, Switzerland.

© Zahid Hussein/Reuters

Sometimes resistance to modernization takes the form of cultural traditionalism and religious fundamentalism, as in Afghanistan during recent decades. This reactionary practice is evident in this family's clothing, the mother's veil, and the father's beard.

Afghanistan known as the Taliban (the Pashto word for "students," specifically of Islam). After helping to force the Russian army out of their country and ending the subsequent civil war, they rose to power in the 1990s and imposed a radical version of traditional Islamic law (Sharia) in an effort to create an Islamic republic based on strict religious values. A somewhat similar, though far less radical, reaction against modernity is taking place in the United States, which, in recent years has elected "born-again" and other fundamentalist politicians dedicated to creating a national culture based on what they see as traditional Christian values.[4]

Cultural Pluralism

Since a single homogenous global culture is not necessarily the wave of the future, what is? Some predict a world in which ethnic groups will become more nation-

alistic in response to globalization, each group stressing its unique cultural heritage and emphasizing differences with neighboring groups. But not all ethnic groups organize themselves politically as distinctive nations with their own state. In fact, it has been common for two or more neighboring ethnic groups or nations to draw together in loose political union while maintaining their particular cultural identities. However, because such pluralistic societies lack a common cultural identity and heritage, and often do not share the same language or religion, political relationships within them can be fraught with tension. When feelings of ethnonationalism are not far from the surface, political pressure may build up and result in separation and independence.

One way of curbing divisive pressures in pluralistic or multi-ethnic societies is the adoption of a collective policy based on mutual respect and tolerance for cultural differences. Known as **multiculturalism,** such an official policy or doctrine asserts the value of different cultures co-existing within a country, and stresses the reciprocal responsibility of all citizens to accept the rights of others to freely express their views and values. In contrast to state policies in which a dominant ethnic group uses its power to impose its own culture as the national standard on other groups within the same state, forcing them to assimilate, multiculturalism involves a public policy for managing a society's cultural diversity.

Examples of long-established multiculturalism may be seen in states such as Switzerland (where German-, French-, Italian-, and Romansh-speaking peoples co-exist under the same government) and Canada (where French- and English-speaking Canadians, as well as dozens of indigenous nations live side by side). Although cultural pluralism is still more common than multiculturalism, several multi-ethnic countries have recently changed their official melting pot ideology and associated policies of assimilation. One example of a country that is moving toward multiculturalism is the United States, which now has over 120 different ethnic groups within its borders (in addition to hundreds of federally recognized American Indian groups). Another is Australia, now counting over 100 ethnic groups and with eighty languages spoken within its territorial boundaries. Similar changes are also under way in many European countries where millions of foreign immigrants have settled during the past few decades. In many pluralistic societies, however, governments lack the ideological commitment or political capacity to successfully structure a national cultural system. As an example

[4]Marsella, J. (1982). Pulling it together: Discussion and comments. In S. Pastner & W. A. Haviland (Eds.), *Confronting the creationists* (pp. 79–80). *Northeastern Anthropological Association, Occasional Proceedings,* 1.

multiculturalism Public policy for managing cultural diversity in a multi-ethnic society, officially stressing mutual respect and tolerance for cultural differences within a country's borders.

Changing attitudes toward the rights of Canada's native people led to the creation of Nunavut, a province roughly the size of western Europe, now governed by the region's Inuit themselves. Here, an Inuit elder lights a traditional "qulluliq" at the dedication of Nunavut's legislature on March 30, 1999.

of one such society—and its attendant problems—we may look at the Central American country of Guatemala.

Guatemalan Cultural Pluralism

Guatemala, like many other pluralistic countries, came into being through conquest—a conquest that was about as violent and brutal as it could be, given the technology of the time (the 1500s). A military expedition of ruthless Spanish adventurers defeated a people whose civilization was far older than Spain's. Their aim was to extract as much wealth as they could for themselves and Spain by seizing the riches of the rulers they overthrew and putting the indigenous population to work mining gold and silver. For the nearly 500 years since, their Ladino (non-Indian) descendants have continued to be motivated by the same interests, even after independence from Spain.

Following its conquest, Guatemala never experienced substantial immigration from Europe. As much as possible, the conquerors and their descendants hoarded the spoils of victory—which, it turned out, included no rich deposits of gold or silver. Guatemala had little else to attract profit-seeking outsiders, so Indians there continued to outnumber non-Indians. Yet, the apparatus of the state, with its instruments of force (the police and army), remained firmly in the hands of the Ladino minority, which demanded tribute and labor from Indian communities.

In the 19th century Guatemala's Ladino population saw coffee and cotton exports as new sources of wealth for themselves. Taking over vast tracts of Indian ground to create their plantations, they deprived the indigenous communities of sufficient land for their own needs. Consequently, many Indians had no alternative but to work on the plantations for pitiful wages. Those who complained faced brutal treatment from plantation authorities.

In the 1940s democratic reforms were introduced in Guatemala. For the first time in over 400 years native peoples could at least hold official positions in their own communities. In the 1950s the Roman Catholic Church began to promote agricultural, consumer, and credit cooperatives in the country's rural areas, inhabited predominantly by Indians. This positive turn toward recog-

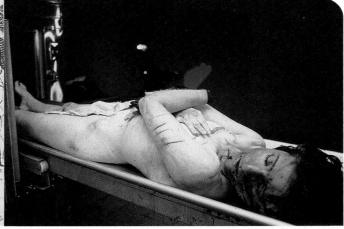

VISUAL COUNTERPOINT In Guatemala, the military and other government-sanctioned groups used violence to maintain the control of one nationality (*Ladino*) over another (*Maya*). There is an eerie similarity between these two images—a 1522 illustration of Spaniards attacking Mayas and a recent photograph of a Maya murdered by Guatemalan government military forces. Although violence has subsided, it has not ended completely.

nizing the social, economic, and cultural rights of Indians came to an abrupt halt in 1954 when the U.S. government engineered a military coup that replaced the democratically elected government with an anticommunist dictatorship. The new regime immediately reversed the land reforms and restored ownership of the vast banana plantations to the U.S.-based United Fruit Company (since then renamed Del Monte). As before, the Indians stayed out of politics except within their own villages. And, for the most part, they remained aloof from the armed rebellion that soon arose in reaction to a succession of military regimes. However, because the confrontations took place in the neighborhoods of Indians who had been distrusted by Ladinos for centuries, the ruling elite came to regard all rural peoples with suspicion. Inevitably, Indians were drawn into the violence.

In the late 1970s and early 1980s, indigenous villages were destroyed, inhabitants killed, and bodies burnt or otherwise mutilated by either the Guatemalan army or secret death squads supported by the army. Military repression came to be seen as the most effective way to maintain political order. Between 1981 and 1983, an estimated 15,000 people "disappeared," at least 90,000 were killed, half a million became refugees inside Guatemala, and 150,000 fled to Mexico while another 200,000 found their way to other countries, including the United States. In the areas hardest hit, the population fell by almost half, and whole towns—some of which had existed for 1,000 years—were destroyed. The overwhelming majority of victims were Indians, but the violence also claimed the life of Guatemalan anthropologist Myrna Mack. She was stabbed to death by the military in 1990 soon after she published a revealing study showing that the government's counterinsurgency policies were responsible for the upheaval and suffering of Guatemala's indigenous peoples.

In the early 1990s, forensic anthropologists, at considerable risk to themselves, began working with local Indian communities, exhuming the bodies of victims in order to bring the killers to account. And an increasing number of Mayas took their struggle for justice to the international arena. In 1992, Rigoberta Menchú, a Maya woman who has worked tirelessly for indigenous rights, won the prestigious Nobel Peace Prize. Receiving this honor in 1992 had particular political significance, because it was the year of the Columbian quincentennial in which people in Europe and the Americas commemorated Columbus' pioneering journey across the Atlantic ocean—a journey that had such devastating consequences for American Indians. The prize focused international attention on the ongoing repression of indigenous peoples in Guatemala and helped pave the way to peace accords in late December 1996. A parallel document, the Accord on Identity and the Rights of Indigenous Peoples, promised that Guatemala would be re-established as a multilingual country where the cultural rights of all indigenous groups would be constitutionally protected.

As of spring 2004, this agreement has yet to be fully implemented. On the positive side, many Maya Indian

Rigoberta Menchú, a Maya woman who won the Nobel Peace Prize in 1992 for her activism on behalf of indigenous rights.

Forensic anthropologists in Guatemala exhume victims of a state-sponsored massacre from a mass grave.

Although a peace agreement in Guatemala has greatly reduced violence against that country's Maya population, anti-Maya violence is on the increase in the neighboring Mexican state of Chiapas. Shown here are coffins with victims of a December 1997 massacre.

refugees have returned to their home villages and towns in Guatemala, where community members have started various educational projects and are pressing for legal recognition of their traditional rights and cultural customs, as called for in the accords. However, Ladinos continue to show little concern and resist attempts to hold the military accountable for past abuses. Moreover, robberies, assaults (including torture), and death threats against journalists, human rights groups, and nongovernmental organizations have increased since 2000.

Guatemala's Ladino elite may be talking more about the need to forge a true national identity in their country, but there is no guarantee that this will be done in a manner that does justice to that country's indigenous peoples. We cannot ignore the fact that, historically, what has been called "nation building" in all parts of the world almost always involves attempts to destroy the cultures of peoples belonging to nations other than those who control the governments in those countries.[5] During the last two decades of the 20th century, states were borrowing more money to fight peoples within their boundaries than for all other programs combined. Nearly all state debt in Africa and nearly half of all other debt in "underdeveloped" countries comes from the cost of weapons purchased by states to fight their own citizens.[6] The more divergent cultural traditions are, the more difficult it seems to make pluralism work.

That said, states as political constructs are products of human imagination, and nothing prevents us from imagining in ways more tolerant of cultural pluralism or multiculturalism. For example, consider once again Switzerland, where multiculturalism has worked out to the satisfaction of all four ethnic groups. In this confederation of small states (cantons), a political tradition of direct democracy is combined with a political organization that does not interfere with the country's regional, linguistic, and religious differences. Obviously, replicating such a success in other political arenas will take a good deal of work, but at least the international community recognizes the concept of *group* rights. Even though it often fails to act on it, the United Nations General Assembly in its 1966 Covenant of Human Rights states unequivocally that: "In those states in which ethnic, religious or linguistic minorities exist, persons belonging to such minorities shall not be denied the rights, in community with the other members of their group, to enjoy their own culture, to profess and practice their own religion or to use their own language."[7] Education has a key

___

[5]Van Den Berghe, P. (1992). The modern state: Nation builder or nation killer? *International Journal of Group Tensions*, 22(3), 194–198.

[6]*Cultural Survival Quarterly* 15(4), p. 38 (1991).

[7]Quoted in Bodley, J. H. (1990). *Victims of progress* (3rd ed., p. 99). Mountain View, CA: Mayfield.

Advocacy for the Rights of Indigenous Peoples

Anthropologists are increasingly concerned about the rapid disappearance of the world's remaining indigenous peoples for a number of reasons, foremost being the basic issue of human rights. The world today is rushing to develop those parts of the planet that have so far escaped industrialization, or the extraction of resources regarded as vital to the well-being of developed economies. These development efforts are planned, financed, and carried out both by governments and businesses (generally the huge multinational corporations) as well as by international lending institutions. Unfortunately, the rights of native peoples generally have not been incorporated into the programs and concerns of these organizations, even where laws exist that are supposed to protect the rights of such peoples.

For example, the typical pattern for development of Brazil's Amazon basin has been for the government to build roads, along which it settles poor people from other parts of the country. This brings them into conflict with Indians already living there, who begin to die off in large numbers from diseases contracted from the new settlers. Before long, the neo-Brazilian settlers learn that the soils are not suited for their kind of farming; meanwhile, outside logging, mining, and agribusiness interests exert pressure to get them off the land. Ultimately, the neo-Brazilians wind up living in disease-ridden slums, while the Indians are decimated by the diseases and violence unleashed upon them by the outsiders. Those who survive are usually relocated to places where resources are inadequate to support them.

In an attempt to do what they can to help indigenous peoples gain title to their lands and avoid exploitation by outsiders, anthropologists in various countries have formed advocacy groups. The major one in the United States is Cultural Survival, Inc., based in Cambridge, Massachusetts. This organization's interest is not in preserving indigenous cultures in some sort of romantic, pristine condition, so that they will be there to study or to serve as "living museum exhibits." Rather, it is to provide the information and support to help endangered groups assess their situation, adapt to the changing circumstances, and practice self-determination in the face of outside political forces. Challenging dominant assumptions that indigenous peoples should be assimilated into mainstream societies, Cultural Survival advocates that they should have the freedom to make their own decisions about how they live. Working as a facilitator, the organization assists with projects initiated by indigenous groups to deal with problems defined by the groups themselves. It may suggest ways to help and has the capability to activate extensive networks of anthropologists, other indigenous peoples who already have faced similar problems, and those government officials whose support can be critical to success. This organization's publications play an important role publicizing the distinct and shared challenges confronting indigenous peoples all around the world.

Cultural Survival funds and other forms of assistance have focused in particular on securing the land rights of indigenous peoples and organizing native federations. It has also identified and funded a number of locally designed experiments in sustainable development. Among these is the Turkmen Weaving Project (which helps Afghan refugees to make profitable income from traditional rug weaving) and the Ikwe Marketing Collective (which helps Minnesota Indians market wild rice and crafts). It also founded Cultural Survival Enterprises, which has developed and expanded markets for such indigenous products as the nuts used in the popular Rain Forest Crunch (itself a creation of Cultural Survival). The organization achieved a major accomplishment in 1982, spearheading a movement that convinced the World Bank to adopt a policy that *guaranteed* the rights and autonomy of tribal peoples and minorities in any project in which the bank is involved. Despite such successes, much remains to be done to secure the survival of indigenous peoples in all parts of the world. ■ ■ ■

role to play in making this acknowledged right a reality. This includes the sort of advocacy work that many anthropologists do on behalf of indigenous peoples—as illustrated in this chapter's Anthropology Applied, above.

MEDIATREK

To find out about Cultural Survival, a leading advocate for the rights, voices, and visions of indigenous peoples, go to MediaTrek 16.2 on the companion Web site or CD-ROM.

Ethnocentrism and Cultural Pluralism

The major problem associated with cultural pluralism has to do with ethnocentrism, a concept introduced in Chapter 2. To function effectively, we may expect a society to embrace at least a degree of ethnocentrism—the idea that its ways are the only proper ones, irrespective of how other cultures do things. Such national self-satisfaction provides individuals with a sense of ethnic pride in and loyalty to their cultural traditions, from which they derive psychological support and a firm bond to their group. In societies where one's self-identification derives from the group, the idea that one's own customary ideas and practices are ideal is essential to a sense of personal worth. As illustrated again and again in this book, the problem with ethnocentrism is that all too easily it can be taken as a charter for condemning other cultures as inferior and as such exploiting them for the benefit of one's own, even though this does not have to be the choice. When it is, however, unrest, hostility, and violence commonly result.

VISUAL COUNTERPOINT A distraught Chechen woman stands next to her home, destroyed by a Russian rocket, and a group of militant Mohawk Indian native rights activists and their indigenous allies face off with Quebec's provincial armed forces at Kahnawake in summer 1990. Both photos exemplify the willingness of states that are controlled by one nationality to use their armies against people of other nationalities within their borders in order to promote the state's interests over those of the other nationality.

In the world today, governments frequently use the idea that no group has the right to stand in the way of "the greater good for the greater number" to justify the expropriation of natural resources in regions traditionally occupied by subsistence farmers, pastoral nomads, or food foragers—without any respect for the rights, concerns, or wishes of those peoples. But is it truly the greater good for the greater number? A look at the rise of global corporations helps to answer this question.

The Rise of Global Corporations

The resistance of the world to political integration seems to be offset to some extent by the ongoing rise and growth of global corporations. Because these cut across the international boundaries between states, they are a force for worldwide integration despite the political, linguistic, religious, and other cultural differences that separate people.

Global corporations are not entirely new in the world. (The Dutch East India Company founded in 1602 was a powerful enterprise, financed by investors and governed by a board of directors, with fortified trading posts all over the world and a large merchant fleet crossing all the oceans for two centuries.) But they became common only in the latter half of the 20th century. Now they are a far-reaching economic and political force in the world. Modern-day business giants such as General Electric, Shell, and Toyota are actually clusters of several corporations joined by ties of common ownership and responsive to a common management strategy. Usually tightly controlled by a head office in one country, these enterprises organize and integrate production across the international boundaries of different countries for interests formulated in corporate boardrooms, irrespective of whether these are consistent with the interests of people in the countries where they operate. In a sense they are products of the technological revolution, for without sophisticated data-processing equipment and electronic communication, these megacorporations could not keep adequate track of their worldwide operations.

Though typically thought of as responding impersonally to outside market forces, large corporations are in fact controlled by an increasingly smaller number of wealthy capitalists who benefit directly from their operations. Yet, the world's largest individual stockholders and most powerful directors, unlike political leaders, are known to few people. For that matter, most people cannot even name the world's major global corporations, which include Wal-Mart, Shell, ExxonMobil, British Petroleum, General Motors, DaimlerChrysler, Toyota, General Electric, and Citigroup (Figure 16.2). Each of these business giants currently generates annual revenues above $120 billion, and one of them—Wal-Mart—is near the $250 billion mark.[8]

So great is the power of large businesses operating all across the globe that they increasingly thwart the wishes of national governments or international organizations such as the United Nations, Red Cross, International Court of Justice, or the World Council of Churches. Because the information these corporations process is kept from flowing in a meaningful way to the population at large, or even to lower levels within the organization, it becomes difficult for governments to get the information they need for informed policy decisions. It took years for the U.S. Congress to extract the information it needed from tobacco companies to decide what to do about tobacco legislation—and it is nearly as slow-going today getting energy and media companies to provide data needed for regulation purposes. Beyond

---

[8]Forbes International 500 List.

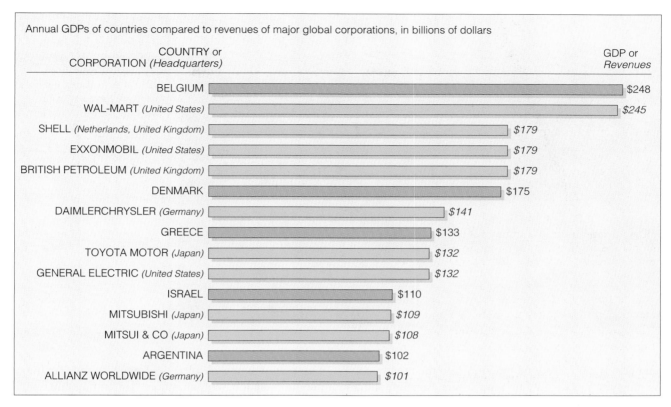

FIGURE 16.2

In today's consumer-driven world, it is not uncommon for the yearly revenues of large multinational corporations to equal and even exceed the total value of all goods and services produced within a country per year, known as a country's Gross Domestic Product (GDP). This graph shows the annual GDPs of selected countries alongside the annual revenues of leading global corporations (Note: GDP says nothing about the unequal distribution of wealth within a country.) (Based on 2002 figures posted on www.forbes.com and www.worldbank.org)

this, the global corporations have repeatedly shown they can overrule foreign policy decisions. While some might see this as a hopeful signal for getting beyond national vices and rivalries, it raises the unsettling issue of whether or not the global arena should be controlled by immensely large and powerful private corporations interested only in financial profits. According to one market research organization,

> Today, the top 100 companies control 33 percent of the world's assets, but employ only one percent of the world's workforce. General Motors is larger than Denmark, Wal-Mart bigger than South Africa. The mega-corporations roam freely around the globe, lobbying legislators, bankrolling elections and playing governments off against each other to get the best deals. Their private hands control the bulk of the world's news and information flows.[9]

If the ability of global corporations to ignore the wishes of sovereign governments is cause for concern, so is their ability to act in concert with such governments. Here, in fact, is where their worst excesses have occurred. One example took place in Brazil, where the situation is hardly unique but is especially well documented. After a 1964 military coup in that country, a partnership emerged between the new government, which was anxious to proceed as rapidly as possible with development of the Amazon rainforest, and a number of global corporations and international lending institutions. (The corporations included ALCOA, Borden, Union Carbide, Swift-Armour, and Volkswagen, among others, and the lending institutions included the Export-Import Bank, the Inter-American Development Bank, and the World Bank.[10])

To help bring about what they liked to call the Brazilian miracle, these allies initiated new road construction projects and introduced inappropriate technology

---

[9]*www.adbusters.org*, accessed January 10, 2003. See also Hertz, N. (2001). *The silent takeover: Global capitalism and the death of democracy* (p. 43). New York: Arrow Books.

[10]Davis, S. H. (1982). *Victims of the miracle*. Cambridge, England: Cambridge University Press.

© Sue Cunningham Photographic

Brazil's Grand Carajas iron ore mine is an example of the kind of project states favor in their drive to develop. Not only does this introduce ecologically unsound technologies, but it also commonly has devastating effects on the indigenous people whose land is seized.

and ecologically unsound practices into the region, converting vast woodlands into semi-desert. Far more shocking, however, has been the practice of uprooting whole human societies because they are seen as obstacles to economic growth. Eager to alleviate acute land shortages in the country's impoverished northeastern region, but unwilling to break up the huge rural estates owned by a powerful elite and embark on much-needed land reform, government officials launched massive resettlement schemes. They lured millions of Brazilian peasants to the Amazon to clear the forest and settle as farmers in territories traditionally owned and long inhabited by many different indigenous nations. Soon, however, it became obvious that few of these newcomers could adequately support their families, so tens of thousands turned to gold mining. This, in turn, resulted in poisoning the rivers with mercury, creating serious health problems. Bad as this is for these poor peasants, the disease, death, and human suffering that such schemes and policies have unleashed upon the native Indians can only be described as massive. Entire indigenous groups have been (and are still being) destroyed with a thoroughness not achieved even by the communist dictator Stalin during his "Great Terror" in the Soviet Union of the 1930s or the Nazis in World War II. Were it not so well documented, it would be beyond belief.

Megacorporations are changing the shape of the world and the lives of individuals from every walk of life, including those they employ. Anthropologist Jules Henry, in a classic 1965 study of life in the United States, observed that working for any large corporation—global or not—tends to generate "hostility, instability,

and fear of being obsolete and unprotected. For most people their job was what they had to do rather than what they wanted to do, . . . taking a job, therefore, meant giving up part of their selves."[11]

Since Henry's day such feelings have grown in the ever more "sprawling, anonymous, networks" of global corporations.[12] Not only are business decisions typically made in corporate headquarters very far removed from where the actual operations of the business take place, but also, because corporations depend on sophisticated data-processing systems, many decisions can be and are being made by computers programmed for particular contingencies and strategies. In the face of such coldly calculating systems for making decisions exclusively in the corporate interest, workers become ever more fearful that, if they ask too much of the company, it simply may shift its operations to another part of the world where it can find cheaper, more submissive personnel.

In their never-ending search for cheap labor, multinational corporations have returned to a practice once seen in the textile mills of 19th-century Britain and New England, but now on a much larger scale. More than ever before, they have come to favor women for low-skilled assembly jobs. In so-called underdeveloped countries, as subsistence farming gives way to mechanical agriculture for production of crops for export, women are less able to

---

[11]Henry, J. (1965). *Culture against man* (p. 127). New York: Vintage Books.

---

[12]Pitt, D. (1977). Comment. *Current Anthropology, 18,* 628.

In so-called underdeveloped countries, women have become a source of cheap labor for large corporations, as subsistence farming has given way to mechanized agriculture. Unable to contribute to their families' well-being in any other way, they have no choice but to take on menial jobs for low wages.

contribute to their families' survival. Together with the devaluation of domestic work, this places pressure on women to seek jobs outside the household to contribute to its support. Since most women in these countries do not have the time or resources to get an education or to develop special job skills, only low-paying jobs are open to them. Corporate officials, for their part, assume female workers are strictly temporary, and high turnover means that wages can be kept low. Unmarried women are especially favored for employment, for it is assumed that they are free from family responsibilities until they marry, whereupon they will leave the labor force. Thus, the increasing importance of the multinationals in developing countries is contributing to the emergence of a marked gender-segregated division of labor. On top of their housework, women hold low-paying jobs that require little skill; altogether, they may work as many as 15 hours a day. Higher-paying jobs, or at least those that require special skills, are generally held by men, whose workday may be shorter since they do not have additional domestic tasks to perform. Men who lack special skills—and many do—are often doomed to lives of unemployment.

Big business has created problems for consumers as well as workers. In a 10-year intensive study of relations between producers and consumers of products and services, anthropologist Laura Nader found repeated and documented offenses by North American businesses that could not be handled by existing complaint mechanisms, either in or out of court. Face-to-faceless relations between producers and consumers, among whom there is a grossly unequal distribution of power, have exacted a high cost: a terrible sense of apathy, even a loss of faith in the system itself.

In recent years, the power of corporations has become all the greater through media expansion. Over the

Maka Indian woman in Paraguay. The poorest people in the world often wear clothing discarded by those who are better off—and people from all walks of life can be found wearing clothes with corporate logos. The power that big business (such as the Disney media corporation) has over individuals is illustrated by the ability of corporations to get consumers to pay for goods that advertise corporate products.

past two decades, a global commercial media system has developed, dominated by a few megacorporations, most based in the United States. One such global media corporation is NBC, now owned by General Electric (GE), which is among the world's leading electronics and manufacturing firms with over $126 billion in sales. In addition to NBC, GE owns various other broadcasting companies, including Paxson Communications and the Telemundo Communications Group. It also owns and operates a host of television stations in major urban markets such as New York, Los Angeles, Chicago, and Washington, DC—not to mention a digital media firm and three cable network companies, including CNBC and MSNBC. Moreover, GE owns companies such as GE Aircraft Engines, GE Commercial Finance, GE Consumer Products, GE Industrial Systems, GE Insurance, GE Medical Systems, GE Plastics, GE Power Systems, GE Specialty Materials, and GE Transportation Systems, and so on.

Having control of television and other media, as well as the advertising industry, gives global corporations such as GE enormous influence on the ideas and behavior of hundreds of millions of ordinary people across the world in ways they little suspect and can hardly imagine. Consider, for example, the powerful marketing messages that shape cultural standards concerning the ideal human body. The widespread nature of this concern is evident in the highly popular U.S. television program *Extreme Makeover,* featuring a few individuals chosen from many thousands of applicants to have their dream come true—to change their looks in an effort to lead better lives. They receive free plastic surgery and other radical cosmetic procedures in exchange for undergoing the knife on camera and allowing the details of their makeover to be broadcast on international television. The following Original Study offers details on what has become a cosmetic surgery trend.

Original Study

Standardizing the Body: The Question of Choice

The question of choice is central to the story of how medicine and business generate controlling processes in the shaping of women's bodies. Images of the body appear natural within their specific cultural milieus. For example, breast implants are not seen as odd within the cultural milieu of the United States, and female circumcision and infibulation (also known as female genital mutilation or fgm) is not considered odd among people from the Sudan and several other African countries. However, many feminist writers differentiate fgm from breast implantation by arguing that North American women *choose* to have breast implants whereas in Africa women are presumably subject to indoctrination [since they experience circumcision as young girls]. One of the most heated debates arising from the public health concern over breast implants is whether the recipients are freely situated—that is, whether their decision is voluntary or whether control is disguised as free will.

An informed response to the free-choice argument requires knowing how the beauty-industrial complex works. Toward this end, corporate accountability researcher Linda Coco carried out fieldwork in multiple sites, gaining insights into the inner-workings of a multibillion-dollar industry that segments the female body and manufactures commodities of and for the body.

Coco's research shows how some women get caught in the official beauty ideology, and in the case of silicone-gel breast implants some hundreds of thousands of women have been ensnared. But who gets caught and when is important to an understanding of the ecology of power. The average age of a woman having breast implantation is 36 years, and she has an average of two children. She is the beauty industry's insecure consumer recast as a patient [with an illness the industry defines as] hypertrophy (small breasts). Coco quotes a past president of the American Society of Plastic and Reconstructive Surgery (ASPRS): "There is substantial and enlarging medical knowledge to the effect that these deformities [small breasts] are really a disease which result in the patient's feelings of inadequacies, lack of self-confidence, distortion of body image, and a total lack of well-being due to a lack of self-perceived femininity. . . . Enlargement . . . is therefore . . . necessary to ensure the quality of life for the [female] patient." In other words, cosmetic surgery is necessary to the patient's psychological health.

The plastic surgeon regards the construction of the official breast as art, the aim being to reform the female body according to the ideals of classic Western art. One surgeon pioneering procedures for correcting deformity took as his ideal female figure that of ancient Greek statues, which he carefully measured, noticing the exact size and shape of the breasts, their vertical location between the third and seventh ribs, the horizontal between the line of the sternal [breast bone] border and the anterior axillary line, and so forth. In Coco's analysis the exercise of the plastic surgeon's techno-art recreates a particular static, official breast shape and applies this creation ostensibly to relieve women's mental suffering. The surgeon becomes a psychological healer as well as an artist.

Along with art and psychology, there is, of course, the business of organized plastic surgery, which responds to the demands and opportunities of market economics (Figure 16.3). By the late 1970s and early 1980s there was a glut of plastic surgeons. The ASPRS began to operate like a commercial enterprise instead of a medical society, saturating the media with ads and even providing low-cost financing. The discourse became a sales pitch. Women "seek" breast implants to keep their husbands or their jobs, to attract men, or to become socially acceptable. Coco calls this "patriarchal capitalism" and questions whether this is free choice or "mind colonization."

Understanding "choice" led Coco to an examination of the power both in the doctor–patient relationship and in the control of information. She found that women "were told by the media, plastic surgeons, women's magazines, other women, and the business world that they could enhance their lives by enhancing their bust lines . . . the social imperative for appearance was personalized, psychologized, and normalized." Social surveys indicate that, to the extent that women internalize the social imperative, they feel they are making the decision on their own.

Not surprisingly, women whose surgery resulted in medical complications often came to recognize the external processes of coercive persuasion that had led them to seek implants. In some ways, they resembled former

cult members who had been deprogrammed: Their disillusionment caused them to question the system that had encouraged them to make the decision in the first place. The result was a gradual building of protest against the industry, expressed in networks, newsletters, support groups, workshops, and seminars. As have some former cult members, women have brought suit, testified before lawmakers, and challenged in other ways some of the largest corporations and insurance companies in the land. The choice of implants, they learn, is part of a matrix of controlling processes in which women are subjects. Given the right circumstances it could happen to anyone. In the Sudan, the young girl is told that fgm procedures are done for her and not to her. In the United States the mutilation

of natural breasts is also done for the re-creation of femininity. Although power is exercised differently in these two cases, Coco notes the similarity: "The operation on the female breast in [North] America holds much of the same social symbolism and expression of cultural mandate as does fgm in Sudan. Thus, the question of why women choose breast augmentation becomes moot."

Breast implantation is now spreading elsewhere, most notably to China. Will it become a functional equivalent to foot-binding in China as part of the competition between patriarchies East and West? Whatever the answer, many social thinkers agree that people are always more vulnerable to intense persuasion during periods of historical dislocation—a break with structures and

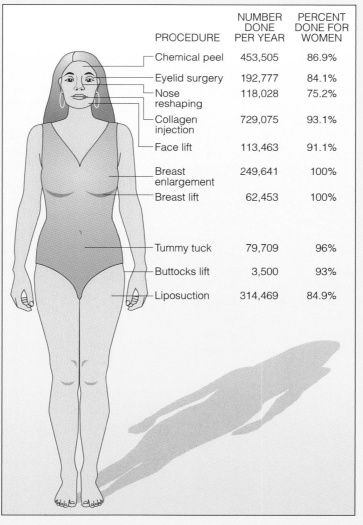

PROCEDURE	NUMBER DONE PER YEAR	PERCENT DONE FOR WOMEN
Chemical peel	453,505	86.9%
Eyelid surgery	192,777	84.1%
Nose reshaping	118,028	75.2%
Collagen injection	729,075	93.1%
Face lift	113,463	91.1%
Breast enlargement	249,641	100%
Breast lift	62,453	100%
Tummy tuck	79,709	96%
Buttocks lift	3,500	93%
Liposuction	314,469	84.9%

FIGURE 16.3

Cosmetic surgical and nonsurgical procedures in the United States (2002) and the percentage carried out for women. In 2002 there were more than 1.4 million cosmetic surgeries done in the United States at a cost of about $5.4 billion, and nearly 4.7 million nonsurgical procedures (chemical peels, collagen injections, and so on) at a cost of over $2.3 billion. From 1997 to 2002, the number of cosmetic procedures performed increased 228 percent.

[CONTINUED]

[CONTINUED]

symbols familiar to the life cycle—in which the media can bring us images and ideas originating in past, contemporary, or even imaginary worlds.

Feminist researchers have sought to crack controlling paradigms such as those that define women's capacities and those that construct a standardized body shape and determine what is beautiful in women. Some of their writings are attempts to free the mind from the beauty constructions of cosmetic industries and fashion magazines. Others relay how the one model of Western beauty is affecting members of ethnic groups who aspire to look the way advertisements say they should. Choice is an illusion, since the restructuring of taste is inextricably linked to shifts in the organization of consumption. *(Adapted from L. Nader. (1997). Controlling processes: Tracing the dynamics of power.* Current Anthropology, 38, 715–717.)

The far-reaching capabilities of modern electronic and digital technologies have led to the creation of a new global media environment. Together with radio and television, the Internet is now the dominant means of mass communication around the world. Today, the global flow of information made possible by fiber optic cables and communications satellites orbiting the earth is almost entirely digital-electronic and takes place in a new boundless cultural space that anthropologist Arjun Appadurai refers to as a "global mediascape" (see Anthropologists of Note).

STRUCTURAL POWER IN THE AGE OF GLOBALIZATION

All of the above makes it clear that a new form of expansive capitalism has emerged since the mid-1900s. Operating under the banner of globalization, it builds on earlier cultural structures of worldwide trade networks, and it is the successor to a system of colonialism in which a handful of powerful, mainly European, capitalist states ruled and exploited foreign nations inhabiting distant territories. Enormously complex and turbulent, globalization is a dynamically structured process in which individuals, business corporations, and political institutions are actively rearranging and restructuring the social field of force to their own competitive advantage, vying for increasingly scarce natural resources, cheap labor, new commercial markets, and ever-larger

profits in a huge political arena spanning the entire globe. Doing this, or course, requires a great deal of power.

As discussed previously, power refers to the ability of individuals or groups to impose their will upon others and make them do things even against their own wants or wishes. Power plays a major role in coordinating and regulating collective behavior toward imposing or maintaining law and order within—and beyond—a particular community or society. There are different levels of power within societies, as well as among societies. Eric Wolf (featured in the Anthropologists of Note in Chapter 15) pointed out the importance of understanding a macro level of power that he referred to as **structural power**—power that organizes and orchestrates the systemic interaction within and among societies, directing economic and political forces on the one hand and ideological forces that shape public ideas, values, and beliefs on the other.[13]

The concept of structural power applies not only to regional political organizations such as chiefdoms or states but also captures the complex new cultural formations currently emerging in the globalization process. It focuses attention on the systemic interaction between the global forces directing the world's changing economies and political institutions on the one hand and those that shape public ideas, values, and beliefs on the other. Joseph Nye, a political scientist, international security specialist, and former Assistant Secretary of Defense in the U.S. government, refers to these two major interacting forces in the worldwide arena as "hard power" and "soft power."[14] **Hard power** is the kind of coercive power that is backed up by economic and military force. **Soft power** is co-optive rather than coercive, pressing others through attraction and persuasion to

structural power Power that organizes and orchestrates the systemic interaction within and among societies, directing economic and political forces on the one hand and ideological forces that shape public ideas, values, and beliefs on the other.
hard power Coercive power that is backed up by economic and military force.
soft power Pressing others through attraction and persuasion to change their ideas, beliefs, values, and behaviors.

---

[13]Wolf, E. (1999). *Envisioning power: Ideologies of dominance and crisis* (p. 5). Berkeley: University of California Press.

---

[14]Nye, J. (2002). *The paradox of American power: Why the world's only superpower can't go it alone.* New York: Oxford University Press.

Anthropologists of Note

Arjun Appadurai (1949–)

Courtesy of Arjun Appadurai

Arjun Appadurai is one of millions of transnational migrants in the world. Growing up in India, he studied at the University of Bombay before heading to the United States, where he continued his education and chose a life in academia. Living abroad, he became interested in the dispersion of ethnic groups around the globe and in the question of how widely scattered members of these groups maintain their sense of cultural identity. His research—including fieldwork in India, South Africa, and the Philippines—shows that migrants form part of strong social networks, which, thanks to modern technology, reach far beyond traditional geographic boundaries.

Appadurai has developed theoretical concepts that help us understand the complex and largely unpredictable processes that are currently rearranging human relations and restructuring cultural systems worldwide. Although most people in today's world still function within geographically defined communities, Appadurai points out that territorial borders have become increasingly irrelevant given the "cultural flows" in our emerging global environment. He marks out five global spaces or dimensions in which transnational cultural flows occur, identifying them as "scapes" (meaning something crafted, configured, or transformed by humans):

■ Ethnoscapes: the fluid and shifting landscape of migrants, refugees, exiles, tourists, and other moving groups and people
■ Technoscapes: the global configuration of technologies moving at high speeds across previously restrictive borders

■ Financescapes: the global crossroads of currency speculation and financial transfers
■ Mediascapes: the distribution of electronic media capabilities to produce and spread information, plus the large complex repertoire of narratives and visual images generated by these media
■ Ideoscapes: ideologies produced by the state and alternative ideologies developed by non-state and counter-hegemonic forces, around which societies organize their political cultures and collective cultural identities

Appadurai earned a Ph.D. from the University of Chicago in 1976 and has taught at the University of Pennsylvania, the University of Chicago, and Yale. Currently, he is provost at the New School University in New York City. Beyond university work, he has served as a consultant/advisor to a wide range of organizations, including the United Nations and the World Bank.

---

change their ideas, beliefs, values, and behaviors. Although propaganda is a form of soft power, the exercise of ideological influence (the global struggle for the hearts and minds) also operates through more subtle means, such as foreign aid, international diplomacy, news media, sports, entertainment, museum exhibits, and academic exchanges.

In today's globalization process, the United States has more hard power at its disposal than any of its allies or rivals worldwide. It is the global leader in military spending—about $340 billion per year, followed by Japan ($47 billion), Britain ($36 billion), France ($34 billion), and China ($31 billion). In fact, as the world's dominant superpower, the United States spends more on its armed forces than the next twenty leading countries combined. And although there are eight other nuclear weapons states (Russia, Britain, France, and China, as well as Israel, India, and Pakistan, and now also Korea), collectively possessing about 30,000 nuclear missiles and bombs, the United States has by far the largest arsenal at its disposal.[15]

In addition to military might, hard power involves the use of economic strength as a political instrument of coercion or intimidation in the global structuring process. Among other things, this means that economic size and productivity, technological capability, and finance capital may be brought to bear on the global market, forcing weaker states to break down trade barriers protecting their workers, natural resources, and local markets. As the world's largest economy and leading exporter, the United States has long pushed for free trade for its corporations doing business on a global scale. Sometimes, it uses military power to impose changes on a foreign political landscape by means of armed interventions or full-scale invasions. For instance, when the United Fruit Company, owner of enormous banana plantations in Guatemala, saw its economic interests threatened by that country's democratically elected government, the U.S. government engineered a military coup in 1954 that resulted in a dictatorship favorable to U.S.-based corporations. Through history, the United States (like several other powerful countries) has engaged in such military interventions around the world. Because of this, many see it as an ever-present threat, apt to use overwhelming military force in order to benefit its corporate interests from fruit to fuel,

---

[15]Sparks, J. (2003, December 22). "The Power Game." *Newsweek, 142*(25).

September 2003 annual meeting of two global banking institutions, the World Bank and the International Monetary Fund. Both institutions have tremendous structural power, for they direct flows of capital to certain regions of the world—resulting in massive economic change.

Courtesy of IMF

from microchips to automobiles. The corporations, in turn, wield enormous political and financial power over governments and international organizations, including the World Trade Organization, headquartered in Geneva, and global banking institutions such as the International Monetary Fund (IMF) and World Bank, both based in Washington, DC.

Specializing in short-term loans to assist poor or developing countries, the IMF's financial resources weigh in at about $300 billion. The five wealthiest countries in the world (United States, Japan, Germany, France, and Britain) control 40 percent of this global fund and dominate its executive board. The IMF's structural power is evident not only in which development projects and policies it chooses to give financial support, but also in its surveillance practices, which involve monitoring a borrower's economic and financial developments. The World Bank invests or makes long-term loans ($20 billion annually) for economic development projects such as roads, schools, and health systems to reduce poverty in about 100 developing countries. Like the IMF, it is largely controlled by a handful of powerful capitalist states. Operating under geopolitical constraints, these global banking institutions strategically direct capital flows to projects in certain parts of the world, financially supporting some governments and withholding capital from others.

Both the IMF and the World Bank have been accused of being insensitive to the political and cultural consequences of the projects they support. For example, in the 1990s the World Bank provided loans to a hydropower project in southern Chile to build dams in the upper Bio-Bio River without any serious consideration the human rights of local Pehuenche Indians.

The dam flooded a large part of the Pehuenche's ancestral lands, forcing hundreds to be resettled against their own will. Likewise, the World Bank approved a $40 million loan to the Chinese government to relocate some of the country's poorest Han Chinese farmers to more fertile land in Qinghai, territory that Tibetans consider part of their homeland. Tibetans protested that the bank was supporting China's effort to dilute the Tibetan ethnic minority population in that region.

Globalization does more than create a worldwide field of force in which megacorporations make megaprofits. It also wreaks havoc in many traditional cultures and disrupts long-established social organizations everywhere. By the early 21st century, the global trend of economic inequality is becoming clear: The poor are becoming poorer and the rich are becoming richer. For the many thousands of big winners or have-lots, there are many millions of losers or have-nots.

As home base to more global corporations than any other country, the United States is endeavoring to protect its interests by investing in creating and controlling what it refers to as a global security environment. Numerous other countries, unable to afford expensive weapons systems (or blocked from developing or acquiring them), have invested in biological or chemical warfare technology. Still others, including relatively powerless political groups, have resorted to guerilla tactics or terrorism as part of their local, regional, or even global warfare strategies.

In addition to reliance on military and economic hard power in the global quest for dominance and profit, competing states and corporations utilize the ideological persuasion of soft power as transmitted by means of electronic and digital media, communications satellites, and other forms of information and communication technology. One of the major tasks of soft power is to package and sell the general idea of globalization as something positive and progressive (as "freedom," "free" trade, "free" market) and to frame or brand anything that opposes capitalism in negative terms. One outcome of this complex interaction between hard and soft power in structuring the global arena is the creation of a new collective awareness of worldwide connectivity, making peoples everywhere understand and possibly accept the new cultural order. Considering existing cultural differences, political divisions, and competing economic interests, combined with growing worldwide resistance against superpower domination, the emerging world system is inherently unstable, vulnerable, and unpredictable.

Structural power and its associated concepts of hard and soft power enable us to better understand the wider field of force in which local communities throughout the world are now compelled to operate. To comprehend it is to realize how unequal the distribution of power is in today's global arena. That said, no matter how effectively a dominant state or corporation combines its hard and soft power, globalization does run into opposition. Pockets of resistance exist within the wealthy industrial and postindustrial states as well as elsewhere in the world. This resistance may manifest itself in the rise of traditionalisms and revitalization movements—efforts to return to life as it was before the familiar order became unhinged and people became unsettled. Some of these reactionary movements may take the form of resurgent ethnonationalism or religious fundamentalist movements. Others may find expression in alternative grassroots movements from radical environmental groups to peace groups. Increasingly, such movements use the Internet to further their causes. While it is true that states and big corporations have expanded their power and influence through electronic communication technologies, it is also true that these same technologies present opportunities to individuals and groups that have traditionally been powerless. They provide a means of distributing information and promoting activities that are distinct from or in opposition to those of dominant society, as illustrated in Chapter 11's Original Study, "Digital Revolution: Indigenous Peoples in Cyberia."

PROBLEMS OF STRUCTURAL VIOLENCE

Based on their capability to harness, direct, and distribute global resources and energy flows, heavily armed states, megacorporations, and very wealthy elites are using their coercive and co-optive powers to structure or rearrange the emerging world system and direct global processes to their own competitive advantage. When such structural power undermines the well-being of others, we may speak of **structural violence**—physical and/or psychological harm (including repression, environmental destruction, poverty, hunger, illness, and premature death) caused by exploitative and unjust social, political, and economic systems. Clearly, the current structures are positioned in a way that leads to more wealth, power, comfort, and glory for the happy few and little more than poverty, subservience, suffering, and death for multitudes. Every day millions of people around the world face famine, ecological disasters, health problems, political instability, and violence rooted in development programs or profit-making maneuvers directed by powerful states or global corporations.

A useful baseline for identifying structural violence is provided by the Universal Declaration of Human Rights, officially adopted by all members of the United Nations in 1948. Anthropologists, including Alfred Metraux, a Swiss-Argentine scholar who headed UNESCO's social science division at the time, played a key role in drafting this important document. The declaration's preamble begins with the statement that "recognition of the inherent dignity and of the equal and inalienable rights of all members of the human family is the foundation of freedom, justice and peace in the world."[16] Generally speaking, structural violence concerns the impersonal systemic violation of the human rights of individuals and communities to a healthy, peaceful, and dignified life.

Although human rights abuses are nothing new, globalization has enormously expanded and intensified structural violence. For instance, it is leading to an ever-widening gap between the wealthiest and poorest peoples, the powerful and powerless. In 1960 the average income for the twenty wealthiest countries in the world was 15 times that of the twenty poorest. Today it is 30 times higher.[17] More remarkable is the fact that the world's 225 richest individuals have a combined wealth equal to the annual income of the poorest 47 percent of the entire world population. In fact, half of all people in the world get by on less than $2 per day, and more than 1.2 billion people live on just $1 a day. Measuring the gap

---

[16] *www.ccnmtl.columbia.edu/projects/mmt/udhr/.*

---

[17] *www.worldbank.org/poverty* (2003 statistics).

---

structural violence Physical and/or psychological harm (including repression, environmental destruction, poverty, hunger, illness, and premature death) caused by exploitative and unjust social, political, and economic systems.

in another way reveals that the poorest 80 percent of the human population make do with 14 percent of all goods and services in the world, the poorest 20 percent with a mere 1.3 percent. Meanwhile, the richest 20 percent enjoy 86 percent.[18]

Structural violence has countless manifestations in addition to widespread poverty. These range from the cultural destruction already described to hunger and obesity, environmental degradation, and emotional discontent, all discussed in the remaining pages of this chapter.

Hunger and Obesity

As frequently dramatized in media reports, hundreds of millions of people face hunger on a regular basis, leading to a variety of health problems, premature death, and other forms of suffering. Today, over a quarter of the world's countries do not produce enough food to feed their populations and cannot afford to import what's needed. The majority of these countries are in sub-Saharan Africa. All told, about 1 billion people in the world are undernourished. Some 6 million children aged 5 and under die every year due to hunger, and those who survive often suffer from physical and mental impairment.[19] For the victims of this situation, the effect is violent, even though it was not caused by the deliberate hostile act of a specific individual. The source of the violence may have been the unplanned yet devastatingly real impact of structural power—for instance, through the collapse of local markets due to subsidized foreign imports—and this is what structural violence is all about.

Ironically, while many millions of people in some parts of the world are starving, many millions of others are overeating—quite literally eating themselves to death. In fact, the number of overfed people now exceeds those who are underfed. According to the World Watch Institute in Washington, DC, more than 1.1 billion people worldwide are now overweight, and 300 million of these are obese. Seriously concerned about the sharp rise in associated health problems (including strokes, diabetes, cancer, and heart disease), the World Health Organization classifies obesity as a global epidemic. Overeating is particularly unhealthy for individuals living in societies where machines have eased the physical burdens of work and other human activities, which helps explain why more than half of the people in some industrial and postindustrial countries are

AP/Wide World Photos

Hunger stalks much of the world as a result of a world food system geared to satisfy an affluent minority in the world's developed nations.

overweight. However, the obesity epidemic is not due solely to excessive eating and lack of physical activity. A key cause is the high sugar and fat content of mass-marketed foods. The problem is spreading and has become a serious concern even in some developing countries. In fact, the highest rates of obesity in the world now exist among Pacific Islanders living in places such as Samoa and Fiji. On the island of Nauru, up to 65 percent of the men and 70 percent of the women are now classified as obese. (That said, not all people who are overweight or obese are so because they eat too much junk food and do too little exercise. In addition to cultural factors, being overweight or obese can also be the result of genetic or other biological causes.)

As for hunger cases, about 10 percent of them can be traced to specific events—droughts or floods, as well as various social, economic, and political disruptions, including warfare. During the 20th century, 44 million people died due to human-made famine.[20] For exam-

---

[18]Kurth, P. (1998, October 14). Capital crimes. *Seven Days,* 7; Swaminathan, M. S. (2000). Science in response to basic human needs. *Science, 287,* 425. See also Human Development Report 2002, *Deepening democracy in a fragmented world,* United Nations ᵊᵖment Program.

:r Project 2003; Swaminathan, p. 425.

[20]Hunger Project 2003; White, M. (2001). *Historical atlas of the twentieth century.* http://users.erols.com/mwhite28/20centry.htm.

ple, in several sub-Saharan African countries plagued by chronic civil strife, it has been almost impossible to raise and harvest crops, for hoards of refugees and soldiers constantly raid fields, often at gunpoint. Another problem is that millions of acres in Africa, Asia, and Latin America once devoted to subsistence farming have been given over to the raising of cash crops for export. This has enriched members of elite social classes in these parts of the world, while satisfying the appetites of people in the developed countries for coffee, tea, chocolate, bananas, and beef. Those who used to farm the land for their own food needs have been relocated—either to urban areas, where all too often there is no employment for them, or to areas ecologically unsuited for farming. In Africa such lands are often occupied seasonally by pastoral nomads, and turning them over to cultivation has reduced pasture available for livestock and led to overgrazing. The increase in cleared land, coupled with overgrazing, has depleted both soil and water, with disastrous consequences to nomad and farmer alike. So it is that more than 250 million people can no longer grow crops on their farms, and 1 billion people in 100 countries are in danger of losing their ability to grow crops.[21]

MEDIATREK

To investigate today's key global problems, from hunger to pollution to ethnic conflict, go to MediaTrek 16.3 on the companion Web site or CD-ROM.

One strategy urged upon so-called underdeveloped countries, especially by government officials and development advisors from the United States, has been to adopt practices that have made North American agriculture so incredibly productive. However, this strategy ignores the crucial fact that these large-scale, commercial farming practices require a financial investment that small farmers and poor countries cannot afford—a substantial outlay of cash for chemical fertilizers, pesticides, and herbicides, not to mention fossil fuels needed to run all the mechanized equipment.

U.S.-style farming has additional problems, including energy inefficiency. For every calorie produced, at least 8—some say as many as 20—calories go into its production and distribution.[22] By contrast, an Asian wet-rice farmer using traditional methods produces 300 calories for each 1 expended. North American agriculture is wasteful of other resources as well: About 30 pounds of

Spraying chemicals on crops, as here in California's Central Valley, trades short-term benefits for long-term pollution and health problems.

fertile topsoil are ruined for every pound of food produced.[23] In the midwestern United States, about 50 percent of the topsoil has been lost over the past 100 years. Meanwhile, toxic substances from chemical nutrients and pesticides pile up in unexpected places, poisoning ground and surface waters; killing fish, birds, and other useful forms of life; upsetting natural ecological cycles; and causing major public health problems. Despite its spectacular short-term success, serious questions arise about whether such a profligate food production system can be sustained over the long run, even in North America.

Yet another problem with the idea of copying U.S. farming styles has to do with subsidies. Despite official rhetoric about free markets, governments of the wealthiest capitalist states in North America and western Europe spend between $100 billion and $300 billion annually on agriculture subsidies. In the United States, the world's largest agricultural exporter, 75 percent of these go to the wealthiest 10 percent of the farmers and large agricultural corporations.

Confronted with such economic forces in the global arena, small farmers in poor countries find themselves in serious trouble when trying to sell their products on markets open to subsidized agricultural corporations dumping mass-produced and often genetically engineered crops and other farm products. Unable to compete under those structural conditions, many are forced to quit farming, leave their villages, and seek other livelihoods in cities or as migrant workers abroad. Such is the fate of many Maya Indians today. Since the early 1980s, when so many fled Guatemala's violence and poverty, thousands have made their way to places like southeastern Florida and taken low-paying jobs as illegal immigrants. Because

[21]Godfrey, T. (2000, December 27). Biotech threatening biodiversity. *Burlington Free Press,* 10A.

[22]Bodley, J. H. (1985). *Anthropology and contemporary human problems* (2nd ed., p. 128). Palo Alto, CA: Mayfield.

[23]Chasin, B. H., & Franke, R. W. (1983). US farming: A world model? *Global Reporter,* 1(2), 10.

of endemic poverty in their homeland where they would face starvation, these victims of structural violence have no choice but to remain where they are, condemned to an uncertain life in exile as cheap laborers without civil rights, Social Security, or health insurance.

Pollution

The effects of big agribusiness practices are part of larger problems of environmental degradation in which pollution is tolerated for the sake of higher profits that benefit select individuals and societies. Industrial activities are producing highly toxic waste at unprecedented rates, and factory emissions are poisoning the air. For example, smokestack gases are clearly implicated in acid rain, which is damaging lakes and forests all over northeastern North America. Air containing water vapor with a high acid content is, of course, harmful to the lungs, but the health hazard is greater than this. As ground and surface and waters become more acidic, the solubility of lead, cadmium, mercury, and aluminum, all of them toxic, rises sharply. For instance, aluminum contamination is high enough on 17 percent of the world's farmland to be toxic to plants—and

has been linked to senile dementia, Alzheimer's, and Parkinson's diseases, three major health problems in industrial countries. Indeed, development itself seems to be a health hazard. It is well known that indigenous peoples in Africa, the Pacific Islands, South America, and elsewhere are relatively free from diabetes, obesity, hypertension, and a variety of circulatory diseases until they adopt the ways of the so-called developed countries.

Finding their way into the world's oceans, toxic substances also create hazards for seafood consumers. For instance, Canadian Inuit face health problems related to eating fish and sea mammals that feed in waters contaminated by industrial chemical waste such as polychlorinated biphenyls (PCBs). Living thousands of miles from the industrial sources poisoning their environment, Inuit women have a right to be alarmed that their breast milk now contains levels of PCBs five to ten times higher than women in southern Canada.[24] Obviously, environmental poisoning affects peoples all across the globe (Figure 16.4).

---

[24]Inuit Tapiirit Kanatami. *http://www.tapirisat.ca/english_text/itk/departments/enviro/ncp/*

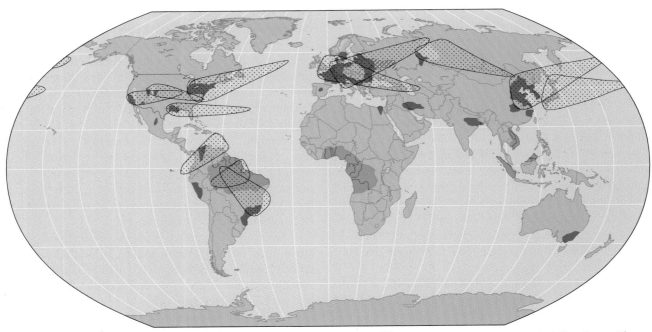

☑ Land areas with significant acid precipitation and atmospheric pollution
■ Land areas with significant atmospheric pollution
☐ Land areas with significant acid precipitation
▨ Land areas of secondary atmospheric pollution

⊡ Air pollution plume: average wind direction and force
(Wind blows in the direction of the tapered end of the air pollution plume and the force of the wind is indicated by the size of the plume.)

FIGURE 16.4

Global pollution. Almost all processes of physical geography begin and end with the flows of energy and matter among land, sea, and air. Because of the primacy of the atmosphere in this exchange system, air pollution is potentially one of the most dangerous human modifications in environmental [...]s. Pollutants such as various oxides of nitrogen or sulfur cause the development of acid precipitation, which damages soil, vegetation, and wild- [...]llution in the form of smog is often dangerous for human health. And most atmospheric scientists believe that the efficiency of the atmos- [...]taining heat—the so-called greenhouse effect—is being enhanced by increased carbon dioxide, methane, and other gases produced by [...] and agricultural activities. The result, they fear, will be a period of global warming that will dramatically alter climates in all parts of the world.

This picture of a flood in Bangladesh exemplifies the structural violence that will result from global warming. As sea levels rise, flooding of low-lying areas will become more extensive and frequent.

The popularity of sports utility vehicles (SUVs) in North America illustrates how consumers in affluent countries contribute to environmental destruction in the world's poorer countries. In Brazil, chainsaws are used to destroy vast tracts of forest in order to procure wood for production of charcoal. This is required to make the pig iron used in the strongest steel to make SUVs. In addition to the environmental devastation, oppressed labor is used to burn the charcoal.

Added to this is the problem of global warming—the greenhouse effect—caused primarily by the burning of fossil fuels. Although much is unknown about the extent of global warming, scientists now overwhelmingly agree it is real. Experts predict that it will lead to an expansion of the geographical ranges of tropical diseases and increase the incidence of respiratory diseases due to additional smog caused by warmer temperatures. Also, they expect an increase in deaths due to heat waves, as witnessed in the 15,000 deaths attributed to the 2003 heat wave in France.[25] Unfortunately, public concern about this is minimal, in large part because energy interests sponsor public relations campaigns to convince people that global warming is not real—just as tobacco companies once ran campaigns claiming that smoking was not hazardous.

Structural violence also manifests itself in the shifting of manufacturing and hazardous waste disposal from developed to developing countries. This trend is encouraged by cheap labor and less stringent safety and environment regulations, which translate into lower production costs and larger profits for corporations. Typically, a few well-placed officials or businesspeople in the developing countries benefit financially from these overseas arrangements, while powerless workers are exploited and environmental pollution is expanded. For instance, not long ago the president of Benin in West Africa signed a contract with a European waste company enabling that company to dump toxic and low-grade radioactive waste on the

lands of his political opposition.[26] In the United States, both government and industry have tried to persuade American Indians on reservations that the solution to their severe economic problems lies in allowing disposal of nuclear and other hazardous waste on their lands.

Given a general awareness of the causes and dangers of pollution, why is it that the human species as a whole is not committed to controlling practices that foul its own nest? At least part of the answer lies in philosophical and theological traditions. As we saw in the chapter on politics, Western industrialized societies accept the Biblical

---

[26]*Cultural Survival Quarterly* 15(4), p. 5 (1991).

Riot police patrol as the prime minister of France addresses the opening of an international conference on global warming in September 2000. Although it is known that the industrialized countries are the greatest contributors to greenhouse gasses, and that the consequences of global warming will be extremely harmful, governments have yet to take effective steps to deal with the problem.

---

[25]World Meteorological Organization, quoted in "Increasing heat waves and other health hazards." Accessed December 2003 at *greenpeaceusa.org/climate/index.fpl/7096/article/907.html*.

assertion (found in the Koran as well) of human dominion over the earth, interpreting that to mean that it is their task to subdue and control the earth and all its inhabitants. These societies are the biggest contributors to global pollution. For example, on average, one North American consumes hundreds of times the resources of a single African, with all that implies with respect to waste disposal and environmental degradation (Figure 16.5). Moreover, each person in North America adds, on average, 20 tons of carbon dioxide (a greenhouse gas) a year to the atmosphere. In "underdeveloped" countries, less than 3 tons per person are emitted.[27] According to botanist Peter Raven, "if everyone lived like Americans, you'd need three planet earths . . . to sustain that level of consumption."[28]

Structural Violence and Population Control

In 1750, 1 billion people lived on earth. Over the next two centuries our numbers climbed to nearly 2.5 billion. And between 1950 and 2000 it soared above 6 billion (Figure 16.6). Today, India and China alone have more than 1 billion inhabitants each. Such increases are highly significant because population growth increases the scale of hunger and pollution—and the many problems tied to these two big issues. Although controlling population growth does not by itself make the other problems go away, it is unlikely those other problems can be solved unless population growth is stopped or even reversed.

---

[27]Broecker, W. S. (1992, April). Global warming on trial. *Natural History*, 14.

---

[28]Quoted in Becker, J. (2004, March). *National Geographic*, 90.

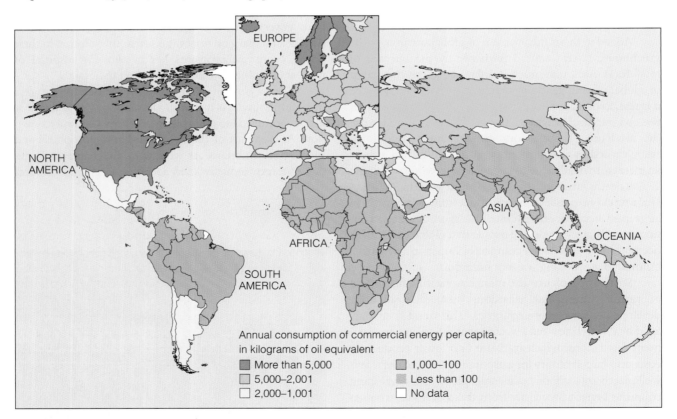

FIGURE 16.5

Global energy consumption. Most of the world's highest energy consumers are in North America and western Europe, where at least 100 gigajoules of commercial energy per year are consumed by each person. (A gigajoule is the equivalent of about 3.5 metric tons of coal.) In some of these countries, such as the United States and Canada, the consumption rates are in the 300 gigajoule range (the equivalent of more than 10 ~etric tons of coal per person per year). At the other end of the scale are low-income countries, whose consumption rates are often less than ~nt of those in the United States. (These figures do not include the consumption of noncommercial energy—the traditional fuels of fire- 'mal dung, and other organic matter widely used in the less developed parts of the world.) (From Allen, J. L., & Shalinsky, A. C., Student ~hropology, p. 126. Copyright © 2004 McGraw-Hill, Inc. A division of the McGraw-Hill Companies.)

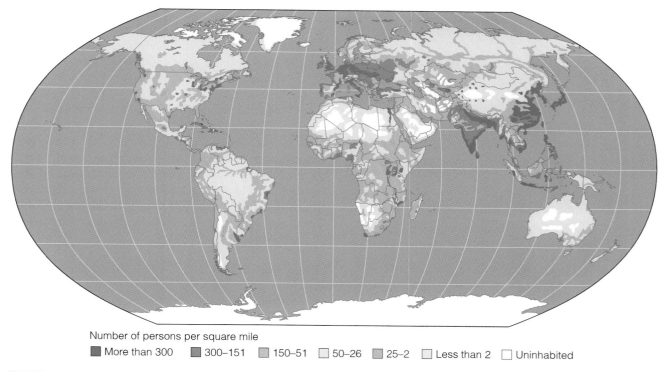

Number of persons per square mile
■ More than 300   ■ 300–151   ■ 150–51   ☐ 50–26   ■ 25–2   ☐ Less than 2   ☐ Uninhabited

FIGURE 16.6

Global population density. Three great concentrations of human population appear on this map—East Asia, South Asia, and Europe—with a fourth, lesser concentration in eastern North America. Population growth is still rapid in South Asia, which is expected to become even more densely populated in the early 21st century. Density in the other three regions is expected to remain about as it now appears due to relatively stable population rates resulting from economic development. The areas of future high density population, in addition to those already existing, are likely to be Central Africa and Central and South America, where growth rates are well above the world average. (From Allen, J. L., & Shalinsky, A. C., Student Atlas of Anthropology, p. 72. Copyright © 2004 McGraw-Hill, Inc. A division of the McGraw-Hill Companies.)

For a population to hold steady, there must be a balance between birthrates and death rates. In other words, people must produce only enough offspring to replace themselves when they die. This is known as **replacement reproduction.** Prior to 1976, birthrates around the world generally exceeded death rates, with the exception of European and North American populations. Poor people, in particular, have tended to have large families because children have been their main resource. Children can provide a needed labor pool to work farms, and they are the only source of security for the elderly. Historically, people were apt to limit the size of their families only when they became wealthy enough that their money replaced children as their main resource; at that point, children actually *cost* them money. Given this, we can see why birthrates remained high for so long in the world's poorer countries. To those who live in poverty, children are seen as the only hope.

Since the mid-1970s, birthrates have dropped below replacement level (which is about 2.1 children per woman) in virtually every industrialized country and also in nineteen "underdeveloped" countries—including China, the world's most populous country. In Africa, as well as much of South Asia and Central and South America (again, the world's poorer countries), birthrates have also declined but far less dramatically.[29]

Despite progress in population control, fertility rates on average remain above replacement, so the number of humans on earth continues to grow overall. Population projections are extremely tricky, given variables such as AIDS, but current projections suggest that global population will peak around 2050 at about 9.37 billion people.

The problem's severity becomes clear when it is realized that the present world population of more than 6 billion people can be sustained only by using up non-renewable resources such as oil, which is like living off

---

[29]Bongaarts, J. (1998). Demographic consequences of declining fertility. *Science, 282,* 419; Wattenberg, B. J. (1997, November 23). The population explosion is over. *New York Times Magazine,* 60.

replacement reproduction When birthrates and death rates are in equilibrium; people produce only enough offspring to replace themselves when they die.

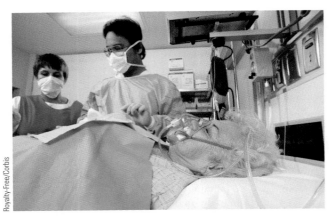

In societies where birthrates drop below replacement level, the number of old people increases relative to the number of productive people of younger age. In North America and other Western industrial countries, care of the elderly is expensive, and increasingly fewer young people are on hand to assume the cost in terms of both money and time.

income-producing capital. It works for a time, but once the capital is gone, so is the possibility of even having an income to live on.

The Culture of Discontent

For the past several decades, the world's poor countries have been sold on the idea they should and actually can enjoy a standard of living comparable to that of the rich countries. Yet, the resources necessary to maintain such a luxurious standard of living are not unlimited. As we saw in the last chapter, this growing gap between expectations and realizations has led to the creation of a culture of discontent. The problem involves not just population growth outstripping available natural resources, but also unequal access to decent jobs, housing, sanitation, health care, leisure, and adequate police and fire protection. It is one in which personal disappointments are echoed in a natural environment degraded by overcrowding, pollution, and soil erosion. This culture of discontent is not limited to people living in poor and overpopulated countries. Because capitalism thrives on growing demands, powerful advertising strategies target people with financial means to purchase more and more luxury goods and services. In the process, even those whose needs are more than met will be made to feel the pinch of discontent and spend their money in pursuit of material dreams.

Some dramatic changes in cultural values and motivations, as well as in social institutions and the types of technologies we employ, are required if humans are going to realize a sustainable future for generations to come. The short-sighted emphasis on consumerism and individual self-interest so characteristic of the world's affluent countries needs to be abandoned in favor of a more balanced social and environmental ethic. These can be created from values still found in many of the world's non-Western cultures. Such values include a worldview that sees humanity as part of the natural world rather than superior to it. Included, too, is a sense of social responsibility that recognizes that no individual, people, or state has the right to expropriate resources at the expense of others. Finally, an awareness is needed of how important supportive ties are for individuals, such as seen in kinship or other associations in the world's traditional societies. Is humanity up to the challenge? And will anthropology play a role in meeting that challenge?

MEDIATREK

To measure how your own life habits are impacting the environment, go to MediaTrek 16.4 on the companion Web site or CD-ROM.

As defined in this book's first chapter, anthropology is the comparative study of humankind everywhere and throughout time. It seeks to produce reliable knowledge about different peoples and cultures, their ideas and behaviors. Since the beginning of the discipline in the mid-1800s, generations of anthropologists have studied our species in all its cultural and biological varieties. In the process, they described in great detail an enormous number of different cultures and biological variations among humans in all parts of the world. They also collected a staggering volume of ethnographic artifacts and used still and motion picture cameras to visually document hundreds of different cultures.

Today, many of the cultures studied by the earliest anthropologists more than a century ago have changed profoundly in response to powerful outside influences and internal dynamics. Others have simply disappeared as a result of deadly epidemics, violent conflicts, acculturation, ethnocide, or even genocide. All too often, the only detailed records we now possess of these altered and vanished cultures are those that some visiting anthropologist was able to document before it was too late. But, anthropologists do much more than trying to preserve precious information about distinctive peoples and cultures. As chronicled in the pages of this book, they also try to explain why cultures are similar or different, why and how they did or did not change. Moreover, they try to identify the particular knowledge and insights that each culture holds concerning the human condition.

Less apt than other scholarly specialists to see facts and activities as separate and unrelated, anthropologists are trained to understand and explain economic/

"Never doubt that a small group of committed people can change the world; indeed it is the only thing that ever has." (Margaret Mead, anthropologist) Many anthropologists do fieldwork that results in information with practical value for the communities in which they do their studies. Not surprisingly, we find anthropologists working for international service organizations such as Oxfam, founded at Oxford University during World War II for famine relief in war-torn Europe. Today, Oxfam offers aid and advocacy worldwide for refugees and others in need. Anthropologists have also long been active in the United Nations Educational, Scientific and Cultural Organization (UNESCO), headquartered in Paris and with offices all over the globe. Founded in 1946, this international forum contributes to peace and security by promoting collaboration among the nations through education, science, and culture. Anthropologists are also likely participants in international human rights organizations such as Amnesty International, founded in London in 1961 to work on behalf of political prisoners. Active in more than 160 countries, Amnesty now has over 1 million members and is more broadly focused on exposing and ending all violations to the Universal Declaration of Human Rights. In 1977, it won the Nobel Peace Prize. Some anthropologists also work with Doctors Without Borders, another Nobel Peace Prize winner. Founded in Paris in 1971 by a group of medical doctors, it has some 2,000 volunteers serving in over eighty countries.

social/political/ideological features and processes as parts of dynamic systems by means of theoretical concepts such as structural power and structural violence. Their cross-cultural and comparative historical perspective on local communities in the age of globalization enables them to make key contributions to our understanding of such troubling problems as overpopulation, food shortages, pollution, and widespread discontent in the world. This is evident, for instance, in hiring choices at the World Bank in the wake of a series of ill-conceived and mismanaged development projects that harmed more than helped local populations. Recognizing the value of anthropological knowledge and methods, the bank now employs and contracts dozens of professional anthropologists for projects all across the world. The same is true for other international organizations, as well as some global corporations and state government agencies.

Some anthropologists go beyond just studying different cultures and reach out to assist besieged groups that are struggling to survive in today's rapidly changing world. In so doing, they seek to put into practice their own knowledge about humankind—knowledge deepened through the comparative perspective of anthropology, which is both cross-cultural and historically informed. The idea that anthropological research is fascinating in itself and also has the potential of helping solve practical problems on local and global levels has drawn and continues to draw a unique group of people into the discipline. Most of these individuals are inspired by the old but still valid idea that anthropology must aim to live up to its ideal as the most liberating of the sciences.

Chapter Summary

■ Anthropologists strive to gain a better understanding of the existing world situation so that decisions affecting humanity's future may be made intelligently. They are especially well suited for this, owing to their experience at seeing things in context, their long-term historical perspective, their ability to recognize culture-bound biases, and their familiarity with cultural alternatives.

■ However humanity changes biologically, culture remains the chief means by which humans try to solve their problems of existence. Rapid developments in communication, transportation, and world trade, some believe, are leading people toward a single world culture that could lessen chances for conflict. Most anthropologists are as skeptical of this as they are critical of the way industrial countries tend to treat traditional societies as obsolete.

■ Ethnic tension, common in pluralistic societies, sometimes turns violent, leading to formal separation. To manage cultural diversity within such societies, some countries have adopted multiculturalism, an official public policy of mutual respect and tolerance for cultural differences.

■ Cutting across international boundaries, global corporations are a powerful force for worldwide integration despite the political, linguistic, religious, and other cultural differences that separate people. Their power and wealth, often exceeding that of national governments, has increased dramatically through media expansion. Major players in the globalization process, these megacorporations have enormous influence on the ideas and behavior of hundreds of millions of people worldwide. In pursuit of wealth and power, states and corporations now compete for increasingly scarce natural resources, cheap labor, new commercial markets, and ever-larger profits in a huge political arena spanning the entire globe.

■ Structural power refers to the global forces that direct economic and political institutions and shape public ideas and values. Hard power is backed up by economic and military force, and soft power is ideological persuasion. The world's largest corporations are almost all based in a small group of wealthy and powerful states, which also dominate international trade and finance organizations. Their development projects in poor countries do not always benefit local populations, including indigenous peoples. Globalization provides megaprofits for large corporations but often wreaks havoc in many traditional cultures and disrupts long-established social organizations. By means of soft power, globalization is marketed as positive and progressive for everyone, but the poor are becoming poorer and the rich richer. Globalization also engenders worldwide resistance against superpower domination. For this reason, the emerging world system is inherently unstable, vulnerable, and unpredictable.

■ One result of globalization is worldwide and growing structural violence-physical and/or psychological harm (including repression, cultural and environmental destruction, poverty, hunger and obesity, illness, and premature death) caused by exploitative and unjust social, political, and economic systems. Uncontrolled population growth makes all of these problems worse. Due to rising expectations created by the media, coupled with limited opportunities, a culture of discontent is growing.

■ Some dramatic changes in cultural values and motivations, as well as in social institutions and the types of technologies we employ, are required if humans are going to realize a sustainable future for generations to come. The shortsighted emphasis on consumerism and individual self-interest so characteristic of the world's affluent countries needs to be abandoned in favor of a more balanced social and environmental ethic. Trained in what has been called the most liberating of the sciences, anthropologists have a contribution to make in bringing about this shift. They are well versed in the dangers of culture-bound thinking, and they bring a holistic and comparative historical perspective to the challenge of understanding and balancing the sometimes conflicting needs and desires of local communities in the age of globalization.

Questions for Reflection

1. Throughout today's world, many pluralistic or multi-ethnic countries face the challenge of "nation building." What would it take for a political organization such as the one developed in Switzerland to work as a model for countries in which minorities have been trampled in efforts to retain their own natural resources, national identities, and cultural traditions?

2. Most of the world's major global corporations are U.S. based, including Wal-Mart, which generates almost $250 billion in annual revenues. Measured in economic terms, this

business is bigger than South Africa, inhabited by 45 million people. In what ways might such a megacorporation use its enormous economic power? Could it influence the U.S. government in terms of world trade policies? If so, would the company benefit more from free trade or protectionism?

3. Considering the relationship between structural power and structural violence, does your own lifestyle in terms of buying clothes and food, driving cars, and so on reflect or have an effect on the globalization process?

4. Anthropologist Arjun Appadurai identified several global "flows," including those involving news media. He refers to the emerging global media environment as a "mediascape." Two of the largest media corporations in the world are Disney (which owns ABC television) and General Electric (which owns NBC television and several cable network companies). With these holdings, both of these global corporations have enormous potential for what has been termed soft power. Do you think their ownership has any influence on the way in which world news is selected and presented to the general public?

Key Terms

Multiculturalism

Structural power

Hard power

Soft power

Structural violence

Replacement reproduction

Multimedia Review Tools

Companion Web Site

Visit **http://www.wadsworth.com/anthropology_d/** and click on the companion Web site for this textbook to access a wide range of material to aid your study of anthropology. Among the options for self-study in each chapter are learning objectives, flash cards, Internet activities, Web links, InfoTrac College Edition exercises, and practice tests that can be scored and emailed to your instructor.

CD-ROM

The *Doing Anthropology Today* CD-ROM supplied with your textbook provides unique and valuable information designed to enhance your learning experience. This interactive multimedia resource includes video clips, interviews with renowned anthropologists, map and timeline exercises, chapter study quizzes, and much more. *Doing Anthropology Today* will not only help you in achieving your grade goals, it will also make your learning experience fun and exciting!

Suggested Readings

Appadurai, A. (1996). *Modernity at large: Cultural dimensions of globalization.* Minneapolis: University of Minnesota Press.

In this fundamental contribution to how globalization works, a leading anthropologist discusses how forces such as migration and electronic mediation acquire shaping roles in the production of contemporary culture.

Bodley, J. H. (2000). *Anthropology and contemporary human problems* (4th ed.). Palo Alto, CA: Mayfield.

Anthropologist Bodley examines some of the most serious problems in the world today: overconsumption, resource depletion, hunger and starvation, overpopulation, violence and war.

Friedman, J. (Ed.). (2003). *Globalization, the state, and violence.* Walnut Creek, CA: Altamira Press.

A vibrant, insightful analysis of globalization and the "lethal explosiveness" that characterizes the current world order. Friedman leads a group of distinguished contributors in examining the global processes and political forces that determine transnational networks of crime, commerce, and terror, leading to economic, social, and cultural fragmentation.

Ginsburg, F. D., Abu-Lughod, L., & Larkin, B. (Eds.). (2002). *Media worlds: Anthropology on new terrain.* Berkeley: University of California Press.

Groundbreaking essays by pioneers of media studies in anthropology, discussing the place and function of film, video, radio, television, and cinema in different cultures and showing that contemporary peoples and cultures cannot be understood without the mediascapes they inhabit.

Lewellen, T. C. (2002). *The anthropology of globalization: Cultural anthropology enters the 21st century.* Westport, CT: Greenwood Publishing Group/Bergin & Garvey.

Readable introduction, summary, and critique of globalization with telling and timely ethnographic examples.

Ong, A. (1999). *Flexible citizenship: The cultural logics of transnationality.* Durham, NC: Duke University Press.

Ong demonstrates how the Chinese transnational community confounds notions of peripheral non-Westerners and argues that the contemporary world is creating the context for the rise of China.

Pitts, V. (2003). *In the flesh: The cultural politics of body modification.* New York: Palgrave Macmillan.

A comprehensive exploration of the connection between body modification practices in the United States and contemporary struggles over sex and gender and techno-consumer culture.

Stiglitz, J. E. (2003). *Globalization and its discontents.* New York: Norton.

A Nobel Prize-winning economist explains clearly the functions and powers of the key institutions governing globalization—the International Monetary Fund, World Bank, World Trade Organization—along with the negative and positive ramifications of their policies.

Trouillot, M. R. (2003). *Global transformations: Anthropology and the modern world.* New York: Palgrave Macmillan.

Examining anthropology's history and discussing future possibilities for the discipline, the author challenges colleagues to question dominant narratives of globalization and to radically rethink key concepts of the discipline.

Glossary

acculturation Massive cultural changes that people are forced to make as a consequence of intensive firsthand contact between their own group and another often more powerful society.

adaptation A series of beneficial adjustments to the environment.

adjudication Mediation with an unbiased third party making the ultimate decision.

affinal kin Relatives by marriage

age grade An organized category of people based on age; every individual passes through a series of such categories over his or her lifetime.

age set A formally established group of people born during a certain time span who move through the series of age grade categories together.

alphabet a series of symbols representing the sounds of a language arranged in a traditional order.

altruism Acts of selflessness or self-sacrificing behavior.

ambilineal descent Descent in which the individual may affiliate with either the mother's or the father's descent group.

ambilocal residence A pattern in which a married couple may choose either matrilocal or patrilocal residence.

animatism A belief that nature is enlivened or energized by an impersonal spiritual power or supernatural potency.

animism A belief that nature is enlivened or energized by distinct personalized spirit beings separable from bodies.

anthropology The study of humankind in all times and places.

applied anthropology The use of anthropological knowledge and methods to solve practical problems, often for a specific client.

archaeology The study of material remains, usually from the past, to describe and explain human behavior.

art The creative use of the human imagination to interpret, express, and enjoy life.

Australopithecus The first well-known hominin; lived between 4.4 and 1 million years ago. Characterized by bipedal locomotion, but with an apelike brain; generally includes seven species: *A. afarensis, A. africanus, A. anamensis, A. boisei, A. robustus, A. aethiopicus,* and *A. gahri.*

avunculocal residence Residence of a married couple with the husband's mother's brother.

balanced reciprocity A mode of exchange in which the giving and the receiving are specific as to the value of the goods and the time of their delivery.

band A relatively small and loosely organized kin-ordered group that inhabits a specific territory and that may split periodically into smaller extended family groups that are politically independent.

bipedalism A special form of locomotion on two feet found in humans and their ancestors. Also called bipedality.

blended family A married couple raising children together from their previous unions.

bride-price Compensation the groom or his family pays to the bride's family upon marriage. Also called "bride wealth."

bride service A designated period of time after marriage when the groom works for the bride's family.

cargo cults Spiritual movements in Melanesia in reaction to disruptive contact with Western capitalism promising resurrection of deceased relatives, destruction or enslavement of white foreigners, and the magical coming of utopian riches.

carrying capacity The number of people that the available resources can support at a given level of food-getting techniques.

caste A closed social class in which membership is determined by birth and fixed for life.

chiefdom A regional polity in which two or more local groups are organized under a single chief, who is at the head of a ranked hierarchy of people.

clan Typically consisting of several lineages, a clan is a noncorporate descent group whose members assume descent from a common ancestor (real or fictive) without actually knowing the genealogical links to that ancestor.

closed-class societies Stratified societies that severely restrict social mobility.

code switching The process of changing from one language or dialect to another.

common-interest associations Associations that result from an act of joining based on sharing particular activities, objectives, values, or beliefs.

conjugal bond The bond between two individuals who are married.

conjugal family A family formed on the basis of marital ties.

consanguineal family Related women, their brothers, and the women's offspring.

consanguineal kin Relatives by birth; so-called blood relatives.

conspicuous consumption A term coined by Thorstein Veblen to describe the display of wealth for social prestige.

contagious magic Magic based on the principle that things once in contact can influence each other after the contact is broken.

convergent evolution A process by which unrelated populations develop similarities to one another. In cultural evolution, the development of similar cultural adaptations to similar environmental conditions by different peoples with different ancestral cultures.

core values Those values especially promoted by a particular culture.

core vocabularies The most basic and long-lasting words in any language—pronouns, lower numerals, and names for body parts and natural objects.

creole A pidgin language that has become the mother tongue of a society.

Crow system Kinship classification usually associated with matrilineal descent in which a father's sister and father's sister's daughter are called by the same term, a mother and mother's sister are merged under another, and a father and father's brother are lumped in a third. Parallel cousins are equated with brothers and sisters.

cultural adaptation A complex of ideas, activities, and technologies that enable people to survive and even thrive in a certain environment.

cultural anthropology The study of customary patterns in human behavior, thought, and feelings. It focuses on humans as culture-producing and culture-reproducing creatures in a particular environment.

cultural control Control through beliefs and values deeply internalized in the minds of individuals.

cultural ecology The dynamic interaction of specific cultures with their environments.

cultural loss The abandonment of an existing practice or trait.

cultural relativism The thesis that one must suspend judgment of other people's ideas and practices in order to understand them in their own cultural terms.

culture A society's shared and socially transmitted ideas, values, and perceptions—which are used to make sense of experience and generate behavior and which are reflected in behavior.

culture area A geographic region in which a number of societies follow similar patterns of life.

culture-bound Theories about the world and reality based on the assumptions and values of one's own culture.

culture core Cultural features that are fundamental in a society's way of making its living—including food-producing techniques, knowledge of available resources, and work arrangements involved in applying those techniques to the local environment.

culture type The view of a culture in terms of the relation of its particular technology to the environment exploited by that technology.

density of social relations Roughly, the number and intensity of interactions among the members of a camp or other residential unit.

dependence training Child-rearing practices that foster compliance in the performance of assigned tasks and dependence on the domestic group, rather than reliance on oneself.

descent group Any publicly recognized social entity requiring lineal descent from a particular real or mythical ancestor for membership.

descriptive linguistics The branch of linguistics that involves unraveling a language by recording, describing, and analyzing all of its features.

dialects Varying forms of a language that reflect particular regions, occupations, or social classes and that are similar enough to be mutually intelligible.

diffusion The spread of certain ideas, things, customs, or practices from one culture to another.

displacement The ability to refer to things and events removed in time and space.

divination A magical procedure or spiritual ritual designed to find out about what is not knowable by ordinary means, such as foretelling the future by interpreting omens.

doctrine An assertion of opinion or belief formally handed down by authority as true and indisputable.

double descent A system tracing descent matrilineally for some purposes and patrilineally for others.

dowry Payment of a woman's inheritance at the time of her marriage, either to her or to her husband.

economic system A means of producing, distributing, and consuming goods.

ecosystem A system, or a functioning whole, composed of both the physical environment and all the organisms living within it.

egalitarian societies Societies in which everyone has about equal access to and power over basic resources.

enculturation The social learning process by which a society's culture is acquired by those who are born into it as well as those who become members of that society in other ways.

endogamy Marriage within a particular group or category of individuals.

entoptic phenomena Bright pulsating geometric forms that are generated by the central nervous system and seen in states of trance.

epic A long oral narrative, sometimes in poetry or rhythmic prose, recounting the glorious events in the life of a real or legendary person.

Eskimo system System of kinship terminology, also called lineal system, which emphasizes the nuclear family by specifically identifying the mother, father, brother, and sister, while lumping together all other relatives into broad categories such as uncle, aunt, and cousin.

ethnic group People who collectively and publicly identify themselves as a distinct group based on various cultural features such as shared ancestry and common origin, language, customs, and traditional beliefs.

ethnicity The expression of the set of cultural ideas held by an ethnic group.

ethnic psychoses Mental disorders specific to particular ethnic groups.

ethnocentrism The belief that the ways of one's own culture are the only proper ones.

ethnography A detailed description of a particular culture primarily based on fieldwork.

ethnohistory The study of cultures of the recent past through oral histories; accounts left by explorers, missionaries, and traders; and through analysis of such records as land titles, birth and death records, and other archival materials.

ethnolinguistics A branch of linguistics that studies the relationship between language and culture.

ethnology The study and analysis of different cultures from a comparative or historical point of view, utilizing ethnographic accounts and developing anthropological theories that help explain why certain important differences or similarities occur among groups.

ethnomusicology The study of a society's music in terms of its cultural setting.

ethnoscientists Anthropologists who focus on identifying the principles behind native idea systems—how they inform people about their environment and what role they play in survival.

evolution Genetic change over successive generations.

exogamy Marriage outside the group.

extended family Several closely related nuclear families clustered together into a large domestic group.

fact An observation verified by several observers skilled in the necessary techniques of observation.

family Two or more people related by blood, marriage, or adoption. The family may take many forms, ranging from a single parent with one or more children, to a married couple or polygamous spouses with offspring, to several generations of parents and their children.

family of orientation The family into which one is born or adopted and raised.

family of procreation The family that one forms by becoming a parent and raising one or more children.

fieldwork The term anthropologists use for on-location research.

fission The splitting of a descent group into two or more new descent groups.

folklore A 19th-century term first used to denote the unwritten stories, sayings, beliefs, and customs of the European peasants (as opposed to the traditions of the literate elite) and later extended to those traditions preserved orally in all societies.

folkloristics The study of folklore (as linguistics is the study of language).

food foraging Hunting, fishing, and gathering animal and wild plant foods.

forensic anthropology Field of applied physical anthropology that specializes in the identification of human skeletal remains for legal purposes.

form classes The parts of speech or categories of words that work the same way in any sentence, such as nouns, verbs, and adjectives.

frame substitution A method used to identify the syntactic units of language. For example, a category called "nouns" may be established as anything that will fit the substitution frame "I see a _____."

fraternal polyandry Marriage of one woman to men who are brothers.

gender The cultural elaborations and meanings assigned to the biological differentiation of the sexes.

gendered speech Distinct male and female syntax exhibited in various languages around the world.

generalized reciprocity A mode of exchange in which the value of the gift is not calculated, nor is the time of repayment specified.

genes Portions of DNA molecules that direct the synthesis of specific proteins.

genocide The extermination of one people by another, often in the name of progress, either as a deliberate act or as the accidental outcome of activities carried out by one people with little regard for their impact on others.

gesture Facial expressions and bodily postures and motions that convey intended as well as subconscious messages.

globalization Worldwide interconnectedness, evidenced in global movements of natural resources, trade goods, human labor, finance capital, information, and infectious diseases.

glottochronology In linguistics, a method for identifying the approximate time that languages branched off from a common ancestor. It is based on analyzing core vocabularies.

grammar The entire formal structure of a language, including morphology and syntax.

group marriage Marriage in which several men and women have sexual access to one another.

hard power Coercive power that is backed up by economic and military force.

Hawaiian system Kinship reckoning in which all relatives of the same sex and generation are referred to by the same term.

historical linguistics The branch of linguistics that studies the histories of and relationships between languages, both living and dead.

holistic perspective A fundamental principle of anthropology, that the various parts of culture must be viewed in the broadest possible context in order to understand their interconnections and interdependence.

hominoid The taxonomic division superfamily within the cattarrhine primates that includes gibbons, siamangs, orangutans, gorillas, chimpanzees, bonobos, and humans and their ancestors.

Homo erectus A species within the genus *Homo* first appearing in Africa and ultimately migrating through out the Old World.

Homo habilis Earliest representative of the genus *Homo;* lived between 2.4 and 1.6 million years ago. Characterized by tool use and expansion and reorganization of the brain, compared to *Australopithecus.*

household The basic residential unit where economic production, consumption, inheritance, child rearing, and shelter are organized and carried out.

Human Relations Area Files (HRAF) An ever-growing catalogue of cross-indexed ethnographic data, filed by geographic location and cultural characteristics. Housed at Yale University, HRAF is also electronically available on the Internet.

hypothesis A tentative explanation of the relation between certain phenomena.

iconic images Visions of people, animals, and monsters seen in the deepest stage of trance.

imitative magic Magic based on the principle that like produces like; sometimes called sympathetic magic.

incest taboo The nearly universal prohibition of sexual relations between specified individuals, usually parent–child and sibling relations at a minimum.

incorporation In rites of passage, reincorporation of the individual into society in his or her new status.

independence training Child-rearing practices that promote independence, self-reliance, and personal achievement on the part of the child.

informal economy The production of marketable commodities that for various reasons escape enumeration, regulation, or any other sort of public monitoring or auditing.

informants Members of a society being studied who provide information that helps the ethnographer make sense of what is being said and done.

infrastructure The economic foundation of a society, including its subsistence practices, and the tools and other material equipment used to make a living.

integrative mechanisms Cultural mechanisms that oppose forces for differentiation in a society; in modernizing societies, they include formal governmental structures, official state ideologies, political parties, legal codes, labor and trade unions, and other common-interest associations.

intensive agriculture Crop cultivation using technologies other than hand tools, such as irrigation, fertilizers, and machinery or the wooden or metal plow pulled by harnessed draft animals.

intersexuals People born with reproductive organs, genitalia, and/or sex chromosomes that are not exclusively male or female.

Iroquois system Kinship terminology wherein a father and father's brother are referred to by a single term, as are a mother and mother's sister, but a father's sister and mother's brother are given separate terms. Parallel cousins are classified with brothers and sisters, while cross cousins are classified separately, but (unlike Crow kinship) not equated with relatives of some other generation.

kindred An individual's close relatives on the maternal and paternal sides of his or her family.

kinesics A system of notating and analyzing postures, facial expressions, and body motions that convey messages.

kinship A network of relatives within which individuals possess certain mutual rights and obligations.

Kula ring A form of balanced reciprocity that reinforces trade relations among the seafaring Trobriand people who inhabit a large ring of islands in the southern Pacific off the eastern coast of Papua New Guinea.

language A system of communication using sounds or gestures that are put together in meaningful ways according to a set of rules.

language family A group of languages descended from a single ancestral language.

law Set of socially approved rules of conduct with formal negative sanctions.

legend A story about a memorable event or figure handed down by tradition and told as true but without historical evidence.

legitimacy The right of political leaders to govern—to hold, use, and allocate power—based on the values a particular society holds.

leveling mechanism A societal obligation compelling persons to distribute goods so that no one accumulates more wealth than anyone else.

levirate A marriage custom according to which a widow marries a brother of her dead husband (a man marries his dead brother's widow).

lineage A corporate descent group—a unified body or corps of consanguineal relatives who trace their genealogical links to a common ancestor and associate with one another for a shared purpose.

linguistic anthropology The study of human languages.

linguistic divergence The development of different languages from a single ancestral language.

linguistic nationalism The attempt by ethnic minorities and even countries to proclaim independence by purging their language of foreign terms.

linguistic relativity The proposition that language plays a fundamental role in shaping the way members of a society think and behave.

linguistics The scientific study of all aspects of language.

Lower Paleolithic The first part of the Old Stone Age; its beginning is marked by the appearance 2.6 million years ago of Oldowan tools.

market exchange The buying and selling of goods and services, with prices set by rules of supply and demand.

marriage A culturally sanctioned union between two or more people that establishes certain rights and obligations between the people, between them and their children, and between them and their in-laws. Such marriage rights and obligations most often include, but are not limited to, sex, labor, property, child rearing, exchange, and status.

matrilateral cross-cousin marriage Marriage of a woman to her father's sister's son, or a man to his mother's brother's daughter (her cross cousin on the paternal side, his cross cousin on the maternal side).

matrilineal descent Descent traced exclusively through the female line to establish group membership.

matrilocal residence A residence pattern in which a married couple lives in the locality associated with the wife's relatives.

mediation Settlement of a dispute through negotiation assisted by an unbiased third party.

medical anthropology A specialization in anthropology that brings theoretical and applied approaches from cultural and biological anthropology to the study of human health and disease.

mobility The ability to change one's class position.

modal personality The body of character traits that occur with the highest frequency in a culturally bounded population.

modernization The process of political and socioeconomic change, whereby developing societies acquire some of the cultural characteristics of Western industrialized societies.

moiety Each group that results from a division of a society into two halves on the basis of descent.

molecular anthropology A branch of biological anthropology that uses genetic and biochemical techniques to test hypotheses about human evolution, adaptation, and variation.

money Anything used to make payments for other things (goods or labor) as well as to measure their value; may be special purpose or multipurpose.

monogamy Marriage in which both partners have just one spouse.

morphemes The smallest units of sound that carry a meaning in language. They are distinct from phonemes, which can alter meaning, but have no meaning by themselves.

morphology In linguistics, the study of the patterns or rules of word formation in a language (including such things as rules concerning verb tense, pluralization, and compound words).

motif A story situation in a folktale and other art forms.

Mousterian tradition Tool-making tradition of the Neandertals and their contemporaries of Europe, western Asia, and northern Africa, featuring flake tools that are lighter and smaller than earlier Levalloisian flake tools.

multiculturalism Public policy for managing cultural diversity in a multi-ethnic society, officially stressing mutual respect and tolerance for cultural differences within a country's borders.

multiregional hypothesis The model for modern human origins through simultaneous local transition from *Homo erectus* to modern *Homo sapiens* with links among these populations through gene flow.

myth A sacred narrative that explains the fundamentals of human existence (where we and everything in our world came from, why we are here, and where we are going).

naming ceremony A special event or ritual to mark the naming of an individual or thing.

nation A people who share a collective identity based on a common culture, language, territorial base, and history.

natural selection The evolutionary process through which factors in the environment exert pressure, favoring some individuals over others to produce the next generation.

Neandertals Representatives of "archaic" *Homo sapiens* in Europe and western Asia, living from about 125,000 years ago to about 30,000 years ago.

negative reciprocity A form of exchange in which the giver tries to get the better of the exchange.

negotiation The use of direct argument and compromise by the parties to a dispute to arrive voluntarily at a mutually satisfactory agreement.

Neolithic revolution The profound culture change associated with the early domestication of plants and animals.

neolocal residence A pattern in which a married couple may establish their household in a location apart from either the husband's or the wife's relatives.

new reproductive technologies Known as NRTs, this term refers to technologically assisted reproduction such as surrogate motherhood and in vitro fertilization.

nuclear family A group consisting of one or more parents and dependent offspring. May include a stepparent, stepsiblings, and adopted children.

Oldowan tool tradition The earliest identifiable stone tools.

open-class societies Stratified societies that permit a great deal of social mobility.

paleoanthropology The study of the origins and predecessors of the present human species.

pantheon The several gods and goddesses of a people.

paralanguage Voice effects that accompany language and convey meaning. These include vocalizations such as giggling, groaning, or sighing, as well as voice qualities such as pitch and tempo.

parallel evolution In cultural evolution, the development of similar cultural adaptations to similar environmental conditions by peoples whose ancestral cultures were already somewhat alike.

participant observation In ethnography, the technique of learning about a group of people through social participation and personal observation within the community being studied, as well as interviews and discussion with individual members of the group over an extended period of time.

patrilateral parallel-cousin marriage Marriage of a man to his father's brother's daughter, or a woman to her father's brother's son (that is, to a parallel cousin on the paternal side).

patrilineal descent Descent traced exclusively through the male line to establish group membership.

patrilocal residence A residence pattern in which a married couple lives in the locality associated with the husband's father's relatives.

personality The distinctive way a person thinks, feels, and behaves.

phonemes The smallest units of sound that make a difference in meaning in a language.

phonetics The systematic identification and description of distinctive speech sounds in a language.

phonology The study of language sounds.

phratry A unilineal descent group composed of two or more clans that assume they share a common ancestry but do not know the precise genealogical links of that ancestry. If only two such groups exist, each is a moiety.

physical anthropology Also known as biological anthropology. The systematic study of humans as biological organisms.

pidgin A language in which the syntax and vocabulary of two other languages are simplified and combined.

pluralistic society A society in which two or more ethnic groups or nationalities are politically organized into one territorial state but maintain their cultural differences.

political organization The way power is distributed and embedded in society; the means through which a society creates and maintains social order and reduces social disorder.

polyandrous family A type of polygamous family involving a woman with multiple husbands and their children.

polyandry Marriage of a woman to two or more men at one time; a form of polygamy.

polygamous family One individual with multiple spouses and all of their children.

polygynous family A type of polygamous family involving a man with multiple wives and their children.

polygyny Marriage of a man to two or more women at the same time; a form of polygamy.

polytheism Belief in several gods and/or goddesses (as contrasted with monotheism—belief in one god or goddess).

potlatch A ceremonial event in which a Native village chief in coastal north-west America publicly gives away stockpiled food and other goods that signify wealth.

power The ability of individuals or groups to impose their will upon others and make them do things even against their own wants or wishes.

prestige economy Creation of a surplus for the express purpose of gaining prestige through a public display of wealth that is given away as gifts.

priest or priestess A full-time religious specialist formally recognized for his or her role in guiding the religious practices of others and for contacting and influencing supernatural powers.

primary innovation The creation, invention, or discovery, by chance, of a completely new idea, method, or device.

primates The group of mammals that includes lemurs, lorises, tarsiers, monkeys, apes, and humans.

primatology The study of living and fossil primates.

progress The notion that humans are moving forward to a higher, more advanced stage in their development toward perfection.

proxemics The cross-cultural study of humankind's perception and use of space.

race In biology, the taxonomic category of subspecies that is not applicable to humans because the division of humans into discrete types does not represent the true nature of human biological variation. In some societies race is an important cultural category.

rebellion Organized armed resistance to an established government or authority in power.

recent African origins hypothesis The model for modern human origins in which anatomically modern humans arose in Africa approximately 200,000 years ago, replacing archaic forms in the rest of the world. Also called the "Eve" or "Out of Africa" hypothesis.

reciprocity The exchange of goods and services, of approximately equal value, between two parties.

redistribution A form of exchange in which goods flow into a central place, where they are sorted, counted, and reallocated.

religion An organized system of ideas about spiritual reality, or the supernatural, along with associated beliefs and ceremonial practices by which people try to interpret and influence aspects of the universe otherwise beyond their control.

replacement reproduction When birthrates and death rates are in equilibrium; people produce only enough offspring to replace themselves when they die.

revitalization movements Movements for radical cultural reform in response to widespread social disruption and collective feelings of anxiety and despair.

revolution Sudden and radical change in a society or culture. In the political arena, it refers to the forced overthrow of an old government and establishment of a completely new one.

rites of intensification Rituals that take place during a crisis in the life of the group and serve to bind individuals together.

rites of passage Rituals that mark important stages in an individual's life cycle, such as birth, marriage, and death.

sanctions Externalized social controls designed to encourage conformity to social norms and rules.

secondary innovation A new and deliberate application or modification of an existing idea, method, or device.

segmentary lineage system A rare form of kin-ordered organization in which a tribal group is split into several branches made up of clans or major lineages, each of which is further divided into minor lineages and minimal lineages.

self-awareness The ability to identify oneself as an indivdual creature, and to reflect, evaluate, and to react to oneself.

separation In rites of passage, the ritual removal of the individual from society.

serial monogamy A marriage form in which a man or a woman marries a series of partners in succession.

shaman A person who enters an altered state of consciousness—at will—to contact and utilize an ordinarily hidden reality in order to acquire knowledge, power, and/or to help others.

signals Instinctive sounds or gestures that have a natural or self-evident meaning.

silent trade A form of barter in which no verbal communication takes place.

social class A category of individuals who enjoy equal or nearly equal prestige according to the system of evaluation.

social control External control over groups through direct or indirect coercion.

social mobility The ability to change one's social class.

social structure The rule-governed relationships—with all their rights and obligations—that hold members of a society together. This includes households, families, associations, and power relations, including politics.

society An organized group or groups of interdependent people who generally share a common territory, language, and culture and who act together for collective survival and well-being.

soft power Pressing others through attraction and persuasion to change their ideas, beliefs, values, and behaviors.

sororal polygyny Marriage of one man to women who are sisters.

sororate A marriage custom according to which a widower marries his dead wife's sister (a woman marries her deceased sister's husband).

species The smallest working unit in the system of classification. Among living organisms, species are populations or groups of populations capable of interbreeding and producing fertile viable offspring.

spirituality Concern with the sacred, as distinguished from material matters. In contrast to religion, spirituality is often individual rather than collective and does not require a distinctive format or traditional organization.

state In anthropology, a centralized political system that may legitimately use force to maintain social order and defend itself.

stratified societies Societies in which people are divided or ranked into social tiers and do not share equally in the basic resources that support life, influence, and prestige.

structural differentiation The division of single traditional roles that embrace two or more functions (for example, political, economic, and religious) into two or more roles, each with a single specialized function.

structural power Power that organizes and orchestrates the systemic interaction within and among societies, directing economic and political forces on the one hand and ideological forces that shape public ideas, values, and beliefs on the other.

structural violence Physical and/or psychological harm (including repression, environmental destruction, poverty, hunger, illness, and premature death) caused by exploitative and unjust social, political, and economic systems.

subculture A distinctive set of standards concerning ideas, values, and behavior patterns by which a group within a larger society operates.

superstructure A society's shared sense of identity and worldview. The collective body of ideas, beliefs, and values by which a group of people makes sense of the world—its shape, challenges, and opportunities—and their place in it. This includes religion and national ideology.

swidden farming Also known as slash-and-burn. An extensive form of horticulture in which the natural vegetation is cut, the slash is subsequently burned, and crops then planted among the ashes, which fertilize the soil.

symbolic indicators In a stratified society, activities and possessions indicative of social class.

symbols Signs, emblems, and other things that represent something else in a meaningful way.

syncretism In culture change, the blending of indigenous and foreign traits to form a new system.

syntax The patterns or rules for the formation of phrases and sentences in a language.

tale A creative narrative recognized as fiction for entertainment.

technology Tools and other material equipment, together with the knowledge of how to make and use them.

theory In science, an explanation of phenomena, supported by a reliable body of data.

tonality In music, scale systems and their modifications.

tonal language A language in which the sound pitch of a spoken word is an essential part of its pronunciation and meaning.

totemism The belief that people are related to particular animals, plants, or natural objects by virtue of descent from common ancestral spirits.

tradition Customary ideas and practices passed on from generation to generation, which in a modernizing society may form an obstacle to new ways of doing things.

transgenders People who crossover or occupy a culturally accepted intermediate position in the binary male–female gender construction.

transition In rites of passage, isolation of the individual following separation and prior to incorporation into society.

tribe In anthropology, refers to a range of kin-ordered groups that are politically integrated by some unifying factor and whose members share a common ancestry, identity, culture, language, and territory.

unilineal descent Descent that establishes group membership exclusively through either the male or female line.

Upper Paleolithic The last part of the Old Stone Age, characterized by the emergence of more modern-looking hominins and an emphasis on the blade technique of tool making.

verbal evaluation What people in a stratified society say about others in their society.

vocal characterizers In paralanguage, vocalizations such as laughing, crying, yawning, or "breaking," which the speaker "talks through."

vocalizations Identifiable paralinguistic noises that are turned on and off at perceivable and relatively short intervals. These include vocal characterizers (giggling, sighing, and so on), vocal qualifiers (volume, tempo, and so on) and vocal segregates ("oh oh," for example).

vocal qualifiers In paralanguage, vocalizations of brief duration that modify utterances in terms of intensity. These include volume, pitch, tempo.

vocal segregates In paralanguage, vocalizations that resemble the sounds of language but do not appear in sequences that can properly be called words. Sometimes called "oh oh expressions."

voice qualities In paralanguage, the background characteristics of a speaker's voice, including pitch, articulation, tempo, and resonance.

witchcraft A practice based on the belief that certain individuals possess an innate psychic power capable of causing harm, including sickness and death.

worldview The collective body of ideas that members of a culture generally share concerning the ultimate shape and substance of their reality.

writing system A set of visible or tactile signs used to represent units of language in a systematic way.

Bibliography

Abbot, E. (2001). *A history of celibacy.* Cambridge, MA: Da Capo Press.

Aberle, D. F., Bronfenbrenner, U., Hess, E. H., Miller, D. R., Schneider, D. H., & Spuhler, J. N. (1963). The incest taboo and the mating patterns of animals. *American Anthropologist, 65,* 253–265.

Abu-Lughod, L. (1986). *Veiled sentiments: Honor and poetry in a Bedouin society.* Berkeley: University of California Press.

Adams, R. E. W. (1977). *Prehistoric Mesoamerica.* Boston: Little, Brown.

Adams, R. M. (1966). *The evolution of urban society.* Chicago: Aldine.

Adams, R. M. (2001). Scale and complexity in archaic states. *Latin American Antiquity, 11,* 188.

Adbusters. *www.adbusters.org.* Accessed January 2003.

AIDS Monthly Surveillance Summary (through July 1997). (1997). San Francisco.

Al-Issa, I., & Dennis, W. (Eds.). (1970). *Cross-cultural studies of behavior.* New York: Holt, Rinehart & Winston.

Alland, A., Jr. (1970). *Adaptation in cultural evolution: An approach to medical anthropology.* New York: Columbia University Press.

Alland, A., Jr. (1971). *Human diversity.* New York: Columbia University Press.

Allen, J. L., & Shalinsky, A. C. (2004). *Student atlas of anthropology.* New York: McGraw-Hill/Dushkin.

Allen, J. S., & Cheer, S. M. (1996). The non-thrifty genotype. *Current Anthropology, 37,* 831–842.

Allen, S. L. (1984). Media anthropology: Building a public perspective. *Anthropology Newsletter, 25,* 6.

Amábile-Cuevas, C. F., & Chicurel, M. E. (1993). Horizontal gene transfer. *American Scientist, 81,* 332–341.

Ambrose, S. H. (2001). Paleolithic technology and human evolution. *Science, 291,* 1,748–1,753.

American Anthropological Association. (1998). Statement on "race." Available at *www.ameranthassn.org.*

Amiran, R. (1965). The beginnings of pottery-making in the Near East. In F. R. Matson (Ed.), *Ceramics and man* (pp. 240–247). Viking Fund Publications, in Anthropology, No. 41.

Anderson, C. M. (1989). Neanderthal pelvis and gestational length. *American Anthropologist, 91,* 327–340.

Andrews, L. B., & Nelkin, D. (1996). The bell curve: A statement. *Science, 271,* 13.

Ankel-Simons, F., Fleagle, J. G., & Chatrath, P. S. (1998). Femoral anatomy of *Aegyptopithecus zeuxis,* an early Oligocene anthropoid. *American Journal of Physical Anthropology, 106,* 413–424.

Appadurai, A. (1996). *Modernity at large: Cultural dimensions of globalization.* Minneapolis: University of Minnesota Press.

Appenzeller, T. (1998). Art: Evolution or revolution? *Science, 282,* 1,451–1,454.

Arensberg, C. M. (1961). The community as object and sample. *American Anthropologist, 63,* 241–264.

Armstrong, D. F., Stokoe, W. C., & Wilcox, S. E. (1993). Signs of the origin of syntax. *Current Anthropology, 34,* 349–368.

Ashmore, W. (Ed.). (1981). *Lowland Maya settlement patterns.* Albuquerque: University of New Mexico Press.

Bailey, R. C., & Aunger, R. (1989). Net hunters vs. archers: Variation in women's subsistence strategies in the Ituri Forest. *Human Ecology, 17,* 273–297.

Balandier, G. (1971). *Political anthropology.* New York: Pantheon.

Balikci, A. (1970). *The Netsilik Eskimo.* Garden City, NY: Natural History Press.

Balter, M. (1998). Why settle down? The mystery of communities. *Science, 282,* 1,442–1,444.

Balter, M. (2001). In search of the first Europeans. *Science, 291,* 1,724.

Balter, M. (1999). A long season puts Çatalhöyük in context. *Science, 286,* 890–891.

Balter, M. (2001). Did plaster hold Neolithic society together? *Science, 294,* 2,278–2,281.

Banton, M. (1968). Voluntary association: Anthropological aspects. In *International encyclopedia of the social sciences* (Vol. 16, pp. 357–362). New York: Macmillan.

Barber, B. (1957). *Social stratification.* New York: Harcourt.

Barfield, T. J. (1984). Introduction. *Cultural Survival Quarterly, 8,* 2.

Barham, L. S. (1998). Possible early pigment use in South-Central Africa. *Current Anthropology, 39,* 703–710.

Barnard, A. (1995). Monboddo's *Orang Outang* and the definition of man. In R. Corbey & B. Theunissen (Eds.), *Ape, man, apeman: Changing views since 1600* (pp. 71–85). Leiden: Department of Prehistory, Leiden University.

Barnett, H. (1953). *Innovation: The basis of cultural change.* New York: McGraw-Hill.

Barnouw, V. (1985). *Culture and personality* (4th ed.). Homewood, IL: Dorsey Press.

Barr, R. G. (1997, October). The crying game. *Natural History, 47.*

Barth, F. (1961). *Nomads of South Persia: The Basseri tribe of the Khamseh confederacy.* Boston: Little, Brown (series in anthropology).

Barth, F. (1962). Nomadism in the mountain and plateau areas of South West Asia. *The problems of the arid zone* (pp. 341–355). Paris: UNESCO.

Barton, R. F. (1919). Ifugao law. Berkeley: *University of California Publications in American Archaeology and Ethnology, XV.*

Bar-Yosef, O. (1986). The walls of Jericho: An alternative interpretation. *Current Anthropology, 27,* 157–162.

Bar-Yosef, O., Vandermeesch, B., Arensburg, B., Belfer-Cohen, A., Goldberg, P., Laville, H., Meignen, L., Rak, Y., Speth, J. D., Tchernov, E., Tillier, A-M., & Weiner, S. (1992). The excavations in Kebara Cave, Mt. Carmel. *Current Anthropology, 33,* 497–550.

Bascom, W. (1969). *The Yoruba of southwestern Nigeria.* New York: Holt, Rinehart & Winston.

Bates, D. G. (2001). *Human adaptive strategies: Ecology, culture, and politics* (2nd ed.). Boston: Allyn & Bacon.

Bates, D. G., & Plog, F. (1991). *Human adaptive strategies.* New York: McGraw-Hill.

Beals, A. R. (1972). Gopalpur: *A South Indian village.* New York: Holt, Rinehart & Winston.

Beattie, J. (1964). *Other cultures: Aims, methods and achievements.* New York: Free Press.

Becker, J. (2004), March). *National Geographic,* 90.

Bednarik, R. G. (1995). Concept-mediated marking in the Lower Paleolithic. *Current Anthropology, 36,* 605–634.

Behrensmeyer, A. K., Todd, N. E., Potts, R., & McBrinn, G. E. (1997). Late Pliocene faunal turnover in the Turkana basin, Kenya, and Ethiopia. *Science, 278,* 1,589–1,594.

Beidelman, T. O. (Ed.). (1971). *The transition of culture: Essays to E. E. Evans-Pritchard.* London: Tavistock.

Bell, D. (1997). Defining marriage and legitimacy. *Current Anthropology, 38,* 241.

Belshaw, C. S. (1958). The significance of modern cults in Melanesian development. In W. Lessa & E. Z. Vogt (Eds.), *Reader in comparative religion: An anthropological approach.* New York: Harper & Row.

Benedict, R. (1959). *Patterns of culture.* New York: New American Library.

Bennett, J. W. (1964). Myth, theory, and value in cultural anthropology. In E. W. Caint & G. T. Bowles (Eds.), *Fact and theory in social science.* Syracuse, NY: Syracuse University Press.

Berdan, F. F. (1982). *The Aztecs of Central Mexico.* New York: Holt, Rinehart & Winston.

Bermúdez de Castro, J. M., Arsuaga, J. L., Cabonell, E., Rosas, A., Martinez, I., & Mosquera, M. (1997). A hominid from the lower Pleistocene of Atapuerca, Spain: Possible ancestor to Neandertals and modern humans. *Science, 276,* 1,392–1,395.

Bernal, I. (1969). *The Olmec world.* Berkeley: University of California Press.

Bernard, H. R. (2002) *Research methods in anthropology: Qualitative and quantitative approaches* (3rd ed.). Walnut Creek, CA: Altamira Press.

Bernard, H. R., & Sibley, W. E. (1975). *Anthropology and jobs.* Washington, DC: American Anthropological Association.

Bernardi, B. (1985) *Age class systems: Social institutions and policies based on age.* New York: Cambridge University Press.

Berra, T. M. (1990). *Evolution and the myth of creationism.* Stanford, CA: Stanford University Press.

Berreman, G. D. (1962). *Behind many masks: Ethnography and impression management in a Himalayan village.* Ithaca, NY: Society for Applied Anthropology (Monograph No. 4).

Berreman, G. D. (1968). Caste: The concept of caste. *International Encyclopedia of the Social Sciences* (Vol. 2, pp. 333–338). New York: Macmillan.

Bicchieri, M. G. (Ed.). (1972). *Hunters and gatherers today: A socioeconomic study of eleven such cultures in the twentieth century.* New York: Holt, Rinehart & Winston.

Binford, L. R. (1972). *An archaeological perspective.* New York: Seminar Press.

Binford, L. R., & Chuan, K. H. (1985). Taphonomy at a distance: Zhoukoudian, the cave home of Beijing man? *Current Anthropology, 26,* 413–442.

Birdsell, J. H. (1977). The recalibration of a paradigm for the first peopling of Greater Australia. In J. Allen, J. Golson, & R. Jones (Eds.), *Sunda and Sahul: Prehistoric studies in Southeast Asia, Melanesia, and Australia* (pp. 113–167). New York: Academic Press.

Blumberg, R. L. (1991). *Gender, family, and the economy: The triple overlap.* Newbury Park, CA: Sage.

Blumer, M. A., & Byrne, R. (1991). The ecological genetics and domestication and the origins of agriculture. *Current Anthropology, 32,* 23–54.

Boas, F. (1962). *Primitive art.* Gloucester, MA: Peter Smith.

Boas, F. (1966). *Race, language and culture.* New York: Free Press.

Bodley, J. H. (2000). *Anthropology and contemporary human problems* (4th ed.). Palo Alto, CA: Mayfield.

Bodley, J. H. (1997). Comment. *Current Anthropology, 38,* 725.

Bodley, J. H. (1998). *Victims of progress* (4th ed.). San Francisco: McGraw-Hill.

Boehm, C. (2000). The evolution of moral communities. *School of American Research, 2000 Annual Report,* 7.

Bohannan, P. (Ed.). (1967). *Law and warfare: Studies in the anthropology of conflict.* Garden City, NY: Natural History Press.

Bohannan, P., & Dalton, G. (Eds.). (1962). *Markets in Africa.* Evanston, IL: Northwestern University Press.

Bohannan, P., & Middleton, J. (Eds.). (1968). *Kinship and social organization.* Garden City, NY: Natural History Press (American Museum Source Books in Anthropology).

Bohannan, P., & Middleton, J. (Eds.). (1968). *Marriage, family, and residence.* Garden City, NY: Natural History Press (American Museum Source Books in Anthropology).

Bolinger, D. (1968). *Aspects of language.* New York: Harcourt.

Bongaarts, J. (1998). Demographic consequences of declining fertility. *Science, 182,* 419.

Bonvillain, N. (2000). *Language, culture, and communication: The meaning of messages* (3rd ed.). Upper Saddle River, NJ: Prentice Hall.

Boone, E. S. (1987). Practicing sociomedicine: Redefining the problem of infant mortality in Washington, D.C. In R. M. Wulff & S. J. Fiske (Eds.), *Anthropological praxis: Translating knowledge into action* (p. 56). Boulder, CO: Westview Press.

Bordes, F. (1972). *A tale of two caves.* New York: Harper & Row.

Bornstein, M. H. (1975). The influence of visual perception on culture. *American Anthropologist, 77*(4), 774–798.

Brace, C. L. (1981). Tales of the phylogenetic woods: The evolution and significance of phylogenetic trees. *American Journal of Physical Anthropology, 56,* 411–429.

Brace, C. L. (1997). Cro-Magnons R us? *Anthropology Newsletter, 38*(8), 1, 4.

Brace, C. L., Nelson, H., & Korn, N. (1979). *Atlas of human evolution* (2nd ed.). New York: Holt, Rinehart & Winston.

Brace, C. L., Ryan, A. S., & Smith, B. (1981). Comment. *Current Anthropology, 22*(4), 426–430.

Brace, C. L. (2000). *Evolution in an anthropological view* (p. 341). Walnut Creek, CA: Altamira.

Bradfield, R. M. (1998). *A natural history of associations.* (2nd ed.). New York: International Universities Press.

Bradford, P. V., & Blume, H. (1992). *Ota Benga: The pygmy in the zoo.* New York: St. Martin's Press.

Braidwood, R. J. (1960). The agricultural revolution. *Scientific American, 203,* 130–141.

Braidwood, R. J. (1975). *Prehistoric men* (8th ed.). Glenview, IL: Scott, Foresman.

Brain, C. K. (1968). Who killed the Swartkrans ape-men? *South African Museums Association Bulletin, 9,* 127–139.

Brain, C. K. (1969). The contribution of Namib Desert Hottentots to an understanding of australopithecine bone accumulations. *Scientific Papers of the Namib Desert Research Station, 13.*

Branda, R. F. & Eatoil, J. W. (1978). Skin color and photolysis: An evolutionary hypothesis. *Science, 201,* 625–626.

Brettell, C. B., & Sargent, C. F. (Eds.). (2000). *Gender in cross-cultural perspective* (3rd ed.). Upper Saddle River, NJ: Prentice-Hall.

Brew, J. O. (1968). *One hundred years of anthropology.* Cambridge, MA: Harvard University Press.

Broecker, W. S. (1992, April). Global warming on trial. *Natural History,* 14.

Brothwell, D. R., & Higgs, E. (Eds.). (1969) *Science in archaeology* (Rev. ed.). London: Thames & Hudson.

Brown, B., Walker, A., Ward, C. V., & Leakey, R. E. (1993). New *Australopithecus boisei* calvaria from East Lake Turkana, Kenya. *American Journal of Physical Anthropology, 91,* 137–159.

Brown, D. E. (1991). *Human universals.* New York: McGraw-Hill.

Brues, A. M. (1977). *People and races.* New York: Macmillan.

Brunet, M., et al. (2002). A new hominid from the Upper Miocene of Chad, Central Africa. *Nature, 418,* 145–151.

Burling, R. (1969). Linguistics and ethnographic description. *American Anthropologist, 71,* 817–827.

Burling, R. (1970). *Man's many voices: Language in its cultural context.* New York: Holt, Rinehart & Winston.

Burling, R. (1993). Primate calls, human language, and nonverbal communication. *Current Anthropology, 34,* 25–53.

Butzer, K. (1971). *Environment and anthropology: An ecological approach to prehistory* (2nd ed.). Chicago: Aldine.

Byers, D. S. (Ed.). (1967). *The prehistory of the Tehuacan Valley: Vol. 1. Environment and Subsistence.* Austin: University of Texas Press.

Cachel, S. (1997). Dietary shifts and the European Upper Paleolithic transition. *Current Anthropology, 38,* 590.

Calloway, C. (1997). Introduction: Surviving the Dark Ages. In C. G. Calloway (Ed.), *After King Philip's War: Presence and persistence in Indian New England* (pp. 1–28). Hanover, NH: University Press of New England.

Campbell, B. G., & Loy, J. D. (1995). *Humankind emerging* (7th ed.). New York: HarperCollins.

Carmack, R. (1983). Indians and the Guatemalan revolution. *Cultural Survival Quarterly, 7*(3), 52–54.

Carneiro, R. L. (1970). A theory of the origin of the state. *Science, 169,* 733–738.

Caroulis, J. (1996). Food for thought. *Pennsylvania Gazette, 95*(3), 16.

Carpenter, E. (1973). *Eskimo realities.* New York: Holt, Rinehart & Winston.

Carroll, J. B. (Ed.). (1956). *Language, thought and reality: Selected writings of Benjamin Lee Whorf.* Cambridge, MA: MIT Press.

Cartmill, M. (1998). The gift of gab. *Discover 19*(11), 64.

Cashdan, E. (1989). Hunters and gatherers: Economic behavior in bands. In S. Plattner (Ed.), *Economic anthropology* (pp. 21–48). Stanford, CA: Stanford University Press.

Catford, J. C. (1988). *A practical introduction to phonetics.* Oxford: Clarendon Press.

Caton, S. C. (1999). *Laurence of Arabia: A film's anthropology.* Berkeley: University of California Press.

Cavalli-Sforza, L. L. (1977). *Elements of human genetics.* Menlo Park, CA: W. A. Benjamin.

Cavallo, J. A. (1990, February). Cat in the human cradle. *Natural History,* 54–60.

Centers for Disease Control. (1997). *Centers for Disease Control Semi-Annual AIDS Report* (through June 1996). Atlanta, GA.

Chagnon, N. A. (1988). *Yanomamo: The fierce people* (3rd ed.). New York: Holt, Rinehart & Winston.

Chagnon, N. A., & Irons, W. (Eds.). (1979). *Evolutionary biology and human social behavior.* North Scituate, MA: Duxbury Press.

Chambers, R. (1983). *Rural development: Putting the last first.* New York: Longman.

Chan, J. W. C., & Vernon, P. E. (1988). Individual differences among the peoples of China. In J. W. Berry (Ed.), *Human abilities in cultural context* (pp. 340–357). Cambridge, England: Cambridge University Press.

Chang, K. C. (Ed.). (1968). *Settlement archaeology.* Palo Alto, CA: National Press.

Chapple, E. D. (1970). *Cultural and biological man: Explorations in behavioral anthropology.* New York: Holt, Rinehart & Winston.

Chase, C. (1998). Hermaphrodites with attitude. *Gay and Lesbian Quarterly, 4*(2), 189–211.

Chasin, B. H., & Franke, R. W. (1983). U.S. farming: A world model? *Global Reporter, 1*(2), 10.

Chatty, D. (1996). *Mobile pastoralists: Development planning and social change in Oman.* New York: Columbia University Press.

Chicurel, M. (2001). Can organisms speed their own evolution? *Science, 292,* 1824–1827.

Childe, V. G. (1951). *Man makes himself.* New York: New American Library. (orig. 1936)

Childe, V. G. (1954). *What happened in history.* Baltimore: Penguin.

Cigno, A. (1994). *Economics of the family.* New York: Oxford University Press.

Ciochon, R. L., & Fleagle, J. G. (Eds.). (1987). *Primate evolution and human origins.* Hawthorne, NY: Aldine.

Ciochon, R. L., & Fleagle, J. G. (1993). *The human evolution source book.* Englewood Cliffs, NJ: Prentice-Hall.

Clark, E. E. (1966). *Indian legends of the Pacific Northwest* (p. 174). Berkeley: University of California Press.

Clark, G. (1967). *The Stone Age hunters.* New York: McGraw-Hill.

Clark, G. (1972). *Starr Carr: A case study in bioarchaeology.* Reading, MA: Addison-Wesley.

Clark, G. A. (1997). Neandertal genetics. *Science, 277,* 1,024.

Clark, G. A. (2002) Neandertal archaeology: Implications for our origins. *American Anthropologist 104*(1), 50–67.

Clark, J. G. D. (1962). *Prehistoric Europe: The economic basis.* Stanford, CA: Stanford University Press.

Clark, W. E. L. (1960). *The antecedents of man.* Chicago: Quadrangle Books.

Clark, W. E. L. (1966). *History of the primates* (5th ed.). Chicago: University of Chicago Press.

Clark, W. E. L. (1967). *Man-apes or ape-men? The story of discoveries in Africa.* New York: Holt, Rinehart & Winston.

Clarke, R. J. (1998). First ever discovery of a well preserved skull and associated skeleton of *Australopithecus. South African Journal of Science, 94,* 460–464.

Clarke, R. J., & Tobias, P. V. (1995). Sterkfontein member 2 foot bones of the oldest South African hominid. *Science, 269,* 521–524.

Clay, J. W. (1987). Genocide in the age of enlightenment. *Cultural Survival Quarterly 12*(3).

Clay, J. W. (1996). What's a nation? In W. A. Haviland & R. J. Gordon (Eds.), *Talking about people* (2nd ed., pp. 188–189). Mountain View, CA: Mayfield.

Clough, S. B., & Cole, C. W. (1952). *Economic history of Europe* (3rd ed.). Lexington, MA: Heath.

Codere, H. (1950). *Fighting with property.* Seattle: University of Washington Press (American Ethnological Society, Monograph 18).

Coe, S. D. (1994). *America's first cuisines.* Austin: University of Texas Press.

Coe, W. R. (1967). *Tikal: A handbook of the ancient Maya ruins.* Philadelphia: University of Pennsylvania Museum.

Coe, W. R., & Haviland, W. A. (1982). *Introduction to the archaeology of Tikal.* Philadelphia: University Museum.

Cohen, J. (1997). Is an old virus up to new tricks? *Science, 277,* 312–313.

Cohen, M., & Armelagos, G. (Eds.). (1°... *Paleopathology at the origins of agr*... Orlando, FL: Academic Press.

Cohen, M. L. (1967). Variations in complexity among Chinese family groups: The impact of modernization. *Transactions of the New York Academy of Sciences, 295,* 638–647.

Cohen, M. L. (1968). A case study of Chinese family economy and development. *Journal of Asian and African Studies, 3,* 161–180.

Cohen, M. N. (1977). *The food crisis in prehistory.* New Haven, CT: Yale University Press.

Cohen, M. N. (1995). Anthropology and race: The bell curve phenomenon. *General Anthropology, 2*(1), 1–4.

Cohen, M. N., & Armelagos, G. J. (1984). Paleopathology at the origins of agriculture: Editors' summation. In M. N. Cohen & G. J. Armelagos (Eds.), *Paleopathology at the origins of agriculture.* Orlando, FL: Academic Press.

Cohen, R., & Middleton, J. (Eds.). (1967). *Comparative political systems.* Garden City, NY: Natural History Press.

Cohen, Y. (1968). *Man in adaptation: The cultural present.* Chicago: Aldine.

Colburn, T., Dumanoski, D., & Myers, J. P. (1996, March). Hormonal sabotage. *Natural History,* 45–46.

Cole, S. (1975). *Leakey's luck: The life of Louis Seymour Bazett Leakey. 1903–1972.* New York: Harcourt Brace Jovanovich.

Collier, J., Rosaldo, M. Z., & Yanagisako, S. (1982). Is there a family? New anthropological views. In B. Thorne & M. Yalom (Eds.), *Rethinking the family: Some feminist questions* (pp. 25–39). New York: Longman.

Collier, J. F., & Yanagisako, S. J. (Eds.). (1987). *Gender and kinship: Essays toward a unified analysis.* Stanford, CA: Stanford University Press.

Connelly, J. C. (1979). Hopi social organization. In A. Ortiz (Ed.), *Handbook of North American Indians, Vol. 9, Southwest* (pp. 539–553). Washington, DC: Smithsonian Institution.

Connor, M. (1996). The archaeology of contemporary mass graves. *SAA Bulletin, 14*(4), 6, 31.

Conroy, G. C. (1997). *Reconstructing human origins: A modern synthesis* (p. 427). New York: Norton.

Constable, G., & the Editors of Time-Life. (1973). *The Neanderthals.* New York: Time-Life.

Co   S. F. (1972). *Prehistoric demography.*
          ling, MA: Addison-Wesley.
    Coon,
         Kno1957). *The seven caves.* New York:

Coon, C. S. (1958). *Caravan: The story of the Middle East* (2nd ed.). New York: Holt, Rinehart & Winston.

Coon, C. S. (1971). *The hunting peoples.* Boston: Little, Brown.

Coon, C. S., Garn, S. N., & Birdsell, J. (1950). *Races: A study of the problems of race formation in man.* Springfield, IL: Charles C Thomas.

Cooper, A., Poinar, H. N., Pääbo, S., Radovci, C. J., Debénath, A., Caparros, M., Barroso-Ruiz, C., Bertranpetit, J., Nielsen-March, C., Hedges, R. E. M., & Sykes, B. (1997). Neanderthal genetics. *Science, 277,* 1,021–1,024.

Coppens, Y., Howell, F. C., Isaac, G. L., & Leakey, R. E. F. (Eds.). (1976). *Earliest man and environments in the Lake Rudolf Basin: Stratigraphy, paleoecology, and evolution.* Chicago: University of Chicago Press.

Corbey, R. (1995). Introduction: Missing links, or the ape's place in nature. In R. Corbey & B. Theunissen (Eds.), *Ape, man, ape-man: Changing views since 1600* (p.1). Leiden: Department of Prehistory, Leiden University.

Cornwell, T. (1995, November 10). Skeleton staff. *Times Higher Education,* p. 20.

Corruccini, R. S. (1992). Metrical reconsideration of the Skhul IV and IX and Border Cave I crania in the context of modern human origins. *American Journal of Physical Anthropology, 87,* 433–445.

Cottrell, F. (1965). *Energy and society: The relation between energy, social changes and economic development.* New York: McGraw–Hill.

Cottrell, L. (1963). *The lost pharaohs.* New York: Grosset & Dunlap.

Courlander, H. (1971). *The fourth world of the Hopis.* New York: Crown.

Cowgill, G. L. (1980). Letter. *Science, 210,* 1,305.

Cowgill, G. L. (1997). State and society at Teotihuacan, Mexico. *Annual Review of Anthropology, 26,* 129–161.

Cox, O. C. (1959). *Caste, class and race: A study in dynamics.* New York: Monthly Review Press.

Crane, L. B., Yeager, E., & Whitman, R. L. (1981). *An introduction to linguistics.* Boston: Little, Brown.

Crocker, W. A., & Crocker, J. (1994). *The canela, bonding through kinship, ritual and sex.* Fort Worth, TX: Harcourt Brace.

Culbert, T. P. (Ed.). (1973). *The Classic Maya collapse.* Albuquerque: University of New Mexico Press.

Culotta, E. (1992). A new take on anthropoid origins, *Science, 256,* 1,516–1,517.

Culotta, E. (1995). Asian hominids grow older. *Science, 270,* 1,116–1,117.

Culotta, E. (1995). New finds rekindle debate over anthropoid origins. *Science, 268,* 1,851.

Culotta, E. (1995). New hominid crowds the field. *Science, 269,* 918.

Culotta, E., & Koshland, D. E., Jr. (1994). DNA repair works its way to the top. *Science 266,* 1,926.

Cultural Survival Quarterly. (1991). 15(4), 5.

Cultural Survival Quarterly. (1991). 15(4), 38.

Dalton, G. (Ed.). (1967). *Tribal and peasant economics: Readings in economic anthropology.* Garden City, NY: Natural History Press.

Dalton, G. (1971). *Traditional tribal and peasant economics: An introductory survey of economic anthropology.* Reading, MA: Addison-Wesley.

Daniel, G. (1970). *The first civilizations: The archaeology of their origins.* New York: Apollo Editions.

Daniel, G. (1975). *A hundred and fifty years of archaeology.* (2nd ed.) London: Duckworth.

Darwin, C. (1936). *The descent of man and selection in relation to sex.* New York: Random House (Modern Library). (orig. 1871)

Darwin, C. (1967). *On the origin of species.* New York: Atheneum. (orig. 1859)

Davenport, W. (1959). Linear descent and descent groups. *American Anthropologist, 61,* 557–573.

Davis, S. H. (1982). *Victims of the miracle.* Cambridge: Cambridge University Press.

Day, G. M. (1972). Quoted in T. C. Vogelman (Director) and Department of Anthropology (Producer). *Prehistoric life in the Champlain Valley* [Film]. Burlington, VT: University of Vermont.

Dean, M. C., Beynon, A. D., Thackeray, J. F., & Macho, G. A. (1993). Histological reconstruction of dental development and age at death of a juvenile *Paranthropus robustus* specimen, SK 63, from Swartkrans, South Africa. *American Journal of Physical Anthropology, 91,* 401–419.

Death and disorder in Guatemala. (1983). *Cultural Survival Quarterly, 7*(1).

DeBeer, Sir G. R. (1964). *Atlas of evolution.* London: Nelson.

Deetz, J. (1967). *Invitation to archaeology.* New York: Doubleday.

Deevy, E. S., Jr. (1960). The human population. *Scientific American, 203,* 194–204.

de Laguna, F. (1977). *Voyage to Greenland: A personal initiation into anthropology.* New York: Norton.

de Laguna, G. A. (1966). *On existence and the human world.* New Haven, CT: Yale University Press.

DeMello, M. (2000). *Bodies of inscription: A cultural history of the modern tattoo community.* Durham, NC: Duke University Press.

De Mott, B. (1990). *The imperial middle: Why Americans can't think straight about class.* New York: Morrow.

de Pelliam, A., & Burton, F. D. (1976). More on predatory behavior in nonhuman primates. *Current Anthropology, 17*(3).

d'Errico, F., Zilhão, J., Julien, M., Baffier, D., & Pelegrin, J. (1998). Neandertal acculturation in Western Europe? *Current Anthropology, 39,* 521.

Desowitz, R. S. (1987). *New Guinea tapeworms and Jewish grandmothers.* New York: Norton.

Dettwyler, K. A. (1997, October). When to wean. *Natural History,* 49.

Devereux, G. (1963). Institutionalized homosexuality of the Mohave Indians. In H. M. Ruitenbeck (Ed.), *The problem of homosexuality in modern society.* New York: Dutton.

DeVore, I. (Ed.). (1965). *Primate behavior: Field studies of monkeys and apes.* New York: Holt, Rinehart & Winston.

de Waal, A. (1994). Genocide in Rwanda. *Anthropology Today, 10*(3), 1–2.

de Waal, F. (1996). *Good natured: The origins of right and wrong in humans and other animals.* Cambridge, MA: Harvard University Press.

de Waal, F., Kano, T., & Parish, A. R. (1998). Comments. *Current Anthropology 39,* 407–408, 410–411, 413–414.

de Waal, F. (2001). Sing the song of evolution. *Natural History, 110*(8), 77.

de Waal, F. (2001). *The ape and the sushi master.* New York: Basic Books.

Diamond, J. (1994). How Africa became black. *Discover, 15*(2), 72–81.

Diamond, J. (1994). Race without color. *Discover, 15*(11), 83–89.

Diamond, J. (1996). Empire of uniformity. *Discover, 17*(3), 78–85.

Diamond, J. (1997). The curse of QWERTY. *Discover, 18*(4), 34–42.

Diamond, J. (1997). *Guns, germs, and steel* (p. 203). New York: Norton.

Diamond, J. (1998). Ants, crops, and history. *Science, 281,* 1,974–1,975.

Dissanayake, E. (2000). Birth of the arts. *Natural History, 109*(10), 89.

Dixon, J. E., Cann, J. R., & Renfrew, C. (1968). Obsidian and the origins of trade, *Scientific American, 218,* 38–46.

Dobyns, H. F., Doughty, P. L., & Lasswell, H. D., (Eds.). (1971). *Peasants, power, and applied social change.* London: Sage.

Dobzhansky, T. (1962). *Mankind evolving.* New Haven, CT: Yale University Press.

Doist, R. (1997). Molecular evolution and scientific inquiry, misperceived. *American Scientist, 85,* 475.

Domestic violence against women and girls. (2000, June). *Innocenti Digest,* 6. p. 4. Florence: United Nations Children's Fund, Innocenti Research Center.

Donnan, C. B., & Castillo, L. J. (1992). Finding the tomb of a Moche priestess. *Archaeology, 45*(6), 38–42.

Douglas, M. (1958). Raffia cloth distribution in the Lele economy. *Africa, 28,* 109–122.

Dozier, E. (1970). *The Pueblo Indians of North America.* New York: Holt, Rinehart & Winston.

Draper, P. (1975). !Kung women: Contrasts in sexual egalitarianism in foraging and sedentary contexts. In R. Reiter (Ed.), *Toward an anthropology of women* (pp. 77–109). New York: Monthly Review Press.

Driver, H. (1964). *Indians of North America.* Chicago: University of Chicago Press.

Dubois, C. (1944). *The people of Alor.* Minneapolis: University of Minnesota Press.

Dubos, R. (1968). *So human an animal.* New York: Scribner.

Dumurat-Dreger, A. (1998, May/June). Ambiguous sex or ambivalent medicine? *The Hastings Center Report, 28*(3), 24–35. (Posted on the Intersex Society of North America Web site: *www.isna.org*.)

Duncan, A. S., Kappelman, J., & Shapiro, L. J. (1994). Metasophalangeal joint function and positional behavior in *Australopithecus afarensis. American Journal of Physical Anthropology, 93,* 67–81.

Dundes, A. (1980). *Interpreting folklore.* Bloomington: Indiana University Press.

Duranti, A. (2001). Linguistic anthropology: History, ideas, and issues. In A. Duranti (Ed.), *Linguistic anthropology: A reader* (pp. 1–38). Oxford: Blackwell.

Durant, J. C. (2000, April 23) Everybody Into the gene pool. *New York Times Book Review,* p. 11.

Durkheim, E. (1964). *The division of labor in society.* New York: Free Press.

Durkheim, E. (1965). *The elementary forms of the religious life.* New York: Free Press.

duToit, B. M. (1991). *Human sexuality: Cross-cultural readings.* New York: McGraw-Hill.

Eastman, C. M. (1990). *Aspects of language and culture* (2nd ed.). Novato, CA: Chandler & Sharp.

Edey, M., & the Editors of Time-Life. (1972). *The missing link.* New York: Time-Life.

Edey, M. A., & Johannson, D. (1989). *Blueprints: Solving the mystery of evolution.* Boston: Little, Brown.

Edmonson, M. S. (1971). *Lore: An introduction to the science of folklore.* New York: Holt, Rinehart & Winston.

Edwards, J. (Ed.). (1999). *Technologies of procreation: Kinship in the age of assisted conception.* New York: Routledge (distributed by St. Martin's Press).

Edwards, S. W. (1978). Nonutilitarian activities on the Lower Paleolithic: A look at the two kinds of evidence. *Current Anthropology. 19*(l), 135–137.

Eggan, F. (1954). Social anthropology and the method of controlled comparison. *American Anthropologist, 56,* 743–763.

Eiseley, L. (1958). *Darwin's century: Evolution and the men who discovered it.* New York: Doubleday.

Eisenstadt, S. N. (1956). *From generation to generation: Age groups and social structure.* New York: Free Press.

Elkin, A. P. (1964). *The Australian aborigines.* Garden City, NY: DoubleDay/Anchor Books.

Ellison, P. T. (1990). Human ovarian function and reproductive ecology: New hypotheses. *American Anthropologist, 92,* 933–952.

Ember, C. R., & Ember, M. (1985). *Cultural anthropology* (4th ed.). Englewood Cliffs, NJ: Prentice–Hall.

Ember, C. R., & Ember, M. (1996). What have we learned from cross-cultural research? *General Anthropology, 2*(2), 5.

Enard, W., et al. (2002). Molecular evolution of FOXP2, a gene involved in speech and language. *Nature, 418,* 869–872.

Epstein, A. (1968). Sanctions. In *International Encyclopedia of the Social Sciences* (Vol. 14, p. 3). New York: Macmillan.

Erasmus, C. J. (1950). Patolli, Pachisi, and the limitation of possibilities. *Southwestern Journal of Anthropology, 6,* 369–381.

Erasmus, C. J., & Smith, W. (1967). Cultu anthropology in the United States *ōgy,* 1900. *Southwestern Journal of Anth* 23, 11–40.

Erickson, P. A. & Murphy, L. D. (2003). *A history of anthropological theory* (2nd ed.). Peterborough, Ontario: Broadview Press.

Errington, F. K., & Gewertz, D. B. (2001). *Cultural alternatives and a feminist anthropology: An analysis of culturally constructed gender interests in Papua New Guinea.* New York: Cambridge University Press.

Ervin-Tripp, S. (1973). *Language acquisition and communicative choice.* Stanford, CA: Stanford University Press.

Esber, G. S., Jr. (1987). Designing Apache houses with Apaches. In R. M. Wulff & S. J.Fiske (Eds.), *Anthropological praxis: Translating knowledge into action* (pp. 187–196). Boulder, CO: Westview Press.

Evans, W. (1968). *Communication in the animal world.* New York: Crowell.

Evans-Pritchard, E. E. (1937). *Witchcraft, oracles, and magic among the Azande.* London: Oxford University Press.

Evans-Pritchard, E. E. (1968). *The Nuer: A description of the modes of livelihood and political institutions of a Nilotic people.* London: Oxford University Press.

Fagan, B. M. (1995). The quest for the past. In L. L. Hasten (Ed.), *Annual Editions 95/96, Archaeology* (p. 10). Guilford, CT: Dushkin.

Fagan, B. M. (1998). *People of the earth* (9th ed.). New York: Longman.

Fagan, B. M. (1999). *Archaeology: A brief introduction* (7th ed.). New York: Longman.

Fagan, B. M. (2000). *Ancient lives: An introduction to archaeology.* (pp. 125–133). Englewood Cliffs, NJ: Prentice-Hall.

Falk, D. (1975). Comparative anatomy of the larynx in man and the chimpanzee: Implications for language in Neanderthal. *American Journal of Physical Anthropology, 43*(1), 123–132.

Falk, D. (1989). Ape-like endocast of "Ape Man Taung." *American Journal of Physical Anthropology, 80,* 335–339.

Falk, D. (1993). A good brain is hard to cool. *Natural History, 102*(8), 65.

Falk, D. (1993). Hominid paleoneurology. In R. L. Ciochon & J. G. Fleagle (Eds.), *The human evolution source book.* Englewood Cliffs, NJ: Prentice-Hall.

Farmer, P. (1992). *AIDS and accusation: Haiti and the geography of blame.* Berkeley: University of California Press.

rnell, B. (1995). *Do you see what I mean? Plains Indian sign talk and the embodiment of tion.* Austin: University of Texas Press.

Farsc S. K. (1970). Family structures and Swe in modern Lebanon. In L. E.), *Peoples and cultures of the*

Middle East (Vol. 2). Garden City, NY: Natural History Press.

Fausto-Sterling, A. (1993, March/April). The five sexes: Why male and female are not enough. *The Sciences, 33*(2), 20–24.

Fausto-Sterling, A. (2000, July/August). The five sexes revisited. *The Sciences.* 40(4),19–24.

Fausto-Sterling, A. (2003, August 2). Personal email communication.

Feder, K. L. (1999). *Frauds, myths, and mysteries* (3rd ed.). Mountain View, CA: Mayfield.

Federoff, N. E., & Nowak, R. M. (1997). Man and his dog. *Science, 278,* 305.

Fedigan, L. M. (1986).The changing role of women in models of human evolution. *Annual Review of Anthropology, 15,* 25–56.

Female genital mutilation. (2000). Fact sheet no. 241. World Health Organization.

Fernandez-Carriba, S., & Loeches, A. (2001). Fruit smearing by captive chimpanzees: A newly observed food-processing behavior. *Current Anthropology, 42,* 143–147.

Ferrie, H. (1997). An interview with C. Loring Brace. *Current Anthropology, 38,* 851–869.

Finkler, K. (2000). *Experiencing the new genetics: Family and kinship on the medical frontier.* Philadelphia: University of Pennsylvania Press.

The First Americans, ca. 20,000 b.c. (1998). *Discover, 19*(6), 24.

Firth, R. (1952). *Elements of social organization.* London: Watts.

Firth, R. (1957). *Man and culture: An evaluation of Bronislaw Malinowski.* London: Routledge.

Firth, R. (1963). *We the Tikopia.* Boston: Beacon Press.

Firth, R. (Ed.). (1967). *Themes in economic anthropology.* London: Tavistock.

Fisher, R., & Ury, W. L. (1991). *Getting to yes: Negotiating agreement without giving in* (2nd ed.). Boston: Houghton Mifflin.

Fishman, J. (1994). Putting a new spin on the human birth. *Science, 264,* 1,082–1,083.

Flannery, K. V. (1973). The origins of agriculture. In B. J. Siegel, A. R. Beals, & S. A. Tyler (Eds.), *Annual Review of Anthropology* (Vol. 2, pp. 271–310). Palo Alto, CA: Annual Reviews.

Flannery, K. V. (Ed.). (1976). *The Mesoamerican village.* New York: Seminar Press.

Fleagle, J. G. (1992, December). *Early anthropoid evolution.* Paper presented at the 91st

annual meeting of the American Anthropological Association.

Folger, T. (1993). The naked and the bipedal. *Discover, 14*(11), 34–35.

Forbes, J. D. (1964). *The Indian in America's past.* Englewood Cliffs, NJ: Prentice-Hall.

Forbes International 500 List. (2003).

Forde, C. D. (1953). *Habitat, economy, and society.* New York: Dutton.

Forde, C. D. (1955). The Nupe. In D. Forde (Ed.), *Peoples of the Niger-Benue confluence.* London: International African Institute (Ethnographic Survey of Africa. Western Africa, part 10).

Forde, C. D. (1968). Double descent among the Yako. In P. Bohannan & J. Middleton (Eds.), *Kinship and social organization* (pp. 179–191). Garden City, NY: Natural History Press.

Fortes, M. (1950). Kinship and marriage among the Ashanti. In A. R. Radcliffe-Brown & C. D. Forde (Eds.), *African systems of kinship and marriage.* London: Oxford University Press.

Fortes, M. (1969). *Kinship and the social order: The legacy of Lewis Henry Morgan.* Chicago: Aldine.

Fortes, M., & Evans-Prichard, E. E. (Eds.). (1962). *African political systems.* London: Oxford University Press. (orig.1940)

Fossey, D. (1983). *Gorillas in the mist.* Burlington, MA: Houghton Mifflin.

Foster, G. M. (1955). Peasant society and the image of the limited good. *American Anthropologist, 67,* 293–315.

Fox, R. (1967). *Kinship and marriage in an anthropological perspective.* Baltimore: Penguin.

Fox, R. (1968). *Encounter with anthropology.* New York: Dell.

Frake, C. O. (1961). The diagnosis of disease among the Subinam of Mindinao. *American Anthropologist, 63,*113–132.

Frake, C. O. (1992). Lessons of the Mayan sky. In A. F. Aveni (Ed.), *The sky in Mayan literature* (pp. 274–291). New York: Oxford University Press.

France, D. L., & Horn, A. D. (1992). *Lab manual and workbook for physical anthropology* (2nd ed.). New York: West.

Frankfort, H. (1968). *The birth of civilization in the Near East.* New York: Barnes & Noble.

Fraser, D. (1962). *Primitive art.* New York: Doubleday.

Fraser, D. (Ed.). (1966). *The many faces of primitive art: A critical anthology.* Englewood Cliffs, NJ: Prentice-Hall.

Frayer, D. W. (1981). Body size, weapon use, and natural selection in the European Upper Paleolithic and Mesolithic. *American Anthropologist, 83,* 57–73.

Frazer, Sir J. G. (1961 reissue). *The new golden bough.* New York: Doubleday, Anchor Books.

Freeman, J. D. (1960). The Iban of western Borneo. In G. P. Murdock (Ed.), *Social structure in Southeast Asia.* Chicago: Quadrangle Books.

Freeman, L. G. (1992). *Ambrona and Torralba: New evidence and interpretation.* Paper presented at the 91st annual meeting of the American Anthropological Association, San Francisco.

Fried, M. (1960). On the evolution of social stratification and the state. In S. Diamond (Ed.), *Culture in history: Essays in honor of Paul Radin.* New York: Columbia University Press.

Fried, M. (1967). *The evolution of political society: An essay in political anthropology.* New York: Random House.

Fried, M. (1972). *The study of anthropology.* New York: Crowell.

Fried, M., Harris, M., & Murphy, R. (1968). *War: The anthropology of armed conflict and aggression.* Garden City, NY: Natural History Press.

Friedl, E. (1975). *Women and men: An anthropologist's view.* New York: Holt, Rinehart & Winston.

Friedman, J. (Ed.). (2003). *Globalization, the state, and violence.* Walnut Creek, CA: Altamira Press.

Fritz, G. J. (1994). Are the first American farmers getting younger? *Current Anthropology, 35,* 305–309.

Frye, M. (1983). *Sexism. In The politics of reality* (pp. 17–40). New York: Crossing Press.

Furst, P. T. (1976). *Hallucinogens and culture* (p. 7). Novato, CA: Chandler & Sharp.

Gamble, C. (1986). *The Paleolithic settlement of Europe.* Cambridge: Cambridge University Press.

Gardner, R. A., Gardner, B. T., & Van Cantfort, T. E. (Eds.). (1989). *Teaching sign language to chimpanzees.* Albany: State University of New York Press.

Gamst, F. C., & Norbeck, E. (1976). *Ideas of culture: Sources and uses.* New York: Holt, Rinehart& Winston.

Garn, S. M. (1970). *Human races* (3rd ed.). Springfield, IL: Charles C Thomas.

Gates, H. (1996). Buying brides in China—again. *Anthropology Today, 12*(4), 10.

Gebo, D. L., Dagosto, D., Beard, K. C., & Tao, Q. (2001). Middle Eocene primate tarsals from China: Implications for haplorhine evolution. *American Journal of Physical Anthropology, 116,* 83–107.

Geertz, C. (1963). *Agricultural involution: The process of ecological change in Indonesia.* Berkeley: University of California Press.

Geertz, C. (1965). The impact of the concept of culture on the concept of man. In J. R. Platt (Ed.), *New views of man.* Chicago: University of Chicago Press.

Geertz, C. (1984). Distinguished lecture: Antirelativism. *American Anthropologist, 86,* 263–278.

Gelb, I. J. (1952). *A study of writing.* London: Routledge.

Gell, A. (1988). Technology and magic. *Anthropology Today, 4*(2), 6–9.

Gellner, E. (1969). *Saints of the atlas.* Chicago: University of Chicago Press (The Nature of Human Society Series).

Gennep, A. Van (1960). *The rites of passage.* Chicago: University of Chicago Press.

Gibbons, A. (1992). Mitochondrial Eve: Wounded, but not yet dead. *Science, 257,* 873–875.

Gibbons, A. (1996). Did Neandertals lose an evolutionary "arms" race? *Science, 272,* 1,586–1,587.

Gibbons, A. (1997). Ideas on human origins evolve at anthropology gathering. *Science, 276,* 535–536.

Gibbons, A. (1997). A new face for human ancestors. *Science, 276,* 1,331–1,333.

Gibbons, A. (1998). Ancient island tools suggest *Homo erectus* was a seafarer. *Science, 279,* 1,635.

Gibbons, A. (2001). Studying humans—and their cousins and parasites. *Science, 292,* 627.

Gibbons, A. (2001). The riddle of coexistence. *Science, 291,* 1,726.

Gibbons, A., & Culotta, E. (1997). Miocene primates go ape. *Science, 276,* 355–356.

Gibbs, J. L., Jr. (1965). The Kpelle of Liberia. In J. L. Gibbs (Ed.), *Peoples of Africa* (pp. 197–240). New York: Holt, Rinehart & Winston.

Giddens, A. (1990). *The consequences of modernity* (p. 64). Stanford, CA: Stanford University Press.

Ginsburg, F. D., Abu-Lughod, L., & Larkin, B. (Eds.). (2002). *Media worlds: Anthropology on new terrain.* Berkeley: University of California Press.

Gleason, H. A., Jr. (1966). *An introduction to descriptive linguistics* (Rev. ed.). New York: Holt, Rinehart & Winston.

Gledhill. J. (2000). *Power and its disguises: Anthropological perspectives on politics* (2nd ed.). Boulder, CO: Pluto Press.

Glob, P. (1969). *The bog people.* London: Faber & Faber.

Gluckman, M. (1955). *The judicial process among the Barotse of Northern Rhodesia.* New York: Free Press.

Goddard, V. (1993). Child labor in Naples. In W. A. Haviland & R. J. Gordon (Eds.), *Talking about people* (pp. 105–109). Mountain View, CA: Mayfield.

Godfrey, T. (2000, December 27). Biotech threatening biodiversity. *Burlington Free Press,* 10A.

Godlier, M. (1971). Salt currency and the circulation of commodities among the Baruya of New Guinea. In G. Dalton (Ed.), *Studies in economic anthropology.* Washington, DC: American Anthro-pological Association (Anthropological Studies No. 7).

Golden, M., Birns, B., Bridger, W., & Moss, A. (1971). Social–class differentiation in cognitive development among black preschool children. *Child Development, 42,* 37–45.

Goodall, J. (1986). *The chimpanzees of Gombe: Patterns of behavior.* Cambridge, MA: Belknap Press.

Goodall, J. (1990). *Through a window: My thirty years with the chimpanzees of Gombe.* Boston: Houghton Mifflin.

Goodall, J. (2000). *Reason for hope: A spiritual journey.* New York: Warner Books.

Goode, W. (1963). *World revolution and family patterns.* New York: Free Press.

Goodenough, W. (1956). Residence rules. *Southwestern Journal of Anthropology, 12,* 22–37.

Goodenough, W. (1961). Comment on cultural evolution. *Daedalus, 90,* 521–528.

Goodenough, W. (Ed.). (1964). *Explorations in cultural anthropology: Essays in honor of George Murdock.* New York: McGraw–Hill.

Goodenough, W. (1965). Rethinking status. and Role: Toward a general model of the cultural organization of social relationships. In M. Benton (Ed.), *The relevance of models for social anthropology.* New York: Praeger (ASA Monographs l).

Goodenough, W. (1970). *Description and comparison in cultural anthropology.* Chicago Aldine.

Goodenough, W. H. (1990) Evolution the human capacity for beliefs. *Amer n Anthropologist* 92:601.

Goodman, M., Bailey, W. J., Hayasaka, K., Stanhope, M. J., Slightom, J., & Czelusniak, J. (1994). Molecular evidence on primate phylogeny from DNA sequences. *American Journal of Physical Anthropology, 94,* 3–24.

Goodman, M. E. (1967). *The individual and culture.* Homewood, IL: Dorsey Press.

Goody, J. (1969). *Comparative studies in kinship.* Stanford, CA: Stanford University Press.

Goody, J. (Ed.). (1972). *Developmental cycle in domestic groups.* New York: Cambridge University Press (Papers in Social Anthropology, No. 1).

Goody, J. (1976). *Production and reproduction: A comparative study of the domestic domain.* Cambridge: Cambridge University Press.

Goody, J. (1983). *The development of the family and marriage in Europe.* Cambridge, MA: Cambridge University Press.

Gordon, R. (1981, December). [Interview for Coast Telecourses, Inc.]. Los Angeles.

Gordon, R. (1990). The field researcher as a deviant: A Namibian case study. In P. Hugo (Ed.), *Truth be in the field: Social science research in southern Africa.* Pretoria: University of South Africa.

Gordon, R. J. (1992). *The Bushman myth: The making of a Namibian underclass.* Boulder, CO: Westview Press.

Gordon, R. J., & Megitt, M. J. (1985). *Law and order in the New Guinea highlands.* Hanover, NH: University Press of New England.

Gorer, G. (1943). Themes in Japanese culture. *Transactions of the New York Academy of Sciences,* series 11, 5.

Gorman, E. M. (1989). The AIDS epidemic in San Francisco: Epidemiological and anthropological perspectives. In A. Podolefsky & P. J. Brown (Eds.), *Applying anthropology, An introductory reader.* Mountain View, CA: Mayfield.

Gornick, V., & Moran, B. K. (Eds.). (1971). *Woman in sexist society.* New York: Basic Books.

Gottlieb, A., & DeLoache, J. S. (Eds.). (2000). *A world of babies: Imagined childcare guides for seven societies.* New York: Cambridge University Press.

Gould, S. J. (1983). *Hen's teeth and horses' toes.* New York: Norton.

Gould, S. J. (1985). *The flamingo's smile: Reflections in natural history.* New York: Norton.

Gould, S. J. (1986). Of kiwi eggs and the Liberty Bell. *Natural History, 95,* 20–29.

Gould, S. J. (1989). *Wonderful life.* New York: Norton.

Gould, S. J. (1991). *Bully for brontosaurus.* New York: Norton.

Gould, S. J. (1994). The geometer of race. *Discover, 15*(11), 65–69.

Gould, S. J. (1996). *Full house: The spread of excellence from Plato to Darwin* (pp. 176–195). New York: Harmony Books.

Gould, S. J. (1996). *The mismeasure of man* (Rev. ed.). New York: Norton.

Gould, S. J. (1997). *Questioning the millennium.* New York: Crown.

Gould, S. J. (2000). The narthex of San Marco and the pangenetic paradigm. *Natural History* 109(6), 29.

Gould, S. J. (2000). What does the dreaded "E" word mean anyway? *Natural History,* 109(1), 34–36.

Graburn, N. H. (1969). *Eskimos without igloos: Social and economic development in Sugluk.* Boston: Little, Brown.

Graburn, N. H. (1971). *Readings in kinship and social structure.* New York: Harper & Row.

Graham, S. B. (1979). Biology and human social behavior: A response to van den Berghe and Barash. *American Anthropologist, 81*(2), 357–360.

Graves, P. (1991). New models and metaphors for the Neanderthal debate. *Current Anthropology, 32*(5), 513–543.

Gray, P. M., et al. (2001). The music of nature and the nature of music. *Science, 291,* 52.

Green, E. C. (1987). The planning of health education strategies in Swaziland. In R. M. Wulff & S. J. Fiske (Eds.), *Anthropological praxis: Translating knowledge into action* (pp. 15–25). Boulder, CO: Westview Press.

Greenberg, J. H. (1968). *Anthropological linguistics: An introduction.* New York: Random House.

Greenfield, L. O. (1979). On the adaptive pattern of Ramapithecus. *American Journal of Physical Anthropology, 50,* 527–547.

Greenfield, L. O. (1980). A late divergence hypothesis. *American Journal of Physical Anthropology, 52,* 351–366.

Griffin, B. (1994). CHAGS7. *Anthropology Newsletter, 35*(1), 12–14.

Grine, F. E. (1993). Australopithecine taxonomy and phylogeny: Historical background and recent interpretation. In R. L. Ciochon & J. G. Fleagle (Eds.), *The human evolution source book,* Englewood Cliffs, NJ: Prentice-Hall.

Grün, R., & Thorne, A. (1997). Dating the Ngandong humans, *Science, 276,* 1,575.

Guillette, E. A., et al. (1998, June). An anthropological approach to the evaluation of preschool children exposed to pesticides in Mexico. *Environmental Health Perspectives 106,* 347.

Gulliver, P. (1968). Age differentiation. In *International encyclopedia of the social sciences* (Vol. 1, pp. 157–162). New York: Macmillan.

Guthrie, S. (1993). *Faces in the clouds: A new theory of religions.* New York: Oxford University Press.

Gutin, J. A. (1995). Do Kenya tools root birth of modern thought in Africa? *Science, 270,* 1,118–1,119.

Haeri, N. (1997). The reproduction of symbolic capital: Language, state and class in Egypt. *Current Anthropology, 38,* 795–816.

Hafkin, N., & Bay, E. (Eds.). (1976). *Women in Africa.* Stanford, CA: Stanford University Press.

Hall, E. T. (1959). *The silent language.* Garden City, NY: Anchor Press/Doubleday.

Hall, E. T., & Hall, M. R. (1986). The sounds of silence. In E. Angeloni (Ed.), *Anthro-pology 86/87* (pp. 65–70). Guilford, CT: Dushkin.

Hall, K. R. L., & DeVore, I. (1965). Baboon social behavior. In I. DeVore (Ed.), *Primate behavior.* New York: Holt, Rinehart & Winston.

Hallowell, A. I. (1955). *Culture and experience.* Philadelphia: University of Pennsylvania Press.

Halperin, R. H. (1994). *Cultural economies: Past and present.* Austin: University of Texas Press.

Halverson, J. (1989). Review of Altimira Revisited and other essays on early art. *American Antiquity, 54,* 883.

Hamblin, D. J., & the Editors of Time-Life. (1973). *The first cities.* New York: Time-Life.

Hamburg, D. A., & McGown, E. R. (Eds.). (1979). *The great apes.* Menlo Park, CA: Cummings.

Hammond, D. (1972). *Associations.* Reading, MA: Addison-Wesley.

Hannah, J. L. (1988). *Dance, sex and gender.* Chicago: University of Chicago Press.

Harlow, H. F. (1962). Social deprivation in monkeys. *Scientific American, 206,* 1–10.

Harner, M. (1980). *The way of the shaman: A guide to power and healing* (p. 20). San Francisco: Harper & Row.

Harpending, J. H., & Harpending, H. C. (1995). Ancient differences in population can mimic a recent African origin of modern humans. *Current Anthropology, 36,* 667–674.

Harris, M. (1965). The cultural ecology of India's sacred cattle. *Current Anthropology, 7,* 51–66.

Harris, M. (1968). *The rise of anthropological theory: A history of theories of culture.* New York: Crowell.

Harrison, G. G. (1975). Primary adult lactase deficiency: A problem in anthropological genetics. *American Anthropologist, 77,* 812–835.

Hart, C. W., Pilling, A. R., & Goodale, J. (1988). *Tiwi of North Australia* (3rd ed.). New York: Holt, Rinehart & Winston.

Hartwig, W. C., & Doneski, K. (1998). Evolution of the Hominid hand and toolmaking behavior. *American Journal of Physical Anthropology, 106,* 401–402.

Hatch, E. (1983). *Culture and morality: The relativity of values in anthropology.* New York: Columbia University Press.

Hatcher, E. P. (1985). *Art as culture, an introduction to the anthropology of art.* New York: University Press of America.

Haviland W. (1967). Stature at Tikal, Guatemala: Implications for ancient Maya, demography, and social organization. *American Antiquity, 32,* 316–325.

Haviland, W. (1970). Tikal, Guatemala and Mesoamerican urbanism. *World Archaeology, 2,* 186–198.

Haviland, W. A. (1972). A new look at Classic Maya social organization at Tikal. *Ceramica de Cultura Maya, 8,* 1–16.

Haviland, W. A. (1974). Farming, seafaring and bilocal residence on the coast of Maine. *Man in the Northeast, 6,* 31–44.

Haviland, W. A. (1975). The ancient Maya and the evolution of urban society. *University of Northern Colorado Museum of Anthropology, Miscellaneous Series, 37.*

Haviland, W. A. (1983). *Human evolution and prehistory* (5th ed.). Fort Worth, TX: Harcourt Brace.

Haviland, W. A. (1991). *Star wars at Tikal, or did Caracol do what the glyphs say they did?* Paper presented at the 90th annual meeting of the American Anthropological Association.

Haviland, W. A. (1997). Cleansing young minds, or what should we be doing in introductory anthropology? In C. P. Kottak, J. J. White, R. H. Furlow, & P. C. Rice (Eds.), *The teaching of anthropology: Problems, issues, and decisions* (p. 35). Mountain View, CA: Mayfield.

Haviland, W. A. (1997). The rise and fall of sexual inequality: Death and gender at Tikal, Guatemala. *Ancient Mesoamerica, 8,* 1–12.

Haviland, W. A., et al. (1985). *Excavations in small residential groups of Tikal: Groups 4F-1 and 4F-2.* Philadelphia: University Museum.

Haviland, W. A., & Moholy-Nagy, H. (1992). Distinguishing the high and mighty from the hoi polloi at Tikal, Guatemala. In A. F. Chase & D. Z. Chase (Eds.), *Mesoamerican elites: An archaeological assessment.* Norman: Oklahoma University Press.

Haviland, W. A., & Power, M. W. (1994). *The original Vermonters: Native inhabitants, past and present* (Rev. and exp. ed.). Hanover, NH: University Press of New England.

Haviland, W. A. (2003). Settlement, society and demography at Tikal. In J. Sabloff (Ed.), *Tikal.* Santa Fe: School of American Research.

Haviland, W. A. (2003). *Tikal, Guatemala: A Maya way to urbanism.* Paper prepared for 3rd INAH/Penn State Conference on Mesoamerican Urbanism.

Hawkes, K., O'Connell, J. F., & Blurton-Jones, N. G. (1997). Hadza women's time allocation, offspring, provisioning, and the evolution of long postmenopausal life spans. *Current Anthropology, 38,* 551–577.

Hawkins, G. S. (1965). *Stonehenge decoded.* New York: Doubleday.

Hays, H. R. (1965). *From ape to angel: An informal history of social anthropology.* New York: Knopf.

Heichel, G. (1976). Agricultural production and energy resources. *American Scientist, 64.*

Heilbroner, R. L. (1972). *The making of economic society* (4th ed.). Englewood Cliffs, NJ: Prentice-Hall.

Heilbroner, R. L., & Thurow, L. C. (1981). *The economic problem* (6th ed.). Englewood Cliffs, NJ: Prentice-Hall.

Helm, J. (1962). The ecological approach in anthropology. *American Journal of Sociology, 67,* 630–649.

Henry, D. O. et al. (2004). Human behavioral organization in the Middle Paleolithic: Were Neandertals different? *American Anthropologist, 107*(1), 17-31.

Henry, J. (1965). *Culture against man.* New York: Vintage Books.

Henry, J. (1966). The metaphysic of youth, beauty, and romantic love. In S. Farber & R. Wilson (Eds.), *The challenge of women.* New York: Basic Books.

Henry, J. (1974). A theory for an anthropological analysis of American culture. In J. G. Jorgensen & M. Truzzi (Eds.), *Anthropology and American life.* Englewood Cliffs, NJ: Prentice-Hall.

Herskovits, M. J. (1952). *Economic anthropology: A study in comparative economics* (2nd ed.). New York: Knopf.

Herskovits, M. J. 1964. *Cultural dynamics.* New York: Knopf.

Hertz, N. (2001). *The silent takeover: Global capitalism and the death of democracy.* New York: Arrow Books.

Hewes, G. W. (1973). Primate communication and the gestural origin of language. *Current Anthropology, 14,* 5–24.

Himmelfarb, E. J. (2000). First alphabet found in Egypt. *Archaeology, 53*(1).

Hodgen, M. (1964). *Early anthropology in the sixteenth and seventeenth centuries.* Philadelphia: University of Pennsylvania Press.

Hoebel, E. A. (1954). *The law of primitive man: A study in comparative legal dynamics.* Cambridge, MA: Harvard University Press.

Hoebel, E. A. (1958). *Man in the primitive world: An introduction to anthropology.* New York: McGraw-Hill.

Hoebel, E. A. (1960). *The Cheyennes: Indians of the Great Plains.* New York: Holt, Rinehart & Winston.

Hoebel, E. A. (1972). *Anthropology: The study of man* (4th ed.). New York: McGraw-Hill.

Hogbin, I. (1964). *A Guadalcanal society.* New York: Holt, Rinehart & Winston.

Holden, C. (1983). Simon and Kahn versus Global 2000. *Science, 221,* 342.

Holden, C. (1996). Missing link for Miocene apes. *Science, 271,* 151.

Holden, C. (1998). *No last word on language origins.* Science, 282, 1,455–1,458.

Holden, C. (1999). Ancient child burial uncovered in Portugal. *Science, 283,* 169.

Hole, F. (1966). Investigating the origins of Mesopotamian civilization. *Science, 153,* 605–611.

Hole, F. & Heizer, R. F. (1969). *An introduction to prehistoric archeology.* New York: Holt, Rinehart & Winston.

Holloway, R. L. (1980). The O. H. 7 (Olduvai Gorge, Tanzania) hominid partial brain endocast revisited. American Journal of *Physical Anthropology, 53,* 267–274.

Holloway, R. L. (1981). The Indonesian Homo erectus brain endocast revisited. *American Journal of Physical Anthropology, 55,* 503–521.

Holloway, R. L. (1981). Volumetric and asymmetry determinations on recent hominid endocasts: Spy I and II, Djebel Jhrou 1, and the Salb Homo erectus specimens, with some notes on Neandertal brain size. *American Journal of Physical Anthropology, 55,* 385–393.

Holloway, R. L., & de LaCoste-Lareymondie, M. C. (1982). Brain endocast asymmetry in pongids and hominids: Some preliminary findings on the paleontology of cerebral dominance. *American Journal of Physical Anthropology, 58,* 101–110.

Holmes, L. D. (2000). Paradise Bent (film review). *American Anthropologist, 102(3),*604–605.

Hostetler, J., & Huntington, G. (1971). *Children in Amish society. New York:* Holt, Rinehart & Winston.

Houle, A. (1999). The origin of platyrrhines: An evaluation of the Antarctic scenario and the floating island model. *American Journal of Physical Anthropology, 109,* 554–556.

Howell, F. C. (1970). *Early man.* New York: Time-Life.

Hsiaotung, F. (1939). Peasant life in China. London: Kegan, Paul, Trench, & Truber.

Hsu, F. L. (1961). *Psychological anthropology: Approaches to culture and personality.* Homewood, IL: Dorsey Press.

Hsu, F. L. (1997). Role, affect, and anthropology. *American Anthropologist, 79,* 805–808.

Hsu, F. L. K. (1977). Role, affect, and anthropology. *American Anthropologist, 79,* 805–808.

Hsu, F. L. K. (1979). The cultural problems of the cultural anthropologist. *American Anthropologist, 81,* 517–532.

Hubert, H., & Mauss, M. (1964). *Sacrifice.* Chicago: University of Chicago Press.

Human development report 2000. *Deepening democracy in a fragmented world.* United Nations Development Program.

Hunger Project. (2003). www.thp.org.

Hunt, R. C. (Ed.). (1967). *Personalities and cultures: Readings in psychological anthropology.* Garden City, NY: Natural History Press.

Hymes, D. (1964). *Language in culture and Society: A reader in linguistics and anthropology.* New York: Harper & Row.

Hymes, D. (Ed.). (1972). *Reinventing anthropology.* New York: Pantheon.

Inda, J. X., & Rosaldo, R. (Eds). (2001). *The anthropology of globalization: A reader.* Malden, MA, and Oxford: Blackwell.

Ingmanson, E. J. (1998). Comment. *Current Anthropology, 39,* 409–410.

Inkeles, A., Hanfmann, E., & Beier, H. (1961). Modal personality and adjustment to the Soviet socio-political system. In B. Kaplan (Ed.), *Studying personality cross-culturally.* New York: Harper & Row.

Inkeles, A., & Levinson, D. J. (1954). *National character: The study of modal personality and socio-cultural systems.* In G. Lindzey (Ed.), *Handbook of social psychology.* Reading, MA: Addison-Wesley.

Inuit Tapiirit Kanatami. http://www.tapirisat.ca/english_text/itk/departments/enviro/ncp/

Interview with Laura Nader. *California Monthly.* November 2000.

Ireland, E. (1991). Neither warriors nor victims, the wauja peacefully organize to defend their land. *Cultural Survival Quarterly, 15(1),* 54–59.

Iroquois constitution. Available at http://www.law.ou.edu/hist/iroquois.html.

It's the law: Child labor protection. (1997, November/December). *Peace and Justice News,* 11.

Jacobs, S. E. (1994). Native American Two-spirits. *Anthropology Newsletter, 35(8),* 7.

Jacoby, R., & Glauberman, N. (Eds.). (1995). *The bell curve.* New York: Random House.

Jennings, F. (1976). *The invasion of America.* New York: Norton.

Jennings, J. D. (1974). *Prehistory of North America* (2nd ed.). New York: McGraw-Hill.

Johanson, D., & Shreeve, J. (1989). *Lucy's child: the discovery of a human ancestor.* New York: Avon.

Johanson, D. C., & Edey, M. (1981). *Lucy, the beginnings of humankind.* New York: Simon & Schuster.

Johanson, D. C., & White, T. D. (1979). A systematic assessment of early African hominids. *Science, 203,* 321–330.

John, V. (1971). Whose is the failure? In C. L. Brace, G. R. Gamble, & J. T. Bond (Eds.), *Race and intelligence.* Washington, DC: American Anthropological Association (Anthropological Studies No. 8).

Johnson, A. (1989). Horticulturalists: Economic behavior in tribes. In S. Plattner (Ed.), *Economic anthropology* (pp. 49–77). Stanford, CA: Stanford University Press.

Johnson, A. W., & Earle, T. (1987). *The evolution of human societies, from foraging group to agrarian state.* Stanford, CA: Stanford University Press.

Johnson, D. (1996). Polygamists emerge from secrecy, seeking not just peace but respect. In W. A. Haviland & R. J. Gordon (Eds.), *Talking about people* (2nd ed., pp. 129–131). Mountain View, CA: Mayfield.

Jolly, A. (1985). The evolution of primate behavior. *American Scientist 73(3),* 230–239.

Jolly, A. (1985). *The evolution of primate behavior* (2nd ed.). New York: Macmillan.

Jolly, A. (1985). Thinking like a Vervet. *Science, 251,* 574.

Jolly, C. J. (1970). The seed eaters: A new model of hominid differentiation based on a baboon analogy. *Man, 5,* 5–26.

Jolly, C. J., & Plog, F. (1986). *Physical anthropology and archaeology* (4th ed.). New York: Knopf.

Jones, S., Martin, R., & Pilbeam, D. (1992). *Cambridge encyclopedia of human evolution.* New York: Cambridge University Press.

Jopling, C. F. (1971). *Art and aesthetics in primitive societies: A critical anthology.* New York: Dutton.

Jorgensen, J. (1972). *The sun dance religion.* Chicago: University of Chicago Press.

Joukowsky, M. A. (1980). *A complete field manual of archeology: Tools and techniques of field work for archaeologists.* Englewood Cliffs, NJ: Prentice-Hall.

Joyce, C. (1991). *Witnesses from the grave: The stories bones tell.* Boston: Little, Brown.

Kahn, H., & Wiener, A. J. (1967). *The year 2000.* New York: Macmillan.

Kaiser, J. (1994). A new theory of insect wing origins takes off. *Science, 266,* 363.

Kalwet, H. (1988). *Dreamtime and inner space: The world of the shaman.* New York: Random House.

Kaplan, D. (1972). *Culture theory.* Englewood Cliffs, NJ: Prentice-Hall (Foundations of Modern Anthropology).

Kaplan, D. (2000). The darker side of the original affluent society. *Journal of Anthropological Research, 53(3),* 301–324.

Karavani, I., & Smith, F. H. (2000). More on the Neanderthal problem: The Vindija case. *Current Anthropology, 41,* 839.

Kardiner, A. (1939). *The individual and his society: The psycho-dynamics of primitive social organization.* New York: Columbia University Press.

Kardiner, A., & Preble, E. (1961). *They studied men.* New York: Mentor.

Kay, R. F., Fleagle, J. F., & Simons, E. L. (1981). A revision of the Oligocene apes of the Fayum Province, Egypt. *American Journal of Physical Anthropology, 55,* 293–322.

Kay, R. F., Ross, C., & Williams, B. A. (1997). Anthropoid origins. *Science, 275,* 797–804.

Kay, R. F., Theweissen, J. G. M., & Yoder, A. D. (1992). Cranial anatomy of Ignacius graybullianus and the affinities of the plesiadapiformes. *American Journal of Physical Anthropology, 89(4),* 477–498.

Keen, B. (1971). *The Aztec image in western thought* (p. 13). New Brunswick, NJ: Rutgers University Press.

Kehoe, A. (2000). *Shamans and religion: An anthropological exploration in critical thinking.* Prospect Heights, IL: Waveland Press.

Kendall, L. (1990, October). In the company of witches. *Natural History,* 92–95.

Kenyon, K. (1957). *Digging up Jericho.* London: Ben.

Kerri, J. N. (1976). Studying voluntary associations as adaptive mechanisms: A review of anthropological perspectives. *Current Anthropology,* 17(1).

Kessler, E. (1975). *Women.* New York: Holt, Rinehart & Winston.

Key, M. R. (1975). *Paralanguage and kinesics: Nonverbal communication.* Metuchen, NJ: Scarecrow Press.

Kirkpatrick R. C. (2000) The evolution of human homosexual behavior. *Current Anthropology* 41:384.

Klass, M. (1995). *Ordered universes: Approaches to the anthropology of religion.* Boulder, CO: Westview Press.

Klass, M., & Weisgrau, M. (Eds.). (1999). *Across the boundaries of belief: Contemporary issues in the anthropology of religion.* Boulder, CO: Westview Press.

Kleinman, A. (1976). Concepts and a model for the comparison of medical systems as cultural systems. *Social Science and Medicine,* 12(2B), 85–95.

Kleinman, A. (1982). The failure of western medicine. In D. Hunter & P. Whitten (Eds.), *Anthropology: Contemporary perspectives.* Boston: Little, Brown.

Kluckhohn, C. (1970). *Mirror for Man.* Greenwich, CT: Fawcett.

Kluckhohn, C. (1994). Navajo witchcraft. Papers of the Peabody Museum of American Archaeology and Ethnology, 22(2).

Knauft, B. (1991). Violence and sociality in human evolution. *Current Anthropology,* 32, 391–409.

Koch, G. (1997). Songs, land rights, and archives in Australia. *Cultural Survival Quarterly,* 20(4).

Konner, M., & Worthman, C. (1980). Nursing frequency, gonadal function, and birth spacing among !Kung hunter-gatherers. *Science,* 207, 788–791.

Koufos, G. (1993). Mandible of Ouranopithecus macedoniensis (hominidae: primates) from a new late Miocene locality in Macedonia (Greece). *American Journal of Physical Anthropology,* 91, 225–234.

Krader, L. (1968). *Formation of the state.* Englewood Cliffs, NJ: Prentice-Hall (Foundation of Modern Anthropology).

Krajick, K. (1998). Greenfarming by the Incas? *Science,* 281, 323.

Kramer, P. A. (1998). The costs of human locomotion: maternal investment in child transport. *American Journal of Physical Anthropology,* 107, 71–85.

Kroeber, A. (1958). Totem and taboo: An ethnologic psycho-analysis. In W. Lessa & E. Z. Vogt (Eds.), *Reader in comparative religion: An anthropological approach.* New York: Harper & Row.

Kroeber, A. L. (1939). Cultural and natural areas of native North America. *American Archaeology and Ethnology* (Vol. 38). Berkeley: University of California Press.

Kroeber, A. L. (1963). *Anthropology: Cultural processes and patterns.* New York: Harcourt.

Kroeber, A. L., & Kluckhohn, C. (1952). *Culture: A critical review of concepts and definitions.* Cambridge, MA: Harvard University Press (Papers of the Peabody Museum of American Archaeology and Ethnology, 47).

Kuhn, T. (1968). *The structure of scientific revolutions.* Chicago: University of Chicago Press (International Encyclopedia of Unified Science, 2[27]).

Kummer, H. (1971). *Primate societies: Group techniques of ecological adaptation.* Chicago: Aldine.

Kunzig, R. (1999). A tale of two obsessed archaeologists, one ancient city and nagging doubts about whether science can ever hope to reveal the past. *Discover,* 20(5), 84–92.

Kuper, H. (1965). The Swazi of Swaziland. In J. L. Gibbs (Ed.), *Peoples of Africa* (pp. 479–511). New York: Holt, Rinehart & Winston.

Kurath, G. P. (1960). Panorama of dance ethnology. *Current Anthropology,* 1, 233–254.

Kurth, P. (1998, October 14). Capitol Crimes. *Seven Days,* 7.

Kurtz, D. V. (2001). *Political anthropology: Paradigms and power.* Boulder, CO: Westview Press.

Kushner, G. (1969). *Anthropology of complex societies.* Stanford, CA: Stanford University Press.

La Barre, W. (1945). Some observations of character structure in the Orient: The Japanese. *Psychiatry,* 8.

LaFont, S, (Ed.). (2003). *Constructing sexualities: Readings in sexuality, gender, and culture.* Upper Saddle River, NJ: Prentice-Hall.

Lai, C. S. L., et al. (2001). A forkhead-domain gene is mutated in severe speech and language disorder. *Nature,* 413, 519–523.

Lampl, M., Velhuis, J. D., & Johnson, M. L. (1992). Saltation and statsis: A model of human growth. *Science,* 258(5083), 801–803.

Lancaster, J. B. (1975). *Primate behavior and the emergence of human culture.* New York: Holt, Rinehart & Winston.

Landau, M. (1991). *Narratives of human evolution.* New Haven, CT: Yale University Press.

Landes, R. (1982). Comment. *Current Anthropology,* 23, 401.

Lanning, E. P. (1967). *Peru before the Incas.* Englewood Cliffs, NJ: Prentice-Hall.

Lanternari, V. (1963). *The religions of the oppressed.* New York: Mentor.

Lasker, G. W., & Tyzzer, R. (1982). *Physical anthropology* (3rd ed.) New York: Holt, Rinehart & Winston.

Laughlin, W. S., & Osborne, R. H. (Eds.). (1967). *Human variation and origins.* San Francisco: Freeman.

Laurel, K. (1990). In the company of witches. *Natural History,* 92.

Lawler, A. (2001) Writing gets a rewrite. *Science* 292, 2,419.

Layton, R. (1991). *The anthropology of art* (2nd ed.). Cambridge: Cambridge University Press.

Leach, E. (1961). *Rethinking anthropology.* London: Athione Press.

Leach, E. (1962). The determinants of differential cross-cousin marriage. *Man,* 62, 238.

Leach, E. (1962). On certain unconsidered aspects of double descent systems. *Man,* 214, 13–34.

Leach, E. (1965). *Political systems of highland Burma.* Boston: Beacon Press.

Leach, E. (1982). *Social anthropology.* Glasgow: Fontana Paperbacks.

Leacock, E. (1981). *Myths of male dominance: Collected articles on women cross culturally.* New York: Monthly Review Press.

Leacock, E. (1981). Women's status in egalitarian society: Implications for social evolution. In *Myths of male dominance: Collected articles on women cross culturally.* New York: Monthly Review Press.

Leakey, L. S. B. (1965). *Olduvai Gorge, 1951–1961* (Vol. 1). London: Cambridge University Press.

Leakey, L. S. B. (1967). Development of aggression as a factor in early human and prehuman evolution. In C. ...ments &

D. Lundsley (Eds.), *Aggression and defense.* Los Angeles: University of California Press.

Leakey, M. D. (1971). *Olduvai Gorge: Excavations in Beds I and II. 1960–1963.* London and New York: Cambridge University Press.

Leakey, M. G., Spoor, F., Brown, F. H., Gathogo, P. N., Kiare, C., Leakey, L. N., & McDougal, I. (2001). New hominin genus from eastern Africa shows diverse middle Pliocene lineages. *Nature, 410,* 433–440.

Leap, W. L. (1987). Tribally controlled culture change: The Northern Ute language revival project. In R. M. Wulff & S. J. Fiske (Eds.), *Anthropological praxis: Translating knowledge into action* (pp. 197–211). Boulder, CO: Westview Press.

Leavitt, G. C. (1990). Sociobiological explanations of incest avoidance: A critical review of evidential claims. *American Anthropologist, 92,* 971–993.

Lee, R. (1993). *The Dobe Ju/boansi.* Ft. Worth, TX: Harcourt Brace.

Lee, R. B., & Daly, R. H. (1999). *The Cambridge encyclopedia of hunters and gatherers.* New York: Cambridge University Press.

Lee, R. B., & DeVore, I. (Eds.). (1968). *Man the hunter.* Chicago: Aldine.

Leeds, A., & Vayda, A. P. (Eds.). (1965). *Man, culture and animals: The role of animals in human ecological adjustments.* Washington, DC: American Association for the Advancement of Science.

Lees, R. (1953). The basis of glottochronology. *Language, 29,* 113–127.

Legros, D. (1997). Comment. *Current Anthropology, 38,* 617.

Lehmann, A. C., & Myers, J. E. (Eds.). (1993). *Magic, witchcraft and religion: An anthropological study of the supernatural* (3rd ed.). Mountain View, CA: Mayfield.

Lehmann, W. P. (1973). *Historical linguistics, An introduction* (2nd ed.). New York: Holt, Rinehart & Winston.

Leigh, S. R., & Park, P. B. (1998). Evolution of human growth prolongation. *American Journal of Physical Anthropology, 107,* 331–350.

Leinhardt, G. (1964). *Social anthropology.* London: Oxford University Press.

Leinhardt, G. (1971). Religion. In H. Shapiro (Ed.), *Man, culture and society* (2nd ed.). London: Oxford University Press.

LeMay, M. (1975). The language capability of Neanderthal man. *American Journal of Physical Anthropology, 43*(1), 9–14.

Lenski, G. (1966). *Power and privilege: A theory of social stratification.* New York: McGraw-Hill.

Lerner, R. N. (1987). Preserving plants for Pomos. In R. M. Wulff & S. J. Fiske (Eds.), *Anthropological praxis: Translating knowledge into action* (pp. 212–222). Boulder, CO: Westview Press.

Leroi-Gourhan, A. (1968). The evolution of Paleolithic art. *Scientific American, 218,* 58ff.

Lestel, D. (1998). How chimpanzees have domesticated humans. *Anthropology Today, 12* (3); Miles, H. L. W. (1993). Language and the orangutan: The "old person" of the forest. In P. Cavalieri & P. Singer (Eds.), *The great ape project* (pp. 45–50). New York: St. Martin's Press.

Lett, J. (1987). *The human enterprise: A critical introduction to anthropological theory.* Boulder, CO: Westview Press.

Levanthes, L. E. (1987). The mysteries of the bog. *National Geographic, 171,* 397–420.

Levine, N. E., & Silk, J. B. (1997). Why polyandry fails. *Current Anthropology, 38,* 375–398.

Levine, R. (1973). *Culture, behavior and personality.* Chicago: Aldine.

Levine, R. P. (1968). *Genetics.* New York: Holt, Rinehart & Winston.

Lévi-Strauss, C. (1963). The sorcerer and his magic. In *Structural anthropology.* New York: Basic Books.

Lewellen, T. C. (2002). *The anthropology of globalization: Cultural anthropology enters the 21st century.* Westport, CT: Greenwood Publishing Group/Bergin & Garvey.

Lewin, R. (1983). Is the orangutan a living fossil? *Science, 222,* 1,223.

Lewin, R. (1985). Tooth enamel tells a complex story. *Science, 228,* 707.

Lewin, R. (1986). New fossil upsets human family" *Science, 233,* 720–721.

Lewin, R. (1987). Debate over emergence of human tooth pattern. *Science, 235,* 749.

Lewin, R. (1987). The earliest "humans" were more like apes. *Science, 236,* 1,062–1,063.

Lewin, R. (1987). Four legs bad, two legs good. *Science, 235,* 969.

Lewin, R. (1987). Why is ape tool use so confusing? *Science, 236,* 776–777.

Lewin, R. (1988). Molecular clocks turn a quarter century. *Science, 235,* 969–971.

Lewin, R. (1993). Paleolithic paint job. *Discover, 14*(7), 64–70.

Lewis, I. M. (1965). Problems in the comparative study of unilineal descent. In M. Banton (Ed.), *The relevance of models for social organization* (A.S.A. Monograph No. 1). London: Tavistock.

Lewis, I. M. (1976). *Social anthropology in perspective.* Harmondsworth, England: Penguin.

Lewis-Williams, J. D. (1990). *Discovering southern African rock art.* Cape Town and Johannesburg: David Philip.

Lewis-Williams, J. D., & Dowson, T. A. (1988). Signs of all times: Entoptic phenomena in Upper Paleolithic art. *Current Anthropology, 29,* 201–245.

Lewis-Williams, J. D., & Dowson, T. A. (1993). On vision and power in the Neolithic: Evidence from the decorated monuments. *Current Anthropology, 34,* 55–65.

Lewis-Williams, J. D., Dowson, T. A., & Deacon, J. (1993). Rock art and changing perceptions of Southern Africa's past: Ezeljagdspoort reviewed. *Antiquity, 67,* 273–291.

Lewontin, R. C. (1972). The apportionment of human diversity. In T. Dobzhansky et al. (Eds.), *Evolutionary biology* (pp. 381–398). New York: Plenum Press.

Lewontin, R. C., Rose, S., & Kamin, L. J. (1984). *Not in our genes.* New York: Pantheon.

Li, X., Harbottle, G., Zhang, J., & Wang, C. (2003).The earliest writing? Sign use in the seventh millennium BC at Jiahu, Henan Province, China. *Antiquity, 77,* 31–44. Ridley, M. (1999). *Genome: The autobiography of a species in 23 chapters* (p. 40). New York: HarperCollins.

Lindenbaum, S. (1978). *Kuru sorcery: Disease and danger in the New Guinea highlands.* New York: McGraw-Hill.

Little, K. (1964). The role of voluntary associations in West African urbanization. In P. van den Berghe (Ed.), *Africa: social problems of change and conflict.* San Francisco: Chandler.

Livingstone, F. B. (1973). The distribution of abnormal hemoglobin genes and their significance for human evolution. In C. Loring Brace & J. Metress (Eds.), *Man in evolutionary perspective.* New York: Wiley.

Lock, M. (2001). *Twice dead: Organ transplants and the reinvention of death.* Berkeley: University of California Press.

Louckey, J., & Carlsen, R. (1991). Massacre in Santiago Atitlán. *Cultural Survival Quarterly, 15*(3), 70.

Lorenzo, C., Carretero, J. M., Arsuaga, J. L., Gracia, A., & Martinez, I. (1998). Intrapopulational body size variation and cranial capacity variation in middle Pleistocene humans: The Sima de los Huesos sample (Sierra de Atapuerca, Spain). *American Journal of Physical Anthropology, 106,* 19–33.

Lounsbury, F. (1964). The structural analysis of kinship semantics. In H. G. Lunt (Ed.), *Proceedings of the Ninth International Congress of Linguists.* The Hague: Mouton.

Lovejoy, C. O. (1981). Origin of man. *Science, 211*(4480), 341–350.

Lowenstein, J. M. (1992, December). Genetic surprises. *Discover 13,* 82–88.

Lowie, R. H. (1948). *Social organization.* New York: Holt, Rinehart & Winston.

Lowie, R. H. (1956). *Crow Indians.* New York: Holt, Rinehart & Winston. (orig. 1935)

Lowie, R. H. (1966). *Culture and ethnology.* New York: Basic Books.

Lustig-Arecco, V. (1975). *Technology strategies for survival.* New York: Holt, Rinehart & Winston.

MacCormack, C. P. (1977). Biological events and cultural control. *Signs, 3,* 93–100.

MacLarnon, A. M., & Hewitt, G. P. (1999). The evolution of human speech: The role of enhanced breathing control. *American Journal of Physical Anthropology, 109,* 341–363.

MacNeish, R. S. (1992). *The origins of agriculture and settled life.* Norman: University of Oklahoma Press.

Mair, L. (1969). *Witchcraft.* New York: McGraw-Hill.

Mair, L. (1971). *Marriage.* Baltimore: Penguin.

Malefijt, A. de W. (1969). *Religion and culture: An introduction to anthropology of religion.* London: Macmillan.

Malefijt, A. de W. (1974). *Images of man.* New York: Knopf.

Malinowski, B. (1922). *Argonauts of the western Pacific.* New York: Dutton.

Malinowski, B. (1945). *The dynamics of culture change.* New Haven, CT: Yale University Press.

Malinowski, B. (1951). *Crime and custom in savage society.* London: Routledge.

Mann, A., Lampl, M, & Monge, J. (1990). Patterns of ontogeny in human evolution: Evidence from dental development. *Yearbook of Physical Anthropology, 33,* 111–150.

Mann, C. C. (2000). Misconduct alleged in Yanomamo studies. *Science, 289,* 2, 253.

Mann C. C. (2002) The real dirt on rainforest fertility. *Science 297,* 920–923.

Marano, L. (1982). Windigo psychosis: The anatomy of an emic-etic confusion. *Current Anthropology, 23,* 385–412.

Marcus, J., & Flannery, K. V. (1996). *Zapotec civilization: How urban society evolved in Mexico's Oaxaca Valley.* New York: Thames & Hudson.

Marks, J. (1995). *Human biodiversity: Genes, race and history.* Hawthorne, NY: Aldine.

Marks, J. (2000, May 12). 98% alike (what our similarity to apes tells us about our understanding of genetics). *Chronicle of Higher Education,* p. B7.

Marks, J. (2002). *What it means to be 98 percent chimpanzee: Apes, people, and their genes.* Berkeley: University of California Press.

Marsella, J. (1982). Pulling it together: Discussion and comments. In S. Pastner & W. A. Haviland (Eds.), *Confronting the creationists.* Northeastern Anthropological Association, Occasiona Proceedings, No. 1, 77–80.

Marshack, A. (1972). *The roots of civilization: A study in prehistoric cognition; the origins of art, symbol and notation.* New York: McGraw-Hill.

Marshack, A. (1976). Some implications of the Paleolithic symbolic evidence for the origin of language. *Current Anthropology, 17*(2), 274–282.

Marshack, A. (1989). Evolution of the human capacity: The symbolic evidence. Year-book of physical anthropology (Vol. 32, pp. 1–34). New York: Alan R. Liss.

Marshall, L. (1961). Sharing, talking and giving: Relief of social tensions among !Kung bushmen. *Africa, 31,* 231–249.

Marshall, M. (1990). Two tales from the Trukese taproom. In P. R. DeVita (Ed.), *The humbled anthropologist* (pp. 12–17). Belmont, CA: Wadsworth.

Martin, E. (1994). *Flexible bodies: Tracking immunity in American culture-from the days of polio to the age of AIDS.* Boston: Beacon Press.

Martorell, R. (1988). Body size, adaptation, and function. *GDP,* 335–347.

Mascia-Lees, F. E., & Black, N. J. (2000). *Gender and anthropology.* Prospect Heights, IL: Waveland Press.

Mason, J. A. (1957). *The ancient civilizations of Peru.* Baltimore: Penguin.

Matson, F. R. (Ed.). (1965). *Ceramics and man.* New York: Viking Fund Publications in Anthropology, No. 41.

Maybury-Lewis, D. (1960). Parallel descent and the Apinaye anomaly. *Southwestern Journal of Anthropology, 16,* 191–216.

Maybury-Lewis, D. (1984). The prospects for plural societies. *1982 Proceedings of the American Ethnological Society.*

Maybury-Lewis, D. (1993, fall). A new world dilemma: The Indian question in the Americas. *Symbols,* 17–23.

Maybury-Lewis, D. (2001). *Indigenous peoples, ethnic groups, and the state.* (2nd ed.). Boston: Allyn & Bacon.

Maybury-Lewis, D. H. P. (1993). A special sort of pleading. In W. A. Haviland & R. J. Gordon (Eds.), *Talking about people* (pp. 16–24). Mountain View, CA: Mayfield.

McCorriston, J., & Hole, F. (1991). The ecology of seasonal stress and the origins of agriculture inthe Near East. *American Anthropologist, 93,* 46–69.

McDermott, L. (1996). Self-representation in Upper Paleolithic female figurines. *Current Anthropology, 37,* 227–276.

McFee, M. (1972). *Modern Blackfeet: Montanans on a reservation.* New York: Holt, Rinehart & Winston.

McGrew, W. C. (2000). Dental care in chimps. *Science, 288,* 1,747.

McHale, J. (1969). *The future of the future.* New York: Braziller.

McHenry, H. (1975). Fossils and the mosaic nature of human evolution. *Science, 190,* 524–431.

McHenry, H. M. (1992). Body size and proportions in early hominids. *American Journal of Physical Anthropology, 87,* 407–431.

McKenna, J. (1999). Co-sleeping and SIDS. In W. Trevathan, E. O. Smith, & J. J. McKenna (Eds.), *Evolutionary medicine.* London: Oxford University Press.

McKenna, J. J. (2002, September-October). Breastfeeding and bedsharing. *Mothering,* 28–37.

Mead, M. (1928). *Coming of age in Samoa.* New York: Morrow.

Mead, M. (1963). *Sex and temperament in three primitive societies* (3rd ed). New York: Morrow. (orig.1935)

Mead, M. (1970). *Culture and commitment.* Garden City, NY: Natural History Press, Universe Books.

Meadows, D. H., Meadows, D. L., Randers, & Behrens, III, W. W. (1974). *The limits to growth* New York: Universe Books.

Medicine, B. (1994). Gender, In M. Davis (Ed.), *Native America in the twentieth century.* New York: Garland.

Melaart, J. (1967). *Catal Hüyük: A Neolithic town in Anatolia*. London: Thames & Hudson.

Mellars, P. (1989). Major issues in the emergence of modern humans. *Current Anthropology, 30* 356–357.

Meltzer, D., Fowler, D., & Sabloff, J. (Eds.). (1986). *American archaeology: Past & future*. Washington, DC: Smithsonian Institution Press.

Merin, Y. (2002). *Equality for same-sex couples: The legal recognition of gay partnerships Europe and the United States*. Chicago: University of Chicago Press.

Merrell, D. J. (1962). *Evolution and genetics: The modern theory of genetics*. New York: Holt, Rinehart & Winston.

Merriam, A. P. (1964). *The anthropology of music*. Chicago: Northwestern University Press.

Mesghinua, H. M. (1966). Salt mining in Enderta. *Journal of Ethiopian Studies, 4*(2).

Michaels, J. W. (1973). *Dating methods in archaeology*. New York: Seminar Press.

Middleton, J. (Ed.). (1970). *From child to adult: Studies in the anthropology of education*. Garden City, NY: Natural History Press (American Museum Source Books in Anthropology).

Miles, H. L. W. (1993). Language and the orangutan: The old person of the forest. In P. Singer (Ed.), *The great ape project* (p. 46). New York: St. Martin's.

Miller, J. M. A. (2000). Craniofacial variation in *Homo habilis:* An analysis of the evidence for multiple species. *American Journal of Physical Anthropology, 112,* 122.

Millon, R. (1973). *Urbanization of Teotihuacán, Mexico: Vol. 1, Part 1. The Teotihuacán map*. Austin: University of Texas Press.

Mintz, S. (1996). A taste of history. In W. A. Haviland & R. J. Gordon (Eds.), *Talking about people* (2nd ed., pp. 79–82). Mountain View, CA: Mayfield.

Minugh-Purvis, N. (1992). The inhabitants of Ice Age Europe. *Expedition, 34*(3), 23–36.

Mitchell, W. E. (1973, December). A new weapon stirs up old ghosts. *Natural History Magazine,* 77–84.

Mitchell, W. E. (1978). *Mishpokhe: A study of New York City Jewish family clubs*. The Hague: Mouton.

Molnar, S. (1992). *Human variation: Races, types, and ethnic groups* (3rd ed.). Englewood Cliffs, NJ: Prentice-Hall.

Montagu, A. (1964). *The concept of race*. London: Macmillan.

Montagu, A. (1964). *Man's most dangerous myth: The fallacy of race* (4th ed.) New York: World Publishing.

Montagu, A. (1975). *Race and IQ*. New York: Oxford University Press.

Moore, J. (1998). Comment. *Current Anthropology, 39,* 412.

Morgan, L. H. (1877). *Ancient society*. New York: World Publishing.

Morse, D., et al. (1979). *Gestures: Their origins and distribution*. New York: Stein & Day.

Moscati, S. (1962). *The face of the ancient orient*. New York: Doubleday.

Mullings, L. (1989). Gender and the application of anthropological knowledge to public policy in the United States. In S. Morgan (Ed.), *Gender and anthropology* (pp. 360–381). Washington, DC: American Anthropological Association.

Murdock, G. (1960). Cognatic forms of social organization. In G. P. Murdock (Ed.), *Social structure in Southeast Asia* (pp. 1–14). Chicago: Quadrangle Books.

Murdock, G. P. (1965). *Social structure*. New York: Free Press.

Murdock, G. P. (1971). How culture changes. In H. L. Shapiro (Ed.), *Man, culture and society* (2nd ed.) New York: Oxford University Press.

Murphy, R. (1971). *The dialectics of social life: Alarms and excursions in anthropological theory*. New York: Basic Books.

Murphy, R., & Kasdan, L. (1959). The structure of parallel cousin marriage. *American Anthropologist, 61,* 17–29.

Murray, G. F. (1989). The domestication of wood in Haiti: A case study in applied evolution. In A. Podolefsky & P. J. Brown (Eds.), *Applying anthropology, an introductory reader*. Mountain View, CA: Mayfield.

Mydens, S. (2001, August 12). He's not hairy, he's my brother. *New York Times,* sec. 4, p. 5.

Myrdal, G. (1974). Challenge to affluence: The emergence of an "under-class." In J. G. Jorgensen & M. Truzzi (Eds.), *Anthropology and American life*. Englewood Cliffs, NJ: Prentice-Hall.

Nader, L. (Ed.). (1965). The ethnography of law, part II. *American Anthropologist, 67*(6).

Nader, L. (Ed.). (1969). *Law in culture and society*. Chicago: Aldine.

Nader, L. (1981, December). [Interview for Coast Telecourses, Inc.]. Los Angeles.

Nader, L. (1997). Controlling processes: Tracing the dynamic components of power. *Current Anthropology, 38,* 714–715.

Nader, L. (2002). *The life of the law: Anthropological projects*. Berkeley: University of California Press.

Nader, L. (Ed.). (1996). *Naked science: Anthropological inquiry into boundaries, power, and knowledge*. New York: Routledge.

Nader, L., & Todd, Jr., H. F. (1978). *The disputing process: Law in ten societies*. New York: Columbia University Press.

Nance, C. R. (1997). Review of Haviland's *Cultural anthropology* (p. 2). [Manuscript in author's possession].

Nanda, S. (1990). *Neither man nor woman: The hijras of India*. Belmont, CA, Wadsworth.

Nanda, S. (1992). Arranging a marriage in India. In P. R. De Vita (Ed.), *The naked anthropologist* (pp. 139–143). Belmont, CA: Wadsworth.

Naroll, R. (1973). Holocultural theory tests. In R. Naroll & F. Naroll (Eds.), *Main currents in cultural anthropology*. New York: Appleton.

Natadecha-Sponsal, P. (1993). The young, the rich and the famous: Individualism as an American cultural value. In P. R. DeVita & J. D. Armstrong (Eds.), *Distant mirrors: America as a foreign culture* (pp. 46–53). Belmont, CA: Wadsworth.

Needham, R. (Ed.). (1971). *Rethinking kinship and marriage*. London: Tavistock.

Needham, R. (1972). *Belief, language and experience*. Chicago: University of Chicago Press.

Neer, R. M. (1975). The evolutionary significance of vitamin D, skin pigment and ultraviolet light. *American Journal of Physical Anthropology, 43,* 409–416.

Nesbitt, L. M. (1935). *Hell-hole of creation*. New York: Knopf.

Netting, R. M., Wilk, R. R., & Arnould, E. J. (Eds.). (1984). *Households: Comparative and historical studies of the domestic group*. Berkeley: University of California Press.

Nettl, B. (1956). *Music in primitive culture*. Cambridge, MA: Harvard University Press.

Newman, P. L. (1965). *Knowing the Gururumba*. New York: Holt, Rinehart & Winston.

Nietschmann, B. (1987). The third world war. *Cultural Survival Quarterly, 11*(3), 1–16.

Norbeck, E., Price-Williams, D., & McCord, W. (Eds.). (1968). *The study of personality: An interdisciplinary appraisal*. New York: Holt, Rinehart & Winston.

Normile, D. (1998). Habitat seen as playing larger role in shaping behavior. *Science, 279,* 1,454.

Nunney, L. (1998). Are we selfish, are we nice, or are we nice because we are selfish? *Science, 281,* 1,619.

Nye, E. I., & Berardo, F. M. (1975). *The family: Its structure and interaction.* New York: Macmillan.

Nye, J. (2002). *The paradox of American power: Why the world's only superpower can't go it alone.* New York: Oxford University Press.

Oakley, K. P. (1964). *Man the tool-maker.* Chicago: University of Chicago Press.

O'Barr, W. M., & Conley, J. M. (1993). When a juror watches a lawyer. In W. A. Haviland & R. J. Gordon (Eds.), *Talking about people* (2nd ed., pp. 44–47). Mountain View, CA: Mayfield.

Oboler, R. S. (1980). Is the female husband a man? Woman/woman marriage among the Nandi of Kenya. *Ethnology, 19,* 69–88.

Offiong, D. (1985). Witchcraft among the Ibibio of Nigeria. In A. C. Lehmann & J. E. Myers (Eds.), *Magic, witchcraft, and religion* (pp. 152–165). Palo Alto, CA: Mayfield.

Okonjo, K. (1976). The dual-sex political system in operation: Igbo women and community politics in midwestern Nigeria. In N. Hafkin & E. Bay (Eds.), *Women in Africa* (pp. 45–58).Stanford, CA: Stanford University Press.

Olszewski, D. I. (1991). Comment. *Current Anthropology, 32,* 43.

O'Mahoney, K. (1970). The salt trade. *Journal of Ethiopian Studies, 8*(2).

Ong, A. (1999). *Flexible citizenship: The cultural logics of transnationality.* Durham, NC: Duke University Press.

Ortiz, A. (1969). *The Tewa world.* Chicago: The University of Chicago Press.

Oswalt, W. H. (1970). *Understanding our culture.* New York: Holt, Rinehart & Winston.

Oswalt, W. H. (1972). *Habitat and technology.* New York: Holt, Rinehart & Winston.

Oswalt, W. H. (1972). *Other peoples other customs: World ethnography and its history.* New York: Holt, Rinehart & Winston.

Otten, C. M. (1971). *Anthropology and art: Readings in cross-cultural aesthetics.* Garden City, NY: Natural History Press.

Otten, M. (2000). On the suggested bone flute from Slovenia. *Current Anthropology, 41,* 271.

Ottenberg, P. (1965). The Afikpo Ibo of eastern Nigeria. In J. L. Gibbs (Ed.), *Peoples of Africa.* New York: Holt, Rinehart & Winston.

Ottenheimer, Martin. (1996). *Forbidden relatives: The American myth of cousin marriage.* Chicago: University of Illinois Press.

Otterbein, K. F. (1971). *The evolution of war.* New Haven, CT: HRAF Press.

Pandian, J. (1991). *Culture, religion, and the sacred self: A critical introduction to the anthropological study of religion.* Englewood Cliffs, NJ: Prentice-Hall.

Parades, J. A., & Purdum, E. J. (1990). Bye bye Ted. . . . *Anthropology Today, 6*(2), 9–11.

Parés, J. M., Perez-Gonzalez, A., Weil, A. B., & Arsuaga, J. L. (2000). On the age of hominid fossils at the Sima de los Huesos, Sierra de Atapuerca, Spain: Paleomagnetic evidence. *American Journal of Physical Anthropology, 111,* 451–461.

Parish, A. R. (1998). Comment. *Current Anthropology, 39,* 413–414.

Parker, R. G. (1991). *Bodies, pleasures, and passions: Sexual culture in contemporary Brazil.* Boston: Beacon Press.

Parker, S., & Parker, H. (1979). The myth of male superiority: Rise and demise. *American Anthropologist, 81*(2), 289–309.

Parkin, R. (1997). *Kinship: An introduction to basic concepts.* Cambridge, MA: Blackwell.

Parnell, R. (1999). Gorilla exposé. *Natural History, 108*(8), 43

Partridge, W. (Ed.). (1984). *Training manual in development anthropology.* Washington, DC: American Anthropological Association.

Pastner, S., & Haviland, W. A. (Eds.). (1982). Confronting the creationists. *Northeastern Anthropological Association Occasional Proceedings, I.*

Patterson, F., & Linden, E. (1981). *The education of Koko.* New York: Holt, Rinehart & Winston.

Patterson, T. C. (1981). *Archeology: The evolution of ancient societies.* Englewood Cliffs, NJ: Prentice-Hall.

Peacock, J. L. (2002). *The anthropological lens: Harsh light, soft focus.* (2nd ed.). New York: Cambridge University Press.

Pease, T. (2000). Taking the third side. *Andover Bulletin,* spring.

Pelliam, A. de, & Burton, F. D. (1976). More on predatory behavior in nonhuman primates. *Current Anthropology, 17*(3), 512–513.

Pelto, G. H., Goodman, A. H., & Dufour, D. L. (Eds.). (2000). *Nutritional anthropology: Biocultural perspectives on food and nutrition.* Mountain View, CA: Mayfield,

Pelto, P. J. (1973). *The snowmobile revolution: Technology and social change in the Arctic.* Menlo Park, CA: Cummings.

Penniman, T. K. (1965). *A hundred years of anthropology.* London: Duckworth.

Peters, C. R. (1979). Toward an ecological model of African Plio-Pleistocene hominid adaptations. *American Anthropologist, 81*(2), 261–278.

Petersen J. B., Neuves, E., & Heckenberger, M. J. (2001). Gift from the past: *Terra preta* and prehistoric American occupation in Amazonia. In C. McEwan and C. Barreo (Eds.) *Unknown Amazon* (pp. 86–105). London: British Museum Press.

Peterson, F. L. (1962). *Ancient Mexico, An introduction to the pre-Hispanic cultures.* New York: Capricorn Books.

Pfeiffer, J. E. (1977). *The emergence of society.* New York: McGraw-Hill.

Pfeiffer, J. E. (1978). *The emergence of man.* New York: Harper & Row.

Pfeiffer, J. E. (1985). *The creative explosion.* Ithaca, NY: Cornell University Press.

Piddocke, S. (1965). The potlach system of the southern Kwakiutl: A new perspective. *Southwestern Journal of Anthropology, 21,* 244–264.

Piggott, S. (1965). *Ancient Europe.* Chicago: Aldine.

Pilbeam, D. (1987). Rethinking human origins. In *Primate evolution and human origins.* Hawthorne, NY: Aldine.

Pilbeam, D., & Gould, S. J. (1974). Size and scaling in human evolution. *Science, 186,* 892–901.

Pimentel, D. (1991). Response. *Science, 252,* 358.

Pimentel, D., Hurd, L. E., Bellotti, A. C., Forster, M. J., Oka, I. N., Sholes, O. D., & Whitman, R. J. (1973). Food Production and the Energy Crisis. *Science, 182.*

Piperno, D. R., & Fritz, G. J. (1994). On the emergence of agriculture in the new world. *CurrentAnthropology, 35,* 637–643.

Pitt, D. (1977). Comment. *Current Anthropology, 18,* 628.

Pitts, V. (2003). *In the flesh: The cultural politics of body modification.* New York: Palgrave Macmillan.

Plane, A. M. (1996). Putting a face on colonization: Factionalism and gender politics in the life history of Awashunkes, the "Squaw Sachem" of Saconnet. In R. S. Grumet (Ed.), *Northeastern Indian Lives, 1632–1816* (pp.140–175). Amherst: University of Massachusetts Press.

Plattner, S. (1989). Markets and market places. In S. Plattner (Ed.), *Economic anthropology.* Stanford, CA: Stanford University Press.

Podolefsky, A., & Brown, P. J. (Eds.). (1989). *Applying anthropology, an introductory reader.* Mountain View, CA: Mayfield.

Pohl, M. E. D., Pope, K. O., & von Nagy, C. (2002). Olmec Origins of MesoAmerican writing. *Science, 298,* 1,984–1,987.

Polanyi, K. (1968). The economy as instituted process. In E. E. LeClair, Jr. & H. K. Schneider (Eds.), *Economic anthropology: readings in theory and analysis* (pp. 122–167). New York: Holt, Rinehart & Winston.

Pope, G. (1989, October). Bamboo and human evolution. *Natural History, 98,* 48–57.

Pope, G. G. (1992). Craniofacial evidence for the origin of modern humans in China. *Yearbook of Physical Anthropology, 35,* 243–298.

Pospisil, L. (1971). *Anthropology of law: A comparative theory.* New York: Harper & Row.

Powdermaker, H. (1966). *Stranger and friend: The way of an anthropologist.* New York: Norton.

Power, M. G. (1995). Gombe revisited: Are chimpanzees violent and hierarchical in the free state? *General Anthropology, 2*(1), 5–9.

Premack, A. J., & Premack, D. (1972). Teaching language to an ape. *Scientific American, 277*(4), 92–99.

Price, T. D., & Feinman, G. M. (Eds.). (1995). *Foundations of social inequality.* New York: Plenam.

Price-Williams, D. R. (Ed.). (1970). *Cross-cultural studies: Selected readings.* Baltimore: Penguin (Penguin Modern Psychology Readings).

Prideaux, T., & the Editors of Time-Life. (1973). *Cro-Magnon man.* New York: Time-Life.

Pringle, H. (1997). Ice Age communities may be earliest known net hunters. *Science, 277,* 1,203 1,204.

Pringle, H. (1998). The slow birth of agriculture. *Science, 282,* 1,446–1,450.

Prins, A. H. J. (1953). *East African class systems.* Groningen, The Netherlands: J. B. Wolters.

Prins, H. E. L. (1996). *The Mi'kmaq: Resistance, accommodation, and cultural survival.* Belmont, CA: Wadsworth/Holt, Rinehart & Winston.

Prins, H. E. L. (1998). Book review of Schuster, C., and Carpenter, E. (1996). *American Anthropologist,100* (3), 841.

Prins, H. E. L. (2002). Visual media and the primitivist perplex: Colonial fantasies, indigenous imagination, and advocacy in North America. In F. D. Ginsburg et al. *Media worlds: Anthropology on new terrain* (pp. 58–74). Berkeley: University of California Press.

Prins, H.E. L., & Carter, K. (1986). *Our lives in our hands.* Video and 16mm. Color. 50 min. Distributed by Watertown, MA: Documentary Educational Resources and Bucksport, ME: Northeast Historic Film.

Profet, M. (1991). The function of allergy: Immunological defense against toxins. *Quarterly Review of Biology, 66*(1), 23–62.

Profet, M. (1995). *Protecting your baby to be.* New York: Addison Wesley.

Puleston, D. E. (1983). *The settlement survey of Tikal.* Philadelphia: University Museum.

Radcliffe-Brown, A. R. (1931). Social Organization of Australian tribes. *Oceania Monographs,* No. 1. Melbourne: Macmillan.

Radcliffe-Brown, A. R., & Forde, C. D. (Eds.). (1950). *African systems of kinship and marriage.* London: Oxford University Press.

Rappaport, R. A. (1969). Ritual regulation of environmental relations among a New Guinea people. In A. P Vayda (Ed.), *Environment and Cultural behavior* (pp. 181–201). Garden City, NY Natural History Press.

Rappaport, R. A. (1984). *Pigs for the ancestors* (Enl. ed.). New Haven, CT: Yale University Press.

Rappaport, R. A. (1994). Commentary. *Anthropology Newsletters, 35*(6), 76.

Rappaport, R. A. (1999). *Holiness and humanity: Ritual in the making of religious life.* New York: Cambridge University Press.

Rathje, W. L. (1974). The garbage project: A new way of looking at the problems of archaeology. *Archaeology, 27,* 236–241.

Rathje, W. L. (1993). Rubbish! In W. A. Haviland & R. J. Gordon (Eds.), *Talking about people: Readings in contemporary cultural anthropology,* Mountain View, CA: Mayfield.

Read, C. E. (1973). *The role of faunal analysis in reconstructing human behavior: A Mousterian example.* Paper presented at the meetings of the California Academy of Sciences, Long Beach.

Read-Martin, C. E., & Read, D. W. (1975). Australopithecine scavenging and human evolution: An approach from faunal analysis. *Current Anthropology, 16*(3), 359–368.

Recer, P. (1998, February 16). *Apes shown to communicate in the wild.* Burlington Free Press, p 12A.

Redfield, R., Linton, R., & Herskovits, M. J. (1936). Memorandum of the study of acculturation. *American Anthropologist, 38,* 149–152.

Redman, C. L. (1978). *The rise of civilization: From early farmers to urban society in the ancient Near East.* San Francisco: Freeman.

Reid, J. J., Schiffer, M. B., & Rathje, W. L. (1975). Behavioral archaeology: Four strategies. *American Anthropologist, 77,* 864–869.

Reina, R. (1966). *The law of the saints.* Indianapolis: Bobbs-Merrill.

Reiter, R. (Ed.). (1975). *Toward an anthropology of women.* New York: Monthly Review Press.

Relethford, J. H. (2001). Absence of regional affinities of Neandertal DNA with living humans does not reject multiregional evolution. *American Journal of Physical Anthropology, 115,* 95–98.

Relethford, J. H., & Harpending, H. C. (1994). Craniometric variation, genetic theory, and modern human origins. *American Journal of Physical Anthropology, 95,* 249–270.

Renfrew, C. (1973). *Before civilization: The radiocarbon revolution and prehistoric Europe.* London: Jonathan Cape.

Reynolds, V. (1994). Primates in the field, primates in the lab. *Anthropology Today, 10*(2), 3–5.

Rice, D. S. & Prudence, M. (1984). Lessons from the Maya. *Latin American Research Review, 19*(3), 7–34.

Rice, P. (2000). Paleoanthropology 2000—part 1. *General Anthropology, 7*(1), 11.

Richmond, B. G., Fleangle, J. K., & Swisher III, C. C. (1998). First Hominoid elbow from the Miocene of Ethiopia and the evolution of the Catarrhine elbow. *American Journal of Physical Anthropology, 105,* 257–277.

Ridley, M. (1999). *Genome, the autobiography of a species in 23 chapters* (p. 142). New York: HarperCollins.

Rightmire, G. P. (1990). *The evolution of Homo erectus: Comparative anatomical studies of an extinct human species.* Cambridge: Cambridge University Press.

Rightmire, G. P. (1998). Evidence from facial morphology for similarity of Asian and African representatives of Homo erectus. *American Journal of Physical Anthropology, 106,* 61–85.

Rindos, D. (1984). *The origins of agriculture: An evolutionary perspective.* Orlando, FL: Academic Press.

Rodman, H. (1968). *Class culture. International encyclopedia of the social sciences* (Vol. 15, pp. 332–337). New York:Macmillan.

Rogers, J. (1994). Levels of the genealogical hierarchy and the problem of hominoid phylogeny. *American Journal of Physical Anthropology, 94,* 81–88.

Romer, A. S. (1945). *Vertebrate paleontology.* Chicago: University of Chicago Press.

Roosevelt, A. C. (1984). Population, health, and the evolution of subsistence: Conclusions from the conference. In M. N. Cohen & G. J. Armelagos (Eds.), *Paleopathology at the origins of agriculture.* Orlando, FL: Academic Press.

Rosas, A., & Bermdez de Castro, J. M. (1998). On the taxonomic affinities of the Dmanisi mandible (Georgia). *American Journal of Physical Anthropology, 107,* 145–162.

Roscoe, P. B. (1995). The perils of "positivism" in cultural anthropology. *American Anthropologist, 97,* 497.

Rowe, T. (1988). New issues for phylogenetics. *Science, 239,* 1,183–1,184.

Ruhlen, M. (1994). *The origin of language: Tracing the evolution of the mother tongue.* New York: Wiley.

Ruvdo, M. (1994). Molecular evolutionary processes and conflicting gene trees: The hominoid case. *American Journal of Physical Anthropology, 94,* 89–113.

Sabloff, J., & Lambert-Karlovsky, C. C. (1973). *Ancient civilization and trade.* Albuquerque: University of New Mexico Press.

Sabloff, J. A. (1989). *The cities of ancient Mexico.* New York: Thomas & Hudson.

Sabloff, J. A., & Lambert-Karlovsky, C. C. (Eds.). (1974). *The rise and fall of civilizations, modern archaeological approaches to ancient cultures.* Menlo Park, CA: Cummings.

Sahlins, M. (1961). The segmentary lineage: An organization of predatory expansion. *American Anthropologist, 63,* 322–343.

Sahlins, M. (1968). *Tribesmen.* Englewood Cliffs, NJ: Prentice-Hall (Foundations of Modern Anthropology).

Sahlins, M. (1972). *Stone age economics.* Chicago: Aldine.

Salthe, S. N. (1972). *Evolutionary biology.* New York: Holt, Rinehart & Winston.

Salzman, P. C. (1967). Political organization among nomadic peoples. Proceedings of the *American Philosophical Society, 3,* 115–131.

Sanday, P. R. (1975). On the causes of IQ differences between groups and implications for social policy. In A. Montagu (Ed.), *Race and IQ.* London: Oxford.

Sanday, P. R. (1981). *Female power and male dominance: On the origins of sexual inequality.* Cambridge: Cambridge University Press.

Sangree, W. H. (1965). The Bantu Tiriki of western Kenya. In J. L. Gibbs (Ed.), *Peoples of Africa.* New York: Holt, Rinehart & Winston.

Sanjek R. (1990). On ethnographic validity. In R. Sanjek (Ed.) *Fieldnotes.* Ithica, New York: Cornell University Press.

Sapir, E. (1921). *Language.* New York: Harcourt.

Savage, J. M. (1969). *Evolution* (3rd ed.). New York: Holt, Rinehart & Winston.

Scaglion, R. (1987). Contemporary law development in Papua New Guinea. In R. M. Wulff & S. J. Fiske (Eds.), *Anthropological praxis: Translating knowledge into action.* Boulder, CO: Westview Press.

Scarr-Salapatek, S. (1971). Unknowns in the IQ equation. *Science, 174,* 1,223–1,228.

Schaller, G. B. (1971). *The year of the gorilla.* New York: Ballantine.

Scheflen, A. E. (1972). *Body language and the social order.* Englewood Cliffs, NJ: Prentice-Hall.

Schepartz, L.A. (1993). Language and human origins. *Yearbook of Physical Anthropology, 36,* 91–126.

Scheper-Hughes, N. (1979). *Saints, scholars and schizophrenics.* Berkeley: University of California Press.

Schlegel, A. (1977). Male and female in Hopi thought and action. In A. Schlegel (Ed.), *Sexual stratification* (pp. 245–269). New York: Columbia University Press.

Schrire, C. (Ed.). (1984). *Past and present in hunter-gatherer studies.* Orlando, FL: Academic Press.

Schurtz, H. (1902). *Alterklassen und Männerbünde.* Berlin: Reimer.

Schusky, E. L. (1975). *Variation in kinship.* New York: Holt, Rinehart & Winston.

Schusky, E. L. (1983). *Manual for kinship analysis* (2nd ed.). Lanham, MD: University Press of America.

Schuster, C., & Edmund Carpenter, E. (1996). *Patterns that connect: Social symbolism inancient & tribal art.* New York: Abrams.

Schwartz, J. H. (1984). Hominoid evolution: A review and a reassessment. *Current Anthropology, 25*(5), 655–672.

Scupin, R. (Ed.). (2000). *Religion and culture: An anthropological focus.* Upper Saddle River, NJ: Prentice-Hall.

Sellen, D.W., & Mace, R. (1997). Fertility and mode of substance: A phylogenetic analysis. *Current Anthropology, 38,* 878–889.

Semenov, S. A. (1964). *Prehistoric technology.* New York: Barnes & Noble.

Sen, G., & Grown, C. (1987). *Development, crisis, and alternative visions: Third World women's perspectives.* New York: Monthly Review Press.

Senut, B., et al. (2001). First hominid from the Miocene (Lukeino formation, Kenya). *C. R. Acad Sci. Paris, 33,*137–144.

Seyfarth, R. M. et al. (1980). Monkey responses to three different alarm calls: Evidence for predator classification and semantic communication. *Science, 210,* 801–803.

Seymour, D. Z. (1986). Black children, black speech. In P. Escholz, A. Rosa & V. Clark (Eds.), *Language Awareness* (4th ed.). New York: St. Martin's Press.

Shapiro, H. (Ed.). (1971). *Man, culture and society* (2nd. ed.). New York: Oxford University Press.

Sharer, R. J., & Ashmore, W. (1993). *Archaeology: Discovering our past* (2nd ed.). Palo Alto,CA: Mayfield.

Sharp, L. (1952). Steel axes for Stone Age Australians. In E. H. Spicer (Ed.), *Human problems in technological change.* New York: Russell Sage.

Shaw, D. G. (1984). A light at the end of the tunnel: Anthropological contributions toward global competence. *Anthropology Newsletter, 25,* 16.

Shearer, R. R. & Gould S. J. (1999) Of two minds and one nature. *Science 286,* 1093.

Sheets, P. (1993). Dawn of a new Stone Age in eye surgery. In R. J. Sharer & W. Ashmore, *Archaeology: Discovering our past* (2nd ed.). Palo Alto, CA: Mayfield.

Shimkin, D. B., Tax, S., & Morrison, J. W. (Eds.). (1978). *Anthropology for the future.* Urbana: Department of Anthropology, University of Illinois, Research Report No. 4.

Shinnie, M. (1970). *Ancient African kingdoms.* New York: New American Library.

Shipman, P. (1981). *Life history of a fossil: An introduction to taphonomy and paleoecology.* Cambridge, MA: Harvard University Press.

Shore, B. (1996). *Culture in mind: Meaning, construction, and cultural cognition.* New York: Oxford University Press.

Shostak, M. (1983). *Nisa: The life and worlds of a !Kung woman.* New York: Vintage.

Shreeve, J. (1994). "Lucy," crucial early human ancestor, finally gets a head. *Science, 264,* 34–35.

Shreeve, J. (1994). Terms of estrangement. *Discover, 15*(11), 56–63.

Shreeve, J. (1995). *The Neandertal enigma.* New York: Morrow.

Shuey, A. M. (1966). *The testing of Negro intelligence.* New York: Social Science Press.

Sillen, A., & Brain, C. K. (1990). Old flame. *Natural History, 4,* 6–10.

Simons, E. L. (1972). *Primate evolution.* New York: Macmillan.

Simons, E. L. (1989) Human origins. *Science 245,* 1,349.

Simons, E. L. (1995). Skulls and anterior teeth of Catopithecus (primates: anthropoidea) from the Eocene and anthropoid origins. *Science, 268,* 1,885–1,888.

Simons, E. L., Rasmussen, D. T., & Gebo, D. L. (1987). A new species of Propliopithecus from the Fayum, Egypt. *American Journal of Physical Anthropology, 73,* 139–147.

Simpson, G. G. (1949). *The meaning of evolution.* New Haven, CT: Yale University Press.

Sjoberg, G. (1960). *The preindustrial city.* New York: Free Press.

Skelton, R. R., McHenry, H. M., & Drawhorn, G. M. (1986). Phylogenetic analysis of early hominids. *Current Anthropology, 27,* 21–43.

Skolnick, A., & Skolnick, J. (Eds.). (2001). *Family in transition* (11th ed.). Boston: Allyn &Bacon.

Slobin, D. I. (1971). *Psycholinguistics.* Glenview, IL: Scott, Foresman.

Small, M. F. (1997). Making connections. *American Scientist, 85,* 503.

Smith, A. H., & Fisher, J. L. (1970). *Anthropology.* Englewood Cliffs, NJ: Prentice-Hall.

Smith, B. D. (1977). Archaeological inference and inductive confirmation. *American Anthropologist, 79*(3), 598–617.

Smith, B. H. (1994). Patterns of dental development in Homo, Australopithecus, Pan, and gorilla. *American Journal of Physical Anthropology, 94,* 307–325.

Smith, F. H., & Raynard, G. C.. (1980). Evolution of the supraorbital region in Upper Pleistocene fossil hominids from South-Central Europe. *American Journal of Physical Anthropology, 53,* 589–610.

Smith, P. E. L. (1976). *Food production and its consequences* (2nd ed.). Menlo Park, CA: Cummings.

Smith, R. (1970). Social stratification in the Caribbean. In L. Plotnicov & A. Tudin (Eds.), *Essays in comparative social stratification.* Pittsburgh: University of Pittsburgh Press.

Smuts, B. (1987). What are friends for? *Natural History. 96*(2), 36–44.

Snowden, C. T. (1990). Language capabilities of nonhuman animals. *Yearbook of Physical Anthropology, 33,* 215–243.

Solomon, R. (2001, February 20). Genome's riddle. *New York Times,* p. D3.

Sparks, J. (2003, December 22). The power game. *Newsweek, 142*(25).

Speck, F. G. (1920). Penobscot shamanism. *Memoirs of the American Anthropological Association, 6,* 239–288.

Speck, F. G. (1935). Penobscot tales and religious beliefs. *Journal of American Folk-Lore, 48*(187), 1–107.

Speck, F. G. (1970). *Penobscot man: The life history of a forest tribe in Maine.* New York: Octagon Books.

Spencer, F., & Smith, F. H. (1981). The significance of Ales Hrdlicka's "Neanderthal phase of man": A historical and current assessment. *American Journal of Physical Anthropology, 56,* 435–459.

Spencer, H. (1896). *Principles of sociology.* New York: Appleton.

Spiro, M. E. (1966). Religion: problems of definition and explanation. In M. Banton (Ed.), *Anthropological approaches to the study of religion* (A.S.A. Monographs). London: Tavistock.

Spitz, R. A. (1949). *Hospitalism. The psychoanalytic study of the child* (Vol. 1). New York: International Universities Press.

Spradley, J. P. (1979). *The ethnographic interview.* New York: Holt, Rinehart &Winston.

Spradley, J. P. (1980). *Participant observation.* New York: Holt, Rinehart & Winston.

Squires, S. (1997). The market research and product industry discovers anthropology. *Anthropology Newsletter, 38*(4), 31.

Stacey, J. (1990). *Brave new families.* New York: Basic Books.

Stahl, A. B. (1984). Hominid dietary selection before fire. *Current Anthropology, 25,* 151–168.

Stanford, C. B. (1998). The social behavior of chimpanzees and bonobos: Empirical evidence and shifting assumptions. *Current Anthropology, 39,* 399–420.

Stanford, C. B. (2001). *Chimpanzee and red colobus: The ecology of predator and prey.* Cambridge, MA: Harvard University Press.

Stanley, S. M. (1979). *Macroevolution.* San Francisco: Freeman.

Stannard, D. E. (1992). *American holocaust.* Oxford: Oxford University Press.

Stanner, W. E. (1968). *Radcliffe-Brown, A. R. International encyclopedia of the social sciences* (Vol. 13). New York: Macmillan.

Steward, J. H. (1972). *Theory of culture change: The methodology of multilinear evolution.* Urbana: University of Illinois Press.

Stewart, D. (1997). Expanding the pie before you divvy it up. *Smithsonian, 28,* 82.

Stiles, D. (1979). Early Acheulean and developed Oldowan. *Current Anthropology, 20*(l), 126–129.

Stiglitz, J.E. (2003). *Globalization and its discontents.* New York: Norton.

Stiles, D. (1992). The hunter-gatherer "revisionist" debate. *Anthropology Today, 8*(2), 13–17.

Stirton, R. A. (1967). *Time, life, and man.* New York: Wiley.

Stocker, T. (1987, spring). A technological mystery resolved. *Invention and Technology,* 64.

Stocking, G. W., Jr. (1968). *Race, culture and evolution: Essays in the history of anthropology.* New York: Free Press.

Stoler, M. (1982). *To tell the truth.* Vermont Visions, 82(3), 3.

Stone, R. (1995). If the mercury soars, so may health hazards. *Science, 267,* 958.

Strasser, B. J. (2003). Who cares about the double helix? Collective memory links the past to the future in science as well as history. *Nature, 422,* 803–804.

Straughan, B. (1996). The secrets of ancient Tiwanaku are benefiting today's Bolivia. In W. A. Haviland & R. J. Gordon (Eds.), *Talking about people* (2nd ed., pp. 76–78). Mountain View, CA: Mayfield.

Straus, W. L., & Cave, A. J. E. (1957). Pathology and the posture of Neanderthal man. *Quarterly Review of Biology, 32.*

Stringer, C. B., & McKie, R. (1996). *African exodus: The origins of modern humanity.* London: Jonathan Cape.

Stuart-MacAdam, P., & Dettwyler, K. A. (Eds.). (1995). *Breastfeeding: Biocultural perspectives.* New York: Aldine.

Suarez-Orozoco, M. M., Spindler, G., & Spindler, L. (1994). *The making of psychological anthropology, II.* Fort Worth, TX: Harcourt Brace.

Sullivan, M. (1999). Chimpanzee hunting habit yield clues about early ancestors. *Chronicle of Higher Education.*

Susman, R. L. (1988). Hand of Paranthropus robustus from Member 1, Swartkrans: Fossil evidence for tool behavior. *Science, 240,* 781–784.

Swadesh, M. (1959). Linguistics as an instrument of prehistory. Southwestern *Journal of Anthropology, 15,* 20–35.

Swaminathan, M. S. (2000). Science in response to basic human needs. *Science, 287,* 425.

Swartz, M. J., Turner, V. W., & Tuden, A. (1966). *Political Anthropology.* Chicago: Aldine.

Swisher III, C. C., Curtis, G. H., Jacob, T., Getty, A. G., Suprijo, A., & Widiasmoro. (1994). Age of the earliest known hominids in Java, Indonesia. *Science, 263,* 1,118–1,121.

Tague, R. G. (1992). Sexual dimorphism in the human bony pelvis, with a consideration of theNeanderthal pelvis from Kebara Cave, Israel. *American Journal of Physical Anthropology, 88,* 1–21.

Tannen, D. (1990). *You just don't understand: Women and men in conversation.* New York: Morrow.

Tapper, M. (1999). *In the blood: sickle-cell anemia and the politics of race.* Philadelphia: University of Pennsylvania Press.

Tax, S. (1953). *Penny capitalism: A Guatemalan Indian economy.* Washington, DC: Smithsonian Institution, Institute of Social Anthropology, Pub. No. 16.

Tax, S. (Ed.). (1962). *Anthropology today: Selections.* Chicago: University of Chicago Press.

Tax, S., Stanley, S., et al. (1975). In honor of Sol Tax. *Current Anthropology. 16,* 507–540.

Taylor, G. (2000). *Castration: Abbreviated history of western manhood* (pp. 38–44, 252–259). New York: Routledge.

Templeton, A. R. (1994). Eve: Hypothesis compatibility versus hypothesis testing. *American Anthropologist, 96*(1), 141–147.

Templeton, A. R. (1995). The "Eve" Hypothesis: A genetic critique and reanalysis. *American Anthropologist 95*(1), 51–72.

Templeton, A. R. (1996). Gene lineages and human evolution. *Science, 272,* 1,363–1,364.

Terashima, H. (1983). Mota and other hunting activities of the Mbuti archers: A socio-ecological study of subsistence technology. *African Studies Monograph* (Kyoto), 3, 71–85.

Thomas, D. H. (1974). *Predicting the past.* New York: Holt, Rinehart & Winston.

Thomas, D. H. (1998). *Archaeology* (3rd ed.). Fort Worth, TX: Harcourt Brace.

Thomas, E. M. (1994). *The tribe of the tiger.* New York: Simon & Schuster.

Thomas, W. L. (Ed.). (1956). *Man's role in changing the face of the earth.* Chicago: University of Chicago Press.

Thompson, S. (1960). *The folktale.* New York: Holt, Rinehart & Winston.

Thomson, K. S. (1997). Natural selection and evolution's smoking gun. *American Scientist, 85,* 516–518.

Thorne, A. G., & Wolpoff, M. D. H. (1981). Regional continuity in Australasian Pleistocene hominid evolution. American *Journal of Physical Anthropology, 55,* 337–349.

Thornhill, N. (1993). Quoted in W. A. Haviland & R. J. Gordon (Eds.), *Talking about people* (p. 127). Mountain View, CA: Mayfield.

Tiffany, S. (Ed.). (1979). *Women in Africa.* St. Albans, VT: Eden Press.

Tobias, P. V. (1980). The natural history of the heliocoidal occlusal plane and its evolution in early Homo. *American Journal of Physical Anthropology, 53,* 173–187.

Tobias, P. V., & von Konigswald, G. H. R. (1964). A comparison between the Olduvai hominines and those of Java and some implications for hominid phylogeny. *Nature, 204,* 515–518.

Togue, R. G. (1992). Sexual dimorphism in the human bony pelvis, with a consideration of the Neanderthal pelvis from Kebara Cave, Israel. *American Journal of Physical Anthropology, 88,* 1–21.

Trevor-Roper, H. (1992). Invention of tradition: The Highland tradition of Scotland. In E. Hobsbawm & T. Ranger (Eds.), *The invention of tradition* (Ch. 2). Cambridge: Cambridge University Press.

Trinkaus, E. (1986). The Neanderthals and modern human origins. *Annual Review of Anthropology, 15,* 197.

Trinkaus, E., & Shipman, P. (1992). *The Neandertals: Changing the image of mankind.* New York: Knopf.

Trouillot, M. R. (2003). *Global transformations: Anthropology and the modern world.* New York: Palgrave Macmillan.

Tuden, A. (1970). Slavery and stratification among the Ila of central Africa. In A. Tuden & L. Plotnicov (Eds.), *Social stratification in Africa.* New York: Free Press.

Tumin, M. M. (1967). *Social stratification: The forms and functions of inequality.* Englewood Cliffs, NJ: Prentice-Hall (Foundations of Modern Sociology).

Turnbull, C. (1983). *Mbuti Pygmies: Change and adaptation.* New York: Holt, Rinehart & Winston.

Turnbull, C. M. (1961). *The forest people.* New York: Simon & Schuster.

Turnbull, C. M. (1983). *The human cycle.* New York: Simon & Schuster.

Turner, T. (1991). Major shift in Brazilian Yanomami policy. *Anthropology Newsletter, 32*(5), 1, 46.

Turner, V. W. (1957). *Schism and continuity in an African society.* Manchester, England: University Press.

Turner, V. W. (1969). *The ritual process.* Chicago: Aldine.

Tylor, E. B. (1871). *Primitive culture: Researches into the development of mythology, philosophy, religion, language, art and customs.* London: Murray.

Tylor, Sir E. B. (1931). Animism. In V. F. Calverton (Ed.), *The making of man: An outline of anthropology.* New York: Modern Library.

Ucko, P. J., & Rosenfeld, A. (1967). *Paleolithic cave art.* New York: McGraw-Hill.

Ucko, P. J., Tringham, R., & Dimbleby, G. W. (Eds.). (1972). *Man, settlement, and urbanism.* London: Duckworth.

Ury, W. L. (1993). *Getting past no: Negotiating your way from confrontation.* New York: Bantum Books.

Ury, W. L. (1999). *Getting to peace: Transforming conflict at home, at work, and in the world.* New York: Viking.

Ury, W. L. (2002). A global immune system. *Andover Bulletin,* winter.

Ury, W. L. (Ed.). (2002). *Must we fight?: From the battlefield to the schoolyard—A new perspective on violent conflict and its prevention.* Hoboken, NJ: Jossey-Bass.

U.S. Department of Commerce, Census Bureau. (2000, January).

Valentine, C. A. (1968). *Culture and poverty.* Chicago: University of Chicago Press.

Van Allen, J. (1979). Sitting on a man: Colonialism and the lost political institutions of Igbo women. In S. Tiffany (Ed.), *Women in society* (pp. 163–187). St. Albans, VT: Eden Press.

Van Den Berghe, P. (1992). The modern state: Nation builder or nation killer? *International Journal of Group Tensions, 22*(3), 191–207.

Van Gennep, A. (1960). *The rites of passage.* Chicago: University of Chicago Press.

Vansina, J. (1965). *Oral tradition: A study in historical methodology* (H. M. Wright, Trans.). Chicago: Aldine.

Van Willigen, J. (1986). *Applied anthropology.* South Hadley, MA: Bergin & Garvey.

Vayda, A. (Ed.). (1969). *Environment and cultural behavior: Ecological studies in cultural anthropology.* Garden City: Natural History Press.

Vayda, A. P. (1961). Expansion and warfare among swidden agriculturalists. *American Anthropologist, 63,* 346–358.

Vincent, J. (1979). On the special division of labor, population, and the origins of agriculture. *Current Anthropology, 20*(2), 422–425.

Vogelman, T. C., et al. (1972). *Prehistoric life in the Champlain Valley* (Film). Burlington, VT: Department of Anthropology, University of Vermont.

Voget, F. W. (1960). Man and culture: An essay in changing anthropological interpretation. *American Anthropologist, 62,* 943–965.

Voget, F. W. (1975). *A history of ethnology.* New York, Holt, Rinehart & Winston.

Vogt, E. Z. (1990). *The Zinacantecos of Mexico, a modern way of life* (2nd ed.). New York: Holt, Rinehart & Winston.

Wagner, P. L. (1960). *A history of ethnology.* New York: Holt, Rinehart & Winston.

Wallace, A. F. C. (1956). Revitalization movements. *American Anthropologist, 58,* 264–281.

Wallace, A. F. C. (1965). The problem of the psychological validity of componential analysis. *American Anthropologist, Special Publication (Part 2), 67*(5), 229–248.

Wallace, A. F. C. (1966). *Religion: An anthropological view.* New York: Random House.

Wallace, A. F. C. (1970). *Culture and personality* (2nd ed.). New York: Random House.

Wallace, E., & Hoebel, E. A. (1952). *The Comanches.* Norman: University of Oklahoma Press.

Ward, C. V., Walker, A., Teaford, M. F., & Odhiambo, I. (1993). Partial skeleton of Proconsul nyanzae from Mfangano Island, Kenya. *American Journal of Physical Anthropology, 90,* 77–111.

Wardhaugh, R. (1972). *Introduction to linguistics.* New York: McGraw-Hill.

Wattenberg, B. J. (1997, November 23). The population explosion is over. New York *Times Magazine,* p. 60.

Washburn, S. L., & Moore, R. (1980). *Ape into human: A study of human evolution* (2nd ed.). Boston: Little, Brown.

Weatherford, J. (1988). *Indian givers: How the Indians of the Americas transformed the world.* New York: Fawcett Columbine.

Weaver, M. P. (1972). *The Aztecs, Maya and their predecessors.* New York: Seminar Press.

Weiner, A. B. (1977). Review of Trobriand cricket: An ingenious response to colonialism. *American Anthropologist, 79,* 506.

Weiner, A. B. (1988). *The Trobrianders of Papua New Guinea.* New York: Holt, Rinehart & Winston.

Weiner, J. S. (1955). *The Piltdown forgery.* Oxford: Oxford University Press.

Weiner, M. (1966). *Modernization: The dynamics of growth.* New York: Basic Books.

Weiss, M. L., & Mann, A. E. (1990). *Human biology and behavior* (5th ed.). Boston: Little, Brown.

Weitzman, L. J. (1985). *The divorce revolution: The unexpected social and economic consequences for women and children in America.* New York: Free Press.

Werner, D. (1990). *Amazon journey.* Englewood Cliffs, NJ: Prentice-Hall.

Wernick, R., & the Editors of Time-Life. (1973). *The Monument Builders.* New York: Time-Life.

Westermarck, E. A. (1926). *A short history of marriage.* New York: Macmillan.

Wheeler, P. (1993). Human ancestors walked tall, stayed cool. *Natural History, 102*(8), 65–66.

Whelehan, P. (1985). Review of Incest, A Biosocial View. *American Anthropologist, 87,* 677–678.

White, D. R. (1988). Rethinking polygyny: Co-wives, codes and cultural systems. *Current Anthropology, 29,* 529–572.

White, E., Brown, D., & the Editors of Time-Life. (1973). *The first men.* New York: Time-Life.

White, L. (1949). *The science of culture: A study of man and civilization.* New York: Farrar, Strauss.

White, L. (1959). *The evolution of culture: The development of civilization to the fall of Rome.* New York: McGraw-Hill.

White, M. (2001). *Historical atlas of the twentieth century.* http://users.erols.com/mwhite28/20century.htm

White, M. (2001). Historical atlas of the twentieth century. http://users.erols.com/mwhite28/20century.htm

White, P. (1976). *The past is human* (2nd ed.). New York: Maplinger.

White, R. (1992). The earliest images: Ice Age "art" in Europe. *Expedition, 34*(3), 37–51.

White, T., Asfaw, B., Degusta, D., Gilbert, H., Richards, G., Suwa, G., Howell, F. C. (2003). Pleistocene Homo sapiens from the Middle Awash, Ethiopia. *Nature, 423,* 742–747.

White, T. D. (1979). Evolutionary implications of Pliocene hominid footprints. *Science, 208,* 175–176.

White, T. D. (2003). Early hominids—diversity or distortion? *Science, 299,* 1,994–1,997.

White, T. D., & Toth, N. (2000). Cutmarks on a Plio-Pleistocene hominid from Sterkfontein, South Africa. *American Journal of Physical Anthropology, 111,* 579–584.

Whitehead, N., & Ferguson, R. B. (Eds.). (1992). *War in the tribal zone.* Santa Fe: School of American Research Press.

Whitehead, N. L., & Ferguson, R. B. (1993, November 10). Deceptive stereotypes about tribal warfare. *Chronicle of Higher Education,* p. A48.

Whiting, B. B. (Ed.). (1963). *Six cultures: Studies of child rearing.* New York: Wiley.

Whiting, J. W. M., & Child, I. L. (1953). *Child training and personality: A cross-cultural study.* New Haven, CT: Yale University Press.

Whiting, J. W. M., Sodergem, J. A., & Stigler, S. M. (1982). Winter temperature as a constraint to the migration of preindustrial peoples. *American Anthropologist, 84,* 289.

Wilk, R. R. (1996). *Economics and cultures: An introduction to economic anthropology.* Boulder, CO: Westview Press.

Willey, G. R. (1966). *An introduction to American archaeology: Vol. 1. North America.* Englewood Cliffs, NJ: Prentice-Hall.

Willey, G. R. (1971). *An introduction to American archaeology, Vol. 2: South America.* Englewood Cliffs, NJ: Prentice-Hall.

Williams, A. M. (1996). *Sex, drugs and HIV: A sociocultural analysis of two groups of gay and bisexual male substance users who practice unprotected sex.* Unpublished manuscript.

Williamson, R. K. (1995). The blessed curse: Spirituality and sexual difference as viewed by Euro-American and Native American cultures. *The College News, 17*(4).

Willigan, J. V. (1986). *Applied anthropology* (pp. 128–129, 133–139). South Hadley, MA: Bergin & Garvey.

Wills, C. (1994). The skin we're in. *Discover, 15*(11), 77–81.

Wilson, A. K., & Sarich, V. M. (1969). A molecular time scale for human evolution. *Proceedings of the National Academy of Science, 63,* 1,089–1,093.

Wingert, P. (1965). *Primitive art: Its tradition and styles.* New York: World.

Winick, C, (Ed.). (1970). *Dictionary of anthropology* (p. 202). Totowa, NJ: Littlefield, Adams.

Wirsing, R. L. (1985). The health of traditional societies and the effects of acculturation. *Current Anthropology 26*(3), 303–322.

Wittfogel, K. A. (1957). *Oriental despotism, a comparative study of total power.* New Haven, CT: Yale University Press.

Wolf, E. R. (1959). *Sons of the shaking earth.* Chicago: University of Chicago Press.

Wolf, E. R. (1966). *Peasants.* Englewood Cliffs, NJ: Prentice-Hall.

Wolf, E. R. (1982). *Europe and the people without history.* Berkeley: University of California Press.

Wolf, E. R. (1999). *Envisioning power: Ideologies of dominance and crisis* (p. 263). Berkeley: University of California Press.

Wolf, M. (1972). *Women and the family in rural Taiwan.* Stanford, CA: Stanford University Press.

Wolf, M. (1985). *Revolution postponed: Women in contemporary China.* Stanford, CA: Stanford University Press.

Wolpoff, M. H. (1971). Interstitial wear. *American Journal of Physical Anthropology, 34,* 205–227.

Wolpoff, M. H. (1977). Review of earliest man in the Lake Rudolf Basin. *American Anthropologist, 79,* 708-711.

Wolpoff, M. H. (1982). Ramapithecus and hominid origins. *Current Anthropology, 23,* 501–522.

Wolpoff, M.H. (1993). Evolution in Homo erectus: The question of stasis. In R. L. Ciochon & J. G. Fleagle (Eds.), *The human evolution source book.* Englewood Cliffs, NJ: Prentice-Hall.

Wolpoff, M. H. (1993). Multiregional evolution: The fossil alternative to Eden. In R. L. Ciochon & J. G. Fleagle (Eds.), *The human evolution source book.* Englewood Cliffs, NJ: Prentice-Hall.

Wolpoff, M. (1996). Australopithecus: A new look at an old ancestor. *General Anthropology, 3*(1), 2.

Wolpoff, M. & Caspari, R. (1997). *Race and human evolution.* New York: Simon & Schuster.

Wolpoff, M. H., Wu, X. Z. & Thorne, A. G. (1984). Modern *Homo sapiens* origins: a general theory of hominid evolution involving fossil evidence from east Asia. In F. H. Smith and F. Spencer (Eds.), *The origins of modern humans.* New York: Alan R. Liss pp. 411–483.

Womack, M. (1994). Program 5: *Psychological anthropology. Faces of culture.* Fountain Valley, CA: Coast Telecourses, Inc.

Wong, K. (1998, January). Ancestral quandary: Neanderthals not our ancestors? Not so fast. *Scientific American,* 30–32.

Wood, B., & Aiello, L. C. (1998). Taxonomic and functional implications of mandibular scaling in early hominines. *American Journal of Physical Anthropology, 105,* 523–538.

Wood, B., Wood, C., & Konigsberg, L. (1994). Paranthropus boisei: An example of evolutionary stasis? *American Journal of Physical Anthropology, 95,* 117–136.

Woodward, V. (1992). *Human heredity and society.* St. Paul, MN: West.

Woolfson, P. (1972). Language, thought, and culture. In V. P. Clark, P. A. Escholz, & A. F. Rosa (Eds.), *Language.* New York: St. Martin's Press.

World Bank. (1982). *Tribal peoples and economic development.* Washington, DC: World Bank.

World Bank. (2003). *www.worldbank.org/poverty.* Accessed January 2003.

World Health Organization. *http://www.who.int/about/definition/en/.*

World Meterological Organization. (2003). Quoted in Increasing heatwaves and other health hazards. Accessed December, 10, 2003, at *greenpeaceusa.org/climatge/index.fpl/7096/article/907.html.*

Wright, R. (1984). Towards a new Indian policy in Brazil. *Cultural Survival Quarterly 8*(1).

Wright, R. M. (1997). Violence on Indian day in Brazil 1997: Symbol of the past and future. *Cultural Survival Quarterly, 21* (2), 47–49.

Wulff, R. M., & Fiske, S. J. (1987). *Anthropological praxis: Translating knowledge into action.* Boulder, CO: Westview Press.

Yip, M. (2002). *Tone.* New York: Cambridge University Press.

Young, A. (1981). The creation of medical knowledge: Some problems in interpretation. *Social Science and Medicine, 17,*1,205–1,211.

Zeder, M. A., & Hesse, B. (2000). The initial domestication of goats (*Capra hircus*) in the Zagros Mountains 10,000 years ago. *Science, 287,* 2,254–2,257.

Zilhão, J. (2000). Fate of the Neandertals. *Archaeology, 53*(4), 30.

Zimmer, C. (1999). New date for the dawn of dream time. *Science, 284,* 1,243.

Zohary, D., & Hopf, M. (1993). *Domestication of plants in the Old World* (2nd ed.). Oxford: Clarenden Press.

Zur, J. (1994). The psychological impact of impunity. *Anthropology Today, 10*(3), 12–17.

Photo Credits

2 © Sandi Fellman 1984; **3** Scala / Art Resource, NY; **4** (top left) © Anup and Manoj Shah; **4** (top) © Jodi Cobb / National Geographic Image Collection; **4** (middle) © James L. Stanfield / National Geographic Image Collection; **4** (bottom) © George H. H. Huey / Corbis; **7** Documentary Educational Resources; **8** (left) Smithsonian Institution Photo No. 56196; **8** (middle) AP / Wide World Photos; **9** (left) © Michael Newman / PhotoEdit; **9** (right) © Maria Stenzel / National Geographic Image Collection; **11** © 1998 Jim Leachman; **12** (left) © Susan Meiselas / Magnum Photos; **12** (right) © Rich Press; **13** U.S. General Services Administration; **15** (left) © Rhoda Sidney / PhotoEdit; **15** (middle) © Laura Dwight / PhotoEdit; **15** (right) © Bruce Broce; **16** Kerry Culllinan; **19** (left) © Mark Richards / PhotoEdit; **19** (right) © Sarah Wesch; **21** (top left) © Bettmann / Corbis; **21** (top middle) The Granger Collection, New York; **21** (top right) Culver Pictures; **21** (bottom right) © Anita Haviland; **25** (right) © Henry S. Hamlin; **25** (left) © Joyce Choo / Corbis; **26** (left) © Gordon Gahan / National Geographic Image Collection; **26** (right) Wartenberg / Picture Press / Corbis; **27** © Alden Pellett / The Image Works; **28** © Patrick Barth / Getty Images; **30** © David Wells / The Image Works; **33** © David Young-Wolff / PhotoEdit; **34** (left) © Elizabeth Crews / The Image Works; **34** (right) © Michael Newman / PhotoEdit; **35** © Dennis MacDonald / PhotoEdit; **36** AP / Wide World Photos; **37** (left) © Monika Graff / The Image Works; **37** (right) United Artists / The Kobal Collection; **41** (left) © Bettmann / Corbis; **41** (right) Photograph by Vance Allen. Courtesy of Claudia Leacock; **42** © David Tejada / Getty Images; **43** Estate of Annette B. Weiner; **46** © Alec Duncan; **47** (top) Courtesy of Phoebe Apperson Hearst Museum of Anthropology and the Regents of the University of California; **47** (bottom left) © Bettmann / Corbis; **47** (bottom middle) AP / Wide World Photos; **47** (bottom right) AP / Wide World Photos; **48** © PhotoEdit; **50** (left) © Sean Cayton / The Image Works; **50** (middle) © A. Ramey / PhotoEdit; **50** (right) © John Neubauer; **52** AP / Wide World Photos; **55** (top) The Kobal Collection / Hammer; **55** (bottom) Courtesy Jonathan Marks; **59** © Jeff Greenberg / Photo Researchers, Inc.; **59** (right) © D. Chivers / Anthro-Photo; **60** (left) © Irven DeVore / Anthro-Photo; **60** (middle) Courtesy Bunataro Imanishi; **61** © Amy Parish / Anthro-Photo; **63** (both) © Anita de Laguna Haviland; **64** (left) © Michael K. Nichols / National Geographic Image Collection; **64** (right) © Bromhall / Animals Animals; **65** © Bromhall / Animals Animals; **67** 1985

David L. Brill by permission of Owen Lovejoy; **68** © 1999 David L. Brill; **69** © J & B Photo / Animals animals; **70** © Gusto / Photo Researchers; **72** National Museums of Kenya; **73** © Javier Trueba / Madrid Scientific Films; **74** (left) © Bettmann / Corbis; **74** (right) The Field Museum, negative number A111668c, Photographer John Weinstein; **75** Paul Jaronski, UM Photo Services. Karen Diane Harvey, Sculptor; **76** (left) © Gianni Dagli Orti / Corbis; **76** (right) Artifact credit: Musee National de Prehistoire, Les Eyzies de Tayac. V 1985 David L. Brill; **78** Negative No. K15806. Courtesy Department of Library Services, American Museum of National History; **79** © 2001 David L. Brill / Brill Atlanta; **80** © Michael Coyne / Getty Images; **82** Kit Kittle / Corbis; **83** (left) © Dinodia Photo Library; **83** (right) A. Ramey / PhotoEdit; **86** © Nepoleon Chagnon / Anthro-Photo; **87** Werner Forman / Art Resource, NY; **88** © Yavuz Arslan / Peter Arnold; **91** H. Lyn Miles; **92** H. Lyn Miles; **95** © Richard Lord / The Image Works; **97** (left) © John Chellmann / Animals Animals; **97** (right) © Jutta Klee / Corbis; **98** (left) © Tim Boyle / Getty Images; **98** (right) Reuters NewMedia Inc. / Corbis; **98** (bottom) © Esbin-Anderson / The Image Works; **99** (left) © 1996 Richard Lord; **99** (middle) © Jeff Greenberg / PhotoEdit; **99** (right) © 1995 Richard Lord; **100** (left) © Frank Pedrick / The Image Works; **100** (right) © Robert Azzi / Woodfin Camp & Associates; **108** (top) James Hill / Getty Images; **108** (bottom) © Klaus Francke / Peter Arnold, Inc.; **109** Orion Pictures Corp. / Courtesy Everett Collection; **110** AP / Wide World Photos; **111** © Archivo Iconografico, S.A. / Corbis ; **112** © Susan Kuklin / Photo Researchers, Inc.; **113** © Bettmann / Corbis; **114** Photograph by Bruce Zuckerman and Marilyn Lundberg, West Semitic Research; **118** © Henry S. Hamlin; **120** © David Young-Wolff / PhotoEdit; **121** James Balog © 1996. Reprinted with permission of Discover Magazine; **122** (left) © 1991 Richard Lord; **122** (right) © David Young-Wolff / PhotoEdit; **124** (left) © Mark Jenike / Anthro-Photo; **124** (right) © Hart / Anthro-Photo; **128** © Gallo Images / Corbis; **129** © Cindy Charles / PhotoEdit; **130** Estate of Jerome Tiger; **131** © Napoleon Chagnon / Anthro-Photo; **133** (left) AP / Wide World Photos; **133** (middle) The Granger Collection, New York; **135** (left) © Michael Nichols / National Geographic Image Collection; **135** (right) AP / Wide World Photos; **137** Smithsonian Institution Photo No. 85-8666; **138** © Heather Croall; **139** William A. Haviland; **140** © John Bishop; **141** © David Young-Wolff / PhotoEdit; **146** © Leslie Hugh Stone / The Image Works; **149** © Mark Richards; **150** (left) Neidhardt Collection / Underwood Archives, SF;

150 (right) ©1993 Kirk Condyles; **151** © National Museum of American Art, Washington, DC / Art Resource, NY; **152** © Nathan Benn / Corbis; **154** © Joe Carini / The Image Works; **155** Courtesy of the University of Illinois at Urbana-Champaign; **157** (top) © Anthony Bannister / ABPL; **157** (middle, both) © Anita de Laguna Haviland; **157** (bottom) © Robert Brenner / PhotoEdit; **159** © Anthony Bannister / ABPL; **160** (both) © Anthony Bannister / ABPL; **163** © Paul Conklin / PhotoEdit; **164** © 1980 James D. Nations / DDB Stock; **167** © Dr. Cynthia M. Beall & Dr. Melvyn C. Goldstein / NGS Image Collection; **168** © Reinhold Loeffler; **169** © Ann Kendall / Cusichaca Trust; **171** © D. Donne Bryant / DDB Stock; **172** Courtesy of the Department of Library Services, The American Museum of Natural History; **173** © Jeff Greenberg / PhotoEdit; **176** © 1991 Richard Lord; **179** (top) Courtesy of Rich Macgurn; **179** (bottom) Estate of Annette B. Weiner; **181** (left) © David H. Wells / The Image Works; **181** (right) © James L. Stanfield / National Geographic Image Collection; **182** (left) © Eric Kroll; **182** (right) © D. Donne Bryant / DDB Stock; **183** © PhotoEdit; **184** © Bruce Dale / National Geographical Image Collection; **185** © 1996 Joel Gordon; **186** © Irven DeVore / Anthro-Photo; **187** © Anthony Bannister / ABPL; **189** © Stan Washburn / Anthro-Photo; **190** (left) © Robert Galbraith / Reuters / Corbis; **190** (right) © Brooks Kraft / Corbis; **191** Courtesy of Karen Stephenson; **192** Estate of Annette B. Weiner; **193** © 2004 Jay Mallin; **194** © 1996 Steve Henrikson; **197** (top) © 1998 Richard Lord; **197** (bottom) © Jack Kurtz / The Image Works; **198** Copyright © The British Museum; **199** © John Moss / Photo Researchers, Inc.; **200** © 1998 Joel Gordon; **204** © Kent Meireis / The Image Works; **205** University of Pennsylvania Museum (neg.#29-94-2); **206** © Richard T. Nowitz / Corbis; **208** (left) Estate of Annette B. Weiner; **208** (right) © Hideo Haga / HAGA / The Image Works; **209** (top) © Irven DeVore / Anthro-Photo; **209** (bottom left) © Lisa Krantz / The Image Works; **209** (bottom right) © Catherine Karnow / Corbis; **213** Omar Khan / Harappa. harappa.com; **215** ©Bill Aron / PhotoEdit; **217** © Brissaud-Figaro / Getty Images; **218** (left) AP / Wide World Photos; **218** (right) © Lauren Goodsmith / The Image Works; **220** © Uppa / Topham / The Image Works; **221** © Reuters / Corbis; **222** (left) © DPA / The Image Works; **222** (right)© SuperStock; **226** (left) Estate of Annette B. Weiner; **226** (right) © Adrian Arbib / Anthro-Photo; **227** (top) © John Eastcott / Yva Momatiuk / Woodfin Camp & Associates; **227** (bottom) © Linda Bartlett / Photo Researchers, Inc.; **229** (1eft) ©

Glenn Russell/Burlington Free Press; **229** (right) Courtesy of Phyllis Austin & Anne Dellenbough 2000; **230** © Jacques M. Chenet/Corbis; **234** Photo by Todd Hoffman; **236** © Bachman/Photo Researchers, Inc.; **237** (top) © Scala/Art Resource; **237** (bottom) © Jim Varney/Science Photo Library/ Photo Researchers; **240** Photo by Todd Hoffman; **241** © Zev Radovan/PhotoEdit; **242** © Aldona Sabalis/Photo Researchers, Inc.; **243** © Vanessa Vick/Photo Researchers; **244** © John Eastcott/Eva Momatiuki/The Image Works; **246** © Joe Cavanaugh/DDB Stock; **247** (top) Courtesy of The Milwaukee Public Museum; **247** (bottom) © Stephen Trimble; **248** Estate of Annette B. Weiner; **249** © Tony Howarth/Woodfin Camp & Associates; **250** © Peter Simon/Stock, Boston; **253** © Andy Levin/Photo Researchers, Inc.; **258** © Wally Turnbull; **261** © The British Museum; **263** (left) Culver Pictures; **263** (right) © Bettmann/Corbis; **265** Gai Ming-sheng/HK China Tourism Press; **266** Arizona State Museum, University of Arizona, Helga Teiwes, Photographer; **268** © Michael Newman/PhotoEdit; **269** © Donald Sanipass; **271** Courtesy of Peggy Reeves Sanday; **273** © Anita de Laguna Haviland; **274** © John Verelst/National Archives of Canada; **275** © Bettmann/Corbis; **278** Photo by Bortell, courtesy Museum of New Mexico Neg. #2631; **279** © PhotoEdit; **282** © David Young-Wolff/PhotoEdit; **284** (both) © Richard Hill; **285** © Daemmrich/The Image Works; **286** © Paul Conklin/PhotoEdit; **287** © Bruce Davidson/Earth Scenes; **288** (left) © Michael Newman/PhotoEdit; **288** (right) PhotoEdit; **569** Courtesy of International Indian Treaty Council; **290** © Chris Trotman/NewSport/Corbis; **291** © Norman Rowan/The Image Works; **294** © Richard Hutchings/Photo Researchers, Inc.; **577** (left) © Anna Clopet/Corbis; **297** (right) © Roman Soumar/Corbis; **299** (top left) © A. Ramey/PhotoEdit; **299** (top right) © 1997 Joel Gordon; **299** (bottom) © Beryl Goldberg; **300** © Gianni Dagli Orti/Corbis; **301** (top) © 1985 Justin Kerr; **301** (bottom right) © Rob Crandall/The Image Works; **301** (bottom left) © Charles & Josette Lenars/Corbis; **302** © 1998 Joel Gordon; **304** © Reuters/Corbis; **305** © Chris Lisle/Corbis; **306** AP/Wide World Photos; **310** Documentary Educational Resources; **311** Ray Baldwin Louis; **312** © George Holton/Photo Researchers, Inc.; **314** Photography by Eleanor Vandevort and Indiana University Libraries' African Studies Collection and Digital Library Program; **315** © Jacques Jangoux/Peter Arnold, Inc.; **319** © Gianni

Dagli Orti/Corbis; **321** © Michael Leckel/ Reuters/Corbis; **322** © Fred McConnaughey/ Photo Researchers, Inc.; **325** © Cunera Buijs, National Museum of Ethnology, Leiden, the Netherlands; **327** © Martin Neptune; **328** © Dr. James Gibbs, Anthropology Department, Stanford University; **328** (right) © Hans Halberstadt/Photo Researchers, Inc.; **329** © Jay Dickman; **330** (left) © Steve Winter/ National Geographic Image Collection; **330** (right) © David Paul Morris; **331** © Napoleon Chagnon/Anthro-Photo; **333** © Dan Connell/The Image Works; **334** Courtesy of Dr. Laura Nader; **335** (left) © Reuters/Corbis; **335** (right) © K. Prouse/ Pressnet/Topham/The Image Works; **338** Photographer: Hester + Hardaway Photographers. The Menil Collection, Houston; **341** (left) © Bettmann/Corbis; **341** (middle) AP/Wide World Photos; **341** (right) © Mike Maple/Woodfin Camp & Associates; **342** AP/Wide World Photos; **344** © Scala/Art Resource; **345** Culver Pictures; **346** © William A. Haviland; **347** (left) © Topham/The Image Works; **347** (right) © Dan Budnick/Woodfin Camp & Associates; **349** © Irven DeVore/Anthro-Photo; **353** AP/Wide World Photos; **354** © Myrleen Cate/PhotoEdit; **355** (top) © Dirk Halstead/Getty Images; **355** (bottom left) © Susan McElhinney/American Image Inc.; **355** (bottom right) Courtesy of the Department of Library Services, The American Museum of Natural History; **356** AP/Wide World Photos; **357** © The Cover Story/Corbis; **361** © Ken Schles Inc. all rights reserved; **362** (left) © Craig Aurness/Woodfin Camp & Associates; **362** (right) AP/Wide World Photos; **366** Vince Hemingson, Courtesy of vanishingtattoo.com; **368** (left) © AFP/Corbis; **368** (right) © M. Antman/The Image Works; **369** (left) © Syndey Byrd; **369** (middle right) Courtesy of the National Museum of the American Indian, Smithsonian Institution, Photo No.4771; **369** (bottom right) © Anita de Laguna Haviland; **370** © Jeff Becom/Photo 20-20; **371** (left) Courtesy of the Burke Museum of Natural History and Culture, catalog # 1163, painted skin tunic with bear design, Tlingit, Ka-gwanta-n Wolf Clan, Sitka, Alaska; **371** (top right, middle right) From *Patterns That Connect*, p. 82. © 1996 The Rock Foundation. Courtesy of Edmund Carpenter; **371** (bottom right) Gemeente Musea Delft, Collectie Museum Nusantara; **372** Photo by Vida Pavesich; **374** (left) © Anita de Laguna Haviland; **374** (right) © J. D. Lewis Williams/Rock Art Research Unit, University of the Witwatersrand; **375**

© Scala/Art Resource, NY; **376** (left, top right) Migraine art reproduced by permission of the Migraine Action Association and Boehringer Ingelheim; **376** (middle right) © Dr. Ronald K. Siegel; **377** © Larry Dale Gordon/The Image Bank; **379** (both) William A. Haviland; **380** © Werner Forman/Art Resource, NY; **382** © Kevin Kelly; **383** © Anthro-Photo; **385** (top) © Paul Souders/ Getty Images; **385** (bottom) © Earl & Nazima Kowall/Corbis; **386** © Michael Newman/PhotoEdit; **387** (top) © Laura Bliss Spaan/AMIPA; **387** (bottom) R. Todd Hoffman; **388** © 2000 Bob Livingston; **389** © Inga Spence/Tom Stack & Associates; **392** © Randy Olson/National Geographic Image Collection; **393** Harald E. L. Prins; **394** Harald E. L. Prins; **397** © Stephen Trimble; **398** © SuperStock; **399** © Steven Ferry/Words & Images; **400** © 1995 Karen Tranberg Hansen; **401** NASA; **402** © Dion Ogust/The Image Works; **405** (top) Chapin Library of Rare Books, Williams College; **405** (middle) © Bettmann/Corbis; **405** (bottom) © Scully/Getty Images; **406** © Robert J. Gordon; **408** AP/Wide World Photos; **409** (top) Arizona State Museum, University of Arizona, Photographer Helga Teiwes; **409** (bottom) © Jerry W. Leach; **410** © Bettmann/Corbis; **411** © Jose Guterres/ Getty Images; **412** © Reuters/Corbis; **413** © A. Ramey/PhotoEdit; **415** (left) © Ewing Galloway/Index Stock; **415** (right) © Robert Brenner/PhotoEdit; **416** © Staffan Widstrand/Corbis; **418** © Nani Gois/Abril Imagens; **420** Courtesy Eric Wolf; **421** © Paul Conklin/PhotoEdit; **424** © Luis Marden/ National Geographic Image Collection; **427** © Allen Green/Photo Researchers, Inc.; **429** © Reuters/Corbis; **430** Jean-Philippe Ksiazek/AFP/Getty Images; **431** © Zahid Hussein/Reuters; **432** (top) AP/Wide World Photos; **432** (bottom right) Jean-Marie Simon; **433** (left) © Karen Kasmauski/Matrix; **433** (right) AP/Wide World Photos; **434** AP/ Wide World Photos; **436** (left) AP/Wide World Photos; **436** (right) © Bettmann/ Corbis; **438** © Sue Cunningham Photo-graphic; **439** (top) © Tom Davenport/Photo Researchers, Inc; **439** (bottom) Harald Prins 1997; **443** Courtesy of Dr. Arjun Appadurai; **444** Courtesy of IMF; **446** AP/Wide World Photos; **447** © Tony Freeman/PhotoEdit; **449** (top left) AP/Wide World Photos; **449** (top right) © Bob Daemmrich/The Image Works; **449** (bottom right) AP/Wide World Photos; **452** © Royalty-Free/Corbis; **453** (top left) © Reuters/Corbis; **453** (top right) © Amnesty International; **453** (middle right, bottom right) AP/Wide World Photos.

Index

L90326